Rick Steves®

BUDAPEST

Rick Steves & Cameron Hewitt

CONTENTS

Budapest

LEGEND

- Pedestrian-Friendly Area
- Ⓜ M1 Metró Stop
- Ⓜ M2 Metró Stop
- Ⓜ M3 Metró Stop
- Ⓜ M4 Metró Stop
- ■ Landmark or Point of Interest
- Tourist Information Offices

BUDA SIGHTS

1. Budapest History Museum
2. Cave Church
3. Chain Bridge
4. Citadella Fortress & Liberation Monument
5. Fishermen's Bastion
6. Funicular to Castle Hill
7. Gellért Baths
8. Church Ruins
9. Hospital in the Rock
10. Hungarian National Gallery
11. Labyrinth Entrance
12. Matthias Church
13. Museum of Military History
14. Royal Palace
15. Rudas Baths
16. St. Mary Magdalene Church Remains
17. Turul Bird Statue

200 Meters
200 Yards

PEST SIGHTS

1. Franz Liszt Museum
2. Franz Liszt Square
3. Great Market Hall
4. Great Synagogue & Jewish Museum
5. Gresham Palace
6. Heroes' Square & Millennium Monument
7. To Holocaust Memorial Center & Applied Arts Mus.
8. House of Terror
9. Hungarian Nat'l Museum
10. Műcsarnok (Hall of Art)
11. Museum of Ethnography
12. Museum of Fine Arts
13. New York Café
14. Opera House
15. Orthodox Synagogue
16. Parliament
17. SMS Leitha
18. St. István's Basilica
19. Synagogue at Rumbach Street
20. Széchenyi Baths
21. Vajdahunyad Castle
22. Vörösmarty Square & Start of Váci Utca Pedestrian Street

Memento Park

Hungarian Parliament

Széchenyi Baths

Great Market Hall

Old Town Sopron

Rick Steves®

BUDAPEST

INTRODUCTION

Budapest (locals say "BOO-daw-pesht") is a unique metropolis at the heart of a unique nation. Here you'll find experiences like nothing else in Europe: Feel your stress ebb away as you soak in hundred-degree water, surrounded by opulent Baroque domes...and by Speedo- and bikini-clad Hungarians. Ogle some of Europe's most richly decorated interiors, which echo a proud little nation's bygone glory days. Perk up your ears with a first-rate performance at one of the world's top opera houses—at bargain prices. Ponder the region's bleak communist era as you stroll amid giant Soviet-style statues designed to evoke fear and obedience. Try to wrap your head around Hungary's colorful history...and your tongue around its notoriously difficult language. Dive into a bowl of goulash, the famous paprika-flavored peasant soup with a kick. Go for an after-dinner stroll along the Danube, immersed in a grand city that's bathed in floodlights.

Budapest excites good travelers...and exasperates bad ones. I love this city for its flaws as much as for its persistent personality. As a tour guide, for years I've introduced travelers to Budapest: walked them step-by-step through the byzantine entry procedure at the thermal baths; handed them a glass of local wine with an unpronounceable name and an unforgettable flavor; and taught them to greet their new Hungarian friends with a robust, *"Jó napot kívánok!"* I've watched them struggle to understand—and gradually succumb to the charms of—this fascinating but beguiling place. And I've taken careful notes. This book represents the lessons I've learned, organized to help you experience Budapest with the wisdom of a return visitor.

Map Legend

⚘	Viewpoint	✈	Airport	)——(	Tunnel
♠	Entrance	Ⓣ	Taxi Stand		Pedestrian Zone
✚	Tourist Info	Ⓜ	Metró Stop	------	Railway
WC	Restroom	Ⓣ	Tram Stop	O++++++++O	Funicular
♜	Castle	Ⓑ	Bus Stop	⊢——⊢——⊣	Tram
⌂	Church	⚓	Boat Stop	▒▒▒▒	Stairs
☾	Mosque	Ⓟ	Parking	• • • •	Walk/Tour Route
✡	Synagogue			------	Trail

Use this legend to help you navigate the maps in this book.

ABOUT THIS BOOK

Rick Steves Budapest is a personal tour guide in your pocket. Better yet, it's actually two tour guides in your pocket: The co-author of this book is Cameron Hewitt, who writes and edits guidebooks for my travel company, Rick Steves' Europe. Inspired by Hungary's epic past, charming people, and delightfully spicy cuisine, Cameron has spent more than a decade closely tracking the exciting changes in this part of the world. Together, Cameron and I keep this book up-to-date and accurate (though, for simplicity, from this point on "we" will shed our respective egos and become "I").

In this book, you'll find the following chapters:

Hungary offers an introduction to this mesmerizing land, including a crash course in its notoriously difficult language.

Orientation to Budapest includes specifics on public transportation, helpful hints, local tour options, easy-to-read maps, and tourist information. The "Planning Your Time" section suggests a day-to-day schedule for how to best use your limited time.

Sights in Budapest describes the top attractions and includes their cost and hours.

The **Thermal Baths** chapter offers step-by-step instructions for enjoying Budapest's quintessential activity like a local.

The **Self-Guided Walks and Tours** cover Budapest's Leopold Town (the banking and business district), Pest Town Center (the down-and-dirty downtown urban zone), Andrássy út (the main boulevard, lined with fine architecture and great sightseeing), Heroes' Square and City Park (the city's playground, including a Who's Who lesson in Hungarian history), and Castle Hill (the city's historic center). The tours lead you through three of Budapest's most compelling sights: the House of Terror Museum, the Great Synagogue and Jewish Quarter, and Memento Park.

Sleeping in Budapest describes my favorite hotels, from good-value deals to cushy splurges.

Key to This Book

Updates
This book is updated regularly—but things change. For the latest, visit www.ricksteves.com/update.

Abbreviations and Times
I use the following symbols and abbreviations in this book:

Sights are rated:

▲▲▲	Don't miss
▲▲	Try hard to see
▲	Worthwhile if you can make it
No rating	Worth knowing about

Tourist information offices are abbreviated as **TI,** and bathrooms are **WC**s. To categorize accommodations, I use a **Sleep Code** (described on page 226).

Like Hungary, this book uses the **24-hour clock.** It's the same through 12:00 noon, then keeps going: 13:00, 14:00, and so on. For anything over 12, subtract 12 and add p.m. (14:00 is 2:00 p.m.).

When giving **opening times,** I include both peak season and off-season hours if they differ. So, if a museum is listed as "May-Oct daily 9:00-16:00," it should be open from 9 a.m. until 4 p.m. from the first day of May until the last day of October (but expect exceptions).

If you see a ✪ in a sight listing, it means that the sight is described in far greater detail elsewhere—either with its own self-guided tour, or as part of a self-guided walk.

For **transit or tour departures,** I first list the frequency, then the duration. So, a train connection listed as "2/hour, 1.5 hours" departs twice each hour, and the journey lasts an hour and a half.

Eating in Budapest outlines one of Hungary's top attractions—its delicious cuisine—and serves up a range of options, from inexpensive take-out joints to fancy restaurants.

Budapest with Children includes my top recommendations for keeping your kids (and you) happy in Budapest.

Shopping in Budapest gives you tips for shopping painlessly and enjoyably, without letting it overwhelm your vacation or ruin your budget.

Entertainment in Budapest is your guide to fun, from a low-key stroll along the Danube embankment to Budapest's most cutting-edge nightspots...and everything in between (opera, tourist concerts, music pubs, river cruises, and more).

Budapest Connections lays the groundwork for your smooth arrival and departure, outlining your options for traveling to destinations by train, bus, plane, car, and Danube riverboat.

Day Trips from Budapest includes the opulent Gödöllő Palace, the lively horse shows at Lázár Lovaspark, the folk village of Hollókő, and the "Danube Bend" river towns of Szentendre, Visegrád, and Esztergom, as well as ideas for farther-flung destinations.

There are also in-depth chapters on Hungary's best attractions outside of Budapest: the towns of **Eger, Pécs,** and **Sopron.** I've also thrown in the nearby Slovak capital of **Bratislava.**

Hungary: Past and Present is an overview of this nation's epic and illustrious history, and a survey of contemporary Hungary.

Practicalities is a traveler's tool kit, with our best travel tips and advice about money, sightseeing, staying connected, and transportation (trains, buses, car rentals, driving, and flights). There's also a list of recommended books and films.

The **appendix** has nuts-and-bolts information, including useful phone numbers and websites, a festival list, climate chart, handy packing checklist, and Hungarian survival phrases.

Browse through this book and select your favorite sights. Then have a great trip! Traveling like a temporary local, and taking advantage of the information here, you'll enjoy the absolute most of every mile, minute, and dollar. As you visit places I know and love, I'm happy that you'll be meeting some of my favorite Hungarians.

Planning

This section will help you get started on planning your trip—with advice on trip costs, when to go, and what you should know before you take off.

TRAVEL SMART

Your trip to Budapest is like a complex play—it's easier to follow and really appreciate on a second viewing. While no one does the same trip twice to gain that advantage, reading this book in its entirety before your trip accomplishes much the same thing.

Design an itinerary that enables you to visit sights at the best possible times. Note holidays, festivals, specifics on sights, and days when sights are closed (all covered in this book). For example, most Hungarian museums close on Mondays. To get between destinations smoothly, read the tips in Practicalities on taking trains and buses, or renting a car and driving. A smart trip is a puzzle—a fun, doable, and worthwhile challenge.

When you're plotting your itinerary, strive for a mix of intense and relaxed stretches. To maximize rootedness, minimize one-night stands. If you're venturing outside Budapest, it's worth taking a long drive after dinner (or a train ride with a dinner picnic) to get settled in a town for two nights. Every trip—and every traveler—needs slack time (laundry, picnics, people-watching, and so on). Pace yourself. Assume you will return.

Reread this book as you travel, and visit local tourist information offices (abbreviated as TI in this book). Upon arrival in a new town, lay the groundwork for a smooth departure; get the schedule for the train, bus, or boat that you'll take when you depart. Drivers can figure out the best route to their next destination.

Update your plans as you travel. You can carry a mobile device (phone, tablet, or laptop) to find out tourist information, learn the latest on sights (special events, tour schedules, etc.), book tickets and tours, make reservations, reconfirm hotels, research transportation connections, and keep in touch with your loved ones. If you don't want to bring a pricey device, you can use guest computers at hotels and make phone calls from landlines.

Enjoy the hospitality of the Hungarian people. Connect with the culture. Set up your own quest for the best thermal bath, bowl of goulash, nostalgic Golden Age interior, or atmospheric café. Slow down and be open to unexpected experiences. Ask questions—most locals are eager to point you in their idea of the right direction. Keep a notepad in your pocket for noting directions, organizing your thoughts, and confirming prices. Wear your money belt, learn the currency, and figure out how to estimate prices in dollars. Those who expect to travel smart, do.

TRIP COSTS

Traveling in Budapest (and throughout Hungary) is a good value. While Budapest has Westernized at an astonishing rate since the Iron Curtain fell, it's still cheaper than most Western European capitals.

Five components make up your trip costs: airfare, surface transportation, room and board, sightseeing and entertainment, and shopping and miscellany.

Airfare: A basic round-trip flight from the US to Budapest can cost, on average, about $1,000-2,000 total, depending on where you fly from and when (cheaper in winter). If Budapest is part of a longer trip, consider saving time and money in Europe by flying into one city and out of another; for instance, into Budapest and out of Prague. Overall, Kayak.com is the best place to start searching for flights on a combination of mainstream and budget carriers.

Surface Transportation: For a typical one-week visit, figure about $100. That includes $22 for a week-long Budapest transit pass, $70 for side-trips to other Hungarian towns (e.g., about $30 round-trip to Eger and $40 round-trip to Pécs), plus an extra $8 for miscellaneous taxi rides. Add around $20 per person for each transfer between the airport and downtown Budapest (cheaper but slower if you take public transportation). If you rent a car for a few days of side-tripping, figure about $100 per day (cheaper per day for longer rentals). To connect farther-flung destinations, train passes normally must be purchased outside Europe but aren't necessarily your best option—you may save money by simply buying tickets as you go. Don't hesitate to consider flying, as budget airlines can be cheaper than taking the train (check www.skyscanner.com for intra-European flights).

Room and Board: You can thrive in Budapest on $100 a day per person for room and board. This allows $10 for lunch, $25 for dinner, and $65 for lodging (based on two people splitting the cost of a $130 double room that includes breakfast). Students and tightwads can enjoy Budapest for as little as $40 a day ($20 per hostel bed, $20 for meals and snacks). If you're traveling beyond Budapest, accommodations cost much less in smaller Hungarian towns and cities (a comfortable double typically costs no more than $90, bringing your budget down to $80 per day per person for two people traveling together).

Sightseeing and Entertainment: Figure about $8-17 per major sight (House of Terror, Memento Park, touring the Parliament or Opera House), $3-6 per minor sight, and $15-25 for splurge experiences (soaking in a thermal bath, taking a nighttime boat cruise on the Danube, going to a tourist concert or opera). You can hire your own private guide for four hours for around $120—a great value when divided between two or more people. An overall average of $20-35 a day works for most people. Don't skimp here. After all, this category is the driving force behind your trip—you came to sightsee, enjoy, and experience Budapest.

Shopping and Miscellany: Figure $1-2 per postcard, coffee, beer, or ice-cream cone. Shopping can vary in cost from nearly nothing to a small fortune. Good budget travelers find that this category has little to do with assembling a trip full of lifelong and wonderful memories.

SIGHTSEEING PRIORITIES

So much to see, so little time. How to choose? Depending on the length of your trip, assuming you're using public transportation, and taking geographic proximity into account, here are my recommended priorities:

3 days:	Budapest
5 days, add:	Eger and one more day in Budapest
7 days, add:	Pécs and another day in Budapest, or choose a day trip
10 days, add:	Bratislava, Sopron, and additional day trips

More days, add: More time in Budapest and more day trips; also see "More Hungarian Destinations" on page 350

Note that Bratislava fits well on the way if you're going between Budapest and Vienna. For more tips, see "Planning Your Time" on page 26.

WHEN TO GO

The "tourist season" runs roughly from May through September. Book ahead for festivals and national holidays that occur throughout the year (for a list, see the appendix).

Summer (July and Aug) has its advantages: very long days, the busiest schedule of tourist fun and special festivals, and virtually no business travelers to compete with for hotel rooms. However, because Hungary has a practically Mediterranean climate, summer temperatures can skyrocket to the 80s or 90s (choose a hotel with air-conditioning). And many cultural events (such as the opera) are on summer vacation.

In spring and fall—May, June, September, and early October—travelers enjoy fewer tourist crowds and milder weather. This is my favorite time to visit Budapest. However, it's also prime convention time (especially September), when hotels tend to fill up and charge their top rates.

Winter travelers find concert season in full swing, with absolutely no tourist crowds, but some accommodations and sights are either closed or run on a limited schedule. Confirm your sightseeing plans locally, especially when traveling off-season. The weather can be cold and dreary, and night will draw the shades on your sightseeing before dinnertime. For weather specifics, see the climate chart in the appendix.

KNOW BEFORE YOU GO

Your trip is more likely to go smoothly if you plan ahead. Check this list of things to arrange while you're still at home.

You need a **passport**—but no visa or shots—to travel in Hungary. You may be denied entry into certain European countries if your passport is due to expire within three months of your ticketed date of return. Get it renewed if you'll be cutting it close. It can take up to six weeks to get or renew a passport (for more on passports, see www.travel.state.gov). Pack a photocopy of your passport in your luggage in case the original is lost or stolen.

Book rooms well in advance if you'll be traveling at busy convention times (Sept-Oct) or during any major holidays (see page 512).

Call your **debit- and credit-card companies** to let them know the countries you'll be visiting, to ask about fees, to request your

PIN code (it will be mailed to you), and more. See page 480 for details.

Do your homework if you want to buy **travel insurance.** Compare the cost of the insurance to the likelihood of your using it and your potential loss if something goes wrong. Also, check whether your existing insurance (health, homeowners, or renters) covers you and your possessions overseas. For more tips, see www.ricksteves. com/insurance.

If you're planning on **renting a car** in Hungary, bring your driver's license and an International Driving Permit (see page 499).

If you plan to hire a **local guide,** reserve ahead by email. Popular guides can get booked up.

If you'd like to **tour the Hungarian Parliament,** consider reserving online a few days ahead to ensure your choice of entrance time (see page 48).

If you're bringing a **mobile device,** download any apps you might want to use on the road, such as translators, maps, and transit schedules. Check out **Rick Steves Audio Europe,** featuring hours of travel interviews and other audio content about Hungary (via the Rick Steves Audio Europe free app, www.ricksteves.com/audioeurope, iTunes, or Google Play; for details, see page 506).

Check the **Rick Steves guidebook updates** page for any recent changes to this book (www.ricksteves.com/update).

Because **airline carry-on restrictions** are always changing, visit the Transportation Security Administration's website (www. tsa.gov) for a list of what you can bring on the plane and for the latest security measures (including screening of electronic devices, which you may be asked to power up).

ATTITUDE ADJUSTMENT

American baby boomers still sometimes approach Hungary—for so long part of the "Evil Empire"—expecting grouchy service, crumbling communist infrastructure, and grimy, depressing landscapes. But visitors are often pleasantly surprised at the color, friendliness, safety, and ease of travel here. Hungary joined the EU in 2004, opened its borders with most of its EU neighbors (Austria, Slovakia, and Slovenia) in 2007, and feels just as "European" as anywhere. Many Hungarians speak excellent English and are forever scrambling to impress their guests. Any remaining rough edges simply add to the charm and carbonate the experience.

The East-West stuff still fascinates many tourists, but to locals, the Soviet regime is old news, Cold War espionage is the stuff of historical documentaries, and oppressive monuments to Stalin are a distant memory. More than 25 years after the fall of the Iron Curtain, Hungarians think about communism only when tourists bring it up. Freedom is a generation old, and—for better or for

> ## How Was Your Trip?
>
> Were your travels fun, smooth, and meaningful? If you'd like to share your tips, concerns, and discoveries, please fill out the survey at www.ricksteves.com/feedback. To check out readers' hotel and restaurant reviews—or leave one yourself—visit my travel forum at www.ricksteves.com/travel-forum. I value your feedback. Thanks in advance—it helps a lot.

worse—McDonald's, Twitter, and mobile phones are every bit as entrenched here as anywhere else in Europe.

With all of these changes in mind, Hungarians bristle at the idea that they live in "Eastern" Europe (which implies a connection to Russia); to them, it's *Central* Europe. Hungarians are looking to the future...and they hope you will, too.

Traveling as a Temporary Local

We travel all the way to Europe to enjoy differences—to become temporary locals. You'll experience frustrations. Certain truths that we find "God-given" or "self-evident," such as cold beer, ice in drinks, bottomless cups of coffee, "first" names first, cigarette smoke being irritating, and bigger being better, are suddenly not so true. One of the benefits of travel is the eye-opening realization that there are logical, civil, and even better alternatives. A willingness to go local ensures that you'll enjoy a full dose of local hospitality. Fortunately for you, hospitality is a Hungarian forte. Hungarian culture is endearingly formal—people really care.

Europeans generally like Americans. But if there is a negative aspect to the image Europeans have of Americans, it's that we are loud, wasteful, ethnocentric, too informal (which can seem disrespectful), and a bit naive.

While Hungarians look bemusedly at some of our Yankee excesses—and worriedly at others—they nearly always afford us individual travelers all the warmth we deserve.

Judging from all the happy feedback I receive from travelers, it's safe to assume you'll enjoy a great, affordable vacation—with the finesse of an independent, experienced traveler.

Thanks, and *jó utat*—happy travels!

Rick Steves

Back Door Travel Philosophy

From *Rick Steves Europe Through the Back Door*

Travel is intensified living—maximum thrills per minute and one of the last great sources of legal adventure. Travel is freedom. It's recess, and we need it.

Experiencing the real Europe requires catching it by surprise, going casual..."through the Back Door."

Affording travel is a matter of priorities. (Make do with the old car.) You can eat and sleep—simply, safely, and enjoyably—anywhere in Europe for $125 a day plus transportation costs. In many ways, spending more money only builds a thicker wall between you and what you traveled so far to see. Europe is a cultural carnival, and time after time, you'll find that its best acts are free and the best seats are the cheap ones.

A tight budget forces you to travel close to the ground, meeting and communicating with the people. Never sacrifice sleep, nutrition, safety, or cleanliness to save money. Simply enjoy the local-style alternatives to expensive hotels and restaurants.

Connecting with people carbonates your experience. Extroverts have more fun. If your trip is low on magic moments, kick yourself and make things happen. If you don't enjoy a place, maybe you don't know enough about it. Seek the truth. Recognize tourist traps. Give a culture the benefit of your open mind. See things as different, but not better or worse. Any culture has plenty to share.

Of course, travel, like the world, is a series of hills and valleys. Be fanatically positive and militantly optimistic. If something's not to your liking, change your liking.

Travel can make you a happier American, as well as a citizen of the world. Our Earth is home to seven billion equally precious people. It's humbling to travel and find that other people don't have the "American Dream"—they have their own dreams. Europeans like us, but with all due respect, they wouldn't trade passports.

Thoughtful travel engages us with the world. In tough economic times, it reminds us what is truly important. By broadening perspectives, travel teaches new ways to measure quality of life.

Globetrotting destroys ethnocentricity, helping us understand and appreciate other cultures. Rather than fear the diversity on this planet, celebrate it. Among your most prized souvenirs will be the strands of different cultures you choose to knit into your own character. The world is a cultural yarn shop, and Back Door travelers are weaving the ultimate tapestry. Join in!

HUNGARY

Magyarország

Hungary is an island of Asian-descended Magyars in a sea of Slavs. Even though the Hungarians have thoroughly integrated with their Slavic and German neighbors in the millennium-plus since they arrived, there's still something about the place that's distinctly Magyar (MUD-jar). Here in quirky, idiosyncratic Hungary, everything's a little different from the rest of Europe—in terms of history, language, culture, customs, and cuisine—but it's hard to put your finger on exactly how.

Travelers to Hungary notice many endearing peculiarities. Hungarians list a person's family name first, and the given name is last—just as in many other Eastern cultures (think of Kim Jong Il). So the composer known as "Franz Liszt" in German is "Liszt Ferenc" in his homeland. (To help reduce confusion, many Hungarian business cards list the surname in capital letters.) Hungarians have a charming habit of using the English word "hello" for both "hi" and "bye," just like the Italians use "ciao." You might overhear a Hungarian end a telephone conversation with a cheery "Hello!" Hungarians even drove on the left side of the road until 1941.

Just a century ago, this country controlled half of one of Europe's grandest realms: the Austro-Hungarian Empire. Today, perhaps clinging to their former greatness, many Hungarians remain old-fashioned and nostalgic. With their dusty museums and bushy moustaches, they love to remember the good old days. Buildings all over the country are marked with plaques boasting *MŰEMLÉK* ("historical monument").

Thanks to this focus on tradition, the Hungarians you'll encounter are generally polite, formal, and professional. Hungarians have class. Everything here is done with a proud flourish. People in the service industry seem to wear their uniforms as a badge of honor rather than a burden. When a waiter comes to your table in a restaurant, he'll say, *"Tessék parancsolni"*—literally, "Please command, sir." The standard greeting, *"Jó napot kívánok,"* means "I wish you a good day." Women sometimes hear the even more formal greeting, *"Kezét csókolom"*—"I kiss your hand." And when your train or bus makes a stop, you won't be alerted by a mindless, blaring beep—but instead, by peppy music. (You'll be humming these contagious little ditties all day.) Perhaps thanks to this artful blending of elegance and formality, Hungarians have a cultural affinity for the French.

Hungarians are also orderly and tidy...in their own sometimes unexpected ways. Yes, Hungary has its share of litter, graffiti, and crumbling buildings, but you'll find great reason within the chaos. The Hungarian railroad has a long list of discounted fares—for seniors, kids, dogs...and monkeys. (It could happen.) My favorite town name in Hungary: Hatvan. This means "Sixty" in Hungarian...and it's exactly 60 kilometers from Budapest. You can't argue with that kind of logic.

This tradition of left-brained thinking hasn't produced many great Hungarian painters or poets who are known outside their homeland. But the Hungarians, who are renowned for their ingenuity, have made tremendous contributions to science, technology, business, and industry. Hungarians of note include Edward Teller (instrumental in creating the A-bomb), John von Neumann (a pioneer of computer science), András Gróf (who, as Andy Grove, emigrated to the US and founded Intel), and George Soros (the billionaire investor famous—or notorious—for supporting left-wing causes). A popular local joke claims that Hungarians are so clever that they can enter a revolving door behind you and exit in front of you.

Perhaps the most famous Hungarian "scientist" invented something you probably have in a box in your basement: Ernő Rubik, creator of the famous cube. Hungarians' enjoyment of a good mind-bending puzzle is also evident in their fascination with chess, which you'll see played in cafés, parks, and baths.

Like their Viennese neighbors, Hungarians know how to enjoy the good life. Favorite activities include splashing and soaking in their many thermal baths (see the Thermal Baths chapter). "Taking the waters," Hungarian-style, deserves to be your top priority while you're here. Though public baths can sound intimidating, they're a delight. In this book I recommend my three favorite baths in Budapest, a fine bath in Eger, and two more just outside of Eger. For each, I've included careful instructions to help you enjoy the warm-water fun like a pro. (To allay your first fear: Yes, you can wear your swimsuit.)

Hungarians have also revived an elegant, Vienna-style café culture that was dismantled by the communists. Whiling away the afternoon at a genteel coffeehouse, as you nurse a drink or a delicate dessert, is a favorite pastime. (For the best options in Budapest, see "Budapest's Café Culture" on page 264.)

Classical music is revered in Hungary, perhaps as nowhere else outside Austria. Aside from scientists and businessmen, the best-known Hungarians are composers: Béla Bartók, Zoltán Kodály, and Franz Liszt. (For more on these figures, see "Hungarian Music" on page 288.)

While one in five Hungarians lives in Budapest, the countryside plays an important role in the country's economy—this has always been a highly agricultural region. The sprawling Great Hungarian Plain (Puszta) that makes up a vast swath of Hungary is the country's breadbasket. You'll pass through fields of wheat and corn, but the grains are secondary to Hungarians' (and tourists') true love: wine. Hungarian winemaking standards plummeted under the communists, but many vintner families are now reclaiming their land, returning to their precise traditional methods, and making wines worth being proud of once more. (For details, see "Hungarian Wines" on page 252.)

Somehow Hungary, at the crossroads of Europe, has managed to become cosmopolitan while remaining perfectly Hungarian. The Hungarians—like Hungary itself—are a cross-section of Central European cultures: Magyars, Germans, Czechs, Slovaks, Poles, Serbs, Jews, Ottomans, Romanians, Roma (Gypsies), and many others. Still, no matter how many generations removed they are from Magyar stock, there's something different about Hungarians—and not just the language. Look a Hungarian in the eye, and

Hungary Almanac

Official Name: Magyarország (Hungary).

Snapshot History: Settled by the Central Asian Magyars in A.D. 896, Hungary became Catholic in the year 1000, and went on to become Christian Europe's front line in fighting against the Ottomans (Muslims from today's Turkey) in the 16th-17th centuries. After serving as co-capital of the vast Austro-Hungarian Empire and losing World Wars I and II, Hungary became a Soviet satellite until achieving independence in 1989.

Population: Hungary's 10 million people (similar to Michigan) are 92 percent ethnic Hungarians who speak Hungarian. One in 50 is Roma (Gypsy). About 40 percent of the populace is Catholic, with nearly 15 percent Protestant and around 30 percent listed as "other" or unaffiliated. Of the world's approximately 12 million ethnic Hungarians, one in six lives outside Hungary (mostly in areas of Romania, Slovakia, Serbia, and Croatia that were once part of Hungary).

Latitude and Longitude: 47°N and 20°E; similar latitude to Seattle, Paris, and Vienna.

Area: 36,000 square miles, similar to Indiana or Maine.

Geography: Hungary is situated in the Carpathian Basin, bound on the north by the Carpathian Mountains and on the south by the Dinaric Mountains. Though it's surrounded by mountains, Hungary itself is relatively flat, with some gently rolling hills. The Great Hungarian Plain—which begins on the east bank of the Danube in Budapest—stretches all the way to Asia. Hungary's two main rivers—the Danube and Tisza—run north-south through the country, neatly dividing it into three regions.

Biggest Cities: Budapest (the capital on the Danube, nearly 2 million), Debrecen (in the east, 206,000), and Miskolc (in the north, 170,000).

you'll see a glimmer of the marauding Magyar, stomping in from the Central Asian plains a thousand years ago.

HUNGARIAN LANGUAGE

Even though Hungary is surrounded by Slavs, Hungarian is not at all related to Slavic languages (such as Polish, Czech, or Croatian). In fact, Hungarian isn't related to *any* European language, except for very distant relatives Finnish and Estonian. It isn't even an Indo-European language—meaning that English is more closely related to Hindi, Russian, and French than it is to Hungarian.

Hungarian is agglutinative: To create meaning, you start with a simple root word and then start tacking on suffixes—sometimes resulting in a pileup of extra sounds. The emphasis always goes on the first syllable, and the following syllables are droned in a kind of

Economy: The Gross Domestic Product is $197 billion (a quarter of Poland's), but the GDP per capita is $19,800 (only slightly less than Poland's). Thanks to its progressive "goulash communism," Hungary had a head start on many other former Soviet Bloc countries and is now thriving, privatized...and largely foreign-owned. In the 1990s, many communist-era workers (especially women) lost their jobs. Today, the workforce is small (only 57 percent of eligible workers) but highly skilled. Grains, metals, machinery, and automobiles are major exports, and about one-quarter of trade is with Germany.

Currency: 225 forints (Ft, or HUF) = about $1 (though the exchange rate can fluctuate significantly).

Government: The single-house National Assembly (199 seats) is the only ruling branch directly elected by popular vote. The legislators in turn select the figurehead president (currently János Áder) and the ruling prime minister (Viktor Orbán); both belong to the right-of-center Fidesz party.

Flag: Three horizontal bands, top to bottom: red (representing strength), white (faithfulness), and green (hope). It's identical to the Italian flag, but flipped 90 degrees counterclockwise. It often includes the Hungarian coat of arms: horizontal red-and-white stripes (on the left); the patriarchal, or double-barred, cross (on the right); and the Hungarian crown (on top).

The Average János: The typical Hungarian eats a pound of lard a week (they cook with it). The average family has three members, and spends almost three-fourths of its income on housing. According to a recent condom-company survey, the average Hungarian has sex 131 times a year (behind only France and Greece), making them Europe's third-greatest liars.

a monotone—giving the language a distinctive cadence that Hungary's neighbors love to tease about.

While the language can be overwhelming for tourists, one easy word is *"Szia"* (SEE-yaw), which means both hello and goodbye (like "ciao" or "aloha"). Confusingly, sometimes Hungarians simply say the English word "hello" to mean either "hi" or "bye." Another handy word that Hungarians (and people throughout Central Europe) will understand is *Servus* (SEHR-voos, spelled *Szervusz* in Hungarian)—the old-fashioned greeting from the days of the Austro-Hungarian Empire. If you draw a blank on how to say hello, just offer a cheery, *"Servus!"*

Hungarian pronunciation is straightforward, once you remember a few key rules. The trickiest: *s* alone is pronounced "sh," while *sz* is pronounced "s." This explains why you'll hear in-the-know travelers pronouncing Budapest as "BOO-daw-pesht." You might catch the *busz* up to Castle Hill—pronounced "boose." And "Franz Liszt" is easier to pronounce than it looks: It sounds just like "list." To review:

s sounds like "sh" as in "shirt"

sz sounds like "s" as in "saint"

Hungarian has a set of unusual palatal sounds that don't quite have a counterpart in English. To make these sounds, gently press the thick part of your tongue to the roof or your mouth (instead of using the tip of your tongue behind your teeth, as we do in English):

gy sounds like "dg" as in "hedge"

ny sounds like "ny" as in "canyon" (not "nee")

ty sounds like "tch" as in "itch"

cs sounds like "ch" as in "church"

As for vowels: The letter *a* almost sounds like o (aw, as in "hot"); but with an accent *(á)*, it brightens up to the more standard "ah." Likewise, while *e* sounds like "eh," *é* sounds like "ay." An accent *(á, é, í, ó, ú)* indicates that you linger on that vowel, but not necessarily that you stress that syllable. Like German, Hungarian has umlauts *(ö, ü)*, meaning you purse your lips when you say that vowel: roughly, *ö* sounds like "ur" and *ü* sounds like "ew." A long umlaut *(ő, ű)* is the same sound, but you hold it a little longer. Words ending in *k* are often plural.

Here are a few other letters that sound different in Hungarian than in English:

c and **cz** both sound like "ts" as in "cats"

zs sounds like "zh" as in "leisure"

j and **ly** both sound like "y" as in "yellow"

OK, maybe it's not *so* simple. But you'll get the hang of it...and Hungarians will appreciate your efforts.

For a complete list of Hungarian survival phrases, see page 517 in the appendix.

BUDAPEST

ORIENTATION TO BUDAPEST

Europe's most underrated big city, Budapest can be as challenging as it is enchanting. The sprawling Hungarian capital on the banks of the Danube is, in so many ways, the capital of Central Europe. It's a city of nuance and paradox—cosmopolitan, complicated, and tricky for the first-timer to get a handle on. Like a full-bodied Hungarian wine, Budapest can overwhelm visitors...even as it intoxicates them with delights.

Think of Budapest as that favorite Hungarian pastime, chess: It's simple to learn...but takes a lifetime to master. This chapter is your first lesson. Then it's your move.

BUDAPEST: A VERBAL MAP

Budapest is huge, with nearly two million people. Like Vienna, the city was built as the head of a much larger empire than it currently governs—which can make it feel a bit too grandiose for the capital of a small country. But the city is surprisingly easy to manage once you get the lay of the land and learn the excellent public transportation network. Those who are comfortable with the Metró, trams, and buses have the city by the tail (see "Getting Around Budapest" on page 35).

The city is split down the center by the Danube River. On the

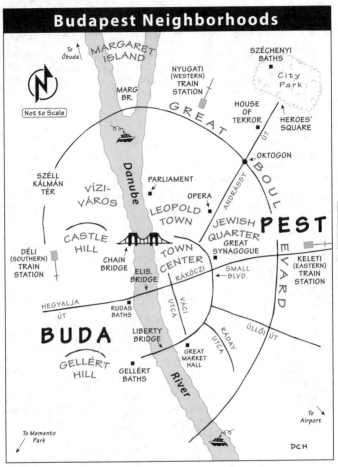

Budapest Neighborhoods

*east side of the Danube is flat **Pest*** (pronounced "pesht"), and on the west is hilly **Buda.** A third part of the city, **Óbuda,** sits to the north of Buda.

Buda and Pest are connected by a series of characteristic bridges. From north to south, there's the low-profile **Margaret Bridge** (Margit híd, crosses Margaret Island), the famous **Chain Bridge** (Széchenyi Lánchíd), the white and modern **Elisabeth Bridge** (Erzsébet híd), and the green **Liberty Bridge** (Szabadság híd). These bridges are fun to cross on foot, but it's faster to go under the river (on the M2/red Metró line), or to cross over it by tram or bus. (Four more bridges lie beyond the tourist zone: the Petőfi and Rákóczi bridges to the south, and Árpád and Megyeri bridges to the north.)

Budapest uses a **district** system (like Paris and Vienna). There are 23 districts *(kerület),* identified by Roman numerals. For ex-

Snapshot History of Budapest

When describing the story of this grand metropolis, it's tempting to fall back on the trusty onion metaphor: Budapest, which has been adored and destroyed by many different groups across the centuries, is layered with history...sometimes stinky, sometimes sweet. The Hungary: Past and Present chapter—and many other tidbits throughout this book—will help you peel back those layers, step-by-step. But here's the quick version:

Budapest is hot—literally. The city sits on a thin layer of earth above thermal springs, which power its many baths. Even the word "Pest" comes from a Slavic word for "oven." Two thousand years ago, the Romans had a settlement (called Aquincum) on the northern edge of today's Budapest. Several centuries later, in A.D. 896, a mysterious nomadic group called the Magyars arrived from the steppes of Central Asia and took over the Carpathian Basin (roughly today's Hungary). After running roughshod over Europe for a time, the Magyars—the ancestors of today's Hungarians—settled down, adopted Christianity, and became fully European. The twin towns of Buda and Pest emerged as the leading cities of Hungary.

In the 16th century, the Ottomans invaded and occupied the region for nearly a century and a half. The Habsburgs (monarchs of neighboring Austria) finally forced them out, but Buda and Pest were in ruins. The cities were rebuilt in a more Austrian style.

After many decades of Hungarian uprisings, the Compromise of 1867 granted Hungary an equal stake in the Austro-Hungarian Empire. Six years later, the cities of Buda, Pest, and Óbuda united to form the capital city of Budapest, which governed a huge chunk of Eastern Europe. For the next few decades, Budapest boomed, and Hungarian culture enjoyed a Golden Age. The expansion reached its peak with a flurry of construction surrounding the year 1896—Hungary's 1,000th birthday.

But with Hungary's defeat in World War I, the city's fortunes reversed. World War II left Budapest in ruins...and in the hands of

ample, Castle Hill is in district I and City Park is in district XIV. Notice that the district number does not necessarily indicate how central a location is: Districts II and III are to the north of Buda, where few tourists go, while the heart of Pest is district V. Addresses often start with the district number (as a Roman numeral). Budapest's four-digit postal codes also give you a clue as to the district: The first digit (always 1) represents Budapest, then a two-digit number represents the district (such as "05" for district V), then a final digit gives more specific information about the location.

the Soviets. A bold uprising in 1956 was brutally dealt with, but before long a milder "goulash communism" emerged in Hungary. Budapest, though still oppressed, was a place where other Eastern Europeans could come to experiment with "Western evils," from Big Macs to Nikes.

Since communism's graceful exit in 1989, Budapest has once again reinvented itself. During this time of transition, the city has struggled with whether to cling to its past glory days, or to leave all that behind and create something new. Budapest has a rich architectural heritage that rivals any European city—but many of those buildings were in a state of horrible disrepair. Now many have been fixed up to their prewar, pre-communist peak, while others have been melded with modern elements.

The latest chapter in Budapest's history has been written by its current prime minister, Viktor Orbán, and his party, Fidesz. Highly controversial both at home and abroad, but also beloved by the majority of Hungarians, Orbán has boldly set about reshaping Budapest and Hungary: restructuring its government, reinterpreting its history, and rebuilding much of the city. Orbán's rule has come with the renaming of squares to honor formerly obscure Hungarian historical-footnote figures, but has also seen an unprecedented burst of urban renewal. Ten years ago, many of Budapest's squares, streets, and parks were miserable, smoggy no-go zones. Today, they are gleaming and filled with happy locals. Orbán's impact on contemporary Hungary is a major theme of this book.

Through it all, Budapest—atmospherically shot through with the crumbling elegance of former greatness—remains the heart and soul of Central Europe. It's a rich cultural stew made up of Hungarians, Germans, Slavs, and Jews, with a dash of Turkish paprika—simmered for centuries in a thermal bath. Each group has left its mark, but through it all, something has remained that is distinctly...Budapest.

As you navigate Budapest, remember these key Hungarian terms: *tér* (pronounced "tehr," square), *utca* (OOT-zaw, street), *út* (oot, boulevard), *körút* (KUR-root, ring road), *híd* (heed, bridge), and *város* (VAH-rohsh, town). To better match what you'll see locally, in this book I've mostly used these Hungarian terms (instead of the English equivalents).

Let's take a tour through the places where you'll be spending your time, neighborhood by neighborhood. This section—like all of the sightseeing, sleeping, eating, and other advice in this book—is divided between Pest and Buda. (It might help to think of these as two separate cities...which, after all, they once were.)

ORIENTATION

Budapest Overview

To Eger

M-3

HUNGÁRIA KÖRÚT

XIV

VÁCI ÚT

See City Park Walk detail map

SZÉCHENYI BATHS

ZOO

DÓZSA

MUSEUM OF FINE ARTS

HEROES' SQUARE

VAJDAHUNYAD CASTLE

CITY PARK

GYÖRGY

MŰCSARNOK (HALL OF ART)

NYUGATI (WESTERN) STATION

VI

See Pest Sights detail map

HOUSE OF TERROR MUSEUM

ANDRÁSSY

FRANZ LISZT MUSEUM

ÚT

1956 MONUMENT

See Andrássy Út Walk detail map

TERÉZ KÖRÚT

"Broadway Quarter"

Oktogon

Franz Liszt Square

ERZSÉBET

OPERA HOUSE

P E S T

KELETI (EASTERN) STATION

See Pest Town Center Walk detail map

JEWISH QUARTER

See detail map

NEW YORK CAFÉ

RÁKÓCZI

KÖRÚT

ÚT

GREAT SYNAGOGUE & JEWISH MUSEUM

HUNGARIAN NATIONAL MUSEUM

VIII

GREAT MARKET HALL

RADAY

JÓZSEF KÖRÚT

APPLIED ARTS MUSEUM

River

BÁLNA CULTURAL CENTER

HOLOCAUST MEMORIAL CENTER

ÜLLŐI ÚT

FERENC KÖRÚT

IX

To Airport

PETŐFI BRIDGE

To "Millennium City"

ORIENTATION

Pest

Pest—the real-world commercial heart of the city—is where most tourists spend the majority of their time.

"Downtown" Pest (district V), just across the river from Castle Hill, is divided into two sections:

The more genteel northern half, called **Leopold Town** (Lipótváros), surrounds the giant red-domed, riverside Parliament building. This is the governmental, business, and banking district, with several fine monuments and grand buildings. Leopold Town is sleepy after hours.

The southern half, the grittier and more urban-feeling **Town Center** (Belváros, literally "Inner Town"), is a thriving shopping, dining, nightlife, and residential zone that bustles day and night. The main pedestrian artery through the Town Center is the famous (and overrated) Váci utca shopping street, which runs parallel to the fine and scenic Danube promenade one block inland. At the southern end of the Town Center is the vast Great Market Hall, with the café street Ráday utca just beyond.

The Town Center is hemmed in by the first of Pest's four concentric **ring roads** (körút). The innermost ring is called the Kiskörút, or "Small Boulevard." The next ring, several blocks farther out, is called the Nagykörút, or "Great Boulevard." These ring roads change names every few blocks, but they are always called körút. Historically, the Nagykörút is subdivided into sections named for Habsburg monarchs, such as Lipótkörút ("Leopold Boulevard"); each of these sections also defines a neighborhood, such as Lipótváros ("Leopold Town"). Beyond the Nagykörút are two more ring roads—the Hungária körút highway, and the M-0 expressway—that few tourists see.

Arterial **boulevards,** called út, stretch from central Pest into the suburbs like spokes on a wheel. One of these boulevards, **Andrássy út,** provides a useful spine for reaching some of outer Pest's best sights, restaurants, and accommodations. It begins at the Small Boulevard (near Deák tér) and extends past several key sights (including the Opera and the House of Terror museum) and dining zones (such as the "Broadway Quarter" and Franz Liszt Square) out to **City Park.** The park has its own collection of attractions, including the monumental Heroes' Square and Budapest's top experience: soaking in the Széchenyi Baths.

Various key sights lie along the **Small Boulevard** ring road (connected by trams #47 and #49), including (from north to south) the Great Synagogue (marking the start of the **Jewish Quarter,** which feels a bit run-down but features several Jewish sights as well as a hopping nightlife zone with cool "ruin pubs"), the National Museum, and the Great Market Hall.

Several other points of interest are spread far and wide along the **Great Boulevard** ring road (circled by trams #4 and #6). From north to south, it passes Margaret Island (the city's playground, in the middle of the Danube); the Nyugati/Western train station; the prominent Oktogon intersection, where it crosses Andrássy út; the opulent New York Café, with the Keleti/Eastern train station just up the street; and the intersection with Üllői út, near the Holocaust Memorial Center and the Applied Arts Museum.

Buda

Sleepy Buda looks pretty (and gets first billing in the city's name), but most tourists spend less time here than in exciting Pest. The Buda side is dominated by two hills: **Castle Hill,** topped by the

green dome of the Royal Palace and the spiny Neo-Gothic spire of the Matthias Church; and to the south, the taller, wooded **Gellért Hill,** capped by a 150-year-old fortress and the Liberation Monument.

The **Castle District,** atop Castle Hill (in district I), is historic but fairly dull. It's packed with tourists by day, and dead at night. The pleasant **Víziváros** (VEE-zee-vah-rohsh) residential neighborhood, or "Water Town," is squeezed between the castle and the river. The square called Batthyány tér, roughly at the north end of Víziváros, is a hub for the neighborhood, with a handy Metró stop (M2/red line), tram stops, market hall, and eateries. Just north of Castle Hill (and Víziváros) is **Széll Kálmán tér,** another transit hub for Buda, with a Metró station (M2/red line), several tram stops, and the giant Mammut shopping mall.

Tucked to the south of **Gellért Hill** is another fine residential district. Here you'll find the Gellért Hotel, with its famous thermal baths; the Rudas Baths are also at the base of Gellért Hill, but farther to the north.

Central Buda is surrounded by a ring road, and the busy Hegyalja út rumbles through the middle of the tourists' Buda (between Castle and Gellért Hills). Behind Castle and Gellért Hills is a low-lying neighborhood of little interest to tourists (except for the Déli/Southern train station), and beyond that rise the **Buda Hills,** a scenic and upscale residential area.

ORIENTATION

ORIENTATION

Outer Budapest

The city doesn't end there. This book also includes tips for the Óbuda district north of central Buda; sights on the outskirts of town (but accessible on the suburban transit network), including Memento Park, Gödöllő Palace, and the small riverside town of Szentendre; and more.

PLANNING YOUR TIME

Visitors attempting to "do" Budapest in just one day leave dazed, exhausted...and yearning for more. Two days are the bare minimum, and force you to tackle the city at a breakneck pace (and you still won't see everything). Three days work, but assume you'll go fast and/or skip some things. Four days are ideal, and a fifth day (or even sixth) gives you time for various day-trip options.

Budapest is quite decentralized: Plan your day ahead to minimize backtracking, and refer to your map frequently. Just about everything is walkable, but distances are far, and public transit can save valuable time.

Each of this book's self-guided walks acts as a sightseeing spine for a particular neighborhood or area: Pest's **Leopold Town,** Pest's **Town Center,** Pest's **Andrássy út,** Pest's **Heroes' Square and City Park,** Pest's **Jewish Quarter** (in the Grand Synagogue chapter), and Buda's **Castle Hill.** Each walk offers an orientation overview, with several in-depth sightseeing opportunities along the way. If you're ambitious, you can do several of these walks in a single day—but you'll have to skip most of the museums. To take your time and dip into each sight, spread the walks over several days.

When divvying your time between Buda and Pest, keep in mind that (aside from the Gellért and Rudas Baths) Buda's sightseeing is mostly concentrated on Castle Hill, and can easily be seen in less than a day, while Pest deserves as much time as you're willing to give it. Start by getting your bearings in Pest (where you'll likely spend most of your time), then head for relatively laid-back Buda when you need a break from the big city.

Below are some possible plans, depending on the length of your trip. Note that these very ambitious itineraries assume you want to sightsee at a speedy pace. In the **evening,** you have a wide range of options (many of which are outlined in the Entertainment in Budapest chapter): enjoying good restaurants, taking in an opera or concert, snuggling on a romantic floodlit river cruise, relaxing in a thermal bath, exploring the city's unique ruin pubs, or simply strolling the Danube embankments and bridges.

Budapest in Two Days

Your time will be full but memorable. Spend Day 1 in Pest. Start

Daily Reminder

Monday: Most of Budapest's museums are closed on Mondays. But you can still take advantage of plenty of other sights and activities: all three major baths, Memento Park, Great Synagogue and Jewish Quarter, Matthias Church on Castle Hill, St. István's Basilica, Parliament tour, Great Market Hall, Opera House tour, City Park (and Zoo), Danube cruises, concerts, and bus, walking, and bike tours. Monday is also a great day to do the Leopold Town and Pest Town Center walks, since their major sights are virtually unaffected.

Tuesday: All major sights are open.

Wednesday: All major sights are open.

Thursday: Some shops are open later (until 20:00 or 21:00), as is the Műcsarnok (Hall of Art, until 20:00).

Friday: All major sights are open. The Orthodox Synagogue and Synagogue at Rumbach Street close early (usually around 13:30 or 15:30).

Saturday: The Great Synagogue, Orthodox Synagogue, and Synagogue at Rumbach Street are closed today. Most shops close early (usually 13:00 or 14:00), and the Great Market Hall closes at 15:00. The Petőfi Csarnok flea market is hopping (8:00-14:00).

Sunday: The Great Market Hall and Franz Liszt Museum are closed today, as are most shops, though large shopping malls remain open. The Petőfi Csarnok flea market is open (8:00-14:00), and the Szimpla ruin pub hosts a morning farmers market (9:00-14:00).

ORIENTATION

with the Leopold Town Walk, then the Pest Town Center Walk. From the Great Market Hall (at the end of that walk), circle around the Small Boulevard to Deák tér and consider the Andrássy út and Heroes' Square/City Park walks. Or, if you're exhausted already, just take the M1/yellow Metró line to Hősök tere, ogle the Heroes' Square statues and Vajdahunyad Castle, and reward yourself with a soak at Széchenyi Baths. (Note that this schedule leaves virtually no time for entering any museums, though you might be able to fit in one or two big sights, such as the Parliament—for which you should book tickets online—Opera House, Great Synagogue, or House of Terror.)

On the morning of Day 2, tackle any Pest sights you didn't have time for yesterday (or take the bus out to Memento Park). After lunch, ride bus #16 from Deák tér to Buda's Castle Hill and follow the Castle Hill Walk. Head back to Pest for some final sightseeing and dinner.

Budapest in Three or Four Days

Your first day is for getting your bearings in Pest. Choose between touring the Parliament or the Opera House; for the Parliament, book your tickets online. Then do the Leopold Town Walk, followed by the Andrássy út and Heroes' Square/City Park walks, ending with a soak at the Széchenyi Baths.

On Day 2, delve deeper into Pest, starting with the Pest Town Center Walk. After visiting the Great Market Hall, you can cross the river to Buda for a soak at the Gellért or Rudas Baths (if you want more spa time), or circle around the Small Boulevard to see the National Museum and/or Great Synagogue and Jewish Quarter.

On Day 3, use the morning to see any remaining sights, then ride from Deák tér out to Memento Park on the park's 11:00 direct bus. On returning, grab a quick lunch and take bus #16 from Deák tér to Castle Hill, where you'll do the Castle Hill Walk.

With a fourth day, spread the Day 1 tours over more time, and circle back to any sights you've missed so far.

If you've got five or more days, consider some of these tempting destinations...

Beyond Budapest

Eger, at the heart of a popular wine region and packed with offbeat sights, is an easy day trip from Budapest (about 2 hours by train or bus each way). **Pécs,** with a gorgeously colorful streetscape and engaging sightseeing, is a bit farther away (3 hours by train), but arguably even more interesting. Roughly between Budapest and Vienna, the small town of **Sopron** (historic and charming) and the Slovak capital of **Bratislava** (big, bustling, and on the move) are both worthy stopovers. Each of these is covered in its own chapter. While any of these could be done as long day trips from Budapest, it's much more satisfying to spend the night (especially in Eger and Pécs).

The Day Trips from Budapest chapter covers excursions that are less appealing than the farther-flung towns mentioned above—but easier to do in a day from Budapest: The **Danube Bend** comprises three towns north of Budapest: the charming, Balkan-flavored artists' colony of **Szentendre;** the castle at **Visegrád;** and Hungary's most impressive church at **Esztergom.** (The Danube Bend is also doable by car on the way to Bratislava or Vienna.) To the east are **Gödöllő Palace** (dripping with Habsburg history, and a very easy side-trip from Budapest), the **Lázár Lovaspark** traditional horse show (a must for horse lovers, or for anyone wanting a peek at a Hungarian farm), and the more distant village of **Hollókő,** an open-air folk museum come to life (by car, these two

Budapest Essentials

English	Hungarian	Pronounced
Budapest	*Budapest*	BOO-daw-pesht
Pest Town Center	*Belváros*	BEHL-vah-rohsh
Pest's Leopold Town	*Lipótváros*	LEE-poht-vah-rohsh
Pest Town Center's Main Pedestrian Street	*Váci utca*	VAHT-see OOT-zaw
Pest Town Center's Main Square	*Vörösmarty tér*	VEW-rewsh-mar-tee tehr
Pest's Grand Boulevard	*Andrássy út*	AWN-drah-shee oot
Heroes' Square	*Hősök tere*	HEW-shewk TEH-reh
City Park	*Városliget*	VAH-rohsh-lee-geht
(Buda) Castle	*(Budai) Vár*	BOO-die vahr
Castle Hill	*Várhegy*	VAHR-hayj
Buda's "Water Town"	*Vízíváros*	VEE-zee-vah-rohsh
Chain Bridge	*Széchenyi Lánchíd*	SAY-chehn-yee LAHNTS-heed
Liberty Bridge (green, a.k.a. Franz Josef Bridge)	*Szabadság híd*	SAW-bawd-shahg heed
Elisabeth Bridge (white, modern)	*Erzsébet híd*	EHR-zay-beht heed
Margaret Bridge (crosses Margaret Island)	*Margit híd*	MAWR-geet heed
Danube River	*Duna*	DOO-naw
Eastern Train Station	*Keleti pályaudvar*	KEH-leh-tee PAH-yuh-uhd-vawr
Western Train Station	*Nyugati pályaudvar*	NYOO-gaw-tee PAH-yuh-uhd-vawr
Southern Train Station	*Déli pályaudvar*	DAY-lee PAH-yuh-uhd-vawr
Suburban Train System	*HÉV*	hayv

can be combined into a single rewarding day, and you'll be back in Budapest in time for dinner).

Budapest Overview

TOURIST INFORMATION

The city of Budapest runs several TIs (www.budapestinfo.hu, tel. 1/438-8080). The main branch is a few steps from the M2 and M3 Métró station at **Deák tér** (daily 8:00-20:00, free Wi-Fi, Sütő utca 2, near the McDonald's, district V). Other locations include **Franz Liszt Square,** a block south of the Oktogon on Andrássy út (daily 12:00-20:00, free Wi-Fi, Liszt Ferenc tér 11, district VII, M1: Oktogon, tel. 1/322-4098), **Heroes' Square** (in the ice rink building facing Vajdahunyad Castle, Sun-Thu 10:00-18:00, Fri-Sat 10:00-20:00), in a small kiosk just inside the main entrance of the **Great Market Hall** (Mon 6:00-17:00, Tue-Fri 6:00-18:00, Sat 6:00-15:00, closed Sun), and in both terminals at the **airport** (TI at Terminal 2A open daily 8:00-22:00; TI at Terminal 2B open daily 10:00-22:00). The helpfulness of Budapest's TIs can vary, but all offer a nice variety of free, useful publications, including a good city map, the information-packed *Budapest Guide* booklet, and various events planners: *Budapest Panorama, Servus,* and the youthful *Budapest Funzine.* At any TI, you can collect a pile of other free brochures (for sights, bus tours, and more) and buy a Budapest Card.

Sightseeing Passes: The **Budapest Card** includes free use of all public transportation, free walking tours of Buda and Pest, a handful of free admissions to lesser museums (including the Budapest History Museum and Hungarian National Gallery), and 10-50 percent discounts on many other major museums and attractions (4,500 Ft/24 hours, 7,500 Ft/48 hours, 8,900 Ft/72 hours; includes handy 100-page booklet with maps, updated hours, and brief museum descriptions; www.budapest-card.com). If you take advantage of the included walking tours, the Budapest Card can be a good value for a very busy sightseer—do the arithmetic.

TourInform: The Hungarian National Tourist Office operates a small TI on Castle Hill. It's located in the circular, white building in the park across from Matthias Church (daily 9:00-19:00, or 10:00-18:00 in winter).

Discover Budapest: Ben Frieday, an American in love with Budapest (and one of its women), runs this agency, which specializes in answering questions Americans have about Budapest and Hungary. It's conveniently located near Andrássy út, behind the Opera House at Lázár utca 16 (district VI, M1: Opera). At their office, you can get online (150 Ft/15 minutes at a terminal, free Wi-Fi) or rent a bike (open daily 9:00-20:00, until 19:00 Nov-March, tel. 1/269-3843, mobile 0620-929-7506, www.discoverbudapest. com). This location is also the meeting point for Ben's various tours: Absolute Walking Tours and Yellow Zebra bike and Segway tours (all described later, under "Tours in Budapest").

ARRIVAL IN BUDAPEST

For a comprehensive rundown on Budapest's train stations, bus stations, airport, driving tips, and boat connections, see the Budapest Connections chapter.

HELPFUL HINTS

Rip-Offs: Budapest feels—and is—safe, especially for a city of its size. While there's little risk of violent crime, and I've rarely had someone try to rip me off here, you might run into a petty crook or two (such as con artists or pickpockets). As in any big city, it's especially important to secure your valuables and wear a money belt in crowded and touristy places, particularly on the Metró and in trams. Keep your wits about you and refuse to be bullied or distracted.

Restaurants on the Váci utca shopping street are notorious for overcharging tourists. Here or anywhere in Budapest, don't eat at a restaurant that doesn't list prices on the menu, and always check your bill carefully. Increasingly, restaurants are adding a (legitimate) service charge of 10 to 12 percent to your bill; if you don't notice this, you might accidentally double-tip (for more on tipping, see page 482).

If you're a male in a touristy area and a gorgeous local girl takes a liking to you, avoid her. She's a *konzumlány* ("consumption girl"), and the foreplay going on here will climax in your grand rip-off. You'll wind up at her "favorite bar," with astronomical prices enforced by a burly bouncer.

Budapest's biggest crooks? Unscrupulous cabbies. For tips on outsmarting them, see "Getting Around Budapest—By Taxi" on page 41. Bottom line: Locals *always* call for a cab, rather than hail one on the street or at a taxi stand. If you're not comfortable making the call yourself, ask your hotel or restaurant to call for you.

Emergency Numbers: The default emergency telephone number in Hungary is 112. You can also dial 107 for police, 104 for ambulance, or 105 for fire.

Medical Help: Near Buda's Széll Kálmán tér, **FirstMed Centers** is a private, pricey, English-speaking clinic (by appointment or urgent care, call first, Hattyú utca 14, 5th floor, district I, M2: Széll Kálmán tér, tel. 1/224-9090, www.firstmedcenters. com). Hospitals *(kórház)* are scattered around the city.

Pharmacies: The helpful **Dorottya Gyógyszertár** pharmacy is dead-center in Pest, between Vörösmarty and Széchenyi squares. Because they cater to clientele from nearby international hotels, they have a useful directory that lists the Hungarian equivalent of US prescription medicines (Mon-Fri 8:00-20:00, closed Sat-Sun, Dorottya utca 13, district V, M1: Vörösmarty tér, for location see map on page 237, tel. 1/317-2374). Each district has one 24-hour pharmacy (these should be noted outside the entrance to any pharmacy).

Calling Mobile Numbers: In Hungary, mobile numbers (generally beginning with 0620, 0630, or 0670) are dialed differently, depending on where you're calling from. I've listed them as you'd dial them from a fixed line within Hungary. From another country, or from a mobile phone in Hungary, omit the initial 06, and replace it with the international access code (011 from the US, 00 from Europe, or + on a mobile phone), then 36, then the number. For more tips on calling, see page 487.

Train Tickets: Ticket-buying lines can be long at train stations, particularly for long-distance international trains. If you want to buy your ticket in advance, **MÁV** (Hungarian Railways) has a very convenient ticket office right in the heart of downtown Pest. They generally speak English and sell tickets for no additional fee (Mon-Fri 9:00-18:00, closed Sat-Sun, just up from the Chain Bridge and across from Erzsébet tér at József Attila utca 16, district V, M1: Vörösmarty tér, for location see map on page 237).

Internet Access: Most hotels offer Wi-Fi or cable Internet (usually free, sometimes for a fee). Internet cafés are common—just look for signs or ask your hotel. In Pest, I like **Discover Budapest,** with fast access and good prices (free Wi-Fi, Internet terminals-150 Ft/15 minutes; see "Discover Budapest" listing on page 30).

Post Offices: These are marked with a smart green *posta* logo (usually open Mon-Fri 8:00-18:00, Sat 8:00-12:00, closed Sun).

Laundry: The handiest option for full service is **Laundromat-Mosómata,** just behind the Opera House (2,400 Ft to wash and dry a big load, generally takes 3-5 hours, Mon-Fri 10:00-18:00, Sat 10:00-14:00, closed Sun; walk straight behind the Opera House and turn right on Ó utca, then look left for signs at #24—you'll go up the main stairs and turn left to find it in the arcade; district VI, M1: Opera, for location see map on page 233, mobile 0670-340-0478). Two self-service launderettes are in the Jewish Quarter/nightlife zone (both charge 800 Ft to wash, 800 Ft to dry): **Laundry Budapest,** a humble but functional option with lots of machines tucked behind an Internet café, sits at the far end of this area, near the Blaha

Tonight We're Gonna Party Like It's 1896

Visitors to Budapest need only remember one date: 1896. For the millennial celebration of their ancestors' arrival in Europe,

 Hungarians threw a huge blow-out party. In the thousand years between 896 and 1896, the Magyars had gone from being a nomadic Central Asian tribe that terrorized the Continent to sharing the throne of one of the most successful empires Europe had ever seen.

On the morning of New Year's Day, 1896, church bells clanged endlessly through the streets of Buda and Pest. In June of that year, the Habsburg royal couple Franz Josef and Sisi were two of the 5.7 million people who came to enjoy the Hungarian National Exhibition at City Park. At Vérmező Park (behind Castle Hill), whole oxen were grilled on the spit to feed commoners.

Budapest used its millennial celebration as an excuse to build monuments and buildings appropriate for the co-capital of a huge empire, including these landmarks:

- **Heroes' Square** and the **Millennium Monument**
- **Vajdahunyad Castle** (in City Park)
- The riverside **Parliament** building (96 meters tall, with 96 steps at the main entry)
- **St. István's Basilica** (also 96 meters tall)
- The M1/yellow Metró line, a.k.a. *Földalatti* ("Underground")—the first subway on the Continent
- The **Great Market Hall** (and four other market halls)
- **Andrássy út** and most of the fine buildings lining it
- The **Opera House**
- A complete rebuilding of **Matthias Church** (on Castle Hill)
- The **Fishermen's Bastion** decorative terrace (by Matthias Church)
- The green **Liberty Bridge** (then called Franz Josef Bridge, in honor of the ruling Habsburg emperor)

Ninety-six is the key number in Hungary—even the national anthem (when sung at the proper tempo) takes 96 seconds. But after all this fuss, it's too bad that the date was wrong: A commission—convened to establish the exact year of the Magyars' debut—determined it happened in 895. But city leaders knew they'd never make an 1895 deadline, and requested the finding be changed to 896.

Lujza tér Metró stop. If you ask nicely and tip them, they may be willing to put it in the dryer and fold it for you (daily 9:00-24:00, last wash at 22:00, Dohány utca 37, tel. 1/781-0098, www.laundrybudapest.hu). **Bazar Hostel,** closer to the Great Synagogue, has just a few machines downstairs from their reception (open daily 24 hours, free Wi-Fi, Dohány utca 22).

English Bookstores: The **Central European University Bookshop** offers the best selection anywhere of scholarly books about this region (and beyond). They also sell guidebooks, literary fiction, and some popular American magazines—all in English (Mon-Fri 10:00-19:00, Sat 11:00-15:00, closed Sun, just down the street in front of St. István's Basilica at Zrínyi utca 12, district V, for location see map on page 237, tel. 1/327-3096).

Bestsellers has a fine selection of new books, mostly in English; it's just around the corner from CEU Bookshop, near St. István's Basilica (Mon-Fri 9:00-18:30, Sat 10:00-17:00, Sun 10:00-16:00, Október 6 utca 11, tel. 1/312-1295).

The **Discover Budapest** office sells a wide range of secondhand books at its location just behind the Opera House at Lázár utca 16 (daily 9:00-20:00, until 19:00 Nov-March, see listing on page 30).

Local Guidebook: András Török's fun, idiosyncratic *Budapest: A Critical Guide* is the best guidebook by a local writer. Its quirky walking tours do a nice job of capturing the city's spirit (available in English at some souvenir stands and bookshops).

Bike Rental: Budapest, whose streets are congested with traffic, isn't the easiest city for bicycling—though things are improving, with more and more bike lanes being included in renovated urban zones. Those comfortable with urban cycling may find that it helps them zip around the city more smoothly. You can rent a bike at **Yellow Zebra,** part of Discover Budapest (2,000-3,000 Ft/all day, 3,000-4,500 Ft/24 hours, price depends on type of bike; see "Discover Budapest" listing on page 30).

Budapest also has a subsidized borrow-a-bike system called **Bubi** (for "**Bu**dapest **Bi**kes"). Bike stations are scattered throughout the Town Center and adjoining areas; you can pick a bike up at any station, and drop it off at any other—making this handy for one-way trips. It's free to use a bike for 30 minutes or less, then costs 500 Ft for each 30 additional minutes. But it requires either a membership card (9,450 Ft for a year) or a short-term "ticket" (500 Ft/24 hours, 1,000 Ft/72 hours, 2,000 Ft/week, plus a 25,000-Ft deposit on your credit card for the duration of the ticket; you can buy a ticket at www.bkk.hu/bubi or at many docking stations; your PIN is sent to your mobile phone). If you'll be using a bike for short rides several times throughout your visit, this system is worth considering. You can get all of the details at www.bkk.hu/bubi, or ask at the TI.

Drivers: Friendly, English-speaking **Gábor Balázs** can drive you around the city or into the surrounding countryside (4,000 Ft/hour, 3-hour minimum in city, 4-hour minimum in country-side—good for a Danube Bend excursion, mobile 0620-936-4317, bgabor.e@gmail.com). **Zsolt Gál** is also available for transfers and side-trips, and specializes in helping people track down Jewish sites in the surrounding areas (mobile 0670-452-4900, forma111562@gmail.com). Note that these are drivers, not tour guides. For tour guides who can drive you to outlying sights, see "Tours in Budapest," later.

Best Views: Budapest is a city of marvelous vistas. Some of the best are from the Citadella fortress (high on Gellért Hill), the promenade in front of the Royal Palace and the Fishermen's Bastion on top of Castle Hill, and the embankments or many bridges spanning the Danube (especially the Chain Bridge). Don't forget the view from the tour boats on the Danube—particularly lovely at night.

Updates to this Book: For updates to this book, check www.ricksteves.com/update.

GETTING AROUND BUDAPEST

Budapest sprawls. Connecting your sightseeing just on foot is tedious and unnecessary. It's crucial to get comfortable with the

public transportation system—Metró lines, trams, buses, trolley buses, and boats that can take you virtually anywhere you want to go. Budapest's well-planned cityscape and thoughtfully coordinated transit network combine to make it one of

the easiest big European cities to zip around. Budapest's transit system website, www.bkk.hu, offers a useful route-planner and a downloadable app for on-the-go transit info.

Tickets: The same tickets work for the entire system. Buy them at kiosks, Metró ticket windows, or machines (with English instructions). As it can be frustrating to find a ticket machine (especially when you see your tram or bus approaching), I generally invest in a multi-day ticket to have the freedom of hopping on at will.

Your options are as follows:

ORIENTATION

ORIENTATION

Budapest Transit

Not to Scale

- --- Metró Line 1
- — Metró Line 2
- ≡ Metró Line 3
- --- Metró Line 4
- ▨ Danube River
- — Tram w/Route #'s
- ···· Bus w/Route #'s
- ⊦⊦⊦ HÉV Rail
- ⊦⊦ Rail
- ⊦⊦⊦ Funicular
- ⭢ Public Riverboat

- **Single ticket** (*vonaljegy,* for a ride of up to an hour on any means of transit; transfers allowed only within the Metró system)—350 Ft (or 450 Ft if bought from the driver)
- **Short single Metró ride** (*Metrószakaszjegy,* 3 stops or fewer on the Metró)—300 Ft
- **Transfer ticket** (*átszállójegy*—allowing up to 90 minutes, including one transfer between Metró and bus)—530 Ft
- **Pack of 10 single tickets** *(10 darabos gyűjtőjegy),* which can be shared—3,000 Ft (that's 300 Ft per ticket, saving you 50 Ft per ticket; note that these must stay together as a single pack—they can't be sold separately)
- Unlimited multi-day travel cards for Metró, bus, and tram,

including a **24-hour travelcard** (*24 órás jegy*, 1,650 Ft/24 hours), **72-hour travelcard** (*72 órás jegy*, 4,150 Ft/72 hours), and **seven-day travelcard** (*hetijegy*, 4,950 Ft/7 days)

• **24-hour group travel card** (*csoportos 24 órás jegy*, 3,300 Ft), covering up to five adults—a great deal for groups of three to five people

• The **Budapest Card**, which combines a multi-day ticket with sightseeing discounts (but it's generally a bad value—see page 30)

Always validate single-ride tickets as you enter the bus, tram, or Metró station (stick it in the elbow-high box). On older buses and trams that have little red validation boxes, stick your ticket in the black slot, then pull the slot toward you to punch holes in your ticket. Multi-day tickets need be validated only once. The stern-looking people with blue-and-green armbands waiting as you enter or exit the Metró want to see your validated ticket. Cheaters are fined 6,000 Ft on the spot, and you'll be surprised how often you're checked—they seem to be stationed at virtually every Metró escalator. All public transit runs from 4:30 in the morning until 23:10.

New Transit Cards: Likely starting in 2016 or 2017, Budapest plans to phase in pay-as-you-go cards, which will replace the paper tickets described previously. As is now common in many major cities worldwide (from London's Oyster Card to New York's Metrocard), public transit passengers will buy a card and load it up with credit, which will be deducted according to how long they ride—so they'll need to "touch in" and "touch out" as they enter and exit the system. For short-time tourists, individual electronic "smart paper" tickets will also be available. See www.bkk.hu for the latest.

Handy Terms: *Á ___ félé* means "in the direction of ___." *Megálló* means "stop" or "station," and *Végállomás* means "end of the line."

By Metró

Riding Budapest's efficient Metró, you really feel like you're down in the guts of the city. There are four working lines:

• **M1/yellow**—The first underground rail line on the Continent, this shallow line runs beneath Andrássy út from the center to City Park (see "Millennium Underground of 1896" on page 144).

• **M2/red**—Built during the communist days, it's 115 feet deep and designed to double as a bomb shelter. This line has undergone a thorough renovation, leaving its stations new and shiny. Going under the Danube to Buda,

ORIENTATION

the M2 connects the Déli/Southern train station, Széll Kálmán tér (where you catch bus #16, #16A, or #116 to the top of Castle Hill), Batthyány tér (Víziváros and the station where you catch the HÉV train to Óbuda or Szentendre), Kossuth tér (behind the Parliament), Astoria (near the Great Synagogue on the Small Boulevard), and the Keleti/Eastern train station (where it crosses the M4/green line).

• **M3/blue**—This line makes a broad, boomerang-shaped swoop north to south on the Pest side. It's noticeably older, but slated for renovation soon. Key stops include the Nyugati/Western train station, Ferenciek tere (in the heart of Pest's Town Center), Kálvin tér (near the Great Market Hall and many recommended hotels; this is also where it crosses the M4/green line), and Corvinnegyed (near the Holocaust Memorial Center).

• **M4/green**—The newest line (opened in 2014) runs from southern Buda to the Gellért Baths, under the Danube to Fővám tér (behind the Great Market Hall) and Kálvin tér (where it crosses the M3/blue line), then up to Rákóczi tér (on the Grand Boulevard) and the Keleti/Eastern train station (where it crosses the M2/red line). Many of its stations boast boldly modern, waste-of-space concrete architecture that's eye-opening to simply stroll through; the one at Gellért tér has a thermal spring-fed waterfall coursing past the main staircase.

The three original lines—M1, M2, and M3—cross only once: at the **Deák tér** stop (often signed as *Deák Ferenc tér*) in the heart of Pest, near where Andrássy út begins.

Aside from the historic M1 line, most Metró stations are at intersections of ring roads and other major thoroughfares. You'll usually exit the Metró into a confusing underpass packed with kiosks, fast-food stands, and makeshift markets. Directional signs (listing which streets, addresses, and tram or bus stops are near each exit) help you find the right exit. Or do the prairie-dog routine: Surface to get your bearings, then head back underground to find the correct stairs up to your destination.

Metró stops themselves are usually very well-marked, with a list of upcoming stops on the wall behind the tracks. Digital clocks either count down to the next train's arrival, or count up from the previous train's departure; either way, you'll rarely wait more than five minutes during peak times.

You'll ride very long, steep, fast-moving escalators to access most Metró stops (except on the shallow M1 line). Hang on tight, enjoy the gale as trains below shoot through the tunnels…and don't make yourself dizzy by trying to read the Burger King ads.

By HÉV

Budapest's suburban rail system, or HÉV (pronounced "hayv," stands for Helyiérdekű Vasút, literally "Railway of Local Interest"), branches off to the outskirts and beyond. Of the four lines, tourists are likely to use only two: the **Szentendre line** (H5/purple), which begins at Batthyány tér in Buda's Víziváros neighborhood (at the M2/red line stop of the same name) and heads through Óbuda to the charming Danube Bend town of Szentendre; and the **Gödöllő line** (H8/pink), which begins at Örs vezér tere (in outer Pest, at the end of the M2/red line) and heads to the town of Gödöllő, with its Habsburg palace. (Szentendre and Gödöllő are both described in the Day Trips from Budapest chapter.)

The HÉV is covered by standard transit tickets and passes for rides within the city of Budapest (such as to Óbuda). But if going beyond—such as to Szentendre or Gödöllő—you'll have to pay more. Tell the ticket-seller (or punch into the machine) where you're going, and you'll be issued the proper ticket. If you have a transit pass, you'll pay only the difference.

By Tram

Budapest's trams are handy and frequent, taking you virtually anywhere the Metró doesn't. Here are some trams you might use (note that all of these run in both directions):

Tram **#2:** Follows Pest's Danube embankment, parallel to Váci utca. From north to south, it begins at the Great Boulevard (near Margaret Bridge) and stops on either side of the Parliament (north side near the visitors center/Országház stop, as well as south side near the Kossuth tér Metró stop), Széchenyi István tér and the Chain Bridge, Vigadó tér, and the Great Market Hall. From there, it continues southward past the Bálna cultural center to the Petőfi Bridge, then all the way to the "Millennium City" complex near Rákóczi Bridge.

Trams **#19** and **#41:** Run along Buda's Danube embankment from Batthyány tér (with an M2/red Metró station, and HÉV trains to Óbuda and Szentendre). From Batthyány tér, these trams run (north to south) through Víziváros to Clark Ádám tér (the bottom of the Castle Hill funicular, near the stop for bus #16 up to Castle Hill; get off here and walk a few minutes to take the Várkert Bazár grand staircase up to the Royal Palace), then under Elisabeth Bridge (get off at Döbrentei tér stop for the Rudas Baths) and around the base of Gellért Hill to the Gellért Hotel and Baths (Gellért tér stop).

Trams **#4** and **#6:** Zip around Pest's Great Boulevard ring road

(Nagykörút), connecting Nyugati/Western train station and the Oktogon with the southern tip of Margaret Island and Buda's Széll Kálmán tér (with M2/red Metró station).

Trams #47 and #49: Connect the Gellért Baths in Buda with Pest's Small Boulevard ring road (Kiskörút), with stops at the Great Market Hall, the National Museum, the Great Synagogue (Astoria stop), and Deák tér (end of the line).

By Bus and Trolley Bus

I use the Metró and trams for most of my Budapest commuting. But some buses are useful for shortcuts within the city, or for reaching outlying sights. Note that the transit company draws a distinction between gas-powered "buses" and electric "trolley buses" (which are powered by overhead cables). Unless otherwise noted, you can assume the following are standard buses:

Buses #16, #16A, and #116: All head up to the top of Castle Hill (get off at Dísz tér, in the middle of the hill—the closest stop to the Royal Palace). You can catch any of these three at Széll Kálmán tér (M2/red Metró line). When coming from the other direction, bus #16 makes several handy stops in Pest (Deák tér, Széchenyi István tér), then crosses the Chain Bridge for more stops in Buda (including Clark Ádám tér, at Buda end of Chain Bridge on its way up to the castle).

Trolley buses #70 and #78: Zip from near the Opera House (intersection of Andrássy út and Nagymező utca) to the Parliament (Kossuth tér).

Bus #178: Goes from Keleti/Eastern train station to central Pest (Astoria and Ferenciek tere Metró stops), then over the Elisabeth Bridge to Buda.

Bus #26: Begins at Nyugati/Western train station and heads around the Great Boulevard to Margaret Island, making several stops along the island.

Bus #27: Runs from either side of Gellért Hill to just below the Citadella fortress at the hill's peak (Búsuló Juhász stop).

Bus #200E: Connects Liszt Ferenc Airport to the Kőbánya-Kispest M3/blue Metró station.

Buses #101 and #150: Run from Keletenföld (the end of the line for the M4/green Metró line) to Memento Park.

Buses #54 and #55: Head from Boráros tér (at the Pest end of the Petőfi Bridge) to the Ecseri Flea Market.

By Boat

Budapest's public transit authority operates a system of Danube riverboats *(hajójárat)* that connect strategic locations throughout the city. The riverboat system has drawbacks: Frequency is sparse (1-2/hour on weekdays, hourly on weekends; off-season weekdays only, hourly), and it's typically slower than hopping on the Metró or a tram. But it's also a romantic, cheap alternative to pricey riverboat cruises, and can be a handy way to connect some sightseeing points.

A 750-Ft ticket covers any trip; on weekdays, it's also covered by a 24-hour, 72-hour, or seven-day travelcards (but not by the Budapest Card; on weekends, you have to buy a ticket regardless of your pass).

Lines #D11 (on weekdays) and #D13 (on weekends) run in both directions through the city, including these stops within downtown Budapest:

• **Margitsziget/Szállodák** and **Margitsziget/Centenáriumi emlékmű,** at the northern and southern ends of Margaret Island (respectively);

• **Jászai Mari tér,** at the Pest end of Margaret Bridge;

• **Batthyány tér,** on the Buda embankment in Víziváros;

• **Kossuth Lajos tér,** near the Parliament on the Pest side;

• **Várkert Bazár,** at the base of the grand entrance staircase to Buda Castle;

• **Petőfi tér,** on the Pest embankment next to the Danube Legenda riverboats (dock 8); and

• **Szent Gellért tér,** at the Buda end of Liberty Bridge, next to the Gellért Baths.

Some stops may be closed if the river level gets very low; as this is a relatively new service, expect changes. For details, see www.bkk.hu.

By Taxi

Budapest's public transportation is good enough that you probably won't need to take many taxis. But if you do, you may run into a dishonest driver. Arm yourself with knowledge: Budapest has recently introduced stringent new regulations. Official taxis must be painted yellow and black, and must charge identical rates, regardless of company: a drop rate of 450 Ft, and then 280 Ft/kilometer, plus 70 Ft/minute for wait time. (The prices go up at night, between 22:00 and 6:00 in the morning.) Prices are per ride, not per passenger. A 10 percent tip is expected. A typical ride within central Budapest shouldn't run more than 2,000 Ft. Despite what some slimy cabbies may tell you, there's no legitimate extra charge for crossing the river.

Instead of hailing a taxi on the street, do as the locals do and call a cab from a reputable company—it's cheaper and you're more

ORIENTATION

likely to get an honest driver. Try **City Taxi** (tel. 1/211-1111), **Taxi 6x6** (tel. 1/266-6666), or **Főtaxi** (tel. 1/222-2222). Most dispatchers speak English, but if you're uncomfortable calling, you can ask your hotel or restaurant to call for you.

Many "cabs" you'd hail on the streets are there only to prey on rich, green tourists. Avoid unmarked taxis (nicknamed "hyenas" by locals), as well as any cabs that wait at tourist spots and train stations. If you do wave down a cab on the street, choose one that's yellow and black, and marked with an official company logo and telephone number (otherwise, it's not official). Ask for a rough estimate before you get in—if it doesn't sound reasonable, walk away. If you wind up being dramatically overcharged for a ride, simply pay what you think is fair and go inside. If the driver follows you (unlikely), your hotel receptionist will defend you.

On a recent trip to Budapest, I arrived late at night at the Keleti/Eastern train station. The lone, unmarked taxi out front wanted 4,000 Ft for the ride to my hotel. Following my own advice, I called a legitimate company and ordered a taxi from the English-speaking dispatcher. A few minutes later, an honest cabbie picked me up and whisked me to my hotel...for 1,500 Ft.

Tours in Budapest

BY FOOT
▲▲▲Local Guides
Budapest has an abundance of enthusiastic, hardworking young guides who speak perfect English and enjoy showing off their city.

Given the reasonable fees and efficient use of your time, hiring your own personal expert is an excellent value. While they might be available last-minute, it's better to reserve in advance by email. I have three favorites, any of whom can do half-day or full-day tours, and can also drive you into the countryside (€90/4 hours, €150/8 hours): **Péter Pölczman** is an exceptional guide who really puts you in touch with the Budapest you came to see (mobile 0620-926-0557, www.budapestyourself. com, polczman@freestart.hu, or peter@budapestyourself.com). **Andrea Makkay** has professional polish and a smart understanding of what visitors really want to experience (mobile 0620-962-9363, www.privateguidebudapest.com, andrea.makkay@gmail. com—arrange details by email; if Andrea is busy, she can arrange to send you with another guide). And **George Farkas** is particularly well-attuned to the hip, stylish side of this fast-changing metropolis (mobile 0670-335-8030, georgefarkas@gmail.com).

Elemér Boreczky, a semi-retired university professor, leads walking tours with a soft-spoken, scholarly approach, emphasizing Budapest's rich tapestry of architecture as "frozen music." Elemér is ideal if you want a walking graduate-level seminar about the easy-to-miss nuances of this grand city (€25/hour, tel. 1/386-0885, mobile 0630-491-1389, www.culturaltours.mlap.hu, boreczky.elemer@gmail.com).

Péter, Andrea, George, and Elemér have all been indispensable help to me in writing and updating this book.

Walking Tours

Budapest has several backpacker-oriented walking-tour companies. While most travelers can get by with the self-guided walks and tours in this book—and I highly recommend hiring one of the excellent local guides listed previously—these outfits are handy for those who want a live guide without paying for a private tour.

Budapest's best-established outfit is **Absolute Walking Tours,** run by Oregonian Ben Frieday and offering tours that are informal but informative. Travelers with this book get a 500-Ft discount on any tour booked in person; or, if you book online, you get a discount (5-30 percent off the full price, depending on tour; enter coupon code "RICK"). The Absolute Walk gives you a good overview of Budapest (4,500 Ft, daily at 10:00, 3.5 hours). The Hammer & Sickle Tour begins at a mini-museum of communist artifacts, then takes you out into the streets to see sites related to the 1956 Uprising (4,500 Ft, 2-3/week, 3.5 hours). The Hungro Gastro Food and Wine Tasting Tour gives you information on traditional recipes and ingredients, and a chance to taste several specialties at the Great Market Hall and nearby specialty shops (21,000 Ft, 6/week, 3.5 hours, reservations required). In the evening, consider the Night Stroll, which includes a one-hour cruise on the Danube (11,000 Ft, 4/week March-Oct, 2/week Nov-Feb, 3 hours). They also offer nightlife tours, pub crawls, a Christmas Market tour (Dec only), and an "Alternative Budapest" tour that visits artsy, edgy, off-the-beaten path parts of town (for details, see www.absolutetours.com or contact the Discover Budapest office at tel. 1/269-3843, mobile 0620-929-7506). Most tours depart from the Discover Budapest office behind the Opera House (see the "Discover Budapest" listing on page 30); however, the food-and-wine tour meets at the Great Market Hall, and the "Alternative" tour departs from the blocky, green-domed Lutheran church at Deák tér, near the Métró station. Note: These prices are for 2015, and may be slightly higher in 2016.

You'll also see various companies advertising **"free" walking tours.** While there is no set fee to take these tours, guides are paid only if you tip (they're hoping for 2,000 Ft/person). They offer a basic 2.5-hour introduction to the city (departing daily at 10:30, and again at 14:00 or 14:30), as well as itineraries focusing on the communist era and the Jewish Quarter. Because they're working for tips, the generally good-quality, certified guides are highly motivated to impress their customers. But because the "free" tag attracts very large groups, these tours tend to be less intimate than paid tours, and (especially the introductory tours) take a once-over-lightly "infotainment" approach. Still, these "free" tours get rave reviews from travelers and offer an inexpensive introduction to the city. As this scene is continually evolving, look for local fliers to learn about the options and meeting points.

BY BOAT
▲▲Danube Boat Tours

Cruising the Danube, while touristy, is a fun and convenient way to get a feel for the city's grand layout. The most established company, **Danube Legenda**, is a class act that runs well-maintained, glassed-in panoramic boats day and night. All cruises include a free drink and romantic headphone commentary. By night, TV monitors show the interiors of the great buildings as you float by.

I've negotiated a special discount with Legenda for my readers (but you must book directly, in person, and ask for the Rick Steves price). By **day,** the one-hour "Duna Bella" cruise costs 3,120 Ft for Rick Steves readers; if you want, you can hop off at Margaret Island to explore on your own, then return after 1.5 hours on a later cruise (6/day May-Aug, 5/day April and Sept, 4/day March and Oct, 1/day Nov-Feb—but no Margaret Island stop in winter). By **night,** the one-hour "Danube Legend" cruise (with no Margaret Island visit) costs 4,400 Ft for Rick Steves readers (4/day March-Oct, 1/day Nov-Feb). On weekends, it's smart to call ahead and reserve a spot for the evening cruises. Note: These special prices are for 2015, and may be slightly higher in 2016.

The Legenda dock is in front of the Marriott on the Pest embankment (find pedestrian access under tram tracks at downriver end of Vigadó tér, district V, M1: Vörösmarty tér, tel. 1/317-2203, www.legenda.hu). Competing river-cruise companies are nearby, but given the discount, Legenda offers the best value.

ORIENTATION

Margaret Island Shuttle

If you just want to get out on the water, but don't care for a full tour with commentary, consider Mahart's cheap hop from Vigadó tér to Margaret Island (800 Ft one-way, 1,500 Ft round-trip, 4/day, 45 minutes, June-Aug daily, Sept and May Sat-Sun only, none Oct-April, boat dock directly in front of Vigadó tér). Mahart's standard sightseeing cruises pale in comparison to Legenda's.

ON WHEELS
Bike and Segway Tours

Various companies offer **bike tours** around the city; as the most interesting part of town (Pest) is quite flat and spread out, this is a good way to see the place. The best-established option is Yellow Zebra, a sister company of Absolute Walking Tours (8,000 Ft, 3.5 hours; April-Oct daily at 11:00; additional shorter tour June-Aug daily at 17:00 for 6,500 Ft; Nov and March only Fri-Sun at 11:00—cancelled in below-freezing temperatures; no tours Dec-Feb).

The same company also offers tours of the city by **Segway** (a stand-up electric scooter). Although expensive, it's a unique way to see Budapest while trying out a Segway. Each tour begins with a 30-minute training; my readers get a 15 percent discount when booking online, or 500 Ft off if booking in person (18,000 Ft/2.5 hours, daily at 9:30 and 15:00, also an evening tour April-Oct daily at 18:00). You can reserve and prepay online (www.yellowzebratours.com, enter coupon code "RICK").

The bike and Segway tours both meet at the Discover Budapest office behind the Opera House (see page 30; tel. 1/269-3843, mobile 0620-929-7506, www.yellowzebratours.com).

Bus Tours

Various companies run hop-on, hop-off bus tours, which make 12 to 16 stops as they cruise around town on a two-hour loop with headphone commentary (generally 5,000/24 hours, 6,000 Ft/48 hours). Most companies also offer a wide variety of other tours, including dinner boat cruises and trips to the Danube Bend. Pick up fliers about all these tours at the TI or in your hotel lobby.

RiverRide

This company offers a bus tour with a twist: Its amphibious bus can actually float on the Danube River, effectively making this a combination bus-and-boat tour. The live guide imparts dry English commentary as you roll (and float). While it's a fun gimmick, the entry ramp into the river (facing the north end of Margaret Island) is far from the most scenic stretch, and the river portion is slow-paced—showing you the same Margaret Island scenery twice, plus a circle in front of the Parliament. The Danube Legenda boat tours, described earlier, give you more scenic bang for your buck (7,500 Ft, 2 hours, 4/day April-Oct, 3/day Nov-March, departs from Széchenyi tér near Gresham Palace, tel. 1/332-2555, www.riverride.com).

TOUR PACKAGES FOR STUDENTS

Andy Steves (Rick's son) runs **WSA Europe,** offering three-day and longer guided and unguided packages—including accommodations, sightseeing, and unique local experiences—for budget travelers across 11 top European cities, including Budapest (from €99, see www.wsaeurope.com for details).

SIGHTS IN BUDAPEST

The sights listed in this chapter are arranged by neighborhood for handy sightseeing. When you see a ✪ in a listing, it means the sight is covered in much more depth in one of my walks or self-guided tours. This is why Budapest's most important attractions get the least coverage in this chapter—we'll explore them later in the book. For tips on sightseeing, see page 484.

Budapest boomed in the late 19th century, after it became the co-capital of the vast Habsburg Empire. Most of its finest buildings

(and top sights) date from this age. To appreciate an opulent interior—a Budapest experience worth ▲▲▲—I strongly recommend touring either the Parliament or the Opera House, depending on your interests. The Opera tour is more crowd-pleasing, while the Parliament tour is a bit drier (with a focus on history and parliamentary process)—but the spaces are even grander. Seeing both is also a fine option. "Honorable mentions" go to the interiors of St. István's Basilica, the Great Synagogue, New York Café, and both the Széchenyi and the Gellért Baths. This diversity—government and the arts, Christian and Jewish, coffee-drinkers and bathers—demonstrates how the shared prosperity of the late 19th century made it a Golden Age for a broad cross section of Budapest society.

The early 21st century has also been a boom time in Budapest. Many formerly dreary squares, parks, and streets have been refurbished, as have many museums. The latest plan is to create an ambitious "Museum Quarter" in City Park, which will be the new home to the National Gallery and museums of contemporary art (Ludwig collection), ethnography, photography, architecture, and music. However, this is unlikely to happen before 2018 (though construction may be underway when you visit—see www. ligetbudapest.org for details).

Remember, most sights in town offer a discount if you buy a Budapest Card (described on page 30). If you have a Budapest Card, always ask about discounts when you buy your ticket.

Pest

Most of Pest's top sights cluster in four neighborhoods: **Leopold Town** and the **Town Center** (together forming the city's "down-town," along the Danube); along **Andrássy út;** and at **Heroes' Square and City Park.** Each of these areas is covered by a sepa-rate self-guided walk (as noted by ✪ below). The **Jewish Quarter** is covered in the Great Synagogue and Jewish Quarter Tour chapter.

Several other excellent sights are not contained in these areas, and are covered in greater depth in this chapter: along the **Small Boulevard** (Kiskörút); along the **Great Boulevard** (Nagykörút); and along the boulevard called **Üllői út.**

LEOPOLD TOWN (LIPÓTVÁROS)

✪ Most of these sights are covered in detail in the Leopold Town Walk chapter. If a sight is covered in the walk, I've listed only its essentials here. These are listed north to south.

▲▲Hungarian Parliament (Országház)

With an impressive facade and an even more extravagant interior, the oversized Hungarian Parliament dominates the Danube riv-erbank. A hulking Neo-Gothic base topped by a soaring Neo-Renaissance dome, it's one of the city's top landmarks. Touring the building offers the chance to stroll through one of Budapest's best interiors. While the guides can be hit-or-miss, the dazzling building speaks for itself.

Cost and Hours: 5,200 Ft, half-price for EU citizens if you show your passport; English tours usually daily at 10:00, 12:00, 13:00, 14:00, and 15:00—but there can be more tours with de-mand, or fewer for no apparent reason, so confirm in advance; on Mon when parliament is in session—generally Sept-May—the only English tour is generally at 10:00 (and likely to sell out).

Getting There: Ride tram #2 to the Országház stop, which is next to the visitors center entrance (Kossuth tér 1, district V, M2: Kossuth tér).

Getting Tickets: Tickets come with an appointed tour time and often sell out. To ensure getting a space, it's worth paying an

extra 200 Ft per ticket to **book online** a day or two in advance at www.jegymester.hu. Select "Parliament Visit," then a date and time of an English tour, and be sure to specify "full price" (unless you have an EU passport). You'll have to create an account, but it's no problem to use a US address, telephone number, and credit card. Print out your eticket and show up at the Parliament visitors center at the appointed time (if you can't print it, show up early enough to have them print it out for you at the ticket desk—which can have long lines, especially in the morning).

If you didn't prebook a ticket, go to the **visitors center**—a modern, underground space at the northern end of the long Parliament building (look for the statue of a lion on a pillar)—and ask what the next available tour time is. While the first English tour of the day is almost always sold out with online tickets, later tours (especially in the afternoon) may have space. The visitors center and ticket desk are open Mon-Fri 8:00-18:00 (or until 16:00 in Nov-March), Sat-Sun 8:00-16:00, and only sell tickets for the same day—if booking in advance, you need to use the website.

Information: Tel. 1/441-4904, www.parlament.hu.

Visiting the Parliament: The visitors center has WCs, a café, a gift shop, and a Museum of the History of the Hungarian National Assembly. Once you have your ticket in hand, be at the security checkpoint inside the visitors center at least five minutes before your tour departure time.

On the 45-minute tour, your guide will explain the history and symbolism of the building's intricate decorations and offer a lesson in the Hungarian parliamentary system. You'll see dozens of bushy-mustachioed statues illustrating the occupations of workaday Hungarians through history, and find out why a really good speech was nicknamed a "Havana" by cigar-aficionado parliamentarians.

To begin the tour, you'll climb a 133-step staircase (with an elevator for those who need it) to see the building's monumental entryway and 96-step grand staircase—slathered in gold foil and frescoes, and bathed in shimmering stained-glass light. Then you'll gape up under the ornate gilded dome for a peek at the heavily guarded Hungarian crown (described on page 106), which is overlooked by statues of 16 great Hungarian monarchs, from St. István to Habsburg Empress Maria Theresa. Finally, you'll walk through

SIGHTS

Budapest at a Glance

In Pest

▲▲▲Széchenyi Baths Budapest's steamy soaking scene in City Park—the city's single best attraction. **Hours:** Swimming pool—daily 6:00-22:00, thermal bath—daily 6:00-19:00. See page 63.

▲▲Hungarian Parliament Vast riverside government center with remarkable interior. **Hours:** English tours usually daily at 10:00, 12:00, 13:00, 14:00, and 15:00. See page 48.

▲▲Great Market Hall Colorful Old World mall with produce, eateries, souvenirs, and great people-watching. **Hours:** Mon 6:00-17:00, Tue-Fri 6:00-18:00, Sat 6:00-15:00, closed Sun. See page 56.

▲▲Great Synagogue The world's second-largest, with fancy interior, good museum, and memorial garden. **Hours:** March-Oct Sun-Thu 10:00-18:00, Fri 10:00-16:30—until 15:30 in March; Nov-Feb Sun-Fri 10:00-16:00; always closed Sat and Jewish holidays. See page 58.

▲▲Hungarian State Opera House Neo-Renaissance splendor and affordable opera. **Hours:** Lobby/box office open Mon-Sat from 11:00 until show time—generally 19:00; Sun open 3 hours before performance—generally 16:00-19:00, or 10:00-13:00 if there's a matinee; English tours nearly daily at 15:00 and 16:00, and maybe at 14:00 June-Oct. See page 59.

▲▲House of Terror Harrowing remembrance of Nazis and communist secret police in former headquarters/torture site. **Hours:** Tue-Sun 10:00-18:00, closed Mon. See page 60.

▲▲Heroes' Square Mammoth tribute to Hungary's historic figures, fronted by art museums. **Hours:** Square always open. See page 61.

▲▲City Park Budapest's backyard, with Art Nouveau zoo, Transylvanian Vajdahunyad Castle replica, amusement park, and Széchenyi Baths. **Hours:** Park always open. See page 62.

▲▲Vajdahunyad Castle Epcot-like replica of a Transylvanian castle and other historical buildings. **Hours:** Always viewable. See page 62.

▲▲Holocaust Memorial Center Excellent memorial and museum honoring Hungarian victims of the Holocaust. **Hours:** Tue-Sun 10:00-18:00, closed Mon. See page 64.

▲**St. István's Basilica** Budapest's largest church, with a saint's withered fist and great city views. **Hours:** Mon 9:00-16:30, Tue-Fri 9:00-17:00, Sat 9:00-13:00, Sun 13:00-17:00; panorama terrace daily June-Sept 10:00-18:30, March-May and Oct 10:00-17:30, Nov-Feb 10:00-16:30. See page 53.

▲**Hungarian National Museum** Expansive collection of fragments from Hungary's history. **Hours:** Tue-Sun 10:00-18:00, closed Mon. See page 57.

▲**Margaret Island** Budapest's traffic-free urban playground, with spas, ruins, gardens, a game farm, and fountains, set in the middle of the Danube. **Hours:** Park always open. See page 68.

▲**Zwack Museum** Venerable Zwack family distillery and samples of Hungary's favorite liquor, Unicum. **Hours:** Mon-Sat 10:00-18:00, closed Sun. See page 67.

In Buda
▲▲**Matthias Church** Landmark Neo-Gothic church with gilded history-book interior and revered 16th-century statue of Mary and Jesus. **Hours:** Mon-Fri 9:00-17:00—possibly also 19:00-20:00 in summer, Sat 9:00-13:00, Sun 13:00-17:00. See page 76.

▲▲**Gellért Baths** Touristy baths in historic Buda hotel. **Hours:** Daily 6:00-20:00. See page 80.

▲▲**Rudas Baths** Half-millennium-old Turkish dome over a series of hot-water pools. **Hours:** Daily 6:00-20:00. See page 80.

▲▲**Memento Park** Larger-than-life communist statues collected in one park, on the outskirts of town. **Hours:** Daily 10:00-sunset. See page 85.

▲**Hungarian National Gallery** Top works by Hungarian artists, housed in the Royal Palace. **Hours:** Tue-Sun 10:00-18:00, closed Mon. See page 70.

▲**Hospital in the Rock** Fascinating underground network of hospital and bomb-shelter corridors from WWII and the Cold War. **Hours:** Daily 10:00-20:00. See page 77.

▲**Buda Castle Park (Várkert Bázar) and Grand Staircase** Lovely Neo-Renaissance people zone from the Danube riverbank to the Royal Palace. **Hours:** Open long hours daily. See page 75.

a cushy lounge—across one of Europe's largest carpets—to see the legislative chamber.

Near the Parliament
Kossuth (Lajos) Tér

The giant square surrounding the Parliament is peppered with monuments honoring great Hungarian statesmen (Lajos Kossuth, Ferenc Rákóczi, Imre Nagy), artists (Attila József), and anonymous victims of past regimes (underfoot is a memorial to the 1956 Uprising, during which protesters were gunned down on this very square).

For more details about Kossuth tér, ✪ see the Leopold Town Walk chapter.

The square is fronted by the...

Museum of Ethnography (Néprajzi Múzeum)

This museum, housed in one of Budapest's majestic venues, feels deserted. Its fine collection of Hungarian folk artifacts (mostly from the late 19th century) takes up only a small corner of the cavernous building. The permanent exhibit, with surprisingly good English explanations, shows off costumes, tools, wagons, boats, beehives, furniture, and ceramics of the many peoples who lived in pre-WWI Hungary (which also included much of today's Slovakia and Romania). The museum also has a collection of artifacts from other European and world cultures, which it cleverly assembles into good temporary exhibits.

Cost and Hours: 1,000 Ft for permanent collection, more for temporary exhibits, Tue-Sun 10:00-18:00, closed Mon, Kossuth tér 12, district V, M2: Kossuth tér, tel. 1/473-2200, www.neprajz. hu.

Between the Parliament and Town Center

For more details on all of the following sights, ✪ see the Leopold Town Walk chapter.

▲Szabadság Tér ("Liberty Square")

One of Budapest's most genteel squares, this space is marked by a controversial monument to the Soviet soldiers who liberated Hungary at the end of World War II, and ringed by both fancy old apartment blocks and important buildings (such as the former Hungarian State Television headquarters, the US Embassy, and the National Bank of Hungary). A fine café, fun-filled playgrounds, statues of prominent Americans (Ronald Reagan and Harry Hill Bandholtz), and yet another provocative monument (to the Hungarian victims of the Nazis) round out the square's many attractions. More architectural gems—including the quintessentially Art Nouveau Bedő-Ház and the Postal Savings Bank in the Hungarian national style—are just a block away.

▲St. István's Basilica (Szent István Bazilika)

Budapest's biggest church is one of its top landmarks. The grand interior celebrates St. István, Hungary's first Christian king. You

can see his withered, blackened, millennium-old fist in a gilded reliquary in the side chapel. Or you can zip up on an elevator (or climb up stairs partway) to a panorama terrace with views over the rooftops of Pest. The skippable treasury has ecclesiastical items, historical exhibits, and artwork.

Cost and Hours: Interior—free but 200-Ft donation strongly suggested, open to tourists Mon 9:00-16:30, Tue-Fri 9:00-17:00, Sat 9:00-13:00, Sun 13:00-17:00, open slightly later for worshippers; panorama terrace—500 Ft, daily June-Sept 10:00-18:30, March-May and Oct 10:00-17:30, Nov-Feb 10:00-16:30; treasury-400 Ft, same hours as terrace; Szent István tér, district V, M1: Bajcsy-Zsilinszky út or M3: Arany János utca.

▲Gresham Palace

This stately old Art Nouveau building, long neglected, has now been renovated to its former splendor. Overlooking Széchenyi tér, it once held the offices of a life-insurance company; today it houses one of Budapest's top hotels. Even if you're not a guest, ogle its glorious facade and stroll through its luxurious lobby (lobby open 24 hours daily, Széchenyi tér 5, district V, M1: Vörösmarty tér or M2: Kossuth tér, www.fourseasons.com/budapest).

▲Chain Bridge (Lánchíd)

The city's most beloved bridge stretches from Pest's Széchenyi tér to Buda's Adam Clark tér (named for the bridge's designer). The gift of Count István Széchenyi to the Hungarian people, the Chain Bridge was the first permanent link between the two towns that would soon merge to become Budapest.

PEST TOWN CENTER (BELVÁROS)

❂ All of these sights are covered in detail in the Pest Town Center Walk chapter. I've listed only the essentials here.

SIGHTS

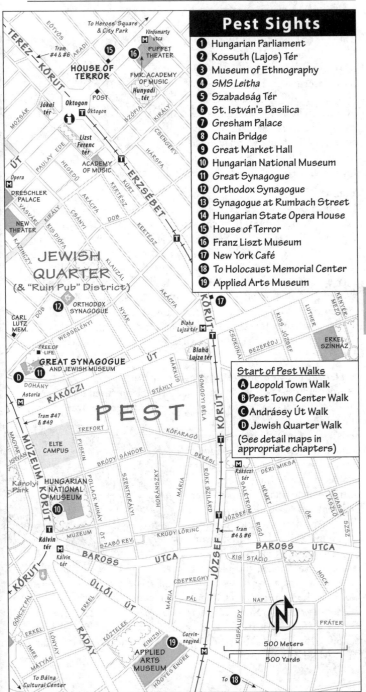

Pest Sights

1 Hungarian Parliament
2 Kossuth (Lajos) Tér
3 Museum of Ethnography
4 SMS Leitha
5 Szabadság Tér
6 St. István's Basilica
7 Gresham Palace
8 Chain Bridge
9 Great Market Hall
10 Hungarian National Museum
11 Great Synagogue
12 Orthodox Synagogue
13 Synagogue at Rumbach Street
14 Hungarian State Opera House
15 House of Terror
16 Franz Liszt Museum
17 New York Café
18 To Holocaust Memorial Center
19 Applied Arts Museum

Start of Pest Walks
A Leopold Town Walk
B Pest Town Center Walk
C Andrássy Út Walk
D Jewish Quarter Walk
(See detail maps in appropriate chapters)

500 Meters
500 Yards

▲Vörösmarty Tér

The central square of the Town Center, dominated by a giant statue of the revered Romantic poet Mihály Vörösmarty and the venerable Gerbeaud coffee shop, is the hub of Pest sightseeing. Within a few steps of here are the main walking street, Váci utca (described next), the delightful Danube promenade,

the "Fashion Street" of Deák utca, and much more.

Váci Utca

In Budapest's Golden Age, Váci Street was where well-heeled urbanites would shop, then show off for one another. During the Cold War, it was the first place in the Eastern Bloc where you could buy a Big Mac or Adidas sneakers. And today, it's an overrated, overpriced tourist trap disguised as a pretty street. I'll admit that I have a bad attitude about Váci utca. It's because more visitors get fleeced by dishonest shops, crooked restaurants, and hookers masquerading as lonely hearts here than anywhere else in town. Like moths to a flame, tourists can't seem to avoid this strip. Walk Váci utca to satisfy your curiosity. But then venture off it to discover the real Budapest.

▲▲Great Market Hall (Nagyvásárcsarnok)

"Great" indeed is this gigantic marketplace on three levels: produce, meats, and other foods on the ground floor; souvenirs up-stairs; and fish and pickles in the cellar. The Great Market Hall has somehow succeeded in keeping local shoppers happy, even as it's evolved into one of the city's top tourist attractions. Goose liver, embroidered tablecloths, golden Tokaji Aszú wine, pickled peppers, communist-kitsch T-shirts, savory *lángos* pastries, patriotic green-

white-and-red flags, kid-pleasing local candy bars, and paprika of every degree of spiciness...if it's Hungarian, you'll find it here. Come to shop for souvenirs, to buy a picnic, or just to rattle around inside this vast, picturesque, Industrial Age hall.

Hours and Location: Mon 6:00-17:00, Tue-Fri 6:00-18:00, Sat 6:00-15:00, closed Sun, Fővám körút 1, district IX, M4: Fővám tér or M3: Kálvin tér.

SIGHTS

Bálna Budapest

This shopping mall and cultural center stands along the riverbank behind the Great Market Hall. Completed in 2013, the complex was created by bridging a pair of circa-1881 brick warehouses with a swooping glass canopy that earns its name, "The Whale" (the meaning of *bálna*). The architecture is striking (especially from the river), and the space inside is sleek and modern, but the building has been controversial for not really having a clear purpose: It's partly filled with boutiques and galleries of local designers (making it worth a browse for items you won't find in the Great Market Hall), but also houses conference and concert space, offices, and several eateries—including several with enticing outdoor seating along the embankment. It still feels unmoored, with several vacant storefronts, but it may eventually live up to its potential. Shoppers and fans of contemporary architecture may find it worth the three-minute stroll beyond the back door of the Great Market Hall.

Cost and Hours: Free to enter, Sun-Thu 10:00-20:00, Fri-Sat 10:00-22:00, www.balnabudapest.hu.

ALONG THE SMALL BOULEVARD (KISKÖRÚT)

These two major sights are along the Small Boulevard, between the Liberty Bridge/Great Market Hall and Deák tér. (Note that the Great Market Hall, listed earlier, is also technically along the Small Boulevard.)

▲Hungarian National Museum (Magyar Nemzeti Múzeum)

One of Budapest's biggest museums features all manner of Hungarian historic bric-a-brac, from the Paleolithic age to a more re-

cent infestation of dinosaurs (the communists). Artifacts are explained by good, if dry, English descriptions.

Cost and Hours: 1,600 Ft—but can change depending on temporary exhibits, audioguide available, Tue-Sun 10:00-18:00, closed Mon, last entry 30 minutes before closing, near Great Market Hall at Múzeum körút 14, district VIII, M3: Kálvin tér, tel. 1/327-7773, www.hnm.hu.

Visiting the Museum: The first floor (one flight down from the entry) focuses on the Carpathian Basin in the pre-Magyar days, with ancient items and Roman remains. The basement features a lapidarium, with medieval tombstones and more Roman ruins.

Upstairs, 20 rooms provide a historic overview from the arrival of the Magyars in 896 up to the 1989 revolution. The museum adds substance to your understanding of Hungary's story—but it helps to have a pretty firm foundation first (read this book's Hungary: Past and Present chapter). The most engaging part is room 20, with an exhibit on the communist era, featuring both pro- and anti-Party propaganda. The exhibit ends with video footage of the 1989 end of communism—demonstrations, monumental parliament votes, and a final farewell to the last Soviet troops leaving Hungarian soil. You'll also see the pen used to un-sign the Warsaw Pact in 1991, and current Prime Minister Viktor Orbán's rucksack—a children's backpack decorated with soccer players—which he carried around throughout his first term as evidence of his connection to the common man. (Now wedded to the gimmick, he's still carrying a bag like this.) Another uprising—the 1848 Revolution against Habsburg rule—was declared from the steps of this impressive Neoclassical building.

JEWISH QUARTER (ZSIDÓNEGYED)

✪ The Great Synagogue and other sights in this area are described in far greater detail in the Great Synagogue and Jewish Quarter Tour chapter.

▲▲Great Synagogue (Nagy Zsinagóga)

The world's second biggest synagogue sits tucked behind a workaday building on the Small Boulevard. Dating from the mid-19th

century—a time when Budapest's Jews were eager to feel integrated with the larger community—this synagogue, with two dominant towers and a longitudinal plan, feels more like a Christian building than a Jewish one. The gorgeously restored, intricately decorated interior is one of Budapest's finest. Attached to the synagogue is the small but well-presented Hungarian Jewish Museum, and behind it is an evocative memorial garden with the powerful *Tree of Life* monument to Hungarian victims of the Holocaust, as well as a symbolic grave for Swedish diplomat Raoul Wallenberg, who worked to save the lives of Hungarian Jews during World War II. The synagogue is also a starting point for various tours both of the building itself, and of the surrounding Jewish sights.

Cost and Hours: 2,500 Ft for Great Synagogue, Hungarian Jewish Museum, and Memorial Garden (or pay 500 Ft just for just the garden), 500 Ft extra to take photos; March-Oct Sun-Thu 10:00-18:00, Fri 10:00-16:30—until 15:30 in March; Nov-Feb Sun-Fri 10:00-16:00; always closed Sat and Jewish holidays, last entry 30 minutes before closing; Dohány utca 2, district VII, near

M2: Astoria or the Astoria stop on trams #47 and #49, tel. 1/344-5131, www.dohanyutcaizsinagoga.hu.

Hungarian Jewish Archives and Family Research Center

At the back of the Great Synagogue's memorial garden, this facility houses a small exhibit about the Jewish Quarter and an archive of Jewish birth, marriage, and death records.

Cost and Hours: Exhibit covered by Great Synagogue ticket, 1,000 Ft to use archives, Mon-Wed 10:00-17:00, Thu 12:00-17:00, Fri 10:00-15:00, closed Sat-Sun, closes one hour earlier Nov-Feb, Wesselényi utca 7, best to call or email ahead to arrange help with archives, tel. 1/413-5547, www.milev.hu, family@milev.hu.

Orthodox Synagogue

This colorfully decorated space is Budapest's second-most-interesting Jewish sight. It's just two blocks behind the Great Synagogue.

Cost and Hours: 1,000 Ft, Sun-Thu 10:00-16:00, Fri 10:00-13:30, closed Sat, enter down little alley, Kazinczy utca 27, district VII, M2: Astoria.

Synagogue at Rumbach Street

This fine house of worship, designed by Otto Wagner and with a faded Moorish-style interior, may close soon for a much-needed restoration.

Cost and Hours: If open—likely 500 Ft, Sun-Thu 10:00-17:30, Fri 10:00-15:30, closed Sat. From the *Tree of Life* it's two blocks down Rumbach utca toward Andrássy út (district VII, M2: Astoria).

ANDRÁSSY ÚT

✪ All of these sights are covered in detail in the Andrássy Út Walk chapter, with the exception of the House of Terror, which is further described in the House of Terror Tour chapter. I've listed only the essentials here.

▲▲Hungarian State Opera House (Magyar Állami Operaház)

This sumptuous temple to music is one of Europe's finest opera houses. Built in the late 19th century by patriotic Hungarians striving to thrust their capital onto the European stage, it also boasts one of Budapest's very best interiors.

You can drop in whenever the box office is open to ogle the ostentatious **lobby** (Mon-Sat from 11:00 until show time—generally 19:00, or until 17:00 if there's no performance; Sun open 3 hours before the performance—generally 16:00-19:00, or 10:00-13:00 if there's a matinee; Andrássy út 22, district VI, M1: Opera).

The 45-minute **tours** of the Opera House are a must for music lovers, and enjoyable for anyone, though the quality of the guides can be erratic: Most spout plenty of fun, if silly, legends, but others can be quite dry. You'll see the main entryway, the snooty lounge area, some of the cozy but plush boxes, and the lavish auditorium. You'll find out why clandestine lovers would meet in the cigar lounge, how the Opera House is designed to keep the big spenders away from the rabble in the nosebleed seats, and how to tell the difference between real marble and fake marble (2,900 Ft, 500 Ft extra to take photos, 600 Ft extra for 5-minute mini-concert of two arias after the tour; English tours nearly daily at 15:00 and 16:00, June-Oct maybe also at 14:00; tickets are easy to get—just

show up 10 minutes before the tour; buy ticket in opera shop—enter the main lobby and go left, shop open daily 11:00-18:00—or until the end of the second intermission during performances, Oct-March closed for lunch 13:30-14:00; tel. 1/332-8197). Since the real appeal is the chance to see the interior, skip the tour if you're going to an opera performance.

▲▲House of Terror (Terror Háza)

The building at Andrássy út 60 was home to the vilest parts of two destructive regimes: first the Arrow Cross (the Gestapo-like en-

forcers of Nazi-occupied Hungary), then the ÁVO and ÁVH secret police (the insidious KGB-type wing of the Soviet satellite government). Now re-envisioned as the "House of Terror," this building uses high-tech, highly conceptual, bombastic exhibits to document (if not proselytize about) the ugliest moments in Hungary's difficult 20th century. Enlightening and well-presented, it rivals Memento Park as Budapest's best attraction about the communist age.

Cost and Hours: 2,000 Ft, possibly more for special exhibits, audioguide-1,500 Ft, Tue-Sun 10:00-18:00, closed Mon, last entry 30 minutes before closing, Andrássy út 60, district VI, M1: Vörösmarty utca—*not* the Vörösmarty tér stop, tel. 1/374-2600, www.terrorhaza.hu.

○ See the House of Terror Tour chapter.

Franz Liszt Museum

In this surprisingly modest apartment where the composer once resided, you'll find a humble but appealing collection of artifacts. A pilgrimage site for Liszt fans, it's housed in the former Academy of Music, which also hosts Saturday-morning concerts (see page 287).

Cost and Hours: 1,300 Ft; dry English audioguide with a few snippets of music-700 Ft, otherwise scarce English information—borrow the information sheet as you enter; Mon-Fri 10:00-18:00, Sat 9:00-17:00, closed Sun, Vörösmarty utca 35, district VI, M1: Vörösmarty utca—*not* Vörösmarty tér stop, tel. 1/322-9804, www.lisztmuseum.hu.

HEROES' SQUARE AND CITY PARK

○ All of these sights are covered in detail in the Heroes' Square and City Park Walk chapter, with the exception of Széchenyi Baths, which are described in the Thermal Baths chapter. I've listed only the essentials here. To reach this area, take the M1/yellow Metró line to Hősök tere (district XIV).

▲▲Heroes' Square (Hősök Tere)

Built in 1896 to celebrate the 1,000th anniversary of the Magyars' arrival in Hungary, this vast square culminates at a bold Millen-

nium Monument. Standing stoically in its colonnades are 14 Hungarian leaders who represent the whole span of this nation's colorful and illustrious history. In front, at the base of a high pillar, are the seven original Magyar chieftains, the Hungarian War Memorial, and young Hungarian skateboarders of the 21st century. It's an ideal place to appreciate Budapest's greatness and to learn a little about its story. The square is also flanked by a pair of museums (described next).

For a statue-by-statue self-guided tour of Heroes' Square, ○ see the Heroes' Square and City Park Walk chapter.

Museum of Fine Arts (Szépművészeti Múzeum)

This collection of Habsburg art—mostly Germanic, Dutch, Belgian, and Spanish, rather than Hungarian—is Budapest's best chance to appreciate some European masters. It's likely closed for renovation through 2017.

SIGHTS

Cost and Hours: If open—likely 1,800 Ft, may be more for special exhibits, audioguide-500 Ft, WC and coat check downstairs, Tue-Sun 10:00-17:30, closed Mon, last entry 30 minutes before closing, Dózsa György út 41, tel. 1/469-7100, www.szepmuveszeti.hu.

Műcsarnok ("Hall of Art")

Facing the Museum of Fine Arts from across Heroes' Square, the Műcsarnok shows temporary exhibits by contemporary artists—of interest only to art lovers. The price varies depending on the exhibits and on which parts you tour.

Cost and Hours: 1,800 Ft, Tue-Wed and Fri-Sun 10:00-18:00, Thu 12:00-20:00, closed Mon, Dózsa György út 37, tel. 1/460-7000, www.mucsarnok.hu.

▲▲City Park (Városliget)

This particularly enjoyable corner of Budapest, which sprawls behind Heroes' Square, is endlessly entertaining. Explore the fantasy castle of Vajdahunyad (described next). Visit the animals and ogle the playful Art Nouveau buildings inside the city's zoo, ride a roller-coaster at the amusement park, or enjoy a circus under the big top (all described in the Budapest with Children chapter). Go for a stroll, rent a rowboat, eat some cotton candy, or challenge a local Bobby Fischer to a game of chess. Or, best of all, take a dip in Budapest's ultimate thermal spa, the Széchenyi Baths (described later). This is a fine place to just be on vacation.

▲▲Vajdahunyad Castle (Vajdahunyad Vára)

An elaborate pavilion that the people of Budapest couldn't bear to tear down after their millennial celebration ended a century ago, Vajdahunyad Castle has become a fixture of City Park. Divided into four parts—representing four typical, traditional schools of Hungarian architecture—this "little Epcot" is free and always open to explore. It's dominated by a fanciful replica of a Renaissance-era Transylvanian castle. Deeper in the complex, a curlicue-covered Baroque mansion houses (unexpectedly) the **Museum of Hungarian Agriculture,** noteworthy for its grand interior (Magyar Mezőgazdasági Múzeum; 1,100 Ft; April-Oct Tue-Sun 10:00-17:00; Nov-March Tue-Fri 10:00-16:00, Sat-Sun 10:00-17:00; closed Mon year-round, last entry 30 minutes before closing, tel. 1/363-1117, www.mezogazdasagimuzeum.hu).

▲▲▲Széchenyi Baths (Széchenyi Fürdő)

My favorite activity in Budapest, the Széchenyi Baths are an ideal way to reward yourself for the hard work of sightseeing and call it

a culturally enlightening experience. Soak in hundred-degree water, surrounded by portly Hungarians squeezed into tiny swimsuits, while jets and cascades pound away your tension. Go for a vigorous swim in the lap pool, giggle and bump your way around the whirlpool, submerge yourself to the nostrils in

water green with minerals, feel the bubbles from an underwater jet gradually caress their way up your leg, or challenge the locals to a game of Speedo-clad chess. And it's all surrounded by an opulent yellow palace with shiny copper domes. The bright blue-and-white of the sky, the yellow of the buildings, the pale pink of the skin, the turquoise of the water...Budapest simply doesn't get any better.

Cost and Hours: 4,500 Ft for locker (in gender-segregated locker room), 500 Ft more for personal changing cabin, cheaper after 19:00, 200 Ft more on weekends; admission includes outdoor swimming pool area, indoor thermal baths, and sauna; swimming pool generally open daily 6:00-22:00, thermal bath daily 6:00-19:00, may be open later on summer weekends, last entry one hour before closing, Állatkerti körút 11, district XIV, M1: Széchenyi fürdő, tel. 1/363-3210, www.szechenyibath.hu.

◐ See the Thermal Baths chapter.

ON THE GREAT BOULEVARD (NAGYKÖRÚT)

▲New York Café

My vote for the most over-the-top extravagant coffeehouse in Budapest, if not Europe, this restored space ranks up there with the city's most impressive old interiors. Springing for a pricey cup of coffee here (consider it the admission fee) is worth it simply to soak in all the opulence.

Cost and Hours: Free to take a quick peek, pricey coffee and meals, daily 9:00-24:00, Erzsébet körút 9, district VII, M2: Blaha Lujza tér, tel. 1/886-6167. For more details, see page 265 of the Eating in Budapest chapter.

SOUTH OF DOWNTOWN PEST

These two areas—a short commute to the south from the center of Pest (10-15 minutes by tram or Metró)—offer a peek at some worthwhile, workaday areas where relatively few tourists venture.

Museums near Üllői Út

These two museums are near the city center, on the boulevard called Üllői út. You could stroll there in about 10 minutes from the Small Boulevard ring road (walking the length of the Ráday utca café street gets you very close), or hop on the M3/blue Metró line to Corvin-negyed (just one stop beyond Kálvin tér).

▲▲Holocaust Memorial Center (Holokauszt Emlékközpont)

This sight honors the nearly 600,000 Hungarian victims of the Nazis...one out of every ten Holocaust victims. The impressive modern complex (with a beautifully restored 1920s synagogue as its centerpiece) is a museum of the Hungarian Holocaust, a monument to its victims, a space for temporary exhibits, and a research and documentation center of Nazi atrocities. Interesting to anybody, but essential to those interested in the Holocaust, this is Budapest's best sight about that dark time—and one of Europe's best, as well. (For background on the Hungarian Jewish experience, see page 186.)

Cost and Hours: 1,400 Ft, Tue-Sun 10:00-18:00, closed Mon, Páva utca 39, district IX, M3: Corvin-negyed, tel. 1/455-3333, www.hdke.hu.

Getting There: From the Corvin-negyed Metró stop, use the exit marked *Holokauszt Emlékközpont* and take the left fork at the exit. Walk straight ahead two long blocks, then turn right down Páva utca.

Visiting the Center: You'll pass through a security checkpoint to reach the courtyard. Once inside, a black marble wall is etched with the names of victims. Head downstairs to buy your ticket.

The excellent permanent exhibit, called "From Deprivation of Rights to Genocide," traces in English the gradual process of disenfranchisement, marginalization, exploitation, dehumanization, and eventually extermination that befell Hungary's Jews as World

War II wore on. From the entrance, a long hallway with shuffling feet on the soundtrack replicates the forced march of prisoners. The one-way route through darkened halls uses high-tech exhibits, including interactive touch screens and movies, to tell the story. By demonstrating that pervasive anti-Semitism existed here long before World War II, the pointed commentary casts doubt on the widely held belief that Hungary initially allied itself with the Nazis partly to protect its Jews. While the exhibit sometimes acknowledges Roma (Gypsy) victims, its primary focus is on the fate of the Hungarian Jews. Occasionally the exhibit zooms in to tell the story of an individual or a single family, following their personal story through those horrific years. One powerful room is devoted to the notorious Auschwitz-Birkenau concentration camp, where some 430,000 Hungarian Jews were sent—most to be executed immediately upon arrival. The main exhibit ends with a thoughtful consideration of "Liberation and Calling to Account," analyzing the impossible question of how a society responds to and recovers from such a tragedy.

The finale is the interior of the synagogue, now a touching memorial filled with glass seats, each one etched with the image of a Jewish worshipper who once filled it. Up above, on the mezzanine level, you'll find temporary exhibits and an information center that helps teary-eyed descendants of Hungarian Jews track down the fate of their relatives.

Applied Arts Museum (Iparművészeti Múzeum)

This remarkable late-19th-century building, a fanciful green-roofed castle that seems out of place in an otherwise dreary urban area, was designed by Ödön Lechner (who also did the Postal Savings Bank—see page 116). The interior is equally striking: Because

historians of the day were speculating about possible ties between the Magyars and India, Lechner decorated it with Mogul motifs (from the Indian dynasty best known for the Taj Mahal). Strolling through the forest of dripping-with-white-stucco arches and columns, you might just forget to pay attention to the exhibits... which would be a shame. This is the third-oldest applied arts institution in the world (after ones in London and Vienna). The small but excellent permanent collection upstairs, called "Collectors and Treasures," displays furniture, clothes, ceramics, and other everyday items, with an emphasis on curvy Art Nouveau (all described in English). This and various temporary exhibits are displayed around

SIGHTS

a light and airy atrium. If you're visiting the nearby Holocaust Memorial Center, consider dropping by here for a look at the building.

Cost and Hours: Ticket price varies with exhibits, but generally around 2,000-3,000 Ft, Tue-Sun 10:00-18:00, closed Mon, Üllői út 33, district IX, M3: Corvin-negyed, tel. 1/456-5100, www.imm.hu.

Getting There: From the Corvin-negyed Metró stop, follow signs to *Iparművészeti Múzeum* and bear right up the stairs.

Millennium City Center

Along the Danube riverbank at the Rákóczi Bridge, you'll find a cutting-edge cultural complex with some of Budapest's best modern venues for music and theater. While there's not much "sightseeing" here (aside from a contemporary art gallery and the quirky distillery museum), it's fun to wander the riverside park amid the impressive buildings. A row of super-modern glass office blocks effectively seals off the inviting park from the busy highway, creating a pleasant place to simply stroll. (Don't confuse this with the similarly named Millenáris Park, at the northern edge of Buda.)

Getting There: Though it looks far on the map, this area is easy to reach: From anywhere along the Pest embankment (including Kossuth tér by the Parliament, Vigadó tér in the heart of Pest's Town Center, or Fővám tér next to the Great Market Hall), hop on tram #2 and ride it south about 10-15 minutes to the Millenniumi Kulturális Központ stop.

National Theater (Nemzeti Színház)

This facility anchors the complex with an elaborate industrial-Organic facade, studded with statues honoring the Hungarian theatrical tradition. The surrounding park is a lively people zone laden

with whimsical art—Hungarian theater greats in stone, a vast terrace shaped like a ship's prow, a toppled colonnade, and a stone archway that evokes an opening theater curtain. Twist up to the top of the adjacent, yellow-brick ziggurat tower for fine views over the entire complex and all the way to downtown Budapest.

Palace of Arts (Művészetek Palotája)

With a sterner facade, this gigantic facility houses the 1,700-seat Béla Bartók National Concert Hall and the smaller 460-seat Festival Theater (free to enter the building, open daily 10:00-20:00 or until end of last performance, www.mupa.hu). The complex is also home to the Ludwig Museum, Budapest's premier collection of contemporary art, with mostly changing exhibits of today's biggest names (price varies depending on exhibits, Tue-Sun 10:00-18:00, temporary exhibits may stay open until 20:00, closed Mon, Komor Marcell utca 1, tel. 1/555-3444, www.ludwigmuseum.hu).

▲Zwack Museum

This museum and visitors center is housed in a corner of the sprawling distillery complex that produces Unicum, the abundantly fla-

vored liquor that's Hungary's favorite spirit (described on page 251). The Zwack family is a Hungarian institution, like the Anheuser-Busch clan in the US. The museum offers a doting look at the Zwacks and their company, which has been headquartered right here since 1892 (with a 45-year break during communism). The Zwacks' story is a fascinating case study in how communism affected longstanding industry—privatization, exile, and triumphant return (see below). And, while the Zwacks' museum feels a bit like a shrine to their own ingenuity, it's worthwhile for Unicum fans, or for anyone who enjoys learning how booze gets made. Hungary's entire production of Unicum—three million liters annually—still takes place right here.

Cost and Hours: 1,800 Ft, Mon-Sat 10:00-18:00, tours in English at 14:00 and likely at other times—call ahead to check, closed Sun, Soroksári út 26, enter around the corner on Dandár utca, tel. 1/215-3575.

Getting There: It's near the Haller utca stop on tram #2 (the stop just before Millennium Park); from the tram stop, walk back a block and head up Dandár utca.

Background: Unicum has a history as complicated as its flavor. Invented by a Doctor Zwack in the late 18th century, the drink impressed Habsburg Emperor Josef II, who supposedly declared: *"Das ist ein Unikum!"* ("This is a specialty!"). The Zwack company went on to thrive during Budapest's late-19th-century Golden Age (when Unicum was the subject of many whimsical Guinness-type ads). Locals enjoy telling the story of how, after all of Budapest's bridges spanning the Danube were destroyed in World War II, a temporary barge bridge was built from Unicum barrels. But when the communists took over in the postwar era, the Zwacks fled to America—taking their secret recipe for Unicum with them. The communists continued to market the drink with their own formula, which left Hungarians (literally and figuratively) with a bad taste in their mouths. In a landmark case, the Zwacks sued the communists for infringing on their copyright...and won. In 1991, Péter Zwack—who had been living in exile in Italy—triumphantly returned to Hungary and resurrected the original family recipe. More recently, to avoid alienating younger palates, they've added some smoother variations: Unicum Next (citrus) and Unicum Szilva ("plum"). But whatever the flavor, Unicum remains a proud national symbol.

Visiting the Museum: Your visit has three parts: a 20-minute film in English (more about the family than about their products); a fine little museum upstairs (glass display cases jammed with old ads, documents, and—up in the gallery—thousands of tiny bottles, includes English audioguide); and—the highlight—a guided tour of the refurbished original distillery building and the cellars where the spirit is aged. On this fascinating tour, you'll be able to touch and smell several of the more than 40 herbs used to make Unicum, and learn about how the stuff gets made (components are distilled in two separate batches, then mixed and aged for six months). Then you'll head down into the cellars where 500 gigantic, 10,000-liter oak casks offer the perfect atmosphere for sampling two types of Unicum straight from the barrel.

The Danube (Duna)

The mighty river coursing through the heart of the city defines Budapest. Make time for a stroll along the delightful riverfront embankments of both Buda and Pest. For many visitors, a highlight is taking a touristy but beautiful boat cruise up and down the Danube—especially at night (see "Tours in Budapest, By Boat" on page 44). Or visit the river's best island...

▲Margaret Island (Margitsziget)

In the Middle Ages, this island in the Danube (just north of the Parliament) was known as the "Isle of Hares." In the 13th century, a desperate King Béla IV swore that if God were to deliver Hungary from the invading Tatars,

SIGHTS

he would dedicate his youngest daughter Margaret to the Church. Hungary was spared...and Margaret was shipped to a nunnery here. But, the story goes, Margaret embraced her new life as a castaway nun, and later refused her father's efforts to force her into a politically expedient marriage with a Bohemian king. She became St. Margaret of Hungary, and this island was named for her.

The island remained largely undeveloped until the 19th century, when a Habsburg aristocrat built a hunting palace here and turned it into his playground. It gradually evolved into a lively garden district, connected to Buda and Pest by a paddleboat steamer. Eventually a bath and hotel complex was built (to take advantage of the island's natural thermal springs), and Margaret Island was connected to the rest of the city in 1901 by the Margaret Bridge. In the genteel age of the late 19th century, a small entrance fee was charged to frolic on the island, to keep the rabble away.

Today, Margaret Island remains Budapest's playground. While the island officially has no permanent residents, urbanites flock to relax in this huge, leafy park...in the midst of the busy city, yet so far away (no cars are allowed on the island—just public buses). The island rivals City Park as the best spot in town for strolling, jogging, biking, and people-watching. Margaret Island is also home to some of Budapest's many baths, one of which (Palatinus Strandfürdő) is like a mini-water park. Rounding out the island's attractions are an iconic old water tower, the remains of Margaret's convent, a rose garden, a game farm, and a "musical fountain" that performs to the strains of Hungarian folk tunes.

Perhaps the best way to enjoy Margaret Island is to rent some wheels. **Bringóhintó** ("Bike Castle"), with branches at both ends

of the island, rents all manner of wheeled entertainment (open daily year-round until dusk; location at Margaret Bridge opens at 10:00, at opposite end opens at 8:00; tel. 1/329-2746, www.bringohinto. hu). The main office is a few steps from the bus stop called "Szállodák (Hotels)." For two or more people, consider renting a fun bike cart—a four-wheeled carriage with two sets of pedals, a steering wheel, handbrake, and canopy (bikes—690 Ft/30 minutes, 990 Ft/1 hour, then 200 Ft/hour; bike carts—2,180 Ft/30 minutes, 3,480 Ft/1 hour; 20,000-Ft deposit or leave your ID). Because they have two locations, you can take bus #26 to the northern end of the island, rent a bike and pay the deposit, bike one-way to the southern tip of the island, and return your bike there to reclaim your deposit. Follow this route (using the helpful map posted inside the bike cart): water tower, monastery ruins, rose garden, past the game farm, along the east side of the island to the dancing fountain; with more time, go along the main road or the west side of the island to check out the baths.

Getting There: Bus #26 begins at Nyugati/Western train station, crosses the Margaret Bridge, then drives up through the middle of the island—allowing visitors to easily get from one end to the other (3-6/hour). **Trams** #4 and #6, which circulate around the Great Boulevard, cross the Margaret Bridge and stop at the southern tip of the island, a short walk from some of the attractions. You can also reach the island by **boat;** the public riverboats have two stops on the island (see page 41), or you can catch a Mahart shuttle boat from Vigadó tér (see page 45). It's also a long but scenic **walk** between Margaret Island and other points in the city.

Buda

Nearly all of Buda's top sights are concentrated on or near its two riverside hills: Castle Hill and Gellért Hill.

CASTLE HILL (VÁRHEGY)

✪ Most of these sights are covered in detail in the Castle Hill Walk chapter. If a sight is covered in the walk, I've listed only its essentials here.

Royal Palace and Nearby
Royal Palace (Királyi Palota)

While imposing and grand-seeming from afar, the palace perched atop Castle Hill is essentially a shoddily rebuilt shell. But the terrace out front offers glorious Pest panoramas, there are signs of life in some of its nooks and crannies (such as a playful fountain depicting King Matthias' hunting party), and the complex houses two museums (described next).

▲Hungarian National Gallery
(Magyar Nemzeti Galéria)

Hungarians are the first to admit that they're not known for their artists. But this collection of Hungarian art—with an emphasis on the 19th and 20th centuries, and an excellent collection of medieval altars—offers even non-art lovers a telling glimpse into the Magyar psyche.

Cost and Hours: 1,400 Ft, may cost more for special exhibits, audioguide-800 Ft, 500 Ft extra to take photos, Tue-Sun 10:00-18:00, closed Mon, required bag check for large bags, café, in the

Buda Sights

1. Royal Palace
2. Hungarian Nat'l Gallery
3. Budapest History Mus.
4. Matthias Church
5. Fishermen's Bastion
6. Remains of St. Mary Magdalene Church
7. Museum of Military History
8. Hospital in the Rock
9. Buda Castle Labyrinth
10. Citadella Fortress
11. Liberation Monument
12. Cave Church
13. Monk House
14. Gellért Hotel & Baths
15. Rudas Baths
16. To Millenáris Park
17. To Children's Railway

500 Meters
500 Yards

Royal Palace—enter from terrace by Eugene of Savoy statue, district I, mobile 0620-439-7325, www.mng.hu.

⊙ Self-Guided Tour: This once-over-lightly tour touches on the most insightful pieces in this sprawling museum.

From the atrium, head up two flights on the grand staircase. When you reach the first floor, go through the second door on the right and walk through a room of gloomy paintings (which we'll return to in a moment). Turn right into the hallway, then take an immediate left to reach the excellent collection of **15th-century winged altars.** The ornately decorated wings could be opened or closed to acknowledge special occasions and holidays. Most of these come from "Upper Hungary," or today's Slovakia—which is more heavily wooded than modern (Lower) Hungary, making woodcarving a popular way to worship there. These date from a time when Hungary was at its peak—before the Ottomans and Habsburgs ruined everything.

Backtrack to the room of **gloomy paintings** from the 1850s and 1860s. We've just gone from one of Hungary's highest points to one of its lowest. In the two decades between the failed 1848 Revolution and the Compromise of 1867, the Hungarians were colossally depressed—and these paintings show it. Take a moment to psychoanalyze this moment in Hungarian history, perusing the paintings in these two rooms.

Begin in the farther room, closer to the atrium. On the left wall is a painting of a corpse covered by a blood-stained sheet—Viktor Madarász's grim *The Bewailing of László Hunyadi*, which commemorates the death of the beloved Hungarian heir-apparent. (The Hungarians couldn't explicitly condemn their Habsburg oppressors, but invoking this dark event from the Middle Ages had much the same effect.) Another popular theme of this era was the Ottoman invasion of Hungary—another stand-in for unwanted Habsburg rule. In this room, two different paintings illustrate the tale of Mihály Dobozi, a Hungarian nobleman who famously stabbed his wife (at her insistence) to prevent her from being raped. In the canvas just to the right, we see her baring her breast, waiting to be slain; across the room, we see a different version, in which Dobozi literally stabs her while on horseback, fleeing from the invaders. While Hungarian culture tends to be less than upbeat, this period took things to a new low.

Flanking the door into the next room are two paintings that are as optimistic as the Hungarians could muster. In both cases, people are preparing to fight off their enemies: On the left, Imre

Thököly takes leave of his father (likely for the last time) as he prepares to take to the battlefield against the Habsburgs; on the right, the women of the town of Eger stand strong against an Ottoman siege (for the full story, see page 363).

More gloominess awaits in the next room, however. On the right wall, the corpse of King Louis II is discovered after the Battle of Mohács, and the hero of the Battle of Belgrade gestures to his compatriots before falling to a valiant death. But on the facing wall, more positive themes come up: Matthias Corvinus is returning from a hunting expedition to his family's Transylvanian palace. Two sculptures of the "Good King Matthias" are also displayed in this room. During dark times, Hungarians looked back to this powerful Renaissance king.

Finally, the large canvas dominating the room represents a turning point: St. István (or Vajk, his heathen name) is being baptized and accepting European Christianity in the year 1000. Not surprisingly, this was painted at the time of the Compromise of 1867, when Hungary was ceded authority within the Catholic Habsburg Empire. Again, the painter uses a historical story as a tip of the hat to contemporary events.

The rest of the collection is spread through several rooms across the atrium. Take a quick spin through these rooms: Begin

by crossing the atrium and angling left, through the glass door at the top of the stairs. In a sharp contrast to what we've just seen, these **Romantics**—who painted mostly after the Great Compromise, when Hungary was feeling its oats—take an idealized view: pristine portraits of genteel city dwellers, bathing beauties with improbable proportions, and bucolic country folk. The best painting in here is straight ahead as you enter the room: the appealing *Picnic in May* by Pál Szinyei-Merse. While this scene is innocent today, the thought of men and women socializing freely was scandalous at the time.

Circling through these rooms, you'll end up back on the other side of the atrium. Cross it once more, this time bearing right into the larger door. This section features a more sober view of the same reality that the Romantics shrouded in gauze. The **genre paintings** here show some of the challenges of both country and city life.

Exiting that section, turn right into an impressive collection of **Realists**. The biggest name here is Mihály Munkácsy, who lived in France alongside the big-name Impressionists and Post-Impressionists. Many of these paintings are gritty slices-of-life, showing the hardships of the poor; notice the sloppier, more Impressionistic brushstrokes. For example, in the second room, on the right, see the hazy, almost Turner-esque *Dusty Road II*.

In the third room, we take a break from Munkácsy with works by László Paál, who primarily painted murky nature scenes—sun-dappled paths through the forest, pondering the connection between man and nature. In the fourth room, on the left (by the door), Munkácsy captures the intensity of English poet John Milton dictating *Paradise Lost* to his daughters. (The wealthy and popular Munkácsy was also frequently hired to paint portraits.)

Backtrack to the atrium, then climb up one more flight of stairs. Straight ahead from the landing are three works by **Tivadar Csontváry Kosztka,** the "Hungarian Van Gogh" (for more on Csontváry, see page 394). Here you see a few of this well-traveled painter's destinations: the giant canvas in the center depicts the theater at Taormina, Sicily; on the left are the water-

falls of Schaffhausen, Germany; and on the right is a cedar tree in Lebanon. Colorful, allegorical, and expressionistic, Csontváry is one of the most in-demand and expensive of Hungarian artists. If you enjoy Csontváry's works and are headed to his hometown of Pécs, don't miss his museum there (see page 393).

Budapest History Museum (Budapesti Történeti Múzeum)

This good but stodgy museum celebrates the earlier grandeur of Castle Hill. It's particularly strong in early history (prehistoric, ancient, medieval; for modern history, the National Museum is better).

Cost and Hours: 1,800 Ft, audioguide-1,200 Ft, some good English descriptions posted; March-Oct Tue-Sun 10:00-18:00, Nov-Feb Tue-Sun 10:00-16:00, closed Mon year-round; last entry 30 minutes before closing, district I, tel. 1/487-8800, www.btm.hu.

Visiting the Museum: On the ground floor (back-right corner, in a darkened room), stroll through the collection of 14th-century sculpture fragments. Many have strong Magyar features—notice that they look Central Asian (similar to Mongolians). In a small room at the end of this wing is a tapestry mixing the coats of arms of the Magyar Árpád dynasty (red-and-white stripes) with the French Anjou dynasty (fleur-de-lis)—the first two royal houses of Hungary—which was found balled up in a wad of mud.

One floor up, the good exhibit called "Budapest: Light and Shadow" traces a thousand years of the city's history, with concise English descriptions. The top floor has artifacts of Budapest's prehistoric residents. The cellar illustrates just how much this hill has changed over the centuries—and how dull today's version is by comparison. You'll wander through a maze of old palace parts, including the remains of an original Gothic chapel, a knights' hall, and marble remnants (reliefs and fountains) of Matthias Corvinus' lavish Renaissance palace.

▲Buda Castle Park and Grand Staircase (Várkert Bazár)

The city has recently refurbished the long-decrepit gateway, gallery, garden, and staircase that stretches from the riverbank up to

the Royal Palace. Originally designed by Miklós Ybl (of Opera House fame) in the 1870s, this Neo-Renaissance people zone evokes a more genteel time.

Cost and Hours: Garden free to enter and open long hours daily; exhibits have their own costs and hours. It's along the Buda embankment, about halfway between the Ádám Clark tér and Döbrentei tér tram stops, at Ybl Miklós tér.

Visiting the Park and Staircase: Walk through the ornate archway (past the bubbling fountain) and climb up the stairs to a cozy plateau with lush, flowery parklands ringed by monumental buildings. Originally, this "Castle Garden Bazaar" was mostly a shopping zone; in its next iteration, the buildings will house cultural institutions, including the National Dance Theater, a convention center, and exhibition space for temporary exhibits (and an exhibit on the architect Ybl and his works). The garden area is divided in half by a long, stately staircase and covered escalator, offering a quick ascent partway up Castle Hill. From the top of the escalator, a series of two elevators bring visitors the rest of the way up to the Royal Palace. Alternatively, you can hike up a long but scenic switchback trail along the ramparts to reach the palace. As this area is still under redevelopment, check www.varkertbazar.hu for the latest.

SIGHTS

Matthias Church and Nearby
▲▲Matthias Church (Mátyás-Templom)

Arguably Budapest's finest church inside and out, this historic house of worship—with a frilly Neo-Gothic spire and gilded Hungarian historical motifs slathered on every in-

terior wall—is Castle Hill's best sight. From the humble Loreto Chapel (with a tranquil statue of the Virgin that helped defeat the Ottomans), to altars devoted to top Hungarian kings, to a replica of the crown of Hungary, every inch of the church oozes history.

Cost and Hours: 1,200 Ft, includes Museum of Ecclesiastical Art (unless closed for renovation), audioguide may be available, Mon-Fri 9:00-17:00—possibly also open 19:00-20:00 in summer, Sat 9:00-13:00, Sun 13:00-17:00, Szentháromság tér 2, district I, tel. 1/488-7716, www.matyas-templom.hu.

For a self-guided tour of the Matthias Church, ✪ see the Castle Hill Walk chapter.

Fishermen's Bastion (Halászbástya)

Seven pointy domes and a double-decker rampart run along the cliff in front of Matthias Church. Evoking the original seven Magyar tribes, and built for the millennial celebra-

tion of their arrival, the Fishermen's Bastion is one of Budapest's top landmarks. This fanciful structure adorns Castle Hill like a decorative frieze or wedding-cake flowers. While some suckers pay for the views from here, parts of the rampart are free and always open. Or you can enjoy virtually the same view through the windows next to the bastion café for free.

Cost and Hours: 700 Ft, buy ticket at ticket office along the park wall across the square from Matthias Church, daily mid-March-mid-Oct 9:00-19:30; after closing time and off-season, no tickets are sold, but bastion is open and free to enter; Szentháromság tér 5, district I.

North Castle Hill
Remains of St. Mary Magdalene Church

Standing like a lonely afterthought at the northern tip of Castle Hill, St. Mary Magdalene was the crosstown rival of the Matthias Church. After the hill was recaptured from the Ottomans, only one church was needed, so St. Mary sat in ruins. But ultimately they rebuilt the church tower—which today evokes the rich but now-missing cultural tapestry that was once draped over this hill (free, always viewable).

Museum of Military History (Hadtörténeti Múzeum)

This fine museum explains various Hungarian military actions through history in painstaking detail. Watch military uniforms and weaponry evolve from the time of Árpád to today. With enough old uniforms and flags to keep an army-surplus store in stock for a decade, but limited English information, this place is of most interest to military and history buffs.

Cost and Hours: 1,400 Ft, April-Sept Tue-Sun 10:00-18:00, Oct-March Tue-Sun 10:00-16:00, closed Mon year-round, Tóth Árpád sétány 40, district I, tel. 1/325-1600.

Under Castle Hill

The hill is honeycombed with caves and passages, which are accessible to tourists in two different locations: The better option (Hospital in the Rock) comes with a fascinating tour illustrating how the caves were in active use during World War II and the Cold War; the Labyrinth offers a quicker visit with only a lightweight, quasi-historical exhibit.

▲Hospital in the Rock and Nuclear Bunker (Sziklakórház és Atombunker)

Bring your Castle Hill visit into modern times with this engaging tour. Sprawling beneath Castle Hill is a 25,000-square-foot labyrinthine network of hospital and fallout-shelter corridors built during the mid-20th century. (Hidden access points are scattered throughout the tourist zone, aboveground.) After decades in mothballs, the complex opened its doors to tourists a few years ago. While pricey, this visit is a must for doctors, nurses, and World War II buffs. I enjoy this as a lively interactive experience to balance out an otherwise sedate Castle Hill visit.

Cost and Hours: 3,600 Ft for required one-hour tour, 10 percent discount with Matthias Church ticket, additional discount if you're in the medical profession and can show your ID, daily 10:00-20:00, English tours at the top of each hour, last tour departs at 19:00, gift shop like an army-surplus store, Lovas utca 4C, district I, mobile 0670-701-0101, www.sziklakorhaz.eu/en.

Getting There: To find the hospital, stand with your back to Matthias Church and the Fishermen's Bastion. Walk straight past the plague column and down the little street (Szentháromság utca), then go down the covered steps at the wall. At the bottom of the stairs, turn right on Lovas utca, and walk 50 yards to the well-marked bunker entrance.

Background: At the outbreak of World War II, in 1939, the

SIGHTS

Hungarian government began building a secret emergency surgical hospital here in the heart of Budapest. When the war finally reached Hungary, in 1945, the hospital was in heavy use. While designed for 200 patients, eventually it held more than triple that number. Later, the forgotten hospital was used for two months to care for those injured in the 1956 Uprising. Then, as nuclear paranoia grew intense in the late 1950s and early 1960s, it was expanded to include a giant bomb shelter and potential post-nuclear-holocaust hospital.

Visiting the Hospital and Bunker: First you'll watch a 10-minute movie (with English subtitles) about the history of the place. Then, on the tour, your guide leads you through the tunnels to see room after room of perfectly preserved WWII and 1960s-era medical supplies and equipment, most still in working order. More than 200 wax figures engagingly bring the various hospital rooms to life: giant sick ward, operating room, and so on. On your way to the fallout shelter, you'll pass the decontamination showers, and see primitive radiation detectors and communist propaganda directing comrades how to save themselves in case of capitalist bombs or gas attacks. In the bunker, you'll also tour the various mechanical rooms that provided water and ventilation to this sprawling underground city.

Labyrinth of Buda Castle (Budavári Labirintus)

Armchair spelunkers can explore these dank and hazy caverns, with some wax figures in period costume, sparse historical information in English, a few actual stone artifacts, and a hokey Dracula exhibit (based on likely true notions that the "real" Dracula, the Transylvanian Duke Vlad Țepeș, was briefly imprisoned under Buda Castle). As this is indeed a labyrinth, expect to get lost—but don't worry; eventually you'll find your way out. After 18:00, they turn the lights out and give everyone gas lanterns. The exhibit loses something in the dark, but it's nicely spooky and a fun chance to startle amorous Hungarian teens—or be startled by mischievous ones. Even so, this hokey tourist trap pales in comparison with the other "underground" option.

Cost and Hours: 2,000 Ft, daily 10:00-19:30, last entry at 19:00, entrance between Royal Palace and Matthias Church at Úri utca 9, district I, tel. 1/212-0207, www.labirintus.com.

GELLÉRT HILL (GELLÉRTHEGY) AND NEARBY

The hill rising from the Danube just downriver from the castle is Gellért Hill. When King István converted Hungary to Christian-

ity in the year 1000, he brought in Bishop Gellért, a monk from Venice, to tutor his son. But some rebellious Magyars had other ideas. They put the bishop in a barrel, drove long nails in from the outside, and rolled him down this hill...tenderizing him to death. Gellért became the patron saint of Budapest and gave his name to the hill that killed him. Today the hill is a fine place to commune with nature on a hike or jog, followed by a restorative splash in its namesake baths. The following sights are listed roughly from north to south.

Monument Hike

The north slope of Gellért Hill (facing Castle Hill) is good for a low-impact hike. You'll see many monuments, most notably the big memorial to Bishop Gellért himself (you can't miss him, standing in a grand colonnade, as you cross the Elisabeth Bridge on Hegyalja út). A bit farther up, seek out a newer monument to the world's great philosophers—Eastern, Western, and in between—from Gandhi to Plato to Jesus. Nearby is

a scenic overlook with a king and a queen holding hands on either side of the Danube.

Citadella

This strategic, hill-capping fortress was built by the Habsburgs after the 1848 Revolution to keep an eye on their Hungarian subjects. There's not much to do up here (no museum or exhibits), but it's a good destination for an uphill hike, and provides the best panoramic view over all of Budapest.

The hill is crowned by the **Liberation Monument,** featuring a woman holding aloft a palm branch. Locals call it "the lady with the big fish" or "the great bottle opener." A heroic Soviet soldier, who once inspired the workers with a huge red star from the base of the monument, is now in Memento Park (see page 85).

Getting There: It's a steep hike up from the river to the Citadella. Bus #27 cuts some time off the trip, taking you up to the Búsuló Juhász stop (from which it's still an uphill hike to the fortress). You can catch bus #27 from either side of Gellért Hill. From the southern edge of the hill, catch this bus at the Móricz Zsigmond körtér stop (easy to reach: ride trams #19 or #41 south from anywhere along Buda's Danube embankment, or trams #47 or #49 from Pest's Small Boulevard ring road; you can also catch any of these trams at Gellért tér, in front of the Gellért Hotel). Alternatively, on the northern edge of the hill, catch bus #27 along the busy highway (Hegyalja út) that bisects Buda, at the intersection with Sánc utca (from central Pest, you can get to this stop on bus #178 from Astoria or Ferenciek tere).

Cave Church (Sziklatemplom)

Hidden in the hillside on the south end of the hill (across the street from Gellért Hotel) is Budapest's atmospheric cave church—burrowed right into the rock face. The communists bricked up this church when they came to power, but now it's open for visitors once again (500 Ft, unpredictable hours, closed to sightseers during frequent services). The little house at the foot of the hill (with the pointy turret) is where the monks who care for this church reside.

▲▲Gellért Baths

Located at the famous and once-exclusive Gellért Hotel, right at the Buda end of the Liberty Bridge, this elegant bath complex has long been the city's top choice for a swanky, hedonistic soak. It's also awash in tourists, and the Széchenyi Baths beat it out for pure fun...but the Gellért Baths' mysterious thermal spa rooms, and its giddy outdoor wave pool, make it an enticing thermal bath option.

Cost and Hours: 4,900 Ft for a locker, 400 Ft more for a personal changing cabin, cheaper after 17:00; open daily 6:00-20:00, last entry one hour before closing; Kelenhegyi út 4, district XI, M4: Gellért tér, tel. 1/466-6166, ext. 165, www.gellertbath.com.

○ See the Thermal Baths chapter.

▲▲Rudas Baths

Along the Danube toward Castle Hill from Gellért Baths, Rudas (ROO-dawsh) offers Budapest's most old-fashioned, Turkish-style bathing experience. The historic main pool of the thermal bath section sits under a 500-year-old Ottoman dome. Bathers move from pool to pool to tweak their body temperature. On weekdays, it's a nude, gender-segregated experience, while it becomes more accessible (and mixed) on weekends, when men and women put on swimsuits and mingle beneath that historic dome. Rudas also has a ho-hum swimming pool, and a state-of-the-art "wellness" section, with a variety of modern massage pools and an inviting hot tub/sun deck on the roof with a stunning Budapest panorama (these two areas are mixed-gender every day).

Cost and Hours: The three parts are covered by separate tickets: thermal baths-3,000 Ft, wellness center-2,900 Ft, combo-ticket for all three-4,500 Ft (or 5,500 Ft on weekends); daily 6:00-20:00, last entry one hour before closing; open for nighttime bathing with nightclub ambience Fri-Sat 22:00-late (4,400 Ft); wellness and swimming pool areas mixed-gender and clothed at all times; thermal baths men-only Mon and Wed-Fri, women-only Tue, mixed Sat-Sun and during nighttime bathing; Döbrentei tér 9, district I, tel. 1/375-8373, www.rudasbaths.com.

○ See the Thermal Baths chapter.

THE REST OF BUDA

There's not much of interest to tourists in Buda beyond Castle and Gellért Hills.

The **Víziváros** area, or "Water Town," is squeezed between Castle Hill and the Danube. While it's a useful home base for

sleeping and eating (see those chapters for details), and home to the Budai Vigadó concert venue (see the Entertainment in Budapest chapter), there's little in the way of sightseeing. The riverfront Batthyány tér area, at the northern edge of Víziváros, is a hub both for transportation (M2/red Metró line, HÉV suburban railway to Óbuda and Szentendre, and embankment trams) and for shopping and dining.

To the north of Castle Hill is **Széll Kálmán tér,** a transportation hub (for the M2/red Metró line, several trams, and buses #16, #16A, and #116 to Castle Hill) and shopping center (featuring the giant Mammut supermall, and many smaller shops that cling to it like barnacles to a boat). This unpretentious zone, while light on sightseeing, offers a chance to commune with workaday Budapest. Its one attraction is **Millenáris Park,** an inviting play zone for adults and kids that combines grassy fields and modern buildings. Though not worth going out of your way for, this park might be worth a stroll if the weather's nice and you're exploring the neighborhood (a long block behind Mammut mall).

Rózsadomb ("Rose Hill"), rising just north of Széll Kálmán tér, was so named for the rose garden planted on its slopes by a Turkish official 400 years ago. Today it's an upscale residential zone.

To the south, the district called the **Tabán**—roughly between Castle Hill and Gellért Hill—was once a colorful, ramshackle neighborhood of sailor pubs and brothels. After being virtually wiped out in World War II, now it's home to parks and a dull residential district.

Beyond riverfront Buda, the terrain becomes hilly. This area—

the **Buda Hills**—is a pleasant getaway for a hike or stroll through wooded terrain, but still close to the city. One enjoyable way to explore these hills is by hopping a ride on the Children's Railway (see the Budapest with Children chapter).

Two other major attractions—the part of town called **Óbuda** ("Old Buda") and **Memento Park**—are on the Buda side of the river but away from the center, and described in the following sections.

Outer Budapest

The following sights, while technically within Budapest, take a little more time to reach.

ÓBUDA

Budapest was originally three cities: Buda, Pest, and Óbuda. Óbuda ("Old Buda") is the oldest of the three—the first known residents of the region (Celts) settled here, and today it's still littered with ruins from the next occupants (Romans). Despite all the history, the district ranks relatively low on the list of Budapest's sightseeing priorities: Aside from a charming small-town ambience on its main square, it offers a pair of good museums on two important 20th-century Hungarian artists, and—a short train ride away—some Roman ruins.

Getting There: To reach the first three sights listed here, go to Batthyány tér in Buda (M2/red Metró line) and catch the HÉV suburban train (H5/purple line) north to the Szentlélek tér stop. The Vasarely Museum is 50 yards from the station (exit straight ahead, away from the river; it's on the right, behind the bus stops). The town square is 100 yards beyond that (bear right around the corner), and 200 yards later (turn left at the ladies with the umbrellas), you'll find the Imre Varga Collection. Aquincum is three stops farther north on the HÉV line.

▲Vasarely Museum

This museum features two floors of eye-popping, colorful paintings by Victor Vasarely (1906-1997), the founder of Op Art. If you're not going to Vasarely's hometown of Pécs, which has an even better museum of his works (see page 399), this place gives you a good taste. The exhibition—displayed in a large, white hall with each piece labeled in English—follows his artistic evolution from his youth as a graphic designer to the playful optical illusions he

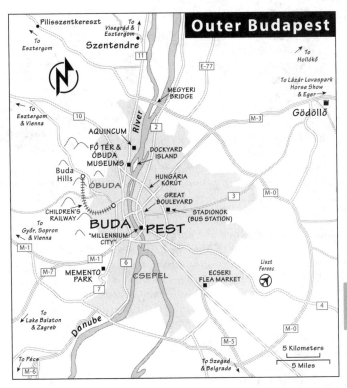

Outer Budapest

was most famous for. You'll find most of these trademark works (as well as temporary exhibits of other artists) upstairs. Sit on a comfy bench and stare into Vasarely's mind-bending world. Let yourself get a little woozy. Think of how this style combines right-brained abstraction with an almost rigidly left-brained, geometrical approach. It makes my brain hurt (or maybe it's just all the wavy lines). Vasarely and the movement he pioneered helped to inspire the trippy styles of the 1960s. If the art gets you pondering Rubik's Cube, it will come as no surprise that Ernő Rubik was a professor of mathematics here in Budapest.

Cost and Hours: 800 Ft, Tue-Sun 10:00-17:30, closed Mon, Szentlélek tér 6, district III, tel. 1/388-7551, www.vasarely.hu. The museum is immediately on the right as you leave the Szentlélek tér HÉV station.

Óbuda Main Square (Fő Tér)

If you keep going past the Vasarely Museum and turn right, you enter Óbuda's cute Main Square. The big, yellow building was the Óbuda Town Hall when this was its own city. Today it's still the

SIGHTS

office of the district mayor. While still well within the city limits of Budapest, this charming square feels like its own small town.

To the right of the Town Hall is a whimsical, much-photographed statue of **women with umbrellas.** Replicas of this sculpture, by local artist Imre Varga, decorate the gardens of wealthy summer homes on Lake Balaton. Varga created many of Budapest's distinctive monuments, including the *Tree of Life* behind the Great Synagogue and a major work that's on display at Memento Park. His museum is just down the street (turn left at the umbrella ladies).

▲Imre Varga Collection (Varga Imre Gyűjtemény)

Imre Varga, who worked from the 1950s through the 2000s, is one of Hungary's most prominent artists, and probably its single best sculptor. This humble museum—crammed with his works (originals, as well as smaller replicas of Varga statues you'll see all over Hungary), and with a fine sculpture garden out back—offers a good introduction to the man's substantial talent. Working mostly with steel, his pieces can appear rough and tangled at times, but are always evocative and lifelike. Unfortunately, English information is virtually nonexistent here.

Cost and Hours: 800 Ft, Tue-Sun 10:00-18:00, closed Mon, Laktanya utca 7, district III, Szentlélek tér HÉV station, tel. 1/250-0274, www.budapestgaleria.hu.

Visiting the Museum: The first room holds a replica of a sculpture of St. István approaching the Virgin Mary, the original of which is in the Vatican. The next room has several small-scale copies of famous Varga works from around the country, including some you might recognize from Budapest (such as the *Tree of Life* from behind the Great Synagogue).

Pause at the statue with the headless, saluting soldier wearing medals. Through the communist times, there were three types of artists: banned, tolerated, and supported. Varga was tolerated, and works like this subtly commented on life under communism. In fact, the medallions nailed to the figure's chest were Varga's own, from his pre-communist military service. Anyone with such medallions was persecuted by communists in the 1950s...so Varga disposed of his this way.

Nearby is the exit to the garden out back, with a smattering of life-size portraits (including three prostitutes leaning against a wall, illustrating the passing of time). The rest of the museum is predominantly filled with portraits (mostly busts) of various important Hungarians. You'll see variations on certain themes that intrigued Varga, including a reclining ballerina.

Aquincum Museum

Long before Magyars laid eyes on the Danube, Óbuda was the Roman city of Aquincum. Here you can explore the remains of the 2,000-year-old Roman town and amphitheater. The museum is proud of its centerpiece, a water organ.

Cost and Hours: 1,600 Ft, grounds open April-Oct Tue-Sun 9:00-18:00, Nov-March Tue-Sun 9:00-16:00, exhibitions open one hour later, closed Mon year-round, Szentendrei út 139, district III, HÉV north to Aquincum stop, tel. 1/250-1650, www.aquincum. hu.

Getting There: From the HÉV stop, cross the busy road and turn to the right. Go through the railway underpass, and you'll see the ruins ahead and on the left as you emerge.

▲▲MEMENTO PARK (A.K.A. STATUE PARK)

Little remains of the communist era in Budapest. To sample those drab and surreal times, head to this motley collection of statues,

which seem to be preaching their Marxist ideology to each other in an open field on the outskirts of town. You'll see the great figures of the Soviet Bloc, both international (Lenin, Marx, and Engels) and Hungarian (local bigwig Béla Kun) as well as gigantic, stoic figures representing Soviet ideals. This stiff dose of Socialist Realist art, while time-consuming to reach, is rewarding for those curious for a taste of history that most Hungarians would rather forget.

Cost and Hours: 1,500 Ft, daily 10:00-sunset, six miles southwest of city center at the corner of Balatoni út and Szabadka út, district XXII, tel. 1/424-7500, www.mementopark.hu.

Getting There: The park runs a handy direct **bus** from Deák tér in downtown Pest to the park (April-Oct daily at 11:00, Nov-March Sat-Mon at 11:00—no bus Tue-Fri, round-trip takes

SIGHTS

2.5 hours total, including a 1.5-hour visit to the park, 4,900-Ft round-trip includes park entry, book online for discount: www. mementopark.hu).

The **public transport** option requires a transfer: Ride the Metró's M4/green line to the end of the line at Kelenföld. Head up to street level and catch bus #101, which takes you to Memento Park in about 15 minutes (second stop, runs every 10 minutes—but only on weekdays). On weekends, when bus #101 doesn't run, take bus #150, which takes longer (2/hour, about 25 minutes). On either bus, be sure the driver knows where you want to get off.

○ See the Memento Park Tour chapter.

BEYOND BUDAPEST

For information on the village of **Szentendre,** the Royal Palace at **Gödöllő,** and the engaging horse shows at **Lázár Lovaspark** (all just outside the city limits), as well as some places farther afield (the royal castles at Visegrád, the great church at Esztergom, and the folk village of Hollókő), see the Day Trips from Budapest chapter.

THERMAL BATHS

Fürdő

Splashing and relaxing in Budapest's thermal baths is the city's top attraction. Though it might sound daunting, bathing with the Magyars is far more accessible than you'd think. The first two thermal baths I've described in this chapter (Széchenyi and Gellért) are basically like your hometown swimming pool—except the water is a hundred degrees, there are plenty of jets and bubbles to massage away your stress, and you're surrounded by scantily clad Hungarians. If you want a more "authentic" and naked experience, I've also described one of those (Rudas, which also has a more modern "wellness" area).

All this fun goes way back. Hungary's Carpathian Basin is essentially a thin crust covering a vast reservoir of hot water. The Romans named their settlement near present-day Budapest Aquincum—"abundant waters"—and took advantage of those waters by building many baths. Centuries later, the occupying Ottomans revived the custom. And today, thermal baths are as Hungarian as can be.

Locals brag that if you poke a hole in the ground anywhere in Hungary, you'll find a hot-water spring. Judging from Budapest, they could be right: The city has 123 natural springs and some two dozen thermal baths *(fürdő)*. The baths, which are all operated by the same government agency, are actually a part of the health-care system. Doctors regularly prescribe treatments that include massage, soaking in baths of various heat and mineral compositions, and swimming laps. For these patients (who you might see carrying a blue ticket), a visit to the bath is subsidized.

But increasingly, there's a new angle on Hungary's hot water:

entertainment. Adventure water parks are springing up all over the country, and even the staid old baths have some enjoyable jets and currents. Overcome your jitters, follow my instructions, and dive in...or miss out on *the* quintessential Budapest experience.

Baths Orientation

American tourists often feel squeamish at the thought of bathing with Speedo-clad, pot-bellied Hungarians. Relax! It's less intimidating than it sounds—and the fun you'll have far outweighs the jitters. I was nervous on my first visit, too. But now I feel like a trip to Hungary just isn't complete without a splish-splash in the bath.

While Budapest has several mostly nude, gender-segregated Turkish baths (such as Rudas), my favorites—Széchenyi and Gellért—are less intimidating: Men and women are usually together, and you can keep your swimsuit on the entire time. (Even at mixed baths, there generally are a few clothing-optional, gender-segregated areas, where locals are likely to be nude—or wearing a *kötény,* a loose-fitting loincloth.)

Bring along these items, if you have them: swimsuit, towel, flip-flops, bottle of water, soap and shampoo for a shower afterward, comb or brush, swim or shower cap (see below), plastic shopping bag or sealable baggie (for your wet swimsuit), and maybe sunscreen and leisure reading. Hotels typically frown on guests taking their room towels to the baths. Try asking nicely if they have some loaner towels just for this purpose (they'll probably tell you to rent one there...but what they don't know won't hurt them). At Budapest's baths, you can usually rent a towel or swimsuit (for men, Speedos are always available, trunks sometimes)—bring enough cash for the deposit, which will be refunded when you leave. A swim cap is required in lap pools at each bath. You can rent or buy a flimsy one there, but if you know you'll be swimming laps, see if you can grab a shower cap from your hotel—it will work fine.

Each bath complex has multiple pools, used for different purposes. Big pools with cooler water are for serious swimming, while the smaller, hotter thermal baths

THERMAL BATHS

(*gyógyfürdő*, or simply *gőz*) are for relaxing, enjoying the jets and current pools, and playing chess. The water bubbles up from hot springs at 77° Celsius (170° Fahrenheit), then is mixed with cooler water to achieve the desired temperatures. Most pools are marked with the water temperature in Celsius (cooler pools are about 30°C/86°F; warmer pools are closer to 36°C/97°F or 38°C/100°F, about like the hot tub back home; and the hottest are 42°C/108°F... yowtch!). Locals hit the cooler pools first, then work their way up to the top temps.

While the lap pools are chlorinated, most of the thermal baths are only lightly chlorinated, or not at all. Unlike swimming pools in the US—where the water is recycled back into the pool—water here is slowly drained out and replaced with fresh water from the hot springs. Locals figure this continuous natural flushing makes chemicals unnecessary. Still, total germophobes may not be entirely comfortable at the baths; either convince yourself to go with the flow, or skip the trip.

You'll also usually find a dry sauna, a wet steam room, a cold plunge pool (for a pleasurable jolt when you're feeling over-

heated), and sunbathing areas (which may be segregated and clothing-optional). Some baths have fun flourishes: bubbles, whirlpools, massage jets, wave pools, and so on.

The most challenging part of visiting a Hungarian bath is the complicated entrance proce-dure. Things have gotten much easier in recent years, but you'll still be confronted with a complex payment scheme, lengthy menus of massages and other treatments, and occasionally monolingual staff. While it seems confusing at first, it's more logical than you might think—and, thankfully, English translations of your ticket options and directions to various parts of the complex are posted. Although I've carefully outlined the specifics for each bath, they can change from year to year. Some general tips: Keep track of any receipt or slip of paper you're given, as you may be asked to show it later (for example, to get your towel deposit back). Hang in there, go where people direct you, and enjoy this unique cultural experience. Remember, they're used to tourists—so don't be afraid to act like one. If you can make it through those first few confusing minutes, you'll soon be relaxing like a pro.

Advance tickets for the baths are sold in hotel lobbies and other sales outlets all over town. But as there's rarely a line to buy

THERMAL BATHS

a bath ticket, prebooking makes little sense—just buy your tickets when you arrive at the bath.

Budapest's baths recently upgraded to a system that uses a plastic, watch-like wristband as your ticket. When you enter, touch the wristband to the entry turnstile, then again to be assigned a changing cabin or to access a locker, then again each time you want to unlock your cabin or locker. When you're done, drop the wristband into a slot as you exit the turnstile.

While enjoying the baths, you can leave your clothing and other belongings in your locked cabin or locker. Although I've found these to be safe, and bath employees assure me that thefts are rare (a cabin is safer than a locker), it's at your own risk. Another option is to leave valuables in a safe (generally costs 600 Ft, ask when you buy ticket). Many locals bring plastic shopping bags to hold their essentials: towels, leisure reading, and sunscreen.

Be aware that the jets, bubbles, waves, waterfalls, and whirlpools sometimes take turns running. For example, a current pool runs for 10 minutes, then a series of jets starts up and the current pool stops for 10 minutes, then the current pool starts up again, and so on. If a particularly fun feature of the pool doesn't seem to be working, just give it a few minutes.

While many treatments require a doctor's prescription, anyone can enjoy a massage. Typically you'll book this when you buy your ticket, and arrange a time; on busy days (especially Mon, Fri, and Sat), you may have to wait an hour or two—if you don't want to spend all day at the baths, ask when the soonest available time is before you book. On other days, you may be able to get your massage immediately (or whenever you want).

You'll be offered a choice of different kinds of massage. There are two basic kinds: A **"relax massage"** or **"aroma massage"** is a restful rubdown, typically using oil (often scented). This is what's sometimes called a Swedish-style massage. The other option is a **"scrub massage"** or **"skin-firming massage."** Similar to a Turkish-style massage, this is (for some) less restful, as it's intended to exfoliate your skin and involves some very hard scrubbing.

Yet another choice is a **Thai massage;** you'll see this advertised at some baths, sometimes in a separate section (since it's operated by a private agency). You'll lie on a mat close to the floor for more of a full-body stretching-and-cracking massage, using feet, knees, and elbows—usually administered by an actual Thai immigrant. Sometimes the Thai massage service also provides a more restful, scented-oils massage as well.

One more word on massages: Remember that the spas are medical facilities, so the massage may be more functional and less serene than what you're used to back home.

After you've changed back to street clothes and are ready to leave the bath, ask whether there's a centrifuge *(centrifuga)* where you can give your soggy swimsuit a spin. (Most baths have one, but they're often hidden.) After just a couple of minutes, it's merely damp rather than dripping—and easier to carry home without making a mess.

Here are some useful phrases:

English	Hungarian	Pronounced
Bath	*Fürdő*	FEWR-dur
Men	*Férfi*	FAYR-fee
Women	*Női*	NUR-ee
Changing Cabin	*Kabin*	KAH-been
Locker	*Szekrény*	SEHK-rayn
Ticket Office	*Pénztár*	PAYNZ-tar
Thermal Bath	*Gyógyfürdő, Gőz*	JODGE-fewr-dur, gorz

Please trust me, and take the plunge. My readers almost unanimously report that the thermal baths were their top Hungarian experience. If you go into it with an easygoing attitude and a sense of humor, I promise you'll have a blast.

The Baths

Budapest's two-dozen baths *(fürdő)* were taken over by the communist government, and they're all still owned by the city. The three baths listed here are the best-known, most representative, and most convenient for first-timers: The Széchenyi Baths are more casual and popular with locals; the Gellért Baths are touristy, famous, and genteel; and the Rudas Baths are old-school Turkish, with more nudity and less "fun" (unless you find public nudity fun...but that's a whole other book). Rudas also has a modern "wellness" section, offering an interesting contrast under one roof. To me, Széchenyi is second to none, but some travelers prefer the Gellért or Rudas experience. As they're all quite different, doing more than one is an excellent option. For more information on all of Budapest's baths, see www.budapestgyogyfurdoi.hu or www.spasbudapest.com.

▲▲▲SZÉCHENYI BATHS (SZÉCHENYI FÜRDŐ)

To soak with the locals, head for this bath complex—the big, yellow, copper-domed building in the middle of City Park. Széchenyi (SAY-chehn-yee) is the best of Budapest's many bath experiences, a place to relax and enjoy some Hungarian good living. Magyars of all shapes and sizes stuff themselves into tiny swimsuits and strut their stuff. Housewives float blissfully in the warm water. Intellectuals and roly-poly elder statesmen stand in chest-high water around chessboards and ponder their next moves. This is Budapest at its best.

Cost: 4,500 Ft for locker (in gender-segregated locker room), 500 Ft more for personal changing cabin, 200 Ft more on weekends, cheaper if you arrive after 19:00. The price includes the outdoor swimming pool area and the indoor thermal bath and sauna (but note that the in-door sections close earlier—see

below). Couples can share a changing cabin: One person pays the cabin rate, the other pays the locker rate, but both use the same cabin. As the cabins are tight, you may need to take turns...or get very cozy.

Hours: Swimming pool (the best part, outdoors) open daily 6:00-22:00, indoor thermal bath and sauna open daily 6:00-19:00, last entry one hour before closing. On some summer weekends, the baths may be open later (see "Night Bathing," later).

Location and Entrances: In City Park at Állatkerti körút 11, district XIV, M1: Széchenyi fürdő. The huge bath complex has

three entrances. The busiest one—technically the **"thermal bath entrance"**—is the grand main entry, facing south (roughly toward Vajdahunyad Castle). I avoid this entrance—there's often a line during peak times, and it's a bit more confusing to find your way once inside. Instead, I prefer the **"swimming pool entrance,"** facing the zoo on the other side of the complex—it's more user-friendly, has shorter lines, and is open later. A third, smaller **"medical entrance,"** to the right as you face the zoo entry (near the Metró station), provides access to either the thermal bath changing rooms or the swimming pool changing rooms, but can also have long lines (tel. 1/363-3210, www.szechenyibath.hu).

Massage: A wide array of massages and other special treatments are offered—find the English menu in the lobby. If you're interested in this, set up an appointment and pay at the office near the towel-rental desk (3,300 Ft/20 minutes, 4,500 Ft/30 minutes, expect 15-30-minute wait for your appointment when it's busy). Remember that these massages are medicinal—not the mellow, soothing variety you might expect back home. You'll pay more for something more hedonistic. There are two other options: a Thai massage parlor at the upper level of the complex (above the swimming pool entrance—just follow the signs) and a separate "infor-

Szechenyi Baths

ZOO
CIRCUS
ZOO

ÁLLATKERTI KÖRÚT

❶

❸ ❼ ❽ ❾ ❽ ❼

Fun Pool

Lap ❺ *Pool*

Relaxation Pool ❻ ❹

To Vörösmarty tér

Ⓜ Széchenyi fürdő

Ⓜ To Mexikói út

❷

50 Meters
50 Yards

KÓS KÁROLY SÉTÁNY

← To Heroes' Square

↙ To Vajdahunyad Castle

City Park

❶ Swimming Pool Entrance
❷ Thermal Bath Entrance
❸ Medical Entrance
❹ Fun Pool (whirlpool, bubbles)
❺ Lap Pool (cap required)
❻ Relaxation Pool (jets, chess)

❼ Changing Cabins (ground floor & upstairs) & Sun Terraces (upstairs)
❽ Locker Rooms & Towel Rental (downstairs)
❾ Grandstand, Fitness Center & Massage (upstairs)

THERMAL BATHS

mation" desk just inside the swimming-pool entrance where you can book a "V.I.P. massage" (either option costs 11,000-14,000 Ft/1 hour).

Night Bathing: The baths are a joy in the evening, when both the price and the crowds are reduced. In cool weather, or even rain or snow, the pools maintain their hot temperatures—making this a delightful after-hours activity. Busy sightseers can be extremely efficient by closing down the museums, then heading to the baths. The only caveat: The indoor (and less appealing) thermal bath sections close after 19:00.

Additionally, Széchenyi is open late into the night on summer weekends, for a "sparty" event called *Szecska* ("Chaff"), where the bath complex basically becomes one big hot-water dance club (about 7,000 Ft if you book online in advance, mid-April-Sept Sat 22:30-late, www.szecska.hu).

Entry Procedure: While the following details might seem intimidating, it's easier than it sounds. Take your time and you'll eventually find your way. These instructions assume that you're using the swimming pool entrance (from this entrance, there are parallel facilities in each direction).

First, in the grand lobby, pay the cashier. You'll be given a waterproof, watch-like wristband with an electronic chip inside. Touch your wristband to the panel on the turnstile to enter the complex. Just after the turnstile, pause to get oriented: Straight ahead is a row of private changing cabins. At the start of this row is a stairwell. If you go **up the stairs,** you'll find another floor of changing cabins (as well as the Thai massage area, gender-segregated "solarium" sun terraces, and a fun grandstand overlooking the main pool—these are ideal vantage points to snap some photos before you change). If you go **down the stairs,** you'll find a long hallway lined with hairdryers and mirrors; the locker rooms are at each end (remember, men are *férfi* and women are *női*). Also downstairs, you'll find the counter where you can rent a towel or swimsuit (do this before you change, as you'll need money: towel-700 Ft plus refundable 1,500-Ft deposit; swimsuit-1,100 Ft plus refundable 4,400-Ft deposit). Renting a small safe for your valuables costs 500 Ft.

Report to the area that you paid for (private cabin or locker room). If you paid for a **cabin,** look for an electronic panel on the wall, and hold your wristband against this panel for a few seconds—you'll automatically be assigned a number for a cabin. Go find your cabin. When you touch your wristband to the lock, the light turns blue and the door unlocks. The door should lock automatically when you close it (but test it to be sure). You can reopen your cabin as often as you like. If you forget the number of your cabin, just touch your wristband to the panel in the hall, and it'll remind you.

If you paid for a **locker,** you can head for the locker room and choose any open one. Once you hold your wristband against it to lock it, it can only be unlocked by that same wristband.

If you get confused, the attendants (who usually speak a few words of English) can help you find your way.

Phew. Now that you've changed into your swimsuit and stored your belongings, let's have some fun.

Taking the Waters: The bath complex has two parts, outside and inside.

For most visitors, the best part is the swimming pool area **outside.** Orient yourself to the three pools (facing the main, domed building): The pool to the left is for fun (cooler water— 30°C/86°F, warmer in winter, lots of jets and bubbles, lively and often crowded, includes circular current pool); the pool on the right is for relaxation (warmer water— 38°C/100°F, mellow atmosphere, a few massage jets, chess); and the main pool in the center is all business (cooler water—28°C/82°F in summer, 26°C/79°F in winter, people doing laps, swim cap required). You get extra credit for joining the gang in a chess match. Stairs to saunas (with cold plunge pools, cold showers, and even an ice maker) are below the doors to the indoor thermal bath complex.

There's a basic **snack bar** right in the middle of the complex, but you're also allowed to bring in your own food if you munch discreetly.

For good **views**—or to use the well-equipped **fitness center**— climb up the stairs near the front of the changing-cabin hallways. There you'll find the grandstand area overlooking the main pool, with the fitness center just above it.

If you're feeling waterlogged and need a break from the baths, it's fun just to explore the sprawling complex. It's a bit of a maze, but don't be afraid to poke around (keep in mind that several areas— such as the solarium sun terraces up top—are clothing-optional; again, men are *férfi* and women are *női*). Go for a photo safari, and don't miss the grandstand.

Inside the main building is the thermal bath section, a series of indoor pools; each of these is designed for a specific medical treatment. You'll notice each one is labeled with the temperature (ranging from 28°C/82°F to 36°C/97°F to 38°C/100°F; you'll also find steam rooms with a 18°C/64°F cold plunge pool nearby). The pools also have varying types and amounts of healthy minerals— some of which can make the water quite green and/or stinky. Hungarians who use Széchenyi Baths medicinally have worked out a specific regimen for moving from pool to pool. But if all of this smelly water is lost on you (as it is on many foreigners), it's totally fine to focus on the fun outdoor pools. (I've had many great visits to Széchenyi Baths without ever going inside the thermal bath complex.)

Exit Procedure: When you leave, be sure to leave your locker open. If you rented a towel or swimsuit, return it to the desk where you got it to reclaim your deposit. Then, as you exit the complex, insert your wristband into the little slot at the turnstile to exit. Now continue your sightseeing...soggy, but relaxed.

If you're heading to the **Metró,** the station is very close, but easy to miss: It's basically a pair of nondescript stairwells in the middle of the park, roughly toward Heroes' Square from the thermal bath entrance (look for the low-profile, yellow *Földalatti* sign; to head for downtown, take the stairwell marked *a Vörösmarty tér felé*).

▲▲GELLÉRT BATHS (GELLÉRT FÜRDŐ)

Using the baths at Gellért (GEH-layrt) Hotel costs a bit more than the Széchenyi Baths, and you won't run into nearly as many locals; this is definitely a more upscale, touristy, spa-like scene. While its thermal areas are smaller, they're arguably even more atmospheric—with exquisite porcelain details and an air of mystery. If you want a soothing, luxurious bath experience in an elegant setting, this is the place. And if it's fun you're looking for, the Gellért Baths have something that Széchenyi doesn't: a huge, deliriously enjoyable wave pool that'll toss you around like a queasy surfer (summer only).

Cost: 4,900 Ft for a locker, 400 Ft more for a personal changing cabin, cheaper if you arrive after 17:00.

Hours: Daily 6:00-20:00, last entry one hour before closing.

Location: It's on the Buda side of the green Liberty Bridge (M4: Szent Gellért tér; or take trams #47 and #49 from Deák tér in Pest, or trams #19 and #41 along the Buda embankment from Víziváros below the castle, Gellért tér stop). The entrance to the

baths is under the stone dome opposite the bridge, around the right side of the hotel (Kelenhegyi út 4, district XI, tel. 1/466-6166, ext. 165, www.gellertbath.com).

Entry Procedure: The grand entry hall is fully open to visitors, so feel free to poke around to get the lay of

THERMAL BATHS

the land before buying your ticket (good views from the gallery up above). The entrance doors are flanked by ticket windows; just past those, on the right, is an information booth that usually has English-speaking staff.

In the summer, they sell two different tickets based on which changing area you'll use (same price for either ticket, and both options allow you to move freely between the thermal baths and swimming pool areas once you're inside). With a **thermal bath ticket,** you'll change in a large, gender-segregated area with wooden stalls separated by curtains. With a **swimming pool ticket,** you'll go to a mixed area where opposite-sex couples can share a cabin (this area also has gender-segregated locker rooms). I prefer the swimming pool section, which has more secure lockers. Couples who want to share a cabin should ask for "swimming pool ticket, one cabin, one locker." As the cabins can be tight, you may have to take turns changing.

A dizzying array of **massages** and other treatment options are also sold at the ticket windows. Most are available only with a doctor's note, but some massages are for anyone (generally 3,500 Ft/20 minutes, 4,700 Ft/30 minutes, 5,700 Ft/40 minutes; arrange a time when you buy your ticket). Upstairs, you can also book a Thai massage.

Buy your ticket (and, if you like, pay for a massage), and you'll be issued a plastic wristband that acts as your ticket. Then glide

through the swanky lobby. The indoor swimming pool is on your right, about halfway down the main hall; look for Gate II. Looking through the window to the pool, visualize the perfectly symmetrical bath complex: The men's thermal bath, changing cabins, and lockers are on the left, while the identical women's facilities are on the right. The two sections meet at this shared pool in the center.

If you bought a swimming pool ticket, you'll touch your wristband to the turnstile and enter here: Men/*férfi* go down the stairs on the left, and women/*női* on the right (either way, you'll head down a long hallway, then up stairs to the changing areas—a mixed-gender area for cabins down below, with a segregated locker area up above). If you have a thermal bath ticket, the entrances are a bit farther away: women to the right, closer to the entrance (Gate I); and men to the left, at the end of the hall (Gate III).

If you want to rent a towel (700 Ft) or swimsuit (1,000 Ft; both with a 4,000-Ft deposit, cash only), look for the desk near the entrance to the changing cabin area.

THERMAL BATHS

Once inside the changing area, if you bought a cabin ticket, hold your wristband against the electronic panel to be assigned a changing cabin number. Once you track it down, touch your wristband to the cabin to open it. The door locks automatically behind you (but test it just to be sure). If you bought a locker ticket, you can choose any open locker, then lock it with your wristband. It can only be unlocked using that same wristband.

Taking the Waters: Once you've changed, you can spend your time either indoors or out. From the locker room, look for signs *to the effervescent bath-pool* (for the indoor section) or *to the swimming-pool with artificial waves* (for the outdoor section).

Inside, the central, genteel-feeling hall is home to a cool-water swimming pool (swim cap required—you can buy a cheap one

for 700 Ft) and a crowded hot-water pool (36°C/97°F). On sunny days, they crank open the retractable roof; for nice views down onto the pool, find the stairs up near the locker rooms. Back toward the main hall are doors to the thermal baths (easy to miss—walk to far end

of pool and look for signs). While the doors may still be marked for men's and women's sections, both sides are now open to both genders. These grand old halls are probably the most atmospheric part of the bath—slathered with colorful porcelain decorations (especially the men's side). There are big pools at either end: 36°C (97°F) and 38°C (100°F) in the men's section, and slightly cooler in the women's section. Notice that these temperatures perfectly flank the normal temperature of the human body, allowing you to toggle your temp at will. At the far end of the bath are a steam room (45-50°C/113-122°F) and a cold plunge pool (18°C/64°F). Back out near the changing cabins is a dry sauna (a.k.a. "dry sweating rooms," 50-70°C/122-158°F). If you paid for a massage, report to the massage room in this section at your appointed time—or just show up and see if they can take you.

Outside, you'll find several sunbathing areas and a warm thermal pool, along with an atmospheric woody sauna and a big

barrel-shaped plunge pool with cold water (all hiding up the stairs on the right). But the main attraction is the big, unheated wave pool in the center (generally closed Oct-April, weather-dependent). Not for the squeamish, this pool thrashes fun-loving swimmers around like driftwood.

The swells in the deeper area are fun and easy to float on, but the crashing waves at the shallow end are vigorous, if not dangerous. If there are no waves, just wait around for a while (you'll hear a garbled message on the loudspeaker five minutes before the tide comes in).

Exit Procedure: When you're finished, return your towel and swimsuit to reclaim your deposit, then insert your wristband into the slot at the exit turnstile.

▲▲RUDAS BATHS (RUDAS FÜRDŐ)

To get to the Turkish roots of Budapest's obsession with thermal baths, head for Rudas (ROO-dawsh). It's the most historic, local,

and potentially intimidating of the three baths I list—but it may also be the most rewarding, as it offers the most variety. Rudas has three sections (covered by separate tickets): the Turkish-style thermal bath zone; the swimming pool area; and the wellness section. While the swimming pool is nothing special, the other two are strikingly different—and equally worthwhile. Read these quick descriptions before your visit, to decide which area(s) you want to experience.

Rudas' **thermal section** feels more like the classic Turkish baths of yore: On most days, the main thermal bath section is men-only, and those men wander around nude or in flimsy loincloths under a 500-year-old dome first built by the Ottoman Turks. These baths are not about splashy fun—there are no jets, bubbles, or whirlpools. Instead, Rudas is about history, and about serious temperature modulation—stepping your body temperature up and down between very hot and very cold. While not for the skittish, Rudas offers adventurous travelers and bath connoisseurs another facet of the Budapest baths experience. Be aware that all of Budapest's single-sex, nude baths are (to varying degrees) a popular meeting point for the local gay community—though Rudas is less so than some others (such as Király Baths). Rudas becomes far more widely accessible to all visitors on weekends (Sat-Sun), when men and women mingle together in swimsuits under the fine old dome; then, at nighttime (Fri-Sat only), this old chamber becomes a modern nightclub until the wee hours.

The newly opened **wellness area**—with a handful of relaxing jet pools—is the modern, accessible yin to the thermal baths' antique yang. The main reason to visit this section is the rooftop terrace, where you can sunbathe or soak while looking out over sweeping views of the Budapest skyline. Imagine: You're up to your

THERMAL BATHS

earlobes in hot water, looking out over commuters slogging across the city's clogged bridges...and feeling pretty happy to be on vacation.

Finally, Rudas' **swimming pool** is similar to, but far less elegant than, Gellért's, and is only worthwhile for those who want to swim laps.

Cost: The various parts are covered by separate tickets. The historic thermal bath alone costs 3,000 Ft, the wellness center alone costs 2,900 Ft, and the swimming pool can be added to either ticket for a few hundred extra forints. But I'd spring for the 4,500-Ft combo-ticket that covers everything—thermal, wellness, and swimming pool—to enjoy the full scope of what Rudas offers. On weekends, the combo-ticket costs 5,500 Ft.

Hours: Daily 6:00-20:00, last entry one hour before closing. While the wellness area is mixed-gender every day, the thermal baths are open only to men Mon and Wed-Fri, only to women Tue, and to both men and women Sat-Sun. The night bathing (described later) is also mixed-gender.

Location: It's in a low-profile building at the foot of Gellért Hill, just south of the white Elisabeth Bridge (Döbrentei tér 9, district I, tel. 1/375-8373, www.rudasbaths.com). From the Döbrentei tér stop on trams #19 and #41 (along the Buda riverfront, between the Gellért Baths and Batthyány tér), walk under the off-ramps for the big white bridge, pass the statue of Elisabeth, and go through the tunnel. The baths are straight ahead. Tram #18 from Szent Gellért tér drops you off right in front. From Pest, you can ride bus #7 or #107 from Astoria or Ferenciek tere to the Rudas Gyógyfürdő stop; in the other direction, these buses also reach Rudas from Szent Gellért tér.

Night Bathing: The baths are open—to both men and women, in swimsuits—with a dance hall ambience Fri-Sat 22:00-late (4,400 Ft).

Entry Procedure: Buy your ticket (see options above), and if you want, rent a towel (400 Ft for a "bath sheet," plus 1,000-Ft refundable deposit) or a swimsuit (1,200 Ft plus 4,000-Ft deposit), or book a massage—either a relaxing "aroma relax massage," or a rougher, exfoliating "water massage with soap" in a noisy, busy room (either costs 3,100 Ft/20 minutes, 4,100 Ft/30 minutes, 5,000 Ft/40 minutes).

You'll be issued a plastic wristband, which you'll use to go through the turnstile into the changing area (two floors of private cabins—there are no lockers in the thermal bath section). If you paid to rent a towel or swimsuit, give your receipt to the attendant to claim it now. Hold your wristband against the electronic panel on the wall for a few seconds to be assigned a cabin number, then find that cabin and touch your wristband to the lock in order to open it. After you change and are ready to explore the complex, lock the cabin door (unlike the other baths in town, it doesn't lock automatically)...then go have fun.

In the wellness and swimming pool areas, you'll wear your swimsuit everywhere, every day. For the thermal bath area, if you're here on a mixed day (Sat-Sun), the dress code is swimsuits. On other days, bathers can go nude, and many of the men wear a flimsy loincloth called a *kötény* (issued as you enter). If you're a self-conscious, gawky tourist (it happens to the best of us), you can wear your swimsuit...although you might get some funny looks.

Taking the Waters: This historic complex was thoroughly renovated a few years ago, making the outer section feel almost institutional. But the innermost section transports you half a millennium back in time.

Rudas' **thermal bath** area is all about modulating your body temperature—pushing your body to its limit with heat, then dousing off quickly with a bucket of cold water, then heating up again, and so on. The different temperatures are designed to let you do this as gradually or quickly as you like.

The central chamber, under an original 35-foot-high Turkish dome supported by eight pillars, is the historic core of the baths. The main, octagonal pool in the center is surrounded by four smaller pools, each in its own corner. Working clockwise from the right as you enter, the four corner pools get progressively hotter: 28°C (82°F), 30° C (86°F), 33°C (91°F), and 42°C (108°F). While the hottest pool feels almost scalding at first, you can ease your way into it, the same way you would into cold water. Conveniently, the largest, central pool—at 36°C (97°F)—is not too hot, not too cold...juuuust right.

Along one wall are entrances to the wet sauna (*nedves gőzkamra*, to the left), with 50°C (122°F) scented steam; and the dry sauna (*hőlégkamra*, to the right), with three progressively hotter rooms ranging from 45°C (113° F) to 72°C (161°F). Near the entrance to each one is a shower or—if you don't want to beat around the bush—a bucket of frigid water (pull the rope for immediate relief if you're feeling overheated).

Surrounding this central chamber are hallways with other areas: resting rooms, tanning beds (*szolarium*, costs extra), massage rooms, a cold plunge pool, and a scale to see how much sweat you've lost.

Float on your back for a while in the main octagonal pool, pondering the faintly glittering translucent tiles embedded in the old Turkish dome. You'll notice that the voices echoing around that dome are mostly Hungarian—there are very few tourists here. You might see people stretching, moving from pool to pool very purposefully, or even doing chin-ups from the metal supports; some are athletes, training for their next event.

When you're ready for a change of pace, head back through the lobby to the other half of the building. First you'll walk along the **swimming pool** (for laps), then enter the turnstile for the **wellness area.** The first room, with a huge window looking out over the busy embankment road, has three small pools of different temperatures (32°C/90°F, 36°C/97°F, and a sweltering 42°C/108°F), all with powerful massage jets. In the cold plunge pool (12-14°C/54-57°F), notice the ice maker that continually drops in a cube or two, every few seconds. Thirsty? Get a drink at the stately ram's-head tiled fountains that line the walls.

But the real highlight of the wellness area is upstairs: At the end of the room, find the staircase and head on up, passing the inviting restaurant (with loaner bathrobes and fine views across the Danube) on your way to the rooftop terrace. While other Budapest baths envelop you in opulent architecture, this is the only one that envelops you in Budapest itself. Whether soaking in rays on the sun deck, or taking a dip in the 36°C/97°F thermal pool, you're surrounded by the bustle of the city. Scanning the horizon, you'll see a workaday burg going about its business...oblivious to the swimsuit-clad barnacle clinging onto the base of Gellért Hill. Your solitude is broken only by the periodic rumble of trams trundling past on the road below you.

Exit Procedure: After changing, return your rental towel and swimsuit to the attendant and get your receipt; present this at the front desk (along with your original towel receipt) to get your deposit back. Then drop your wristband through the little slot at the turnstile, head out the door, and stumble along the Danube...as relaxed as you'll ever be.

Aaaaahhh.

THERMAL BATHS

LEOPOLD TOWN WALK

*Lipótváros, from the Parliament to
the Chain Bridge*

The Parliament building, which dominates Pest's skyline, is the centerpiece of a banking and business district that bustles by day, but is relatively quiet at night and on weekends. Called Lipótváros ("Leopold Town"), this area is one of Budapest's most genteel quarters, and features some of the best of Budapest's many monuments. This walk also takes in several of the city's most grandiose landmarks: the Parliament, St. István's Basilica, the Gresham Palace, and the Chain Bridge.

Note: If you're planning to tour the Parliament interior, get tickets before you begin this walk (as explained on page 48). Then do the first part of this walk while waiting for your Parliament tour to begin.

Orientation

Length of This Walk: Allow 1.5 hours, not including time to enter the sights.

Getting There: We'll begin on Kossuth tér, behind the Parliament. You can take the M2/red line to the Kossuth tér stop; or, from southern Pest (such as the Great Market Hall—at the end of the Pest Town Center Walk; or Vigadó tér near Vörösmarty tér), take tram #2 along the Danube embankment, and hop off at the looming Parliament building (you can get off either at the Kossuth tér stop, at the south end of the Parliament, or at the Országház stop, at the north end, near the visitors center). From near the Opera House, hop on trolley bus #70 or #78.

Parliament: 5,200 Ft; English tours usually daily at 10:00, 12:00, 13:00, 14:00, and 15:00—confirm times and book online in advance; Kossuth tér 1, tel. 1/441-4904, www.parlament.hu.

St. István's Basilica: Interior—free, but 200-Ft donation strongly suggested, open to tourists Mon 9:00-16:30, Tue-Fri 9:00-17:00, Sat 9:00-13:00, Sun 13:00-17:00, open later for worshippers; panorama terrace—500 Ft, daily June-Sept 10:00-18:30, March-May and Oct 10:00-17:30, Nov-Feb 10:00-16:30; treasury—400 Ft, same hours as terrace; Szent István tér, district V, M1: Bajcsy-Zsilinszky út or M3: Arany János utca.

Starring: Grand buildings, fine facades, contemporary politics, and monuments, monuments, monuments.

The Walk Begins

• *Start in the vast square on the non-river side of the gigantic, can't-miss-it, red-domed Parliament building. Position yourself near the bottom of the very tall, pointy flagpole, near the stiff guards. Follow their gaze to the...*

Hungarian Parliament (Országház)

The Parliament was built from 1885 to 1902 to celebrate the Hungarian millennium year of 1896 (see sidebar on page 33). Its elegant,

frilly spires and riverside location were inspired by its counterpart in London (where the architect studied). When completed, the Parliament was a striking and cutting-edge example of the mix-and-match Historicist style of the day—just as Frank Gehry's undulating buildings are examples of today's bold new aesthetic. Like the Hungarian people, this building is at once grandly ambitious and a somewhat motley hodge-podge of various influences—a Neo-Gothic palace topped with

a Neo-Renaissance dome, which once had a huge, red communist star on top of the tallest spire. Fittingly, it's the city's top icon. The best views of the Parliament are from across the Danube—especially in the late-afternoon sunlight.

The enormous building—with literally miles of stairs—was appropriate for a time when Budapest ruled much of Eastern Europe. The Parliament was built in an exuberant age, when Hungary was part of the Dual Monarchy—the "Austro-Hungarian Empire"—and triple the size it is today. Look at the Parlia-

Leopold Town Walk

1 Hungarian Parliament
2 Tisza Pillar & Parl. Visitors Ctr.
3 Kossuth Monument
4 Museum of Ethnography
5 Ministry of Agriculture & 1956 Monument
6 Rákóczi Statue
7 Stairs to 1956 Museum
8 Buda Viewpoint
9 József Statue
10 Holocaust Monument
11 Nagy Statue
12 Szabadság Tér
13 Reagan Statue
14 Soviet War Memorial
15 Apt. Buildings (4)
16 Bedő-Ház Building
17 Bandholtz Statue
18 Market Hall
19 Postal Savings Bank
20 National Bank
21 Monument to the Hungarian Victims of the Nazis
22 St. István's Basilica
23 Police Officer Statue
24 Central Euro. Univ.
25 Duna Palota
26 Széchenyi István Tér
27 Gresham Palace
28 Chain Bridge

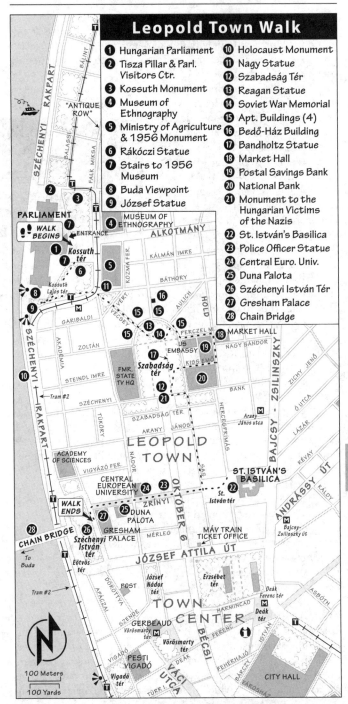

LEOPOLD TOWN

ment with an 1896 Hungarian state of mind. The building is a celebration of Hungary, built with Hungarian hands and of Hungarian materials. But now it feels just plain too big—the legislature only occupies an eighth of the space.

The interior—decorated with 84 pounds of gold—is even more glorious than the facade. Apart from all that opulence, it also holds the **Hungarian crown** (directly under the dome—surrounded, as if at a tribal summit, by over a thousand years' worth of Hungary's great kings). This quintessential symbol of Hungarian sovereignty is supposedly the original one that Pope Sylvester II sent to Hungary to crown István on Christmas Day in the year 1000.

Since then, the crown has been hidden, stolen, lost, and found again and again...supposedly bending the cross on top in the process. That original, simple crown has been encrusted with jewels and (as a gift from a Byzantine emperor) adorned with a circlet. This makes the crown look like a hybrid of East and West—perhaps appropriately, as for much of history Budapest was seen as the gateway to the Orient. In modern times, the crown actually spent time in Fort Knox, Kentucky, where the US government kept it safe between the end of World War II and 1978, when Jimmy Carter returned it to Hungary. (For details on touring the Parliament, see page 48).

During the 20th century, this building saw monarchists, nationalists, democrats, fascists, and communists. Today, the Hungarian Parliament is controlled by the Fidesz party, led by Viktor Orbán. In addition to introducing you to old buildings and monuments, this tour will familiarize you with some of the contemporary politics in Hungary—including the controversial reforms of Orbán and Fidesz. A highly nationalistic, right-wing party, which swept to power after Hungarians grew weary of the bumblings of the poorly organized, shortsighted left-wing opposition party, Fidesz has exerted its influence over every walk of Hungarian life... beginning with the look of this building and square.

• *The vast square behind the Parliament is studded with attractions. Stay where you are for a quick...*

Kossuth Tér Spin-Tour

This square is sprinkled with interesting monuments and packed with Hungarian history. But it's gone through a lot of changes in the last few years, at the hands of architects and urban planners working under the steady guidance of Fidesz. The first big change was the square itself, which used to be a more higgledy-piggledy mix of ragged asphalt, parks, monuments, and trees. But Fidesz wanted the mighty Parliament building to stand bold and unobstructed. Several ragtag older monuments (including, ironically, an "eternal" flame honoring victims of the communists) were swept away. Trees were cut down overnight, before would-be protesters could make a peep. And today the square has a scrubbed-clean look that some critics consider almost fascist.

Check out the **flags** that are being flown from the Parliament building. In addition to the Hungarian flag (red, white, and green stripes), you may also see the flag of Transylvania (blue flag with a yellow stripe, and a star and crescent moon in the corner). Like many Hungarians, the leaders of Fidesz cling to the memory of a much larger, pre-WWI Hungary, which included Transylvania. Although the treaty ceding Transylvania to Romania was signed nearly a century ago, Fidesz stubbornly flies this flag to bolster their suggestion that Romania grant Transylvania its independence (an idea that almost nobody takes seriously). Meanwhile, Fidesz has refused to fly the European Union's flag (a circle of yellow stars on a blue background). The particular flags you see today serve as a barometer of Fidesz's current level of feistiness.

Look to the right end of the Parliament. Poking up is a **pillar** topped by a lion being strangled and bitten by a giant snake—a proud, noble nation laid low by an insidious enemy. At the base of the pillar stands István Tisza, who was prime minister of Hungary when the Austro-Hungarian Empire was pulled into World War I—which, despite Tisza's best efforts, led to the loss of Hungary's outlying territories. This pillar marks the entrance to the Parliament visitors center; if you want to check on the availability of tours today, now's a good time (for details, see page 48).

Looking a bit to the right, at the end of the park you'll see another stony tribute, this one to the square's namesake, **Lajos**

Kossuth, who led the 1848 Revolution against the Habsburgs. A previous monument to Kossuth on this very spot showed him rallying people from all walks of life to join him in the revolution. The current version, from Fidesz, isolates the great patriot with a downcast, almost lonesome gaze. (Some suggest that the earlier version was a bit too populist for the liking of the hardline Fidesz.) For more on Kossuth, see page 177.

The street that leaves this square behind Kossuth's right shoulder is Falk Miksa utca, Budapest's **"antique row"**—a great place to browse for nostalgic souvenirs (see page 280).

Panning right from the Kossuth statue, across the tram tracks you'll see the stately home of the **Museum of Ethnography.** While its collection of Hungarian folk artifacts is good (closed Mon, see page 52), the building is even more notable. The design was the first runner-up for the Parliament building, so they built it here, where it originally housed the Supreme Court.

To the right, the **Ministry of Agriculture** was the second runner-up for the Parliament. Today it features a very low-profile, but poignant, monument to the victims of the 1956 Uprising against Soviet rule (see the "1956" sidebar): At the right end of the protruding arcade, notice that the walls are pockmarked with little metal dollops (you may have to walk closer to see these clearly). Two days into the uprising, on October 25, the ÁVH (communist police) and Soviet troops on the rooftop above opened fire on demonstrators gathered in this square—massacring many and leaving no doubt that Moscow would not tolerate dissent. In the monument, each of the little metal knobs represents a bullet.

Spin farther to the right, where a dramatic equestrian statue of **Ferenc Rákóczi** stands in the park. Rákóczi valiantly—but unsuccessfully—led the Hungarians in their War of Independence (1703-1711) against the Habsburgs. (For more on this leader, see page 176.) Although they lived more than a century apart, Rákóczi and Kossuth—who now face each other across this square—were aligned in their rebellion against the Habsburgs.

Complete your 360 and face the Parliament again. Every so often, costumed soldiers appear on the front steps for a brief "changing of the guard" ceremony set to recorded music...another very new, very patriotic custom, compliments of Fidesz.

Along the two grassy parks that flank the dome, look for low-profile black walls marked *1956*, which enclose staircases leading down under the square. These lead to a new museum dedicated to the 1956 Uprising (which may be open during your visit).

• *Now we'll head to a nice riverfront viewpoint—and, of course, more monuments. Circle around the left side of the giant Parliament building, passing another statue on a pillar (Gulya Andrássy, described in the sidebar on page 145). Belly up to the bannister overlooking a spectacular...*

View of Buda

Slowly scan the skyline to get oriented to the older, hillier half of

LEOPOLD TOWN

City of Monuments

There's a reason why Budapest is so monument-crazy. In 1897, German Emperor Wilhelm II came to visit his ally and rival,

Habsburg Emperor Franz Josef, here in Budapest. Wilhelm commented on how few monuments graced the city streets, prompting a jealous Franz Josef to fund the immediate creation of 10 new statues around town. The Budapesters' enjoyment of a good monument continues today. Here are a few favorites, scattered around the city:

- **Attila József,** the brooding young poet, on the riverbank by the Parliament (see page 110).
- **Imre Nagy,** the brave anti-communist leader, standing pensively on a bridge just behind Parliament (see page 111).
- **Empty Shoes** lining the Danube riverbank between the Parliament and the Chain Bridge, honoring Jews who stood there before being executed by the Nazis (see page 110).
- **Anonymous,** the first scribe to chronicle the history of the Hungarian people, in City Park's Vajdahunyad Castle (see page 182).
- **George Washington,** minding his own business deep in City Park near Vajdahunyad Castle (see page 182).
- **1956,** a gigantic rusted-metal hull in City Park, honoring the way Hungarians came together to attempt to throw off Soviet rule (see page 179).
- **Heroes' Square,** where 21 Hungarian leaders (and one angel) stand sternly as a Who's Who of Hungarian history (see page 169).
- **Memento Park,** a collection of surviving communist-era statues and monuments that evoke the Red old days (see page 215).

Buda-Pest. Far to the left, the Gellért Hill is topped by the Soviet-era Liberation Monument. Castle Hill is dominated by the sprawling Royal Palace (with its green dome). Across the river from you, the pointy hilltop spires mark the Matthias Church and Fishermen's Bastion; below that is the riverbank neighborhood called Víziváros. Just to the right, the two onion-domed churches bookend Batthyány tér, a local transportation hub. And far to the right, in the middle of the Danube, sits the tree-filled city park of Margaret Island, connected to both Pest and Buda by Margaret Bridge.

• *Now walk along the banister to the left until you come upon a statue of a young man, lost deep in thought, gazing into the Danube.*

Attila József (1905-1937)

This beloved modern poet lived a tumultuous, productive, and short life before he killed himself by jumping in front of a train at

age 32. József's poems of life, love, and death—mostly written in the 1920s and 1930s—are considered the high point of Hungarian literature. His birthday (April 11) is celebrated as National Hungarian Poetry Day.

Here József re-enacts a scene from one of his best poems, "At the Danube." It's a hot day—his jacket lies in a heap next to him, his shirtsleeves are rolled up, and he cradles his hat loosely in his left hand. "As I sat on the bank of the Danube, I watched a watermelon float by," he begins. "As if flowing out of my heart, murky, wise, and great was the Danube." In the poem, József uses the Danube as a metaphor for life—for the way it has interconnected cities and also times—as he reflects that his ancestors likely pondered the Danube from this same spot. Looking into his profound eyes, you sense the depth of this artist's tortured inner life.

• *Walk down the steps next to József, and stand at the railing just above the busy road. If you visually trace the Pest riverbank to the left about 100 yards, just before the tree-filled, riverfront park, you can just barely see several low-profile dots lining the embankment. This is a...*

Holocaust Monument

Consisting of 50 pairs of bronze shoes, this monument commemorates the Jews who were killed when the Nazis' puppet government, the Arrow Cross, came to power in Hungary in 1944. While many Jews were sent to concentration camps, the Arrow Cross massacred some of them right here, shooting them and letting their bodies fall into the Danube.

• *If you'd like a closer look at the shoes, use the crosswalk (50 yards to your right) to cross the busy embankment road and follow the waterline. I'll wait right here.*

When you're ready to move on, turn your back to the Danube and walk inland, along the ugly building (with an entrance to the Metró), up to the *back corner of Kossuth tér. Cross the street in a little park (at Vértanúk tere), where you'll see a monument to...*

Imre Nagy (1896-1958)

The Hungarian politician Imre Nagy (EEM-ray nodge), now thought of as an anti-communist hero, was actually a lifelong communist. In the 1930s, he allegedly worked for the Soviet secret police. In the late 1940s, he quickly moved up the hierarchy of Hungary's communist government, becoming prime minister during a period of reform in 1953. But when his proposed changes alarmed Moscow, Nagy was quickly demoted.

When the 1956 Uprising broke out on October 23, Imre Nagy was drafted (reluctantly, some say) to become the head of the movement to soften the severity of the communist regime. Because he was an insider, it briefly seemed that Nagy might hold the key to finding a middle path (represented by the bridge he's standing on) between the suffocating totalitarian model of Moscow and the freedom of the West. Some suspect that Nagy himself didn't fully grasp the dramatic sea change represented by the uprising. When he appeared at the Parliament building on the night of October 23 to speak to the reform-craving crowds for the first time, he began by addressing his countrymen—as communist politicians always did—with, "Dear comrades..." When the audience booed, he amended it: "Dear friends..."

But the optimism was short-lived. The Soviets violently put down the uprising, arrested and sham-tried Nagy, executed him, and buried him disgracefully, face-down in an unmarked grave. The regime forced Hungary to forget about Nagy.

Later, when communism was in its death throes in 1989, the Hungarian people rediscovered Nagy as a hero. His body was located, exhumed, and given a ceremonial funeral at Heroes' Square. (It was also something of a coming-out party for Viktor Orbán—now the prime minister—who, as a twentysomething rebel, delivered an impassioned speech at the ceremony.) This event is considered a pivotal benchmark in that year of tremendous change. By the year's end, the Berlin Wall would fall, and the Czechs and Slovaks would stage their Velvet Revolution. But Nagy's reburial was the first in that series of toppling dominoes. And today, thanks to this monument, Nagy keeps a watchful eye on today's lawmakers in the Parliament across the way. Since Fidesz took power, democracy-loving locals swear that every so often, they see Nagy wince.

1956

The year 1956 is etched into the Hungarian psyche. In that year, the people of Budapest staged the first major uprising against the communist regime. It also marked the first time that the Soviets implicitly acknowledged, in brutally putting down the uprising, that the people of Eastern Europe were not "communist by choice."

The seeds of revolution were sown with the death of a tyrant: Josef Stalin passed away on March 5, 1953. Suddenly the choke-hold that Moscow had held on its satellite states loosened. During this time of "de-Stalinization," Hungarian premier Imre Nagy presided over two years of mild reform, before his political opponents (and Moscow) became nervous and demoted him. (For more on Nagy, see page 111.)

In 1955, Austria declared its neutrality in the Cold War. This thrust Hungary to the front line of the Iron Curtain, and raised the stakes both for Hungarians who wanted free-dom and for Soviets who wanted to preserve their buffer zone. When Stalin's successor, Ni-kita Khrushchev, condemned Stalin's crimes in a "secret speech" to communist leaders in February of 1956, it emboldened the Soviet Bloc's dissidents. A workers' strike in Poznań, Poland, in October inspired Hungarians to follow their example.

On October 23, 1956, the Hungarian uprising began. A stu-dent union group gathered in Budapest at 15:00 to articulate a list of 16 demands against the communist regime. Then they marched toward Parliament, their numbers gradually swelling. One protest-er defiantly cut the Soviet-style insignia out of the center of the Hungarian flag, which would become the uprising's symbol.

By nightfall, some 200,000 protesters filled Kossuth tér be-hind Parliament, calling for Imre Nagy, the one communist leader they believed could bring change. Nagy finally appeared around 21:00. Ever the pragmatic politician, he implored patience. Fol-lowing the speech, a large band of protesters took matters into their own hands, marched to City Park, and tore down the hated Stalin statue that stood there (see page 179).

Another group went to the National Radio building to read their demands on the air. The ÁVH (communist police) refused to let them do it, and eventually opened fire on the protesters. The peaceful protests evolved into an armed insurrection, as fright-ened civilians gathered weapons and supplies.

Overnight, Moscow decided to intervene. Budapesters awoke on October 24 to find Red Army troops occupying their city. That morning, Imre Nagy—who had just been promoted again to prime minister—promised reforms and tried to keep a lid on the simmer-ing discontent.

The next day, October 25, a huge crowd gathered on Kossuth tér behind the Parliament to hear from Nagy. In the hubbub, shots rang out as Hungarian and Soviet soldiers opened fire on the (mostly unarmed) crowd. At least 70 protesters were killed and more than 100 injured.

The Hungarians fought back with an improvised guerilla resistance. They made use of any guns they could get their hands on, as well as Molotov cocktails, to strike against the Soviet occupiers. Many adolescents (the celebrated "Pest Youth") participated. The fighting tore apart the city, and some of the fallen were buried in impromptu graves in city parks.

Political infighting in Moscow paralyzed the Soviet response, and an uneasy ceasefire fell over Budapest. For 10 tense days, it appeared that the Soviets might allow Nagy to push through some reforms. Nagy, a firmly entrenched communist, had always envisioned a less repressive regime...but within limits. While he was at first reluctant to take on the mantle of the uprising's leadership, he gradually began to echo what he was hearing on the streets. He called for free elections, the abolishment of the ÁVH, the withdrawal of Soviet troops, and Hungary's secession from the Warsaw Pact.

But when the uprisers attacked and killed ÁVH officers and communist leaders in Budapest, it bolstered the case of the Moscow hardliners. On November 4, the Red Army launched a brutal counterattack in Budapest that left the rebels reeling. At 5:20 that morning, Imre Nagy's voice came over the radio to beg the world for assistance. Later that morning, he sought asylum at the Yugoslav Embassy across the street from City Park. He was never seen alive in public again.

János Kádár—an ally of Nagy's who was palatable to the uprisers, yet firmly loyal to Moscow—was installed as prime minister. The fighting dragged on for about another week, but the uprising was eventually crushed. By the end, 2,500 Hungarians and more than 700 Soviets were dead, and 20,000 Hungarians were injured. Communist authorities arrested more than 15,000 people, of whom at least 200 were executed (including Imre Nagy). Anyone who had participated in the uprising was blacklisted; fearing this and other forms of retribution, some 200,000 Hungarians fled to the West.

Though the 1956 Uprising met a tragic end, within a few years Kádár did succeed in softening the regime, and the milder, so-called "goulash communism" emerged. And today, even though the communists are long gone, the legacy of 1956 pervades the Hungarian consciousness. Some Budapest buildings are still pockmarked with bullet holes from '56, and many Hungarians who fled the country in that year still have not returned. October 23 remains Hungary's most cherished holiday.

• *Go up the short, diagonal street behind Nagy, called Vécsey utca. After just one block, you emerge into...*

Szabadság Tér (Liberty Square)

"Liberty Square"—one of Budapest's most inviting public spaces—was so named when a Habsburg barracks here was torn down after the Hungarians gained some autonomy in the late 19th century.

• *The first person you'll see as you enter the square, striding confidently and charismatically away from the Parliament, is an actor-turned-politician you may recognize...*

Ronald Reagan is respected in Hungary for his role as a Cold Warrior. But don't take this monument as a sign that he's universally adored by Hungarians. In truth, this statue, the result of a political stunt, was erected in 2011 to deflect attention from a brewing scandal: When Fidesz took power in 2010, they quickly began rolling back previous democratic reforms and placing alarming constraints on the media. Many international observers—including the US government—spoke out against what they considered an infringement on freedom of the press. In an effort to appease American concerns, Prime Minister Viktor Orbán erected this statue on one of his capital's main squares—and then, perhaps not quite grasping the subtleties of American political divisions, invited Secretary of State Hillary Clinton to the unveiling. While Reagan played a role in ending the Cold War, many Hungarian patriots are offended that this monument overshadows the contributions and sacrifices of so many other important figures, including Imre Nagy. Either way, it's fun to watch the steady stream of passersby (both Hungarians and tourists) do a double-take, chuckle, then snap a photo with The Gipper.

• *Walk around the stout obelisk to the center of the square. Stand facing the obelisk.*

This is the **Soviet War Memorial,** commemorating "Liberation Day": April 4, 1945, when the Soviets officially forced the Nazis out of Hungary. As a very rare reminder of the Soviet days—you almost never see hammers-and-sickles in the streets of Hungary anymore—it has often been defaced. Some Budapesters feel that the memorial should be removed. Ponder for a moment this complex issue: Soviet troops did liberate Hungary from the

LEOPOLD TOWN

Nazis. Does their leaders' later oppression of the Hungarians make these soldiers' sacrifice less worthy of being honored? One way or another, there's a certain irony now that Ronald Reagan stands just a few yards from the Soviet War Memorial—perhaps a fittingly schizophrenic metaphor for this city's complex history and allegiances.

Ringing the top of Szabadság tér (behind the memorial) are **four ornate apartment buildings,** typical of high-class townhouses from Budapest's Golden Age in the late 1800s. While each one is strikingly different from the next, they are all typical of Historicism— the mix-and-match aesthetic that was popular at the time. Like residential buildings throughout Pest, the ground

floor has particularly high ceilings. But the second and third floors were more desirable—up away from the rabble of street life, but with relatively few stairs (in a time before elevators were common). Notice that in each of these buildings, those are the only floors with balconies.

Here's an optional detour for architecture buffs: If you go up the middle street between these buildings (Honvéd utca, straight ahead from the middle of Szabadság tér), a few doors down on the right you'll find one of Budapest's finest Art Nouveau buildings, **Bedő-Ház.** The curvy green facade is a textbook example of the Hungarian Secession style. Built in 1903, the building was dilapidated for decades before a studs-out restoration in 2007. Inside is a small café and three floors with a modest but interesting exhibit of elegantly delicate Art Nouveau furniture, dishes, and other decorative arts (2,000 Ft, Mon-Sat 10:00-17:00, closed Sun, Honvéd utca 3, tel. 1/269-4622). For just a peek, duck into the next-door Secessió Café & Delikat, which occupies part of the building (Mon-Fri 8:00-19:00, Sat 10:00-17:00, closed Sun).

• *Back in the middle of Szabadság tér, turn with your back to the Soviet memorial, and look down to the far end of the square.*

On the right is a giant, twin-spired building that once housed the stock exchange and, later, **Hungarian State Television,** or MTV—not music television, but Magyar television. Now the building has been converted into luxury offices and apartments.

The genteel open-air **café** in the middle of the park is an inviting place for a coffee break.

On the left side of the square, behind car-bomb barriers and a heavily fortified fence, the yellow corner building is the **US Embassy.**

This is where Cardinal József Mindszenty holed up for 15 years during the Cold War to evade arrest by the communist authorities (see page 347). A hundred yards down the left side of the square (and worth a detour for military buffs) stands a statue of **Harry Hill Bandholtz,** a US officer from World War I who prevented treasured Hungarian art from being taken by Romania. This statue stood inside the US Embassy for 40 chilly years (1949-1989), but now it's back out in the open.

• *We're headed down Perczel Mór utca, the street next to the US Embassy—but you'll have to detour a bit to the left (and tiptoe around some barricades) to get there. Follow the oversized fortifications one block along Perczel Mór utca, and you'll run right into...*

Hold Utca

Look for the big *Belvárosi Piac* sign over the door, and step inside. This **market hall** was built around the same time as the Great Market Hall, but it's smaller and less touristy—worth poking around inside. If you're hungry, sit down at one of several dirt-cheap market eateries upstairs, or gather a picnic here to eat at nearby Szabadság tér (Mon 6:30-17:00, Tue-Fri 6:30-18:00, Sat 6:30-14:00, closed Sun).

Exit the market building and turn left onto Hold utca. As you walk down this street, keep your eyes high on the green-and-yellow roofline of the building on the right. This **Postal Savings Bank,** designed by Ödön Lechner in the late 19th century, combines

traditional folk motifs with cutting-edge Art Nouveau in an attempt to forge a new, distinctly Hungarian national style. A key element of this emerging style was the use of colorful mosaic tiles to decorate the roof. (In its truest form, this style uses pyrogranite ceramic tiles from the famous Zsolnay porcelain factory in the city of

Pécs—see page 400.) The beehives along the rooftop are an appropriate symbol for a bank—where people store money as bees store honey. When asked why he lavished such attention on the rooftop, which few people can see, Lechner said, "To please the birds." The next building is the grand **National Bank of Hungary,** with entertaining reliefs tracing the history of money.

• *Return to Liberty Square by taking the street between these two banks, Kiss Ernő utca. Again you'll be following an almost comically heavy-duty fence for the US Embassy. (Ponder for a moment why the US feels the need to build a fortress in the most tranquil corner of a relatively powerless European nation's capital.) Emerging back into the square, angle left past the playground to reach yet another controversial monument, at the end of the square, near the fountain.*

Monument to the Hungarian Victims of the Nazis

This recent addition to the square—another heavy-handed Fidesz production—commemorates the German invasion of Hungary on March 19, 1944. Standing in the middle of a broken colonnade, an immaculate angel holds a sphere with a double cross (part of the crown jewels and a symbol of Hungarian sovereignty). Overhead, a mechanical-looking black eagle (a traditional symbol of Germany) screeches in, its talons poised to strike. In case the symbolism weren't clear enough, the eagle wears a hit-you-over-the-head armband that says *1944*.

Although offensive enough for its lack of artistry, this monument was instantly controversial for the way it whitewashes Hungarian history. Viewing this, you might imagine that Hungary was a peaceful land that was unwittingly caught up in the Nazi war machine. In fact, the Hungarian government was an ally of Nazi Germany for more than three years before this invasion. While many Hungarians today emphasize that Jews here were not executed before the Germans arrived, tens of thousands of Jews did die from forced labor or through being exported to Nazi-controlled lands. And there's no question that, after the invasion, many Hungarians enthusiastically collaborated with their new Nazi overlords.

Mindful of the old adage about people who forget their own history, locals have created a **makeshift memorial** to the victims of the World War II-era Hungarians (not just Germans) in front of this official monument. (If this informal memorial—a gathering of faded photographs and handwritten signs—is nowhere to be seen, it's a safe guess that Fidesz is cracking down on free speech.)

On a lighter note, the **fountain** that faces the monument is particularly entertaining. Sensors can tell when you're about to walk through the wall of water...and the curtain of water automatically parts just long enough for you to pass. Try it.

• *Turning your back to the monument, go left, then take the first right (before the big, blocky bank building), and head down Sas utca for two blocks. Sas utca and neighboring streets are home to several good and trendy restaurants (including the recommended Café Kör and Borkonyha). Consider window-shopping here and reserving a place for dinner tonight.*

You'll emerge into a broad plaza in front of Budapest's biggest Catholic church...

St. István's Basilica (Szent István Bazilika)

The church is only about 100 years old—like most Budapest landmarks, it was built around the millennial celebrations of 1896. Designed by three architects over more than 50 years, St. István's is particularly eclectic. Each architect had a favorite style: Neoclassical, Neo-Renaissance, and Neo-Baroque. Construction was delayed for a while when the giant dome collapsed midway through.

Head up the grand stairs to get oriented. To the right is the ticket desk, the elevator to the treasury, and the entrance to the church. To the left is the elevator to the panoramic tower.

The church's **interior** is dimly lit but gorgeously restored; all the gilded decorations glitter in the low light. You'll see not Jesus, but St. István (Stephen), Hungary's first Christian king, glowing above the high altar.

The church's main claim to fame is the **"holy right hand"** of St. István. The sacred fist—a somewhat grotesque, 1,000-year-old withered stump—is in a jeweled box in the chapel to the left of the main altar (follow signs for *Szent Jobb Kápolna*, chapel often closed). Pop in a 200-Ft coin for two minutes of light. Posted information describes the hand's unlikely journey to this spot (chapel open April-Sept Mon-Sat 9:00-16:30, Sun 13:00-16:30; Oct-March Mon-Sat 10:00-16:00, Sun 13:00-16:30).

LEOPOLD TOWN

On your way out, in the exit foyer, you'll find a small exhibit about the building's history.

There are two other attractions at St. István's, each covered by a separate ticket. The **panoramic tower** offers views over Buda-

pest's rooftops that are pretty distant (and disappointing without a good zoom lens), but it does provide a good sense of the sprawl of the city. You have various options: You can walk up the entire way (302 steps); or you can take an elevator to midlevel (with WCs), where you can follow signs to another elevator (plus 42 steps) or climb 137 steps to the top. To the right as you face the church, an elevator zips up to the skippable church **treasury,** a small collection of vestments, ecclesiastical gear, a model of the building, exhibits about its construction, a porcelain replica of the Hungarian crown, and a fine Murillo *Holy Family*—all well-described in English.

The church also hosts regular **organ concerts** (advertised near the entry).

• *The square in front of the church is called, logically…*

St. István Tér

This grand plaza is a classic example of how Budapest has spiffed up its once-gloomy downtown. A decade ago, this space was an ugly parking lot. Then, a few years back, a German engineering firm created an experimental, cutting-edge parking garage beneath this square. Instead of finding a parking space, drivers simply leave their car on a pallet and walk up to the square—while the car-loaded pallet is moved with a series of giant elevators and conveyor belts to a parking space. This futuristic system is all going on underfoot. Meanwhile, over the last few years, the streets around this plaza—once sleepy—have been transformed into one of Budapest's trendiest nightlife zones, with lots of bars, restaurants, and cafés catering to local yuppies. The **DiVino wine bar,** on your left as you leave the church, is a perfect place to sample a variety of Hungarian vintages by the glass; this and other nearby eateries are recommended on page 256.

• *From here, you have two options. If you'd like to skip ahead to my* ***Andrássy Út Walk,*** *you're very close: Walk around the right side of the basilica, turn right on busy Bajcsy-Zsilinszky út, and you're one block from the start of Andrássy út (across the street, on your left).*

Or you can complete this walk to Vörösmarty tér, where you can begin the ***Pest Town Center Walk.*** *For this option, walk straight ahead from St. István's main staircase down…*

Zrínyi Utca

Traffic-free Zrínyi utca is a fine people zone, and a handy way to connect St. István's to the river. Plans are in the works to redevelop other central Pest streets to be as pedestrian-friendly as this one.

At the start of Zrínyi utca, on the right-hand corner (in front of the gelato shop), look for the **red fire hydrant** with a blue attachment on one end. This contraption—called *ivócsap* ("drinking tap"), the winner of a recent citywide design competition—allows passersby to use the hydrant as a drinking fountain. It's a typically clever Hungarian solution.

At the next corner (on the right), look for the bushy-mustachioed **police officer** statue, evoking the grand old days of the Austro-Hungarian Empire (just before World War I). There's no particular story for this character: he's just for fun. In keeping with their rich tradition of monuments, the local district sponsors a contest each year to come up with the best statues.

Farther down this block, on the right-hand corner, is **Central European University.** Offering graduate study for Americans and students from all over Central and Eastern Europe, this school is predominantly funded by George Soros, a Hungarian who escaped communism by emigrating to the US, then became a billionaire through shrewd investments. Today Soros is loved by the left and loathed by the right as a major contributor to liberal campaigns. But he hasn't forgotten worthy causes back home. In addition to funding this university, he is at the forefront of a movement for Central Europeans to better protect the rights of their huge Roma (Gypsy) population. The university's CEU Bookshop, a few steps up Zrínyi utca toward the basilica, is the best place in town to find academic books about the region in English (listed on page 34).

Continue down Zrínyi utca. After crossing Nádor utca, on the left you'll see **Duna Palota** ("Danube Palace")—a former casino, and today a venue and ticket office for Hungária Koncert's popular tourist shows. If you're up for a crowd-pleasing show of either classical or folk music, drop in here to check your options (see page 286 in the Entertainment in Budapest chapter).

Zrínyi utca dead-ends at the big traffic circle called **Széchenyi**

István tér. For decades, this was called Roosevelt tér, in honor of the American statesman who helped defeat the Nazis in World War II. But in 2010, Fidesz went on a renaming binge around the city, and decided to christen this square for the Hungarian statesman whose statue stands on the right: István Széchenyi, the early 19th-century nobleman who, among other deeds, built the Chain Bridge and founded the Hungarian Academy of Sciences (both of which face this square). On the left is the statesman Ferenc Deák, who fought for Hungarian autonomy using peaceful means.

· *Turn left and walk a half-block to the entrance (on the left) of the...*

Gresham Palace

The Gresham Palace was Budapest's first building in the popular Historicist style, and also incorporates elements of Art Nou-

veau. Budapest boomed at a time when architectural eclecticism—mashing together bits and pieces of different styles—was in vogue. But because much of the city's construction was compressed into a short window of time, even these disparate styles enjoy an unusual harmony.

Damaged in World War II, the building was an eyesore for decades. (Reportedly, an aging local actress refused to move out, so developers had to wait for her to, ahem, vacate before they could reclaim the building.) In 1999, the Gresham Palace was meticulously restored to its former glory. Even if you can't afford to stay here (see page 239 in the Sleeping in Budapest chapter), saunter into the lobby and absorb the gorgeous details. For example, not only did they have to re-create the unique decorative tiles—they had to rebuild the original machines that made the tiles.

· *Be sure to get a good look at the Gresham Palace's fine facade—consider circling around the park and looking back. This also puts you right next to the bridge that grandly spans the Danube from here.*

Chain Bridge (Széchenyi Lánchíd)

One of the world's great bridges connects Pest's Széchenyi tér and Buda's Clark Ádám tér. This historic, iconic bridge, guarded by lions (symbolizing power), is Budapest's most enjoyable and convenient bridge to cross on foot.

Until the mid-19th century, only pontoon barges spanned the Danube between Buda and Pest. In the winter, the pontoons had to be pulled in, leaving locals to rely on ferries (in

LEOPOLD TOWN

good weather) or a frozen river. People often walked across the frozen Danube, only to get stuck on the other side during a thaw, with nothing to do but wait for another cold snap.

Count István Széchenyi was stranded for a week trying to get to his father's funeral. After missing it, Széchenyi commissioned Budapest's first permanent bridge—which was also a major symbolic step toward another of Széchenyi's pet causes, the unification of Buda and Pest. The Chain Bridge was built by Scotsman Adam Clark between 1842 and 1849, and it immediately became an important symbol of Budapest. Széchenyi—a man of the Enlightenment—charged both commoners and nobles a toll for crossing his bridge, making it an emblem of equality in those tense times. Like all of the city's bridges, the Chain Bridge was destroyed by the Nazis at the end of World War II, but was quickly rebuilt.

• *Our walk is over. From Széchenyi tér, you can catch bus #16 from in front of the Hungarian Academy of Sciences (at the right end of the square) to Castle Hill, or simply walk across the Chain Bridge for great views.*

If you'd like to wind up in the heart of Pest, Vörösmarty tér (and the start of my **Pest Town Center Walk**—*see next chapter) is just two long blocks away: Turn left out of the Gresham Palace, and walk straight on Dorottya utca.*

PEST TOWN CENTER WALK

Belváros, from Vörösmarty Tér to the Great Market Hall

Pest's Belváros ("Inner Town") is its gritty urban heart—simultaneously its most beautiful and ugliest district. You'll see fancy facades, some of Pest's best views from the Danube embankment, richly decorated old coffee houses that offer a whiff of the city's Golden Age, parks tucked like inviting oases between densely populated streets, recently pedestrianized streets that ooze urbane sophistication, and a cavernous, colorful market hall filled with Hungarian goodies. But you'll also experience crowds, grime, and pungent smells like nowhere else in Budapest. Remember: This is a city in transition. Local authorities plan to ban traffic from more and more Town Center streets in the coming years. If construction and torn-up pavement (common around here) impede your progress, be thankful that things will be nicer for your next visit. Within a decade, all of those rough edges will be sanded off...and tourists like you will be nostalgic for the "authentic" old days. (If you want the sanitized version today, stick with the other tourists on Váci utca.)

Even if this whole walk doesn't appeal to you, don't miss the spectacular Great Market Hall, described on page 135.

Orientation

Length of This Walk: Allow 1.5 hours.

Getting There: Take the M1/yellow Metró line to the Vörösmarty tér stop.

Károlyi Park: Free, open daily 8:00-dusk.

Great Market Hall: Free, Mon 6:00-17:00, Tue-Fri 6:00-18:00, Sat 6:00-15:00, closed Sun, Fővám körút 1.

Starring: The urban core of Budapest, a gorgeous riverfront promenade, several of the city's top cafés, and a grand finale at the Great Market Hall.

The Walk Begins

• *Start on the central square of the Town Center, Vörösmarty tér (at the M1 Metró stop of the same name). Face the giant, seated statue in the middle of the square.*

Vörösmarty Tér

As we begin exploring the central part of Pest, consider its humble history. In the mid-1600s, Pest was under Ottoman occupation and nearly deserted. By the 1710s, the Habsburgs had forced out the Ottomans, but this area remained a rough-and-tumble, often-flooded quarter just outside the Pest city walls. Peasants came here to enjoy bearbaiting (watching brutal, staged fights between blood-hounds and bears—like cockfights, only bigger and angrier, with more fur and teeth). The rebuilding of Pest was gradual; most of the buildings you'll see on this walk are no older than 200 years.

Today this square—a hub of activity in the Town Center—is named for the 19th-century Romantic poet **Mihály Vörösmarty**

(1800-1855), whose statue dominates the little park in the square's center. Writing during the time of reforms in the early 19th century, Vörösmarty was a Romantic whose poetry still stirs the souls of patriotic Hungarians—he's like Byron, Shelley, and Keats rolled into one. One of his most famous works is a patriotic song whose popularity rivals the national anthem's: "Be faithful to your country, all Hungarians." At Vörösmarty's feet, as if hearing those inspiring words chiseled into the stone, figures representing the Hungarian people rise up together. During Vörösmarty's age, the peasant Magyar tongue was, for the very first time, considered worthy of literature. The people began to think of themselves not merely as "subjects of the Habsburg Empire"...but as Hungarians.

• *Survey the square with a spin tour. First, facing the statue of Vörösmarty, turn 90 degrees to the left.*

At the north end of the square is the landmark **Gerbeaud café** and pastry shop. Between the World Wars, the well-to-do ladies of Budapest would meet here after shopping their way up Váci utca. Today it's still *the* meeting point in Budapest...for tourists, at least. Consider stepping inside to appreciate the elegant old decor, or for a cup of coffee and a slice of cake (but meals here are overpriced). Better yet, hold off for now—even more appealing cafés await later on in this walk.

The yellow **M1 Metró stop** between Vörösmarty and Gerbeaud is the entrance to the shallow *Földalatti*, or "underground"—the first subway on the Continent (built for the Hungarian millennial celebration in 1896). Today, it still carries passengers to Andrássy út sights, running under that boulevard all the way to City Park (it basically runs beneath the feet of people following my Andrássy Út Walk).

• *Turn another 90 degrees to the left.*

This super-modern **glass building** is the newest addition to Vörösmarty tér. If you think its appearance is jarring, then you should have seen the communist-style eyesore it replaced. Downstairs is upscale shopping; higher up are offices; and at the top are luxury apartments. Early plans called for a Mediterranean garden spiraling up inside this building, but it never materialized—so now it's just a beautiful waste of space.

• *Turn another 90 degrees to the left, and walk to the beginning of the Váci utca pedestrian street. Look up the street that's to your left (with the yellow, pointy-topped building at the end).*

This traffic-free street (Deák utca)—also known as **"Fashion Street,"** with top-end shops—is the easiest and most pleasant way to walk to Deák tér and, beyond it, through Erzsébet tér to Andrássy út (❂ see the Andrássy Út Walk chapter).

• *Extending straight ahead from Vörösmarty tér is a broad, bustling, pedestrianized shopping street. For now, look—but do not walk—down this street; we'll stroll a different stretch of it later on this walk.*

Dating from 1810-1850, **Váci utca** (VAHT-see OOT-zah) is one of the oldest streets of Pest. Váci utca means "street to Vác"—a

town 25 miles to the north. This has long been the street where the elite of Pest would go shopping, then strut their stuff for their neighbors on an evening promenade. Today, the tourists do the strutting here—and the Hungarians go to American-style shopping malls.

This boulevard—Budapest's tourism artery—was a dreamland for Eastern Bloc residents back in the 1980s. It was here that they fantasized about what it might be like to be free, while drooling

Pest Town Center Walk

1. Vörösmarty Tér
2. Gerbeaud Café
3. "Fashion Street"
4. Start of Váci Utca
5. Danube Promenade
6. Pesti Vigadó Concert Hall
7. Little Princess Sculpture
8. Historic McDonald's
9. Adidas Shop
10. March 15 Square
11. Town Center Parish Church
12. Sándor Petőfi Statue
13. Orthodox Church
14. Ferenciek Tere
15. Jégbüfé Café
16. Párisi Udvar Gallery
17. Károlyi Mihály Utca
18. Centrál Kávéház
19. Károlyi Park
20. University Square
21. Serbian Orthodox Church
22. Great Market Hall

over Nikes, Adidas, and Big Macs before any of these "Western evils" were introduced elsewhere in the Warsaw Pact region.

Ironically, this street—once prized by Hungarians and other Eastern Europeans because it felt so Western—is what many Western tourists today mistakenly think is the "real Budapest." Visitors mesmerized by this people-friendly stretch of souvenir stands, tourist-gouging eateries, and upscale boutiques are likely to miss some more interesting and authentic areas just a block or two away.

Don't fall for this trap. You can have a fun and fulfilling trip to this city without ever setting foot on Váci utca. In fact, this walk is designed to give you only the briefest taste of this famous street's tackiness. (If you're dying to saunter down Váci utca, this walk concludes at its far end—it takes about 20 minutes to walk back to its start.) Instead, we'll zigzag through the heart of Pest's Town Center for a look at the *real* "real Budapest."

• *Head for the river: Take the street that runs along the left side of the big glass building at the bottom of Vörösmarty tér. Cross the street and continue all the way to the railing and tram tracks. Swing about 30 yards to the right along the tracks, pausing by the statue of the girl with the dog. You're on the most colorful stretch of the...*

Danube Promenade (Dunakorzó)

Some of the best views in Budapest are from this walkway facing Castle Hill—especially this stretch, between the white Elisabeth Bridge (left) and the iconic Chain Bridge (right). This is a favorite place to promenade *(korzó)*, strolling aimlessly and greeting friends. Imagine the days before World War II, when—instead of mid-century monstrosities Marriott and InterContinental—this strip was lined with elegant grand hotels: Hungaria, Bristol, Carlton.

Take in the views of Buda, across the river (left to right): Gellért Hill, topped with its distinctive Liberation Monument; the green-domed Royal Palace, capping Castle Hill; and, farther along the hilltop, the colorful tile roof and spiny spire of the Matthias Church, surrounded by the cone-shaped decorations of the Fishermen's Bastion.

Behind you (fronting the little park) is a big concert hall, which dominates this part of the promenade. This is the Neo-Romantic-style **Pesti Vigadó**—built in the 1880s, and recently restored. Charmingly, the word *vigadó*—used to describe a concert hall—literally means "joyous place." In front, the playful statue of **the girl with her dog** captures the fun-loving spirit along this drag. At the gap in the railing, notice the platform

to catch **tram #2**, which goes frequently in each direction along the promenade—a handy and scenic way to connect riverside sights in Pest. (You can ride it to the right, to the Parliament and the start of my Leopold Town Walk; or to the left, to the Great Market Hall—where this walk ends.)

• *About 30 more yards toward the Chain Bridge, find the little statue wearing a jester's hat. She's playing on the railing, with the castle behind her.*

The ***Little Princess*** is one of Budapest's symbols and a favorite photo-op for tourists. While many of the city's monuments have interesting back-stories, more recent statues (like this one) are simply whimsical and fun.

• *Now walk down the promenade to the left (toward the white bridge). Directly in front of the corner of the Marriott Hotel, watch for the easy-to-miss stairs leading down under the tram tracks, to a crosswalk that leads safely across the busy road to the riverbank. From the top of these stairs, look along the river.*

Lining the **embankment** are several long boats: Some are excursion boats for sightseeing trips up and down the Danube (especially pleasant at night), while others are overpriced (but scenic) restaurants. Kiosks along here dispense info and sell tickets for the various boat companies—look for Danube Legenda (their dock is just downstream from here—go down the stairs, cross the road, then walk 100 yards left; for details, see page 44).

• *For now, continue walking downstream (left) along the promenade, passing in front of the blocky, dirty-white Marriott. When you reach the end of the Marriott complex, at the little parking lot, turn inland (left), cross the street, and walk up the street called Régi Posta utca. Head for the Golden Arches. You deserve a break today.*

Historic McDonald's

The fancy McDonald's (on the left) was a landmark in Eastern Europe—the first McDonald's behind the Iron Curtain. Budapest has always been a little more rebellious, independent, and cosmopolitan than other Eastern European cities, whose citizens flocked here

PEST TOWN CENTER

during the communist era. Váci utca (which we'll see next) was a showcase street during those grim times, making this a strategic location for Ronald McDonald and Co. Since you had to wait in a long line—stretching around the block—to get a burger, it wasn't "fast food"...but at least it

was "West food." Váci utca also had a "dollar store," where you could buy hard-to-find imported and luxury items as long as you had Western currency. During the Cold War, Budapest was sort of the "Sin City" of the Eastern Bloc. (What happened in Budapest, stayed in Budapest. Unless the secret police were watching...which they always were...uh-oh.)

• After the McDonald's, Régi Posta utca crosses...

Váci Utca

We'll follow this crowded drag for two blocks to the right. As we stroll, be sure to look up. Along this street and throughout Pest, spectacular facades begin on the second floor, above a plain entryway (in the 1970s, the communist government made ground-floor shop windows uniformly dull). Locals like to say these buildings are "wearing socks." Pan up above the knees to see some of Pest's best architecture. These were the townhouses of the aristocracy, whose mansions dotted the countryside. You might notice that some of the facades are plain. Many of these used to be more ornate, like their neighbors, but were destroyed by WWII bombs and rebuilt in the stripped-down style of the austere years that followed.

As you head to the right down Váci utca, notice two buildings in particular. The second building on the right, at #15 (marked Sörorrás), features beautiful carved wood on the bottom and tile-and-stone decorations on the top. Combining everything that was typically thought of as "beautiful" in the late 19th century, this building exemplifies Historicism. Across the street and down one door (at #18), we see another architect's response to that facade: stern Jugendstil (Vienna's answer to Art Nouveau). Based in a movement called "The Secession" for the way it broke away from past conventions, this building almost seems to be having a conversation with the one across the street: "Dude, tone it down. Be cool."

A few doors down (past the modern Mercure Hotel), on the left at #24, is any old **Adidas** shop...except, like the "any old McDonalds" we just saw, this was the first Adidas shop behind the Iron Curtain. And, like the McDonald's, 30 years ago you'd have to stand in an hours-long line just to get in the door.

Continue strolling down the street. Here and elsewhere along Váci utca, you'll see restaurants touting Hungarian fare. Avoid these places. Any restaurant along this street is guaranteed to be at least half as good and twice as expensive as other eateries nearby. (For better options—some just a few steps from Váci utca—see the Eating in Budapest chapter.)

• *After about two blocks, turn right down the little lane called Piarista utca. You'll emerge into a charming square called...*

March 15 Square (Március 15. Tér)

This fine riverfront square—facing the graceful modern lines of the Elisabeth Bridge and Gellért Hill—sits upon some serious history. This was the site of **Contra-Aquincum,** a third-century fortress built across *(contra)* the Danube from Aquincum, the main Roman settlement just a few miles up the river, in today's Óbuda (see page 85). Contra-Aquincum fortified the narrowest Danube crossing, where the river is constricted at the base of Gellért Hill. Like so many others who have viewed Budapest as a boundary between West and East, the Romans considered the Danube the natural border of their empire—and fortresses like Contra-Aquincum helped keep the barbarian hordes at bay. For decades, the partially excavated ruins of Contra-Aquincum made this square an ugly jumble of fences and scaffolding, and it gained a reputation as one of downtown Budapest's most dangerous corners. But now it has been gorgeously restored as a fine park, and those ancient ruins are neatly displayed under glass in the middle of the square.

The inland part of the square is enlivened by entertaining, kid-friendly fountains and a sprawling outdoor café, called simply **Kiosk.** While this walk passes a few genteel, old-fashioned coffee houses, these days young urbanites flock to places like this instead. Just order at the bar, then take the scenic seat of your choice.

The twin spires belong to the **Town Center Parish Church** (Belvárosi Plébániatemplom). The oldest building in Pest, this church was founded in 1046, and has lived through many iterations: Romanesque basilica, Gothic hall church, Ottoman mosque. Today, the Gothic foundations are topped with frilly, Baroque, onion-domed steeples. When Franz Josef and Sisi, the Habsburg monarchs, were crowned as the Hungarian king and queen in 1867, they did it right here on this square (for more on the couple and their coronation, see page 320).

Closer to the river (to the right as you face it), you can see a stirring statue of Hungary's national poet, **Sándor Petőfi**—sort of the Hungarian Lord Byron. On the morning of March 15, 1848, a collection of local intellectuals and artists—who came to be known as the "Pest Youth"—gathered at the Pilvax Café (just three blocks up from here, at the corner of Pilvax köz and Városház utca; it's now an Irish pub) to listen to their friend Sándor Petőfi read a new poem. Petőfi's call to arms so inspired the group that they decided to revolt against their Habsburg oppressors...right away. Later that day, Petőfi read his poem again on the steps of the National Museum, rebels broke a beloved patriot out of jail at the castle, the group printed up their list of 12 demands...and the 1848 Revolution had begun. The revolution was ultimately crushed—and Petőfi was killed fighting at the front line—but Hungarians still feel pride about their valiant defeat. (While powerful nations have the luxury of celebrating great military victories, underdogs like the Hungarians cherish their Alamos.) March 15—the namesake of this square—remains one of Hungary's national holidays. (For more on 1848, see page 463.)

The **Orthodox Church** facing Petőfi has noticeably mismatched steeples. The right one was blown off during World War II and never replaced.

• *At the top of March 15 Square, find the grandly arcaded passage called Piarista köz, between the café and the church. Take this one block up to Váci utca, then proceed straight ahead one more block up Kígyó utca. Emerging into a busy urban zone, walk up to the Jégbüfé café near the corner, and survey...*

Ferenciek Tere

"Franciscan Square"—so named for the church across the highway—is the perfect place to take in some of Pest's best "diamond in the rough" architecture...fantastic facades that stand grim and caked with soot. The boulevard was developed (like so much of Budapest) in the late 19th century, to connect the Keleti/Eastern train station (to the left, not visible from here) with the Elisabeth Bridge (to the right). Looking toward the Elisabeth Bridge, you'll see that the busy

highway is flanked by twin apartment blocks called the **Klotild Palaces.** Recently both of these have been purchased by investors and turned into new hotels (you may see them working on the one on the left)—but other nearby buildings remain soot-caked. Imagine this area before 20th-century construction routed a major thoroughfare through it, when people could stroll freely amidst these elaborate facades. Someday, you might not have to imagine. But for now, breathe in the real Budapest.

The **Jégbüfé,** which you're standing in front of, is an increasingly rare artifact of communist times. This *bisztró* serves stand-up coffee and cakes to urbanites on the go. For more details on this place, including how and what to order, see page 266.

Continue about 30 yards back the way you came, toward the right-hand Klotild Palace. On the right (at Kossuth Lajos út 11) is the low-profile entrance to the **Párisi Udvar** ("Parisian Courtyard")—a grand, hidden gallery with delicate woodwork, fine mosaics that glitter evocatively in the low light, and a breathtaking stained-glass dome. Like the streets around it, this fine space sat neglected for decades, rotting all around its tenants. Now everybody has moved out, it has been purchased, and it's slated to become yet another fancy hotel. While it's likely closed for your visit, peek (or, if possible, walk) through the gate to appreciate the grand space...and daydream about the day when it's returned to its former glory.

This gallery is a reminder that if you only experience what's on the main streets in Budapest, you'll miss a big part of the story. Behind most of Pest's once-grand, now-crumbling facades, you'll find cozy courtyards where residents carry out much of their lives. These courtyards, shared among neighbors and ringed by a common balcony, stay cool through the summer. Poking into some of these courtyards (which are generally open to the public, offering a handy shortcut through city blocks) is an essential Back Door experience for understanding the inner life of Budapest.

• *Facing the gallery door, turn 180 degrees and head straight down the stairs into the pedestrian underpass. Surfacing on the other side, turn left, walk to the end of the block, then (at the church) turn right and walk along...*

Károlyi Mihály Utca

As you walk up the street, appreciate the pretty corner spires on the buildings. The yellow one marks the university library.

At the end of the block, cross Irányi utca, and you'll be face-to-face with the entrance to the recommended **Centrál Kávéház** (on the right-hand corner)—another of Budapest's newly rejuvenated, old-style café/restaurants (see page 266). Step inside to be transported to another time. If you haven't taken a coffee break yet, now's a good time.

Continue along Károlyi Mihály utca. Just past Centrál Kávéház, on the left (at #12), is the recently restored **Ybl Palace**, designed by and named for the prominent architect Miklós Ybl (who also did the Opera House).

You can usually pop inside the palace and step into its fine inner courtyard to see the impressive remodel job.

• *Continue along Károlyi Mihály utca to the end of the block, then take the first left up Ferenczy István utca. After the long building, dip through the green fence on the right, into...*

Károlyi Park (Károlyi Kert)

This delightful, flower-filled oasis offers the perfect break from loud and gritty urban Pest. Once the private garden of the aris-

tocratic Károlyi family from eastern Hungary (whose mansion it's behind), it's now a public park beloved by people who live, work, and go to school in this neighborhood. The park is filled with tulips in the spring, potted palm trees in the summer, and rich colors in the fall. On a sunny summer day, lo-

cals escape here to read books, gossip with neighbors, or simply lie in the sun. Many schools are nearby. Teenagers hang out here after school, while younger kids enjoy the playground. (If you need a potty break after all that coffee, a pay WC is in the green pavilion in the far-right corner.)

• *Exit the park straight ahead from where you entered, and turn right down Henszimann utca. At the end of the street, you'll come to a church with onion-dome steeples. The big plaza in front of it is...*

University Square (Egyetem Tér)

This square is one of Budapest's most recent to enjoy a makeover. An initiative called the "Heart of the City" is directing EU and

Hungarian funds at renovating city-center streets and squares like this one (as well as Károlyi Mihály utca, which we were walking down earlier). Traffic is carefully regulated. Notice the automatic bollard that goes up and down to let in approved vehicles: buses, taxis, and local residents only. The modern lampposts and barriers are an interesting (and controversial) choice in this nostalgic city, where the priority is usually on re-creating the city exactly as it was a century ago. The idea in this case is to keep the original buildings, but surround them with a modern streetscape.

The colonnaded building on the left is the law school for ELTE

University (Hungary's biggest, with 30,000 students and colleges all over the city). The letters stand for "Eotvös Lorand Technical University," named for an influential physicist. As in much of the former Soviet Bloc, the university system in Hungary is still heavily subsidized by the government. It's affordable to study here...*if* you can get in (competition is fierce).

• *Facing the university building, turn left, then take the first right down Szerb utca. After one long block, on the right, in the park behind the yellow fence, is a...*

Serbian Orthodox Church

This used to be a strongly Serbian neighborhood—there's still some Cyrillic writing on some of the buildings nearby. The church is rarely open, but if it is, step inside to be transported to the far-eastern reaches of Europe...heavy with incense and packed with icons.

The Serbs are just one of many foreign groups that have coexisted here. Traditionally, Hungary's territory included most of Slovakia and large parts of Romania, Croatia, and Serbia—and people from all of those places (along with Austrians, Jews, and Roma/Gypsies) flocked to Buda and Pest. And yet, most of the residents of this cosmopolitan city still speak Hungarian. Throughout centuries of foreign invasions and visitors, new arrivals have undergone a slow-but-sure process of "Magyarization"—"becoming" Hungarian (often against their will). This has made Budapest one of the greatest "melting pot" cities in Europe, if not the world.

• *Continue down Szerb utca, until it runs into Váci utca. Turn left, and set your sights on the colorful tiled roofs two blocks directly ahead. Across the street is the...*

Great Market Hall (Nagyvásárcsarnok)

This market hall (along with four others) was built—like so much of Budapest—around the millennial celebration year of 1896 (see

page 33). Appreciate the colorful Zsolnay tiles lining the roof—frostproof and harder than stone, these were an integral part of the Hungarian national style that emerged in the late 19th century.

Tunnels connect this hall to the Danube, where goods could be unloaded at the customs house (now Budapest Corvinus University of Economics, formerly Karl Marx University, next door) and easily transported into the market hall. Along the river behind the market hall and university—not quite visible from here—is the sleek, glass-roofed Bálna ("Whale"), a super-modern cultural center (with an extension of the Great

Market Hall's vendors, and art gallery, and inviting public spaces) that opened in late 2013 (for details, see page 56).

To the right, the green **Liberty Bridge**—formerly named for Habsburg Emperor Franz Josef—spans the Danube to the Gellért Baths, in the shadow of Gellért Hill. And to the left, the Small Boulevard (here named Vámház körút) curls around toward Deák tér, passing Kálvin tér, the National Museum, and the Great Synagogue along the way.

Step inside the market and get your bearings: The cavernous interior features three levels. The ground floor has produce stands, bakeries, butcher stalls, heaps of paprika, goose liver, and salamis. Upstairs are stand-up eateries and souvenirs. And in the basement are a supermarket, a fish market, and piles of pickles.

Main Floor

Before exploring, take this guided stroll along the market's "main drag" (straight ahead from the entry). Notice the floor slopes slightly downhill to the left. Locals say that the vendors along the right wall are (appropriately enough) higher-end, with more specialty items, while the ones along the left wall are cheaper. Just inside the door, to the right as you enter, notice the small electronic scale—so shoppers can double-check to be sure the merchants didn't cheat them.

In the first "block" of stalls, the corner showcase on the left explains how this stall has been in the same family since 1924, and includes photos of three generations. At the end of this set of stalls, in the dairy case, they sell **Túró Rudi** (TOO-roh ROO-dee), a semi-sweet cottage cheese covered in chocolate (in the red-and-white polka-dot wrapper). This is a favorite treat for young Hungarians—mothers get their kids to behave here by promising to buy them one. Across the "street," the corner showcase on the right (at the end of this block) displays some favorite **Hungarian spirits:** Tokaji Aszú, colored (and priced) like gold and called "the wine of kings, and the king of wines" (see page 252); Unicum, the secret-recipe herbal liquor beloved by Hungarians and undrinkable to everyone else (see page 251); and the local version of schnapps, *pálinka*, in several fruit flavors.

In the second block, meat is on the right, and produce is on the left. At the end of this section on the left, you have a good opportunity to sample homemade **strudels** *(rétesek)* of various flavors for 230 Ft.

In the third block, you'll see paprika on both sides. To sample before you buy, turn left before entering this block, go down the street, then turn right at the next corner. The **Csárdi és Csárdi** stall (on the right) lets you sample both types of

paprika: sweet (*édes,* used for flavor) and hot (*csípós,* used sparingly to add some kick). Note the difference, choose your favorite, and buy some to take home (for more information, see "Paprika Primer"

on page 251). They also sell fun little wooden spice spoons.

Back on the main paprika drag, just after the stairs on the right, hung high amidst the paprika (at the Kmetty & Kmetty stall), is a photo of **Margaret Thatcher** visiting this market in 1989. She expected atrocious conditions compared to English markets, but was pleasantly surprised to find this place up to snuff. This was, after all, "goulash communism" (Hungary's pragmatic

mix, which allowed a little private enterprise to keep people going). On the steps of this building, she delivered a historic speech about open society, heralding the impending arrival of the market economy.

At the fourth block, on the right, the corner showcase features another favorite Hungarian food: **goose liver** *(libamáj)*—not to be confused with the cheaper and less typical duck liver *(kacsamáj);* see the geese standing above the case. Goose liver comes in various forms: most traditional is packaged whole (*naturel* or *blokk*), others are pâté (*parfé* or *püré*). Hungary is, after France, the world's second-biggest producer of foie gras.

In the fifth block, on the left, look for another local favorite: Hungarian *szalámi* (Pick, a brand from the town of Szeged, is a favorite here).

Reaching the sixth block, above the corner showcase on the right, you'll see a poster showing two types of uniquely Hungarian **livestock**. *Mangalica* is a hairy pig (with a thick, curly coat resembling a sheep's fleece) that almost went extinct, but became popular again after butchers discovered it makes great ham—and has a lower fat content than other types of pork (look for this on local menus). *Szürkemarha* are gray longhorn cattle. Keeping an eye on all that livestock, but not pictured here, is the distinctive *Puli* (or larger *Komondor*)—a Hungarian sheepdog with tightly curled hair that resembles dreadlocks.

• *Head up the escalator at the back of the market (on the left).*

Upstairs

Along the upstairs back wall are historic photos of the market hall (and pay WCs).

If you're in the mood for some shopping, this is a convenient place to look—with a great selection of souvenirs both traditional (embroidery) and not-so-traditional (commie-kitsch T-shirts). While there are no real bargains here, the prices are a bit better than out along Váci utca. For tips on shopping here, see the Shopping in Budapest chapter.

The left wall (as you face the front) is lined with fun, cheap, stand-up, Hungarian-style fast-food joints and six-stool pubs. About two-thirds of the way along the hall (after the second bridge), the **Lángos** stand is the best eatery in the market, serving up the deep-fried snack called *lángos*—similar to elephant ears, but savory rather than sweet. The most typical version is *sajtos tejfölös*—with sour cream and cheese. You can also add garlic *(fokhagyma)*. The **Fakanál Étterem** cafeteria above the main entrance is handy but pricey.

• *For a less glamorous look at the market, head down the escalators near the front of the market (below the restaurant) to the...*

Basement

The market basement is pungent with tanks of still-swimming carp, catfish, and perch, and piles of pickles (along the left side of the supermarket). Stop at one of the pickle stands and take a look. Hungarians pickle just about anything: peppers and cukes, of course, but also cauliflower, cabbage, beets, tomatoes, garlic, and so on. They use particularly strong vinegar, which has a powerful flavor but keeps things very crispy.

Until recently—before importing fruits and vegetables became more common—most "salads" out of season were pickled items like these. Vendors are usually happy to give you a sample; consider picking up a colorful jar of mixed pickled veggies for your picnic.

• *When your exploration is finished...so is this walk. Exit the hall the way you came in. Near the Great Market Hall, you have several sight-*

*seeing options. If you'd like to stroll back to Vörösmarty tér—this time along the fashionable Váci utca—you can walk straight ahead from the market. In the opposite direction, along the river behind the Great Market Hall, you can poke into the Bálna Budapest cultural center. The green Liberty Bridge next to the market leads straight to Gellért Hotel, with its famous hot-springs bath, at the foot of Gellért Hill (see the Thermal Baths chapter; **trams #47** and **#49** zip you right there, or it's one stop on the M4/green Metró line).*

*Convenient trams connect this area to the rest of Budapest: **Tram #2** runs from under the Liberty Bridge along the Danube directly back to Vigadó tér (at the promenade by Vörösmarty tér), the Chain Bridge, and the Parliament (where my **Leopold Town Walk** begins). **Trams #47** and **#49** (catch them directly in front of the market) zip to the right around the Small Boulevard to the National Museum (see page 57) and, beyond that, the Great Synagogue (for my **Great Synagogue and Jewish Quarter Tour**) and Deák tér (the starting point of my **Andrássy Út Walk**)—or you can simply walk around the Small Boulevard to reach these sights in about 15 minutes.*

ANDRÁSSY ÚT WALK

From Deák Tér to Heroes' Square

Connecting downtown Pest to City Park, Andrássy út is Budapest's main boulevard, lined with plane trees, shops, theaters, cafés, and locals living very well. Budapesters like to think of Andrássy út as the Champs-Elysées and Broadway rolled into one. While that's a stretch, it is a good place to stroll, get a feel for today's urban Pest, and visit a few top attractions (most notably the Opera House and the House of Terror) on the way to Heroes' Square and City Park.

Orientation

Length of This Walk: Allow an hour, not including time to enter the sights.

Overview: Andrássy út is divided roughly into thirds. The most interesting first section (from Deák tér to the Oktogon) is the focus of this walk. The middle section (between the Oktogon and Kodály körönd) features one major sight, the House of Terror. The final third (Kodály körönd to Heroes' Square), while pleasant and comparatively low-key, offers fewer sight-seeing opportunities.

Shortcut: The M1/yellow Metró line runs every couple of minutes just under the street—so it's easy to skip several blocks ahead, or to backtrack (stops marked by yellow signs).

Getting There: The walk begins at Deák tér—easy to reach from anywhere in the city, as it's on three Metró lines. If you're coming from Vörösmarty tér in central Pest, simply hop the M1/yellow Metró line one stop, or walk five minutes up Deák utca. If you want to skip to the start of Andrássy út itself, you can ride the M1 to the Bajcsy-Zsilinszky út stop and start this walk at the "Millennium Underground of 1896" section.

Opera House: Lobby free to enter Mon-Sat 11:00 until show time—generally 19:00, or until 17:00 if there's no performance, on Sun open 3 hours before the performance—generally 16:00-19:00, or 10:00-13:00 if there's a matinee; tours-2,900 Ft, 600 Ft extra for 5-minute mini-concert following the tour, 45 minutes, in English nearly daily at 15:00 and 16:00, June-Oct maybe also at 14:00—buy tickets at shop inside lobby and to the left, shop has slightly shorter hours than lobby; Andrássy út 22, tel. 1/332-8197.

House of Terror: 2,000 Ft, possibly more for special exhibits, audioguide-1,500 Ft, Tue-Sun 10:00-18:00, closed Mon, last entry 30 minutes before closing, Andrássy út 60, tel. 1/374-2600, www.terrorhaza.hu.

Franz Liszt Museum: 1,300 Ft, audioguide-700 Ft; Mon-Fri 10:00-18:00, Sat 9:00-17:00, closed Sun; performances in concert hall Sat at 11:00, Vörösmarty utca 35, tel. 1/322-9804, www.lisztmuseum.hu.

Starring: Budapest's most elegant drag, with fine architecture, upscale shopping, great restaurants, and top-notch sightseeing—from opulent (Opera House) to sobering (House of Terror).

The Walk Begins

• *Begin in the middle of the paved square (near the M2 and M3 Metró entrances) called...*

Deák Tér

This square is named for **Ferenc Deák** (1803-1876), a statesman who pushed for persistent international pressure on the Habsburgs to improve Hungary's status after his rabble-rousing compatriots failed in the 1848 Revolution. (The peace-loving Deák was sort of a Hungarian Jimmy Carter.) It worked. With the Compromise of 1867, Hungary was granted an impressive measure of autonomy in the empire.

Sitting unassumingly on the square is the blocky, typically austere **Lutheran church,** with its Neoclassical colonnade entry and shallow green dome. Looming over the square across the street is the landmark, but sadly neglected, yellow office block called the **Ankerház.** Like the square it dominates, this building isn't as important as it might seem.

On the upper part of the square (up the stairs) is an angular

Andrássy Út Walk

To **17** & END OF WALK

SZINYEI MERSE

BAJNOK

SZÍV

RÓZSA

IZABELLA

VÖRÖSMARTY

CSENGERY

EÖTVÖS

HOUSE OF TERROR

To Nyugati/Western Train Station

Tram #4 & #6

TERÉZ KÖRUT

JÓKAI

Jókai tér

WEINER LEÓ

LOVAG

DESSEWFFY

NAGYMEZŐ

"Broadway Quarter"

OPERA HOUSE

DISCOVER BUDAPEST

US EMBASSY

POSTAL SAVINGS BANK

NATIONAL BANK

Arany János utca

CROSSWALK

KÁLDY GYULA

Bajcsy-Zsilinszky út

AKVÁRIUM KLUB

Deák Ferenc tér

Kodály körönd

FELSŐ ERDŐSOR

Kodály körönd

SZÍV

SZEGFŰ

SZALMÁS

Lövölde tér

100 Meters
100 Yards

ARADI

SZONDI

Vörösmarty utca

PUPPET THEATER

Hunyadi tér

KIRÁLY

VÖRÖSMARTY

DOB

CSENGERY

HÁRSFA

POST

SZÓFIA

To New York Café

Oktogon

ERZSÉBET KÖRUT

Oktogon

Liszt Ferenc tér

KÜRT

KERTÉSZ

PAULAY EDE

HEGEDŰ

AKÁCFA

CSÁNYI

MOZSÁR

ZICHY JENŐ

HAJÓS

Opera

VASVÁRI

DRESCHLER PALACE

NEW THEATER

SZÉKELY

KIS DIÓFA

ORTHODOX SYNAGOGUE

KAZINCZY

JEWISH QUARTER
(& "Ruin Pub" District)

HOLLÓ

GOSZDU UDVAR

RUMBACH STREET SYNAGOGUE

RUMBACH SEBESTYÉN

To Great Synagogue

ASBÓTH

ANKERHÁZ

KÁROLY KÖRUT

WALK BEGINS

Deák tér

ISTVÁN

SEMMELWEIS

CITY HALL

COUNTY HALL

GERLÓCZY

BAJCSY-ZSILINSZKY

VADÁSZ

NAGY SÁNDOR

BANK

Ó UTCA

LÁZÁR

RÉVAY

1. Deák Tér
2. Erzsébet Tér
3. Underground Station
4. Herend Porcelain Shop
5. Callas Café
6. Hungarian State Opera House
7. "Broadway Quarter"
8. Művész Kávéház
9. Párisi Nagy Áruház Café
10. Writer's Bookshop
11. Franz Liszt Square
12. Franz Liszt Acad. of Music
13. Oktogon
14. House of Terror
15. Former Academy of Music & Franz Liszt Museum
16. Kodály Körönd
17. To Diplomatic Quarter, Heroes' Square & City Park

memorial to **Gábor Sztehlo,** a Lutheran pastor who rescued approximately 2,000 local Jews from the Arrow Cross regime during the Holocaust. Hungarian officials understandably love to celebrate these (relatively rare) "righteous Gentiles" who came to the rescue of the Jews. (For more on the Holocaust in Hungary, see page 186.)

• *From Deák tér, cross Harmincad street— the one with all the bus stops (including one to Memento Park, explained on page 215)—and head for...*

Erzsébet Tér

This pretty, leafy park was Pest's main market square. It's named for one of Deák's contemporaries: Elisabeth, the wife of the Habsburg Emperor Franz Josef. While Deák pressed Franz Josef with diplomacy, Empress Elisabeth (a.k.a. Sisi) pressured him at home... Hungarian autonomy was one of her pet issues (for more on this "royal and imperial" couple, see page 320).

The park was long marred by the presence of a gloomy, polluting, communist-era international bus station. But now it has been reclaimed as a welcoming public zone, and the bus station has been converted into the Design Terminal (with a gallery and studios) and lively Fröccsterasz outdoor bar/café. Deeper in the park, in the summertime you may see the Budapest Eye, a Ferris wheel that offers an overpriced (but scenic and romantic) spin over the rooftops of the city center.

Notice there are two parts to Erzsébet tér: the more traditional park behind the former bus station and a sleek, modern new area in front of it. A few years ago, the government planned to build a new national theater in this spot, and they even began to dig the foundation. But when the parliament changed hands, construction was aborted—leaving a giant hole that locals called "The National Ditch."

Eventually they came up with a creative use for the space: an underground parking garage and a unique café/nightclub. Walk closer to the low wall at the end of the park near the busy street and look down (at the end facing Deák tér): A long series of terraces filled with café tables leads down into the **Akvárium** nightclub. On balmy summer nights, outdoor performances take place here, and this whole area is filled with young locals. The incline leads to the indoor, underground part of the café. Walk a little farther through the park to reach the artificial pond that covers part of the ditch. Look closely: Especially at night, you can see through the glass floor of the very shallow pond and spot people walking around in the underground nightclub. (For more, see page 291.)

• *At the far corner of Erzsébet tér (past the ditch and the rack of loaner Bubi bikes), cross the busy Small Boulevard (here called Bajcsy-Zsilinszky*

út) to the beginning of Andrássy út. For now, stay on the right side of the boulevard. You'll pass a heavenly smelling stand selling a delicious Hungarian treat, **kürtőskalács**—*a "pastry horn" that's slow-cooked on a rotisserie, then rolled in cinnamon, coconut, or other toppings. Be sure to get one that's hot and fresh. A few steps farther along, look for the yellow railings on either side of the street with the low-profile* Földalatti *sign. This marks the Bajcsy-Zsilinszky út Metró stop. Go down the steps and back more than 100 years (if they ask you for your Metró ticket, just take a peek, then head back up).*

Millennium Underground of 1896

Built to get the masses conveniently out to Heroes' Square for the millennium festivities, this fun and extremely handy little

Metró line follows Andrássy út from Vörösmarty tér (Pest's main square) to City Park. It was originally dubbed the "Franz Josef Underground Line"—in honor of the then-emperor—but later simply became known as the Underground *(Földalatti)*. Just 20 steps below street level, it's so shallow that you must follow the signs on

the street (listing end points—*ua Mexikói út felé* takes you toward City Park) to gauge the right direction, because there's no underpass for switching platforms. The first underground on the Continent (London's is older), it originally had horse-drawn cars. Trains depart every couple of minutes. Though recently renovated, the M1 line retains its 1896 atmosphere, with fun black-and-white photos of the age.

• *From the top of the stairs here, notice the great view across the street to St. István's Basilica. Now continue...*

Gyula Andrássy (1823-1890)

A key player in the 1848 Revolution, Count Gyula (Julius) Andrássy went on to help forge (along with Ferenc Deák) the Dual Monarchy of the Austro-Hungarian Empire. As Budapest boomed, Andrássy also served as an urban planner who championed the idea of building a grand boulevard from downtown to City Park. Andrássy was also the Hungarian prime minister and Austro-Hungarian foreign minister (1871-1879). Eventually he was forced to step down after his unpopular campaign to appropriate Bosnia-Herzegovina (and consequently boost the Slav population of the empire, which destabilized its delicate ethnic balance). But to most Hungarians, Andrássy is best known for his alleged relationship with Empress Sisi, who adored all things Hungarian (see page 320). Her third daughter—who some believed to be the count's—was known as the Little Hungarian Princess.

Strolling up Andrássy Út

This grand boulevard—140 feet wide and nearly 2 miles long—was begun in 1871, when city bigwigs decided that on-the-rise Budapest needed an answer to Paris' Champs-Elysées. But instead of leading to an Arc de Triomphe, Andrássy út culminates at the similarly triumphal Heroes' Square. The boulevard also provided a convenient link between the dense urban center of Pest and the green expanse of City Park, allowing city-dwellers to zip out for a break from the bustle without plodding along congested narrow streets. The boulevard was officially inaugurated with much fanfare in 1885. Because most of the buildings were built within about 15 years, Andrássy út enjoys a pleasant architectural harmony. Historicism—a creative merging of various complementary styles—was all the rage at the time. Look up as you stroll to see the heroic statuary adorning the tops of buildings.

Since being built, this boulevard (and the major intersections along its length) has constantly changed names with the tenor of the times. Originally called Radial Boulevard (Súgarút), it was later christened for Count Andrássy, who had strongly promoted its construction (see sidebar). When the Soviets moved in, they renamed it Sztálin út; after the 1956 Uprising, it was briefly called Hungarian Youth Boulevard, before they re-dubbed it People's Republic Boulevard. And finally, with the fall of communism, it regained its historical name: Andrássy út.

Running parallel to Andrássy út, two blocks to the right, is **Király utca,** which is lined with home-improvement shops (a hot commodity in this swiftly gentrifying city, where so many people are fixing up flats). This area—formerly the Jewish Quarter, and now more seedy than most parts of central Pest—is also home to the city's distinctive "ruin pubs" (described on page 292).

• *At your first opportunity—about a block and a half up from the underground station—cross to the left side of Andrássy út to find the next few attractions. As you cross, look to the far end of the street, where you can already faintly see the column that marks Heroes' Square.*

Once across the street, peek into the window of the **Miniversum**—a model railroad that curls its way through miniature buildings from Budapest and around Hungary. While you could pay to enter, you can see most of it from here.

This first stretch of Andrássy út is a cancan of big-money stores featuring international brands, such as Gucci and Louis Vuitton. But there are still some local shops—on the left, at #16, is a **Herend** shop, selling very expensive pieces of Hungary's top porcelain (see page 279).

Upscale as it has become, Andrássy út remains an artery for the city, often clogged with traffic...except during "critical mass," when 80,000 bikers take back the street twice a year (though these days it's occurring more and more often—generally on weekends). During these times, the street is closed to traffic for a full day and given over to cyclists, in-line skaters, skateboarders, and pedestrians...a tempting taste of what could be.

On the left side of the street, on the corner at #20, look for the recommended **Callas café,** with sumptuous *Jugendstil* decor (for details, see page 267).

It was along this stretch of Andrássy út that Steven Spielberg filmed much of the 2005 film *Munich,* since the street has fine architecture that can stand in for many great European cities.

• *On the left, just after Callas, is the can't-miss-it...*

Hungarian State Opera House (Magyar Állami Operaház)

The Neo-Renaissance home of the Hungarian State Opera features performances (almost daily

except during outdoor music season, late June-early Sept) and delightful tours. The building dates from the 1890s, not long after Budapest had become co-capital of the Habsburg Empire. The Hungarians wanted to put their city on the map as a legitimate European capital, and that meant they needed an opera house. Emperor Franz Josef provided half the funds...on the condition that it be smaller than the opera house in his hometown of Vienna. And so, Miklós Ybl designed a building that would exceed Vienna's famous Staatsoper in opulence, if not in size. (Franz Josef was reportedly displeased.) It was built using almost entirely Hungarian materials. After being damaged in World War II, it was painstakingly restored in the early 1980s. Today, with lavish marble-and-gold-leaf decor, a gorgeous gilded interior slathered with paintings of Greek myths, and high-quality performances at bargain prices, this is one of Europe's finest opera houses.

You have a few options for seeing this place. To just get a taste, slip in the front door when the box office is open and check out the sumptuous entryway. For the full story (and to get into the remarkable auditorium), take one of the guided tours in English (see page 59). To see the Opera House in action, take in an excellent (and refreshingly affordable) performance—for specifics, see page 283.

• *The Opera House marks the beginning of an emerging dining-and-nightlife zone dubbed the...*

"Broadway Quarter"

• *Cross to the right side of Andrássy út for the next few sights.*

Across the street from the Opera House, and echoing its shape (although in a different style), is the **Dreschler Palace.** It was co-de-

signed by Ödön Lechner, a leading architect whose works also include the Postal Savings Bank (see page 116). In this building's late-19th-century heyday, one of Budapest's top cafés filled its gallery. More recently, it housed the Ballet Institute. And not long ago, the beautiful but neglected building was purchased by a luxury hotel chain...but their plans fell through, and it's still waiting for a new tenant. Tucked behind it is the **New Theater** (Új Szinház, with a fine *Jugendstil* facade), one of many popular venues around here for Hungarian-language plays (Paulay Ede utca 35, tel. 1/269-6021, www.ujszinhaz.hu).

A few steps up Andrássy út on the right (at #29) is another fine historic café, **Művész Kávéház.** As it's a hangout for actors and musicians, this is your best chance to rub elbows with actual drama queens and divas (described on page 267).

The next major cross-street, **Nagymező utca,** features a chic cluster of restaurants, bars, and theaters (especially on the left side of Andrássy). This is an enjoyable place to stroll on a summer evening. While you might be tempted to attend a show along Budapest's answer to Broadway, note that most of the plays and musicals here are in Hungarian only. So unless you want to hear "Music of the Night" sung in Hungarian (as it was meant to be), keep looking. (The Entertainment in Budapest chapter offers several more accessible alternatives.)

Continue straight across Nagymező utca, staying on the right side of Andrássy út. A half-block down on the right (at #39) is

a grand old early-20th-century building marked **Párisi Nagy Áruház** (Paris Department Store), with a fine recommended café inside. Go in, and head up the escalator. One of the city's first department stores, this was a popular shopping stop for years, even through communism. But as was common in Budapest, the store closed down and sat deserted and glum for years until investors came along to rescue it. The new owners, the Alexandra bookstore chain, turned the main area into a great bookshop, created office space above, and—inside, up the escalator at the back—fully restored the sumptuous Lotz Hall to create an excellent café with tinkling-piano ambience and reasonable prices (free entry, daily 10:00-22:00; for more details, see page 266). Upstairs is an art gallery and antique shop.

At the end of the block on the right (at #45) is a much humbler (but arguably more historic) bookstore: the **Writer's Bookshop** (Írók Boltja). During Budapest's late-19th-century glory days, the Japan Café at this spot was the haunt of many of the great artistic minds that populated the city, including architect Ödön Lechner and poet Attila József. Today the management still encourages loitering (and sells some English books).

• *Just after the bookshop is a popular outdoor-dining area.*

Franz Liszt Square (Liszt Ferenc Tér)

This leafy square is surrounded by hip, expensive cafés and restaurants. (The best is the recommended, kitschy, communist-themed restaurant **Menza**.)

Strangely, neither the statue on this square nor the one facing it, across Andrássy út, is of Franz Liszt. But deeper in the park, you'll find a modern statue of Liszt energetically playing an imaginary piano. And at the far end of the square is the **Franz Liszt Academy of Music,** founded by and named for this half-Hungarian, half-Austrian composer who had a Hungarian name and passport. Liszt loved his family's Magyar heritage (though he didn't speak Hungarian) and spent his last six years in Budapest. His Academy of Music has been stunningly restored inside and out—step into the sumptuous lobby. This space, though smaller, gives the Opera House a run for its money...and speaking of money, the concerts here are much more affordable even than at the already reasonably priced Opera (for details, see page 287; for more on Liszt, see page 288).

• *One block up from Franz Liszt Square is the gigantic crossroads known as the...*

Oktogon

This vast intersection with its corners snipped off—where Andrássy út meets the Great Boulevard ring road (Nagykörút)—was

called Mussolini tér during World War II, then November 7 tér in honor of the Bolshevik Revolution. Today kids have nicknamed it American tér for the fast-food joints littering the square and streets nearby.

From here, if you have time to delve into workaday Budapest, hop on tram #4 or #6, which trundle in both directions around the ring road. If you've got time for a short detour to the most opulent coffee break of your life, head for the recommended **New York Café** (see page 265): Just hop on a tram to the right (tram #6 toward Móricz Zsigmond körtér or tram #4 toward Fehérvári út), and get off at the Wesselényi utca stop.

• *There's one more major sight between here and Heroes' Square. Walk two more blocks up Andrássy út to reach the...*

House of Terror (Terror Háza)

The building at Andrássy út 60 (on the left) has been painted a lifeless blue-gray, and the word "TERROR" is carved into the overhanging eaves. This is the place where two evil regimes tortured their Hungarian subjects. Now a modern museum documenting the terror of Hungary's "double occupation"—first at the hands of the Nazis, then the Soviets—this is essential sightseeing for those intrigued by Budapest's dark 20th century, and interesting to anyone. ♦ See the House of Terror Tour chapter for a self-guided tour of the museum.

In the tree-lined sidewalk strip in front of the House of Terror, notice two other symbolic landmarks of that dark time: a chunk of the **Berlin Wall,** and an actual **iron curtain** of heavy, rusted chains.

• *Two significant buildings stand across the boulevard from the House of Terror (on the right side of Andrássy út, just behind the Metró stop).*

Former Academy of Music (Franz Liszt Museum) and Puppet Theater

The yellow building on the corner of Vörösmarty utca (at Andrássy #67) is the **former Academy of Music**—founded by Franz Liszt and later moved to the building we just saw on his square. Upstairs is the small but endearing

Franz Liszt Museum, in the old flat where the composer spent much of his time for the last six years of his life. This dusty collection might interest classical music buffs but will probably underwhelm most others. After putting on shoe covers, you glide through three rooms filled with period furniture and pianos (including ones custom-made for Liszt, and—on the lower shelf of a glass case—a "composing desk" with a small three-octave keyboard built by famous piano-maker Ludwig Bösendorfer).

Liszt's bedroom (to the right as you enter) contains his actual bed and a little personal altar where he knelt to pray. Look for the lithographs of Liszt sitting in this very room. The cupboard contains personal belongings, including a plate that belonged to writer (and Liszt friend) George Sand, and locks of the composer's hair that were saved by his fans. In his heyday, Liszt was as adored as much as today's biggest-name rock stars.

On Saturdays at 11:00, **performances** take place in the building's small concert hall (for specifics, see page 287).

The next building is the **Puppet Theater** (Bábszinház), a venue for top-notch puppet shows (see page 274 for details).

• *While you can hoof it from here to Heroes' Square (visible in the distance, about a 15-minute walk), there's less to see along the rest of Andrássy út. If you prefer, hop on the Metró here (from right in front of the Puppet Theater) and ride it three stops to Hősök tere.*

Or, if you continue walking up Andrássy út, after four blocks you'll reach the grand intersection called...

Kodály Körönd

This circular crossroads—which seems to echo the octagonal one we passed through earlier—is named for another great Hungar-

ian composer, Zoltán Kodály (who lived in a mansion here, at #1, now a museum; for more on Kodály, see page 288). During the Nazi occupation, it had the jarring name Hitler tér.

Standing in the four wedge-shaped parks—overshadowed by the stately mansions surrounding them—are statues of four Hungarian heroes who fought against Ottoman invaders. Think of these as rejects from the Millennium Monument at Heroes' Square just up the boulevard. In fact, two of the original statues from Kodály körönd were eventually "promoted" to the colonnade there, and their spots here were taken by two different heroes.

• *After Kodály körönd, Andrássy út enters its final third, the...*

Diplomatic Quarter

Continuing up the street, notice that the buildings lining Andrássy út shrink and pull back from the busy boulevard, huddling behind trees. Instead of boasting bulky four- and five-story apartment blocks, it turns into a sleepy, leafy residential zone. These villas were formerly occupied by aristocrats, diplomats, and wealthy Jews. Today this is where many foreign states maintain their embassies. If you'd like to skip the final stretch, you can hop on the Metró at Kodály körönd. Or, to complete your stroll, keep going.

• *Andrássy út terminates at Heroes' Square. See the* **Heroes' Square and City Park Walk** *chapter.*

HOUSE OF TERROR TOUR

Terror Háza

Along one of the prettiest stretches of urban Budapest, in the house at 60 Andrássy Boulevard, some of the most horrific acts in Hungarian history took place. The former headquarters of two of the country's darkest regimes—the Arrow Cross (Nazi-occupied Hungary's version of the Gestapo) and the ÁVO/ÁVH (communist Hungary's secret police)—is now, fittingly, an excellent museum that recounts those times of terror. The high-tech, conceptual, and sometimes over-the-top exhibits attempt to document the atrocities endured by Hungary during the 20th century. This is a powerful experience, particularly for elderly Hungarians who knew both victims and perpetrators and have personal memories of the terrors that came with Hungary's "double occupation."

Orientation

Cost: 2,000 Ft, possibly more for special exhibits.

Hours: Tue-Sun 10:00-18:00, closed Mon, last entry 30 minutes before closing.

Getting There: It's located at Andrássy út 60, district VI, near the Vörösmarty utca stop of the M1/yellow Metró line. Note that this is Vörösmarty utca, not Vörösmarty tér (which is a different stop). Outside, an overhang casts the shadow outline of the word "TERROR" onto the building.

Audioguide and Information: The 1,500-Ft English audioguide is good but almost too thorough, and can be difficult to hear over the din of Hungarian soundtracks in each room. You can't fast-forward through the dense and sometimes long-winded commentary. As an alternative, my self-guided tour covers the key points. A silver plaque in each room provides the basics (in English), and each room is stocked with free English fliers providing more in-depth information (very similar to what's covered by the audioguide). Tel. 1/374-2600, www.terrorhaza. hu.

Length of This Tour: 1.5-2 hours.

Services: Café, good bookshop, and WCs.

Photography: Not allowed inside.

Starring: Fascism, communism, and the resilient Hungarian spirit.

BACKGROUND

In the lead-up to World War II, Hungary initially allied with Hitler—both to retain a degree of self-determination and to try to regain its huge territorial losses after World War I's devastating Treaty of Trianon (see page 466). As the rest of Europe fell into war, Hungary tiptoed between supporting the Nazis and, wherever possible, charting its own course. The Hungarians found themselves in the unenviable position of providing a buffer between Nazi Germany to the west and the Soviet Union to the east. They did just enough to stay in the Nazis' good graces (the Hungarian Second Army invaded the Soviet Union in 1941), while attempting to maintain what autonomy they could.

Hitler finally got fed up with Hungary's less-than-whole-hearted support, and in March of 1944, the Nazi-affiliated Arrow

Cross Party was forcibly installed as Hungary's new government. The Arrow Cross immediately set to work exterminating Budapest's Jews (most of whom had survived until then, although they had suffered under the earlier regime's anti-Semitic laws). The Nazi surrogates deported nearly 440,000 Jewish people to Auschwitz, murdered thousands more on the streets of Budapest, and executed hundreds in the basement of this building. (For more on this ugly time, see page 186.)

The Red Army entered Hungary from the USSR in late August of 1944. After a hard-fought battle (and a devastating siege), they took Budapest on February 13, 1945, and forced the last Nazi soldier out of Hungary on April 4. Although the USSR characterized this as the "liberation" of Hungary, it soon became clear that the Hungarians had merely gone from the Nazi frying pan into the Soviet fire. Here in Budapest, the new communist leaders took over the same building as headquarters for their secret police (the ÁVO, later renamed ÁVH). To keep dissent to a minimum, the secret police terrorized, tried, deported, or executed anyone suspected of being an enemy of the state.

Critics of this museum point out that it doesn't draw a very fine distinction between these two very different phases of the "double occupation." As you tour the exhibits, remember that as similar as their methods might seem, the Nazis and the communists represented opposite extremes of the political spectrum. Hungarians, like so many others in the 20th century, got caught in the cross fire.

The Tour Begins

• *Buy your ticket (and rent an audioguide, if you wish) and head into the museum.*

Atrium

The atrium features a Soviet T-54 tank, symbolizing the looming threat of violence that helped keep both regimes in power. Tanks like this one rolled into Hungary to crush the 1956 Uprising. Behind the tank, stretching to the ceiling, is a vast wall covered with 3,200 portraits of people who were murdered by the Nazis or the communists in this very building.

• *The one-way exhibit begins two floors up, then spirals down to the cellar—just follow signs for* Kiállítás/ Exhibition. *To begin, you can either take the elevator (to floor 2), or walk up the red stairwell nearby, decorated with old Socialist Realist sculptures from the communist days (including, near the base of the stairs, two subjects you won't find at Memento Park: Josef Stalin and Mátyás Rákosi, the most severe communist leader of Hungary).*

Once upstairs, the first room gives an overview of the...

Double Occupation (Kettős Megszállás)

The video by the entrance sets the stage for Hungary's 20th century: its territorial losses after World War I; its alliance with, then invasion by, the Nazis; and its "liberation," then occupation, by the USSR (described earlier, under "Background").

The TV screens on the partition in the middle of the room show grainy footage of both sides of the "double occupation": the Nazis on the black side and the Soviets (appropriately) on the red side. Do a slow counterclockwise loop, starting with the black (Nazi) side. See Hitler speaking and saluting in occupied Hungary, and Nazis goose-stepping down Andrássy út. The giant, ironic quote reads, "Last night I dreamed that the Nazis were gone...and nobody else came."

But come they did. The giant picture of the destroyed Chain Bridge (on the far wall) shows the passing of the torch between the two regimes and is a chilling reminder that these two equally brutal groups, which employed similar means of terror, were sworn enemies: As the Soviets' Red Army approached from the east to liberate Hungary, the Nazis made a last stand in Budapest (Hitler, who considered the Danube a natural border, ordered them never to retreat). The Nazis destroyed all of the bridges across the Danube (some without warning, while they were filled with civilians), then holed up on Castle Hill. The Soviets laid siege for 100 days, gradually devastating the city.

Circling around to the red (Soviet) side, you see Budapest in the aftermath of World War II and the early days of Soviet rule. The telephones on the wall play Hungarian sound clips from the time.

• *Go through the* **Passage of Hungarian Nazis,** *decorated with the words of a proclamation by Arrow Cross leader Ferenc Szálasi (there's also a WC). Continue into the room of...*

Hungarian Nazis (Nyilas Terem)

The table is set with Arrow Cross china, bearing a V-for-victory emblem with a laurel wreath. At the head of the table stands an

Arrow Cross uniform. Examine the armband: The red and white stripes are an old Hungarian royal pattern, dating from the days of St. István, and the insignia combines arrows, a cross, and an "H" for Hungary. On the loudspeaker, Arrow Cross leader Ferenc Szálasi preaches about reclaiming a "Greater Hungary" and about fighting against the Jews and the insidious influence of their Bolshevism. On the far wall, the footage of the frozen river shows where many of those Jews ended up: unceremoniously shot into the icy Danube. Listen for the sickening, periodic splash...splash...splash....

• *As you leave the room, the exhibit subtly (perhaps too subtly) turns the page from the Nazi period to the communist one.*

Gulag

After the Red Army drove the Nazis out of Hungary, they quickly set to work punishing people who had backed their enemies. Being sent to a gulag was one particularly hard fate.

The word "gulag" refers to a network of secret Soviet prison camps, mostly in Siberia. These

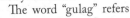

were hard-labor camps where potential and actual dissidents were sent in order to punish them, remove their dangerous influence from society, and make an example of those who would dare to defy the regime. The Soviets euphemistically told them they were going away for "a little work" *(malenki robot)*. It was an understatement.

On the carpet, a giant map of the USSR shows the locations of some of these camps, where an estimated 600,000 to 700,000 Hungarian civilians and prisoners of war were sent...about half of whom never returned. And that only represents a tiny fraction of the millions of people from throughout Europe and the USSR thought to have perished in the gulag system. The lighted cones locate specific camps, with artifacts from those places. Video screens show grainy footage of transfer trains clattering through an icy countryside, gruesome scenes from the camps, and prisoner testimony. (For more on the atrocious conditions in the gulag, see sidebar on page 164.)

People of Germanic heritage living in Hungary were targeted for deportation, but—due to a strict Moscow-imposed quota system—nobody was immune. Among the gulag victims was the Swedish diplomat Raoul Wallenberg, who had rescued many Hungarian Jews from the Nazis (see page 192).

Those who survived their experience with "corrective forced labor" were often not allowed to return to their families, and if they did, were sworn to secrecy...never allowed to tell of the horrors of the gulag until after 1989. The last Hungarian gulag prisoner, András Toma, finally returned from Siberia in 2000, having been interned in a mental hospital for decades after the gulags were dissolved—two years in a gulag followed by 53 years in an asylum.

The doctors, unfamiliar with his tongue-twisting Hungarian language, assumed he was simply mad.

Changing Clothes (Átöltözés)

This locker room—with rotating figures dressed alternately in Arrow Cross and communist uniforms—satirizes the readiness of many Hungarians to align themselves with whomever was in power. The sped-up video shows turncoat guards changing their uniforms. While it seems absurd that someone's allegiance could shift so quickly, many of these people were told that they'd be executed if they did not switch...or they could "change clothes," admit their mistake in joining the Arrow Cross, and pledge allegiance to the new communist regime. For most, it was an easy choice. Many people (including Cardinal József Mindszenty) were imprisoned by both regimes—and it's entirely plausible that they saw the same guards dressed in both uniforms.

The Fifties ('50-es Évek)

Of course, the transition was not always so straightforward. The insinuation of the communist regime into the fabric of Hungary was a gradual process. From the Red Army's "liberation" in 1945 until 1948, a power struggle raged between pro-democracy factions and the Soviet-backed communist puppet leaders. The voting booths at the beginning of this room symbolize that, at first, the Soviets fostered an illusion of choice for the Hungarian people. Elections were held throughout the Soviet satellite states in the mid-1940s, with the assumption that the communist Hungarian Workers' Party would sweep into power. But in the 1945 parliamentary elections, the communists won only 17 percent of the vote. After this, the Soviets gradually eliminated opposition leaders by uncovering "plots," then executing the alleged perpetrators. In the following two elections, they also stacked the deck by allowing workers to vote as often as they liked—often five or six times apiece (using the blue ballot cards you'll see in the voting booths). Even so, in the 1947 election, the communists still had to disqualify 700,000 opposition votes in order to win. (And you thought "hanging chads" were aggravating.)

Once in power, the Hungarian Workers' Party ruled with an iron fist and did away with the charade of elections entirely. Hungary became a "People's Republic" and was reorganized on the Soviet system. Private property was nationalized, the economy became fully socialistic, and the country fell into poverty.

Not that you'd know any of this from the sanitized, state-sponsored images of the time. In the voting booths, screens show

a loop of communist propaganda from the 1950s. Lining the walls are glossy communist-era paintings, celebrating the peasants of the "people's revolution" (farmers, soldiers, and sailors looking boldly to the future), idyllic scenes of communities coming together, and romanticized depictions of communist leaders (Lenin as the brave sailor; Mátyás Rákosi—the portly, bald communist leader of Hungary—as the kindly grandfather, gladly receiving flowers from a sweet young girl). Imagine the societal schizophrenia bred by the communists' good-cop, bad-cop methods: pretending to be a bunch of nice guys while at the same time terrorizing the people.

The distorted stage separates these two methods of people-control. The stretched-out images of Lenin, Rákosi, and Stalin imply the false-hood of everything we've just seen; backstage is the dark underbelly of the regime—the constant surveillance that bred paranoia among the people. The cases at the end display documentation for show trials. We'll learn more about these means of terror as we progress.

Soviet "Advisors" (Szovjet Tanácsadók)

These "advisors" were more like supervisors. On the wall plaque is a list of the Soviet ambassadors to Hungary, who wielded ter-

rific influence over the communist leaders here. Yuri Andropov, the ambassador during the 1956 Uprising, helped set up the ÁVH secret police and later became the Soviet premier. So shocked was Andropov at how quickly the uprising had escalated, that he later advocated for cracking down violently at the first signs of unrest in the empire (think of the Soviet tanks rolling into Czechoslovakia during the 1968 Prague Spring).

The desk displays items from the ambassador's office, and the video screens show footage of the ambassador garnering goodwill by visiting families, factories, and so on. A portrait of Stalin slyly surveys the scene.

In the passage, a TV plays an idyllic propaganda video of happy and productive farmers, with swelling music to rouse the Hungarian patriotic spirit.

Resistance (Ellenállás)

It wasn't all upbeat and shiny. This room—empty aside from three very different kitchen tables—symbolizes the way that resistance to the regime emerged in every walk of life. Each table and chair represents a different social class: countryside peasant, middle-class urbanite, and bourgeoisie. On each table is a propaganda message that was printed by that dissident (and now used as evidence in their interrogation). Notice that, like the furniture, these messages evolve in sophistication from table to table. A screen facing each table shows footage of an accused person from that class, labeled with how many years *(év)* each one spent in prison.

• *Go down the stairs, and enter the room about...*

Resettlement and Deportation (Kitelepítés)

The creation of small nations from sprawling empires at the end of World War I had also created large minority groups, which could upset the delicate ethnic balance of a new country. Having learned this lesson, the Soviets strove to create homogenous states without minorities. Ethnic cleansing on a staggering scale—or, in the more pleasant parlance of the time, "mutual population exchange"—took place throughout Central and Eastern Europe in the years following World War II (for example, three million ethnic Germans were forced out of Czechoslovakia). In Hungary, 230,000 Germans were uprooted and deported. Meanwhile, Hungarians who had become ethnically "stranded" in other nations after the Treaty of Trianon were sent to Hungary (100,000 from Slovakia, 140,000 from Romania, and 70,000 from Yugoslavia). Most have still not returned to their ancestral homes.

Notice the doorbell on the plaque at the beginning of the room. Press the white button to hear the jarring sound that hundreds of thousands of people heard in the middle of the night, when authorities showed up at their doorstep to tell them they had to pack up and move. These people were forced to sign an "official agreement of repatriation" (see the deportation paperwork on the wall), and then were taken away by the ÁVO. They were strictly limited in the number of belongings they could bring; the rest was left behind, carefully inventoried, and folded into the wealth of the upwardly mobile Party bureaucrats—represented by the fancy black sedan with plush hammer-and-sickle upholstery draped in black in the middle of the room.

In the hallway at the end of this section (after the WCs), peer into the haunting **torture cell.** Inside you'll see original items used to beat and torture prisoners.

Surrender of Property and Land (Beszolgáltatás)

With the descent of the communist cloak, people were forced to surrender their belongings to the government. Land was redistributed. Even those who came out ahead in this transaction—formerly landless peasants—found that it was a raw deal, as they were now expected to meet often-impossible production quotas. The Soviet authorities terrorized the peasant class in order to pry as many people as possible away from their old-fashioned farming lifestyles (not to mention deeply held Hungarian traditions), and embrace the industrialization of the new regime. Some 72,000 wealthy peasants called *kulaks,* who did not want to turn over their belongings, ended up on a list to be deported; all told, some 300,000 people were eventually ejected. (Eventually the regime sidestepped the peasant-farmer "middleman" completely, as farms were simply collectivized and run as giant units.)

Of the produce grown in Hungary, a significant amount was sent to other parts of the Soviet Bloc, leading to rampant shortages. The Hungarian people had to survive on increasingly sparse rations. Enter the labyrinth of pork-fat bricks, which remind old-timers of the harsh conditions of the 1950s (lard on bread for dinner). Look for the ration coupons, which people had to present before being allowed to buy even these measly staples. The pig hiding out in the maze is another symbol of these tough times. Traditionally, peasants would slaughter a pig in order to sustain themselves through the winter. But the communist authorities could seize that pig for their own uses, leaving the farmers to rely on the (unreliable) government to provide for their families. To avoid this, many farmers would slaughter their pigs illegally in the cellar, instead of out in the open.

ÁVO

The communist secret police (State Security Department, or ÁVO, later called the State Security Authority, or ÁVH) began as a means to identify and try war criminals. But the organization quickly mutated into an apparatus for intimidating the common people of Hungary—equivalent to the KGB in the Soviet Union. Before they were finished, the ÁVO/ÁVH imprisoned, abused, or murdered one person from every third Hungarian family. On the wall are pictures of secret police leaders and a Rákosi quote: "The ÁVH is the fist of the Party." This organization infiltrated every walk of Hungarian life. Factory workers and farmers, writers and singers, engineers and doctors, teenagers and senior citizens, even Party leaders and ÁVO/ÁVH officers were vulnerable. Their power came from enlisting untold numbers of civilians as informants (see sidebar, next page).

Gábor Péter's Office

Gábor Péter was the first director of the ÁVO/ÁVH. Like many former communist leaders, Péter wound up a prisoner himself

Victims and Victimizers

The foot soldiers of the secret police were civilians—workaday people who informed on their friends and neighbors in vast

numbers. Anything could be cause for suspicion, even just not clapping quite hard enough at a Hungarian Workers' Party rally. The regime routinely turned family members against one another. They were just as likely to compel you to implicate your father or brother as your neighbor or co-worker. Pavlik Morozov, a Soviet boy, was the literal poster child for this, after he informed on his own father. It was common to simultaneously be an informant and be informed upon by someone else.

Imagine being a man or woman on the street in 1950s Budapest. Like most people on this planet, you are basically apolitical—you couldn't care less who's in charge, as long as you can raise your family in peace and prosperity. One day on your way to work, a black van pulls up next to you, and in a blur, you're pulled

inside. An intimidating agent asks you to report on your friends' watercooler conversations—particularly any statements against the regime, no matter how casual. When you hesitate, the agent says, "Your son András is so very bright. It would be a shame if he could not attend university." Or maybe, "You appear to have a promising career in engineering ahead of you. And yet, it is so difficult to find employment in your chosen field. Well, there's always ditch-digging."

The decision about whether to collaborate with the secret police suddenly becomes muddled. (Which would you choose? Are you *sure*?) Some people refused and endured years or decades of misery. Others capitulated, enjoyed relatively fulfilling lives, but regretted selling out their friends and even their families. In post-communist Hungary, both groups wonder if they made the right choice.

(notice the prison motif lurking around the edges of the room). It became an almost expected part of the life cycle of a communist bigwig to eventually be fingered as an enemy...the more power you gained, the better an example you became. (In Péter's case, it didn't help that he was Jewish—anti-Semitism didn't leave Hungary when the Arrow Cross left.) It was abundantly clear that nobody was safe. Péter went to his grave in 1993 without remorse for his participation in the Soviet regime.

"Justice" (Igazságszolgálatás)

This room explores the concept of "show trials"—high-profile, loudly publicized, and completely choreographed trials of people

who had supposedly subverted the regime. The burden of proof was on the accused, not on the accuser, and coerced confessions were fair game. From 1945 until the 1956 Uprising, more than 71,000 Hungarians were accused of political crimes, and 485 were executed.

The TV screen shows various show trials, including the one for Imre Nagy (leader of the 1956 Uprising—see page 112) and his associates. Nagy was found guilty and executed in 1958.

In some cases—as in Nagy's—the defendants had defied the regime. But in many cases, the accused were innocent. (The authorities simply wanted to make an example of someone—guilt or innocence was irrelevant.) For example, if there was a meat shortage, they'd arrest and try slaughterhouse workers, ferreting out the ones who "didn't do their best." They might even execute the foreman. Not only did this intimidate all of the others to work harder, it also kept people who had gained some small measure of power in check.

The area behind the stage names the judges of these trials, with photos of some of them. Looking at these people, consider that it was not unusual for judges who had conducted show trials to later go on trial themselves.

Propaganda

Next you'll encounter another, more upbeat method for controlling the people: bright, cheery communist propaganda. The motivational film (on the right) extols the value of productivity. Find the chalkboard where workers would keep track of the "work competition" *(munkaverseny hiradó)* by noting the best workers and how far above the average productivity they achieved.

The next room shows how advertising became more colorful in the 1970s and 1980s. (Because there was no real competition in

the marketplace, glossy posters were relatively rare.) Look at a few of the posters: Several tout Bambi Narancs, the first Hungarian soft drink (from a time when Coke and Pepsi were pipe dreams). The poster about the Amerikai Bogár warns of the threat of the "American Beetle" (from Kolorádó), which threatened Hungarian crops. When the communists collectivized traditional family farm plots, they removed the trees and hedgerows that separated them—thereby removing birds that had kept pest populations in check. When a potato beetle epidemic hit, rather than acknowledging their own fault, the communists blamed an American conspiracy.

"Hungarian Silver" (Magyar Ezüst)

This was a nickname for aluminum, which was produced in large quantities from local bauxite (the pile of rocks in the middle of the room). The items that line the walls, made of this communist equivalent of "silver," lampoon the low-brow aesthetic of that era.

Religion (Felekezetek)

In 1949, nearly 7 out of every 10 Hungarians identified themselves as Catholics. Over the next four decades, that number de-

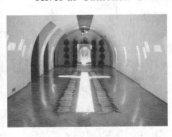

clined precipitously. The communist regime infiltrated church leadership, and bishops, priests, monks, and nuns filled Hungarian prisons. Many people worshipped in private (hence the glowing cross hidden under the floorboards). Those who were publicly faithful were discriminated against, closely supervised by

the secret police, and often arrested. As things mellowed in the 1960s and 1970s, it was easier to be openly religious, but people of faith were still considered an "enemy of the class" and risked being blacklisted (they might have difficulty finding a job, or their children could be denied an education). Hungarians had to choose

Gulag and Work Camps

The stories that later emerged from the Soviet gulag system and the equivalent Hungarian work camps are unthinkably nauseating. Prisoners lived in makeshift barracks with wide gaps between the boards, allowing freezing winter winds to howl through. They were forced to do backbreaking manual labor (such as quarrying stone) and were punished when they failed to meet their impossible daily quotas. Nutrition was laughable—prisoners would become walking skeletons in short order. While the gulags were not formally "death camps," many prisoners died of exposure, overwork, accidents, punishment, and disease. Two unlucky prisoners, who had served time both at the Nazi-run Dachau Concentration Camp and at the communist Recsk work camp in Hungary, reported that conditions had been better at Dachau.

It's particularly appalling to think that many innocent people were sent to work camps. One prisoner explained that he was accidentally arrested because his name was similar to a suspect's; however, by the time the mistake was sorted out, it was too late to let him go...so off he went to the camp. Another prisoner was

between church and success. The loudspeakers at the end of the room, which belched communist propaganda, stand at odds with the vestments.

The next hallway contains a tribute to **Cardinal József Mindszenty,** who was arrested and beaten by the communists and later sought refuge in the US embassy for 15 years (see sidebar on page 347).

• *Now head down to the basement in a creepy...*

Elevator

The elevator gradually lowers into the cellar. As it descends, you'll watch a three-minute video of a guard explaining the grotesque execution process.

• *When the door opens, you're in the...*

Prison Cellar (Pincebörtön)

As you exit the elevator, a movie shows this cellar when it was first reclaimed in the 1980s. It's chilling to think of this space's history: In the early 1950s, it was the scene of torture; in 1956, it became recruited by the secret police to make a list of the people he knew to be dissidents. Instead he made a list of the people he disliked the most, then signed his own name at the bottom. Later, a black van pulled up to him on the street and he was thrown in the back—face-to-face with all of the people he'd turned in.

And yet, for some prisoners, their time in a work camp was strangely enjoyable. They were surrounded by other intelligent people, with nothing to do all day but engage in enlightening conversation while they worked. Think of the Greek myth of Sisyphus, who is condemned to spend eternity rolling a stone up a hill again and again. Some philosophers optimistically believe that the only thing Sisyphus could do was to resolve to be happy. (One good book about the work camp experience, by George Faludy, has the insightful title *My Happy Days in Hell*.)

One university professor was not actually imprisoned but became unemployable because he was outspoken. He could find work only as a ditch-digger...and looked forward to going to his job every day, so he could engage in long conversations with his fellow ousted professors, who dug ditches alongside him.

Hungary's work camps were closed soon after Stalin's death in 1953. The regime denied their existence, and the topic was taboo through the 1980s. People whose relatives had perished in these camps could not speak of it for decades. Only after 1989 have these families been allowed to mourn publicly.

a clubhouse of sorts for the local communist youth. It has been reconstructed and now looks as it might have circa 1955.

Wander through **former cells** used for different purposes. On the right side of the hall are a "wet cell" (where the prisoner was

forced to sit in water) and a cramped "foxhole cell" (where the prisoner was forced to crouch). On the left side are a "standing cell" (where the prisoner was forced to stand 24 hours a day) and a padded cell. On both sides, you'll also see standard cells with photos of the men who once filled them.

In the large room after the cells, you'll see a stool with a lamp; nearby are the **torture** devices: hot pads and electrical appliances. The bucket and hose were used to revive torture victims who had blacked out. Interrogations would normally happen at night, after food, water, and sleep had been withheld from the prisoner for days. Communist interrogators employed techniques still beloved by some torture connoisseurs today, such as "stress positions"...though waterboarding was still just a glimmer in some young sadist's eye. Simple beatings, however, were commonplace.

After the torture room, a small room on the right contains a **gallows** that was used for executions (described earlier on your journey, in the elevator video).

As you think of the people who were imprisoned and murdered here, feel the vibration of traffic on Andrássy út just outside—these victims were so close to the "normal" world, yet so far away.

Internment (Internálás)

While the most notorious gulag network was in Siberia, a similar system also emerged in the Soviet satellites, such as Hungary, which had its own network of prison camps (including a secret one at a quarry overlooking the village of Recsk, not far from Eger—symbolized by the pile of rocks in the center of the room). In just three years (1945-1948), more than 40,000 people were sent to such camps, and the practice continued until 1953. The subtitled video shows a wealthy woman talking about her own experience being sent to one such camp to "learn how to work."

1956 Uprising ('56 Forradalom)

This room commemorates the 1956 Uprising (see page 112). The Hungarian flag with a hole cut out of the middle (a hastily removed Soviet emblem) and the slogan *Ruszkik Haza!* ("Russkies go home!") are important symbols of that time. The clothes and bicycle recall the "Pest Youth," teenagers and preteens who played a major role in the uprising. The Molotov cocktail—a bottle of flammable liquid with a cloth wick—was a weapon of choice for the uprisers. Screens show the events of '56.

In the next room (**Megtorlás**) stand six symbolic gallows—actually used for executions (though not in this building). Children's voices quietly read aloud the names of some of those killed in the aftermath of 1956. Some 230 were formally executed, while another 15,000 were indicted. (On the gallows, see the legal paperwork for execution.)

Emigration (Kivándorlás)

More than 200,000 Hungarians simply fled the country after the uprising. A wall of postcards commemorates these emigrants, who flocked to every corner of the Western world. Once they reached Austrian refugee camps, these desperate Hungarians could choose where to go—the US offered to fly them anywhere in America to get them started. A video screen shows people leaving Hungary and arriving at their destination, with the help of the United States. Only 11,000 of them would eventually return to their homeland.

Hall of Tears (Könnyek Terme)

This somber memorial commemorates all of the victims of the communists from 1945 to 1967 (when the final prisoners were released from this building).

Room of Farewell (Búcsú Terme)

This room shows several color video clips that provide a (relatively) happy ending: the festive and exhilarating days in 1991 when the Soviets departed, making way for freedom; the reburial of the Hungarian hero, Imre Nagy, at Heroes' Square; and the dedication of this museum. In the film that shows the Soviets' goodbye, watch for the poignant moment when the final Russian officer crosses the bridge on foot, with a half-hearted salute and a look of relief.

Victimizers (Tettesek)

The chilling finale: walls of photographs of the "victimizers"—members and supporters of the Arrow Cross and ÁVO, many of whom are still living and who were never brought to justice. The Hungarians have a long way to go to reconcile everything they lived through in the 20th century. For many of them, this museum is an important first step.

HEROES' SQUARE AND CITY PARK WALK

Hősök Tere és Városliget

The grand finale of Andrássy út, at the edge of the city center, is also one of Budapest's most entertaining quarters. Here you'll find the grand Heroes' Square, dripping with history (both monumental and recent); the vast tree-filled expanse of City Park, dressed up with fanciful buildings that include a replica Transylvanian castle and an Art Nouveau zoo; and, tucked in the middle of it all, Budapest's finest thermal spa and single best experience, the Széchenyi Baths. If the sightseeing grind gets you down, take a mini-vacation from your busy vacation and relax the way Budapesters do: Escape to City Park.

Orientation

Construction Alert: The city has embarked on ambitious plans to build a new "Museum Quarter" in the corner of the City Park along Dózsa György út (a.k.a. "Parade Street," near today's 1956 Monument). Eventually this will consolidate several far-flung museum collections, including the National Gallery and museums of contemporary art (Ludwig collection), ethnography, photography, architecture, and music. The historic building of the Hungarian Technical and Transportation Museum—sloppily rebuilt after World War II as a shadow of its former self—may also be rebuilt. The plans also include a complete redevelopment of the park itself. As work will likely be ongoing through at least 2018, you may find part of this area torn up. For the latest updates, see www.ligetbudapest.org.

Length of This Walk: One hour, not including museum visits or the baths.

What to Bring: If taking a dip in the Széchenyi Baths, bring your swimsuit and a towel from your hotel (or rent these items there). You may also want to bring flip-flops, sunscreen, and soap and shampoo to shower afterward.

Getting There: If you walk the full length of Andrássy út (see the Andrássy Út Walk chapter), you'll run right into Heroes' Square. But most visitors hightail it out here on the M1/yellow Metró line, and hop off at the Hősök tere stop. You'll exit the Metró in the middle of busy Andrássy út. Cross the street three times (making three-quarters of a circle) to work your way to the middle of Heroes' Square, with a great view of the Millennium Monument. (If you're heading directly for the baths, you could ride the M1 line one stop farther, to the Széchenyi fürdő stop.)

Museum of Fine Arts: Likely closed for renovation through 2017; if open likely 1,800 Ft, audioguide-500 Ft, Tue-Sun 10:00-17:30, closed Mon, last entry 30 minutes before closing, Dózsa György út 41, tel. 1/469-7100, www.szepmuveszeti.hu.

Műcsarnok ("Hall of Art"): 1,800 Ft, Tue-Wed and Fri-Sun 10:00-18:00, Thu 12:00-20:00, closed Mon, Dózsa György út 37, tel. 1/460-7000, www.mucsarnok.hu.

Museum of Hungarian Agriculture (in Vajdahunyad Castle): 1,100 Ft; April-Oct Tue-Sun 10:00-17:00; Nov-March Tue-Fri 10:00-16:00, Sat-Sun 10:00-17:00, closed Mon year-round, last entry 30 minutes before closing; tel. 1/363-1117, www.mezogazdasagimuzeum.hu.

Széchenyi Baths: 4,500 Ft for locker (in gender-segregated locker room), 500 Ft more for personal changing cabin, 200 Ft more on weekends, cheaper after 19:00; admission includes outdoor swimming pool area, indoor thermal baths, and sauna; swimming pool generally open daily 6:00-22:00, thermal baths and sauna daily 6:00-19:00, may be open later on summer weekends, last entry one hour before closing, Állatkerti körút 11, district XIV, tel. 1/363-3210, www.szechenyibath.hu.

Starring: A lineup of looming Hungarian greats, a faux-Transylvanian castle, Budapest's best baths, and the city's most enticing green patch.

The Walk Begins

• *Stand in the middle of...*

HEROES' SQUARE (HŐSÖK TERE)

Like much of Budapest, this Who's Who of Hungarian history at the end of Andrássy út was commissioned to celebrate the country's 1,000th birthday in 1896 (see page 33). Ironically, it wasn't finished until 1929—well after Hungary had lost World War I and two-thirds of its historical territory, and was facing its darkest hour. Today, more than just the hottest place in town for skateboarding, this is the site of several museums and the gateway to City Park.

• *The giant colonnades and tall column that dominate the square make up the...*

Millennium Monument

Step right up to meet the world's most historic Hungarians (who look to me like their language sounds). Take a moment to explore this monument, which offers a step-by-step lesson in the story of the Hungarians. (Or, to skip the history lesson, you can turn to "Museum of Fine Arts" on page 177.)

Central Column: The Magyars

The granddaddy of all Magyars, **Árpád** stands proudly at the bottom of the pillar, peering down Andrássy út. He's surrounded by

six other chieftains; altogether, seven Magyar tribes first arrived in the Carpathian Basin (today's Hungary) in the year 896. Remember that these ancestors of today's Hungarians were from Central Asia and barely resembled the romanticized, more European-looking figures you see here. (Only one detail of these statues is authentically Hungarian: the bushy moustaches.) Magyar horsemen were known and feared for their speed: They rode sleek Mongolian horses (rather than the powerful beasts shown here), and their use of stirrups—revolutionary in Europe at the time—allowed them to ride fast and turn on a dime in order to quickly overrun their battlefield opponents. Bows and spears were their weapons of choice; they'd have had little interest in the chain mail and heavy clubs and battle axes that Romantic sculptors gave them. They used these skills to run roughshod over the Continent, laying waste to Europe.

The 118-foot-tall pillar supports the archangel **Gabriel** as he offers the crown to Árpád's great-great-grandson, István (as we'll learn, he accepted it and Christianized the Magyars).

In front of the pillar is the **Hungarian**

War Memorial (fenced in to keep skateboarders from enjoying its perfect slope).

The **sculptures** on the top corners of the two colonnades represent, in order from left to right: Work and Welfare, War, Peace, and the Importance of Packing Light.

Each statue in the two colonnades represents a great Hungarian leader, with a relief below showing a defining moment in his life. Likewise, each one represents a trait or trend in the colorful story of this dynamic people. (For all the details, see the Hungary: Past and Present chapter.)

• *Behind the pillar, look to the...*

First (Left) Colonnade

The first colonnade features rulers from the early glory days of Hungary.

St. István (c. 967-1038)

After decades of terrorizing Europe, the Magyars were finally defeated at the Battle of Augsburg in 955. King Géza realized that

unless they could learn to get along with their neighbors, the Magyars' military might only garner them short-term prosperity. Géza decided to baptize his son, Vajk, gave him the Christian name István (Stephen), and married him off to a Bavarian princess. On Christmas Day in the year 1000, commissioners of the pope (pictured in the relief below) brought to István the same crown that still sits under the Parliament dome. To

historians, this event marks the beginning of the Christian—and therefore European—chapter of Magyar history. (For more on István, see page 211.)

St. László I (c. 1040-1095)

Known as Ladislas in English, László was a powerful knight/king who carried the Christian torch first taken up by his cousin István. Joining the drive of his fellow European Christian leaders, he led troops into battle to expand his territory into today's Croatia. Don't let the dainty chain-mail skirt fool you... that axe ain't for chopping wood. In the relief below, see László swing the axe against a pagan soldier who had taken Christian women hostage. László won a chunk of Croatia, then lost it...but was sainted anyway (hence the halo). László's story is the first of many we'll hear about territorial expansion and loss—a crucial issue to Hungarian leaders across the centuries (and even today).

Kálmán (c. 1070-1116)

Kálmán (Coloman) traded his uncle László's bloody axe for a stack of books. Known as "the Book Lover," Kálmán was enlightened

before his time, acclaimed as being the most educated king of his era. He was the first European ruler to prohibit the trial or burning of women as witches (on the relief, see him intervening to save the cowering woman in the bottom-right corner). He was also the king who retook Croatia yet again, bringing it into the Hungarian sphere of influence through the early 20th century. Kálmán reminds us that the Hungarians pride themselves on being a highly intellectual people, as demonstrated by the many scientists, economists, and other great minds they've produced. (As you walk through City Park in a few minutes, keep an eye out for chess players.)

András II (c. 1177-1235)

András (Andrew) II is associated with the golden charter he holds in his hand (with the golden medallion dangling from it)—the

Golden Bull of 1222. This decree granted some measure of power to the nobility, releasing the king's stranglehold and acknowledging that his power was not absolute. This was the trend across Europe at the time (the Magna Carta, a similarly important document, was signed in 1215 by England's King John). András demonstrates the importance Hungarians place on self-determination: Like many small Central European nations, Hungary has often been dominated by a foreign power...but has always shown an uncrushable willingness to fight back. (We'll meet some modern-day Hungarian freedom fighters shortly.) It's no

surprise that so many place names in Hungary include the word *Szabadság* ("Liberty"). The relief shows that the Hungarians are willing to fight for this ideal for others, as well: András is called "The Jerosolimitan" for his success in the Fifth Crusade, in which his army liberated Jerusalem. Here he is depicted alongside the pope kissing the rescued "true cross."

Despite his achievements, András is far less remembered today than his daughter **Elisabeth** (1207-1231, not depicted here), who was sent away to Germany for a politically expedient marriage. She is the subject of an often-told legend: The pious, kindly Elisabeth was known to sneak scraps of food out of the house to give to poor people on the street. One evening, her cruel confessor saw her leaving the house and stopped her. Seeing her full apron (which was loaded with bread for the poor), he demanded to know what she was carrying. "Roses," she replied. "Show me," he growled. Elisabeth opened her apron, the bread was gone, and rose petals miraculously cascaded out onto the floor. In her short life, Elisabeth went on to found hospitals and carry out other charitable acts, and (unlike her father) became a saint. Elisabeth remains a popular symbol of charity not only in Hungary, but also in Germany. (It's easy to confuse St. Elisabeth with the equally adored Empress Elisabeth, a.k.a. Sisi, the Habsburg monarch, described on page 320.)

Béla IV (1206-1270)

Having governed over one of the most challenging periods of Hungarian history, the defiant-looking Béla—St. Elisabeth's

brother—is celebrated as the "Second Founder of the Country" (after István). Béla led Hungary when the Tatars swept in from Central Asia, devastating Buda, most of Hungary, and a vast swath of Central and Eastern Europe. Because his predecessors had squandered away Hungary's holdings, Béla found himself defenseless against the onslaught. In the relief, we see Béla surveying the destruction left by the Tatars. Béla made a deal with God to send his daughter Margaret to a nunnery (on the island that would someday bear her name— see page 68) in exchange for sparing Hungary from complete destruction. After the Tatars left, he rebuilt his ruined nation. It was Béla who moved Buda to

its strategic location atop Castle Hill and built a wall around it, to be better prepared for any future invasion. This was the first of many times that Budapest (and Hungary) was devastated by invaders; later came the Ottomans, the Nazis, and the Soviets. But each time, like Béla, the resilient Hungarian people rolled up their sleeves to rebuild.

Károly Róbert (1288-1342)

Everyone we've met so far was a member of the Árpád dynasty—descendants of the tough guys at the base of the big column. But when that line died out in 1301, the Hungarian throne was left vacant. The Hungarian nobility turned to "Charles Robert," a Naples-born prince from the French Anjou (or Angevin) dynasty, which had married into Hungarian royalty. (His shield combines the red-and-white stripes of Hungary with the fleur-de-lis of France.) The Hungarians were slow to accept Robert—he had to be crowned four different times to convince everybody, and he was actually banned from Buda. (He built his own palace, which still stands, at Visegrád up the Danube—see page 341.) Eventually he managed to win them over and stabilize the country, even capturing new lands for Hungary (see the relief). Károly Róbert represents the many Hungarian people who are not fully, or even partially, Magyar. Today's Hungarians are a cultural cocktail of the various peoples—German, Slavic, Jewish, Roma (Gypsy), and many others—that have lived here and been "Magyarized" to adopt Hungarian language, culture, and names.

Nagy Lajos (1326-1382)

"Louis the Great" built on his father Károly Róbert's successes and presided over the high-water mark of Hungarian history. He expanded Hungarian territory to its historical maximum—including parts of today's Dalmatia (Croatia), Bulgaria, and Bosnia-Herzegovina—and even attempted to retake his father's native Naples (pictured in the relief). Hungarians still look back with great pride on these days more than six centuries ago, when they were a vast and mighty kingdom.

• *Now turn your attention to the...*

Second (Right) Colonnade

The gap between the colonnades coincides with some dark times for the Hungarians. The invading **Ottomans** swept up the Balkan Peninsula from today's Turkey, creeping deeper and deeper into Hungarian territory...eventually even taking over Buda and Pest for a century and a half. Hungarian nobility retreated to the farthest corners of their lands, today's Slovakia and Transylvania, and soldiered on.

Salvation came in the form of the **Habsburgs**, rulers of a fast-expanding

Austrian Empire, who presented Hungary with a classic "good news, bad news" scenario: They forced out the Ottomans, then claimed Hungary as part of their realm. While the Habsburgs eventually granted the Hungarians some leadership in the empire, the Habsburg era was a time of frustration and rebellion. In fact, at the time of this monument's construction—when Budapest was controlled from Vienna—Habsburg rulers stood in the last five slots of the right-hand colonnade. (The statue of Empress Maria Theresa now stands in the lobby of the Museum of Fine Arts, across the street.) But after the monument was damaged in World War II, locals seized on the opportunity to replace the Habsburgs with Hungarians...who were famous for fighting *against* those slots' former occupants. The lineup begins with...

János Hunyadi (c. 1387-1456)

A military hero who achieved rare success fighting the Ottomans, Hunyadi won the fiercest-fought skirmish of the era, the Battle of Belgrade (Nándorfehérvár in Hungarian). The relief depicts a

particularly violent encounter in that battle. (The guy holding the cross is János Kapisztran, a.k.a. St. John Capistrano, an Italian friar and Hunyadi's right-hand man.) This victory halted the Ottomans' advance into Hungary for decades. Owing largely to his military prowess, Hunyadi was extremely popular among the people and became wealthier than even the king. He led Hungary for a time as regent, when the preschool-age king was too young to rule. After he died of the plague, Hunyadi's reputation allowed his son Mátyás to step up as ruler....

Mátyás Corvinus (1443-1490)

Perhaps the most beloved of all Hungarian rulers, Mátyás (Matthias) Corvinus was a Renaissance king who revolutionized the monarchy. He was a clever military tactician and a champion of the downtrodden, known among commoners as "the people's king." The long hair and laurel wreath (instead of a crown) attest to his knowledge and enlightenment. And most importantly, he was the first (and last) Hungarian-blooded king from the death of the Árpád dynasty in 1301 until today. Building on his father's military success against the Ottomans,

Matthias achieved a diplomatic peace with them—allowing him to actually expand his territory while other kings of this era were losing it. (He even had time for some vanity building projects—the relief shows him appreciating a model of his namesake church, which still stands atop Castle Hill.) Matthias' death represented the death of Hungarian sovereignty. After him, Hungary was quickly swallowed up by the Ottomans, then the Habsburgs. For more on King Matthias, see page 204.

Appropriately, Matthias is the final head of state at Heroes' Square. Reflecting the sea change after his death, the rest of the heroes here are freedom-fighters who rallied against Habsburg influence.

István Bocskai (1557-1606), Gábor Bethlen (1580-1629), and Imre Thököly (1657-1705)

After Matthias, the Ottomans took over most of Hungary. Transylvania, the eastern fringe of the realm, was fragmented and in a state of ever-fluctuating semi-independence—sometimes under the firm control of sovereign princes, at other times controlled by the Ottomans. The three Hungarian dukes depicted here helped to unify their people through this difficult spell (see the reliefs): Bocskai and Thököly

found rare success on the battlefield against the Habsburgs, while Bethlen made peace with the Czechs and united with them to fight against the Habsburgs.

The next two statues are of Ferenc Rákóczi and Lajos Kossuth, arguably the greatest Hungarian heroes of the Habsburg era and the namesakes of streets and squares throughout the country.

Ferenc Rákóczi II (1676-1735)

Although he was a wealthy aristocrat educated in Vienna, Rákóczi (Thököly's stepson) resented Habsburg rule over Hungary. When his countrymen mobilized into a ragtag peasant army to stage a War of Independence (1703-1711), Rákóczi reluctantly took charge. (The relief depicts an unpleasant moment in Rákóczi's life, when he realizes just how miserable his army will be.) Allied with the French (who were trying to wrest power from the Habsburgs' western territory, Spain), Rákóczi mounted an attack that caught the Habsburgs off-guard. Moving west from his home region of Transylvania, Rákóczi succeeded in reclaiming Hungary all the way to the Danube. But the tide turned when, during a pivotal battle, Rákóczi fell from his horse and was presumed dead by his army. His officers retreated and appealed to the Habsburgs for mercy, effectively ending the revolution. Rákóczi left Hungary in disgrace and rattled around Europe—to like-minded Habsburg enemies Poland, France, and the Ottoman Empire—in a desperate attempt to gain diplomatic support for a free Hungary. He died in exile in a small Turkish town, but his persistence still inspires Hungarians today.

Lajos Kossuth (1802-1894)

Kossuth was a nobleman and parliamentarian known for his rebellious spirit. When the winds of change swept across Europe in 1848, the Hungarians began to murmur once again about more independence from the Habsburgs—and Kossuth emerged as the movement's leader (in the relief, he's calling his countrymen to arms). After a bitterly fought revolution, Habsburg Emperor Franz Josef enlisted the help of the Russian czar to put down the Hungarian uprising, shattering Kossuth's dream. (For more on the 1848 Revolution, see page 463.) Kossuth went into exile and traveled the world, tirelessly lobbying foreign governments to support Hungary's bid for independence. He even made his pitch to the US Congress...and today, a bust of Kossuth

is one of only three sculptures depicting non-Americans in the US Capitol. After Kossuth died in exile in 1894, his body was returned to Budapest for an elaborate three-day funeral. The Habsburg Emperor Franz Josef—who knew how to hold a grudge—refused to declare the former revolutionary's death a national holiday, so Catholic church bells did not toll...but Protestant ones did.

The less-than-cheerful ending to this survey of Hungarian history is fitting. Hungarians tend to have a pessimistic view of their past...not to mention their present and future. In the Hungarian psyche, life is a constant struggle, and you get points just for playing your heart out, even if you don't win.

• *Two fine museums flank Heroes' Square. As you face the Millennium Monument, to your left is the...*

Museum of Fine Arts (Szépművészeti Múzeum)

This giant collection of mostly European art—likely closed for renovation through 2017—is the underachieving cousin of the famous Kunsthistorisches Museum in Vienna. Like that collection, it's strong in art from areas in the Habsburgs' cultural orbit: Germanic countries, the Low Countries, and especially Spain. (For the best Hungarian art, head for the National Gallery on Castle Hill—see page 203.) The collection belonged to the noble Eszterházy family, and was later bought and expanded by the Hungarian government.

If you enjoy European art (particularly Spanish Golden Age), consider visiting this museum. After buying your ticket, grab a floor plan and head up the stairs on the right, go to the end of the hall and through the door on the right, and do a clockwise spin through the good stuff: German and Austrian (including some works by Albrecht Dürer); early Dutch and Flemish (including paintings by both Brueghels); and finally Spanish. The Spanish collection features works by Murillo, Zubarán, and Velázquez, along with five El Grecos and several Goyas, including *The Water Carrier*.

• *Across Heroes' Square (to the right as you face the Millennium Monument) is the...*

Műcsarnok ("Hall of Art")

Used for cutting-edge contemporary art exhibits, the Műcsarnok (comparable to a German *"Kunsthalle"*) has five or six temporary exhibits each year. While art lovers enjoy this place, it's more difficult to appreciate than some other Budapest museums.

The Műcsarnok was also the site of a major event in recent history. On June 16, 1989, several anti-communist heroes who had been executed by the regime were finally given a proper funeral on the steps of this building. The Műcsarnok was draped in black-and-white banners, and in front were four actual coffins (including one with the recently exhumed remains of reformist hero Imre Nagy—see page 111), and a fifth, empty coffin to honor others who were lost. One of the most memorable speakers from that occasion was a 25-year-old, shaggy-haired burgeoning politician named Viktor Orbán—who now leads the right-of-center Fidesz Party that's attempting to reshape modern Hungary. The Yugoslav Embassy, which was in the building across the busy ring road from Heroes' Square (on the left-hand corner), was the last place Imre Nagy was seen alive in public.

• *Before continuing into the park, consider an optional 15-minute detour down Dózsa György út, a.k.a...*

"PARADE STREET"

The area along the busy street beyond the Műcsarnok was once used for communist parades. While the original communist monuments are long gone, two new monuments have replaced them. You'll also likely see lots of construction in this zone (which may impede your access to these monuments). They're working on turning this corner of City Park into a state-of-the-art campus of museums, in order to consolidate several small collections that are currently scattered around the city (for details, see "Construction Alert," earlier).

As you walk behind the Műcsarnok, first you'll see the giant, circular **Time Wheel** (Időkerék). Notice the sand inside the circle, which acts like a giant hourglass. Unveiled with much fanfare when Hungary joined the European Union on May 1, 2004, the wheel is manually rotated 180 degrees to restart the hourglass every year. Unfortunately, unexpected condensation has gummed up the mechanism (hardly an auspicious kickoff for Hungary's EU membership). While most Budapesters laugh it off as an eyesore, it's cheaper to leave it here than to tear it down. We'll see if it survives the latest round of redevelopment.

Across the street, notice the shiny, undulating **ING Bank Headquarters.** ING has invested heavily in Budapest in recent years, building both this and the shiny glass mall on Vörösmarty tér.

Continuing along the parking lot, you'll soon see the impressive **1956 Monument,** celebrating the historic uprising against the communists (see page 112). During the early days of the Soviet regime, this was the site of a giant monument to Josef Stalin that towered 80 feet high (Stalin himself was more than 25 feet tall). While dignitaries stood on a platform at Stalin's feet, military parades would march past. From the inauguration of the monument in 1951, the Hungarians saw it as a hated symbol of an unwanted regime. When the

1956 Uprising broke out, the removal of the monument was high on the protesters' list of 16 demands. On the night the uprising began, October 23, some rebels decided to check this item off early. They came here, cut off Stalin just below the knees, and toppled him from his platform. (Memento Park has a reconstruction of the original monument's base, including Stalin's boots—see page 223.) The current monument was erected in 2006 to commemorate the 50th anniversary of the uprising. Symbolizing the way Hungarians came together to attempt the impossible, it begins with scattered individuals at the back (rusty and humble), gradually coming together and gaining strength and unity near the front—culminating in a silver ship's prow boldly plying the ground. To fully appreciate the monument, walk up the middle of it from the back to the front. Think about how comforting it is to realize you're not alone, as others like you gradually get closer and closer.

• *Head back to the Műcsarnok at Heroes' Square. The safest way to reach City Park is to begin in front of the Műcsarnok, then use the crosswalk to circle around across the street from the Millennium Monument to reach the bridge directly behind it. (There's no crosswalk from the monument directly to the bridge.)*

Begin walking over the bridge into...

CITY PARK (VÁROSLIGET)

Budapest's not-so-central "Central Park" was the private hunting ground of wealthy aristocrats until the mid-19th century, when it was opened to the public. Soon after, it became the site of the overblown 1896 Millennium Exhibition, celebrating Hungary's 1,000th birthday. It's still packed with huge party decorations from that bash: a zoo with quirky Art Nouveau buildings, a replica of a Transylvanian castle, a massive bath/swimming complex, walking paths, and an amusement park. City Park is also filled with unwinding locals.

Orient yourself from the bridge: The huge Vajdahunyad Castle is across the bridge and on your right. Straight into the park and on the left are the big copper domes of the fun, relaxing Széchenyi Baths. And the zoo is on the left, beyond the lake and the recommended waterfront Robinson restaurant. Near the zoo (not quite visible from here) is the world-famous Gundel restaurant, where visiting bigwigs have dined—though it was recently bought out by an international hotel chain and has gone downhill.

The area in front of the castle seems to shift constantly: It's

City Park Walk

HEROES' SQUARE AND CITY PARK

1. Heroes' Square
2. Millennium Monument
3. Hungarian War Memorial
4. Museum of Fine Arts
5. Műcsarnok ("Hall of Art")
6. "Parade Street"
7. Vajdahunyad Castle
8. Museum of Hungarian Agriculture
9. Petőfi Csarnok (Flea Market)
10. Széchenyi Baths
11. Zoo
12. Circus
13. Robinson Restaurant

generally used as a paddleboat pond in summer and a skating rink in winter, but it can also be drained to create a festival ground at any time.

• *Cross the bridge, take the immediate right turn, and follow the path to the entrance of...*

Vajdahunyad Castle (Vajdahunyad Vára)

Many of the buildings for Hungary's Millennial National Exhibition were erected with temporary materials, to be torn down at the end of the festival—as was the case for most world fairs at the time. But locals so loved Vajdahunyad Castle that they insisted it stay, so it was rebuilt in brick and stone. The complex actually has four parts, each representing a high point in Hungarian architectural style: Romanesque chapel, Gothic gate, Renaissance castle, and Baroque palace (free and always open to walk around the grounds).

From this direction, the **Renaissance castle** dominates the view. It's a replica of a famous castle in Transylvania that once belonged to the Hunyadi family (János and Mátyás Corvinus—both of whom we met back on Heroes' Square).

Cross over the bridge and through the **Gothic gateway.** Once inside the complex, on the left is a replica of a 13th-century Roman-

esque **Benedictine chapel.** Consecrated as an actual church, this is Budapest's most popular spot for weddings on summer weekends. Farther ahead on the right is a big Baroque mansion housing the **Museum of Hungarian Agriculture** (Magyar Mezőgazdasági Múzeum). It brags that it's Europe's biggest agriculture museum, but most visitors will find the lavish interior more interesting than the exhibits.

Facing the museum entry is a monument to **Anonymous**—specifically, the Anonymous from the court of King Béla IV who penned the first Hungarian history in the Middle Ages.

For an optional detour to yet another monument (of György—er, George—Washington), consider going for a walk in the park. Continue across the bridge at the far end of Vajdahunyad Castle, then turn right along the main path. **George Washington** (funded by Central European immigrants to the US) is about five minutes down, on the left-hand side.

Deeper in the park is the giant **Petőfi Csarnok,** which is used for big rock concerts (tel. 1/363-3730, www.petoficsarnok.hu) as well as a weekend flea market (see page 280).

• *Time for some fun. Head back out to the busy main road, and cross it. Under the trees, you'll pass some red outdoor tables where you'll likely see elderly locals playing chess. Beyond the tables and a bit to the right, the pretty gardens and copper dome mark the famous...*

Széchenyi Baths (Széchenyi Fürdő)

Budapest's best thermal baths, and (for me) its single best experience, period, the Széchenyi Baths offer a refreshing and culturally enlightening Hungarian experience. Reward yourself with a soak. ✪ For all the details, see the Thermal Baths chapter.

• *The best entrance to the baths is around the back side. That's also where you'll find...*

Attractions Behind Széchenyi Baths

Lining the street behind the baths are two kid-friendly attractions. From the steps of the swimming pool entrance, look through the

fence across the street to see the **zoo's** colorful Art Nouveau elephant house (pictured at left), slathered with Zsolnay tiles outside and mosaics inside. The zoo was recently expanded to take over the adjacent amusement park; they incorporated some of the most popular rides into the zoo itself. To the right is Budapest's 120-year-old **circus** (marked *Nagycirkusz*). For more details on these attractions, see the Budapest with Children chapter.

• *Our walk is over. Your options are endless. Soak in the bath, visit the zoo, rent a rowboat, buy some cotton candy...enjoy City Park any way you like.*

If you're ready for some food, cheap snack stands are scattered around the park; for something fancier, consider the recommended Robinson restaurant (see page 260).

When you're ready to head home, the M1/yellow Metró line (with effortless connections to the House of Terror, Opera, the Metró hub of Deák tér, or Vörösmarty tér in downtown Pest) has two handy stops here: The entrance to the Széchenyi fürdő stop is at the southwest corner of the yellow bath complex (easy to miss—to the left and a bit around the side as you face the main entry, just a stairway in the middle of the park); and the Hősök tere stop is back across the street from Heroes' Square, where we began this walk.

GREAT SYNAGOGUE AND JEWISH QUARTER TOUR

Zsinagóga / Zsidónegyed

With an elegant history cut brutally short by the Holocaust, Pest's Jewish Quarter is gradually restoring its once-grand sights and embracing its long-dormant heritage. Today's Jewish Quarter is a ramshackle neighborhood—still quite run-down despite its city-center location—that contains several synagogues, Jewish-themed restaurants, and other remnants of a once-thriving Jewish community. And in the last few years, this neighborhood has emerged as Budapest's most lively nightlife zone. Each year, there seem to be more and more distinctive "ruin pubs" (convivial, youthful bars with ramshackle furniture that sprawls through should-be-condemned buildings and courtyards), art galleries, fashion boutiques, and all the trappings of hipster culture. This means that two very different cultures coexist in these streets: traditional Jewish heritage, and cutting-edge, hard-partying trendiness. Somehow, it works.

The area's main attraction is the spectacular Great Synagogue, which I cover in Part 1 of this tour. Some might find it worthwhile to also explore the nearby sights and monuments, including two other synagogues, which I've linked with a short walk in Part 2.

Orientation

Length of This Tour: 1.5 to 2 hours.

Dress Code: To visit the interiors of the Great Synagogue and the Orthodox Synagogue, men will need to cover their heads, and women, their shoulders (loaner yarmulkes and scarves are available at the door).

Getting There: The Great Synagogue is at Dohány utca 2, district VII. From M2: Astoria (or the Astoria stop on trams #47 and #49), it's a five-minute walk—but it can be hard to find since the synagogue hides behind a line of modern buildings. Just follow the Small Boulevard (called Károly körút at this point) and keep an eye to the right.

Great Synagogue, Hungarian Jewish Museum, and Memorial Garden: 2,500 Ft includes all three sights or pay 500 Ft for just the garden; 500 Ft to take photos. Open March-Oct Sun-Thu 10:00-18:00, Fri 10:00-16:30—until 15:30 in March; Nov-Feb Sun-Fri 10:00-16:00; closed Sat year-round and Jewish holidays, last entry 30 minutes before closing, tel. 1/344-5131, www.dohanyutcaizsinagoga.hu.

Hungarian Jewish Archives and Family Research Center: Exhibit covered by Great Synagogue ticket, 1,000 Ft to use archives with some help from the staff. Open Mon-Wed 10:00-17:00, Thu 12:00-17:00, Fri 10:00-15:00, closed Sat-Sun, closes one hour earlier Nov-Feb. If you plan to do research here, it's best to contact them in advance to let them know you're coming: tel. 1/413-5547, www.milev.hu, family@milev.hu.

Orthodox Synagogue: 1,000 Ft, Sun-Thu 10:00-16:00, Fri 10:00-13:30, closed Sat.

Printa Café: Mon-Fri 11:00-19:00, Sat-Sun 12:00-18:00—except closed Sun Sept-May, Rumbach 10, www.printa.hu.

Synagogue at Rumbach Street: May be closed for renovation; otherwise 500 Ft, Sun-Thu 10:00-17:30, Fri 10:00-15:30, closed Sat.

Tours: Aviv Travel, with a kiosk just outside the Great Synagogue entrance, leads tours of the synagogue, museum, and related sights. You have three options: A quick 45-minute tour combines the Great Synagogue and Memorial Garden (2,850 Ft). A longer 80-minute tour covers the above, plus a guided visit to the Hungarian Jewish Museum (3,200 Ft). The 90-minute version includes the Great Synagogue, Memorial Garden, and the nearby synagogue on Rumbach Street, plus free time in the museum (5,650 Ft). Since these tours include admission, you're paying only a small price for the guiding—making this an affordable way to really understand the place (shorter tours leave every 30 minutes during the Great Synagogue's open hours, other tours depart less frequently, last tour departs one hour before closing).

Jewish Quarter by Night: This walk—which you'll presumably do during the day (when the sights are open)—leads past several streets that seem decrepit and sleepy in the sunlight, but 12 hours later are hopping with rollicking nightlife. Get your bearings in this neighborhood during the day, then consider returning here at night to experience this fascinating and accessible Budapest phenomenon. My self-guided "Ruin Pub

Crawl" (see page 293) passes many of these same streets, but focuses on a very different slice of life.

Starring: Budapest's rich tapestry of Jewish history.

BACKGROUND

As the former co-capital of an empire that included millions of Jews, Budapest always had a high concentration of Jewish residents. Before World War II, 5 percent of Hungary's population and 25 percent of Budapest's were Jewish (the city was often nicknamed "Judapest").

In the 1780s, the progressive Habsburg Emperor Josef II emancipated the Jews of his empire, allowing them to live and do business in the city of Pest. Because they were still not allowed to purchase property within the city, many settled in the area just outside the city wall (today marked by the Small Boulevard ring road), in what would become the Jewish Quarter. At the same time, many Jews (like other minorities) were compelled to undergo "Magyarization"—taking on Hungarian language and culture, and even adopting Hungarian spellings of their names. And many Jews were eager to win the acceptance of their Catholic neighbors—which might explain why the Great Synagogue, built in the mid-19th century, almost feels more like a Christian house of worship than a Jewish one.

The anti-Semitism that infected Europe around the turn of the 20th century also tainted Budapest. In fact, Hungary—and not Germany—was the first European country to enforce "Jewish laws" in the 1920s. A long tradition of resentment toward Jews had been amplified by a more recent perception of the Jewish connection to the "dangerous" influence of communism. Furious and humiliated after losing two-thirds of their territory in the Treaty of Trianon that ended World War I, the Hungarians sought a handy scapegoat—and Jews filled that role.

When Hitler was on the rise in Germany, Hungary allied with him, allowing local politicians some degree of self-determination. The Hungarians sometimes interned or deported their Jewish citizenry, but refused to execute them—even as the Nazis began to institute their "Final Solution" of Jewish genocide in the lands they controlled. On the other hand, Nazi-allied Hungary was hardly blameless. Military service was compulsory, but Jews weren't allowed in the armed forces—so instead, many joined forced-labor brigades; tens of thousands died from the horrific conditions.

Hitler grew impatient and invaded Hungary in March of

1944, installing the Arrow Cross regime. Jews were forced to live in a small, walled ghetto surrounding the Great Synagogue, and allowed no contact with the outside world. By May—just two months after the Nazi takeover—trains began heading for Auschwitz; by the middle of July, about 430,000 Hungarian Jews had already been deported. (For more on the Arrow Cross, see the House of Terror Tour chapter.)

As the end of the war neared, Hungarian Nazi collaborators resorted to desperate measures, such as lining up Jews along the Danube and shooting them into the river (now commemorated by a monument near the Parliament—see page 110). To save bullets, they'd sometimes tie several victims together, shoot one of them, and throw him into the freezing Danube—dragging the others in with him. Hungary lost nearly 600,000 Jews to the Holocaust. Today, only 0.5 percent of Hungarians are Jewish, and most of them live in Budapest. But that still represents the largest Jewish population of any city in Central Europe.

After the Holocaust, the Great Synagogue sat neglected for 40 years. But since the thawing of communism, Hungarian Jews have taken a renewed interest in preserving their heritage. In 1990, the Great Synagogue was painstakingly rebuilt, largely with financial support from the Hungarian-American cosmetics magnate Estée Lauder. Theodor Herzl, a pioneer of Zionism, was born in a house next door to the Great Synagogue (now gone). Other people of Hungarian-Jewish descent include big names from every walk of life: Harry Houdini (born Erich Weisz), Elie Wiesel, Joseph Pulitzer, Tony Curtis (and his daughter Jamie Lee), Goldie Hawn, Peter Lorre, and Eva and Zsa Zsa Gabor. A visit to the Great Synagogue and surrounding Jewish Quarter offers insight into this vital facet of Hungarian history and contemporary life.

The Tour Begins

PART 1: GREAT SYNAGOGUE TOUR
• *Stand in front of the...*

Great Synagogue (Nagy Zsinagóga)
Also called the Dohány Street Synagogue, Budapest's gorgeous synagogue is the biggest in Europe and the second biggest in the world (after the Temple Emanu-El of New York). A visit here has three parts: touring its ornately decorated interior; exploring the attached muse-

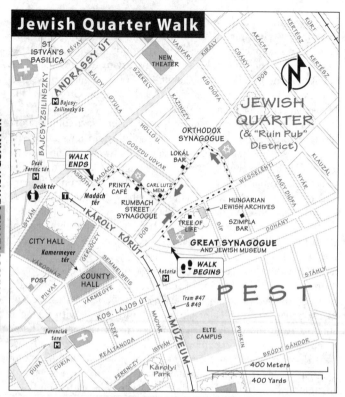

Jewish Quarter Walk

um, which offers a concise lesson in the Jewish faith; and lingering in the evocative memorial garden, with its weeping-willow *Tree of Life* sculpture and other poignant monuments.

• *You might see a long ticket and tour line to the left of the main entrance gate. You may be able to skip this line and buy tickets and tours inside the courtyard (at the far-right end, in front of the synagogue entrance)—ask at the security checkpoint.*

Synagogue Exterior

Before going inside, check out the synagogue's striking facade, which captures the rich history of the building and the people it

represents: The synagogue was built in 1859 just outside what was then the city limits. Although Budapest's Jews held fast to their own faith, they also wished to demonstrate their worth and how well-integrated they were with the greater community. Building this new synagogue was partially an attempt to impress the city's Gentile majority.

The religious leaders commissioned the Austrian (and non-Jewish) architect Ludwig Förster to create a synagogue in Budapest that would top the Stadttempel recently built in Vienna (also designed by a Gentile). The synagogue is loosely based on biblical descriptions of the Temple of Solomon in Jerusalem. This explains the two tall towers, which are not typical of traditional synagogues. These towers—along with the rosette (rose window)—also helped the synagogue resemble Christian churches of the time. In fact, when it was built, the synagogue was dubbed by one observer as "the most beautiful Catholic synagogue in the world."

• *Now step inside.*

Synagogue Interior

Notice that the synagogue interior really feels like a church with the symbols switched—with a basilica floor plan, three naves, two pulpits, and even a pipe organ. The organ—which Franz Liszt played for the building's inauguration—is a clue that this synagogue belonged to the most progressive of the three branches of Judaism here at the time. (Orthodox Jews would never be able to do the "work" of playing an organ on the Sabbath.) Of the various synagogues in this district, this one belonged to the Neolog Jewish congregation (close to Conservative Judaism in the US).

The Moorish-flavored decor—which looks almost Oriental—is a sign of the Historicist style of the time, which borrowed eclectic elements from past styles. Specifically, it evokes the Sephardic Jewish culture that flourished in Iberia; many Hungarian Jews are descended from that group, who fled here after being expelled from Spain in 1492.

In the ark, behind the white curtain, 25 surviving Torah scrolls are kept. Catholic priests hid these scrolls during World War II (burying them temporarily in a cemetery). The synagogue itself, while damaged, avoided being completely destroyed in the war. While it might have been luck, or divine intervention, it was likely also because the occupying Nazis protected it for their own uses: They put radio antennas in the two towers, stabled horses in the nave, and (according to some reports) might have even had a Gestapo base in the balcony above the main entrance.

The two biggest chandeliers are typical neither of synagogues nor of churches; they were likely inspired by concert halls of the day. During the war, the chandeliers were melted down and used to make bullets, but have since been recast. The pews are original, as are the kneelers—another borrowed Christian feature not typically used in Jewish worship.

The two-tiered balconies on the sides of the nave were originally for women, who worshipped separately from the men. (These galleries are accessed by separate staircases, from outside.) Today, men and women can sing together in the choir, but they still sit apart: men in the two inner rows, and women in the two outer rows. (Women sit in the balconies only on important holy days.) The service, attended by several hundred local Jews each Sabbath (and a couple thousand on high holidays), is still said in Hebrew. However, due to security concerns, people who are not members of the local congregation are generally not invited to attend.

• *When you're finished inside, exit through the main doors, turn right, and go to the opposite end of the front courtyard. Here you'll find the entrance to the...*

Hungarian Jewish Museum (Magyar Zsidó Múzeum)

This small but informative museum illuminates the Jewish faith, with artifacts and succinct but engaging English explanations. Pick up the audioguide as you enter (included with ticket). In the long hall, you'll find descriptions of **rituals and holidays,** from Rosh Hashanah and Yom Kippur to Passover and Chanukah. The exhibit also explains the symbolism of **objects** such as prayer shawls, the mezuzah, and so on.

The next room focuses on **family life,** tracing the Jewish lifeline from birth to marriage to death. The marriage contracts posted on the wall show the relative equality between the sexes: Like an old-fashioned form of "prenups," they provide for how property would be divided equitably between both spouses in the event of a divorce. In the funeral section, notice the bowl filled with wooden knobs: If a person died without kin, the Jewish community would provide proper burial. This bowl was a sort of lottery system for randomly determining which person was responsible for burying the deceased.

The final room holds a small, powerful exhibit about the **Holocaust.** Follow the exhibit chronologically as it wraps clockwise around the room: The first few panels are a reminder that the roots of the Holocaust existed in Hungary long before the Nazis took over. In one photo, Hungarian leader Miklós Horthy shakes hands with Hitler—the two nations were allied early in World War II. As the war raged on, the Hungarians proved more benevolent toward their Jewish population than the Germans, but some Jews were still forced to leave the cities and move to the countryside. Then came the horrific time after the Nazis invaded Hungary and installed the Arrow Cross regime, which swiftly began to send Jews to death camps. One display case shows drums made out of Torah scrolls (see photo, facing page). In another is a bar of soap made of human fat—a grotesquely "efficient" use of "resources" from the Nazi concentration-camp system. In the same case is a menorah made by a resourceful inmate out of scraps of bread. Then comes a series of disturbing images of this very neighborhood during World War II, including bodies lined up waiting to be buried in the park next to this synagogue (we'll see that area soon). The final photo shows the hanging of Arrow Cross leader Ferenc Szálasi, who was executed in 1946. In the middle of the room is an exhibit honoring non-Jews who risked everything to rescue Jews during this dark time. (We'll find out more about some of these people later on this tour.) Stairs lead down to a small Holocaust memorial. (For more about this tragic chapter of the Hungarian Jewish experience, don't miss the outstanding Holocaust Memorial Center—see page 64.)

• *Exiting back into the front courtyard, go down the passageway between the synagogue and the museum (straight ahead from the security checkpoint, past the gift shop).*

Tree of Life and Memorial Garden

As you walk alongside the Great Synagogue, notice the small **park** on your left. During the Soviet siege that ended the Nazi occupation of Budapest in the winter of 1944-1945, many Jews in the ghetto here died of exposure, starvation, and disease. Soon after the Soviets liberated the city, a mass grave was dug here for an estimated 2,281 Jews. The trees and headstones (donated by survivors) were added later. The pillars you'll pass have historical photos of the synagogue and Jewish Quarter.

At the far end of the cemetery, look for the small, angular **sculpture** on the pedestal by renowned artist Imre Varga (for more on Varga, see page 84). This represents a forced march—with clearly defined figures at the front, melting into a blocky form at the back. When the Nazi-puppet Arrow Cross regime took over Hungary, they wanted to quickly transport as many Jews as possible to death camps. The trains couldn't take the Jews away fast enough, so the Arrow Cross made them march hundreds of miles to their final destination. Among the victims was a poet named Miklós Radnóti, who was compelled to fight with the Hungarian Army, and then forced to march back to Hungary after a defeat. He died and was buried along the way. A year and a half later, his body was exhumed. In his pocket was a notebook with poignant handwritten poems about his experience. In one, Radnóti daydreams about a life to which (he seems to suspect) he would never return:

> *If only once again I heard the quiet hum*
> *Of bees on the veranda, the jar of orchard plums*
> *Cooling with late summer, the gardens half asleep,*
> *Voluptuous fruit lolling on branches dipping deep,*
> *And she before the hedgerow stood with sun-bleached hair,*
> *The lazy morning scrawling vague shadows on the air...*
> *Why not? The moon is full, her circle is complete.*
> *Don't leave me, friend, shout out, and see! I'm on my feet!*

The building just past the garden is the **Heroes' Temple,** built in 1929 to honor Hungarian Jews who had fought in World War I.

In the garden behind the synagogue is the *Tree of Life*, also created by Imre Varga. This weeping willow, cast in steel, was erected in 1990, soon after the fall of communism made it

possible to acknowledge the Holocaust. The willow makes an upside-down menorah, and each of the 4,000 metal leaves is etched with the name of a Holocaust victim. New leaves are added all the time, donated by families of the victims. Notice that at the end of each branch is a Roman numeral, to assist people in finding their relatives' names. The large black-marble gateway represents a temple; the Hebrew inscription reads, "Is there a bigger pain than mine?" The plaques embedded in the base of the sculpture bear messages (many in English) from donors.

In the center of the garden is a symbolic grave of **Raoul Wallenberg** (1912-1947). An improbable hero, this ne'er-do-well Swedish playboy from a prominent family was sent as a diplomat to Hungary because nobody else wanted the post. He was empowered by the Swedish government to do whatever he could—bribe, threaten, lie, or blackmail—to save as many Jews as possible from the Nazis. He surpassed everyone's low expectations by dedicating (and ultimately sacrificing) his life to the cause. By giving Swedish passports to Jews and admitting them to safe houses, he succeeded in rescuing tens of thousands of people from certain death. Shortly after the Soviets arrived, Wallenberg was arrested, accused of being a US spy, sent to a gulag...and never seen alive again. Russian authorities recently acknowledged he was executed, but have not revealed the details.

The grave is also etched with the names of other "righteous Gentiles" who went above and beyond to save Jews. According to the Talmud, "Whoever saves one life, saves the world entire." The small stones placed on graves are typical of Jewish cemeteries: Each stone is a sign of remembrance, indicating that someone has visited the grave. Surrounding the grave are four rose-colored pillars with the names of other non-Jews who saved individuals or families. The list is still growing, with periodic new additions. In the big stained-glass window that stands near the grave, the fire symbolizes the Holocaust (the Hebrew word is *Shoah,* literally, "catastrophe"), and the curling snake represents fascism.

Along the back wall behind the stained glass, find the little **alcoves** labeled for victims, with lights that go on after dark. The alcoves—like other memorials in this garden—are filled with small stones.

• *The building that defines the far end of the memorial garden is the...*

Hungarian Jewish Archives (Magyar Zsidó Levéltár)

This facility, worth a visit only for those with a special interest, has a **prayer room** on the ground floor and, on the first floor, the **Family Research Center**—with birth, marriage, and death records for Jews from Budapest and much of Hungary. For 1,000 Ft, you're welcome to use their archives. They'll point you in the right direction and can help with basic translations. (Ideally, bring not just your family name, but also—if possible—ancestors' birth and death dates, and any other data you have. It's also best to notify them a few days ahead of your visit—see contact information at the beginning of this chapter.)

Upstairs on the second floor of the same building is a small **virtual exhibition** about the Jewish Quarter, with a few historical artifacts from everyday life, touchscreens with maps and documents to help you learn more about topics of your choice, and a screening room for English-subtitled films about the local Jewish experience, past and present.

• *The exit is through the fence, near the* Tree of Life.

PART 2: JEWISH QUARTER WALK

If you're interested in exploring the rest of the Jewish Quarter, consider the following sights.

• *Exiting the Great Synagogue grounds by the* Tree of Life, *turn right up Wesselényi utca. After two blocks, you reach the intersection with Kazinczy utca. If you're curious about Budapest's burgeoning ruin-pub nightlife scene, detour here a half-block to the right to see* **Szimpla**, *the first and best of those ramshackle nightspots. (While it's pretty dead—and often closed—during the daytime, the space hosts a farmers market on Sunday mornings.)*

To head for the next sight, turn left on Kazinczy utca. Where the road curves, on the right you'll see the...

Orthodox Synagogue

Built in the Vienna-inspired Secession style in 1912, damaged and deserted for decades after World War II, and now renovated, today this temple invites visitors to see its colorful, sumptuously decorated interior (completed in 2006). While grandly opulent, this place is far more typical of synagogue architecture than the Great Synagogue.

Inside, the green pillars at the front flanking the ark evoke the Torah scrolls, and the red columns (with Zsolnay tile decorations)

echo the Temple of Solomon. The seat on the left was filled by the synagogue's first rabbi, Koppel Reich (1838-1929), who was a pillar of the community: He advised Habsburg Emperor Franz Josef and was a member of the Hungarian Parliament. Out of deference to him, nobody has sat in this seat since his death. The temple is still used by a small but dedicated local Orthodox congregation of about 50 people.

• *From the Orthodox Synagogue, turn right onto Kazinczy utca. At the end of the block, turn left onto Dob utca. After about a block and a half on your right, just past the Lokál ruin pub, is the easy-to-miss entrance to...*

Gozsdu Udvar

This long series of courtyards burrows through the middle of a city block, between Dob utca 16 and Király utca 13. When this

neighborhood hosted a fast-growing Jewish population and space was at a premium, courtyards like this one were filled with community life: restaurants, shops, and other businesses. After decades of neglect, this passage was recently spruced up and opened to the public. This genteel space—which evokes the Golden Age of Jewish life in Budapest—is filled with cafés and bars, and after hours it's a bustling nightlife hub.

• *A few steps down from the courtyard, on the right side of Dob utca (where the street widens), keep an eye out for the...*

Monument to Carl Lutz

Born in Switzerland and educated in the US, Carl Lutz (1895-1975) became a Swiss vice-consul to Hungary during World War

II. After the Nazis invaded and began sending Hungarian Jews to death camps, Lutz set up safe houses around the city (which he formally registered as "Swiss soil"), and issued permission for tens of thousands of Jews to emigrate. In the monument, the figure on the side of the building (representing Lutz) is extending a lifeline to the vulnerable figure lying on the ground below him. Lutz is credited, ultimately, with saving 62,000 Jewish lives.

This monument also marks the edge of the WWII-era Jewish ghetto.

• *A few steps beyond the Lutz monument, on the left at #9, notice another long series of courtyards like Gozsdu Udvar—but this one's still deserted and under lock and key.*

At the end of the block, turn right on Rumbach utca. Just before the synagogue, on the left at #10, is the creative...

Printa Café

This inviting design shop/silkscreen studio/art gallery/coffeehouse offers a perfect glimpse at the hipster culture that's taking over this area of Budapest—designer fair-trade coffee, local artists exhibiting their works, and a wide array of "trashion" accessories made from reused materials (stylish bags made from old leather jackets, belts made from discarded shirts, and so on).

• *Across the street is the...*

Synagogue at Rumbach Street

This synagogue's colorful but faded Moorish-style interior survives from the Golden Age of Jewish culture in Budapest. The late-19th-century building was designed by the great Viennese architect Otto Wagner. It was abandoned for years, and rumor has it that Yoko Ono nearly bought it as a studio space—but backed out when she realized its proximity to the tram tracks would cause unacceptable background noise. Today the building awaits a desperately needed renovation. In the meantime, if it's open and you enjoyed the Great Synagogue, it's worth a look. You'll wander through the relatively small but very tall space, and peruse a few scant posted plans (in Hungarian only) about what the renovated synagogue will look like someday.

• *From the synagogue, turn right and walk to the end of the block. On the left, you'll see a giant ceremonial gateway built into a drab red-brick apartment building. Pass through here into...*

Madách Imre Tér

This gateway was designed to be the entrance of an elaborate boulevard that would have connected the Small and Great Boulevards (similar—and parallel—to Andrássy út). But this great road was never built, leaving this impressive gateway to an underwhelming, narrow street with a parking garage and office building. However, the zone in front of the gateway—formerly a jumble of parked cars—has recently been turned into an inviting plaza where locals enjoy lounging and relaxing on sunny days.

• *Our tour is finished. You're facing the Small Boulevard (the former city wall). The Great Synagogue, where we started our walk, is just two long blocks along here to the left.*

From here, you have several options. Diagonally across the busy street (and past the tram stop in the middle of the parklike strip) is Deák tér—a handy Metró hub (where lines M1, M2, and M3 intersect) and the starting point for the ❂ Andrassy Út Walk. The tram stop is the terminus for trams #47 or #49, which zip around the Small Boulevard to the National Museum, Great Market Hall, and Gellért Baths.

CASTLE HILL WALK

Várhegy

Once the seat of Hungarian royalty, and now the city's highest-profile tourist zone, Castle Hill is a historic spit of land looming above the Buda bank of the Danube. Scenic from afar, but (frankly) a bit soulless from up close, it's best seen quickly. The major landmarks are the huge, green-domed Royal Palace at the south end of the hill (housing a pair of museums) and the frilly-spired Matthias Church near the north end (with the hill's best interior). In between are tourist-filled pedestrian streets and historic buildings. This walk gives you the lay of the land and leads you to the hill's most worthwhile attractions and museums, including the Matthias Church, the Fishermen's Bastion, the Hungarian National Gallery, and the WWII-era Hospital in the Rock. You'll also appreciate the bird's-eye views that a visit to Castle Hill offers across the Danube to Pest.

Orientation

Length of This Walk: Allow about two hours, including a visit to Matthias Church; you'll need more time for additional sights (especially the Hungarian National Gallery and the Hospital in the Rock).

When to Visit: Castle Hill is packed with tour groups in the morning, but it's much less crowded in the afternoon. Since restaurants up here are touristy and a bad value, Castle Hill is an ideal after-lunch activity.

Getting There: The Metró and trams won't take you to the top of Castle Hill. Instead, you can hike, taxi, catch a bus, or ride the funicular.

For most visitors, the easiest bet is to hop on **bus #16,** with handy stops in both Pest (at the Deák tér Metró hub—on

Harmincad utca alongside Erzsébet tér, use exit "E" from the station underpass; and at Széchenyi tér at the Pest end of the Chain Bridge) and Buda (at Clark Ádám tér at the Buda end of the Chain Bridge—across the street from the lower funicular station, and much cheaper than the funicular). Or you can go via Széll Kálmán tér (on the M2/red Metró line or by taking tram #4 or #6 around Pest's Great Boulevard); from here, bus **#16,** as well as buses **#16A** and **#116,** head up the hill (at Széll Kálmán tér, catch the bus just uphill from the Metró station—in front of the red-brick, castle-looking building). All buses stop at Dísz tér, at the crest of the hill, about halfway along its length (most people on the bus will be getting off there, too). From Dísz tér, cross the street and walk five minutes along the row of flagpoles toward the green dome, then bear left to find the big Turul bird statue at the start of this walk.

The **funicular** (*sikló*, SHEE-kloh), which lifts visitors from the Chain Bridge to the top of Castle Hill, is a Buda-

pest landmark. Built in 1870 to provide cheap transportation to Castle Hill workers, today it's a pricey little tourist trip. Read the fun first-person history in glass cases at the top station (1,200 Ft one-way, 1,800 Ft round-trip, not covered by transit pass, daily 7:30-22:00, departs every 5-10 minutes, closed for maintenance every other Mon). It leaves you right at the Turul bird statue, where this walk begins.

If you'd like to **hike** up, the most interesting approach is through the castle gardens called Várkert Bazár. From the monumental gateway facing the Danube embankment (just below the Royal Palace, between the Clark Ádám tér and Döbrentei tér stops for trams #19 and #41), head up the stairs into a fine Renaissance garden, then walk (or ride the long escalator) about two-thirds of the way up the hill. From there, a series of two elevators takes you directly up to the palace promenade with minimal climbing—or you can take the scenic route, walking up the delightful switchback ramparts. Either way, you'll wind up at the Royal Palace (begin the walk at ❷, the viewpoint in front of the palace, and see the Turul bird on your way back across the hill later). For more on Várkert Bazár, see page 75.

To **leave the hilltop,** most visitors find it easiest just to walk down after their visit (see the end of this tour). But if you'll be taking the bus down, it's smart to buy tickets for the return trip before you ascend Castle Hill—the only place to buy them up top is the post office near Dísz tér (Mon-Fri until 16:00, closed Sat-Sun).

Changing of the Guard: On the hour, uniformed soldiers do a changing-of-the-guard ceremony at Sándor Palace (the president's residence, near the top of the funicular), with a more elaborate show at 12:00. While not worth planning your day around (it's just a few guys in modern military uniforms slinging rifles), it's fun to watch if you happen to be nearby.

Hungarian National Gallery: 1,400 Ft, may be more for special exhibits, 500 Ft extra to take photos, audioguide-800 Ft, Tue-Sun 10:00-18:00, closed Mon, Szent György tér 2.

Budapest History Museum: 1,800 Ft, audioguide-1,200 Ft; March-Oct Tue-Sun 10:00-18:00, Nov-Feb Tue-Sun 10:00-16:00, closed Mon year-round; Szent György tér 2.

Matthias Church: 1,200 Ft, Mon-Fri 9:00-17:00, Sat 9:00-13:00, Sun 13:00-17:00, Szentháromság tér 2.

Fishermen's Bastion: 700 Ft, daily mid-March-mid-Oct 9:00-19:30; after closing time and off-season, no tickets are sold but bastion is open and free to enter; Szentháromság tér 5.

Eateries: In the Eating in Budapest chapter, I've suggested a few lunch options up here—but for more (and cheaper) choices, head just downhill to Batthyány tér.

Starring: Budapest's most historic quarter, with a palace (and a top collection of Hungarian art), a gorgeous church interior, sweeping vistas over city rooftops, and layers of history.

BACKGROUND

This hilltop has a history as complex and layered as Hungary's. Originally, the main city of Hungary wasn't Buda or Pest, but Esztergom (just up the river—see page 345). In the 13th century, Tatars swept through Eastern Europe, destroying much of Hungary. King Béla IV, who was forced to rebuild his kingdom, re-envisioned Buda as a fortified hilltop town, and moved the capital to this more protected location in the interior of the country. The city has dominated the region ever since.

Over the years, the original Romanesque fortress here was rebuilt and accentuated with a textbook's worth of architectural styles: Gothic, Renaissance, and Baroque. It was one of Europe's biggest palaces by the early 15th century, when King Mátyás (Matthias) Corvinus made the palace even more extravagant, putting Buda—and Hungary—on the map.

Just a few decades later, the invading Ottomans occupied Buda and turned the palace into a military garrison. When the Habsburgs laid siege to the hill for 77 days in 1686, gunpowder stored in the cellar exploded, destroying the palace. The Habsburgs (with a motley, pan-European army that included few Hungarians) took the hill, but Buda was deserted and in ruins. The town was resettled by Austrians, who built a new Baroque palace, hoping that the Habsburg monarch would move in—but none ever did. The useless palace again became a garrison, then the viceroy's residence. It was damaged yet again during the 1848 Revolution, but was repaired and continued to grow right along with Budapest's prominence.

As World War II drew to a close, Budapest became the front line between the Nazis and the approaching Soviets. The labyrinth of natural caves under the hill was even adapted for use as a secret military hospital (the tourable Hospital in the Rock). The Nazis, who believed the Danube to be a natural border for their empire, destroyed bridges across the river and staged a desperate "last stand" on Castle Hill. The Red Army laid siege to the hill for 100 days. They eventually succeeded in taking Budapest...but the city—and the hill—were devastated once again. Since then, the Royal Palace and hilltop town have been rebuilt once more, with a mix-and-match style that attempts, with only some success, to evoke the site's grand legacy.

The Walk Begins

• *Orient yourself from the top of the funicular, enjoying the views over the Danube. (We'll get a full visual tour from a better viewpoint later.) At the top of the nearby staircase, notice the giant bird that looks like a vulture. This is the...*

❶ Turul Bird

This mythical bird of Magyar folktales supposedly led the Hungarian migrations from the steppes of Central Asia in the ninth century. He dropped his sword in the Carpathian Basin, indicating that this was to be the permanent home of the Magyar people. While the Hungarians have long since integrated into Europe, the Turul remains a symbol of Magyar pride. During a surge of nationalism in the 1920s, a movement named after this bird

Castle Hill Walk

Walk

1. Turul Bird
2. Pest Panorama
3. Hungarian Nat'l Gallery
4. King Matthias Fountain
5. Palace Courtyard
6. Budapest History Museum
7. Golden Pharmacy Museum
8. Matthias Church
9. Fishermen's Bastion
10. Statue of St. István
11. Szentháromság Utca
12. Hilton Hotel
13. Remains of St. Mary Magdalene Church

Eateries

14. CBA Grocery Store
15. Rétesbár Strudel
16. Ruszwurm Café

CASTLE HILL

helped revive traditional Hungarian culture. And today, the bird is invoked by right-wing nationalist politicians.

• We'll circle back this way later. But for now, go through the monumental gateway by the Turul and climb down the stairs, then walk along the broad terrace in front of the...

Royal Palace (Királyi Palota)

The imposing palace on Castle Hill barely hints at the colorful story of this hill since the day that the legendary Turul dropped

his sword. It was once the top Renaissance palace in Europe...but that was several centuries and several versions ago. The current palace—a historically inaccurate, post-WWII reconstruction—is a loose rebuilding of previous versions. It's big but soulless. The most prominent feature of today's palace—the green dome—didn't even exist in earlier versions. Fortunately, the palace does house some worthwhile museums (described later), and boasts the fine terrace you're strolling on, with some of Budapest's best views.

Walk all the way down the terrace to the big **equestrian statue** in front of the dome. This depicts Eugene of Savoy, a French general who had great success fighting the Hungarians' hated enemies, the Ottomans. First he helped break the Turkish Siege of Vienna in 1683, then he led the successful Siege of Belgrade in 1717; together, these victories marked the beginning of the end of the Ottoman advance into Europe. Eugene—who fought under three successive Habsburg emperors—was hugely popular across a Europe that was terrified of the always-looming Ottoman threat. He was the Patton or Eisenhower of his day—a great war hero admired and ap-

preciated by all. This explains why a Frenchman gets a place of honor in front of Hungary's Royal Palace.

• With the palace at your back, notice the long, skinny promontory sticking out from Castle Hill (on your right). Walk out to the tip of that promontory to enjoy Castle Hill's best...

❷ Pest Panorama

From here, you can see how topographically different the two halves of Budapest really are. The hill you're on is considered one of the last foothills of the Alps, which ripple from here all the way to France. But immediately across the Danube, everything is oh so flat. Here begins the so-called Great Hungarian Plain, which comprises much of the country—a vast expanse that stretches all the way to Asia. For this reason, Budapest has historically been thought of as being on the bubble between West and East. From the ancient Romans to Adolf Hitler, many past rulers have viewed the Danube through Budapest as a natural border for Europe.

Scan Pest on the horizon, from left to right. Tree-filled Margaret Island, a popular recreation spot, sits in the middle of the

Danube. Following the Pest riverbank, you can't miss the spiny Parliament, with its giant red dome. Straight ahead, you enjoy views of the Chain Bridge, with Gresham Palace and the 1896-era St. István's Basilica lined up just beyond it. (The Parliament and St. István's are both exactly 96 meters tall, in honor of the auspicious millennium celebration in 1896—see page 33.) The Chain Bridge cuts downtown Pest in two: The left half, or "Leopold Town," is administrative, with government ministries, embassies, banks, and so on; the right half is the commercial and touristic center of Pest, with the best riverside promenade. (Each of these is covered by a different self-guided walk in this book.) To the right is the white Elisabeth Bridge, named for the Austrian empress ("Sisi") who so loved her Hungarian subjects. Downriver (to the right) is the green Liberty Bridge, formerly named for Elisabeth's hubby Franz Josef. (If you squint, you might be able to see the Turul birds that top the pillars of this bridge.) And the tall hill to the right, named for the martyred St. Gellért (who patiently attempted to convert the rowdy Magyars after their king adopted Christianity), is topped by the Soviet-era Liberation Monument. At your feet, to the right, sprawl the inviting Renaissance gardens of the recently restored Várkert Bazár terrace (described on page 75).

• *Head back to the statue on the terrace. Facing Eugene's rear end is the main entrance to the...*

❸ Hungarian National Gallery (Magyar Nemzeti Galéria)

The best place in Hungary to appreciate the works of homegrown artists, this art museum offers a peek into the often-morose Hungarian worldview. The collection includes a remarkable

Mátyás (Matthias) Corvinus: The Last Hungarian King

The Árpád dynasty—descendants of the original Magyar tribes—died out in 1301. For more than 600 years, Hungary would be ruled by foreigners...with one exception.

In the mid-15th century, two of Hungary's foreign kings died unexpectedly within seven years. Meanwhile, homegrown military general János Hunyadi was enjoying great success on the battlefield against the Ottomans. When five-year-old László V was elected king, Hunyadi was appointed regent and essentially ruled the country.

Hunyadi defeated the Ottomans in the crucial 1456 Battle of Belgrade, which kept them out of Hungary (at least for another 70 years) and made him an even greater hero to the Hungarian people. But soon afterward, Hunyadi died from the plague. When the young king also died (at age 16), the nobles looked for a new leader. At first they settled on Hunyadi's eldest son, László. But the Habsburgs—who were trying to project their influence from afar—had László killed.

At this dark moment, the Hungarians turned to the younger Hunyadi son, Mátyás (or Matthias in English). At the time, Matthias was at court in Prague (his first wife was a Czech princess). According to legend, Matthias' mother sent for him with a raven with a ring in its beak. The raven supposedly flew nonstop from Transylvania to Prague. The raven-with-ring motif became part of the family crest, as well as the family name: Corvinus (Latin for "raven").

---

group of 15th-century, wood-carved altars from Slovakia (then "Upper Hungary"); piles of gloomy canvases dating from the dark days after the failed 1848 Revolution; several works by two great Hungarian Realist painters, Mihály Munkácsy and László Paál; and paintings by the troubled, enigmatic, and recently in-vogue Post-Impressionist Tivadar Csontváry Kosztka. While not quite a must-see, the collection's highlights can be viewed quickly. For a self-guided tour of the top pieces, see page 70.

• *Head back out to the Eugene statue and face the palace. Go through the passage to the right of the National Gallery entrance (next to the café). You'll emerge into a courtyard decorated with the...*

❹ King Matthias Fountain

This fountain depicts King Matthias enjoying one of his favorite pastimes, hunting. (Notice the distinctive, floppy-eared Hungarian hound dog, or Vizsla.) At the bottom of the fountain, the guy on

Matthias Corvinus returned to Buda, becoming the first Hungarian-descended king in more than 150 years. Progressive and well-educated in the Humanist tradition, Matthias Corvinus (r. 1458-1490) was the quintessential Renaissance king. A lover of the Italian Renaissance, he patronized the arts and built palaces legendary for their beauty. As a benefactor of the poor, he dressed as a commoner and ventured into the streets to see firsthand how the nobles of his realm treated his people.

A strong, savvy leader, Matthias created Central Europe's first standing army—30,000 mercenaries known as the Black Army. No longer reliant on the nobility for military support, Good King Matthias was able to drain power from the nobles and make taxation of his subjects more equitable—earning him the nickname the "people's king."

Matthias was also a shrewd military tactician. Realizing that squabbling with the Ottomans would squander his resources, he made peace with the Ottoman sultan to stabilize Hungary's southern border. Then he swept north, invading Moravia, Bohemia, and even Austria. By 1485, Matthias moved into his new palace in Vienna, and Hungary was enjoying a Golden Age.

Five years later, Matthias died mysteriously at the age of 47, and his empire disintegrated. It is said that when Matthias died, justice died with him. To this day, Hungarians rank him the greatest of all kings, and they sing of his siege of Vienna in their national anthem. They're proud that for a few decades in the middle of half a millennium of foreign oppression, they had a truly Hungarian king—and a great one at that.

CASTLE HILL

the left is Matthias' scribe, while the woman on the right is Ilonka ("The Beautiful"). While Matthias was on an incognito hunting

trip, he wooed Ilonka, who fell desperately in love with him—oblivious to the fact he was the king. When he left suddenly to return to Buda, Ilonka tracked him down and realized who he was. Understanding that his rank meant they could never be together, Ilonka committed suicide. This is typical of many Hungarian legends, which tend to be melancholic and end badly.

• *On that cheerful note, go around the right side of the fountain and through the passage, into the...*

❺ Palace Courtyard

This space, while impressive, somehow feels like an empty husk...a

too-big office building. The entrance to the Budapest History
Museum (described next) is at
the far end of the courtyard. But
first, duck through the door and
down the hallway on your right
as you go through the passage
(free entry). This hall is lined
with minor artifacts from the

museum, giving you a free glimpse (and English descriptions) of
the evolution of this site over the centuries, including artifacts,
paintings, drawings, and photographs of the palace in different eras
(plus an ATM). If you like what you see here, consider visiting the
museum; if not, skip ahead to "Walk to Matthias Church."

❻ Budapest History Museum (Budapesti Történeti Múzeum)

This earnest but dusty collection strains to bring the history of this
city to life. If Budapest really intrigues you, this is a fine place to
explore its history. Otherwise, skip it. The dimly lit fragments of
14th-century sculptures, depicting early Magyars, allow you to see
how Asian those original Hungarians truly looked. The "Budapest:
Light and Shadow" exhibit deliberately but effectively traces the
union between Buda and Pest. Rounding out the collection are exhibits on prehistoric residents and a sprawling cellar that unveils
fragments from the oh-so-many buildings that have perched on
this hill over the centuries. For a rundown of its collection, see
page 74.

Walk to Matthias Church

Leaving the palace courtyard, walk straight up the slight incline.
In good weather, you might see an opportunity to try your hand

at shooting an old-fashioned
bow and arrow. Then you'll
pass under a gate with a
raven holding a ring in its
mouth (a symbol of King
Matthias). As you continue
along the line of flagpoles,
the big white building on
your right (near the funicular station) is the **Sándor Palace**. This
mansion underwent a very costly renovation under the previous
Hungarian prime minister, who hoped to make it his residence.
But in 2002, the same year it was finished, he lost his bid for re-
election. The spunky new PM refused to move in. By way of compromise, this is now the president's office. This is where you can see

the relatively low-key changing of the guard each hour on the hour, with a special show at noon.

After Sándor Palace is the yellow former **Court Theater** (Várszínház), which has seen many great performances over the

centuries—including a visit from Beethoven in 1800. Until recently, this housed the National Dance Theater. But current Hungarian Prime Minister Viktor Orbán (not known for humble gestures) grew jealous of the president's swanky digs, kicked out the dancers, and ren-

ovated this building as the prime minister's residence. The bizarre back-and-forth—one PM wanting to live at the castle, the next refusing, and the next again wanting to—is perfectly illustrative of the swaying pendulum that is Hungarian politics.

In the field in the middle of this terrace, you'll notice the **ruins** of a medieval monastery and church. Along the left side (past the flagpoles) is the ongoing excavation of the medieval Jewish quarter—more reminders that most of what you see on today's Castle Hill has been destroyed and rebuilt many times over.

Notice the bridge on the left, crossing over some of those ruins, as well as a trench around the castle wall. Go over that bridge to a viewpoint for a look at the **Buda Hills**—the "Beverly Hills" of Hungary, draped with orchards, vineyards, and the homes of the wealthiest Budapesters.

Walk along this outer terrace, enjoying the views, then hook right to reach the **former Ministry of War.** Until 2013, this was

still a bombed-out shell, with war damage from both World War II and the brutal Soviet response to the 1956 Uprising (see page 112). Now it has been converted into a fine space for special exhibits—head to the front door to see what's on (likely 2,000 Ft, Tue-Sun 10:00-18:00, closed Mon). To the left of the door, you can see

the faint bullet holes and shrapnel scars—intentionally left here as a memorial (see the *Memento 1944-1945* plaque).

Cross the street in front of the former Ministry of War to reach **Dísz tér** (Parade Square). Here you'll see convenient bus stops for connecting to other parts of Budapest (bus #16, #16A, or #116 to Széll Kálmán tér; or bus #16 to the Pest side of the Chain Bridge). On the left is a handy post office (bus tickets sold here Mon-Fri before 16:00, closed Sat-Sun). On the right, behind the yellow wall, is a courtyard with an open-air Hungarian **folk-art market.** While it's fun to browse, prices here are high (haggle away). The Great Market Hall has a better selection and generally lower prices (see page 56).

Continue straight uphill on **Tárnok utca** (noticing, on the left, the recommended Vár Bistro—a handy lunch cafeteria). This area often disappoints visitors. After being destroyed by Ottomans, it was rebuilt in sensible Baroque, lacking the romantic time-capsule charm of a medieval old town. But if you poke your head into some courtyards, you'll almost always see some original Gothic arches and other medieval features.

As you continue along, ponder the fact that there are miles of **caves** burrowed under Castle Hill—carved out by water, expanded by the Ottomans, and used by locals during the siege of Buda at the end of World War II. If you'd like to spelunk under Castle Hill, there are two different sightseeing options: To learn about how the caves were used during the 20th century, it's worth going on the lengthy Hospital in the Rock tour (see page 77); for just a quick look, you can check out the touristy Buda Labyrinth cave, with a sparse, hokey historical exhibit (see page 78).

As you approach the plague column, on your left at #18 is the low-profile entrance to the ❼ **Golden Pharmacy Museum** (dark-orange building). Consider dipping into this modest three-room collection of historic pharmaceutical bric-a-brac, including a cute old pharmacy counter and an alchemist's lab (500 Ft, borrow English descriptions, Tue-Sun 10:30-18:00, closed Mon, last entry 30 minutes before closing, Tárnok utca 18).

Finally, you'll come to a little park. The white, circular building in the park, marked *TourInform*, is a **TI** that can answer questions and has a handy pictorial map of the castle area (daily 10:00-18:00).

Across the street from the park (on the left), the **CBA grocery store** sells reasonably priced cold drinks, and has a coffee shop upstairs (open daily). A good spot for dessert is just around the corner: **Rétesbár,** selling strudel *(rétes)* with various fillings for 300 Ft each (just down the little lane—Balta köz—next to the grocery store, daily 8:00-19:30).

Just beyond the park, a warty plague column from 1713 marks **Szentháromság tér** (Holy Trinity Square), the main square of old Buda.

• *Dominating the square is the...*

❽ Matthias Church (Mátyás-Templom)

Budapest's best church has been destroyed and rebuilt several times in the 800 years since it was founded by King Béla IV. Today's version—renovated at great expense in the late 19th century and restored after World War II—is an ornately decorated lesson in Hungarian history. The church's actual name is the Church of Our Lady, or the Coronation Church (because its unofficial namesake, Matthias Corvinus, isn't a saint, it can't be formally named for him). But everyone calls it the Matthias Church, for the popular Renaissance king who got married here—twice.

Ɔ **Self-Guided Tour:** Examine the **exterior.** While the nucleus of the church is Gothic, most of what you see outside—including the frilly, flamboyant steeple—was added for the 1896 celebrations. At the top of the stone corner tower facing the river, notice the raven—the ever-present symbol of King Matthias Corvinus.

Buy your ticket across the square from the church's side door, at the ticket windows embedded in the wall. Then enter the church. The good English descriptions posted throughout will amplify this tour.

The sumptuous **interior** is wallpapered with gilded pages from a Hungarian history textbook. Different eras are represented by symbolic motifs. Entering the side door, turn left and go to the back end of the church. The wall straight ahead represents the Renaissance, with a giant coat of arms of beloved King Matthias Corvinus. (The tough guys in armor on either side are members of his mercenary Black Army, the source of his power.) Notice another raven, with a ring in its beak.

Work your way clockwise around the church. The first chapel (in the back corner, to the left as you face the closed main doors)—the **Loreto Chapel**—holds the church's prize possession: a 1515 statue of Mary and Jesus. Anticipating Ottoman plundering, locals walled over its niche. The occupying Ottomans used the church as their primary mosque—oblivious to the precious statue hidden behind the plaster. Then, a century and a half later, during the siege of Buda in 1686, gunpowder stored in the castle up the street detonated, and the wall crumbled. Mary's triumphant face showed through, terrifying the Ottomans. Supposedly this was the only part of town taken from the Ottomans without a fight.

Facing the doors, look to the top of the stout pillar on the right to see a **carved capital** showing two men gesturing excitedly at a book. Dating from 1260, these carvings are some of the earliest surviving features in this church, which has changed much over the centuries.

As you look down the **nave,** notice the banners. They've hung here since the Mass that celebrated Habsburg monarch Franz Josef's coronation at this church on June 8, 1867. In a sly political compromise to curry favor in the Hungarian part of his territory, Franz Josef was "emperor" *(Kaiser)* of Austria, but only "king" *(König)* of Hungary. (If you see the old German phrase "K+K"—still used today as a boast of royal quality—it refers to this *"König und Kaiser"* arrangement.) So, after F. J. was crowned emperor in Vienna, he came down the Danube and said to the Hungarians, "King me." (For more on the K+K system, see page 320.)

Continue circling around the church. Along the left aisle (toward the main altar from the gift shop) is the **altar of St. Imre,** the son of the great King (and later Saint) István—who is standing to the left of him. This heir to the Hungarian throne was mysteriously killed by a boar while hunting when he was only 19 years old. Though Imre didn't live long enough to do anything important, he rode his father's coattails to sainthood. Lacking a direct heir, István dedicated his country to Mary—which is why she's wearing the Hungarian crown in this altar, and at this church's main one (which we'll see soon).

The next chapel is the **tomb of Béla III,** utterly insignificant except that this is one of only two tombs of Hungarian kings that still exist in the country. The rest—including all of the biggies—were defiled by the Ottomans.

Up next to the main altar is the **chapel of László**—King István's nephew, who stepped in as king of Hungary when the rightful heir, Imre, was killed.

Now stand at the modern altar in the middle of the church, and look down the nave to the **main altar.** Mary floats above it all, and hovering over her is a full-scale replica of the Hungarian crown, which was blessed by Pope John Paul II. More than a millennium after István, Mary still officially wears this nation's crown.

Climb the circular stone staircase (in the corner, near the chapel of László) up to the **gallery.** Walk along the royal oratory to

CASTLE HILL

a small room that overlooks the altar area. Here, squeezed in the corner between luxurious vestments, is another replica of the Hungarian crown (the original is under the Parliament's dome, and described on page 106). Then you'll huff up another staircase for more views down over the nave, and an exhibit on the church's recent restoration, displaying original statues and architectural features. You'll exit back down into the nave.

• *Back outside, at the end of the square next to the Matthias Church, is the...*

❾ Fishermen's Bastion (Halászbástya)

This Neo-Romanesque fantasy rampart offers beautiful views over the Danube to Pest. In the Middle Ages, the fish market was just below here (in today's Víziváros, or "Water Town"), so this part of the rampart actually was guarded by fishermen. The current structure, however, is completely artificial—yet another example of Budapest sprucing itself up for 1896. Its seven pointy towers represent the seven Magyar tribes. The cone-headed arcades are reminiscent of tents the nomadic Magyars called home before they moved west to Europe.

Paying 700 Ft to climb up the bastion makes little sense. Enjoy virtually the same view through the windows (left of café) for free. (The café offers a scenic break if you don't mind the tour groups.) There's a pay WC to the right of the bastion.

Explore the full length of the bastion, and you'll find that several other sections are also open and free to the public—as well as more scenic cafés, sometimes with live "Gypsy" music. Note that the (free) grand staircase leading down from the bastion offers a handy shortcut to the Víziváros neighborhood and Batthyány tér (for affordable restaurants there, see page 262).

Tucked around the far side of the bastion, at the back of a pastry shop in the modern, glassy building, is the **Szabó Marzipan Museum,** where you can pay 400 Ft to see two rooms crammed full of little sculptures created from this almond-paste confection (daily 9:00-18:00). While it's not as impressive as the similar sight in Eger (see page 369), it's worth a peek if you're curious.

• *Between the bastion and the church stands a...*

❿ Statue of St. István

Hungary's first Christian king tamed the nomadic, pagan Magyars and established strict laws and the concept of private property. In the late 900s, King Géza of Hungary lost a major battle against the forces of Christian Europe—and realized that he must raise his son Vajk (c. 967-1038) as a Catholic and convert his people, or they would be forcefully driven out of Europe. Vajk took the Christian name István (EESHT-vahn, "Stephen") and was baptized in the year 1000. The reliefs on this statue show the commissioners of the pope crowning St. István, bringing Hungary into the fold of Christendom. This put Hungary on the map as a fully European kingdom, forging alliances that would endure for centuries. Without this pivotal event, Hungarians believe that the Magyar nation would have been lost. A passionate evangelist—more for the survival of his Magyar nation than for the salvation of his people—István beheaded those who wouldn't convert. To make his point perfectly clear, he quartered his reluctant uncle and sent him on four separate, simultaneous tours of the country to show Hungarians that Christianity was a smart choice. Gruesome as he was, István was sainted within 30 years of his death.

· *Directly across from Matthias Church is a charming little street called...*

⓫ Szentháromság Utca

Halfway down this street on the right, look for the venerable, recommended **Ruszwurm** café—the oldest in Budapest (see listing on page 267). At the end of the street is an equestrian statue of the war hero **András Hadik.** If you examine the horse closely, you'll see that his, ahem, undercarriage has been polished to a high shine. Local students rub these for good luck before a big exam. I guess you could say students really have a ball preparing for tests.

Continue out to the terrace and appreciate more views of the Buda Hills. If you go down the stairs here, then turn right up the street, you'll reach the entrance of the World War II-era **Hospital in the Rock,** which you can tour to learn about the Nazi and Cold War era of Castle Hill (excellent tours at the top of each hour, described on page 77).

· *Retrace your steps back to Matthias Church. Some visitors will have had their fill of Castle Hill; if so, you can make a graceful exit down the big staircase below the Fishermen's Bastion. You'll wind up in Víziváros, on the embankment.*

But if you'd like to extend your walk to the northern part of Castle Hill, start at the plague column, and go up the street next to the modern building. This is the...

⓬ Hilton Hotel

Built in 1976, the Hilton was the first plush Western hotel in town. Before 1989, it was a gleaming center of capitalism, offering a cushy

refuge for Western travelers and a stark contrast to what was, at the time, a very gloomy city. To minimize the controversy of building upon so much history, architects thoughtfully incorporated the medieval ruins into their modern design. Halfway down the hotel's facade (after the first set of doors, at the base of the tower), you'll see fragments of a 13th-century wall, with a monument to King Matthias Corvinus. After the wall, continue along the second half of the Hilton Hotel facade. Turn right into the gift-shop entry, and then go right again inside the second glass door. Through yet another glass door, stairs on the left lead down to a reconstructed 13th-century Dominican cloister (now housing a wine cellar). For an even better look at what was here back then, continue past the cloister stairs and enter the lobby café-bar. Look out the back windows to see fragments of the 13th-century Dominican church incorporated into the structure of the hotel. If you stood here eight centuries ago, you'd be looking straight down the church's nave. You can even see tomb markers in the floor.

Back out on the street, cross the little park and duck into the entryway of the **Fortuna Passage.** Along the passageway to

the courtyard, you can see the original Gothic arches of the house that once stood here. In the Middle Ages, every homeowner had the right to sell wine without paying taxes—but only in the passage of his own home. He'd set up a table here, and his neighbors would come by to taste the latest vintage. These passageways evolved into very social places, like the corner pub.

Leaving the passage, turn left down Fortuna utca and walk toward the mosaic roof (passing the recommended 21 Magyar Vendéglő on your right—a good place for an upscale meal). Reaching the end of the street, look right to see the low-profile **Vienna Gate.** If you go through it and walk for about 10 days, you'll get to Vienna. (For now, settle for climbing up to the top for a view of some of Buda's residential neighborhoods.) Just inside the Vienna Gate, notice the bus stop—handy for leaving Castle Hill when you're finished.

CASTLE HILL

• *Now turn left and walk along the hulking, mosaic-roofed National Archive building (with your back to the Danube) until you reach the...*

⑱ Remains of St. Mary Magdalene Church

This was once known as the Kapisztrán Templom, named after a hero of the Battle of Belgrade in 1456, an early success in the strug-

gle to keep the Ottomans out of Europe. (King Matthias' father, János Hunyadi, led the Hungarians in that battle.) The pope was so tickled by the victory that he decreed that all church bells should toll at noon in memory of the battle—and, technically, they still do. (Californians might recognize Kapisztrán's Spanish name: San Juan Capistrano.) This church was destroyed by bombs in World War II, though no worse than Matthias Church. But, since this part of town was depopulated after the war, there was no longer a need for a second church. The remains of the church were torn down, the steeple was rebuilt as a memorial, and a carillon was added—so that every day at noon, the bells can still toll...and be enjoyed by the monument of János Kapisztrán, just across the square.

• *Our walk is finished, but there are a few more options nearby. You can walk out to the terrace just beyond the big building for another look at the Buda Hills. From here, just to the right (near the flagpole), is the entrance to the **Museum of Military History**, with a mountain of army-surplus artifacts from Hungary's gloriously unsuccessful military past (described on page 77). If you continue around the terrace past the museum, at the northern point of Castle Hill you'll find an old **Turkish grave**, honoring a pasha who once ruled here during Ottoman times.*

If you're ready to leave Castle Hill, you can backtrack to the Fishermen's Bastion and walk down the grand staircase there (into the Víziváros neighborhood). Or, from the square just inside Vienna Gate, you can catch bus #16, #16A, or #116 to Széll Kálmán tér— or head out through the gate and follow the road downhill. You'll run into bustling Széll Kálmán tér, which has a handy Metró stop (M2/red line) and the huge, modern, popular Mammut shopping complex.

MEMENTO PARK TOUR

a.k.a. Statue Park (Szoborpark)

When regimes fall, so do their monuments...literally. Just think of all those statues of Stalin and Lenin that crashed to the ground in late 1989, when people throughout Eastern Europe couldn't wait to get rid of these reminders of their oppressors. But some clever entrepreneur hoarded Budapest's, collecting them in a park in the countryside just southwest of the city—where tourists flock to get a taste of the communist era. Though it can be time-consuming to visit, this collection is worth ▲▲▲ for those fascinated by Hungary's commie past.

Orientation

Name-Change Warning: Confusingly, this attraction—which for years had been called Statue Park—was later re-branded as Memento Park. The names are still occasionally used interchangeably; they refer to the same sight.

Cost: 1,500 Ft.

Hours: Daily 10:00-sunset.

Getting There: It's in the countryside six miles southwest of the city center, at the corner of Balatoni út and Szabadka út, in district XXII.

The park runs a convenient **direct bus** from Deák tér in downtown Budapest (where three Metró lines converge; bus stop is at corner of busy Bajcsy-Zsilinszky út and Harmincad utca). The trip takes 2.5 hours total, including a 1.5-hour visit to the park (4,900-Ft fee includes round-trip and park entry, 33 percent discount if you prebook online at www.mementopark. hu, runs April-Oct daily at 11:00, Nov-March Sat-Mon at 11:00—no bus Tue-Fri off-season).

The **public transport** option requires a transfer, but is doable: Ride the Metró's M4/green line to the end of the line at Kelenföld. Head up to street level and catch bus #101, which takes you to Memento Park in about 15 minutes (second stop, runs every 10 minutes—but only on weekdays). On weekends, when bus #101 doesn't run, you'll have to take bus #150, which takes longer (2/hour, about 25 minutes). On either bus, be sure the driver knows where you want to get off.

Hiring a **taxi** for the round-trip, including about an hour of waiting time at the park, should cost around 15,000 Ft (ask your hotel to call one for you, and confirm the price before you set out).

Tours and Information: This chapter's self-guided tour gives you all the information you need. Alternatively, 50-minute English tours depart from the entrance (1,200 Ft, 33 percent discount if you prebook online; April-Oct daily at 11:45, May-Sept also generally daily at 13:00 and 14:00; Nov-March Sat-Mon at 11:45—no tours Tue-Fri off-season). The 1,500-Ft English guidebook, *In the Shadow of Stalin's Boots*, is very informative. Tel. 1/424-7500, www.mementopark.hu.

Starring: Marx, Engels, Lenin, stiff soldiers, passionate patriots... and other ghosts of Hungary's communist past.

BACKGROUND

Under the communists, creativity was discouraged. The primary purpose of art was to further the goals of the state, with creative expression only an afterthought. This **Socialist Realist** art served two purposes: It was Realistic, breaking with the "decadent" bourgeois art that came before it (Impressionism, Post-Impressionism, and other modern -isms); and Socialistic, encouraging complicity with the brave new world the commu-

Memento Park

BRICK WALL

20 Meters
20 Yards

LOOP VI
LOOP V
LOOP IV
LOOP III
LOOP II
LOOP I

BALATONI ÚT

Public Bus Stop

TICKET OFFICE & GIFT SHOP

TRABANT CAR

ENTRY FACADE

7

Official/Direct Bus Stop

REPLICA BARRACKS

"Witness Square"

STALIN'S TRIBUNE

To Budapest

SZABADKA ÚT

Note:
These numbers correspond to the official Memento Park map. Numbers filled in black are described on this tour.

MEMENTO PARK

nists were forging. From 1949 until 1956, Socialist Realism was legally enforced as the sole artistic style of the Soviet Bloc.

As propaganda was an essential weapon in the Soviet arsenal, the regime made ample use of Socialist Realist art. Aside from a few important figureheads, individuals didn't matter. Everyone was a cog in the machine—strong, stoic, doing their job well and proudly for the good of the people. Individual characteristics and distinguishing features were unimportant; people were represented as automatons serving their nation. Artistic merit was virtually ignored. Most figures are trapped in stiff, unnatural poses that ignore the 3,000 years of artistic evolution since the Egyptians. Sculptures and buildings alike from this era were designed to evoke feelings of power and permanence.

The Tour Begins

• *The numbers in the following tour match the statue labels in the park, the official park map, and the map in this chapter.*
> *As you approach the park, you encounter the imposing red-brick...*

Entry Facade

You're greeted by three of the Communist All-Stars: ❶ **Vladimir Lenin,** a leader of Russia's Bolshevik Revolution; and ❷ **Karl Marx** and **Friedrich Engels,** the Ger-man philosophers whose *Communist Manifesto* first articulated the principles behind communism in 1848. (These three figures weren't offensive enough to be destroyed, but very few statues survive anywhere of the biggest "star" of all, the hated Josef Stalin.)

Like the rest of the park, this gate's design is highly conceptual: It looks impressive and monumental...but, like the rotted-out pomp of communism, there's nothing behind it. It's a glossy stage-set with no substance. If you try to go through the main, central part of the gate, you'll run into an always-locked door. Instead, as with the communist system, you have to find another way around (in this case, the side gate to the left). Etched in the door is the Hungarian poem "Where seek out tyranny?", published after the 1956 Uprising.

Inside the gate, buy your ticket and head into the park. Surveying the layout, notice that the main road takes you confidently toward...a dead end (the brick wall). Once again, as with life under the communists, you'll have to deviate from this main axis to actually accomplish anything. Even so, notice that the six walkways branching off the main road all loop you right back to where you started—representing the endless futility of communism. The loops are thematically tied together in pairs: Roughly, the first figure-eight focuses on Hungarian-Soviet friendship; the second figure-eight celebrates the heroes of communism; and the third figure-eight shows off the idealized concepts of communism. The statues are also organized very loosely chronologically; the statues near the entrance are generally older than the ones farther into the park.

• *Now we'll zigzag back and forth through each of the six loops. Begin with the loop to the right as you enter the park.*

Liberation Monuments (Loop I)

All of these statues celebrate the Soviet Army's triumphant rescue of Hungary from the Nazis in 1945.

Dominating this loop is a ❸ **giant soldier** holding the Soviet flag. This statue once stood at the base of the Liberation Monument that still overlooks the Danube from Gellért Hill (see page 79). Typical of Socialist Realist art, the soldier has a clenched fist (symbolizing strength) and a face that is inspired by his egalitarian ideology. After the fall of communism, some critics wanted the entire monument torn down. As a compromise, they removed the overt communist themes (the red star and this soldier), covered what remained with a sheet for a while to exorcise the communist mojo, then re-unveiled it.

To the left of this soldier, see the ❹ **two comrades** stiffly shaking hands: the Hungarian worker thrilled to meet the Soviet soldier—protector of the proletariat.

Beyond them is a ❺ **long wall,** with a triumphant worker breaking through the left end—too busy doing his job to be very excited. Just another brick in the wall.

(The three big blocks protruding from the wall were for hanging commemorative wreaths.)

The big ❼ **panel** came from an apartment building in a conservative Buda Hills neighborhood. Each neighborhood had a similar monument to the liberation. The nail holes once held letters that proclaimed in Hungarian and Russian: "Everlasting praise for the freedom of the Soviet Union, for its independence, and for its fallen heroes in the battle to liberate Hungary."

• *Cross "main street" to a group of statues commemorating the key communist holiday of...*

April 4, 1945 (Loop II)

On this date, the Soviets forced the final Nazi soldier out of Hungary. The tall panel nearest the entrance shows a Hungarian woman and a Soviet woman setting free the ❽ **doves of peace.** According to the inscription, "Our freedom and peace is founded upon the enduring Hungarian-Soviet friendship." (With friends like these....)

The ❾ **woman holding the palm leaf** is reminiscent of the Liberation Monument back

MEMENTO PARK

on the Danube—which, after all, celebrates the same glorious day. Check out the size of that palm leaf: Seems like she's overcompensating...

At the back of the loop, the ❿ **Hungarian worker and Soviet soldier** (who appear to be doing calisthenics) are absurdly rigid even though they're trying to be dynamic. (Even the statues couldn't muster genuine enthusiasm for communist ideals.)

• *Cross over and head up to the next loop to pay homage to...*

Heroes of the Workers' Movement (Loop III)

Look for the ⓮ bust of the Bulgarian communist leader **Georgi Dimitrov** (ruled 1946-1949)—one of communist Hungary's many Soviet Bloc comrades. During the 1956 Uprising, protesters put a noose around this bust's neck and hung it from a tree. Next is a ⓯ full-size statue of Dimitrov, a gift from "the working people of Sofia." (Talk about a white elephant.)

At the back of this loop are ⓰ three blocky portraits. The middle figure is the granddaddy of Hungarian communism: **Béla Kun** (1886-1938) fought for the Austro-Hungarian Empire in World War I. He was captured by the Russian Army, taken to a prisoner of war camp inside Russia, and became mysteriously smitten with communism. After proving himself too far left even for Lenin, Kun returned to Hungary in 1918 and formed a Hungarian Communist Party at a time when communism was most definitely not in vogue. We'll see more of Kun later in the park.

To the left is one of the park's best-loved, most-photographed, and most artistic statues: ⓱ **Vladimir Lenin,** in his famous "hailing a cab" pose. It once stood at the entrance to the giant industrial complex in Budapest's Csepel district.

• *Cross over—passing the giant red star made of flowers (resembling one that was once planted in the middle of the roundabout at the Buda end of the Chain Bridge)—to meet...*

More Communist Heroes (Loop IV)

This group—which includes a ㉕ statue of an interior minister made a foot shorter at the bottom when the Iron Curtain fell—is

dominated by a ㉔ dramatic, unusually emotive sculpture by a genuine artist, **Imre Varga** (described on page 84). Designed to commemorate the 100th anniversary of Béla Kun's birth, this clever statue accomplishes seemingly con-

tradictory feats. On the one hand, it reinforces the communist message: Under the able leadership of Béla Kun (safely overlooking the fray from above), the crusty, bourgeois old regime of the Habsburg Empire (on the left, with the umbrellas and fancy clothes) was converted into the workers' fighting force of the Red Army (on the right, with the bayonets). And yet, those silvery civilians in back seem more appealing than the lunging soldiers in front. And notice the lamppost next to Kun: In Hungarian literature, a lamppost is a metaphor for the gallows. This reminds viewers that Kun—in spite of his groundbreaking and heroic work for the communist movement in Hungary—was ultimately executed by the communists during Stalin's purges of the late 1930s.

• *Zig and head up again, for a lesson in...*

Communist Concepts (Loop V)

Look for a rusty pair of ㉛ **workers' hands** holding a sphere (which was once adorned with a red star). This represented the hard-won ideals of communism, carefully protected by the hands—but also held out for others to appreciate.

The ㉜ **monument to Hungarian soldiers** (who look like saluting Rockettes) honors those who fought against the fascist Francisco Franco in the Spanish Civil War.

Dominating this group is a ㉝ **communist worker** charging into the future, clutching the Soviet flag. Budapesters of the time had a different interpretation: a thermal bath attendant running after a customer who'd forgotten his towel. This is a favorite spot for goofy posed photos.

To the left is a monument to the communist version of the Boy Scouts: the elementary-school-age ㉞ **Little Drummers** and the older **Pioneers.** While these organizations existed before the communists, they were slowly infiltrated and turned into propaganda machines by the regime. These kids—with their jaunty red and blue neckerchiefs—were sent to camp to be properly raised as good little communists; today, many of them have forgotten the brainwashing but still have fond memories of the socializing.

• *Now zag once more to learn about...*

More Communist Concepts (Loop VI)

The ③⑦ long, **white wall** at the back of this section tells quite a story (from left to right): The bullet holes lead up to a jumbled, frightful clutter (reminiscent of Pablo Picasso's *Guernica*) representing World War II. Then comes the bright light of the Soviet system, and by the end everyone's properly regimented—striking *Charlie's Angels* poses—and looking boldly to the future (and enjoying a bountiful crop, to boot). The names in the center represent "heroes" who stayed true to the ideology, Party, and nation and died in "defense of proletarian power" in 1956. Some became household names to older locals, who show their age by still referring to places using their communist titles (from 1956 until 1990, many Budapest streets were named in honor of these "heroes").

Next is a ③⑧ **fallen hero** with arm outstretched, about to collapse to the ground—mortally wounded, yet victorious. This monument to "the Martyrs of the Counter-Revolution" also commemorates those who died attempting to put down the 1956 Uprising.

Finally you'll see a ③⑨ **plundered monument.** Missing its figures and red star, it was destroyed in 1989 by jubilant Hungarians celebrating their freedom.

• *Now continue down the main drag to, um, a....*

Dead End

The main path dead-ends at the wall, symbolizing life's frustrations under communism. Here stand statues of two Soviet officers who negotiated with the Nazis to end the WWII siege of Budapest. ④⓪ **Captain Miklós Steinmetz** (on the right) was killed by a Nazi land mine, while ④① **Ilja Ostapenko** (on the left) was shot under mysterious circumstances as he returned from the successful

summit. Both became heroes for the communist cause. Were they killed by wayward Nazi soldiers, as the Soviets explained—or by their own Red Army, to create a pair of convenient martyrs? These two statues once flanked the road out of Budapest toward the popular resort area at Lake Balaton. Locals eager to get out of town would hitchhike "at Ostapenko."

Heading back out to the entry gate, peruse the fun parade of communist kitsch at the **gift shop.** The stirring music may just move you to pick up the CD of *Communism's Greatest Hits,* and maybe a model of a Trabant (the classic two-stroke commie-mobile). A real **Trabant** is often parked just inside the gate.

• *Now head out across the parking lot to find...*

Stalin's Tribune

This section of the complex is a re-creation of the giant grandstand that once stood along Parade Street (the boulevard next to City

Park; the original site is described on page 179). Hungarian and Soviet leaders stood here, at the feet of a giant Stalin statue, to survey military and civilian processions. But during the 1956 Uprising, protesters cut Stalin off at the knees... leaving only the boots. (The entire tribune was later dismantled, and Stalin disappeared without a trace.) If you circle around behind the tribune, you'll find stairs up top for a view over the park.

• *Flanking the lot in front of the tribune are replica...*

Barracks

These are reminiscent of the ramshackle barracks where political prisoners lived in communist-era work camps (sometimes called gulags, described on page 164). These hold special exhibits, often including a good explanation of "Stalin's Boots" (with a plaster replica, and photos of the original tribune) and the events of 1956. Sit down for the creepy film, *The Life of an Agent*—a loop of four training films (10-15 minutes each) that were actually used to teach novice spies about secret-police methods and policies.

• *Our tour is over. Now, inspired by the bold propaganda of your Hungarian comrades, march proudly into the dawn of a new day.*

MEMENTO PARK

SLEEPING IN BUDAPEST

Contents

I favor hotels and restaurants that are handy to your sightseeing activities. Rather than list hotels scattered throughout a city, I describe my favorite neighborhoods and recommend the best accommodations values in each, from dorm beds to fancy doubles with all of the comforts.

A major feature of this book is its extensive and opinionated listing of good-value rooms. I like places that are clean, central, relatively quiet at night, reasonably priced, friendly, small enough to have a hands-on owner and stable staff, run with a respect for Hungarian traditions, and not listed in other guidebooks. Obviously, a place meeting every criterion is rare, and all of my recommendations fall short of perfection—sometimes miserably. But I've listed the best values for each price category. I'm more impressed by a convenient location and a fun-loving philosophy than flat-screen TVs and a pricey laundry service.

Book your accommodations well in advance, especially if you'll be traveling during busy times. September is extremely tight (because of conventions), with October close behind. The Formula 1 races (one weekend in late July or early Aug) send rates through the roof (see page 512 for a list of major holidays and festivals in Hungary). Most rates drop 10-25 percent in the off-season (generally Nov-March). For tips on making reservations, see page 230.

Sleep Code

(€1 = $1.40, 225 Ft = about $1, country code: 36, area code: 1)

Price Rankings

To help you easily sort through my listings, I've divided the accommodations into three categories, based on the highest price for a standard double room with bath during high season:

$$$ **Higher Priced**—Most rooms €100 or more.

$$ **Moderately Priced**—Most rooms between €70-100.

$ **Lower Priced**—Most rooms €70 or less.

I always rate hostels as $, whether or not they have double rooms, because they have the cheapest beds in town. Prices can change without notice; verify the hotel's current rates online or by email. For the best prices, always book directly with the hotel.

Abbreviations

To pack maximum information into minimum space, I use the following code to describe the accommodations in this book. Prices listed are per room, not per person. When a price range is given for a type of room (such as double rooms listing for €100-120), it means the price fluctuates with the season, size of room, or length of stay; expect to pay the upper end for peak-season stays.

S = Single room (or price for one person in a double).

D = Double or twin room. "Double beds" are often two twins sheeted together and are usually big enough for nonromantic couples.

T = Triple (generally a double bed plus a single).

Q = Quad (usually two double beds; adding an extra child's bed to a T is usually cheaper).

b = Private bathroom with toilet and shower or tub.

s = Private shower or tub only (the toilet is down the hall).

According to this code, a couple staying at a "Db-€100" hotel would pay a total of €100 (about $140) for a double room with a private bathroom. Unless otherwise noted, breakfast is included but not the 4 percent tourist tax, English is spoken, and credit cards are accepted. There's almost always Wi-Fi and/or a guest computer available, either free or for a fee. Some hotel rooms have high-speed Internet jacks that you can plug into with an Ethernet cable (sometimes called "WLAN").

RATES AND DEALS

I've described my recommended accommodations using a Sleep Code (see sidebar). Prices listed are for one-night stays in peak season, include breakfast (unless specified), and assume you're booking directly with the hotel (not through an online hotel-booking engine or TI). Booking services extract a commission from the hotel, which logically closes the door on special deals. Book direct.

My recommended hotels each have a website (often with a built-in booking form) and an email address; you can expect a response in English within a day (and often sooner).

In Budapest, most hotels quote their rates in euros (for the convenience of international guests), and I've followed suit. (Outside of the capital, hotels more often quote rates in forints.) However, most places prefer to be paid in forints (figured at the exchange rate on the day of payment). Unless I note otherwise in the listing, you can assume the hotel accepts credit cards—though smaller places always prefer cash. I've listed prices per room, not per person.

The majority of hotels don't include the 4 percent tourist tax in their rates. Be warned that some big chains also don't include the whopping 22 percent sales tax, which can make your hotel cost nearly a quarter more than you expected. (Independent hotel rates typically do include sales tax.)

While most hotels listed in this chapter cluster at about €70-105 per double, they range from €20 bunks to €500-plus splurges (maximum plumbing and more). Rooms outside the capital—such as in Eger, Pécs, and Sopron—are much cheaper. Hoteliers know what their beds are worth, so generally you get what you pay for. Since my €100 listings are substantially nicer than my €85 listings, I'd spring for the extra expense to have a comfortable home base. In general, a triple room is cheaper than the cost of a double and a single. Traveling alone can be expensive: A single room can be close to the cost of a double.

For each hotel in this chapter, I've listed the average price during relatively busy periods (though not peak-of-peak times). At most hotels, you'll find these rates vary dramatically with demand. A few years back, Budapest built a few too many new hotels; with Hungary's recent economic woes, many—including some luxury hotels—routinely offer deeply discounted rates to attract guests. Use my prices as a rough guideline, but check the hotel's own website or try emailing them to ask for their best price. Comparison-shop and make your choice. This is especially helpful when dealing with the larger hotels that use "dynamic pricing," a computer-generated system that predicts the demand for particular days and sets prices accordingly: High-demand days will often be more than double the price of low-demand days. This makes it impossible for a guidebook to list anything more accurate than a wide range of prices. I regret this trend. While you can assume that hotels listed in this book are good, it's very difficult to say which ones are the better value unless you email to confirm the price.

In general, prices can soften if you do any of the following: offer to pay cash, stay at least three nights, or mention this book. You can also try asking for a cheaper room or a discount, or offer to skip breakfast.

If you're on a tight budget, consider one of Budapest's many hostels (described on page 241). But don't overlook the good-value **Bellevue B&B** (page 244) and **Mária and István**'s place (page 240). At any hotel, three or four people can save money by requesting one big room.

Types of Accommodations

HOTELS

If you're arriving early in the morning, your room probably won't be ready. You can drop your bag safely at the hotel and dive right into sightseeing. When packing, keep in mind that hotel elevators, while becoming more common, are often very small—pack light, or you may need to take your bags up one at a time.

Hoteliers can be a great help and source of advice. Most know their city well, and can assist you with everything from public transit and airport connections to finding a good restaurant, the nearest launderette, or a Wi-Fi hotspot. Of my recommended hotels, all of the places in Budapest (and virtually all those outside of Budapest) have English-speaking staff. In the rare instance where they do not, you'll find a note in my listing.

For environmental reasons, towels are often replaced only when you leave them on the floor. In some cheap hotels, they aren't replaced at all during your stay, so hang them up to dry and reuse. You might be tempted to borrow your hotel towel for your visit to the thermal baths (saving the towel-rental cost). Some hotels frown on this, others forbid it, and a few will loan you a special towel for this purpose.

Most hotels listed here include a buffet breakfast. Some smaller budget places serve no breakfast at all, while larger chain hotels charge (too much) extra for it; in these cases, I've noted it in the listing. Consider having breakfast instead at one of two good cafés I've recommended in the Eating in Budapest chapter: Gerlóczy Café or Callas (see "Budapest's Café Culture" on page 264).

Even at the best places, mechanical breakdowns occur: Air-conditioning malfunctions, sinks leak, hot water turns cold, and toilets gurgle and smell. Report your concerns clearly and calmly at the front desk. For more complicated problems, don't expect instant results.

If you suspect night noise will be a problem (if, for instance, your room is over a nightclub), ask for a quieter room in the back or on an upper floor. To guard against theft in your room, keep valuables out of sight. Some rooms come with a safe, and other hotels have safes at the front desk. I've never bothered using one.

Checkout can pose problems if surprise charges pop up on your bill. If you settle your bill the afternoon before you leave, you'll have time to discuss and address any points of contention (before 19:00, when the night shift usually arrives).

The only tip my recommended accommodations would like is a friendly, easygoing guest. And, as always, I appreciate feedback on your experiences.

Above all, keep a positive attitude. Remember, you're on vacation. If your hotel is a disappointment, spend more time out enjoying the city you came to see.

HOSTELS

You'll pay about €20 per bed to stay at a hostel. Travelers of any age are welcome if they don't mind dorm-style accommodations and meeting other travelers. Most hostels offer kitchen facilities, guest computers, Wi-Fi, and a self-service laundry. Nowadays, concerned about bedbugs, hostels are likely to provide all bedding, including sheets. Family and private rooms may be available on request.

Independent hostels, which Budapest is full of, tend to be easygoing, colorful, and informal (no membership required); see www.hostelz.com and www.hostels.com.

Official hostels are part of Hostelling International (HI) and share an online booking site (www.hihostels.com); these are fairly rare in Hungary. HI hostels typically require that you either have a membership card or pay extra per night.

OTHER ACCOMMODATION OPTIONS

It's easy, and often cheaper than a hotel room, to rent a furnished apartment in Budapest (I've listed a few apartments in this chapter). Consider this option if you're traveling as a family or with friends, staying at least a few days, and like the option of cooking some of your own meals to save money. Most rental apartments are squirrelled away in big, dank buildings; the proprietors can't do much about a gloomy entrance and stairwell, but the apartments themselves are generally bright and nicely furnished.

Websites such as HomeAway and its sister sites VRBO and GreatRentals let you correspond directly with European property owners or managers. When you reserve, you'll typically arrange a meeting time with the proprietor, who will greet you to hand over

Making Hotel Reservations

Reserve your rooms several weeks in advance—or as soon as you've pinned down your travel dates. Note that some national holidays merit your making reservations far in advance (see page 512), and that hotels fill up fast in convention season (mainly September and, to a lesser degree, October).

Requesting a Reservation: It's easiest to book your room through the hotel's website. (For the best rates, always use the hotel's official site and not a booking agency's site.) If there's no reservation form, or for complicated requests, send an email (see the sample request). Most recommended hotels take reservations in English.

The hotelier wants to know:

- the number and type of rooms you need
- the number of nights you'll stay
- your date of arrival (use the Hungarian style for writing dates: year/month/day)
- your date of departure
- any special needs (such as bathroom in the room or down the hall, cheapest room, twin beds vs. double bed, and so on)

Remember to ask for the hotel's best price—many are eager to offer discounts. It can't hurt to mention this book.

Confirming a Reservation: Most places will request a credit-card number to hold your room. If they don't have a secure online reservation form—look for the *https*—you can email it (I do), but it's safer to share that confidential info via a phone call or two emails (splitting your number between them).

Canceling a Reservation: If you must cancel, it's courteous—

the keys. Remember that you'll be basically on your own after that first meeting, so ask any questions up front.

Airbnb and Roomorama make it reasonably easy to find a place to sleep in someone's home. Beds range from air-mattress-in-living-room basic to plush-B&B-suite posh. If you want a place to sleep that's free, Couchsurfing.org is a vagabond's alternative to Airbnb. It lists millions of outgoing members, who host fellow "surfers" in their homes.

Budapest Accommodations

IN PEST

Most travelers find staying in Pest more convenient than sleeping in Buda. Most sights worth seeing are in Pest, which also has a much higher concentration of Metró and tram stops, making it a snap to get around. Pest feels more lively and local than stodgy,

From:	rick@ricksteves.com
Sent:	Today
To:	info@hotelcentral.com
Subject:	Reservation request for 19-22 July

Dear Hotel Central,

I would like to reserve a room for 2 people for 3 nights, arriving 19 July and departing 22 July. If possible, I would like a quiet room with a double bed and a bathroom inside the room.

Please let me know if you have a room available and the price.

Thank you!
Rick Steves

and smart—to do so with as much notice as possible, especially for smaller family-run places—at least three days. Be warned that cancellation policies can be strict; read the fine print or ask about these before you book. Internet deals may require prepayment, with no refunds for cancellations.

Reconfirming Your Reservation: Always call to reconfirm your room reservation a few days in advance. For smaller hotels and pensions, I call again on my day of arrival to tell my host what time I expect to get there (especially important if arriving late—after 17:00).

Phoning: For tips on how to call hotels overseas, see page 487.

touristy Buda, but it's also much more urban (if you don't enjoy big cities, sleep in Buda instead). I've arranged my listings by neighborhood, clustered around the most important sightseeing sectors.

Near Andrássy Út

Andrássy Boulevard is handy, local-feeling, and endlessly entertaining. With its ample restaurants, upscale-residential vibe, and easy connection to downtown (via the M1/yellow line), it's the neighborhood where I prefer to sleep. Most of the hotels listed here are within a two-block walk of this main artery. For locations, see the map on page 233.

$$$ K+K Hotel Opera is wonderfully situated beside the Opera House in the fun "Broadway Quarter"—my favorite home-base location in Budapest. It's a regal splurge, with 200 classy rooms and helpful, professional service. The published rates are sky-high (Sb-€215, Db-€265), but most of the time you can score a better

The Good and Bad of Online Reviews

User-generated travel review websites—such as TripAdvisor, Booking.com, and Yelp—have quickly become a huge player in the travel industry. These sites give you access to actual reports—good and bad—from travelers who have experienced the hotel, restaurant, tour, or attraction.

My hotelier friends in Europe are in awe of these sites' influence. Small hoteliers who want to stay in business have no choice but to work with review sites—which often charge fees for good placement or photos, and tack on commissions if users book through the site instead of directly with the hotel.

While these sites work hard to weed out bogus users, my hunch is that a significant percentage of reviews are posted by friends or enemies of the business being reviewed. I've even seen hotels "bribe" guests (for example, offer a free breakfast) in exchange for a positive review. Also, review sites can become an echo chamber, with one or two flashy businesses camped out atop the ratings, while better, more affordable, and more authentic alternatives sit ignored farther down the list. (For example, I find review sites' restaurant recommendations skew to very touristy, obvious options.)

Remember that a user-generated review is based on the experience of one person. That person likely stayed at one hotel and ate at a few restaurants, and doesn't have much of a basis for comparison. A guidebook is the work of a trained researcher who has exhaustively visited many alternatives to assess their relative value. I recently checked out some top-rated TripAdvisor listings in various towns; when stacked up against their competitors, some are gems, while just as many are duds.

Both types of information have their place, and in many ways, they're complementary. If a hotel or restaurant is well-reviewed in a guidebook or two, and also gets good ratings on one of these sites, it's likely a winner.

deal (often Sb-€110, Db-€125 in summer and on weekends; €25 more for bigger and fancier "executive" rooms, non-smoking floors, air-con, elevator, guest computer, Wi-Fi, parking garage-€16/day, Révay utca 24, district VI, M1: Opera, tel. 1/269-0222, www.kkhotels.com, hotel.opera@kkhotels.hu).

$$$ Kapital Inn is an upscale boutique B&B tucked behind the House of Terror. Its six rooms are pricey but perfectly stylish—there's not a pillow out of place. Albert, who lived in Boston, gives his B&B a sense of real hospitality. You'll enjoy the public spaces, from the restful, momentum-killing terrace to the giant kitchen, where Albert serves breakfast at a huge shared counter (D-€89—a particularly good value, Db-€125, bigger Db-€149, 2-bedroom suite-€199, cheaper Nov-March, air-con, guest computer, Wi-Fi,

Andrássy Út Hotels & Restaurants

1 K+K Hotel Opera
2 Kapital Inn
3 Casati Budapest Hotel
4 easyHotel
5 Hotel Queen Mary
6 To Aventura Boutique Hostel
7 Home Made Hostel
8 Belvárosi Lugas Étterem
9 Menza Restaurant
10 Klassz Bistro
11 Pesti Disznó
12 Bock Bisztró
13 Két Szerecsen
14 Millennium da Pippo
15 Shalimar Rest.
16 Macesz Huszár
17 Kőleves
18 Soul Food
19 Főzelékfaló Ételbár
20 Hummus Bar
21 Duran Szendvics
22 Alexandra Bookstore Café
23 Callas Café
24 Müvész Kávéház
25 Laundry
26 Discover Budapest

SLEEPING

free communal minibar, up several flights of stairs with no elevator, Aradi utca 30, district VI, M1: Vörösmarty utca, mobile 0630-915-2029, www.kapitalinn.com, kapitalinn@kapitalinn.com).

$$$ Casati Budapest Hotel is a solid value, and conveniently located a block off Andrássy út (across the boulevard from the Opera House, then down a side street—just steps from the edge of the ruin-pub zone). This classy, Swiss-run hotel has 25 rooms in four different styles, ranging from "classic" to "cool" (all the same price—review your options online and choose your favorite). Many rooms surround a peaceful courtyard—in this potentially noisy neighborhood, it's worth requesting one of these (prices change constantly, but generally Db-€110-130, cheaper Nov-mid-March, air-con, elevator, guest computer, Wi-Fi, free sauna and fitness room, Paulay Ede utca 31, district VI, M1: Opera, tel. 1/343-1198, www.casatibudapesthotel.hu, info@casatibudapesthotel.hu).

The **$ easyHotel** chain follows a similar model to its parent company, the no-frills easyJet airline: They charge you very little up front, then nickel-and-dime you with optional extras—so you pay only for what you want (pick up the list at entry: TV access-€7.50/24 hours; hairdryer-€1/24 hours; laundry-€10/load; room-cleaning during your stay-€10; €10 extra if arriving before 8:00 or checking out after 14:00, and so on). The 59 rooms feel popped out of a plastic mold, with a nauseating orange color scheme, sterile quasi-linoleum floors, and tiny prefab ship's-head bathrooms. But it's conveniently located (just a block off the busy Great Boulevard and around the corner from the Oktogon), well-run by Zoltán, and the price is right...if you can resist the extras (Sb/Db-€19-69 depending on demand, average rate is €31 for a small room and €35 for a standard room, no breakfast, 24-hour reception, non-smoking, air-con, elevator, free slow Wi-Fi—or pay for faster access, cable Internet access-€2/hour or €10/24 hours, two wheelchair-accessible rooms, Eötvös utca 25A, district VI, M1: Oktogon, tel. 1/411-1982, www.easyhotel.com, info@budapestoktogon.easyhotel.com).

Pest Town Center (Belváros), near Váci Utca

Most hotels on the very central and convenient Váci utca come with overly inflated prices. But these less expensive options—just a block or two off Váci utca—offer some of the best values in Budapest.

$$$ Gerlóczy Café & Rooms, which also serves good meals in its recommended café, is the best spot in central Budapest for affordable elegance. The 19 rooms, set around a classy old spiral-staircase atrium with a stained-glass ceiling, are thoughtfully and stylishly appointed. This gem is an exceptional value (cozy low-beamed attic Db-€104, standard Db-€119, Sb for €12 less, rates include great à la carte breakfast in café, some restaurant noise on lower floors until 23:00, air-con, elevator, Wi-Fi, free minibar, 2 blocks from Váci utca, just off Városház utca at Gerlóczy utca 1, district V, M3: Ferenciek tere or M2: Astoria or M1/M2/M3: Deák tér, tel. 1/501-4000, www.gerloczy.com, info@gerloczy.com).

$$ Butterfly Home, run with care by András (OHN-drash) and Timea, is a B&B with seven spacious, contemporary-style rooms overlooking a quiet pedestrianized lane a block from the happening University Square (Egyetem tér). You'll enjoy the (included) à la carte breakfast in the neighboring restaurant. András really hustles to help you fully appreciate Budapest (Sb-€72-82, Db-€99-112, price depends on size, top-floor "economy" room with bathroom down a half-flight of stairs-Sb-€62/Db-€79, 25 percent cheaper Nov-March, book directly with hotel for the best rates, air-con, guest computer, Wi-Fi, Képíró utca 3, district V, M3/M4: Kálvin tér, mobile 0630-964-7287, www.butterflyhome. hu, info@butterflyhome.hu).

$$ Peregrinus Hotel, just a block off Váci utca, has 25 high-ceilinged, spacious, old-fashioned, parquet-floored rooms (most of which lack air-conditioning—in summer, request a third-floor room with air-con for the same price). Because it's owned by the big ELTE university, many of its guests are visiting professors and lecturers (Sb-€60, Db-€85, Tb-€95, cheaper June-Aug and Nov-March, rates very soft—email to ask about deals, elevator, guest computer, Wi-Fi, free loaner bikes, Szerb utca 3, district V, M4: Fővám tér, tel. 1/266-4911, www.peregrinushotel.hu, peregrinushotel@elte.hu).

$$ Kálvin-Ház, a long block up from the Great Market Hall, has quirky management, a nice classic feel, and 36 big rooms with old-fashioned furnishings and squeaky parquet floors. The newer top-floor rooms have a bit less classic character, but are air-conditioned and tidier than the older rooms (all rooms cost the same, slippery rates vary with demand—generally around Sb-€59, Db-€79, extra bed-€20, elevator, guest computer, Wi-Fi, Gönczy Pál utca 6, district IX, M4: Fővám tér, tel. 1/216-4365, www. kalvinhouse.hu, info@kalvinhouse.hu).

$$ Loft V65 is a peaceful oasis of an apartment right on Váci utca, rented by the family that also runs the recommended Butterfly Home (described earlier). The large, well-appointed apartment has two double bedrooms, one-and-a-half baths, and a kitchen. You can rent just one bedroom (for 2 people, €85 mid-March-mid-Oct, €60-75 off-season) or both bedrooms (for up to 4 people, €95 mid-March-mid-Oct, €75-85 off-season). After you reserve, Gábor and András will arrange a meeting time to give you the keys (non-smoking, air-con, elevator, Wi-Fi, Váci utca 65, district V, M4: Fővám tér or M3: Ferenciek tere, in the mornings call András at mobile 0630-964-7287, in the afternoons call Gábor at US tel. 917-880-3656, www.LoftV65.com, LoftV65@gmail.com).

ACADEMY OF SCI.

To Parliament & 15

23

CENTRAL EUROPEAN UNIVERSITY

27 33 22

To 32

LEOPOLD

VIGYÁZÓ FER.

32

41

ST. ISTVÁN'S BASILICA

26

ANDRÁSSY ÚT

RÉVAY

KÁLDY

SZEKELY

GYULA

To Heroes' Square & City Park

Széchenyi István tér

ZRÍNYI

11

40

DUNA PALOTA

OKTÓBER 6

SAS

24

Bajcsy-Zsilinszky út

M

GOSZDU UDVAR

HOLLÓ

CHAIN BRIDGE

GRESHAM PALACE

13

MÉRLEG

25

12

TOWN

33

RUMBACH STREET SYNAGOGUE

8

To Buda & Castle Hill

Eötvös tér

T

JÓZSEF ATTILA ÚT

BÉCSI

BAJCSY-ZSILINSZKY

AKVÁRIUM KLUB

ANKERHÁZ

RUMBACH SEBESTYÉN

Tram #2

POST

38

József Nádor tér

GERBEAUD CAFÉ

Erzsébet tér

HARMINCAD

Deák Ferenc tér

Deák tér

ASBÓTH

BELGRÁD

DOROTTYA

APÁCZAI

SZENDE

Vörösmarty tér

M

39

FERENC

FERENCIEK ISTVÁN

M

T

KÁROLY KÖRÚT

PESTI VIGADÓ

DEÁK

Vörösmarty tér

FEHÉRHAJÓ ISTVÁN

VÁROSHÁZ

CITY HALL

GERLÓCZY

SEMMELWEIS

Vigadó tér

T

RÁKPART

VIGADÓ

CSERE

TÜRR I.

Kamermayer tér

1

COUNTY HALL

MAHART BOAT DOCK

ARANY J.

JANÓS PETŐFI

RÉGIPOSTI

HISTORIC MCDONALD'S

POST

PILVAX

FORMER PILVAX CAFÉ

VÁRMEGYE

KOSSUTH LAJOS UTCA

SZÉP

LEGENDA BOAT DOCK

"SORRARAS HISTORICISM BLDG. (#15)"

JUGENDSTIL BLDG. (#18)

31

TOWN

KIGYÓ

36

Ferenciek tere

M

FRANCISCAN CHURCH

REÁLTANODA

Petőfi tér

PIARISTA UTCA

Danube

Petőfi tér

PIARISTA KÖZ

KLOTILD PALACES

KÁROLY MIHÁLY

FERENCZY

Károlyi Park

Tram #19 & #41

SZABAD SAJTÓ ÚT

CENTER

35

18

PAPNÖV.

Egyetem

32

Döbrentei tér

ELISABETH BRIDGE

Március 15 tér

P

IRÁNYI

VÁCI UTCA

PÁL

VERES PÁLNÉ

ELTE LAW FACULTY

KIR. PÁL

RUDAS BATHS

IRÁNYI

Tram #2

NYÁRI

SÖRHÁZ

Serbian CHURCH

SZERB

G. GYÖRGY

17

Gellért Hill

CITADELLA

BELGRÁD RÁKPART

21

5

MOLNÁR

3

16

SZARKA

SÓ

BÁSTYA

CITADELLA

River

HAVAS

POST

SÉTÁNY

SZT. GELLÉRT RÁKPART

Fővám tér

M

T

VÁMHÁZ KÖRÚT

i

PIPA

19

GREAT MARKET HALL

BUDA

CAVE CHURCH

VEREJTÉK

UNIV. OF ECONOMICS

SÓHÁZ

N

200 Meters

200 Yards

LIBERTY BRIDGE

Szent Gellért tér

GELLÉRT HOTEL & BATHS

KELENHEGYI

Szent Gellért tér

KEMENES

SLEEPING

Pest Town Center Hotels & Restaurants

1. Gerlóczy Café & Rooms
2. Butterfly Home
3. Peregrinus Hotel
4. Kálvin-Ház Hotel
5. Loft V65
6. Brody House
7. Budapest Rooms
8. ROOMbach Hotel Budapest Center
9. Danube Guest House
10. BudaBaB
11. Four Seasons Gresham Palace
12. Hotel Central Basilica
13. Starlight Suiten
14. Mária & István Rooms
15. To GuestBed Budapest
16. Halkakas Halbisztró
17. Borssó Bistro
18. BorLabor Restaurant
19. Great Market Hall
20. Café Intenzo
21. Trattoria Toscana & Taverna Dionysos
22. Café Kör
23. Mák Bistro
24. DiVino Wine Bar
25. Borkonyha Wine Bar
26. Belvárosi Lugas Étterem
27. Első Pesti Rétesház
28. Macesz Huszár
29. Kőleves
30. Soul Food
31. Főzelékfaló Ételbár
32. Hummus Bar (4)
33. Duran Szendvics (2)
34. To Laundry Budapest & New York Café
35. Centrál Kávéház
36. Jégbüfé Café
37. Bazar Hostel (Laundry)
38. Dorottya G. Pharmacy
39. MÁV Train Ticket Office
40. CEU Bookshop
41. Bestsellers Bookstore

SLEEPING

Map labels: KIRÁLY, KIS DIÓFA, CSÁNYI, KLAUZÁL, KERTÉSZ, KAZINCZY, AKÁCFA, JEWISH QUARTER (& "Ruin Pub" District), ORTHODOX SYNAGOGUE, WESSELÉNYI, DOB, NYÁR, NAGY DIÓFA, To 34, GREAT SYNAGOGUE AND JEWISH MUSEUM, SÍP, DOHÁNY, DOHÁNY ÚT, RÁKÓCZI, Astoria, STÁHLY, PEST, TREFORT, GYULAI, VAS, ELTE CAMPUS, PUSKIN, BRÓDY SÁNDOR, SZENTKIRÁLYI, HORÁNSZKY, POLLACK MIHÁLY, HUNGARIAN NATIONAL MUSEUM, MÚZEUM KÖRÚT, MÚZEUM, KRÚDY LŐRINC, Kálvin tér, SZABÓ REV., BAROSS, ÜLLŐI ÚT, GONCZY PÁL, ERKEL, IMRE, LÓNYAY, MÁTYÁS, CZUCZOR, RÁDAY, ERKEL, KÖZTELEK, KINIZSI, APPLIED ARTS MUSEUM, KŐZRAKTÁR UT, BÁLNA CULTURAL CENTER, To Petőfi Bridge, ZSIL, BAKÁTS, KEMECH, TŰZOLTÓ, POST, To Corvin-negyed, To Petőfi Bridge, HOLOCAUST MEMORIAL CENTER, Tram #47 & #49

Near the National Museum

These two places are within a block or two of the National Museum, just across the Small Boulevard from the Town Center, near M3/M4: Kálvin tér (district VIII).

$$ Brody House comes from artistic DNA—it began as an art gallery that provided a place for its guests to crash, and has evolved into a comfortable, full-service B&B. It fills three spacious floors of a townhouse with eight rooms and three apartments that all ooze a funky, idiosyncratic style. The sprawling public spaces may tempt you to just hang out. Each room is named for an artist who once used it as a studio; they're wildly different and thoughtfully described on their website (Db-€70-120 depending on size, 2-room apartment with kitchenette-€100-130, continental breakfast-€8, air-con in most of the rooms, two stories up with no elevator, Wi-Fi, Bródy Sándor utca 10, tel. 1/266-1211, www.brodyhouse.com, reception@brodyhouse.com).

$ Budapest Rooms is a great budget option, where the Boda family rents five simple but surprisingly stylish, nicely appointed rooms in a dreary residential zone (Sb-€48, Db-€62, Tb-€74, Qb-€84, all have en-suite bathrooms except one room with private bathroom across the hall, includes continental breakfast, Wi-Fi, Szentkirályi 15, tel. 1/630-4743, mobile 0620-569-9513, www.budapestrooms.eu, info@budapestrooms.eu).

In the Jewish Quarter

District VII—the city's Jewish Quarter—has emerged as one of Budapest's most happening nightlife zones, with ramshackle "ruin pubs" popping up all over. These three options offer proximity to the fun, which means they also come with some noise.

$$ ROOMbach Hotel Budapest Center, tucked down a gloomy but central street facing the Rumbach Street Synagogue, has 51 sleek, basic, smallish rooms with a stylish industrial-mod design. Part of a good-value chain, it feels fresh and modern, and the triple-glazed windows work hard to keep out the ruin-pub noise (Db-€85-95 in high season, can be as low as €75 off-season, air-con, elevator, Wi-Fi, parking-€12, Rumbach Sebestyén utca 14, tel. 1/413-0253, www.roombachhotel.com, info@roombach.com).

$ Danube Guest House's six basic, tidy, gaudily decorated rooms can be noisy for light sleepers (more so in warm weather, as open windows are the only "air-conditioning" here—ask for a quieter courtyard room). But if you want proximity to one of the city's liveliest nightlife areas, this place is a great value (Sb-€45, small Db-€49, bigger Db-€59, guest computer, Wi-Fi, Dohány utca 16, district VII, M2/red: Astoria, tel. 1/788-2891, mobile 0620-419-

3986, www.danubeguesthouse.com, danube.guesthouse@upcmail.hu).

$ At **BudaBaB**, thoughtful Americans Ryan and Ron rent two rooms in their apartment. You'll feel like you're a houseguest, as everybody shares the bathrooms and the comfy living room; they appreciate conscientious guests (smaller room: S-€30, D-€45, T-€55; larger room: S-€40, D-€55, T-€70, Q-€85; cash or pre-pay with PayPal for 3 percent surcharge, Akácfa utca 18, district VII, M2: Blaha Lujza tér, or tram #4 or #6 to Wesselényi stop, tel. 1/267-5240, www.budabab.com, info@budabab.com).

In Leopold Town, near the Chain Bridge

The first listing below is the city's most prestigious address; the next two are business-class options that are nicely located and worth booking if you can get a discounted rate. All of these are a short stroll from the delightful St. István tér/Zrínyi utca restaurant zone.

$$$ Four Seasons Gresham Palace is Budapest's top hotel—and one of its most expensive. Stay here only if money is truly no object. You'll sleep in what is arguably Budapest's finest Art Nouveau building. Damaged in World War II, the Gresham Palace sat in disrepair for decades. Today it's sparkling from a recent head-to-toe renovation, and every detail in its lavish public spaces and 179 rooms is perfectly in place. Even if you're not sleeping here, dip into the lobby and café to soak in the elegance (non-view Db-€420-510, Danube-view Db-€630, prices don't include 22 percent tax—not a typo, breakfast-€30-35, non-smoking rooms, air-con, elevator, guest computer, Wi-Fi, top-floor spa, Széchenyi tér 5, district V, between M1: Vörösmarty tér and M2: Kossuth tér, tel. 1/268-6000, www.fourseasons.com/budapest, budapest.reservations@fourseasons.com). For more on the building's history, see page 121.

$$ Hotel Central Basilica has 47 forgettable business-class rooms in the heart of the tidy and sane Leopold Town, near St. István's Basilica and the surrounding yuppie dining and nightlife zone. The location makes it worth considering if you can score a good price (Sb-€99, Db-€109, superior Db-€139, but prices very soft—usually more like Db-€89, even cheaper Nov-March, air-con, elevator, pay Wi-Fi, Hercegprímás utca 8, district V, M1: Bajcsy-Zsilinszky út, tel. 1/328-5010, www.hotelcentral-basilica.hu, info@hotelcentral-basilica.hu).

$$ Starlight Suiten has 54 spacious suites—each with a living room, bedroom, and kitchenette—on a quiet but dull street directly behind the Gresham Palace (listed earlier). While rates can range widely (€80-130), suites often go for €90—at that price, this place is a great deal (includes small breakfast—or pay for a bigger one, air-con, elevator, guest computer, pay Wi-Fi, free fitness room and sauna, Mérleg utca 6, district V, M1: Vörösmarty tér, tel. 1/484-3700, www.starlighthotels.com, manager.merleg@starlighthotels.com).

On or near the Great Boulevard

All of these places are on or near Budapest's Great Boulevard (Nagykörút) ring road—though they are spread far and wide. Tram #4 and #6 travel around the Great Boulevard, connecting all of these, and most are also near a Metró stop.

Friendly Budget Beds near Üllői Út: **$ Mária and István,** your chatty Hungarian aunt and uncle, are saving a room for you in their Old World apartment. For warmth and hospitality at youth-hostel prices, you can bunk in one of their two simple, old-fashioned rooms, which share a bathroom. The smaller room is cheaper and quieter; the bigger room gets some street noise on weekends (S-€20-22, D-€30-34, T-€39-42, price depends on size of room and length of stay—longer is cheaper, no breakfast but guests' kitchen, cash only, elevator plus a few stairs, Ferenc körút 39, district IX, M3 or tram #4/#6: Corvin-negyed, tel. 1/216-0768, www.mariaistvan. hu, mariaistvan@upcmail.hu). From the Corvin-negyed Metró stop, follow signs for exit "E," bear right up the stairs, and walk straight about a block and a half, looking for #39 (on the left; dial 19 at the door and ride the elevator to floor 4).

Near Margaret Bridge: **$ GuestBed Budapest** has five apartments—two in a mellow residential zone near the Margaret Bridge and the Great Boulevard, north of downtown Pest, and three more in the Andrássy út area (one in the Jewish Quarter, another near the Nyugati/Western train station, and another near St. István's Basilica—all well-described on their website). The straightforward apartments, all with full kitchens, are not luxurious—they're an old-fashioned mix of parquet floors and Ikea furniture. But this place is distinguished by its welcoming and conscientious owners, János and József. When you book, arrange a time to meet to check in and get oriented. They also rent a "B&B" room in their own apartment (sharing their bathroom)—you'll really feel like you're staying with local friends (B&B room-€45, apartment-€60, 2-bedroom apartment-€65, for best rates book directly with hotel, Wi-Fi, airport pick-up service, János also offers bike and walking tours, Katona József utca 39, district XIII, tram #4/#6: Jászai Mari tér, mobile 03670-258-5194, www.guestbudapestapartment.com, budapestrentapartment@gmail.com).

Near the Oktogon: **$ Hotel Queen Mary** (named not for the

British monarch, but for the owner's wife) is mysteriously cheap and often empty, with impersonal service and 26 unimaginative rooms. The neighborhood is dingy and gloomy (two blocks beyond the end of the happening Franz Liszt Square), but the place is affordable for those on a tight budget and also likely to have rooms when other hotels are full (Sb-€50, Db-€60, Tb-€70, prices vary with demand, 20 percent cheaper Nov-March, air-con, elevator, Wi-Fi, Kertész utca 34—for location see map on page 233, district VII, between M1: Oktogon and M2: Blaha Lujza tér, closer to tram #4/#6: Király utca, tel. 1/413-3510, www.hotelqueenmary.hu, info@hotelqueenmary.hu).

Hostels

Budapest has seemingly dozens of apartments that have been taken over by young entrepreneurs, offering basic, rough-around-the-edges hostel charm. You'll buzz in at the door and climb up a creaky, dank, and smelly staircase to a funky little enclave of fellow backpackers. Most of these places have just three rooms (one double and two small dorms) and feel more like communes than the finely tuned, high-capacity youth-hostel machines common in many other cities. As each of these fills a niche (party, artsy, communist-themed, etc.), it's hard to recommend just one—read reviews on a hostel site (such as www.hostels.com) and find one that suits your hosteling philosophy. For hostel locations, see the map on page 233.

$ Aventura Boutique Hostel is a low-key, colorful, and stylish place in a dreary urban neighborhood near the Nyugati/Western train station. Well-run by friendly Ágnes, it's both homey and tastefully mod, with clean, imaginatively decorated rooms (4 rooms, bed in 4- to 8-bed dorm-€20, D-€42, price can be much less off-season and if you book in advance, breakfast-€2-5, includes sheets, towel rental-450 Ft, guest computer, Wi-Fi, kitchen, laundry service, massage available, across the busy Great Boulevard ring road and a very long block from Nyugati train station at 12 Visegrádi utca, district XIII, M3: Nyugati pu., tel. 1/239-0782, www.aventurahostel.com, info@aventurahostel.com). They also rent several apartments—two nearby, the other near St. István's Basilica (all Db-€84).

$ Home Made Hostel is a fun-and-funky slumbermill artfully littered with secondhand furniture. It's run and decorated with a sense of humor. With 20 beds in four rooms located near the Oktogon, it's another good option (bunk in 8-bed dorm-€14, in 4-bed dorm-€16, D-€39, apartment Db-€42, includes sheets and towels, no breakfast, guest computer, Wi-Fi, kitchen, laundry service, Teréz körút 22, district VI, M1: Oktogon, tel. 1/302-2103, www.homemadehostel.com, info@homemadehostel.com).

IN BUDA
Víziváros

The Víziváros neighborhood—or "Water Town"—is the lively part of Buda squeezed between Castle Hill and the Danube, where fishermen and tanners used to live. Víziváros is the most pleasant central area to stay on the Buda side of the Danube, with fine views across the river toward the Parliament building and bustling Pest. It's expensive and a little less convenient than Pest, but feels less urban.

The following hotels are in district I, between the Chain Bridge and Buda's busy Margit körút ring road. Trams #19 and #41 zip along the embankment in either direction. Batthyány tér, a few minutes' walk away, is a handy center with lots of restaurants (see next page), a Metró stop (M2/red line), and the HÉV train to Óbuda and Szentendre. All of these places come with professional, helpful staff.

$$$ Hotel Victoria, with 27 stylish, business-class rooms—each with a grand river view and attention to detail—is a class act.

This tall, narrow place (three rooms on each of nine floors) is run with pride and attention to detail by on-the-ball manager Zoltán and his friendly staff (Sb-€129, Db-€134, extra bed-€30, 20 percent cheaper Nov-March, air-con, elevator, guest computer, Wi-Fi, cheap international phone calls, free sauna, free afternoon tea for guests 16:00-17:00, reserve ahead for €16/day parking garage or park free on street, Bem rakpart 11, tel. 1/457-8080, www.victoria.hu, victoria@victoria.hu). The painstakingly restored 19th-century Hubay Palace behind the hotel (entrance next to reception) is used for concerts and other events. It feels like a museum, with inlaid floors, stained-glass windows, and stuccoed walls and ceilings—even if you're not staying at Hotel Victoria, drop in and ask to see it.

$$$ art'otel impresses New York City sophisticates. Every detail—from the breakfast dishes to the carpets to the good-luck blackbird perched in each room—was designed by American artist Donald Sultan. This stylish, fun hotel has 165 rooms spread between two attached buildings: the new section fronting the Danube and a restored older house just behind it (high rack rates, but usually Sb/Db-€99-165 depending on season, figure Sb/Db-€129 in summer, Danube view-€20 more, bigger "art rooms plus"-€35 more, deluxe "art suites"-€60 more, breakfast-€14, non-smoking rooms, air-con, elevator, guest computer, Wi-Fi, free sauna and

Buda Hotels & Restaurants

1. Hotel Victoria
2. art'otel
3. Bellevue B&B
4. St. George Residence
5. Hotel Castle Garden
6. Burg Hotel
7. Vár Bistro
8. Ruszwurm Café
9. 21 Magyar Vendéglő
10. Baltazár
11. Batthyány tér Eateries
12. To Csalogány 26
13. CBA Grocery

SLEEPING

mini-exercise room, bike rental, Bem rakpart 16-19, tel. 1/487-9487, www.artotels.com, budapest@artotels.com).

$ Bellevue B&B is one of Budapest's best deals. It hides in a quiet residential area on the Víziváros hillside just below the Fishermen's Bastion staircase. This gem is run by retired economists Judit (YOO-deet) and Lajos (LIE-yosh) Szuhay, who lived in Canada for four years and speak flawless English. The breakfast room and some of the six straightforward, comfortable rooms have views across the Danube to the Parliament and Pest. Judit and Lajos love to chat, and pride themselves on offering genuine hospitality and a warm welcome (let them know what time you're arriving). As this B&B is understandably popular, book ahead (Sb-€50-65, Db-€60-75; price depends on room size, view, and length of stay; 20-30 percent cheaper Nov-March, cash only, non-smoking, air-con, Wi-Fi; M2: Batthyány tér plus a 10-minute uphill walk, or bus #16 from Deák, Széchenyi, or Adam Clark squares to Dónati utca plus a 2-minute walk uphill, then downhill—they'll email you detailed directions; Szabó Ilonka utca 15/B, mobile 0630-370-8678 or 0630-951-5494, www.bellevuebudapest.com, judit@bellevuebudapest.com).

Castle Hill

Romantics may enjoy calling Castle Hill home (district I). These places couldn't be closer to the Castle Hill sights, but they're in a tourist zone—dead at night, and less convenient to Pest than other listings.

$$$ St. George Residence, just a couple of short blocks from Matthias Church, rents 24 elegant rooms around a restful garden courtyard. Each room is different and comes with a kitchenette (Db-€129, more for bigger rooms, air-con, Wi-Fi, Fortuna utca 4, tel. 1/393-5700, www.stgeorgehotel.hu, info@stgeorgehotel.hu).

$$ Hotel Castle Garden huddles above an Italian restaurant in a tranquil, park-like neighborhood just outside the castle's Vienna Gate (north end). As it's roughly on the way between the castle and Széll Kálmán tér, it's relatively handy, though still less convenient than the Víziváros listings. But its 39 tastefully appointed, contemporary rooms are a good value for the quality (Sb-€79, Db-€89, maybe less June-Aug and Nov-April, "superior" room with terrace for €20 more, air-con, elevator, guest computer, Wi-Fi, parking garage-€10, Lovas út 41, M2: Széll Kálmán tér; exit the castle through the Vienna Gate and turn left along the wall, or hike up from Széll Kálmán tér and turn right along the castle wall; tel. 1/224-7420, www.castlegarden.hu, hotel@castlegarden.hu).

$$ Burg Hotel, with 26 overpriced rooms on Holy Trinity Square (Szentháromság tér), is simply efficient: concrete, spacious, and comfy, if a bit worn, with a professional staff. You'll find more conveniently located hotels for less money elsewhere, but if you simply *must* stay in a modern hotel across the street from Matthias Church, this is it (official rates: Sb-€105, Db-€115, Db apartment-€134, but rates very soft—usually more like €85-99, extra bed-€15, 10 percent discount off their official online rate if you book direct and mention this book—unless they're very busy, 20 percent cheaper Nov-March, request view room for no extra charge, entirely non-smoking, no elevator, air-con, top-floor rooms are extremely long, family rooms, guest computer, Wi-Fi, Szentháromság tér 7, tel. 1/212-0269, www.burghotelbudapest.com, hotel.burg@mail.datanet.hu).

EATING IN BUDAPEST

Contents

Hungarian cuisine is one of Europe's most delightful—rich, spicy, smooth, and delicious. And Budapest specializes in trendy restaurants that mix Hungarian flavors with international flair, making the food here even tastier. Best of all, the prices are reasonable, especially if you venture off the main tourist trail. This is affordable sightseeing for your palate.

Dining Tips

When restaurant-hunting, choose a spot filled with locals, not the place with the big neon signs boasting, *"We Speak English and Accept Credit Cards."* Most restaurants have an English menu posted (or you can ask to see one). Any restaurant specializing in purely "traditional Hungarian food" is catering almost entirely to tourists. Locals prefer international-slash-Hungarian places, which is what I've emphasized in my listings.

If the place isn't full, you can usually just seat yourself (get a server's attention to be sure your preferred table is OK)—the American-style "hostess," with a carefully managed waiting list, isn't common here.

Once seated, feel free to take your time. In fact, it might be difficult to dine in a hurry. Only a rude waiter will rush you. Hungarian service is polite, but formal; don't expect "Hi, I'm László and I'll be your server—how you folks doin' tonight?" chumminess. At traditional places, your tuxedoed server might bring your food to the table, bow with a formal click of the heels...then go back to the kitchen to apply more wax to his moustache. At any eatery, good service is deliberate (slow to an American).

An *étterem* ("eatery") is a nice sit-down restaurant, while a *vendéglő* is usually more casual (similar to a tavern or an inn). A

söröző ("beer place") is a pub that sells beer and food, ranging from a small selection of snacks to a full menu. A *kávéház* ("coffeehouse"), or café, is where Budapesters gather to meet friends, get a caffeine fix...and sometimes to have a great meal. (I've listed my favorite cafés—including a few that are also some of Budapest's best eateries—on page 264.) Other cafés serve only light food, or sometimes only desserts. But if you want a wide choice of cakes, look for a *cukrászda* (pastry shop—*cukr* means "sugar").

Ethnic restaurants provide a break from Hungarian fare (in the unlikely event you need one). Budapest has abundant vegetarian, Italian, Indian, Chinese, and other non-Hungarian eateries; I've listed my favorites. Once you leave the capital, the options are fewer, and the food gets even heartier and cheaper.

Occasionally, when you order a main course, it includes only the item itself (with no garnishes, side dishes, or starches). In these cases, you can order your choice of sides—listed on a separate page of the menu, and paid for separately. If you see a page listing these extras, ask the server if anything is included with your main dish.

Menus usually list drink prices by the tenth of a liter, or deciliter (dl), not by the glass; this is an honest and common practice, but can trip up visitors.

When the server comes to take your order, he might say *"Tessék"* (TEHSH-shayk), or maybe the more formal *"Tessék parancsolni"* (TEHSH-shayk PAW-rawn-chohl-nee)—"Please command, sir." When they bring the food, they will probably say, *"Jó étvágyat!"* (yoh AYT-vah-yawt)—"Bon appétit." When you're ready for the bill, you can simply say, *"Fizetek"* (FEE-zeh-tehk)—"I'll pay."

At any restaurant, it's smart to check the bill and count your change carefully. While most Hungarian restaurateurs are honest, rip-off joints abound in downtown Budapest's tourist zone—especially along the main walking street, Váci utca. (Frankly, I'd never eat on Váci utca, which practically guarantees bad food and service for high prices.) Avoid any place with a menu that doesn't list prices, and tune in to the fine print (such as the service charge—explained next).

TIPPING

Hungarians tip less than Americans do. Most restaurants in Budapest automatically add a 10 percent service charge to the bill.

(A few of the more tourist-oriented eateries have nudged this up to 12 or even 15 percent, which Hungarian diners consider excessive.) The extra charge should be noted on the menu (if it's not, complain), and appears as a line item after the subtotal on the bill (look for "service," "tip," *felszolgálási díj,* or *szervízdíj*). In these cases, an additional tip is not necessary for adequate service.

If the service fee is not included, waiters expect a tip of about 10 percent (or a little less; more than 10 percent is reserved for exceptional service).

For more on tipping, see page 482.

Hungarian Cuisine

Most Eastern Europeans dine on a starchy meat-and-potatoes cuisine to maximize calories and carbs through a harsh winter. But, as with many things, Hungary is different. Hungarians don't just eat to live—they live to eat. This makes Hungarian cuisine the undisputed best in Central Europe. It delicately blends Magyar peasant cooking (with rich spices), refined by the elegance of French preparation, with a delightful smattering of flavors from the vast, multiethnic Austro-Hungarian Empire (including Germanic, Balkan, Jewish, and Carpathian). Everything is heavily seasoned: with paprika, tomatoes, and peppers of every shape, color, size, and flavor.

When foreigners think of Hungarian cuisine, what comes to mind is goulash. But tourists are often disappointed when "real Hungarian goulash" isn't the thick stew that they were expecting. The word "goulash" comes from the Hungarian *gulyás leves,* or "shepherd's soup"— a tasty, rustic, nourishing dish originally eaten by cowboys and shepherds on the Great Hun-

EATING

garian Plain. Here in its homeland, it's a clear, spicy broth with chunks of meat, potatoes, and other vegetables. Elsewhere (such as in the Germanic and Slavic countries that are Hungary's neighbors), the word "goulash" does describe a thick stew. The hearty Hungarian stew called *pörkölt* is probably closer to what most people think of as goulash.

Aside from the obligatory *gulyás*, make a point of trying another unusual Hungarian specialty: cold fruit soup *(hideg gyümölcs leves)*. This sweet, cream-based treat—generally eaten before the meal, even though it tastes more like a dessert—is usually made with *meggy* (sour cherries), but you'll also see versions with *alma* (apples) or *körte* (pears). Other Hungarian soups *(levesek)* include *bableves* (bean soup), *zöldségleves* (vegetable soup), *gombaleves* (mushroom soup), *halászlé* (fish broth with paprika), and *húsleves* (meat or chicken soup). The ultimate staple of traditional Hungarian home-cooking, but rarely served in restaurants, is *főzelék*—a simple but tasty wheat flour-thickened stew that can be supplemented with various vegetables and meats (served at cheap restaurants around Budapest—see the Főzelékfaló Ételbár listing on page 263).

Hungarians adore all kinds of meat. *Hús* or *marhahús* is beef, *csirke* is chicken, *borjú* is veal, *kacsa* is duck, *liba* is goose, *sertés* is

pork, *sonka* is ham, *kolbász* is sausage, *szelet* is schnitzel (*Bécsi szelet* means Wiener schnitzel)—and the list goes on. One trendy ingredient you'll see on menus is *mangalica*. This uniquely Hungarian, free-range woolly pig (basically a domesticated boar) is high in unsaturated fat—which fits perfectly with the current foodie culture that elevates the mighty pig. *Libamáj* is goose liver, which shows up everywhere (anything prepared "Budapest style" is topped with goose liver). Lard is used extensively in cooking, making Hungarian cuisine very rich and filling.

Meat is often covered with delicious sauces or garnishes, from rich cream sauces to spicy pastes to fruit jam. For classic Hungarian flavors, you can't beat chicken or veal *paprikás* (described in the "Paprika Primer" sidebar).

Vegetarians have a tricky time in traditional Hungarian restaurants, many of which offer only a plate of deep-fried vegetables. A traditional Hungarian "salad" is composed mostly or entirely of pickled vegetables (pickles, cabbage, peppers, and others); even many modern restaurants haven't quite figured out how to do a good, healthy, leafy salad. Fortunately, the more modern, trendy eateries in the capital often offer excellent vegetarian options.

Starches *(köretek)*—which you'll sometimes order separate from the meat course—can include *nokedli* (small potato dumplings, a.k.a. *Spätzle*), *galuska* (noodles), *burgonya* (potatoes), *krumpli* (French fries), *krokett* (croquettes), or *rizs* (rice). *Kenyér* (bread) often comes with the meal. A popular snack—especially to accompany a wine-tasting—is a *pogácsa*, a deep-fried savory doughnut.

Sometimes your main dish will come with steamed, grilled, or deep-fried vegetables. A common side dish is *káposzta* (cabbage, often prepared like sauerkraut). You may also see *töltött káposzta* (cabbage stuffed with meat) or *töltött paprika* (stuffed peppers). *Lescó* (LEH-chew) is the Hungarian answer to ratatouille: a richly flavorful stew of tomatoes, peppers, and other vegetables.

Thin, crêpe-like pancakes *(palacsinta)* are sometimes served as a main dish. A delicious traditional Hungarian dish is *Hortobágyi palacsinta* (Hortobágy pancakes, named for the Hungarian Great Plain where the dish originates). This is a savory crêpe wrapped around a tasty meat filling and drenched with creamy paprika sauce.

Pancakes also appear as desserts, stuffed and/or covered with fruit, jam, chocolate sauce, walnuts, poppy seeds, or whipped cream. Most famous is the *Gundel palacsinta*, named for the top-of-the-line Budapest restaurant—stuffed with walnuts and raisins in a rum sauce, topped with chocolate sauce, and flambéed.

Pastries are a big deal in Hungary. In the late 19th century, pastry-making caught on here in an attempt to keep up with the

renowned desserts of rival Vienna. Today Hungary's streets are still lined with *cukrászda* (pastry shops) where you can simply point to whichever treat you'd like. Try the *Dobos torta* (a many-layered chocolate-and-caramel cream cake), *somlói galuska* (a dumpling with vanilla, nuts, and chocolate), anything with *gesztenye* (chestnuts), and *rétes* (strudel with various fillings, including *túrós*, curds). And many *cukrászda* also serve *fagylalt* (ice cream, *fagyi* for short), sold by the *gomboc* (ball).

DRINKS

Kávé (KAH-vay) and *tea* (TEH-aw) are coffee and tea. (Confusingly, *tej* is not tea—it's milk.) As for water (*víz*, veez) it comes as *szódavíz* (soda water, sometimes just carbonated tap water) or *ásványvíz* (spring water, more expensive).

Hungary is first and foremost a wine country. For the complete rundown on Hungarian wines, see the next section.

Hungary isn't particularly well-known for its beer (*sör*, pro-

Paprika Primer

The quintessential ingredient in Hungarian cuisine is paprika. In Hungarian, the word *paprika* can mean both peppers (red or

green) and the spice that's made from them. Peppers can be stewed, stuffed, sautéed, baked, grilled, or pickled. For seasoning, red shakers of dried paprika join the salt and pepper on tables.

Locals say paprika is best from the sunny south of Hungary. There are more than 40 varieties of paprika spice, with two main types: hot (*csípős* or *erős*) and sweet (*édesnemes* or simply *édes*, often comes in a white can; sometimes also called *csemege*—"delicate"). Hungarians typically cook with sweet paprika to add flavor and color. Then, at the table, they put out hot paprika so each diner can adjust the

heat to his or her preferred taste. A can or bag of paprika is a handy and tasty souvenir of your trip (see the Shopping in Budapest chapter).

On menus, anything cooked *paprikás* (PAW-pree-kash) comes smothered in a spicy, creamy red stew. Most often you'll see this option with *csirke* (chicken) or *borjú* (veal), and it's generally served with dumpling-like boiled egg noodles called *nokedli* (similar to German *Spätzle*). This dish is *the* Hungarian staple—if you sample just one dish in Hungary, make it chicken or veal *paprikás*.

To add even more kick to your food, ask for a jar of the bright-red paste called *Erős Pista* (EH-rewsh PEESH-taw). Literally "Spicy Steve," this Hungarian answer to Tabasco is best used sparingly. Or try *Édes Anna* (AY-desh AW-naw, "Sweet Anna"), a variation that's more sweet than spicy.

nounced "shewr"), but Dreher and Borsodi are two of the better brands. *Villagos* is lager; if you prefer something darker, look for *barna* (brown).

Hungary is almost as proud of its spirits as its wines. The local firewater, *pálinka*, is a powerful schnapps made from various fruits (most often plum, *szilva*; or apricots, *barack*). Also look for the pear-flavored Vilmos brandy.

Unicum is a unique and beloved Hungarian bitter liquor made

of 40 different herbs and aged in oak casks. Look for the round bottle with the red cross on the label. The flavor is powerfully unforgettable—like Jägermeister, but harsher. Unicum started out as a medicine and remains a popular digestif for easing an upset stomach (especially if you've eaten too much rich food—not an uncommon problem in Hungary). Purists claim it's better to drink it at room temperature (so you can fully appreciate its bouquet), but novices find it easier to slug back when chilled. If the original Unicum overwhelms your palate, try one of the newer variations: Unicum Next, with more of a citrus flavor, and Unicum Szilva (with a golden plum on the label), which is aged in plums that cut some of the bitterness with a rich sweetness (www.zwack.hu). For more on the epic story behind Unicum, see page 67.

If you're drinking with some new Magyar friends, impress them with the standard toast: *Egészségedre* (EH-gehs-shay-gehdreh; "to your health").

HUNGARIAN WINES

Wine *(bor)* is an essential part of Hungarian cuisine. Grapes have been cultivated here since Roman times, and Hungarian wines had an excellent reputation (winning raves from the likes of France's King Louis XIV and Ludwig von Beethoven) up until World War II. Under communism, most vineyards were collectivized, and the quality suffered terribly. But since the end of that era, many wine-growing families have reclaimed their property and gone back to their roots (literally). Today they're attempting to resuscitate the reputation of Hungarian wines. They're off to a great start.

Hungary boasts 22 designated wine-growing regions. The area around Eger is the most famous, but that's only the beginning. The Villány Hills south of Pécs—with a semi-Mediterranean climate at the same latitude as Bordeaux, France—produce full-bodied, tannic reds. The Sopron region near the Austrian border produces both reds and whites. (Northern reds like these tend to be fruity and light.) The hillsides above Lake Balaton (west of Budapest) and the Szekszárd area (along the Danube in southern Hungary) also produce well-respected wines.

Whites *(fehér)* can be sweet *(édes)*, half-dry *(félszáraz)*, or dry *(száraz)*. Whites include the standards (riesling, chardonnay), as well as some wines made from more typically Hungarian grapes: **leányka** ("little girl"), a half-dry, fairly heavy, white table wine; **cserszegi fűszeres**, a spicy, light white that can be fruity; the half-dry, full-bodied *hárslevelű* ("linden leaf"); and the dry *furmint* and *kéknyelű* ("blue stalk").

Reds *(vörös)* include the familiar varieties (cabernet sauvignon, cabernet franc, merlot, pinot noir), and some that are less familiar. *Kekporto* is better known as *blauer Portugieser* in German-speaking countries. In Eger, don't miss **Bull's Blood,** a.k.a. Egri Bikavér, a distinctive blend of reds that comes with a fun local legend (described on page 375). The spicy, medium-body *kékfrankos* ("blue Frankish") supposedly got its name because when Napoleonic sol-

diers were here, they could pay either with valuable blue-colored bank notes or unstable white ones...and local vintners wanted the blue francs. (Like most wine origin legends, this story is untrue— *kékfrankos* wasn't cultivated here until after Napoleon's time.)

Probably the most famous Hungarian wine is **Tokaji Aszú,** a sweet, late-harvest, honey-colored dessert wine made primarily from *furmint* grapes. Known as the "wine of kings, and the king of wines," Tokaji Aszú is a D.O.C. product, meaning that to have that name, it must be grown in a particular region. Tokaj is a town in northeastern Hungary, while *aszú* is a "noble rot" grape. The wine's unique, concentrated flavor is made possible by a fungus *(Botrytis cinerea)* that thrives on the grapes in the late fall. The grapes are left on the vine, where they burst and wither like raisins before they are harvested in late October and November. This sucks the water out of the grape, leaving behind very high sugar content and a deep golden color. Tokaji Aszú wines are numbered, from three to six, indicating how many eight-gallon tubs *(puttony)* of these "noble rot" grapes were added to the base wine—the higher the number, the sweeter the wine. Other variations on Tokaji can be less sweet. (This might sound like another bizarre Hungarian custom, but the French Sauterne and German Beerenauslese wines are also made from "noble rot" grapes. The similarly named French Tokay wine— which derives from the same word—is a different story altogether.)

Finally, note that, except for Bull's Blood and Tokaji Aszú, Hungarian wines are not widely available in the US. Packing home a bottle or two (in your checked luggage) is a unique souvenir.

EATING

Restaurants in Budapest

Thanks to Budapest's ever-evolving culinary scene, there's no shortage of places to dine. I can barely keep track of what's new—and scouting new restaurants is the highlight of my research chores. The broad range of options and healthy sense of one-upmanship among local chefs keep prices reasonable and quality high. The foodie scene here is boom-and-bust: A place quickly acquires a huge and enthusiastic following, but soon falls from grace as an even more enticing competitor opens up shop.

While you'll find the standard Hungarian fare, most big-city restaurants like to dabble in international cuisine. Many of my listings feature an international menu with some Hungarian flourishes. (If you want truly traditional Hungarian fare, you'll actually do better in smaller towns.) The good news: Most Hungarian chefs are so skilled that any cuisine is well-executed here.

Most Hungarians dine between 19:00 and 21:00, peaking around 20:00; trendy zones such as St. István Square and Franz Liszt Square, which attract an after-work crowd, are lively earlier in the evening.

Lunch Specials: Many Budapest restaurants offer lunch specials, called *napimenü*, on weekdays. As these are designed for local office workers on their lunch breaks rather than for tourists, they're often not advertised in English—but if you see the magic word *napimenü*, ask about it. Even at trendy, otherwise pricey eateries, you'll generally pay around 1,000 Ft for a fixed menu (soup and main dish or main dish and dessert; no choices—take it or leave it).

IN PEST

I've listed these options by neighborhood, for easy reference with your sightseeing.

In Pest's Town Center (Belváros), near Váci Utca

When you ask natives about good places to eat on Váci utca, they just roll their eyes. Budapesters understand that only rich tourists who don't know better would throw their money away on the relatively bad food and service along this high-profile pedestrian drag.

But wander a few blocks off the tourist route, and you'll discover alternatives with fair prices and better food. For locations, see the map on page 237.

Gerlóczy Café is tucked on a peaceful little square next to the giant City Hall. This classy café features French, Hungarian, and international cuisine with several seating options (out on the square, in the coffee-house interior, or upstairs). There's a good permanent menu, plus changing specials (Friday is fish day). The clientele is a mix of tourists and upscale-urban Budapesters, including local politicians and actors from several nearby theaters. With a take-your-time ambience that's arguably more Parisian than Hungarian—and with live harp or piano music inside from 19:00 to 23:00—this is a particularly inviting spot (3,000-5,000-Ft main dishes, 1,900-Ft two-course or 2,500-Ft three-course lunch specials available Mon-Thu, good breakfasts, fresh-baked pastries and bread, daily 7:00-23:00, 2 blocks from Váci utca, just off Városház utca at Gerlóczy utca 1, district V, M3: Ferenciek tere, tel. 1/501-4000). They rent good rooms, too (see page 234).

Halkakas Halbisztró ("Fishrooster Fish Bistro") is a tight, tidy, cheery, colorful French-style bistro serving up mostly Hungarian fish with a variety of sauces. In this landlocked country, that means freshwater fish (catfish, pikeperch, trout, and so on)—better than it sounds, and very local (1,600-2,000-Ft main dishes, Mon-Sat 12:00-22:00, closed Sun, Veres Pálné utca 33, mobile 0630-226-0638).

Borssó Bistro, in the newly spiffed-up area near University Square (Egyetem tér), is a trendy eatery offering small portions of delicately assembled modern French cuisine with a bit of Hungarian flair. The cozy two-story interior's ambience, like the cuisine, is an elegant yet accessible blend of old and new. They also have outdoor tables and occasional live music. Reservations are important at this pricey, popular place (3,600-5,000-Ft main dishes, Tue 18:00-23:00, Wed-Sun 12:00-23:00, closed Mon, Király Pál utca 14, district V, M3/M4: Kálvin tér, tel. 1/789-0975, mobile 0620-807-7087).

BorLabor ("Wine Lab") features traditional, regional, updated Hungarian specialties at reasonable prices in a warm, mod, romantic wine-cellar atmosphere. It's not as trendy as many other Budapest eateries...but that's the point (2,500-3,000-Ft main dishes, daily 12:00-24:00, a block north of Váci utca at Veres Pálné utca 7, district V, M3: Ferenciek tere, tel. 1/328-0382).

Great Market Hall: At the far south end of Váci utca, you can eat a quick lunch on the upper floor of the Great Market Hall (Nagyvásárcsarnok). **Fakanál Étterem**—the glassed-in, sit-down cafeteria above the main entrance—is touristy, but offers good seating (2,000-3,200-Ft main dishes, Mon-Fri 10:00-17:00, Sat 10:00-14:00, closed Sun; live music most days 12:00-15:00). The sloppy, stand-up stalls along the right side of the building are cheaper, but quality can vary (grab a bar stool or you'll stand while you munch). Locals love the **Lángos** stand for deep-fried bread slathered with sour cream and cheese (add garlic for some kick). Or you can assemble a **picnic**—produce and butcher stands line the main floor, and an Aldi supermarket is in the basement (the end nearest Váci utca; market hall open Mon 6:00-17:00, Tue-Fri 6:00-18:00, Sat 6:00-15:00, closed Sun; supermarket open longer hours, Fővám körút 1-3, district IX, M4: Fővám tér).

Ráday Utca: This mostly pedestrianized street is lined with a variety of cafés and restaurants, mostly catering to tourists and specializing in big portions of listlessly executed traditional Hungarian fare. But while its trendy heyday has largely passed, Ráday utca is still a marginally better alternative to the tourist traps along nearby Váci utca. To reach Ráday utca, take the M3/blue or M4/green Metró line to Kálvin tér—a five-minute walk from the Great Market Hall—and head south (district IX). For something a bit better than the rest, stop by **Café Intenzo,** hiding around the corner from the start of Ráday utca, where it meets the busy ring road. Low-key and with a loyal local following, they serve Hungarian and international cuisine, either in a nondescript interior or out in a pleasant courtyard garden (1,400-Ft sandwiches, 1,700-2,000-Ft pastas, 2,000-4,000-Ft main dishes, Mon-Fri 11:00-24:00, Sat-Sun 12:00-23:00, Kálvin tér 9, tel. 1/219-5243).

Danube Promenade

The riverbank facing the castle is lined with hotel restaurants and permanently moored restaurant boats. You'll find bad service, mediocre food, mostly tourists, and sky-high prices...but the atmosphere and people-watching are enticing.

For a more affordable and more local experience, head a bit farther south, near the green Liberty Bridge. Along the embankment road called Belgrád Rakpart is a cluster of fun and lively ethnic restaurants (including good Italian at **Trattoria Toscana,** #13, and a mini-Santorini with Greek fare at **Taverna Dionysos,** #16).

Various companies run **dinner cruises** along the Danube, including Legenda (see page 44) and Hungária Koncert (see page 286), both of which offer a discount to Rick Steves readers. While these can be romantic, Budapest's real restaurants are too tempting to pass up. Instead, dine at your choice of eateries, then take the Legenda nighttime cruise.

Near St. István's Basilica

The streets in front of St. István's Basilica are jammed with upscale, dressy, yuppie-oriented eateries. You could simply browse the options along Zrínyi utca (which stretches straight down to the Danube from the basilica's front door) and its cross streets. But the following choices are worth seeking out. For locations, see the map on page 237.

Café Kör ("Circle") has long been a mainstay in this fast-emerging zone. This stylish but unsnooty eatery serves up mostly Hungarian and some Mediterranean fare in a tasteful, tight one-room interior and at a few sidewalk tables. It prides itself on being friendly and providing a good value. Because it's beloved by local foodies, reservations are smart anytime—and essential on weekends (2,000-4,000-Ft main dishes, small portions for 30 percent less, good salads, daily specials, cash only, Mon-Sat 10:00-22:00, closed Sun, Sas utca 17, district V, between M3: Arany János utca and M1: Bajcsy-Zsilinszky út, tel. 1/311-0053).

Mák Bistro is pricey but unpretentious, with a loyal local following (reservations are smart, especially on weekends). It feels like a well-kept secret, tucked down a forgotten side street parallel to the bustling Zrínyi utca main drag. Inside, it has a lively brasserie ambience under white-painted brick vaults. The short, carefully selected seasonal menu is based on what's fresh (5,500-7,500-Ft main courses, Tue-Sat 12:00-15:00 & 18:00-23:00, closed Sun-Mon, Vigyázó Ferenc 4, mobile 0630-723-9383, www.mak.hu).

Wine-Focused Eateries: Two wine bars—one casual, the other upscale—have helped turn this neighborhood into a happening nightspot. **DiVino** is all about the wine, serving 130 different types of exclusively Hungarian wines, listed by region on the chalkboard—all of them available either by the glass or by the bottle. The well-versed staff can help introduce you to Hungary's underrated wines—just tell them what you like and let them guide you to something to try. While DiVino doesn't do flights or "tastings" per se, couples are invited to share glasses to try several varieties. The interior has a hip black-chalkboard atmosphere, and there's also very inviting seating out on the square (many glasses affordable at around 600-1,000 Ft, also 1,300-2,500-Ft meals, daily 16:00-24:00, later on weekends, St. István tér 3, mobile 0670-935-3980; they also have another, bigger location in the Gozsdu Udvar passage in the Jewish Quarter). Just around the corner, **Borkonyha** ("Winekitchen") focuses both on its list of high-quality (and pricey) Hungarian wines, and on its modern Hungarian cuisine ("Hungarian dishes—but less paprika, less fat"). Because they're enthusiastic about their wines, they sell even pricey bottles by the glass (about 45 types—700-3,000 Ft per glass). The menu—especially the adventurous chalkboard specials—ventures into "nose-to-tail" cooking, using ingredients you won't find everywhere. The decor is sophisticated black, white, and gold—it's a dressy place where wine snobs feel at home. As this place has received a lot of international press, reservations are smart (3,800-4,200-Ft main dishes, Mon-Sat 12:00-24:00, closed Sun, Sas utca 3, tel. 1/266-0835, www.borkonyha.hu).

Behind St. István's Basilica: **Belvárosi Lugas Étterem** is your cheap-and-charming, no-frills option. *Lugas* is a Hungarian word for a welcoming garden strewn with grape vines, and the cozy dining room—with a dozen tables of happy eaters under overhanging vines—captures that spirit. Or sit at one of their sidewalk tables outside on busy Bajcsy-Zsilinszky. The food is simply good Hungarian (1,500-3,200-Ft main dishes, order starches separately, daily 12:00-23:30, directly behind and across the street from St. István's Basilica at Bajcsy-Zsilinszky út 15, district VI, M1: Bajcsy-Zsilinszky út, tel. 1/302-5393).

Homemade Strudel: **Első Pesti Rétesház** is a favorite among fans of *rétes* (strudel). Step inside to watch them roll out the long, paper-thin sheets of dough, then wrap them around a variety of fillings. Get a 300-Ft piece to go at the takeaway counter, or sit and enjoy your *rétes* with a cup of coffee (also has a full food menu, daily 9:00-23:00, Október 6 utca 22, tel. 1/428-0134).

Near Andrássy Út and the Oktogon

Some of Budapest's best eateries are in this area—a hotbed for capable chefs and restaurateurs. For locations, see the map on page 233.

Franz Liszt Square (Liszt Ferenc Tér): Franz Liszt Square, a leafy park on the most interesting stretch of Andrássy út, boasts a

stylish cluster of pricey, pretentious, yuppie restaurants, many with outdoor seating (lively on a summer evening; most places have main dishes around 3,000-5,000 Ft). My favorite Liszt Square eatery, **Menza** (the old communist word for "School Cafeteria"), wins the "Best Design" award. Recycling 1970s-era furniture and an orange-brown-gray color scheme, it's a postmodern parody of an old communist café—half kitschy-retro, half contemporary-stylish. When old-timers come in here, they can only chuckle and say, "Yep. This is how it was." With tasty and well-priced updated Hungarian and international cuisine, embroidered leather-bound menus, brisk but efficient service, breezy jazz on the soundtrack, and indoor or outdoor seating, it's a memorable spot (2,300-3,500-Ft main dishes, daily 10:00-24:00, halfway up Andrássy út at Liszt Ferenc tér 2, district VII, tel. 1/413-1482, www.menza.co.hu). If you like the Franz Liszt Square scene, you'll find a similar energy on Kertész utca beyond the end of the square, and in the "Broadway Quarter" near the Opera House (on Hajós utca and Nagymező utca).

Right on Andrássy út: **Klassz** is a trendy bistro with a similarly postmodern "eclectic-mod" aesthetic, both in its decor and its food. Serving surprisingly affordable international/nouvelle cuisine with Hungarian flair, it's a favorite among Budapest's value-seeking foodies (1,900-4,600-Ft main dishes, daily 11:30-22:30, Andrássy út 41, district VI, between M1: Opera and M1: Oktogon, no reservations possible).

In the "Broadway Quarter": **Pesti Diszno** ("Pest Pig"), set right along the liveliest stretch of theaters in town, is dedicated to serving delicious and surprisingly affordable food that celebrates Hungarian pork: the prized hairy pig called *mangalica*. The menu ranges from well-executed Hungarian classics to international fare to creative fusion dishes—like a *mangalica* hamburger. While the interior, with tall tables surrounding the open kitchen, is fine, I'd rather sit out under the red-and-white striped awnings facing the bright lights of Budapest's theater scene (2,000-3,500-Ft main dishes, daily 11:00-24:00, Nagymező 19, tel. 1/951-4061).

On the Great Boulevard: **Bock Bisztró,** run by a prominent Hungarian vintner from Villány, offers traditional Hungarian staples presented with modern flourish—almost "deconstructed" but still recognizable. The ambience is that of an unpretentious wine bar, with cork-filled tables. Pricey and well-regarded, with 250 different wines on the menu (including 60 by the glass), it's a good opportunity to sample food and wine from around the country. The service can be a bit stuffy, but the food lives up to its reputation. Reservations are essential (3,700-4,700-Ft main dishes, Mon-Sat 12:00-24:00, closed Sun, in the Corinthia Grand Royal Hotel, a couple of blocks west of the Oktogon on the Great Boulevard, Erzsébet körút 43-49, district VII, M1: Oktogon, right by Király utca stop on trams #4 and #6, tel. 1/321-0340, http://bockbisztropest.hu).

On Nagymező utca: **Két Szerecsen** ("Two Saracens"), named for a historic coffee shop at this location a century ago that a trader filled with exotic goods, features eclectic and well-executed international cuisine—including Mediterranean and Asian. With good indoor and outdoor seating, reasonable prices, and relatively small portions, it's a reliable choice (1,600-2,000-Ft pastas and salads, 2,200-3,800-Ft main dishes, daily 9:00-24:00, a block off Andrássy út at Nagymező utca 14, district VI, M1: Opera, tel. 1/343-1984).

Italian: **Millennium da Pippo,** run by a Sicilian who speaks only Italian, greets you with a robust *"Buona sera!"* A neighborhood favorite for pasta and pizza, it's a handy choice near the House of

Terror (1,900-2,800-Ft pizza and pastas, daily 12:00-24:00, Andrássy út 76, district VI, M1: Vörösmarty utca, tel. 1/374-0880).

Indian: Hungarians seem to have an affinity for Indian cuisines, which, like Hungarian cuisine, smooth together powerful spices. **Shalimar**'s high-ceilinged, nondescript dining room hides in a dreary neighborhood two blocks beyond the end of Franz Liszt Square. Everything about this place is unexceptional...except the food, which is my favorite for a break from pork and kraut. I can never resist the *murg makhani*...and I'm never disappointed (1,600-3,000-Ft main dishes, half-portions 40 percent less, daily 11:30-16:00 & 18:00-23:00, Dob utca 33, district VII, between M1: Oktogon and M2: Blaha Lujza tér, tel. 1/352-0305).

In the Jewish Quarter and "Ruin Pub" Nightlife Zone

Along with the rise of "ruin pubs" (see page 292), Budapest's Jewish Quarter has seen the arrival of several good restaurants in recent years. While some of these feature Jewish food (either kosher or updated), others are more eclectic, catering to a younger clientele. As this is a fast-emerging scene, you could just explore here. The following are some reliably good options. For locations, see the maps on pages 233 and 237.

Macesz Huszár is a grandma's-dining-room-cozy corner restaurant serving traditional Jewish recipes with modern attention to ingredients and technique. It's a good value and has quickly gained a loyal following, so reserve ahead (2,300-3,500-Ft main courses, daily 11:30-24:00, Dob utca 26, tel. 1/787-6164, www.maceszhuszar.hu).

Kőleves ("Stone Soup") runs a ruin-pub garden, but their restaurant feels upscale and put-together without being stuffy. The eclectic, international menu includes several Jewish (though not kosher) dishes. This is a good place to try if Macesz Huszár (listed above) is full (2,000-3,600-Ft main dishes, daily 12:00-24:00, Kazinczy utca 41, mobile 0620-213-5999).

Soul Food is a casual Cajun and creole-inspired eatery run by Attila, who's a well-traveled singer by profession and a chef by passion. It feels like a creative college dive: Create your own rice or noodle bowl, or order a sandwich or burger (1,300-1,800-Ft meals, daily 12:00-23:00, later on weekends, takeaway also available, Kazinczy utca 32, mobile 0670-313-8804).

In City Park

I wouldn't go out of my way to eat in City Park, but if you're enjoying a day here and would like a scenic meal, Robinson is a good option. For the location, see the map on page 181.

Robinson, stranded on an island in City Park's lake, is a hip, playful, mellow theme restaurant. With island-castaway ambience and more outdoor seating than indoor, it's made to order for lazing away a sunny afternoon at the park. The terrace and elegant, glassed-in dining room feature pricey international and Hungarian cuisine, and upstairs is a swanky steak house. In good weather, I'd come here for the terrace, to just sip a coffee or have a slice of cake (3,500-Ft pastas, 4,000-5,000-Ft main dishes, daily 11:00-17:00 & 18:00-23:00, reserve ahead and ask for lakefront seating, Városligeti tó, district XIV, M1: Hősök tere, tel. 1/422-0222).

For something quicker and more casual, closer to the end of the lake, look for the **BRGR** burger stand.

IN BUDA

Eateries on Castle Hill are generally overpriced and touristy—as with Váci utca, locals never eat here. The Víziváros ("Water Town") neighborhood, between the castle and the river, is a bit better. Even if sleeping in Buda, try to dine in Pest—that's where you'll find the city's best restaurants. All of the restaurants listed here (except Szent Jupát) are in district I. For locations, see the map on page 243.

Castle Hill

If you must eat atop Castle Hill, and just want a quick bite, visit the handy, affordable **CBA** grocery store (Mon-Fri 7:00-20:00, Sat 8:00-20:00, Sun 9:00-18:00).

For coffee and cakes, try the historic **Ruszwurm** (described later, under "Budapest's Café Culture"). If you'd rather have a meal—and don't want to head down to Víziváros—try the following choices:

Vár Bistro is a convenient, affordable cafeteria that makes for an easy and quick way to grab a meal between sightseeing; best of all, it has delightful outdoor seating overlooking a pretty park (1,000-2,500-Ft main dishes, 1,300-Ft "tourist menu" main dish and soup combo available at lunch, open daily 8:00-20:00, Dísz tér 8, mobile 0630-237-0039).

21 Magyar Vendéglő ("21 Hungarian Kitchen") features traditional Hungarian fare that's updated for the 21st century (hence the name). While the mod interior is pleasant, it's also fun to sit out on pretty Fortuna utca (near the north end of the hill). Most restaurants on Castle Hill are overpriced, and this is no exception—but the quality is also good. This is a rare castle-zone eatery that really takes pride in its food rather than being a crank-'em-out tourism machine (2,300-3,800-Ft light meals, 3,500-5,400-Ft bigger meals, chalkboard specials, daily 11:00-24:00, Fortuna utca 21, tel. 1/202-2113).

Baltazár, near the ruins of St. Mary Magdalene Church (a few short blocks from the main sights), is singlehandedly trying to inject some youthful liveliness into the staid, sleepy north end of Castle Hill. It's a fun choice, with bright, brash decor, pleasant outdoor seating, and a wood-fired charcoal grill that churns out smoky dishes. They also have an inviting beer garden just up the street, under the church tower (2,700-3,800-Ft main dishes, daily 7:30-24:00, Országház utca 31, tel. 1/300-7050).

Batthyány Tér and Nearby

This bustling square—the transportation hub for Víziváros—is overlooked by a recently renovated, late-19th-century market hall (today housing a big Spar supermarket and various shops). Several worthwhile, affordable eateries—nothing fancy, just practical—cluster around this square. Survey your options before settling in.

Nagyi Palacsintázója ("Granny's Pancakes")—just to the right of the market hall entrance—serves up cheap and tasty crêpes *(palacsinta)* to a local crowd (200-400-Ft sweet or savory small crêpes—order more than one for a filling meal, ask for English menu, open 24 hours daily, Batthyány tér 5).

As you face the market hall, go up the street that runs along its left side (Markovits Iván utca) to reach more good eateries: At the end of the block on the right is **Édeni Végan,** a self-service, point-and-shoot vegetarian cafeteria (main dishes less than 1,000 Ft, daily 8:00-20:00, tel. 1/375-7575). And tucked behind the market hall is **Bratwursthäusle/Kolbászda,** a fun little beer hall/beer garden with Bavarian specialties and blue-and-white checkerboard decor to match. Sit outside, or in the woody interior (900-1,200-Ft sausages, daily 11:00-23:00, Gyorskocsi utca 6, tel. 1/225-3674).

Fine Dining near Batthyány Tér: **Csalogány 26** is a stylish, upscale bistro a few short blocks from Batthyány tér in an otherwise dull urban neighborhood. Its modern international cuisine, served in a classy contemporary dining room, has earned it raves as one of the best eateries in this part of town. You can order à la carte (2,600-5,000-Ft main dishes), or go for one of their *menus:* 9,000 Ft/four courses, 13,000 Ft/eight courses (Tue-Sat 12:00-15:00 & 19:00-22:00, closed Sun-Mon, Csalogány utca 26, tel. 1/201-7892, www.csalogany26.hu).

SNACKS AND LIGHT MEALS

When you're in the mood for something halfway between a restaurant and a picnic meal, look for takeout food stands, bakeries (with sandwiches to go), grocers willing to make you a sandwich, and simple little eateries for fast and easy sit-down restaurant food.

A popular snack is *lángos*—a savory deep-fried doughnut (similar to an elephant ear or Native American fry bread). Sold at stands on the street, the most typical versions are spread with cheese and sour cream, and sometimes topped with garlic. Some restaurants serve a fancier version (often with meat) as an entrée. The Lángos stand upstairs in the Great Market Hall is a local favorite (see page 56).

For quick, inexpensive, and very local grub, head for the chain called **Főzelékfaló Ételbár** (roughly, "Soup Slurper Eating Bar"). This self-service cafeteria dishes up simple fare to businesspeople on their lunch break. *Főzelék,* a simple soup that's thickened with roux (wheat flour mixed into lard or butter) and can be supplemented with various vegetables, is a staple of Hungarian home cooking. Go to the counter, choose your *főzelék* soup (various flavors, 400 Ft), then choose from a variety of basic meat dishes (chicken, pork, meatballs, and more for 500-1,000 Ft apiece; some English spoken, but pointing also works). A filling meal here typically runs 1,000-2,000 Ft. Because of the limited seating, most people get their grub to go (though the location near Andrássy út has fine outdoor tables). There are two locations in central Pest: One is just off Andrássy út in the "Broadway Quarter" (Mon-Fri 9:00-21:00, Sat 10:00-21:00, Sun 11:00-18:00, Nagymező utca 22, a block north of the Opera House, district VI, M1: Opera); the other is in a big building along the busy highway at Ferenciek tere (Mon-Fri 10:00-21:30, Sat 12:00-20:00, closed Sun, Kossuth Lajos utca 2A, district V, M3: Ferenciek tere).

Hummus Bar, while not authentically Hungarian, is a popular expat-run chain that offers cheap Middle Eastern vegetarian meals to grateful backpackers and young locals. Their falafel is tasty (800-1,300 Ft for a pita-wrapped sandwich, combination plates for 1,000-1,900 Ft). You can either eat in or get it to go. They have several locations: in the Town Center on Egyetem tér at Kecskeméti utca 1, district V, M3/M4: Kálvin tér; in Leopold Town at Alkotmány utca 20, district V, M2: Kossuth tér; between Liberty Square and St. István Square at Október 6 utca 19; and in the ruin-pub district at the corner of Síp and Wesselényi. All are open roughly the same hours (Mon-Fri 10:00-22:00, Sat-Sun 12:00-22:00).

All around town, you'll see cheery **open-face sandwich shops,** each displaying a dozen or so tempting little treats in its front window—thin slices of bread piled with egg salad, veggies, cold cuts, cream spreads, cheese, salmon, affordable caviar, or other toppings for 180-300 Ft apiece. There's no English menu—just point at what looks good. Two sandwiches and a drink make a quick and healthy meal for about $5 (they'll also box things to go for a classy picnic). The selection wanes as the day goes on, making these a better option for lunch or a light, early dinner. Of the various chains, **Duran Szendvics** is the dominant operation, with a convenient location near the start of Andrássy út (Mon-Fri 8:00-19:00, Sat

8:00-15:00, Sun 8:00-12:00, Bajcsy-Zsilinszky út 7, district VII, M1: Bajcsy-Zsilinszky út, tel. 1/267-9624) and another branch in Leopold Town (Mon-Fri 8:00-17:00, Sat 9:00-13:00, closed Sun, Október 6 utca 15, district V, M3: Arany János utca).

For a fast snack, you'll see **Fornetti** stands everywhere (on street corners and Metró underpasses). This Hungary-based chain, which is becoming wildly popular across Central and Eastern Europe, sells small, tasty, freshly baked phyllo dough-based pastries by weight. They have both sweet and savory varieties. For a bite on the go, just point to what you want and hold your fingers up for how many you'd like of each type (around 30 Ft apiece). If you smell something heavenly in the Metró passages...it's probably a Fornetti.

COOKING CLASS

Chefparade's cooking classes offer a fun, if pricey, way to delve into Hungarian cuisine. A local chef walks you through preparing a traditional Hungarian menu of your choos-ing. Not a stuffy cooking school, they use fun, casual teachers with lively personalities; it's more about the experience of cooking and eating together, rather than just learning how to cook. Sign up for a class, and they'll set you up with others interested in the same menu. Their modern studio also has a well-stocked shop with cookbooks, spices, and cooking tools (€70/person, 3-hour class; "premium package" for €39 extra gets you an apron, cookbook, bottle of wine, and taxi transfer to the class; add a tour of the Great Market Hall to shop for ingredients for €19; Páva utca 13 in Pest, district IX, M3: Corvin-negyed; occasionally you might go instead to second location at Bécsi út 27 in Buda, district II, HÉV suburban train from Batthyány tér to Szépvölgyi út stop; mobile 0620-316-1876, www.cookingbudapest.com).

Budapest's Café Culture

In the late 19th century, a vibrant café culture boomed here in Budapest, just as it did in Vienna and Paris. The *kávéház* ("coffeehouse") was a local institution. By 1900, Budapest had more than 600 cafés. In this crowded and fast-growing cityscape, a neighborhood café allowed urbanites to escape their tiny flats (or get a jolt of caffeine to power them through a 12-hour workday). Local people (many of whom had moved to the city from the countryside) didn't want to pay to heat their homes during the day. So instead, for the price of a cup of coffee, they could come to a café to enjoy warmth, companionship, and loaner newspapers.

Realizing that these neighborhood living rooms were breeding grounds for dissidents, the communists closed the cafés or converted them into *eszpresszós* (with uncomfortable stools instead of easy chairs) or *bisztrós* (stand-up fast-food joints with no chairs at all). Today, nostalgia is bringing back the *kávéház* culture—both as a place to get coffee and food, and as a social institution. While some serve only coffee and cakes, most serve light meals, and some serve full meals (as noted below).

***On the Great Boulevard:* New York Café** makes the others listed here look like Starbucks. Originally built in 1894 as part of

the "New York Palace" (and it really is palatial), this fanciful, over-the-top explosion of Neo-Baroque and Neo-Renaissance epitomizes the "mix and match, but plenty of everything" Historicist style of the day. In the early 20th century, artists, writers, and musicians came here to

sip overpriced coffee and bask in opulence. After decades of neglect, Italian investors completely restored it in 2006, and now it once again welcomes guests. You'll be met at the door and asked if you want a table; they'll typically let you gape at the inside for a few minutes if you ask nicely, but only paying customers may take photos. The food is drastically overpriced and disappointing—don't bother eating a meal here, but do consider coffee and cake. If you're up for a coffee break, this place might actually be worth an $8 cup of coffee. Be sure to read the fun history in the menu (4,000-6,500-Ft main dishes, 1,000-1,500-Ft coffee and hot chocolate drinks, 1,800-2,300-Ft desserts). While it's a few blocks beyond the tourist zone, it's worth the trip out here for the ultimate in turn-of-the-20th-century Budapest elegance (daily 9:00-24:00, inside the Boscolo Hotel at Erzsébet körút 9-11, district VII, tel. 1/886-6167). Take the M2/red Metró line to Blaha Lujza tér, and exit toward *Erzsébet körút* and walk a block. You can also take tram #4 or #6 from the Oktogon (at Andrássy út) around the Great Boulevard to the Wesselényi utca stop. For location, see the color map at the front of this book.

***Two blocks up from Váci utca:* Gerlóczy Café,** listed as a restaurant on page 254, nicely recaptures Budapest's early-1900s ambience, with loaner newspapers on racks and a management that encourages loitering. Nearby, another good choice for coffee and cakes is the similarly old-fashioned **Centrál Kávéház.** While the food here is pricey and hit-or-miss (don't bother having a meal), it has an enjoyable and atmospheric two-story interior and a handy central location (daily 8:00-23:00, Károlyi Mihály utca 9, district V, M3: Ferenciek tere, tel. 1/266-2110). For location, see the map on page 237.

Near Ferenciek tere: **Jégbüfé** is where Pest urbanites get their quick, cheap, stand-at-a-counter fix of coffee and cakes. And for those feeling nostalgic for the communist days, little has changed at this typical *bisztró.* First, choose what you want at the counter. Then explain it to the cashier across the aisle. Finally, take your receipt back to the appropriate part of the counter (figure out the four different zones: coffee, soft drinks, ice cream, cakes), trade your receipt for your goodie, go to the bar, and enjoy it standing up (cakes for under 400 Ft, Mon-Sat 7:00-21:30, Wed until 20:30, Sun 8:00-21:30, Ferenciek tere 10, district V, M3: Ferenciek tere—for location, see the map on page 237). Not sure what to get? Here are some traditional Hungarian favorites: *krémes* (KRAY-mesh) is custard sandwiched between delicate wafers. *Rákóczi turós* (RAH-koht-see TOO-rohsh) is a cake of sweet cottage cheese (a Hungarian dessert staple) with jam on top. *Dobos torta* (DOH-bohsh TOR-taw) has alternating layers of chocolate and vanilla cake topped with caramelized sugar. *Somlói galuska* (SHOM-lowee GAW-losh-kaw) is made of pieces of moist sponge cake soaked in rum and drizzled with chocolate. And *flódni* (FLOHD-nee)—in the pie section (in this area, you can pay directly at the counter)—has layers of nut paste and poppy seeds...another Hungarian dessert staple. For a simpler procedure, get in line at the waffle *(gofry)* window facing the street, where you can pay cash for a steaming-hot Belgian waffle with toppings (window open daily 10:00-18:00).

On Andrássy út, near the Opera House: Three fine and very different cafés are within a block of the Opera (for locations, see the map on page 233). The **Alexandra** bookstore—in the Lotz Hall of the newly refurbished Párisi Nagy Áruház (Paris Department Store)— hides a spectacular gilded café that immerses you in turn-of-the-century splendor (walk straight in and go up the escalator). Because this prominent local chain encourages loitering, the service here is no-pressure, and the drinks and desserts are bargain-priced (600-1,000-Ft coffee drinks and cakes). Rounding out this café's appeal are the occasional live piano music, periodic evening concerts, and mirrors at either end that make the hall seem to go on forever (daily 10:00-22:00, can close unexpectedly for private events, Andrássy út 39, district VI, M1: Opera, tel. 1/461-5835). **Callas** features ideal outdoor seating facing the Opera House, and one of the finest Art Nouveau interiors in town, with gorgeous *Jugendstil* chandeliers. While their full meals are pricey (4,000-5,000 Ft), this is a wonderful spot on Andrássy út for a coffee break, a tasty dessert, or breakfast (ham and eggs plus coffee for around 2,000 Ft, 800-Ft pastries; daily 10:00-24:00, Andrássy út 20, district VI, M1: Opera, tel. 1/354-0954). Across the street and a block toward the Oktogon, **Művész Kávéház** ("Artists Coffee House") is a classic café with 19th-century elegance, a hoity-toity high-ceilinged interior, snobby staff, and fine outdoor seating on Andrássy út. True to its name, this institution in the "Broadway Quarter" is a favorite after-rehearsal haunt of locally famous actors and musicians (700-900-Ft cakes, 1,500-Ft sandwiches, 3,400-Ft main dishes, 900-1,600-Ft breakfasts, Mon-Sat 9:00-22:00, Sun 10:00-22:00, Andrássy út 29, district VI, M1: Opera, tel. 1/333-2116).

In Buda, atop Castle Hill: **Ruszwurm** lays claim to being Budapest's oldest café (since 1827). Tiny but classy, with old-style Biedermeier furnishings and fine sidewalk seating, it upholds its venerable reputation with pride. Its dead-central location—a block in front of Matthias Church in the heart of the castle district—means that it has become a popular tourist spot (though it remains dear to locals' hearts). Look for gussied-up locals chatting here after the 10:00 Sunday-morning Mass at the church (700-Ft coffees, 400-600-Ft desserts, daily 10:00-19:00, Szentháromság utca 7, district I, for location see map on page 243, tel. 1/375-5284).

EATING

BUDAPEST WITH CHILDREN

Despite its reputation as a big, gloomy metropolis, Budapest is surprisingly kid-friendly. Many of the city's best experiences—such as splashing around in a warm-water whirlpool at Széchenyi Baths, or ogling giant monuments from the communist days at Memento Park—bring out the kid in any traveler.

Trip Tips

EATING

Try these tips to keep your kids content throughout the day.

- Hungarian food is generally flavorful, filling, and easy to enjoy. But a few ingredients (like liver and spicy paprika) are liberally used and may gross out finicky eaters.
- Make sure to start the day with a good breakfast (at hotels and B&Bs, breakfast is nearly always included).
- Picnic lunches and dinners work well. Supermarkets and grocery stores abound in the city center, and assembling a picnic at one of the city's many turn-of-the-century market halls (especially the Great Market Hall) is a cultural experience. Having snacks on hand can prevent meltdowns.
- Choose easy eateries. All of the places listed under "Snacks and Light Meals" on page 262—including cafeterias, open-face sandwich shops, hummus bars, and Fornetti pastry kiosks—are quick and easy, and kids can see what they're getting before they order. If you're browsing the Great Market Hall, the food stands upstairs are another easy choice. Eating al fresco is great with kids.
- Eat dinner relatively early (around 18:00) to miss the romantic crowd. Skip fancy or famous places, which are too formal for kids to really enjoy.

DISCOUNTS

- While I haven't listed kids' prices in this book, most sights charge much less for children than for adults—always ask.
- Budapest's hotels often give price breaks for kids (and when it's hot, air-conditioning is worth the splurge).
- If you're taking the train outside of the city, ask about family or child discounts.

SIGHTSEEING

The key to a successful Budapest family vacation is to slow down. Tackle one or two key sights each day, mix in a healthy dose of pure fun at a park or thermal bath, and take extended breaks when needed.

- Incorporate your child's interests into each day's plans. Let your kids make some decisions: choosing lunch spots or deciding which stores to visit. Turn your kid into your personal tour guide and navigator of the Metró system. Deputize your child to lead you on my self-guided walks and museum tours.
- Public WCs can be hard to find. Try shopping malls, museums, cafés, and restaurants, particularly fast-food places.
- Follow this book's crowd-beating tips to a T. Kids hate lines even more than you do.
- Give your child a money belt and an expanded allowance; you are on vacation, after all. Let your children budget their funds by comparing and contrasting the dollar and forint.
- Buy your kids a trip journal and encourage them to write down their observations, thoughts, and favorite memories. This journal could end up being their favorite souvenir.
- Have a "what if" procedure in case something goes wrong. Give each child a business card from your hotel, along with your contact information and taxi fare, to use if you get separated. If they have a mobile phone, make sure they know how to use it in Hungary.

Top Sights and Activities

THERMAL BATHS

The top attraction for kids is the same as it is for adults: thermal baths (✪ see the Thermal Baths chapter). **Széchenyi Baths**—with colorful outdoor pools and mostly mixed-gender areas—are fun for families (though children under 14 are not allowed in the indoor thermal pools). **Gellért Baths'** outdoor area and fun wave pool offer the best thermal bath thrills for kids in Budapest. At both of these baths, children over two years old pay full price. I'd skip the **Rudas Baths** with kids.

For a more kid-oriented water park, you have two good options in or near Budapest: **Aquaworld** is about nine miles north of downtown, but still in the city limits (www.aqua-world.hu); **Aquaréna** is about 20 miles northeast of town, in the countryside near Gödöllő Palace and the Lázár Lovaspark horse show (on the way to Eger, in the village of Mogyoród, www.aquarena.hu).

There are also fun-for-kids thermal baths in and near **Eger** (see page 371).

PLAYGROUNDS

Local parents filled me in on their favorite playgrounds. Many of these are in parks also described in more detail in this book, and are fun for moms and dads, too.

Szabadság Tér

A pair of inviting playgrounds flank the bottom (south) end of this square, which is ringed with some of Budapest's grandest buildings. Nearby is a fun, interactive fountain, where kids step on panels to make the fountains start and stop. The café in the middle of the park is perfect for parents to sit out in the sun and sip a coffee. (This square is described in detail on page 114.)

Híld Tér

Tucked in the very heart of downtown Pest, kitty-corner from Elisabeth Square (with its summer Ferris wheel—see later), this small, leafy square has a handy playground that's popular with local kids and their parents.

City Park

Enjoyable playgrounds are scattered throughout this park, as well as other attractions listed below.

Millenáris Park

This highly conceptual park is tucked behind the Mammut shopping center (near M2: Széll Kálmán tér). In addition to a fun playground, entertaining exhibits called "House of the Future" and "Palace of Miracles" might appeal to older kids.

PARKS

On a sunny day, there's no better place to have fun than in City Park or on Margaret Island.

City Park

The fun, dynamic statues at Heroes' Square help bring Hungarian history to life. The fairy-tale Vajdahunyad Castle—a striking ensemble of Hungarian buildings—also captures young imaginations. You can rent bikes or bike carts, and the big artificial pond near Vajdahunyad Castle usually offers paddleboats in summer and ice skating in the winter. If the weather's good, just spread out a picnic blanket and enjoy the park like a local. The park is slated for renovation through the next few years, which should result in even better facilities for kids (but in the meantime, it may be a bit torn up). With a little more energy, tackle one of the following attractions. (For more on this area, ✪ see the Heroes' Square and City Park Walk.)

Budapest Zoo and Botanical Garden
(Fővárosi Állat- és Növénykert)

Budapest has an entertaining big-city zoo complex, with a "safari park," butterfly house, petting zoo, baby rhino, and more. It also

has redeeming sightseeing value: Many of its structures are playful bits of turn-of-the-20th-century Art Nouveau. (To reach the beautiful Art Nouveau elephant house, turn right inside the main entry, then right again at the fork, and look for the white-and-turquoise tower.) Sometimes on summer weekends, kids can feed the animals.

Cost and Hours: Adults-2,500 Ft, kids ages 2-14-1,800 Ft, 7,300-Ft family ticket covers two adults and two kids; May-Aug Mon-Thu 9:00-17:00, Fri-Sun 9:00-18:00; these are last entry times—zoo stays open one hour later; shorter hours Sept-March; Állatkerti körút 6-12, district XIV, M1: Hősök tere, tel. 1/364-0109, www.zoobudapest.com.

Nearby: The zoo recently expanded, nearly doubling its territory and taking over an old amusement park next door. This area, called the **Holnemvolt Park** ("Once Upon a Time Park"), displays exotic animals, hosts puppet shows, offers pony rides, and boasts some fun rides—from a rickety wooden roller coaster to a beautifully restored, century-old merry-go-round (each ride costs 1-2 tokens for 200 Ft apiece). While none of it will thrill Americans who've been to Six Flags, it's good fun and also has attractions for younger visitors. Holnemvolt Park—which can be accessed directly from the zoo, or separately (find the entrance to the right of the old circus building)—is included in a zoo ticket, or 500 Ft on its own, but may be closed off-season (Nov-March).

The **Játék Mester Zoo Playhouse,** described later, is also in the middle of the zoo action.

Circus (Nagycirkusz)

This old-fashioned big-top act includes clowns, gymnasts, and animals. In operation since 1891, the circus moved into its current City Park home—nestled between the two parts of the zoo, facing the swimming pool entrance for Széchenyi Baths—in 1970.

Cost and Hours: Adults-1,900-4,500 Ft, kids-1,500-3,100 Ft, show schedule changes depending on season but typically 2-3 shows per day on weekends, M1: Széchenyi fürdő, tel. 1/343-8300, www.fnc.hu.

Margaret Island

This delightful island in the Danube is filled with diversions, including baths/swimming pools, a small petting zoo, great bike trails, and fun bike-cart rentals. For details, see page 68.

Károlyi Park

Right in the heart of Pest's Town Center, this inviting garden is a favorite place for local urbanites to simply relax with their children. Small but beautifully landscaped, it's a popular after-school hangout for local kids. For a full description, see page 134.

Elisabeth Square (Erzsébet tér)

This leafy, restful square—also in Pest's Town Center—is a fine place to get a break from the city anytime. But in recent summers, it has also hosted an enjoyable 215-foot-tall Ferris wheel called the **Budapest Eye.** Operating only in good weather (typically mid-May-mid-Oct), it offers three slow spins up and over the rooftops of downtown Budapest (adult-2,400 Ft, child-1,500 Ft, generally runs daily 10:00-24:00 or later in summer, until 22:00 in shoulder season). While it's pricey (and the nearby view terrace at St. István's Basilica is cheaper and equally scenic), it's a fun ride.

Gellért Hill

Kids with hill-climbing stamina might enjoy the trails that twist up this peak overlooking the Danube to great views.

PLAYHOUSES AND ADVENTURE PARK

Budapest has several playhouses *(játszóház)* for young kids—basically big, colorful, indoor jungle gyms with lots of hands-on activities. While most of the clientele are Hungarian tots, others are welcome, and it could be a good opportunity for your child to make a Magyar buddy. You'll generally pay 1,000-2,500 per child, they're typically open daily from 9:00 or 10:00 until 20:00, and adults are free or deeply discounted. Popular choices include the following: The **Játék Mester Zoo Playhouse** (Állatkert Játszóház), in City Park, is wedged down a narrow path between the back end of the zoo and the circus (just across from Széchenyi Baths entry, M1: Széchenyi fürdő, www.jatek-mester.hu). The **Millipop Játszóház**—on the Buda side, in the Millenáris Park near the Mammut shopping mall—is bigger and more extensive, with laser tag (Kis Rókus utca 16-20, M2: Széll Kálmán tér, www.millipopjatszo.hu).

And for something even more exciting—especially for bigger kids— the outdoor **Római Kalandpark** (Adventure Park) has high-ropes courses, a giant sandbox, and laser tag (at the north end of Óbuda, past Aquincum and on the way to Szentendre at Szentendrei út 189, take the Szentendre/H5/purple HÉV line from Batthyány tér to the Rómaifürdő stop, www.romaikalandpark.hu).

CHILDREN'S RAILWAY (GYERMEKVASÚT)

This unusual attraction in the Buda Hills is a holdover from the communist days, when kids were primed from an early age to eagerly work for the betterment of their society. While the commies are long gone, their railway's kid-friendly message of "work is fun!" is full steam ahead—and the line is still manned entirely by children (aside from driving the engines, of course). Children get a kick out of seeing fellow kids selling tickets, acting as conductor, and so on.

The only drawback is that it's on the outskirts of town and requires a few transit changes, but if you—and your kids—have a spirit of adventure, it's a fun ride through the Buda Hills (see map on page 83). The easiest trip is this: From Buda's Széll Kálmán tér (on the M2/red Metró line), hop on tram #59 or #61 and ride two stops to Városmajor (or simply walk 10 minutes along the busy road called Szilágyi Erzsébet fasor away from the Danube). Here you can switch to the rack railway *(fogaskerekű vasút)*, which climbs up in about 15 minutes to the end of the line at Széchenyi-hegy. From this stop, it's a short walk to the starting station of the Children's Railway line, which putters seven miles in about 40 minutes through the hills (part of a national park) to the other end at Hűvösvölgy. Near this station is a stop for tram #61 back to Széll Kálmán tér.

Cost and Hours: Public transit covered by regular transit tickets; Children's Railway tickets: free for kids under 6, 350 Ft one-way for kids 6-14, 700 for adults; 3,500-Ft "family day ticket" covers two adults and three kids or one adult and four kids; train runs about hourly, sometimes 2/hour on summer weekends; May-Aug daily 9:00-19:00; Sept-April Tue-Sun 9:00-17:00, closed Mon; old-fashioned steam engine runs occasionally for an extra charge, confirm schedules on website: www.gyermekvasut.hu.

OTHER ACTIVITIES

The **Lázár Lovaspark horse show**—near Gödöllő Palace, about 33 miles northeast of downtown—is entertaining for the entire family, and gives your kids the chance to explore a real, working, traditional Hungarian farm, complete with all of the unique livestock this country is known for (wooly pigs, giant longhorn cattle, twisty-antlered goats, dreadlocked dogs, and so on). The public-transit option for getting here is probably too much of a hassle with kids; consider making it easier with taxi rides to and from the Gödöllő train station, or hire a driver for the entire day. Notice that this is also close to **Gödöllő Palace** (with some upper-crust history that could bore some kids—but the Empress Sisi stories may fascinate others) and to the **Aquaréna** waterpark mentioned earlier; these could be combined into a very busy, but fun, day out from the big city. The horse show and palace are explained in the Day Trips from Budapest chapter.

Memento Park, with its gigantic statues, captures kids' imaginations—and offers a good springboard for a lesson about the communist days. (Teenagers might enjoy learning more at the **House of Terror**—though that engaging exhibit is too powerful for most young children.) ✪ See the individual tour chapters for details.

The **Puppet Theater** (Bábszínház) offers frequent morning and afternoon performances. The playful "children" shows feature light Hungarian folk tales, while the "youth/adult" shows can include weightier opera performances and avant-garde modern puppetry (1,000-1,600 Ft depending on show and time). Performances are typically not in English, but the puppets still entertain (across from the House of Terror at Andrássy út 69, district VI, M1: Vörösmarty utca, tel. 1/342-2702, www.budapest-babszinhaz.hu).

Kids might also enjoy the touristy, crowd-pleasing Hungarian folk music and dancing shows presented by **Hungária Koncert** (see page 286).

The **Labyrinth of Buda Castle,** while a bit too hokey for serious adults, might entertain children with the opportunity to explore the caves beneath Castle Hill. It's especially enjoyable (and a bit spooky) after 18:00, when it's lit only by lanterns. For details, see page 78.

SHOPPING IN BUDAPEST

While it's not quite a shopper's mecca, Budapest does offer some enjoyable opportunities to hunt for that perfect Hungarian souvenir.

For a look at local life and a chance to buy some mementos, Budapest's single best shopping venue is the **Great Market Hall** (described in detail on page 56). In addition to all the colorful produce downstairs, the upstairs gallery is full of fiercely competitive souvenir vendors. There's also a **folk-art market on Castle Hill** (near the bus stop at Dísz tér), but it's generally more touristy and a little more expensive. And, while **Váci utca** has been Budapest's main shopping thoroughfare for generations, today it features the city's highest prices and worst values.

For something a bit less touristy—but still evolving—drop by the **Bálna ("Whale") Cultural Center**, which sits along the Danube just behind the Great Market Hall (described on page 57). This modern space is a combined cultural center and shopping mall, but has yet to figure out its commercial identity. You'll see some souvenir stands similar to what's upstairs in the Great Market Hall, but you'll also find unique, one-off designers who are still just establishing their reputation. While it may be potluck for shoppers, it's worth exploring—and the architecture is interesting.

As a big, cosmopolitan capital, Budapest has its share of international fashion boutiques. Most of these are along or near **Deák utca** (called "Fashion Street," connecting Vörösmarty tér and Deák tér), or along the first stretch of **Andrássy út.** A few more big-ticket shops are along and near **Váci utca,** with an intriguing cluster along the cross-street **Irányi utca** (just south of Ferenciek tere, near the river in the Town Center). A block over, at Nyáry Pál utca 7, **Eventuell Gallery** displays and sells the works of local designers (www.eventuell.hu).

To see how Hungarian urbanites renovate their crumbling concrete flats, don't miss the home-improvement shops that line **Király utca,** which runs parallel to Andrássy út (two short blocks south). For a taste of the good old days—which somehow just feels right, here in nostalgic Budapest—wander up the city's **"antique row,"** Falk Miksa utca, just north of the Parliament (described later).

Budapesters do most of their shopping in big, American-style **shopping malls**—three of which (WestEnd City Center, Mammut, and Arena Plaza) are downtown and described later.

Budapest has several excellent **English bookstores.** For details, see page 34.

Hours: Smaller shops tend to be open Mondays through Fridays from 10:00 to 18:00 (sometimes later—until 20:00 or 21:00—on Thu), Saturdays from 10:00 to 13:00 or 14:00, and are closed Sundays. Big malls have longer hours.

Bargaining: At touristy markets (but not established shops), haggling is common for pricier items (more than about 4,000 Ft)—but you'll likely get the merchant to come down only about 10 percent (maybe down to 20 percent for multiple items). If you pay with a credit card, you're less likely to snare a discount.

VAT Refunds and Customs Regulations: For tips on getting a VAT (Value-Added Tax) refund, and getting your purchases through customs, see page 483.

SOUVENIR IDEAS

The most popular souvenir is that quintessential Hungarian spice, **paprika.** Sold in metal cans, linen bags, or porcelain vases—and

often accompanied by a tiny wooden scoop—it's a nice way to spice up your cooking with memories of your trip. (But remember that only sealed containers will make it through customs on your way back home.) For more, see "Paprika Primer" on page 251.

If you want a top-notch Hungarian **cookbook,** the pricey *Culinaria Hungary* beautifully describes and illustrates Hungary's culinary tradition (though a cheaper paperback edition is available online or at bookstores in North America).

Special drinks are a fun souvenir, though they're tricky to bring home (you'll have to wrap them very carefully and put them in your checked luggage—not permitted in carry-on; for customs regulations, see page 484). Good choices include the unique Hungarian spirit **Unicum** (described on page 251), or a bottle of Hungarian **wine** (see page 252).

Another popular local item is a hand-embroidered **linen tablecloth.** The colors are often red and green—the national colors of Hungary—but white-on-white designs are also available (and classy). If the thread is thick and the stitching is very even, it was probably done by machine, and obviously is less valuable.

Other handicrafts to look for include **chess sets** (most from Transylvania) and **nesting dolls.** While these dolls have more to

do with Russia than with Hungary, you'll see just about every modern combination available: from classic girl dolls, to Russian heads of state, to infamous terrorists, to American presidents. Tacky...but fun.

Fans of **communist kitsch** can look for ironic T-shirts that poke fun at that bygone era. But remember that the best selection is at the Memento Park gift shop, which also sells communist memorabilia and CDs of commie anthems (see page 223).

Music lovers can shop for a CD of **Hungarian music** at the Opera House gift shop (see page 288).

For a wearable souvenir, **Tisza shoes** (Tisza Cipő) are retro and newly hip. The company dates from communist times, but went bust when Western brands became widely available. Recently, the brand was rescued by an investor with a renewed dedication to quality. They make both athletic and work shoes, as well as bags, shirts, and accessories. While you'll find Tisza products sold around the country, their flagship store is along the Small Boulevard near the Great Synagogue (at Károly körút 1, www.tiszacipo. hu).

HIPSTER DESIGN AND VINTAGE

Budapest is becoming a hipster mecca, and that means fun and idiosyncratic design, home decor, and vintage shops are popping up all around town. The fast-evolving scene makes it tricky to recommend a specific shop, but many intriguing boutiques have emerged in the **Jewish Quarter/"Ruin Pub" zone.** Scout the possibilities on Király (with an emphasis on home decor), Dob, Rumbach, Dohány, Wesselényi, Kazinczy, and neighboring streets. **Printa,** the print shop described on page 195, is one reliable place to get a taste of the neighborhood's vendors; they may sell a map directing you to what's hot in the area right now. **Kék Ló** ("Blue Horse"), a recommended ruin pub, also has a fine gallery of affordable clothes designed by the owner (Kazinczy utca 10, www.keklo.hu). Just across the street, **Szimpla**—the original ruin pub—hosts a colorful farmers market each Sunday (9:00-14:00, Kazinczy utca 14, www.szimpla.hu).

Very nearby—just across Andrássy út from the Jewish Quarter—you'll also find a smattering of intriguing shops along **Hajós utca,** behind the Opera House.

Another space worth checking for this sort of design is the **Bálna Cultural Center,** described earlier (and on page 57), which has an intriguing selection of local fashion and home designers.

Check to see if you're in town for the **Wamp Design Fair.** One or two Sundays each month, dozens of local artists and designers gather to show off their products (free entry, 11:00-19:00, schedule at www.wamp.hu). In summer, this takes place in the city-center Elisabeth Square, while off-season it moves to Millenáris Park (on the Buda side, near M2: Széll Kálmán tér).

HUNGARIAN PORCELAIN

Hungary has two major porcelain manufacturers. While very pricey, their works might interest collectors.

Herend, arguably the best (and most expensive) of all, produces tableware with intricately detailed color patterns on a white base.

They've created porcelain for Queen Victoria, Emperor Maximilian of Mexico, and other historic heads of state. Herend, produced in a town of the same name near Lake Balaton, is also exported (including to the US). In Budapest, the main shop—with the best selection—is in central Pest, just off Vörösmarty tér (go around the right side of Gerbeaud café, József Nádor tér 11, www.herend.com). There are also locations at Castle Hill (in front of the Matthias Church, Szentháromság utca 5), on Váci utca (at #19-21), on Andrássy út (at #16), and in various shopping malls (including WestEnd City Center and Mammut).

Zsolnay also produces tableware, but it's better known for its decorative tiles, which adorn the facades and roofs of many major

Budapest buildings. You can buy Zsolnay pieces at several shops in Budapest (see www.zsolnay.hu). For more about Zsolnay, see the sidebar on page 400 in the chapter on the city of Pécs, where the porcelain originates.

For **antique porcelain,** check the several shops along Pest's "antique row" (described later). However, don't buy porcelain (or any glass) at the Great Market Hall, as it will include a significant mark-up.

MODERN SHOPPING MALLS

Budapest has a range of modern, American-style shopping malls in the city center (most shops generally open Mon-Sat 10:00-21:00, Sun 10:00-18:00). The biggest and most convenient options include **WestEnd City Center,** next door to Nyugati/Western train station (Váci út 1-3, district VI, M3: Nyugati pu., tel. 1/374-6573, www.westend.hu); **Mammut** ("Mammoth"), two separate malls a few steps from Buda's Széll Kálmán tér (Lövőház utca 2-6, district II, M2: Széll Kálmán tér, tel. 1/345-8020, www.mammut.hu); and **Arena Plaza,** near Keleti/Eastern train station (Kerepesi út 9, district XIV, M2: Keleti pu., tel. 1/880-7000, www.arenaplaza.hu).

PEST'S "ANTIQUE ROW": FALK MIKSA UTCA

Get into the nostalgic spirit of Budapest with a stroll down Falk Miksa utca, which extends from Kossuth tér (behind the Parliament) four blocks north to the Great Boulevard (near the end point of tram #2; also at Jászaí Mari tér stop for trams #4 and #6 around the Great Boulevard). Browse your way up and down this drag, with several hole-in-the-wall shops selling furniture, porcelain, and other antiques (most shops generally open Mon-Fri 10:00-18:00, Sat 10:00-13:00 or 14:00, closed Sun). Look for signs that say *antik* or *antikvitás*. There's also a fun vintage poster shop at #28. (The hulking building on the east side of the street is the Defense Ministry—sort of the "Hungarian Pentagon.") At the far end of Falk Miksa utca are a pair of particularly interesting shops, both facing the Great Boulevard. On the left is **BÁV**, the state-run antique shop. On the right, look for **Kieselbach Galéria,** which specializes in top-notch modern and contemporary works by Hungarian artists.

FLEA MARKETS (BOLHAPIAC)

The gigantic **Ecseri Flea Market** (sometimes called "Tangó"), on the outskirts of town, is an authentic, down-and-dirty scene where the fringes of society meet to swap goods (free entry, Mon-Fri 8:00-16:00, Sat 6:00-15:00, Sun 8:00-13:00, best on Sat-Sun, mostly under cover, entrance at Nagykörösi út 156, district XIX). The public transit connection is tricky (from Boráros tér, at the Pest end of the Petőfi Bridge, catch bus #54 or #55 and ride it for about 25 minutes, get off at Autópiac stop); it's easier to take a taxi. This is prime pickpocket territory—keep an eye on your valuables.

For something smaller but much more central, drop by the **Petőfi Csarnok** (or "Pecsa," PEH-chaw, for short) concert venue in City Park, which hosts a flea market on weekend mornings (cheap entry fee, Sat-Sun 8:00-14:00, www.bolhapiac.com).

For an easier-to-reach (and much smaller) flea-market experience in the city center, consider **Bolhapalota** ("Flea Palace"), a tourist-oriented consignment shop right on Ferenciek tere (at #5, www.bolhapalota.net).

ENTERTAINMENT IN BUDAPEST

Budapest, the cultural capital of Hungary (and much of Central Europe), is endlessly entertaining. Whether it's opera, folk music and dancing, a twilight stroll or boat trip, raving at a nightclub 'til the break-a break-a dawn, or holing up in one of the city's uniquely ramshackle "ruin pubs," Budapest offers something for everybody. The scene here has already grabbed international attention: A recent poll of Lonely Planet readers ranked two Budapest nightspots as the first and third "great bars in the world" (the A38 party ship and Szimpla ruin pub, respectively).

For **event schedules,** pick up the free, monthly *Budapest Panorama*, which makes things easy—listing performances with dates, venues, performers, and contact information for getting tickets (get it at the TI, or visit www.budapestpanorama.com). The TI also hands out two other helpful guides with a more youthful slant: *Servus* and *Budapest Funzine* (www.funzine.hu). Other helpful websites include www.wherebudapest.hu (general), www.welovebudapest.com (general), www.xpatloop.com (expat news), and www.muzsikalendarium.hu (classical). Hungarian-only websites—easy enough to translate using Google Translate or the Google Chrome browser—include www.varosban.blog.hu (what's new in town, with an emphasis on food), www.pestiest.hu (nightlife), and www.pestimusor.hu (cutting-edge arts).

To buy **tickets,** I've given strategies for the top options (Opera House and Hungária Koncert), and listed telephone numbers and (where possible) websites for others. Resources such as *Budapest Panorama* usually explain how you can get tickets for specific performances. You can search for information about—and buy tickets for—many Budapest events at www.jegymester.hu and www.kulturinfo.hu.

What's on can vary by **season.** Some of the best nightclubs and bars are partly or entirely outdoors, so they're far more enjoyable in the summer. Meanwhile, the Hungarian State Opera and other indoor cultural events tend to take a summer break from late June into early September (though that's prime time for outdoor music and Hungária Koncert's touristy shows).

For a list of some local **festivals,** which often include excellent live music, see page 512 in the appendix.

Budapest's Music Scene

Budapest is a great place to catch a good—and inexpensive—musical performance. In fact, music lovers from Vienna often make the three-hour trip here just to take in a fine opera in a luxurious setting at a bargain price. Options range from a performance at one of the world's great opera houses to light, touristy Hungarian folk concerts. The tourist concerts are the simplest option—you'll see the fliers everywhere—but you owe it to yourself to do a little homework and find something that really appeals to you. See the resources listed earlier, including the good classical music schedules at www.muzsikalendarium.hu.

Locals dress up for the more "serious" concerts and opera, but many tourists wear casual clothes—as long as you don't show up in shorts, sneakers, or flip-flops, you'll be fine.

A NIGHT AT THE OPERA

Take in an opera by one of the best companies in Europe, in one of Europe's loveliest opera houses, for bargain prices. The Hun-

garian State Opera performs almost nightly, both at the main Opera House (Andrássy út 22, district VI, M1: Opera, see page 146) and in the Erkel Színház theater (not nearly as impressive—described under "Other Venues," later). If you want classical opulence, be careful to get a performance in the Opera House—not the Erkel Színház. Note that there are generally no performances from late June into early September. Most performances are in the original language with Hungarian and English supertitles.

Ticket prices range from 1,200 to 20,000 Ft, but the best music deal in Europe may be the 500-Ft, obstructed-view tickets (easy to get, as they rarely run out—even when other tickets are sold out). If you buy one of these $2.25 opera tickets, you'll get a seat in one of two places: If you're sitting at the back of one of the

ENTERTAINMENT

Entertainment in Pest

ENTERTAINMENT

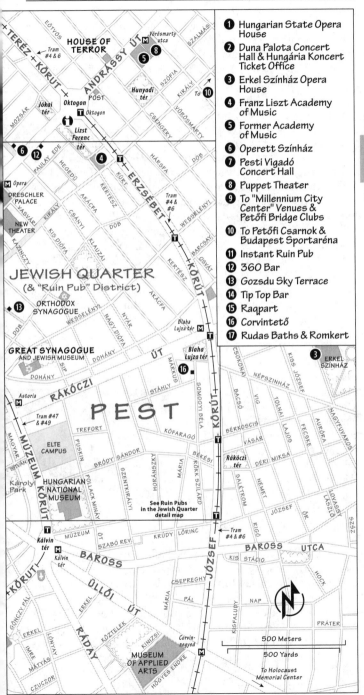

1. Hungarian State Opera House
2. Duna Palota Concert Hall & Hungária Koncert Ticket Office
3. Erkel Színház Opera House
4. Franz Liszt Academy of Music
5. Former Academy of Music
6. Operett Színház
7. Pesti Vigadó Concert Hall
8. Puppet Theater
9. To "Millennium City Center" Venues & Petőfi Bridge Clubs
10. To Petőfi Csarnok & Budapest Sportaréna
11. Instant Ruin Pub
12. 360 Bar
13. Gozsdu Sky Terrace
14. Tip Top Bar
15. Raqpart
16. Corvintető
17. Rudas Baths & Romkert

boxes along the side of the theater, you can either sit comfortably, and see nothing; or stand and crane your neck to see about half the stage. If you sit on the top of the side balcony, you can stand near the door for a view of the stage. If the seats in front of you don't fill up, scooting up to an empty seat when the show starts is less than a capital offense. Either way, you'll hear every note along with the big spenders.

To get tickets, book online (www.opera.hu or www.jegymester.hu), print your eticket, and waltz right in. Or you can book by phone with a credit card (tel. 1/332-7914, phone answered Mon-Fri 10:00-17:00), then pick up your ticket at the Opera House before the performance. Maybe best of all, just drop by in person and see what's available during your visit. There are often a few tickets for sale at the door, even if it's supposedly "sold out" (box office open Mon-Sat from 11:00 until show time—generally 19:00, or until 17:00 if there's no performance; Sun open 3 hours before the performance—generally 16:00-19:00, or 10:00-13:00 if there's a matinee). If you're desperate to attend a specific performance and it looks sold out online, don't give up: Try calling or stopping by the Opera House, or ask your hotelier. There's almost always a way to get a ticket.

TOURIST CONCERTS BY HUNGÁRIA KONCERT

Hungária Koncert offers a wide range of made-for-tourists performances of traditional music. These take place in one of two historic venues: the Budai Vigadó ("Buda Concert Hall," on Corvin tér in Víziváros, between Castle Hill and the Danube, district I, M2: Batthyány tér—for location, see map on page 201); or in the former Budapest Ritz, now called the Duna Palota ("Danube Palace," 3 long blocks north of Vörösmarty tér in Pest, behind Széchenyi tér and the Gresham Palace at Zrínyi utca 5, district V, M1: Vörösmarty tér).

While highbrow classical music buffs will want a more serious concert, these shows are crowd-pleasers. The most popular options are **Hungarian folk music-and-dance shows** by various interchangeable troupes (3,900-6,500 Ft, June-Oct Sun-Fri at 20:00, can be at either theater) and **classical "greatest hits"** by the Danube Symphony Orchestra (with some traditional Hungarian instruments as well; 6,700-9,200 Ft, June-Oct Sat at 20:00, always at Duna Palota). Or you can take in an **organ concert** (usually mixing Bach and Mozart with Liszt or Bartók) in the impressive St.

István's Basilica (4,800-8,100 Ft, May-Oct Thu at 20:00; see page 53).

If you book direct, you'll get a 10 percent Rick Steves discount on anything they offer (must book in person, by phone, or by email; on their website, you can book the "student rate"; discount may not be honored if you buy your tickets through your hotel). The main office is in the Duna Palota at Zrínyi utca 5 (daily April-Dec 8:00-21:00, Jan-March 8:00-18:00, open later during concerts, tel. 1/317-2754 or 1/317-1377, www.ticket.info.hu, hunkonc@ticket.info.hu). Hungária Koncert also offers lunch and dinner cruises on the Danube, in-depth tours of the Jewish Quarter, and (pointless) advance tickets for the baths.

OTHER VENUES

Budapest has many other grand spaces for enjoying a performance. Notice that *Színház* ("scene house") means "Theater."

The **Franz Liszt Academy of Music** (Liszt Ferenc Zeneművészeti Egyetem, a.k.a. Zeneakadémia), on Franz Liszt Square, hosts high-quality professional concerts every night, and occasional free concerts by its students. Recently restored to its stunning late-19th-century splendor, this venue rivals even the Opera House for opulence; if you can't take in an opera while you're in Budapest, this is a suitable substitute—and can be much more affordable. There are five different halls in this building, but the main attraction is the Grand Hall (Nagyterem)—if attending a concert, try to make sure it's there (1,500-10,500-Ft tickets in Grand Hall depending on performance—many have tickets averaging 3,000-5,000 Ft, can be much less expensive in other venues, fewer performances when school's out July-Aug, Liszt Ferenc tér 8, just off of Andrássy út, district VI, M1: Oktogon, tel. 1/342-0179, www.zeneakademia.hu).

The **former Academy of Music** (Régi Zeneakadémia)—just up Andrássy út near the House of Terror—houses the Franz Liszt Museum and hosts performances on Saturday mornings at 11:00 (1,300 Ft, or 2,000-Ft combo-ticket with museum, Vörösmarty utca 35, tel. 1/322-9804, www.lfze.hu).

The **Pesti Vigadó** ("Pest Concert Hall"), gorgeously restored and sitting proudly on the Pest embankment, is another fine place for a concert in elegant surroundings (mostly classical, 4,000-Ft tickets, Vigadó tér 1, district V, M1: Vörösmarty tér, tel. 1/266-6177, www.vigado.hu).

The **National Dance Theater** (Nemzeti Táncszínház) puts on performances ranging from ballet to folk to contemporary at various venues around town, including the Palace of Arts (at the Millennium City Center—see later), the MOM Cultural Center (near the Great Synagogue, at Csörsz utca 18), and the Royal Garden

Hungarian Music

As a leading city of the music-loving Habsburg Empire, where so many great composers thrived, Budapest has seen a steady parade of great musical talent waltz through its streets. And, for such a small country, Hungary boasts an exceptional musical tradition. The local music is typified by a unique mingling of powdered-wig classical influences and down-home campfire hoedowns. Even the great classical Hungarian composers freely admitted to drawing inspiration from their humble Magyar heritage.

Hungary's traditional music—like its language, cuisine, and everything else—still shows the influence of its Central Asian roots. Almost hauntingly discordant to foreign ears, it makes ample use of stringed instruments, especially violins and the cimbalom (*czembalom*, similar to a hammered dulcimer). These soulful melodies seem to pluck the strings of the Hungarian soul; more than once I've seen Hungarians (especially after sipping some local wine) spontaneously break into a traditional *csárdás* or *verbunkos* dance, with the womenfolk periodically punctuating the proceedings with an excited little yelp. Popular tunes include the lively "Az a Szép" ("He is Handsome") and the downbeat "Virágom, Virágom" ("My Flower, My Flower").

Another Asian-descended group, the Roma (Gypsies), have also had a strong influence on Hungarian music. Because of the similarities in these two peoples' music, and the convergence of their cultures in the Hungarian countryside, "Hungarian folk" music and "Gypsy" music are virtually indistinguishable to the casual listener. For example, Roma composer Grigoraș Dinicu's "The Lark"—a high-speed violin piece that replicates a bird's chirp—is a favorite show-off song for Hungarian violin virtuosos. The rollicking high spirits that accompany a lively music session are described with the Roma term *mulatság*.

The "big three" Hungarian composers all borrowed tunes from their Magyar ancestors:

Franz Liszt (pronounced "list," 1811-1886) was raised speaking German, but had a Hungarian surname and ancestry, and loved what he considered his homeland of Hungary. This master composer, conductor, pedagogue, and (above all) pianist was prodigiously talented and traveled far and wide to share his skill ("Liszt played here" signs are plastered on buildings all over Hungary). He died never having mastered the Magyar tongue, but his countrymen embrace him anyway. Liszt composed what's probably the definitive piece of Magyar music, Hungarian Rhapsody No. 2 in D Minor (famously employed by various cartoons, most notably conducted by Bugs Bunny). His former Budapest apartment now hosts a modest museum to the composer (see page 150).

Béla Bartók (BAR-tohk, 1881-1945), from Transylvania, was as much an ethnomusicologist as a composer. He collected and catalogued folk songs from the distant corners of the Hungarian realm and beyond. In addition to composing the well-known choral work *Cantata Profana* and the symphonic *Concerto for Orchestra*, he penned the opera *Bluebeard's Castle*. His erotic ballet, *The Miraculous Mandarin*, caused a scandal at its 1926 debut; after that he wrote only concert pieces. Bartók is particularly well-known to Americans because he fled to New York City during World War II. He never again set foot in Hungary, dying of leukemia before the war ended.

Zoltán Kodály (KOH-dye, 1882-1967) was also an ethnomusicologist, who strove to analyze folk music on a scientific basis. Like Bartók, he harvested many songs in the fertile soil of rustic Transylvania, where rural traditions thrived. But unlike Bartók, Kodály focused on understanding and forging a uniquely Hungarian folk sound. Kodály was also a composer, but he's best-known today as the namesake of the solfège sight-singing method called the "Kodály Method"—the principle behind "do, re, mi..."

Other (non-Hungarian) composers were also inspired by Magyar music. For example, Johannes Brahms (1833-1897), from Germany, composed a series of Hungarian Folk Dances (the most famous is No. 5/Allegro, which the Hungarians have adopted as an anthem).

Traditional Hungarian music was discouraged by the communists because it stoked Magyar patriotism, but it was kept alive by the underground *táncház* ("dance house") movement. Today, traditional music thrives once more out in the open—not only becoming a draw for visitors (touristy Budapest restaurants often have live "Gypsy music"), but also popular among locals. Muzsikás is a well-respected band that performs classic folk music with a very old-fashioned sound (www.muzsikas.hu), while the Roma bands Ando Drom (www.andodrom.hu) and Besh o droM each have a following of their own.

If you're in the market for some Hungarian music, you'll find music stores around town (including in the Opera House gift shop). For a good local recording, look for the well-regarded Hungaroton label.

ENTERTAINMENT

Pavilion in the Várkert Bázár complex, along the Buda riverbank just below the Royal Palace (tel. 1/201-4407, www.dancetheatre. hu).

As noted earlier, the modern **Erkel Színház** is the State Opera's "second venue" (near the Keleti/Eastern train station at Köztársaság tér 30, district VIII, M2: Keleti pu., tel. 1/333-0540, www.opera.hu).

In the heart of the "Broadway Quarter," the **Operett Színház** specializes in operettas and modern musical theater performances, but these are usually in Hungarian (just off Andrássy út at Nagymező utca 17, district VI, M1: Opera, tel. 1/312-4866, www.operettszinhaz.hu).

For something a bit more playful, consider the **Puppet Theater** (Bábszínház; across from the House of Terror), which offers puppet performances that please old and young alike (see page 274).

The **"Millennium City Center"** complex, sitting on the Pest riverbank near the Rákóczi Bridge south of downtown (district IX), is a state-of-the-art facility with multiple venues. The **Palace of Arts** (Művészetek Palotája) features art installations as well as musical performances in two venues: the 1,700-seat Béla Bartók National Concert Hall and the 460-seat Festival Theater (tel. 1/555-3001, www.mupa.hu). The **National Theater** (Nemzeti Színház) presents mostly Hungarian-language drama and lectures (tel. 1/476-6868, www.nemzetiszinhaz.hu). For more information on this complex, including how to ride the tram there from downtown, see page 66.

Major rock acts perform at the **Petőfi Csarnok** (in City Park, district XIV, M1: Széchenyi fürdő, tel. 1/363-3730, www. petoficsarnok.hu; also hosts a flea market—see page 281), or at the newly renovated **Budapest Sportaréna** (a.k.a. Papp László Sportaréna; southeast of City Park at intersection of Hungária körút and Kerepesi út, district XIV, M2: Stadionok, www.budapestarena.hu).

Nightlife in Budapest

Budapest is a youthful and lively city, with no shortage of after-hours fun. I've listed these options roughly in increasing order of edginess, from "asleep by 10:00 (p.m.)" to "asleep by 10:00 (a.m.)."

LOW-IMPACT NIGHTLIFE

This beautiful city is gorgeously lit after dark. Strolling along either the Buda or the Pest **promenade** along the Danube rewards you with wonderful views.

NIGHTTIME DANUBE CRUISE

For a different angle on Budapest, consider joining one of these fun, romantic, crowd-pleasing boat trips. **Legenda**'s cruises include two drinks and evocative

commentary about the floodlit buildings you pass (for details, see page 44).

BATHING AFTER DARK

If you need some rejuvenation after a busy day of sightseeing, soak and splash at **Széchenyi Baths**. The indoor thermal baths close

down at 19:00, but the outdoor pools—which are the best part anyway—stay open until 22:00 (last entry at 21:00). And both Széchenyi and the historic, Turkish-style **Rudas Baths** become nightclubs each weekend until the wee hours (22:00-late; at Széchenyi it's only during summer—mid-April-Sept—and only on Sat; at Rudas it's Fri and Sat year-round; at either, wear your bathing suit). ✪ See the Thermal Baths chapter.

YUPPIE DRINKING ZONES

The plaza in front of **St. István's Basilica** has recently become Budapest's most fashionable locale for a glass of wine. Of the many upscale restaurants and bars in this area, DiVino—a bar with contemporary decor and a wide range of Hungarian wines by the glass—is a good choice (see page 257).

Young locals also meet up for happy hour after work at the many trendy bars on **Franz Liszt Square** (Liszt Ferenc tér, on page 258). **Ráday utca** (described on page 256) has a similar scene, but has become touristy in recent years. Many of these places also serve food.

For something a bit more genteel—evocative of this city's late-19th-century Golden Age—locals pass their evenings sipping wine or nibbling dessert at a **café** (see "Budapest's Café Culture" on page 264).

IN THE "NATIONAL DITCH"

Akvárium fills the foundation for the never-completed new National Theater, in the very center of Pest at Erzsébet tér (next to

Deák tér, where three Metró lines converge). It's a café by day and a music club by night, when the sprawling subterranean space (which is faintly visible below the surface of the park's shallow pond) hosts an eclectic range of concerts (from DJs and rock bands to folklore shows and electronica). In the summer, people fill the tables on the terraces that lead down into the club, and hang out on the lawn nearby—creating a fun and engaging scene (concert tickets generally 1,000 Ft, doors open at 21:00, music starts at 22:00, also open earlier for drinks, Erzsébet tér, district V, M1/M2/M3: Deák tér, mobile 0630-860-3368, www.akvariumklub.hu). For more on the history of this odd site—nicknamed the "National Ditch"—see page 143.

RUIN PUBS

If you're looking for memorable, lively, smoke-filled, trendy pubs crammed with twentysomething Budapesters and backpackers, explore the dingy streets of the Jewish Quarter, behind the Great Synagogue. (This area is between the Small and Great Boulevards, south of Király utca and north of Rákóczi út.) Damaged (like most of the city) in World War II, this neighborhood sat, dilapidated and forgotten, for decades—and remained neglected even when other parts of town were rejuvenated in the 1990s

and early 2000s. Now it's finally getting some attention from innovative young people—though it retains a certain endearing scruffiness, still lacking the spit and polish of central neighborhoods just across the Small Boulevard. This unusual combination of a very central location and low rents has attracted a funky new breed of bars, dubbed "ruin pubs" *(romkocsma);* some also bill themselves as *kert* (garden), *mulató* (club), or *kávézó* (coffeehouse). The low-profile entryways look abandoned, but once you walk back through a maze of hallways, you'll emerge into large halls and open-air courtyards filled with people huddled around ramshackle tables...rickety-chic.

Most of the clientele is in their 20s or 30s, but hip oldsters feel welcome; there's a wide variety of ruin pubs, ranging from rollicking to mellow, so survey several to find your favorite. While dingy and gloomy, this neighborhood is generally considered safe by locals. And at night, the streets can be jammed with bar-hoppers. But it's always smart to be prudent; stick to well-lit streets. Note that most ruin pubs have vast outdoor zones, but small interiors—so they're better in good weather. In addition to the places noted here, you can find a partial listing at www.ruinpubs.com.

Ruin Pub Crawl in the Jewish Quarter

I've connected several of Budapest's most interesting ruin pubs on this pub crawl through the core of Budapest's Jewish Quarter. While this area has several synagogues and other Jewish heritage sights (see the Great Synagogue and Jewish Quarter Tour), it's also *the* hottest place for Budapest nightlife. This walk is designed to give you your bearings, leading you past several of the most appealing streets. If you try to stop at each place, you'll never make it to the end: Pace yourself, keeping in mind that the first, best, and quintessential ruin pub is Szimpla, near the end of this walk. This area can be very lively any night of the week (especially in good weather), but it's best Thursday through Saturday. During the peak of summer (July-Aug), most Budapesters are out of town on holiday, so you'll encounter mostly tourists here; at other times, it has a largely local vibe.

Begin by making your way to **Király utca** (it runs parallel to Andrássy út, two blocks south; for this tour, it's handiest to ride the M1 Metró line to the Opera stop, then walk south). Király utca itself is lined with a few bars and ruin-pub-type nightspots, but the best scene is just south and east of here.

From Király utca, head down **Kazinczy utca,** at the intersection with a delightful little urban park made much bigger by a cheery parklands mural painted on the adjacent wall. Heading down Kazinczy, after one short block, poke down the unnamed alley on the right (after Piritós). This strip is lined with several enticing places, the best of which is probably **Négyszáz** ("400"), flanking the alley (officially at Kazinczy 52). **My Way,** near the end on the right (just before the cross street), is also lively, but with an older clientele. Continuing straight ahead to the end of the lane, you can enter right into the middle of the long series of courtyards called **Gozsdu Udvar,** which is jammed with lively bars and cafés—and worth exploring in its own right, either now or later. Also in here is the entrance to **Gozsdu Sky Terrace,** a summer-only rooftop bar (described later).

Head back out to Kazinczy. Directly across the street from the alley is **Mika Tivadar Mulató** (Kazinczy 47)—fun, but with a little less personality. Continuing (to the right) along Kazinczy, however, you'll quickly spot its adjacent and much more characteristic **Mika Kert,** filling a vacant lot with happy drinkers. Across the street is **Ellátó Kert** ("Supplier," Kazinczy 48), a mostly outdoor pub with mismatched furniture under tents, and with Latino flair and food. A bit farther down on the left (at #41), **Kőleves** ("Stone Soup") is another fine garden, this one also well-regarded for its food (see page 260).

Just after Kőleves, Kazinczy utca crosses Dob street. You could detour left to find a few options, including **Rácskert**—with big

ENTERTAINMENT

Ruin Pubs in the Jewish Quarter

1. Négyszáz ("400")
2. Mika Tivadar Mulató & Mika Kert
3. Ellátó Kert
4. Kőleves
5. Rácskert
6. Lokál
7. Szóda
8. Szimpla Kert
9. Szimpla Kávézó
10. Kék Ló
11. El Rapido
12. Kirakat
13. Csendes
14. Telep
15. Anker't
16. Gozsdu Sky Terrace
17. Tip Top Bar
18. Corvintető

water-tubs-turned-tables and multicolored light tubes, a half-block north of the main ruin-pub zone at Dob 40. But for more variety, turn right onto Dob, which is lined with more ruin pubs. A block and a half down, on the right (at #18, facing the intersection with Síp street), **Lokál** expertly combines cool and ramshackle, with tables made of repurposed shipping pallets. It has a few indoor rooms, but most of the action happens in the graffitied garden. Just past Lokál, also on the right, is another entrance to the **Gozsdu Udvar** passageway described earlier.

Continuing past Gozsdu Udvar on Dob utca, turn left when you reach Rumbach utca (if you went right on Rumbach, it's a one-block detour to the lively **Telep** pub, described later). You'll take Rumbach utca one short block, which leads you right to the gate of the memorial garden for the **Great Synagogue** (and an evocative view of the floodlit weeping-willow Holocaust monument).

Turn left at the gate and head up **Wesselényi utca,** which is also lined with appealing bars and cafés. A block and a half up Wesselényi utca on the left (at #18) is **Szóda**—named for the seltzer bottles that line the wall. It maintains a healthy reverence for the Red old days, with secondhand communist furniture and a sprawling open-air courtyard in good weather (dance floor in cellar, www.szoda.com).

Take the first right turn after Szóda, putting you back on **Kazinczy utca.** This next block is the home of the first—and still best—of the ruin pubs, Szimpla Kert (described next); but since Szimpla set the trend, about a dozen copycats have sprung up along the same street. Feel free to explore the other options, but first head for the top dog.

Szimpla Kert ("Simple Garden," on the right at #14) sprawls through an old building that ought to be condemned, and spills out into an equally shoddy courtyard. Sur

rounding the garden is a warren of tiny rooms—each one different. This place oozes nostalgia for young Budapesters who have fond memories of their communist-era childhoods. Even the snacks are communist kitsch, and along with a full range of alcohol, they serve the old commie soft drinks (such as grape-flavored Traubi *szóda* and sour cherry Meggymárka). Although it's on the route of the tourist pub-crawls, Szimpla is still mostly frequented by locals (www.szimpla.hu). This space also hosts a farmers market on Sunday mornings (9:00-14:00). They have a second, smaller, far less impressive café, Szimpla Kávézó, a few blocks north near the Franz Liszt Academy of Music (Kertész utca 48).

Across the street from Szimpla, **Kék Ló** ("Blue Horse," at #10) combines a fashion boutique with a low-key bar. A few doors down on the same side of the street as Szimpla, the *Taco on Grill* sign (at #11) marks **El Rapido,** a small ruin pub-slash-taquería with a bodega upstairs and a junk-crammed cellar. A few doors down, across the street on the left (at #3), **Kirakat** ("Shop Window") has a white, minimalist-with-graffiti, open-feeling interior and a crowded sidewalk out front.

If you're still vertical, head back to the place(s) that caught your eye. Or, to see a different side of the ruin-pub scene, venture to the options listed next; each one is within about a 10- to 15-minute walk from this area.

More Ruin Pubs in Other Parts of Town

Csendes ("Silent"), with two adjacent branches, is a mellower, more grown-up-feeling (but still artistically ramshackle) ruin pub tucked behind Károlyi Park, right in the heart of the Town Center (across the Small Boulevard from the heart of the ruin-pub zone). The junk-cluttered main "art bar" is at Ferenczy István utca 7, while the Csendes Társ ("Silent Partner") wine bar—a bit more upmarket and snooty—has delightful outdoor tables across the street at the gate to the park (Magyar utca 16; both open Mon-Fri 8:00 until late, Sat-Sun 14:00 until late).

Instant—a few blocks away, closer to the Opera House and the "Little Broadway" quarter—fills three floors and a warren of dozens of rooms and alcoves in a historic-feeling (but appropriately run-down) building. Each room is decorated differently, but always creatively (I like the upside-down room, with furniture on the ceiling). Find your own little private room, and just chill. Choose between the louder dance halls or the quieter café vibe. While there is an outdoor garden, the real appeal here is all those little rooms (daily 16:00 until late, Nagymező utca 38, www.instant.co.hu).

Telep ("Site") is a tumble-down secondhand bar incongruously located in a residential and office-block neighborhood just around the corner from the heart of the ruin-pub scene. There's an art gallery upstairs, they often host live music, and the semi-rowdy crowd out front gives this otherwise sleepy street a lively ambience (Madách Imre utca 8, just off Rumbach utca, http://telepgaleria. tumblr.com).

Anker't, a young, brash, and slightly snooty offshoot of a popular nightclub (Anker), has a minimalist charm. It's conveniently located a short block off Andrássy út—look for the

> ## Escape Room Games
>
> If you enjoy haunted houses at Halloween, you'll love the latest trend in Budapest: "escape room games." Taking root in the fertile soil of the ruin-pub scene, dozens of local tour operators are setting up this fun (for some) and terrifying (for others) experience: Your small group is locked in a room in a spooky, derelict building. To escape, you'll have to solve a series of clues and puzzles (in English) within the allotted time. Various hazards and hurdles pop up as you go, and you'll need to work together to achieve the goal. The escape room game concept—popular for team-building outings, but accessible to curious tourists—has taken off in a big way, and Hungary is now exporting the games to other European cities. Companies come and go, but well-established options include www.claustrophilia.hu, www.trap.hu, www.exitpointgames.hu, and www.parapark.hu. As the lineup is constantly changing and each outfit has its own personality, read some online reviews to find the one that suits your interests. Then book ahead, have fun…and good luck.

|A| sign (across the street from the Opera House at Paulay Ede utca 33).

SUMMER TERRACES (TETŐ)

In addition to *kert* ("garden"), a key term for enjoying Budapest in the summer is *tető* ("roof"). Rooftop terraces—offering laid-back scenery high above the congested city—are the newest wave of hangouts. Most roof terraces are open only in the summer (typically May-Sept), in good weather, and start serving drinks and light food around mid-afternoon. Several offer live music. While this is an emerging scene, here are a few places worth checking out:

360 Bar has rustic-chic tables high above Andrássy út; to reach it, you'll go in the door just to the right of the Alexandra bookstore (with an outrageously opulent café) in the old Párisi Nagy Áruház department-store building (Andrássy út 39, M1: Opera, mobile 0670-259-5153, www.360bar.hu).

Gozsdu Sky Terrace is high above the Gozsdu Udvar gallery in the heart of the Jewish Quarter (M1/M2/M3: Deák tér or M1: Opera, find easy-to-miss entrance near the vintage car collection inside Gozsdu Udvar, www.gozsduudvar.hu).

The smaller, more rustic **Tip Top Bar** is in the Town Center, overlooking University Square (Egyetem tér) at Kecskeméti utca 3/ Királyi Pál utca 4 (M3/M4: Kálvin tér, tel. 0670-333-2113).

Raqpart, lower than the rest, sits just one story above ground— but its setting, on the Pest side of the Chain Bridge, overlooking the beautiful Buda panorama, is stunning (in front of the Hotel InterContinental on Jane Haining rakpart, mobile 0630-464-0646, www.raqpart.hu).

Corvintető ("Corvin Roof"), one of the original rooftop bars, feels a bit dingier. It fills the top floor of an old department store. You'll hike up several flights of stairs to a maze of bars and dance halls, eventually emerging onto an outdoor terrace looking out over the rooftops of Pest (on top of the Corvin department store, across from New York Café at Blaha Lujza tér 1-2, enter on Somogyi Béla utca, district VII, M2: Blaha Lujza tér; www.corvinteto.hu).

NIGHTCLUBS AND DISCOS

Budapest has a thriving nightlife scene for twentysomethings. In general, places are hopping Wednesday through Saturday nights—and pretty dead Sunday through Tuesday. Remember, in the summer, many Budapesters head to nearby Lake Balaton for the weekend (which has its own share of nightspots)—leaving Budapest's clubs mostly for tourists. To mingle with Hungarians, Thursday nights are best. Many of the places I mention here are outdoor and summer-only—look for the words *kert* (garden), *terasz* (terrace), *udvar* (courtyard), or "beach." Off-season (Oct-April) or in questionable weather, skip the trip. Note that some clubs charge a cover (usually for men only). While this scene is constantly changing, the places listed here are well-established. But before venturing to any specific place, ask around for the latest advice (youth hostels and backpackers are a great source of tips). Look around town (including at some TIs and hotels) for the free weeklies *Budapest Funzine* (in English, www.funzine.hu) and *Pesti Est* (in Hungarian, www.pestiest.hu). *Time Out Budapest* is also helpful (sold at newsstands).

Warning: Gentlemen, read and heed my warning about the extremely attractive women nicknamed ***konzumlány*** who hit on green and goofy tourists in order to lure them into dangerously overpriced bars (see page 31). In general, be highly suspicious if a very attractive local woman fawns all over you. (Sorry, you're not *that* handsome, even here in upside-down Hungary.) Many of the city's strip clubs—whether recommended by *konzumlány* or ones you find on your own—are expert at semi-legally extorting enormous sums of cash from out-of-towners. Even if you're accustomed to visiting strip clubs back home, it's best to steer clear here. (If you're looking for advice on which specific strip clubs are better than others...you bought the wrong book, buddy.)

In Buda

At the foot of Gellért Hill, **Romkert** is a very posh option, sexy and filled with plastic-surgery success stories. This is where Budapest's beautiful people go to see and be seen; it's more popular for its aesthetics than for its music (next to Rudas Baths at

Buda end of Elisabeth Bridge, Döbrentei tér 9, district I, www.rudasromkert.hu).

Near Széll Kálmán tér, **Jam Pub** often features live performances by has-been bands from the 1990s (otherwise "retro disco," in the second building of the giant Mammut shopping mall, Lövőház utca 1-3, district II, M2: Széll Kálmán tér, www.jampub.hu).

On Margaret Island

Budapest's playground island has several summer-only clubs near the southern tip of the island (within a 5-minute walk of Margaret Bridge, district XIII). The mod and classy **Holdudvar** is in the courtyard of an old mansion (www.holdudvar.net).

On "Dockyard Island" (Hajógyári Sziget)

One of the most happening zones—especially in the summer—is the island in the Danube just north of Margaret Island (near Óbuda, a.k.a. Óbudai Island, district III). However, this area can be dangerous and is known for its drug scene. An ever-changing lineup of several clubs keeps this island throbbing. This is a thriving and sprawling scene, with imported beaches, rental boats, and a meat-market vibe. You can take the HÉV suburban railway from Batthyány tér and get off at the Filatorigát stop, then walk across the bridge to the island—or just take a taxi from downtown. This island is also the site of Budapest's biggest bash, the **Sziget Festival**, which attracts huge-name, mid-level, and small-name acts for a week each August (www.sziget.hu). This "Hungarian Lollapalooza," typically attended by nearly 400,000 people, is one of Europe's top parties.

On the Southern Edge of Downtown Budapest, near the Petőfi Bridge (Petőfi Híd)

More summer-only options cluster just south of downtown, next to the Petőfi Bridge (near Boráros tér, district IX, take tram #2 south from Pest Town Center, or tram #4 or #6 around the Great Boulevard). Floating in the river on the Pest side is the party barge/live music venue called **A38** (generally a 3,000-Ft ticket, known for its big-name local acts, www.a38.hu).

BUDAPEST CONNECTIONS

Budapest is the hub of transportation for all of Hungary; from here, train lines and expressways fan out like spokes on a wheel. This chapter covers arrivals and departures by train, bus, plane, car, and riverboat.

By Train

Budapest has three major train stations (*pályaudvar*, abbreviated *pu.*): Keleti ("Eastern") Station, Nyugati ("Western") Station, and Déli ("Southern") Station. A century ago, the name of the station indicated which part of Europe it served. But these days, there's no correlation: Trains going to the east might leave from the Western Station, and vice versa. Even more confusing, the station used by a particular train can change from year to year. Before departing from Budapest, it's essential to carefully confirm which station your train leaves from.

The Keleti/Eastern train station and the Nyugati/Western train station are both cavernous, slightly run-down, late-19th-century Erector-set masterpieces in Pest. The Déli/Southern train station—behind Castle Hill in Buda—mingles its dinginess with modern, concrete flair.

All three stations are seedy and overdue for renovation. This makes them a bit intimidating—not the most pleasant first taste of Budapest. But once you get your bearings, they're easy to navigate. A few key words: *pénztár* or *jegypénztár* is ticket window, *vágány* is track, *induló vonatok* is departures, and *érkező vonatok* is arrivals. At all stations, access to the tracks is monitored: You might have to show your ticket to reach the platforms (though this is very loosely enforced).

The taxi stands in front of each train station are notorious for ripping off tourists; it's better to call for a taxi (or, better yet, stick to public transit). For tips on this—and on using the Metró system to connect into downtown Budapest—see "Getting Around Budapest" on page 35.

Here's the rundown, station by station:

KELETI/EASTERN STATION

Keleti train station (Keleti pu.) is just south of City Park, east of central Pest. The station faces a pretty, split-level, newly renovated

plaza called Baross tér, with stops for two different Metró lines (M2/red and M4/green).

On arrival, go to the front of long tracks 6-9 to reach the exits and services. Several travel agencies masquerading as TIs cluster near the head of the tracks. A handy **ATM** is just to the left of the main door (and

two more ATMs are inside banks that face the square out front). There's no official TI at the station, but the railroad runs a customer service office with train advice and basic city info (near the front of track 9, in the left corner, near the ATM).

Along track 6, from back to front, you'll see a side door (leading to a beautifully restored arrivals hall, and an exit to a taxi stand), Interchange exchange booth (with bad rates—use the ATM instead), international ticket windows *(nemzetközi jegypénztár)*, grubby gyro stands, and the classy Baross Restaurant (described later). Pay WCs are down the hall past the gyro places.

Across the main hall, more services run **along track 9,** including domestic ("inland") ticket windows and lockers. The big staircase at the head of the tracks leads down to more domestic ticket windows, WCs, telephones, and more lockers.

To get **into the city center,** the easiest option is to take the Metró: Heading down the main stairs where the tracks dead-end, you'll pass through a grubby ticket area, and then (on your right) a public transit ticket and information office (a handy place to pick up a transit ticket, if you need one). Just beyond that, the underpass opens up: Turn left to reach the M2/red Metró line, or right to reach the M4/green Metró line.

I'd avoid taxis—the ones waiting alongside the station (through the exit by track 6) are likely to be dishonest, but you can try asking for a rough estimate: the fair rate to downtown should be no more than 2,000 Ft. If you must take a taxi, it's far more reliable to phone for one (call 211-1111 or 266-6666, tell the English-speaking dispatcher where you are, and go outside to meet your taxi).

Eating at Keleti Station: **Baross Restaurant,** at the head of track 6, captures some of the turn-of-the-20th-century gentility that this grand station once enjoyed. A time warp with dingy woodwork, chandeliers, and fake marble, it serves up tired Hungarian classics worth considering if you want a meal while waiting for your train (2,000-3,000-Ft main dishes, daily 8:00-20:00). Your other eating options inside the station are a nearby bakery and some unappealing gyro stands.

Shopping near Keleti Station: Roughly across the street from the station is the **Arena Plaza** shopping mall (Mon-Sat 10:00-21:00, Sun 10:00-18:00, Kerepesi út 9, tel. 1/880-7000, www.arenaplaza.hu).

NYUGATI/WESTERN STATION

Nyugati train station (Nyugati pu.) is the most central of Budapest's stations, facing the Great Boulevard on the northeast edge of downtown Pest. The square in front of Nyugati Station is slated for a complete renovation over the next few years. Expect the station area to be torn up, and many of the services or tram stops mentioned here may be temporarily relocated. Look for signs or ask officials for help.

Most international arrivals use tracks 1-9, which are set back from the main entrance. From the head of these tracks, use the stairs or escalator just inside the doors to reach an underpass and the Metró (M3/blue line), or exit straight ahead into a parking lot with buses and taxis. Note that the taxi drivers here are often crooked—it's far better to call for your own cab (see instructions and taxi phone numbers described previously for Keleti Station).

Ticket windows are through an easy-to-miss door across the tracks by platform 13 (marked *cassa* and *információ;* once you enter the ticket hall, international windows are in a second room at the far end—look for *nemzetközi jegypénztár,* daily 7:30-19:00). Lockers are down the hall next to the international ticket office, on the left. An **ATM** is just inside the main door, on the right.

From the head of tracks 10-13, exit straight ahead and you'll be on Teréz körút, the very busy Great Boulevard—and, quite likely, a chaotic, torn-up construction zone. In front of the building should be the stop for the handy trams #4 and #6 (which zip around Pest's Great Boulevard ring road); to the right are stairs leading to an underpass (use it to avoid crossing this busy intersection, or to reach the Metró's M3/blue line); and to the left is the classiest

Art Nouveau McDonald's on the planet, filling the station's former waiting room. (Seriously. Take a look inside.)

Shopping near Nyugati Station: Next door is the huge, American-style **WestEnd City Center** mall (complete with a Starbucks; most shops open Mon-Sat 10:00-21:00, Sun 10:00-18:00, entrance next to track 1, www.westend.hu).

DÉLI/SOUTHERN STATION

In the late 19th century, local newlyweds caught the train at Déli train station (Déli pu.) for their honeymoon in Venice. Renovated by the heavy-handed communists, today the station—tucked behind Castle Hill on the Buda side—is dreary, dark-stone, smaller, and more modern-feeling than the other train stations. From the tracks, go straight ahead into the vast, empty-feeling main hall, with well-marked domestic and international ticket windows at opposite ends. A left-luggage desk is outside beyond track 1. Downstairs, you'll find several shops and eateries, and access to the very convenient M2/red Metró line, which takes you to several key points in town: Batthyány tér (on the Buda embankment, at the north end of the Víziváros neighborhood), Deák tér (the heart of Pest, with connections to two other Metró lines), and Keleti train station (where you can transfer to the M4/green Metró line).

TRAIN CONNECTIONS FROM BUDAPEST

There's no telling which station any given train will use, especially since it can change from year to year—always confirm carefully which station your train leaves from. Remember, for specific schedules, check www.bahn.com or www.mav-start.hu.

From Budapest by Train to Destinations in Hungary: Eger (every 2 hours direct, 2 hours, more with transfer in Füzesabony, usually from Budapest's Keleti/Eastern Station), **Pécs** (every 2 hours direct, 3 hours; a few more connections possible with transfer at suburban Budapest-Kelenföld station), **Sopron** (6/day direct, 3 hours, more with transfer in Győr), **Visegrád** (trains arrive at Nagymaros-Visegrád station, across the river—take shuttle boat to Visegrád; hourly, 50 minutes, usually from Budapest's Nyugati/Western Station), **Esztergom** (hourly, 1.5 hours, usually from Budapest's Nyugati/Western Station, may be discontinued due to construction—if so, take the bus, described later), **Kecskemét** (hourly, 1.5 hours), **Szeged** (hourly, 2.5 hours). Note that Nagymaros (the station for Visegrád) and Esztergom are on opposite sides of the river—and on different train lines. To reach **Szentendre** and **Gödöllő**, take the suburban HÉV line (see "By HÉV," later).

By Train to International Destinations: Bratislava (that's **Pozsony** in Hungarian, 7/day direct, 2.75 hours; more with transfers), **Vienna** (that's **Bécs** in Hungarian, every 2 hours direct on express RailJet, 3 hours; more with transfers), **Prague** (3/day direct, 7 hours, more with transfers in Győr and/or Vienna; plus 1 night train/day, 8 hours), **Kraków** (1 direct night train/day, 10.5 hours; otherwise transfer in Břeclav, Czech Republic), **Zagreb** (2/day direct, 6-7 hours), **Ljubljana** (1/day direct, 9 hours; additional options with transfers, 8-10 hours, no convenient night train), **Munich** (5/day by express RailJet, 7.5 hours, additional options with transfers; 1 direct night train/day, 9 hours), and **Berlin** (1/day direct, 12 hours; 1 night train/day, 13 hours).

By HÉV: Budapest has its own suburban rail network, called HÉV. For tourists, this is mostly useful for reaching **Szentendre** (from M2: Batthyány tér) and **Gödöllő** (from M2: Örs vezér tere). For more on the HÉV system, see page 39.

By Bus

Buses can be relatively inexpensive, but are typically slower and less convenient than trains. You can search bus schedules at the (Hungarian-only) website www.menetrendek.hu (click on "VOLÁN Menetrend"). Budapest lacks a single, consolidated bus station; instead, buses fan out from several points around town, each one next to—and named for—a Metró stop. (While these aren't all "bus stations" in the strict sense, they are handy transit hubs.) A few are particularly useful for tourists:

From the **Újpest-Városkapu** bus station (on the M3/blue line), buses depart about hourly to trace the Danube Bend around to **Szentendre** (30 minutes), **Visegrád** (1.25 hours), and **Esztergom** (2 hours).

The **Stadionok** bus station (on the M2/red line) serves **Eger** (2/hour, 1.75-2.25 hours) and **Lázár Lovaspark** (sporadic departures, ride about 50 minutes to Domonyvölgy stop).

The **Árpád híd** bus station (on the M3/blue line) has buses taking the faster overland route to **Esztergom** (1-2/hour, 1.25 hours).

The **Népliget** bus station (on the M3/blue line) is mostly used by international buses (including to **Bratislava:** 2/day, 3 hours), as well as buses to **Pécs** (5/day direct, 3.5-4.5 hours). Trains are faster to these destinations.

Orange Ways Buses: For long-distance international journeys, consider Orange Ways buses, which offer affordable express connections from Budapest to **Bratislava** (1-4/day, 2.5 hours), **Vienna** (3-4/day, 3 hours), **Kraków** (5/week, 6.5 hours), **Prague** (1-4/day, 6.5-7.5 hours; this same bus sometimes continues to **Dresden** and **Berlin**), and more (www.orangeways.com).

By Plane

BUDAPEST LISZT FERENC AIRPORT

Budapest's airport is 10 miles southeast of the center (airport code: BUD, tel. 1/296-7000, www.bud.hu). Many Hungarians still call the airport by its former name, "Ferihegy." The airport's lone passenger terminal is, perhaps optimistically, called "Terminal 2" ("Terminal 1" closed in 2012). The terminal has two adjacent parts, which you can easily walk between in just a few minutes: the smaller Terminal 2A is for flights from EU/Schengen countries (no passport control required), while Terminal 2B is for flights from other countries. Both sections have ATMs and TI desks (open daily 8:00-23:00 in 2A, and daily 10:00-22:00 in 2B). Car rental desks are in the arrivals area for 2B.

From the Airport to Budapest: The fastest door-to-door option is to take a **taxi.** Főtaxi has a monopoly at the taxi stand out front; figure about 6,000-7,000 Ft to downtown, depending on traffic.

The **airport shuttle** minibus is cheaper for solo travelers, but two people will pay only a few dollars more to share a taxi (3,200 Ft/1 person, 4,790 Ft/2 people; minibus ride to any hotel in the city center takes about 30-60 minutes depending on hotel location, plus waiting time; tel. 1/296-8555, www.airportshuttle.hu; if arranging a minibus transfer *to* the airport, call at least 24 hours in advance). To save time, you can book your transfer at their handy desk inside the baggage claim area, or wait until you're out in the arrivals lobby. Because they prefer to take several people at once, you may have to wait awhile at the airport for a quorum to show up (about 20 minutes in busy times, up to an hour when it's slow—they can give you an estimate).

Finally, there's the cheap but slow **public bus #200E.** This stops at both Terminal 2A and 2B, and runs in about 25 minutes to the Kőbánya-Kispest station on the M3/blue Metró line; from there, take the Metró the rest of the way into town (entire journey covered by basic 350-Ft transit ticket, allow about an hour total for the trip to the center).

To Eger: Eger makes an enjoyable small-town entry point in Hungary for getting over your jet lag. Unfortunately, there is no direct connection there from Budapest's airport. The easiest plan is to ride the airport shuttle minibus to Budapest's Keleti/Eastern train station, then catch the Eger-bound train from there. Or, to save a little money, you could take public bus #200E to Kőbánya-Kispest, ride the M3/blue Metró line to Deák tér, and transfer to the M2/red Metró line, which stops at both Keleti Station (for the train to Eger) and Stadionok (for the bus to Eger).

By Car

Avoid driving in Budapest if you can—roads are narrow, and fellow drivers, bikes, and pedestrians make the roads feel like an obstacle course. Especially during rush hour (7:00-9:00 and 16:00-18:00), congestion is maddening, and since there's no complete expressway bypass, much of the traffic going through the city has to go *through* the city—sharing the downtown streets with local commuters. The recent wave of roadwork and other construction around Budapest only complicates matters. Signage can be confusing. Don't drive down roads marked with a red circle, or in lanes marked for buses; these can be monitored by automatic traffic cameras, and you could be mailed a ticket.

There are three concentric ring roads, all of them slow: the Small Boulevard (Kiskörút), Great Boulevard (Nagykörút), and outermost Hungária körút, from which highways and expressways spin off to other destinations. Farther out, the M-0 expressway makes a not-quite-complete circle around the city center, helping to divert some traffic.

Parking: While in Budapest, unless you're heading to an out-of-town sight (such as Memento Park), park the car at or near your hotel and take public transportation. Public street parking costs 175-525 Ft per hour (pay in advance at machine and put ticket on dashboard—watch locals and imitate). Within the Great Boulevard, it's generally free to park from 20:00 until 8:00 the next morning (farther out, it's free after 18:00). But in some heavily touristed areas, you may have to pay around the clock—in any event, check signs carefully, and confirm with a local (such as your hotelier) that you've parked appropriately. Also, be sure to park within the lines—otherwise, your car is likely to get "booted" (I've seen more than one confused tourist puzzling over the giant red brace on his wheel). A guarded parking lot is safer, but more expensive (figure 3,000-4,000 Ft/day, ask your hotel or look for the blue *P*s on maps). As rental-car theft can be a problem, ask at your hotel for advice.

ROUTE TIPS FOR DRIVERS

To Eger and Other Points East: Head out of the city center on Andrássy út, circling behind Heroes' Square to access Kós Károly sétány through the middle of City Park. You'll pass Széchenyi Baths on the left, then (exiting the park) go over the Hungária körút ring road, before getting on M-3. This expressway zips you conveniently to Eger (exit #114 for Füzesabony; go north on road 33, then follow road 3, then road 25 into Eger). Between Budapest and Eger, M-3 also passes Gödöllő (with its Royal Palace; also exit here for the Lázár Lovaspark horse show) and Hatvan (where you can exit for Hollókő).

To Bratislava, Vienna, and Other Points West: From central Pest, head over the Danube on the white, modern Elisabeth Bridge (Erzsébet híd). Once in Buda, the road becomes Hegyalja út; simply follow *Bécs-Wien* signs to get on M-1.

To the Danube Bend: For tips on driving around the Danube Bend (Szentendre, Visegrád, and Esztergom), see page 349.

By Boat

In the summer, Mahart runs high-speed hydrofoils up the Danube to **Vienna.** It's not particularly scenic, and it's slower than the train, but it's a fun alternative for nautical types. The boat leaves Budapest at 9:00 and arrives in Vienna at 15:30; on the return trip, a boat leaves from Vienna at 9:00 and reaches Budapest at 14:30 (May-late Sept only, departs from Budapest Tue, Thu, and Sat; from Vienna Wed, Fri, and Sun). The trip costs €99 one-way between Budapest and Vienna (or €109 the other direction). To confirm times and prices, and to buy tickets, contact Mahart in Budapest (tel. 1/484-4010, www.mahartpassnave.hu) or DDSG Blue Danube in Vienna (Austrian tel. 01/58880, www.ddsg-blue-danube.at).

For details on taking the boat to **Danube Bend** towns (Szentendre, Visegrád, and Esztergom), see page 333.

BEYOND BUDAPEST

DAY TRIPS FROM BUDAPEST

Gödöllő Palace • Lázár Lovaspark • Hollókő • Szentendre • Visegrád • Esztergom • More Hungarian Destinations

The most rewarding destinations outside Budapest are Eger, Pécs, Sopron, and Bratislava (Slovakia). But each of those (covered in their own chapters) is more than two hours away; for a shorter visit, the region immediately surrounding Budapest offers some enticing options for a break from the big city.

I've arranged these in geographical clusters, east and west of the capital. To the east, just outside Budapest, Gödöllő Palace is the best spot in Hungary to commune with its past Habsburg monarchs, the larger-than-life Franz Josef and Sisi. Nearby, Lázár Lovaspark is the handiest opportunity to take in a traditional Hungarian cowboy show. The tiny village of Hollókő, tucked in the hills northeast of Budapest, combines a living community with an open-air folk museum.

Meanwhile, west of Budapest, three river towns along the Danube Bend offer an easy escape: the charming town of Szentendre is an art colony with a colorful history to match; the castles of Visegrád boast a sweeping history and equally grand views over the Bend; and Esztergom is home to Hungary's top church.

At the end of this chapter, I've briefly outlined two areas that—while a bit too far for a day trip—are worth knowing about for those who want to extend their Hungarian explorations: the Great Hungarian Plain (including the city of Szeged) and Lake Balaton.

PLANNING YOUR TIME

Of this chapter's main attractions, Gödöllő Palace and Szentendre are the easiest to reach from Budapest (each one is a quick ride away on the suburban train, or HÉV). These sights—which are also the best attractions in this chapter—can be done in just a few hours each. Lázár Lovaspark is an easy taxi ride from Gödöllő. The other sights (Hollókő, Visegrád, and Esztergom) are farther afield and less rewarding; do these only if you have extra time or they're on the way to your next stop.

For efficient sightseeing, cluster your visits to these sights strategically. If you have a car, some combination of Gödöllő Palace, Lázár Lovaspark, and Hollókő can be done in a day (round-trip from Budapest, or on a long day driving between Budapest and Eger; for details, see page 307). The Danube Bend sights (Szentendre, Visegrád, and Esztergom) also go well together if you have a car, and line up conveniently between Budapest and Bratislava or Vienna.

East of Budapest

These three attractions—Gödöllő Palace, Lázár Lovaspark horse show, and the folk village of Hollókő—line up east of Budapest. Each one is a detour from the M-3 expressway that heads northeast; consider stopping at one or more of these on your way to Eger, or seeing two or three as a side-trip from Budapest. Gödöllő Palace is also easy to reach by train from Budapest.

Budapest Day Trips at a Glance

If you only have a day or two to venture outside of Budapest, this overview might help you decide where to go. I've listed these sights roughly in order of worthiness.

▲▲**Eger** This appealing midsized town, packed with gorgeous Baroque architecture, has one of Hungary's most historic castles, some pleasantly quirky museums, excellent local wines, and fine thermal baths (including two in the nearby countryside). Eger is the best look at workaday Hungary outside Budapest. Allow a full day or overnight. See the Eger chapter.

▲▲**Pécs** A medium-sized city in southern Hungary, Pécs features a rich history (typified by the unique mosque-turned-church on its main square), surprisingly top-notch museums, and beautiful buildings slathered with colorful local Zsolnay tiles. Allow a full day or overnight. See the Pécs chapter.

▲▲**Bratislava, Slovakia** The Slovak capital—conveniently situated between Budapest and Vienna—is worth a look for its increasingly rejuvenated Old Town, taste of Slovak culture, and evocative sea of construction cranes, which are hard at work reinventing the city as an economic capital of the New Europe. Allow a half-day to a full day (most convenient on the way to Vienna). See the Bratislava chapter.

▲▲**Gödöllő Palace** This summer palace of the Habsburg monarchs is the best place in Hungary to get to know the "royal and imperial" couple, Franz Josef and Sisi (closed Mon). It's easy to see in a half-day from Budapest (or, by car, combine with Lázár Lovaspark or Hollókő for a full day). See page 314.

▲▲**Esztergom Basilica** Hungary's biggest and most important church, packed with history, looms above the Danube (open daily). Allow a full day combined with other Danube Bend sights (Szentendre and possibly Visegrád). See page 346.

▲**Szentendre** This colorful, Balkan-feeling artist colony is the easiest (and most touristy) small town to visit from Budapest.

DAY TRIPS

Allow a half-day from Budapest, or combine with a full-day trip around the Danube Bend. See page 334.

▲**Lázár Lovaspark** This entertaining demonstration of traditional Hungarian equestrian arts includes some thrilling horseback tricks, and a chance to meet local livestock (shows daily in summer, but confirm times before making the trip). Allow about two hours for the complete visit, ideally combined with nearby Gödöllő Palace. See page 322.

▲**Sopron** A small-town alternative that's also between Budapest and Vienna, Sopron has a charmingly well-preserved Old Town peppered with dusty museums and historic buildings. Allow a half-day to a full day (most convenient on the way to Vienna). See the Sopron chapter.

▲**Hollókő** This intriguing village-meets-open-air folk museum hides in the middle of nowhere an hour and a half northeast of Budapest. Visit only if you have a car and are interested in the culture and architecture of the Hungarian countryside. Allow a full day (by car, it can be combined with Gödöllő Palace and/or Lázár Lovaspark for a full-day side-trip, or visited en route between Budapest and Eger). It's closed Mondays and completely dead off-season. See page 325.

Visegrád The least engaging of the Danube Bend sights, Visegrád offers a small riverside palace museum and a dramatic hilltop castle with fine views over the Bend. Visit only if it's on the way of your Danube Bend day. See page 341.

Great Hungarian Plain Hungary's "Big Sky Country" boasts cowboy shows, the bustling cultural capital of Szeged, colorful Kecskemet, the wild Organic architecture of Makó, and an easy side-trip to Subotica, Serbia. This area is worth considering if you have more time (or a special interest) and want to see more of Hungary. See page 350.

Lake Balaton The freshwater "Hungarian Riviera" has lots of beach resorts, the historic hill-capping town of Tihany, the unique thermal lake of Hévíz, and the Herend porcelain factory. Consider stopping off here on your way between Budapest and regions to the southwest. See page 355.

DAY TRIPS

Gödöllő Palace

Holding court in an unassuming town on the outskirts of Budapest, Gödöllő Royal Palace (Gödöllői Királyi Kastély; pronounced roughly "GER-der-ler") is Hungary's largest Baroque palace and most interesting royal interior to tour. The pink-and-white, U-shaped Baroque complex is haunted by Habsburg ghosts: Once the residence of Habsburg Emperor Franz Josef and his wife, Empress Elisabeth (known as Sisi), Gödöllő has recently been restored to its

"*K und K*" (royal and imperial) splendor. Compared to other Habsburg properties, Gödöllő is compact, well-presented, and pleasantly uncrowded. If you want a Habsburg fix and aren't going to Vienna—or if you're a Habsburg completist—Gödöllő is worth ▲▲, and well worth a half-day visit from Budapest.

Orientation

Cost and Hours: Permanent exhibit (main palace apartments)-2,200 Ft; April-Oct daily 10:00-18:00, last entry one hour before closing; Nov-March open only by guided tour at :30 past each hour Mon-Fri 10:30-14:30 (palace closes at 16:00), Sat-Sun 10:00-17:00; tel. 28/410-124, www.kiralyikastely.hu. For the cost and hours of the other palace attractions, see later.

Getting There: Gödöllő Palace is an easy side-trip from Budapest, by HÉV suburban train or by car. By **public transit,** take the M2/red Metró line to the end of the line at Örs vezér tere, then go under the street to the HÉV suburban train (H8/pink line) and hop a train marked for Gödöllő (2/hour). Once in Gödöllő, get off at the Szabadság tér station (about an hour total from central Budapest). The palace is across the street, kitty-corner from the station. **Drivers** will find the palace 17 miles east of Budapest, just off the M-3 expressway (on the way to Eger and other points east). You'll find pay-and-display parking directly in front of the palace.

Audioguide: You can rent an 800-Ft audioguide for the permanent exhibit, but this chapter's self-guided tour covers the basics, and enough English descriptions are posted throughout to bring meaning to each of the rooms and exhibits.

Services: The palace houses a café that Sisi would appreciate.

There's also baggage storage (no bags are allowed within the tourable parts of the palace).

Time to Allow: By public transportation, figure an hour each way from central Budapest, plus another hour or so to tour the palace. You'll need additional time to visit the other sights at the palace (such as the Baroque theater or WWII-era bunker).

Starring: That quintessential royal and imperial couple, Franz Josef and Sisi.

BACKGROUND

The palace was built in the 1740s by Count Antal Grassalkovich, a Hungarian aristocrat who was loyal to Habsburg Empress Maria Theresa (at a time when most Hungarians were chafing under her rule). When the Compromise of 1867 made Habsburg rulers Franz Josef and Sisi "king and queen of Hungary" (see page 320), the couple needed a summer home where they could relax in their Hungarian realm—and Gödöllő Palace was that place. Sisi adored Hungary (in many ways preferring it to Vienna) and spent much of her time here; Franz Josef especially enjoyed hunting in the surrounding woods. The family spent many Christmases at Gödöllő. More than 900 servants worked hard to make this a pleasant second home for just that one family.

After the fall of the monarchy, Gödöllő Palace became a residence of Admiral Miklós Horthy, who led Hungary between the World Wars. The palace fell into disrepair during the communist period (when the Soviets gutted it of period furniture and used it as military barracks, and then a nursing home). But it was recently rehabilitated to Habsburg specifications and opened to the public.

Two wings of the palace are still in ruins, and renovations are ongoing.

The most interesting part of the palace is its permanent exhibit, which fills several wings: the Grassalkovich wing, Franz Josef wing, Sisi wing, and Gisella wing, which you'll visit in that order. Pleasant gardens stretch behind the palace. Various other parts of the palace—such as a Baroque theater, the stables, and Admiral Horthy's bunker—are also tourable, but not really geared for English-speakers. See the details for these after the self-guided tour.

The Tour Begins

PERMANENT EXHIBIT

• *After buying your ticket, head upstairs and go left, following the marked tourist route. To help you find your way, the numbers noted below correspond to the audioguide numbers you'll see posted in each room.*

Franz Josef and Grassalkovich Wings

You'll begin in the **small dining room** (#4)—where the table is set with exquisite Herend porcelain made specifically for this palace—then see the **butler's pantry** (#5), displaying more porcelain. The actual kitchens were in another building, across the park, because Sisi didn't care for the smell of cooking food.

Head down the long hallway, bypassing the small side-rooms for now; at the end of the hall, do a quick clockwise loop through the adjoining **Grassalkovich wing,** named for the aristocratic family that built the original palace. (When this family died out in 1841, the palace went to the Habsburgs.) If this obscure blue blood doesn't thrill you, take the opportunity to simply appreciate the opulent apartments. From Room #7 (displaying a countess' robin's-egg-blue gown), you'll hook to the right, through a small armory collection, to reach the oratory (#10/#11), which gives you a peek down into the chapel. This room allowed the royal couple to "attend" Mass without actually mingling with the rabble. Notice the chapel's perfect Baroque symmetry: two matching pulpits, two matching chandeliers, and so on. Continue your loop, watching on the right for the hidden indoor toilet, and then—built into the door frame—the secret entrance to passages where servants actually scurried around inside the walls like mice, serving their masters unseen and unheard. (Notice that the stoves have no doors—they were fed from behind, inside the walls.)

Circling the rest of the way around to the blue gown, turn left, then head back down the long hallway. Turn left near the end of the hall into the **Franz Josef wing,** starting in the Adjunct General's Quarters (#15). In the next room, the **coronation chamber**

(#16), we finally catch up with the Habsburgs. Look for the giant painting of Franz Josef being crowned king of Hungary at Matthias Church, on top of Buda's Castle Hill, in 1867. (On the right side, hat in hand, is Count Andrássy. He gestures with the air of a circus ringmaster—which makes sense, as he was a kind of MC of both this coronation and the Hungarian government in general. Andrássy is the namesake of Pest's main drag—and was the reputed lover of Franz Josef's wife Sisi.) Across the room is a painting of another Franz Josef coronation, this time at today's March 15 Square in Pest. Back then, Buda and Pest were separate cities—so two coronations were required.

In the **study of Franz Josef** (#17), on the right wall, we see a portrait of the emperor, with his trademark bushy 'stache and 'burns. The painting of the small boy (to the left) depicts Franz Josef's great-great-nephew Otto von Habsburg, the Man Who Would Be Emperor, if the empire still existed. Otto (1912-2011) was an early proponent of the creation of the European Union. (The EU's vision for a benevolent, multiethnic state bears striking similarities to the Habsburg Empire of Franz Josef's time.) Otto celebrated his 90th birthday (in 2002) here at Gödöllő Palace. The bust is Otto's father—Austrian Emperor Charles I, aka Hungarian King Károly IV. He was the last Habsburg emperor, ruling from the death of Franz Josef in 1916 to the end of World War I (and the end of that great dynasty) in 1918. Sisi looks on from across the room.

The **reception room of Franz Josef** (#18) displays a map of the Habsburg Empire at its peak, flanked by etchings featuring 12 of the many different nationalities it ruled. The big painting on the right wall shows the Hungarian Millennium celebrations of 1896 at the Royal Palace at Buda Castle. Also in this room, near the smoking area, notice the very colorful reconstructed stove.

The lavishly chandeliered **grand ballroom** (#19) still hosts concerts. Above the main door, notice the screened-in loft where musicians could play—heard, but not seen. This placement freed up floor space for dancing in this smaller-than-average ballroom.

• *At the far end of the grand ballroom, you enter the...*

Sisi Wing

This wing—where the red color scheme gives way to violet—is dedicated to the enigmatic figure that most people call "Empress

Elisabeth," but whom Hungarians call "our Queen Elisabeth." Sisi adored her Hungarian subjects, and the feeling was mutual. At certain times in her life, Sisi spent more time here at Gödöllő Palace than in Vienna. While the Sisi fixation is hardly unusual at Habsburg sights, notice that the exhibits here are particularly doting...and always drive home Sisi's Hungarian affinities.

In the **reception room** (#20), along with the first of many Sisi portraits, you'll see the portrait of Count Gyula Andrássy. Sisi's enthusiasm for all things Hungarian reportedly extended to this dashing aristocrat, who enjoyed riding horses with Sisi...and allegedly sired her third daughter, Marie Valerie—nicknamed the "Little Hungarian Princess."

In Sisi's **study** (#21), see the engagement portraits of the fresh-faced Franz Josef (age 23) and Sisi (age 16). Although they supposedly married for love, Sisi is said to have later regretted joining the imperial family. The book by beloved Hungarian poet Sándor Petőfi, from Sisi's bedside, is a reminder that Sisi could read and enjoy the difficult Magyar tongue. (It's also a reminder of Sisi's courageous empathy for the Hungarian cause, as Petőfi was killed—effectively by Sisi's husband—in the Revolution of 1848.)

You'll then pass through Sisi's **dressing room** (#23, with small family portraits) and **bedroom** (#24, with faux marble decor). Habsburg Empress Maria Theresa spent two nights here in 1751, a century before it became Sisi's bedroom. Next up are three more rooms with exhibits on Sisi. In the second room, look for the letter in Hungarian, written in Sisi's own hand (marked as *item #17* in the display case) and an invitation to her wedding (set with the fancy lace collar). The third room, with a bust of Sisi, is filled with images of edifices throughout Hungary that are dedicated to this beloved Hungarian queen (such as Budapest's Elisabeth Bridge).

• *Now proceed into the...*

Gisella Wing

Explore these six rooms, which are filled with an exhibit that brings the palace's history up to the 21st century. In the first room, you'll see a huge painting of Sisi mourning Ferenc Deák, the statesman who made great diplomatic strides advocating for Hungarian interests within the Habsburg realm. There's also a more-intimate-than-usual portrait of Franz Josef, with the faint echoes of a real personality (for a change).

Also in this wing are interactive children's exhibits. The blue room introduces you to Sisi's children, including Gisella (the wing's namesake), Rudolf (whose suicide caused his cousin Franz Ferdinand to become the Habsburg heir apparent), and Maria Valeria (the so-called "Little Hungarian Princess").

Finishing your tour, you'll learn how, in the post-Habsburg

era, this building became a summer home for Admiral Miklós Horthy, and later a military base and nursing home, with photographs showing the buildings during each of those periods. The final room displays impressive before-and-after photos illustrating how this derelict complex was only recently restored to its past (and current) glory. You'll exit into a gallery with (surprise, surprise) even more Habsburg portraits.

• *The permanent collection is enough for most visitors. But there are also several intriguing...*

OTHER SIGHTS AT GÖDÖLLŐ PALACE

These extra activities add different dimensions to your experience here. Unfortunately, they're primarily geared toward Hungarian visitors—most require joining a guided tour, which rarely run in English. You can call to ask if an English tour is scheduled; also, some palace guides speak English, and may be willing to tell you a few details after their Hungarian spiel.

Baroque Theater

This reconstructed, fully functional, 120-seat theater can be visited only with a 30-minute guided tour. You'll go backstage to get a good look at the hand-painted scenery, and below the stage to see the pulleys that move that scenery on and offstage. While it's fascinating to theater buffs, the facility feels new rather than old (it's computer-operated), diminishing the "Baroque" historical charm.

Cost and Hours: 1,400 Ft, or 1,100 Ft with palace ticket, English tour may be possible 1-2/day on weekends but unlikely on weekdays, otherwise join Hungarian tour and use English handout.

Stables, Riding Hall, and 3-D Movie

One ticket covers a 40-minute tour of these three sights. The equestrian sights may interest horse lovers, and the movie is interesting to anyone.

The beautifully restored **stables** lead to the high-ceilinged, chandeliered **riding hall** that can still seat 400 people for special events. Upstairs is a small, good **museum** (in English) on Hungary's proud equestrian tradition, with high-tech displays and lots of old uniforms, saddles, and other equipment.

The 10-minute **3-D movie** does a good job of illustrating the history of the royal palace, including virtual re-creations of past versions of the building and its gardens, and dramatic re-enactments of Franz Josef and Sisi's favorite pastimes here. While normally shown in Hungarian, you can try requesting a showing of the English version.

Cost and Hours: 1,200 Ft, or 900 Ft with palace ticket, tours

Franz Josef (1830-1916) and Sisi (1837-1898): Emperor and Empress of Austria, King and Queen of Hungary

In a unique power-sharing compromise, the emperor and empress of the Austrian realm were only the "king" and "queen" of Hungary. (This was known as "*K und K*" in German, for *König und Kaiser*, king and emperor...same guy.) From the beginning of this "K+K" arrangement in 1867 through World War I, this "royal and imperial" couple was Franz Josef and Sisi.

Franz Josef I—who ruled for 68 years (1848-1916)—was the embodiment of the Habsburg Empire as it finished its six-century-long ride. Born in 1830, Franz Josef had a stern upbringing that instilled in him a powerful sense of duty and—like so many men of power—a love of all things military.

His uncle, Ferdinand I, suffered from profound epilepsy, which prevented him from effectively ruling. As the revolutions of 1848 (including Hungary's) were rattling royal families throughout Europe, the Habsburgs forced Ferdinand to abdicate, and put 18-year-old Franz Josef on the throne. Ironically, as one of his first acts as emperor, Franz Josef—whose wife would later become closely identified with Hungarian independence—marched into Budapest to put down the 1848 Revolution. He spent the beginning of his long reign understandably paranoid, as social discontent continued to simmer.

Franz Josef was very conservative. But worse, he wrongly believed that he was a talented military tactician, and led Austria into catastrophic battles. Wearing his uniform to the end, he couldn't see what a dinosaur his monarchy was becoming, and never thought it strange that the majority of his subjects didn't even speak German. Like Queen Victoria, his contemporary, Franz Josef was the embodiment of his empire—old-fashioned but sacrosanct. His passion for low-grade paperwork earned him the nickname "Joe Bureaucrat." Mired in these petty details, he missed the big picture. In 1914, he helped start a Great War that ultimately ended the age of the divine monarchs.

Empress **Elisabeth**—Franz Josef's mysterious, narcissistic, and beautiful wife—has been compared to Princess Diana because of her beauty, bittersweet life, and tragic death.

Sisi, as she's lovingly called, was mostly silent. Her main

goals in life seem to have been preserving her reputation as a beautiful empress, maintaining her Barbie-doll figure, and tending to her fairy-tale, ankle-length hair. In the 1860s, she was considered one of the most beautiful women in the world. But, in spite of severe dieting and fanatical exercise, age took its toll. After turning 30, she allowed no more portraits to be painted of her and was generally seen in public with a delicate fan covering her face (and bad teeth).

Complex and influential, Sisi was adored by Franz Josef, whom she respected. Although Franz Josef was supposed to marry her sister Helene (in an arranged diplomatic marriage), he fell in love with Sisi instead. It was one of the Habsburgs' few marriages for love. (The family was famously adept at strategic marriages.) Still, Sisi never felt fully accepted by her mother-in-law...which made the Hungarians—who also felt misunderstood and not taken seriously by the Habsburgs—appreciate her even more.

Sisi's personal mission and political cause was promoting Hungary's bid for autonomy within the empire. While she was married to Emperor Franz Josef, she spent seven years in Budapest and at Gödöllő, enjoying horseback riding, the local cuisine... and the company of the dashing Count Gyula Andrássy. (For more on the count, see page 145.) Hungarians, who call Sisi their "guardian angel," partly credit her for the Compromise of 1867, which elevated their status within the Habsburg Empire.

Sisi's personal tragedy was the death of her son Rudolf, the crown prince, in an apparent suicide. Disliking Vienna and the confines of the court, Sisi traveled more and more frequently. As years passed, the restless Sisi and her hardworking husband became estranged. In 1898, while visiting Geneva, Switzerland, she was murdered by an Italian anarchist.

A final note: While for simplicity in this book I've referred to these figures as history knows them—"Emperor Franz Josef" and "Empress Sisi"—Hungarians might bristle at these imperial titles. After all, they (and *only* they) called the couple "King Franz Josef" and "Queen Sisi."

DAY TRIPS

at :30 past each hour Thu-Sun 10:30-16:30, no tours Mon-Wed, generally in Hungarian with English handout.

▲WWII-Era Bunker Tour

Gödöllő was a summer residence of Miklós Horthy, the sea admiral who ruled this landlocked country between the World Wars (during Hungary's "kingdom without a king" period). Near the end of his reign, soon before the Nazis invaded, Horthy had a stout bunker built underneath the palace. On the 30-minute required tour, you'll see the two oddly charming, wood-paneled rooms where Horthy and his family would have holed up in case of invasion. (The hominess was designed to make the space more tolerable for Horthy's deeply claustrophobic wife.) The bunker wasn't even finished until after the Nazis took over, and the communist government stored gasoline here for decades—you can still smell the fumes.

Cost and Hours: 800 Ft, or 700 Ft with palace ticket, tours daily year-round at 10:30 and 14:00, generally in Hungarian with an English handout.

Falconry and Archery Show

On summer Sunday afternoons, the palace hosts a one-hour presentation of its trained birds and talented archers. As with most activities here, it's in Hungarian only—but still plenty entertaining.

Cost and Hours: 1,500 Ft, May-Sept Sun only at 15:00.

Lázár Lovaspark Horse Show

Hungary has a rich equestrian tradition dating back to the time when those first Magyars rode across the Asian steppes to Central Europe. And, like the American West, Hungary's rugged Great Plain was settled by brave cowboys (here called *csikós*). As in the US, a world of vivid folklore surrounds these rough-and-tumble cattle wranglers, who are romantically thought of as camping out under the stars and slow-sim-

mering a rich paprika broth in a copper kettle over an open fire (the origin of *gulyás leves,* "shepherd's soup"—a.k.a. goulash). Today, several places around Hungary offer the chance to see a working farm with Hungary's many unique livestock, and take in a thrilling presentation that telescopes a millennium of show-off equestrian talent into one big extravaganza. While authentic, these traditions are kept alive today mostly for curious tourists—so Hungarian horse shows can feel a little hokey. But if you surrender yourself to the remarkable horsemanship, and the connection riders have with their magnificent animals, it's a hoot.

Most horse shows are performed in places where real-life Hungarian cowboys roamed: on the Great Hungarian Plain at Hortobágy National Park (for details, see page 350). But seeing one of those requires an all-day side-trip from Budapest. A handy alternative, the family-run Lázár Lovaspark, worth ▲, is in Budapest's northeastern suburbs—27 miles from the capital, and just nine miles from Gödöllő, making it easy to combine with the royal palace or Hollókő folk village for a busy but fun day out.

GETTING TO LÁZÁR LOVASPARK

It's workable by **public transportation,** but taxis are helpful to connect the dots. From the train station in Gödöllő (connected by frequent trains to downtown Budapest—see page 314), you can take a taxi to Lázár Lovaspark (figure about 2,000 Ft one-way, 15 minutes). You can also reach Lázár Lovaspark directly by public bus from Budapest (runs sporadically Mon-Fri, less Sat-Sun): From the Stadionok bus station (on the M2/red Metró line), ride the bus about 50 minutes, get off at the Domonyvölgy stop (with a small wooden bus shelter), and walk about a half-mile to the park (from the bus stop, cross the street to the other bus stop, and walk down the road—Fenyő utca).

Drivers can exit the M-3 expressway east of Budapest for *Gödöllő,* then follow signs for *Domonyvölgy.* Consider hiring a driver for a day trip to both Gödöllő and Lázár Lovaspark, or stop off on the drive from Budapest to Eger.

ORIENTATION TO LÁZÁR LOVASPARK

Lázár Lovaspark, in the village of Domonyvölgy, is a working farm that's picturesquely set at the base of gently rolling hill. The Lázár brothers have won 16 world championships in carriage riding, and *lovas* is a term meaning, roughly, "equestrian arts."

Cost: 4,000 Ft, includes welcome snack and schnapps, horse show, brief tour, and carriage ride—about 1.5 hours in total.

Hours: Shows generally take place April-Sept daily at 11:30 or 12:00, and at 15:00 and 17:00. But the schedule can vary, so it's essential to call ahead to confirm the time before planning your day around it (and to let them know you're coming). Off-season, shows are often held for private groups (others are welcome to join), but the schedule is less predictable—call ahead.

Information: It's at Fenyő utca 47 in Domonyvölgy, tel. 28/576-510, mobile 0630-871-3424, www.lazarteam.hu, lazarteam@lazarteam.hu.

VISITING LÁZÁR LOVASPARK

Your visit to the park has several parts.

Museum, Stables, and Barnyard Tour: A 20-minute tour takes you to a small "hall of champions" museum celebrating the Lázár clan's illustrious history, and the stables where the horses live (each stall marked with its occupant's prestigious bloodlines). Then you'll visit the barnyard—strangely fascinating for the chance to meet several only-in-Hungary animals: the woolly pig, *mangalica;* the giant gray longhorn cattle, *szürkemarha;* and the corkscrew-antlered goat, *racka.* The farm even has a *puli* sheepdog, with its dreadlock-like coat.

Horse Show: The main event is a 40-minute presentation neatly designed to show off various aspects of Hungary's long equestrian tradition. While there may be commentary during the show, it might not be in English—here's what to watch for: First come the Magyar-style archers, who ride fast as they shoot arrows and throw spears with deadly accuracy at a target (at first stationary, and then moving). Then Hungarian cowboys, clad in blue uniforms, crack their whips as they ride in. They'll show how the whips could be used to disarm an enemy, as well as to train horses not to be startled by gunshots. To demonstrate how well-trained the horses are, the cowboys get their horses to kneel, then lie down—all while the rider is still seated. They explain that nights spent out on the Great Hungarian Plain were far more comfortable when the cowboy could lie on top of his reclining horse. And the cowboys stage a competition to see who can spill the least amount of suds from a full mug of beer while galloping around the track. For comic relief, a rodeo-clown-type "shepherd boy" attempts to get his donkey to do some of the tricks he's seen the horses tackle. Then a carriage rumbles in, pulled by the gigantic grey longhorn cattle called *szürkemarha*—which, it's believed, accompanied those original Magyars on their initial trip here from Asia. A costumed "Sisi" rides out sidesaddle on a clever Lipizzaner stallion, who elegantly do-si-dos a brief routine. Then comes the stirring climax of the show: the famous "Puszta five," where a horseman stands with one foot on each of two horses, while leading three additional horses with reins—galloping at breakneck speed around the track as if waterskiing. Finally the entire gang takes a victory lap.

Carriage Ride: After the show, you'll have the option to hop on an open carriage for a bumpy but fun 15-minute ride through the surrounding plain and forest.

Hollókő

Worth ▲, remote, minuscule Hollókő (HOH-loh-ker), nestled in the hills a 1.5-hour drive from Budapest, survives as a time capsule

of Hungarian tradition. This proud village is half living hamlet, half open-air folk museum; unlike many such places around Europe, people actually reside in quite a few of Hollókő's old buildings. To retain its "real village" status, Hollókő has its own mayor, elementary school, general store, post office, and doctor (who visits twice a week). The village is a treasured part of Hungarian cultural history; an extensive renovation project—which may open some new sights beyond those mentioned here—is due to wrap up in mid-2015.

Hollókő is worth a visit for those who are interested in Hungarian folk culture, especially if you have a car. Note that most of the village shuts down off-season (Oct-Easter) and on Mondays; at these times, skip Hollókő.

GETTING THERE

Hollókő is in a distant valley about 60 miles northeast of Budapest. By **car,** it's about a 1.5-hour drive (assuming light traffic): Take the M-3 expressway east, exit at Hatvan (exit 55), and follow road #21 north toward Salgótarján. Keep an eye out (on the left) for the turnoff for Hollókő and Szécsény, then carefully track *Hollókő* signs. From Eger, figure about 1.5 hours (fastest via the M-3 expressway west, then follow the directions above).

In the summer, and on Sundays year-round, it's possible (but more time-consuming) to reach Hollókő by public transit: A **bus** leaves from Budapest's Stadionok bus station daily year-round at 15:15; on weekends only (Sat-Sun), a second bus departs at 8:30. Buses return to Budapest on a similar schedule (May-Aug daily at 14:00; year-round Sat-Sun at 16:00; plus one early-morning departure at 5:00 on weekdays). The trip takes about two hours each way. Notice that this schedule makes a same-day round-trip from Budapest impossible on weekdays.

PLANNING YOUR TIME

Hollókő deserves at least a couple of hours; a half-day is about right for most visitors. With a car, consider detouring to Hollókő between Budapest and Eger. Remember, Gödöllő Palace and Lázár Lovaspark (which are also off the M-3 expressway) connect well with Hollókő; you could see some combination of these as a side-trip from Budapest, or on the way between Budapest and Eger.

The village is particularly worthwhile on festival days (listed at www.holloko.hu). Don't bother on a Monday or off-season, when nearly everything is closed.

If choosing what to visit at Hollókő, the Village Museum is the most worthwhile, followed by the Doll Museum. The others sights are skippable, but it's worth poking into several shops. Hike up to the castle only if you've got time and energy to burn.

Orientation to Hollókő

Hollókő (total pop.: about 350) is a village squeezed into a dead-end valley overlooked by a castle. The hamlet is divided into two parts: the Old Village (with all the protected old houses, shops, and museums, and about 35 residents) and the New Village. The bus stop and big parking lot are just above the entry point to the Old Village. There's an ATM and a WC behind the pub that overlooks the entrance to the Old Village.

TOURIST INFORMATION

Hollókő's useful TI is at the entrance to the Old Village, at the Hollóköves Infocafé. They can give you a brochure and help you find a room (summer daily 8:00-18:00, sometimes until 20:00; winter Mon-Fri 8:30-16:00, Sat-Sun open only briefly or closed entirely; Kossuth utca 50, mobile 0620-626-2844, www.holloko.hu).

Local Guide: Since English-speakers get little respect at Hollókő (only a few borrowable translations in some museums), you owe it to yourself to hire a local guide. **Ádám Kiss** is a young city slicker who fell in love with Hollókő and moved here with his wife and kids to become part of the community. Ádám, who lived in Montana and speaks good English, will enthusiastically make your time here more meaningful, and he's a great value. He also works as a driver/guide in nearby destinations, including Gödöllő Palace and Eger (6,500 Ft/2-hour tour, does not include entrance fees, more for multi-day driving tours, mobile 0620-379-6132, adamtheguide@gmail.com).

Sights in Hollókő's Old Village

The Old Village at Hollókő is a perfectly preserved enclave of the folk architecture, dress, and traditions of the local Palóc culture. Because it's in a dead-end valley, Hollókő's folk traditions survived here well into the 20th century. (Only when villagers began commuting to other towns for work in the 1950s did they realize how "backward" they seemed to other Hungarians.)

Cost and Hours: It's free to enter the Old Village, but each sight inside has its own modest entry fee (generally around 250 Ft). Unless otherwise noted, sights here are open Easter-Sept Tue-Sun 10:00-17:00, closed Mon; off-season, most places close entirely or are only open Sat-Sun in good weather. Assume that no English is spoken, but at most places you can ask to borrow English translations.

• *I've listed these sights roughly in the order of an easy self-guided orientation walk. Start at the entry point into the Old Village, which begins where the cobbles do. Get oriented with the big wooden map posted nearby (which stands directly in front of the Hollóköves Infocafé—housing the TI). Across the paved street is the...*

Barnyard (Pajtakert)

A local agency coordinates special events here for visiting groups. If you see the ladies in their colorful folk dresses (generally a few

times each day in summer), feel free to gawk from over the fence. Hollókő's men, who tended to go elsewhere for work, abandoned their old-fashioned outfits earlier; but the women, who remained in the valley, kept wearing traditional dress much longer. Their costume is marked by a big, round abdomen (a sign of fertility, created by layering many petticoats), an embroidered vest, and a colorful headdress. In this courtyard, you can pay 300 Ft to enter the weaving room and see an old loom.

• *Now head down the village's main street. As you walk, take a closer look at the...*

Traditional Houses

The exteriors of these houses cannot be changed without permission, but interiors are modern (with plumbing, electricity, Internet access, phones, and so on). They once had thatched roofs with no chimneys (to evade a chimney tax), but a devastating fire in 1909 compelled residents to replace the thatch with tiles and add little chimneys. The thick walls are made of a white-

washed, adobe-type mix of mud and dung (which keeps things cool in summer and warm in winter). Thick walls, small doors (watch your head), small windows...small people back then. The big, overhanging roof (nicknamed the house's "skirt") prevents rain from damaging this fragile composition. Most began as one simple house along the road; as children grew and needed homes of their own, a little family compound evolved around a central courtyard.

• *Continuing down through the village, pause at the fork in the road, in front of Hollókő's...*

Church

A traveling priest says Mass here twice weekly. This is a popular wedding spot for Budapest urbanites charmed by its simplicity.

• *Take the fork to the right (Petőfi út) and wander past a few more shops until the road rejoins. Continue a few yards down the street. On the left, you'll see a* vár/castle *sign leading very steeply up to the town's castle (which is prominent overhead; for a more gradual approach, read on). Across the street is the...*

People and Landscape Museum

This little collection displays photos of Hollókő in the olden days—with thatched roofs and dirt roads...but otherwise looking much the same (250 Ft, closed Mon and Wed).

• *Now backtrack and head back up on the other road (Kossuth út). On the right is the...*

Doll Museum

Step inside to see some 200 dolls dressed in traditional costumes of the area. Each is labeled with the specific place of origin and a basic English description, allowing you to see the subtle changes from village to village (250 Ft, daily 10:00-17:00).

• *Farther up on the right is the...*

▲Village Museum

The Old Village's highlight, this is the only house here with an authentic interior (250 Ft, March-mid-Dec daily 10:00-18:00, closed off-season). Take a trip back a hundred years as you stroll through the house.

Visiting the Museum: You enter into the **kitchen.** Most of the family (including piles of kids) would sleep on the floor here, near the warmth of the stove. The doors on the back wall (behind the stove) lead to a smoker. This very efficient design allowed them to heat the house, cook, bake, and smoke foods all at the same time.

Then head into the **main room** (to the left as you enter). Even today, many older Hungarians have a "nice room" where they keep their most prized possessions and decorations. They let visitors peek in to see their treasures...then make them sit in the kitchen to socialize. In here you'll see plates and clocks proudly displayed. Looking around this room also gives you clues to the family's status. The pillows and linens piled on the bed (stored there during the day, as most family members bunked on the floor) indicate that this was a middle-class home. The linens were traditionally given by the bride's father as a dowry to the groom, allowing the couple to start their life together. The matching furniture is delicately painted. The dresser is well-built and intricate, indicating that a carpenter was paid to make it (other furniture would have been more roughly built by the head of the household). The glass in the windows is not authentic; back then, they would have stretched pig bladders over the windows instead. Turn your attention to the ceiling: The rafters are painted blue to ward off flies (the blue hue contains copper sulfate, a natural insecticide). People would hang their boots (their most expensive item of clothing) up high to prevent mice from ruining them.

Now cross back over to the **third room,** used for storing tools and food. The matriarch of the house slept in here (on the uncomfortable-looking rope bed) and kept the key for this room, doling out the family's ration of food—so in many ways, Grandma was the head of the household. When Granny wasn't watching, and while the rest of the family slept elsewhere in the house, a young woman of courting age could come here to meet up with a suitor, who'd sneak in through the window. (The Hungarians even have a verb for these premarital interactions—roughly, "storaging.") Find the crude crib, used to bring a baby along with adults working the

fields (notice it could be covered to protect from the sun's rays). In other parts of Hungary, peasants were known to partially bury their babies in the ground to prevent them from moving around while they worked. (These days, we use TV—is that really so much more humane?) Look up to find the bread rack suspended from the ceiling—again, to rescue the bread from those troublesome mice. Out back, you'll see the old wine press.

• *Continue up the street. A bit farther up on the right, look for the...*

Post Office Museum

This shows off old postal uniforms, equipment, stamps, and currency (500 Ft, April-Oct daily 10:00-18:00, closed off-season).

• *A few more steps up, and you've completed your circle—you're back at the town church. There's one more sight in town. If you're up for a 15-20-minute uphill hike, consider going up to the* **castle:** *First hike up to the big parking lot; from there, follow the rough path marked* vár/ castle *(a bit uphill at first, then mostly level).*

Castle

Hollókő's castle originally dates from the 13th century. By the 16th century, it was on the frontier between Habsburg-held Hun-

gary and the Ottoman invaders (who eventually conquered the castle and used it for their own defense for a century and a half). After the Habsburgs had retaken Hungary, Emperor Leopold I destroyed the castle prophylactically (in 1711, just after the failed War of Independence) to ensure his Hungarian subjects wouldn't use it against him. It sat in ruins until 1966, when it underwent an extensive, 30-year-long renovation. There are only a few small exhibits to see inside, but it's enjoyable enough to hike around to ever-higher and better panoramas (700 Ft, April-Oct daily 10:00-17:30, may be open in winter on good-weather Sat-Sun). Views over the Old Village give you a sense of how minuscule the town is. The nearby

fields are used to graze Hollókő's livestock, which stay out to pasture at all times rather than being stabled. The high hills on the horizon are across the border, in Slovakia.

The castle is also tied to the legend of how Hollókő ("Hill of the Ravens") got its name: Supposedly the owner of a castle that stood on the hill above this one once kidnapped a girl from the village. The girl's nanny, who was a witch, sent ravens to pick the castle apart, stone by stone.

Sleeping in Hollókő

This is a very sleepy place to spend the night, but those who really want to delve into village Hungary might enjoy it (and its accommodations are far cheaper than other cities or towns in this book).

The **TI** rents several rooms in nine traditional buildings right in the Old Village (figure Db-12,000 Ft including breakfast; see "Tourist Information," earlier).

Tugári Vendégház, run by local guide Ádám Kiss and his wife, has four rooms in a nicely restored old building in the New Village, a five-minute walk from the main sights (8,500-10,500 Ft depending on room size, breakfast-1,200 Ft, Rákóczi út 13, tel. 32/379-156, mobile 0620-379-6132, www.holloko-tugarivendeghaz.hu, tugarivendeghaz@gmail.com).

Eating in Hollókő

Two restaurants near the entrance to Hollókő's Old Village sling traditional, well-priced Hungarian food: **Muskátli Restaurant** and **Vár Restaurant.** Be warned that they both close early (by 18:00 or 19:00, just after the day-trippers go home), so don't wait too long for dinner. At the start of the village, you'll also see a **pub.** A humble **grocery store** is upstairs above the pub (Mon-Sat 7:30-15:30, closed Sun).

The Danube Bend

The Danube, which begins as a trickle in Germany's Black Forest, becomes the Mississippi River of Central Europe—connecting 10 countries and four capitals (Vienna, Bratislava, Budapest, Belgrade) as it flows southeast through the Balkan Peninsula toward the Black Sea. Just south of Bratislava, the river squeezes between mountain ranges, which force it to loop back on itself—creating the scenic "Danube Bend" (Dunakanyar). Here Hungarians sunbathe and swim along the banks of the Danube, or hike in the rugged hills that rise up from the river. Hungarian history hides around every turn of the Bend: For centuries, Hungarian kings ruled not from Buda or Pest, but from Visegrád and Esztergom. And during the Ottoman occupation of Hungary, this area was a buffer zone between Christian and Muslim Europe.

Today, three river towns north of Budapest on the Danube Bend offer a convenient day-trip getaway for urbanites who want a small-town break. Closest to Budapest is Szentendre, whose colorful, storybook-cute Baroque center is packed with tourists. The ruins of a mighty castle high on a hill watch over the town of Visegrád. Esztergom, birthplace of Hungary's first Christian king, has the country's biggest and most important church. All of this is within a one-hour drive of the capital, and also reachable (up to a point) by public transportation.

PLANNING YOUR TIME

Remember, Szentendre is the easiest Danube Bend destination—just a quick suburban-train (HÉV) ride away, it can be done in a few hours. Visegrád and Esztergom are more difficult to reach

DAY TRIPS

The Danube Bend

by public transportation; either one can require a substantial walk from the train or bus stop to the town's major sight.

By **public transportation,** don't try to see all three towns in one day; focus on one or two. (I'd skip Visegrád, whose castle is a headache to reach without a car.) To do the whole shebang, take a tour, rent a car, or hire a driver (see page 35) or local guide (page 42).

With a **car,** try this ambitious one-day plan:

    9:00 Leave Budapest.
    9:30 Arrive at Szentendre and see the town.
  12:00 Leave Szentendre.
  12:30 Lunch in Visegrád.
  13:30 Tour Visegrád Royal Palace and Citadel.
  15:30 Leave Visegrád.
  16:00 Visit Esztergom Basilica.
  17:00 Head back to Budapest.

With extra time, add a visit to the Hungarian Open-Air Folk Museum ("Skanzen") near Szentendre.

If you're driving between Budapest and Vienna (or Bratislava), the Danube Bend towns are a fine way to break up the journey, but seeing all three en route makes for a very long day—get an early start, or skip one.

GETTING AROUND THE DANUBE BEND

Going north from Budapest, the three towns line up along the same road on the west side of the Danube—Szentendre, Visegrád, Esztergom—each spaced about 15 miles apart.

By Car: It couldn't be easier. Get on road #11 going north out of Buda, which will take you through each of the three towns—the road bends with the Danube. As you approach Szentendre (at the traffic light, just before the train station—watch for *Suzuki Szentendre* and various hotel signs), branch off to the right, toward the old center and the river promenade. To return from Esztergom to Budapest, see "Route Tips for Drivers" at the end of this chapter.

By Boat: In the summer, Mahart runs boats from Budapest up the Danube Bend. The slower **riverboats** run to Szentendre (1.5 hours, May-Sept daily except Mon), Visegrád (3 hours, May-Aug daily except Mon, Sept Sat only), and Esztergom (5 hours, May-Aug daily except Mon, Sept Sat only); the faster **hydrofoils** (none to Szentendre, 1 hour to Visegrád, 1.5 hours to Esztergom) run only on summer weekends (May-Sept Sat-Sun). No boats run off-season (Oct-April). Check schedules and buy tickets at the Mahart office in Budapest (dock near Vigadó tér in Pest, tel. 1/484-4010, www.mahartpassnave.hu).

By Train: The three towns are on three separate train lines. Szentendre is truly handy by train, while Visegrád and Esztergom are less convenient.

Getting to **Szentendre** is a breeze by train—the HÉV, Budapest's suburban rail, zips you right there (catch train on H5/purple line at Batthyány tér in Buda's Víziváros neighborhood, easy connection via M2/red Metró line; 4-7/hour, 40 minutes each way, last train returns from Szentendre around 23:00).

The nearest train station to **Visegrád** is actually across the river in Nagymaros (this station is called "Nagymaros-Visegrád"; don't get off at the station called simply "Nagymaros"). From the station, you'll walk five minutes to the river and take a ferry across to Visegrád (see "Arrival in Visegrád" on page 342). Trains run hourly between Nagymaros-Visegrád and Nyugati/Western Station in Budapest (trip takes about 50 minutes).

To **Esztergom,** trains run hourly from Budapest's Nyugati/Western Station (1.5 hours), but the Esztergom train station is a 45-minute walk from the basilica—I'd take a bus or boat instead.

By Bus: Without a car, buses are the best way to hop between the three towns. They're as quick as the train if you're coming from Budapest, but can be standing room only. There are two main routes. The **river route** runs hourly from Budapest along the Danube through Szentendre (30 minutes) and Visegrád (1.25 hours), then past Esztergom Basilica (2 hours, Iskola Utca stop) to the Esztergom bus station (more frequent during weekday rush hours). This bus leaves from Budapest's Újpest-Városkapu bus station (at the M3/blue line Metró station of the same name). A different bus takes the **overland shortcut** (skipping Szentendre and Visegrád) to directly connect Budapest and Esztergom (1-2/hour, 1.25 hours, departs from Budapest's Árpád híd station on the M3/blue Metró line). Buses make many stops en route, so you'll need to pay attention for your stop (ask driver or other passengers for help).

By Tour from Budapest: If you want to see all three towns in one day but don't have a car and don't want to shell out for a private driver, a bus tour is the most convenient way to go. All of the companies are about the same (all 3 towns in about 10 hours, including lunch and shopping stops, plus return by boat, for around 20,000 Ft); look for fliers at the Budapest TI or in your hotel's lobby.

Szentendre

Worth ▲, the Old Town of Szentendre (SEHN-tehn-dreh, "St. Andrew" in English) rises gently from the Danube, a postcard-pretty village with a twisty Medi- terranean street plan filled with Habsburg Baroque houses. Argu- ably the most "Balkan-feeling" town of Hungary—thanks to the many diverse immigrants who settled the community—Szentendre promises a taste of Hungarian village life with- out having to stray far from Buda- pest...but it sometimes feels like too many other people have had the same idea. Szentendre is where Budapesters bring their sig- nificant others for that special weekend lunch. The town has a long tradition as an artists' colony, and it still has more than its share of museums and galleries. It's also packed with corny, gimmicky museums—a few of which (such as the Micro Art collection) are actually worthwhile. But the best plan is this: Venture off the sou- venir-choked, tourist-clogged main streets...and you'll soon have the quiet back lanes under colorful Baroque steeples all to yourself.

Orientation to Szentendre

Little Szentendre (pop. 23,000) is easy to navigate. It clusters along a mild incline rising from the Danube, culminating at the main square (Fő tér) at the foot of Church Hill (Templomdomb). From the embankment—where most tourists arrive—various streets lead

up to Fő tér, none more touristy than the souvenir gauntlet of Bog-
dányi utca.

TOURIST INFORMATION

The TI sits at the southern end of the old center, near the blocky
modern tower of the Evangelical Church. Pick up the good town
map, with sights and services well-marked (unpredictable hours but
typically daily 10:00-17:30, Fri-Sun until 18:00, less off-season,
Dumtsa Jenő utca 22, tel. 26/317-965, www.iranyszentendre.hu).

ARRIVAL IN SZENTENDRE

By Train or Bus: The combined **train/HÉV and bus station** is
at the southern edge of town. To reach the town center from the
station (about a 10-minute walk), go through the pedestrian underpass at the head of the train tracks. (A handy map of town is
posted by the head of the tracks.) The underpass funnels you onto
the small Kossuth Lajos utca. After a long block, you'll pass the
yellow Pozsarevacska Serbian Orthodox church, then cross the
bridge; the TI is on the right, and the main square is three blocks
straight ahead.

    By Boat: Some boats arrive right near the main square, but
most come to a pier about a 15-minute walk north of the center.
After you get off the boat, take the first path to your left; stay on it,
and it'll lead you straight into town.

    By Car: Approaching on road #11 from Budapest, turn right
at the traffic light just after several signs directing you to hotels
(also watch for the *Suzuki Szentendre* arrow). Park anywhere along
the embankment road (pay and display); if you can't find any free
spaces, continue on to the large bus parking lot near the boat dock.
From the embankment, it's an easy uphill walk into town; all roads
lead to the main square.

DAY TRIPS

Sights in Szentendre

Sightseeing in Szentendre is low-impact. While
there are museums and churches to visit, the
best plan for most is to simply stroll and peo-
ple-watch through town and along the elevated
Danube riverbank. Head off to the back streets,
and you'll be surprised at how quickly you'll find
yourself alone with Szentendre.

ON OR NEAR FŐ TÉR
▲Main Square (Fő Tér)

Szentendre's top sight is the town itself. Start at
the main square (Fő tér). Take a close look at

A Taste of the Balkans: Szentendre's History

Szentendre feels more Balkan than Hungarian. That's because it was built as a melting pot of Serbs, Greeks, and Dalmatians.

The Habsburgs forced the Ottomans out of Hungary in the late 17th century, and pushed them farther south in the Balkan Peninsula. Especially after the Ottomans' successful 1690 siege of Belgrade, a flood of 40,000 refugee families—Serbs, Dalmatians (from today's Croatia), and Greeks—sought shelter up the Danube. Many settled here in Szentendre.

At first, these Balkan transplants built temporary houses and shops, following the narrow-alley street plan of their homeland.

They tended to settle in regional enclaves, each of which maintained its heritage and traditions: four neighborhoods representing different regions of Serbia, and two from other ethnic backgrounds (Greeks and Dalmatians). Each of the six neighborhoods had its own church, plus the original, medieval Catholic church.

While they were waiting to return home, the Balkan refugees supported the Habsburgs (who were facing down the Hungarians in Ferenc Rákóczi's War of Independence). This earned Szentendre the favor of the emperor, who rewarded the town with special trade privileges, including the right to make and sell wine—a tradition still evidenced by the vineyards blanketing the hillsides around town.

the **cross,** erected in 1763 to give thanks for surviving the plague. Notice the Cyrillic lettering at the monument's base. This is a reminder that in many ways, Szentendre is more of a Serbian town than a Hungarian one (see sidebar).

Face the cross and get oriented: Behind the cross, the square narrows as it curls around Church Hill, with its hilltop Catholic church; just behind that is the Orthodox Cathedral. Through a narrow alley to the left (between the red and yellow houses) is the fun Micro Art Museum. The street to the left (Dumtsa Jenő utca) leads to the Marzipan Museum and TI. To the right, the church fronting the square is Orthodox (called Blagovestenszka); it's been closed for a lengthy restoration, but might reopen as a museum. And directly behind you (facing the cross) is the ticket office for Szentendre's top art collection, the Margit Kovács Museum. All of these sights are described next.

By the time the Ottomans were forced out of the Balkans, the former refugees in Szentendre had decided to stick around. They benefited from the increased trade flowing up the Danube (from lands recently liberated from the Ottomans), and replaced their temporary houses and churches with permanent ones—mostly in the snazzy, colorful Baroque and Rococo styles popular in Habsburg lands at the time. This explains why so many churches in town are Baroque Catholic on the outside, but have strikingly different Orthodox interiors.

The fortunes of the people here began to change in the 1770s, when the reformist Emperor Josef II revoked Szentendre's special rights. The town's prominence declined, as commerce shifted down the Danube to Buda and Pest. Then, a phylloxera pest infestation in the 1880s devastated the town's vineyards.

By the late 19th century, Szentendre was a semi-ghost town, still populated by the now-poor descendants of those original Balkan immigrants. Artists began to discover the village, and were inspired by its colorful cultural pastiche, unusual-for-Hungary narrow lanes, low rents, and closeness to nature—all within close proximity to the bustling metropolis of Budapest. A "Szentendre School" of artists emerged, putting the town on the map of art history and luring Budapesters to come for a visit. Today Szentendre has six different museums dedicated to local artists (the best is Margit Kovács), with many more starving art students who toil away, hoping to fill their own gallery someday. Szentendre is also a bedroom community for wealthy Budapesters—near the big city, but still in a tranquil and beautiful setting.

Margit Kovács Museum (Kovács Margit Múzeum)

The best of Szentendre's small art museums celebrates the local artist Margit Kovács, highly regarded for her whimsical, primitive-looking, wide-eyed pottery sculptures. Kovács (1902-1977) was the first female Hungarian artist to be accepted as a major talent by critics and by her fellow artists. She came from a close-knit family, and had a religious upbringing, both themes that would appear frequently in her work. The down-to-earth Kovács, who never married, lived with her mother—her best friend and most constructive critic. This collection of her ceramic sculptures, displayed on several floors and explained in English, is organized by theme. You'll see Christian, mythological, and folkloric subjects depicted side by side; even in many biblical scenes, the subjects wear traditional Hungarian clothing. Look for the room of sorrowful statues dating from after her mother's death. On the top floor, in the replica of Kovács' study, find the gnarled tree stump. This tree, which once stood on Budapest's Margaret Island, had been struck by lightning, and its twisted forms inspired Kovács.

Cost and Hours: 1,000 Ft, daily 10:00-18:00, www.pmmi.hu. First buy your tickets at the office at the bottom of Fő tér (at #2-5). Then, you might be able to pass directly into the museum, or you might have to go around the block to get there (jog down Görög utca and take your first right to Vastagh György utca 1).

Micro Art Museum (Mikro Csodák Múzueuma)

This charming and genuinely fascinating "Micro Miracles" collection, while a bit of a tourist trap, is worth a squint. Ukrainian artist Mikola "Howdedoodat" Szjadrisztij has crafted an array of 15 literally microscopic pieces of art—a detailed chessboard on the head of a pin, a pyramid panorama in the eye of a needle, a swallow's nest in half a poppy seed, a golden lock on a single strand of hair, and even a minuscule portrait of Abe Lincoln. You'll go from microscope to microscope, peering at these remarkably detailed sculptures.

Cost and Hours: 700 Ft, English descriptions, daily 9:00-18:00, down the appropriately tiny alley called Török föz at Fő tér 18-19, tel. 26/313-651.

ON DUMTSA JENŐ UTCA

This street, which leads away from Fő tér, is where you'll find the...

Marzipan Museum

This collection (attached to a popular candy and ice-cream store) features two floors of sculptures made of marzipan. Feast your eyes on Muppets, cartoon characters, Russian nesting dolls, an over-the-top wedding cake, a life-size Michael Jackson, and, of course, Hungarian patriotic symbols (the Parliament, the Turul bird, and so on). While fun for kids, this is skippable for adults. Note that there are similar marzipan museums in Eger and on Budapest's Castle Hill; visiting more than one is redundant.

Cost and Hours: Free to enter shop, small fee for museum, daily 10:00-18:00, Dumtsa Jenő utca 12, enter from Batthyány utca, tel. 26/311-931, www.szamosmarcipan.hu.

CHURCH HILL LOOP

For a representative look at Szentendre's seven churches, visit the best two, connected by a loop walk.

• Begin on the main square (Fő tér). Go a few steps up the street at the top of the square (behind the cross). Just before the white Town Hall, climb the stairs on your right, and work your way up to the hilltop park, called...

DAY TRIPS

Church Hill (Templomdomb)

This hill-capping perch offers some of the best views over the jum-

bled, Mediterranean-style roofline of old Szentendre. (See how many steeples you can count in this church-packed town.) Looking down on Fő tér, you can see how the town's market square evolved at the place where its three trade roads converged.

• *The hill's centerpiece is...*

St. John Catholic Church (Keresztelő Szent János)

This was the first house of worship in Szentendre, around which the Balkan settlers later built their own Orthodox churches. If it's open, step into the humble interior (free, sporadic hours). Pay special attention to the apse, which was colorfully painted by starv-
ing artists in the early 20th century.

• *Exiting the church, take the downhill lane toward the red-and-yellow steeple. Find the gate in the wall (along Alkot-mány street) to enter the yard around this church. Pay a visit to the...*

DAY TRIPS

▲Belgrade Serbian Orthodox Cathedral (Belgrádi Székesegyház)

This offers perhaps Szentendre's best opportunity to dip into an Orthodox church.

Cost and Hours: 600 Ft, also includes museum, Tue-Sun 10:00-18:00, closed Mon, shorter hours off-season; during winter, go to the museum first, then they'll let you into the church.

Visiting the Church: Standing in the gorgeous **church interior,** ponder the Ortho-dox faith that dominates in most of the Balkan Peninsula (starting just south and east of the Hungarian border). Keep in mind that these churches carry on the earliest traditions of the Christian faith. Notice the lack of pews—wor-shippers stand through the service, with men separate from women, as a sign of respect before God. The Serbian Orthodox Church uses essentially the same Bible as Catholics, but it's written in the Cyrillic alphabet (which you'll see displayed around many Orthodox churches). Following Old Testament Judeo-Christian tradition, the Bible is kept on the altar behind the iconostasis—the big screen in the middle of the room covered with icons (golden paintings of saints), which separates the material world from the spiritual one.

Orthodox icons are typically not intended to be lifelike. Packed with intricate symbolism, and cast against a shimmering golden background, they're meant to remind viewers of the metaphysical nature of Jesus and the saints rather than their physical form. However, this church, which blends pure Orthodoxy with Catholic traditions of Hungary, features some Baroque-style statues that are unusually fluid and lifelike.

Orthodox services generally involve chanting (a dialogue that goes back and forth between the priest and the congregation), and the church is filled with the evocative aroma of incense. The incense, chanting, icons, and standing up are all intended to heighten the experience of worship. While many Catholic and Protestant services tend to be more of a theoretical and rote consideration of religious issues, Orthodox services are about creating an actual religious experience.

Don't miss the adjacent **museum,** covered by the same ticket. You'll see religious objects, paintings, vestments, and—upstairs—icons, with good English descriptions.

• *For a scenic back-streets stroll before returning to the tourist crush, go through the yard around the church, exit through the gate, turn left up the little alley, and then turn right at the T-junction, which takes you through what was the Dalmatian neighborhood to charming Rab-Ráby tér. The lanes between here and the waterfront are among the most appealing and least crowded in Szentendre.*

NEAR SZENTENDRE
Hungarian Open-Air Folk Museum
(Szabadtéri Néprajzi Múzeum, aka Skanzen)

Three miles northwest of Szentendre is an open-air museum featuring examples of traditional Hungarian architecture from all over the country. As with similar museums throughout Europe, these aren't replicas—each building was taken apart at its original location, transported piece by piece, and reassembled here. The museum is huge and spread out, so a thorough visit could take several hours. The admission price includes a map in English, and the museum shop sells a good English guidebook for 1,000 Ft. Because it's so large, the museum is worth visiting only if you can give it the time it deserves. Skip it unless you can arrange your visit to coincide with one of their frequent special-events-laden "festival days" (listed on their website).

Cost and Hours: 1,500 Ft, 100 Ft more on "festival days"; April-Oct Tue-Sun 9:00-17:00, closed Mon; mid-Feb-March Sat-Sun only 10:00-16:00, closed Mon-Fri; closed Nov-mid-Feb; last entry 30 minutes before closing, Sztaravodai út, tel. 26/502-500, www.skanzen.hu.

Getting There: It takes about five minutes to **drive** from Szentendre to Skanzen (pay parking). **Bus** #7 heads from Szentendre to Skanzen when the museum's open (runs sporadically—see Skanzen website for specific schedule). A **taxi** from Szentendre to the museum should cost no more than 2,000 Ft; the TI can call one for you (mobile 0626-314-314).

Eating in Szentendre

Interchangeable, touristy restaurants abound in Szentendre. I enjoy the ambience at **Promenade Vendéglő,** with charming courtyard or indoor seating. They serve Hungarian and Balkan cuisine with take-your-time service (2,000-4,000-Ft main dishes, daily 10:00-22:00, Futó utca 4, along the Dunakorzó embankment, tel. 26/312-626).

Visegrád

Visegrád (VEE-sheh-grahd, Slavic for "High Castle," pop. 1,600) is a small village next to the remains of two major-league castles: a hilltop citadel and a royal riverside palace. While the town itself disappoints many visitors, others enjoy the chance to be close to these two chapters of history.

The Romans were the first to fortify the steep hill overlooking the river. Later, Károly Róbert (Charles Robert), from the French/Neapolitan Anjou dynasty, became Hungary's first non-Magyar king in 1323. He was so unpopular with the nobles in Buda that he had to set up court in Visegrád, where he built a new residential palace down closer to the Danube. (For more on this king, see page 204.) Later, King Mátyás (Matthias) Corvinus—notorious for his penchant for Renaissance excess—ruled from Buda but made Visegrád his summer home, and turned the riverside palace into what some called a "paradise on earth." Matthias knew how to party; during his time here, red-marble fountains flowed with wine. (To commemorate these grand times, the town hosts a corny Renaissance restaurant, with period cookware, food, costumed waitstaff, and live lute music—you can't miss it, by the palace and Hotel Vár.)

Today, both citadel and palace are but a shadow of their former splendor. The citadel was left to crumble after the Habsburg reoccupation of Hungary in 1686, while the palace was covered by a mudslide during the Ottoman occupation, and is still being excavated. The citadel is more interesting, but difficult to reach by public transport. Non-drivers may be better off skipping this town.

Orientation to Visegrád

The town of Visegrád is basically a wide spot in the riverside road, squeezed between the hills and the riverbank. At Visegrád's main intersection (coming from Szentendre/Budapest), the crossroads leads to the left through the heart of the village, then hairpins up the hills to the citadel. To the right is the dock for the ferry to Nagymaros (home to the closest train station, called Nagymaros-Visegrád—see "Arrival in Visegrád").

The town has two sights. The less interesting, riverside Royal Palace is a 15-minute walk downriver (toward Szentendre/Budapest) from the village center. The hilltop citadel, high above the village, is the focal point of a larger recreational area best explored by car.

TOURIST INFORMATION

The town doesn't have an official TI. You can get information at the giant **Hotel Visegrád** complex, which caters to passing tour groups at the village crossroads. They answer basic questions, sell maps, and hand out a few free leaflets. In summer, check in at the **Visegrád Tours** travel agency (May-Oct daily 8:00-17:30, generally closed Nov-April, Rév utca 15, tel. 26/398-160, www.visegrad. hu or www.visegradtours.hu); at other times, ask at the hotel reception desk (at the opposite end of the complex, through the unappealing Sirály restaurant).

ARRIVAL IN VISEGRÁD

Train travelers arrive across the river at the Nagymaros-Visegrád station (don't get off at the station called simply "Nagymaros"). Walk five minutes to the river and catch the ferry to Visegrád, which lands near the village's main crossroads (hourly, usually in sync with the train, last ferry around 20:30). **Buses** to Visegrád make several stops: the Királyi Palota stop is most convenient for the Royal Palace near the entrance to town, while the Nagymarosi Rév stop is at the main crossroads in the heart of town.

Sights in Visegrád

Visegrád Citadel (Fellegvár)

The remains of Visegrád's hilltop citadel, while nothing too exciting, can be fun to explore. Only a few exhibits have English labels, but headsets allow you to hear information in English. Perhaps best of all, the upper levels of the citadel offer commanding views over the Danube Bend—which, of course, is exactly why they built it here.

Cost and Hours: 1,700 Ft, save 300 Ft if you skip the waxworks; daily May-Sept 10:00-18:00, March-April and Oct 9:00-17:00, may be open shorter hours Nov-Feb but always closes in icy winter weather, last entry 30 minutes before closing, tel. 26/398-101, www.parkerdo.hu/visegradi_var.

Getting There: To **drive** to the citadel, follow *Fellegvár* signs down the village's main street and up into the hills (parking-300 Ft). Otherwise, you have two options: Get a map at Visegrád Tours/Hotel and **hike** 45 steep minutes up from the village center; or take the **taxi service** misleadingly called "City Bus." This minivan trip costs 2,600 Ft one-way, no matter how many people ride along (ask at Visegrád Tours/Hotel, or call 26/397-372, www.city-bus.hu).

Visiting the Castle: Buy your ticket and hike up the path toward the castle entry. On the way up, you can pay extra to try your hand at a bow and arrow, or pose with a bird of prey perched on your arm.

Belly up to the viewpoint for sweeping **Danube Bend views.** From here, you can see that the Danube actually does a double-bend—a smaller one (upstream), then a bigger one (downstream)—creating an S-shaped path before settling into its southward groove. It's easy to understand why the Danube, constricted between mountains, is forced to bend here. The river nar-rows as it passes through this gorge, then widens again below the castle, depositing sediment that becomes the islands just downstream. Just upstream from Visegrád, the strange half-lake on the riverbank is all that's left of an aborted communist-era dam project to tame the river.

Climb up to the top of the complex. In the **castle museum,** you'll see a replica of the Hungarian crown. The real one (now safely stored under the Parliament dome in Budapest) was actually kept here, off and on, for some 200 years, when this was Hungary's main castle.

Deeper into the complex, you reach the **waxworks** *(panopti-kum)*, illustrating a scene from an important medieval banquet: In 1335, as Habsburg Austria was rising to the west, the kings of Hungary, Poland, and Bohemia converged here to strategize against this new threat. Centuries later, history repeated itself: In February of 1991, after the fall of the Iron Curtain, the heads of state of basically the same nations—Hungary, Poland, and Czechoslovakia—once again came together here, this time to compare notes about Westernization. To this day, Hungary, Poland, the Czech Republic, and Slovakia are still sometimes referred to collectively as the "Visegrád countries."

Continue up to the very top of the complex, the **inner castle.** Here you'll find a hunting exhibit (dioramas with piles of stuffed animals) and the armory (with a few weapons, and coats of arms of knights). To conquer the castle, climb up to the very top tower, where you can scramble along the ramparts.

Near the Citadel: Around the citadel is a recreational area that includes restaurants, a picnic area, a luge and toboggan run, a network of hiking paths, a Waldorf school, and a children's nature-education center and campground.

Eating near the Citadel: Eating options in Visegrád are limited; most restaurants are big operations catering to tour groups. By the luge run (a lengthy-but-doable walk from the citadel), the **Nagyvillám restaurant** is elegant, with breathtaking views from the best tables (2,000-3,300-Ft main dishes, Mon-Thu 11:30-18:00, Fri-Sun 11:30-20:00, tel. 26/398-070). Only drivers can reach the **picnic area** (called Telgárthy-rét), in a shady valley with paths and waterfalls.

Royal Palace (Király Palota)

Under King Matthias Corvinus, this riverside ruin was one of Europe's most elaborate Renaissance palaces. During the Ottoman occupation, it was deserted and eventually buried by a mudslide. For generations, the palace's existence faded into legend, so its rediscovery in 1934 was a surprise. Today, the partially excavated remains are tourable, with sparse English descriptions.

Cost and Hours: 1,100 Ft, Tue-Sun 9:00-17:00, closed Mon, tel. 26/398-026, www.visegradmuzeum.hu.

Visiting the Palace: The palace courtyard, decorated with a red-marble fountain, evokes its Renaissance glory days. Upstairs, look for the giant green ceramic stoves, and at the top level, find the famous canopied fountain with lions. This "Hercules Fountain"—pictured on the back of the 1,000-Ft note—once had wine spouting from the lions' mouths, with which Matthias used to ply visiting dignitaries to get the best results.

The small Solomon's Tower up the hill from the Royal Palace (not worth the 700-Ft admission) once held a vampire... sort of. Vlad the Impaler, a nobleman who terrorized villagers in Transylvania (back when it was part of Hungary), was arrested and imprisoned here during the time of Matthias. Centuries later, Bram Stoker found inspiration in Vlad's story while writing his novel *Dracula*.

Esztergom

Esztergom (EHS-tehr-gohm, pop. 29,000) is an unassuming town with a big Suzuki factory. You'd never guess it was the first capital of Hungary—until you see the towering 19th-century Esztergom Basilica, built on the site where István (Stephen) I, Hungary's first Christian king, was crowned in A.D. 1000.

ARRIVAL IN ESZTERGOM

Esztergom's **boat dock** is more convenient to the basilica than the bus or train stations are (can't miss the basilica as you disembark—hike on up).

If arriving on the **riverside bus** from Visegrád, get off by the basilica (Iskola Utca stop)—not at the bus station.

If you're coming by **train,** or on the **overland bus** from Budapest, you're in for a longer walk. To reach the basilica on foot from the train station, allow at least 45 minutes. Continue in the same direction as the train tracks, and when the street forks, go straight along the residential Ady Endre utca. After a few minutes, you'll pass the bus station, from which it's 30 minutes farther to the basilica. Local buses run between the train station and the basilica roughly hourly. On Wednesdays and Fridays, an open-air market enlivens the street between the bus station and the center.

Sights in Esztergom

▲▲Esztergom Basilica (Esztergomi Bazilika)

This basilica, on the site of a cathedral founded by Hungary's beloved St. István, commemorates Hungary's entry into the fold of Western Christendom. St. István was born in Esztergom, and

on Christmas Day in the year 1000—shortly after marrying the daughter of the king of Bavaria and accepting Christianity—he was crowned here by a representative of the pope (for more on St. István, see page 211). Centuries later, after Esztergom had been retaken from the retreating Ottomans, the Hungarians wanted to build a "small Vatican" complex to celebrate the Hungarian Catholic Church and their triumphant return to the region. The Habsburgs who controlled the area at the time (and were also good Catholics) agreed, but did not want to be upstaged, so progress was sluggish. The Neoclassical basilica was erected slowly between 1820 and 1869, on top of the remains of a ruined hilltop castle. With a 330-foot-tall dome, this is the tallest building in Hungary.

Cost and Hours: Basilica—free, daily April-Oct 8:00-18:00, Nov-March 8:00-16:00. Tower climb—700 Ft, daily April-Oct 9:30-17:00, closed Nov-March and in bad weather. Crypt—200 Ft, daily March-Oct 9:00-17:00, Nov-Feb 10:00-16:00. Treasury—900 Ft, same hours as crypt. Tel. 33/402-354, www.bazilika-esztergom.hu.

⊘ Self-Guided Tour: Approaching the church is like walking toward a mountain—it gets bigger and bigger, yet you never quite reach it. In front of the church is a **statue of Mary,** the "Head, Mother, and Patron" of the Hungarian Church.

Enter through the side door (on the left as you face the front of the basilica, under the arch). In the foyer, the stairway leading down to the right takes you to the **crypt.** This frigid space, with tree-trunk columns, culminates at the tomb of Cardinal József Mindszenty, revered and persecuted for standing up to the communist government (see sidebar). Also in the main chamber, look for original tombstones of 15th-century archbishops.

Back upstairs in the foyer, a stairway leads up to the church **tower,** which has fine views.

Enter the cavernous **nave.** Take in the enormity of the third-biggest church in Europe (by square footage). The lack of supporting pillars in the center of the church further exaggerates its vastness. This space was consecrated in 1856—before the entire

Cardinal József Mindszenty
(1892-1975)

József Mindszenty was a Hungarian priest who rose through the ranks to become Archbishop of Esztergom, cardinal, and head of the Hungarian Catholic Church. This outspoken cleric was arrested several times, by very different regimes: in 1919 for defying the early Hungarian communist leader Béla Kun; during World War II, for criticizing the Arrow Cross's deportation of Jews; and again in 1948, for speaking out against the communist regime.

Upon his arrest in 1948, Mindszenty was relentlessly tortured to extract a confession. He became the subject of a high-profile "show trial," and was convicted to life in prison. (An enraged Pope Pius XII excommunicated those who had tried and convicted Mindszenty.) Mindszenty's plight was dramatized in the 1955 film *The Prisoner*, starring Alec Guinness as the cardinal.

During the 1956 Uprising, Mindszenty was freed for a brief time. But when the uprising was put down with violence, he sought refuge in the US Embassy on Budapest's Szabadság tér—where he stayed for 15 years, unable to leave for fear of being recaptured. Many Catholic Americans who grew up during this time remember praying for Cardinal Mindszenty every day when they were kids. In 1971, he agreed to step down from his position, then fled to Austria.

On his deathbed, in 1975, Mindszenty said that he did not want his body returned to Hungary as long as there was a single Russian soldier still stationed there. As the Iron Curtain was falling in 1989, Mindszenty emerged as an important hero to post-communist Hungarians, who wanted to bring his remains back to his homeland. But Mindszenty's secretary, in accordance with the cardinal's final wishes, literally locked himself to the coffin—refusing to let the body be transported as long as any Soviet soldier remained in Hungary. In May of 1991, when only a few Russians were still in Hungary, Mindszenty's remains were finally brought to the crypt in the Esztergom Basilica.

building was finished—at a Mass with music composed by Franz Liszt.

As you face the altar, find the chapel on the left before the transept. This Renaissance **Bakócz Chapel,** part of an earlier church that stood here, predates the basilica by 350 years. It was commissioned by the archbishop during King Matthias Corvinus' reign. The archbishop imported Italian marble-workers to create a fitting space to house his remains. Note the typically Renaissance red marble—the same marble that decorates Matthias' palace at Visegrád. When the basilica was built, the chapel was disassembled into 1,600 pieces and rebuilt inside the new structure. The heads around the chapel's altar were defaced by the Ottomans, who, as Muslims, believed that only God—not sculptors—can create man.

Continue to the **transept.** On the right transept wall, St. István offers the Hungarian crown to Mary—seemingly via an angelic DHL courier. There's a depiction of this very church towering on the horizon. Mary is particularly important to Hungarians, because István—the first Christian king of Hungary—had no surviving male heir, so he appealed to Mary for help. (Eventually one of István's cousins, András I, took the crown and managed to keep his kingdom in the fold of Christianity.)

And one more tour-guide factoid: Above the **altar** is what's reputed to be the biggest single-canvas oil painting in the world. (It's of the Assumption, by Michelangelo Grigoletti.)

Finish your visit with the **treasury,** to the right of the main altar (do this last, as you'll exit outside the building; no English descriptions—pick up the illustrated listing at the entrance or, if they're out, at the gift shop at the end). Head up the spiral staircase to view the impressive collection. After a display of vestments, you'll wander a long hall tracing the evolution of ecclesiastical art styles: Gothic, Renaissance, Baroque, Rococo, and Modern. In the first (Gothic) section, find the giant drinking horns, used by kings at royal feasts. The second (Renaissance) section shows off some intricately decorated chalices. A close look at the vestments here shows that they're embroidered with 3-D scenes, and slathered with gold and pearls. In the case on the wall, find the collection's prized possession: an incredibly ornate example of Christ on the cross—but Jesus here bears an unmistakable likeness to King Matthias Corvinus. In the third (Baroque) and fourth (Rococo) sections, notice things getting frilly—and bigger and bigger, as the church got more money. The fifth (Modern) section displays an array of kissable bishop rings.

The exit takes you out to a **Danube-view terrace.** For the best river-bend view, walk a hundred yards or so downstream (right) to the modern statue of St. István. It shows Hungary's favorite saint being crowned by the local bishop after converting to Christianity; St. István symbolically holds up the arches of the Hungarian Church. (Until this statue was built in 2003, this was *the* choice spot for Esztergom teens to kiss.) Between the statue and the river, you can see the ruins of an Ottoman bath and the evocative stub of a ruined minaret, with its spiral staircase exposed and going nowhere.

That's **Štúrovo, Slovakia,** across the river, connected to Hungary by the Mária Valéria Bridge—destroyed in World War II and rebuilt only in 2001. Before its reconstruction, no bridges spanned the Danube between Budapest and Bratislava. If you have time, you can walk or drive across the bridge to Slovakia for the best views back to this basilica (no passport checks).

Near the Basilica: This hilltop was once heavily fortified, and some ruins of its castle survive—now part of the **Castle Museum** next to the basilica (opposite side from the István statue). In 2007, restorers discovered a fresco of the four virtues, likely by Sandro Botticelli. The complex also includes the chapel where St. István was supposedly born. Unfortunately, both of these areas are closed for restoration (work has stalled due to lack of funding). For now, all there is to see is lots of dusty old exhibits about arcane Hungarian history, from the Stone Age through the Ottoman period (500-Ft "walking ticket" to tour the grounds; 1,300 Ft to join a Hungarian tour of the interior, or pay 500 Ft extra if there's an English tour; April-Oct Tue-Sun 10:00-18:00, Nov-March Tue-Sun 10:00-16:00, closed Mon year-round, www.mnmvarmuzeuma.hu).

Eating in Esztergom

A few restaurants cluster near the basilica (including one built into the fortifications underneath it), but these cater to tour groups and serve mediocre food. It's more interesting to venture down the hill to the **Víziváros** ("Water Town") neighborhood on the riverbank below the basilica. This area has a pleasant, old-town ambience and some fine local-style eateries. You can either walk down on the path from the basilica, or (in summer) catch a handy tourist train for 500 Ft.

Esztergom Connections

BY BUS
For connections, see "Getting Around the Danube Bend" on page 333. When choosing between the riverside bus and the direct overland bus, note that the overland bus—while faster and offering different scenery—departs much farther from the basilica than the riverside bus.

ROUTE TIPS FOR DRIVERS:
RETURNING FROM ESZTERGOM TO BUDAPEST
The easiest choice is to retrace your route on road #11 around the Bend to Budapest. But to save substantial time and see different

scenery, I prefer "cutting the Bend" and taking a shortcut through the Pilis hills (takes just over an hour total, depending on traffic).

To Cut the Bend: From the basilica in Esztergom, continue along the main road #11 (away from Budapest) to the roundabout with the round, yellow, Neoclassical church (built as a sort of practice before they started on the basilica). Here you can choose your exit: If you exit toward **Budapest/Dorog,** it'll take you back on road #11 for a while, then route you onto the busier road #10 (which can have heavy traffic—especially trucks—on weekdays). Better yet, if you head for **Dobogókő,** you'll follow a twistier but faster route via the town of Pilisszentkereszt to Budapest. After about 30 minutes on this road, in the town of Pomáz, follow signs to road #11 to the left, then turn right toward Budapest at the next fork to join road #11 into the city. (Don't follow signs at the Pomáz intersection for Budapest, which takes you along a more heavily trafficked road.)

More Hungarian Destinations

The destinations I've covered in depth will keep you busy for at least two weeks in Hungary. But if you have more time or a special interest, there's much more of Hungary to experience. Here are some ideas to get you started on planning a visit to other parts of the country.

South of Budapest:
The Great Hungarian Plain

More than half of Hungary (essentially everything southeast of the Danube) constitutes the Great Hungarian Plain, or Puszta. Broad, flat, desolate, and parched in the late summer and autumn, the Great Hungarian Plan is the Magyar version of Big Sky Country. Most of the sights listed here (except Hortobágy National Park) line up along the M-5 expressway south of Budapest; a train line also connects them (trains depart Budapest hourly, 1.5 hours to Kecskemét, 2.5 hours to Szeged).

▲▲Traditional Horse Shows

If the idea of the Lázár Lovaspark horse show (described earlier) intrigues you, consider experiencing a similar performance in its original setting, on the Great Hungarian Plain. Various farms around the Puszta put on these shows frequently in summer, and by request off-season. The various options all hew pretty close to the same format: performance, tour of stables and farm, carriage ride, and sometimes a traditional goulash lunch from a copper pot over an open fire. (Read the description on page 324 so you know roughly what to expect.) One popular choice is in the village of **Bugac,** deep in the countryside roughly halfway between Kecskemét and Szeged (about 45 minutes from either town; www.bugacpuszta.hu). Another option is in **Hortobágy National Park,** two hours' drive due east of Budapest (www.hnp.hu). It's important to call or email them in advance to confirm the schedule and let them know you're coming.

Kecskemét

This low-impact, charming city (pop. 115,000, www.kecskemet.hu) is handy for a stretch-your-legs break on your drive south (about an hour south of Budapest on M-5; follow *Centrum* signs and park in the garage for the big Malom shopping mall adjacent to the main square).

Kecskemét (KETCH-keh-mayt) has a downtown core made up of a series of wide, interlocking squares with a mix of beautiful Art Nouveau and Secessionist architecture, as well as some unfortunate communist-era drabness. Sometimes called the "garden city," Kecskemét is ringed by inviting parks and greenbelts. The city is also known for producing wine as well as apricot brandy *(barackpálinka).* While there aren't many "sights" to enter, Kecskemét gives you a taste of a largely untouristy midsize city.

If taking a lunch break in Kecskemét, do it at **Kecskeméti Csárda,** a traditional, almost folksy, borderline kitschy restaurant that hides just a few blocks off of the main drag. The service is warm, and the Hungarian specialties are executed as well here as anywhere (daily for lunch and dinner, Kölcsey utca 7, tel. 76/488-686, www.kecskemeticsarda.hu).

Near Kecskemét: Just off of M-5 between Kecskemét and Szeged, **Ópusztaszer Heritage Park** celebrates those original Hungarians who arrived in the Great Plain more than 11 centuries ago: the Magyars. This complex has an open-air museum of traditional village architecture, a wrap-around panorama painting of the arrival of the Magyars, a cluster of "Csete-yurts" in the distinctive Organic architecture style, and frequent special events that include equestrian shows (www.opusztaszer.hu).

▲Szeged

Szeged (SEH-gehd; pop. 160,000, including 23,000 university students) is the leading city of the Great Hungarian Plain. It boasts a livable town center with gorgeous Art Nouveau architecture, some impressive sights and baths, and a fascinating multiethnic collage.

Historically and culturally, Szeged is southern Hungary's main crossroads. It sits along the Tisza River, at the intersection of three countries: From here, Serbia and Romania are both within a 15-minute drive. Remember that well into the 20th century, Hun-

DAY TRIPS

gary was triple the size it is now, and Szeged was quite central rather than a southern outpost. The neighboring regions of Vojvodina (now in Serbia) and Transylvania (now in Romania) still have substantial Hungarian populations.

Weighty history aside, Szeged is simply enjoyable. It's a purely late-19th-century city. After a devastating 1879 flood (known locally as "The Great Catastrophe"), Szeged was swiftly rebuilt in the eye-pleasing Art Nouveau and Secessionist styles that were so popular during that age. Today, Szeged's wealth of Hungarian Art Nouveau masterpieces is second only to Budapest's. And, as Szeged enjoys a particularly sun-drenched climate, it's also synonymous with both paprika (Szeged is one of Hungary's two main paprika production centers) and with spicy salami (the Pick brand, made here, is sold at grocery stores nationwide).

While Szeged's outer sprawl is disheartening—especially the heavily industrialized Új-szeged ("New Szeged") district, purpose-built by the communists to increase the city's output—its central core is a delight. The very center of town is a grid of **pedestrianized streets** with finely restored old buildings, abundant outdoor cafés, and whimsical statues. Stroll the perpendicular main drags, Kölcsey utca and Kárász utca, and linger over an al fresco coffee or strudel.

This pedestrian zone is flanked by pretty squares: At the north end, the café-ringed Klauzál tér is just across the street from Szeged's "main square": **Széchenyi tér.** This vast space feels more like a park than a square, with a broad, traffic-free boulevard flanked by stately, towering plane trees; civic buildings (including the City Hall); and a smattering of dynamic monuments celebrating great Hungarians.

At the southern edge of the pedestrian zone is **Dugonics tér**—a leafy square wrapped around a large, communist-style fountain built in 1979 for the centennial of Szeged's big flood. This lively people zone is also home to the main branch of the **TI** (www.szegedtourism.hu). Just north from here along the ring road, facing its own little square, is the **Reök Palace,** a decadent high-water mark (no pun intended) of Szeged's post-flood Art Nouveau flourishing.

Just to the south of the traffic-free core, **Cathedral Square** (Dóm tér)—which, locals are eager to point out, has identical dimensions to St. Mark's Square in Venice—is home to the soaring twin spires of the cathedral. Officially called the **Votive Church** (Fogadalmi Templom), it was built as a "thank the Lord anyway" gesture after the devastating 1879 flood (www.szegedidom.hu). Although relatively new (completed in 1930), it feels ancient inside: Its interior is a riot of lavish, gilded, Neo-Byzantine mosaics that trumpet the greatness of Hungarian culture. The Orthodox-looking icons also evoke the cultural connection to Szeged's Balkan neighbors—the Romanians, Serbs, and Bulgarians. The Virgin Mary who floats ethereally on the dome above the altar wears a pair of Szeged's unique red-velvet slippers. Outside, the square is ringed by a brick arcade with more than a hundred small plaques and monuments honoring local and national big shots.

The inner ring road that hems in the town center (Tisza Lajos körút) links several other fine sights. A block west of the ring road, on Gutenberg utca, is Szeged's most impressive sight, its lavish **New Synagogue**—which takes a backseat to Budapest's in size (it's the third-biggest in the world), but not in opulence (www.zsinagoga.szeged.hu). Designed in Moorish Art Nouveau style in 1903, its unassuming exterior hides a stunning blue-hued interior with Zsolnay tile decorations, glittering chandeliers, stained-glass windows illustrating the Jewish faith, and menorahs that were modeled after engravings of Jerusalem on Rome's Arch of Titus. Typical of the Historicist style of the day, the synagogue mashes up a variety of historical features: Gothic windows, Romanesque columns, a Renaissance Greek-cross floor plan, a Baroque exterior, and Byzantine decorations.

Along the northwestern edge of the ring road are the **Anna Thermal Baths,** a beautifully restored late-19th-century palace that nearly approaches the elegance of Budapest's baths (www.szegedsport.hu). Roughly across the ring road and a block up Vidra utca, **Szent István tér** is an inviting urban park with a gorgeous circa-1904 water tower as its centerpiece.

The riverfront is sleepy, but gives a chance to sample the local specialty, *halászlé* ("fishermen's soup")—a paprika-flavored fish goulash. While several places around town sell this, the best option is **Halászcsárda** ("Fishermen's Inn"), on Roosevelt tér facing the town's main bridge (2,000 Ft for a big shareable pot, Roosevelt tér 12-14—look for the big terrace on the corner closest to the river, www.sotarto-halaszcsarda.hu).

Sleeping and Eating in Szeged: **Tiszavirág** ("Tisza Flower") is a hotel/restaurant imbued with both class and hipster modernity. Its 12 rooms are stylish and upscale, but still affordable; the public areas—from the hangout café to the cozy lounge to the well-respected restaurant—make this a delightful home base (near the synagogue at Hajnóczy utca 1B, just across the ring road from the pedestrian core, restaurant closed Sun, www.tiszaviragszeged.hu).

Local Guide: **István Koteczki** has a passion for his hometown

DAY TRIPS

and shares it well (5,000 Ft/hour or 25,000 Ft for all day, mobile 0630-400-8898, koteczki@hotmail.com).

▲Makó

A small town of less than 30,000 people, Makó (MAH-koh) sits just east of Szeged—it's practically a suburb. (It's a 30-minute drive; if you make a wrong turn, you'll wind up in Romania.) In most regards unassuming, Makó has two big claims to fame: It was the birthplace of Joseph Pulitzer (who emigrated stateside as a teenager) and has the highest concentration anywhere of buildings by Hungary's foremost

postcommunist architect, Imre Makovecz, whose Organic style defines Hungarian architecture over the last 20 years (for more on Makovecz and Organic style, see page 373). The most stunning Makovecz work in Makó—and perhaps in Hungary—is the **Makó Hagymatikum Thermal Baths.** Typical of Organic works, the bath complex looks like it's rising up out of the ground—a bulbous, bulging mushroom hiding an array of hot-water fun. While the otherworldly architecture is reason enough for a visit, the bath's modern facilities—with indoor and outdoor sections, both relaxing and fun zones, and everything from massages to water slides—also make it one of the best options outside of Budapest for just splashing around (www.hagymatikum.hu). The **TI** inside the bath complex's main entry can tell you more about the nine Makovecz buildings scattered around town; architecture pilgrims enjoy going on a scavenger hunt (also see www.makoinfo.hu).

Subotica, Serbia (Суботица/Szabadka)

If you appreciate Szeged's Art Nouveau architecture, go to Serbia. Before 1920, Subotica (SOO-boh-teet-seh, pop. 98,000) was a Hungarian burg, and fully participated in the architectural boomtime of the late 19th century. Many of Szeged's top architects designed equally stunning works in Subotica. Today part of Serbia, Subotica is worth a visit for adventurous travelers who'd enjoy seeing a different facet of Hungarian culture (as the city still has a large Hungarian population)—and getting another stamp for their passport. You can side-trip from Szeged to Subotica, or use it as a scenic international detour on the ride between Szeged and Pécs (to avoid needless delays or disappointment at the border, make sure you have the car-rental company's permission to cross into Serbia). For more on Subotica, see the town's excellent website: www.visitsubotica.rs. The lakeside resort of **Palić** (Палић in Cyrillic, Palics in Hungarian)—which sits along the road from Szeged to

Subotica—also has some fine Art Nouveau buildings, and is worth a quick stop (www.palic.rs).

West of Budapest:
Lake Balaton and Nearby

Landlocked Hungary doesn't have a seafront, but it does have the next best thing: Lake Balaton, the "Hungarian Riviera." Balaton—bigger than Switzerland's Lake Geneva—is one of Europe's largest freshwater lakes. The long, skinny lake—48 miles long, and never wider than about 9 miles across—begins an hour's drive west of Budapest, then stretches to the southwest. Its long shoreline and shallow waters harbor a staggering variety of tourist attractions, almost all of them catering to vacationing Hungarians. Many Budapest urbanites have humble summer cottages on or near Balaton, and in July and August, the capital empties out as people hit the beach.

Beloved as it is among Hungarians, Balaton has less to offer international tourists. (It'd be a bit like a Hungarian traveling all the way to the US just to see Fort Lauderdale.) But if you're driving in western Hungary, you might consider a quick stopover at one or more of the attractions near Lake Balaton. I've listed a few good options below.

DAY TRIPS

BALATON'S NORTH BANK
Balaton's scenic north bank enjoys several worthwhile attractions. Rolling hills rise up from the lakeshore, forming the Balaton-Felvidéki (Highland) National Park as well as a thriving wine-growing region. The lakeside road is punctuated with several resorty towns, the biggest of which is Balatonfüred. The attractions noted below are the most worthwhile.

▲Tihany
Near Balatonfüred, the bulbous peninsula called Tihany (TEE-hayn) juts out into the lake. At the crest of the peninsula's hill, overlooking virtually the entire lake, is the extremely tidy, scenic village of Tihany, with the highest property values in the country. Tihany village is capped by a Benedictine abbey and church, with the 11th-century tomb of King András I (one of only two Hungarian royal tombs that were not desecrated by Ottoman invaders) and finely carved 18th-century decorations. The surrounding terrace offers sweeping views over

the waters of Balaton. Count the sailboats in the marina, and ponder a Hungarian seaside holiday. From the tip of the peninsula, ferries make the quick crossing to the south bank (less than a mile away).

▲Hévíz Thermal Lake

The town of Keszthely (with its fine, Baroque Festetics Palace) anchors the western tip of Lake Balaton. Nearby is the thermal lake

and spa of Hévíz (HAY-veez), which fills a volcanic crater. The world's second-largest thermal lake (*gyógytó*, about 500,000 square feet), Hévíz is continually fed by thermal waters that bubble up from springs a hundred feet below. All of this constant, natural flushing ensures that the lake's waters refresh completely every two days, and the temperature never drops below about 70°F (and stays closer to 95°F in summer). Extremely popular with aging Russians and Germans, the lake's unique mineral composition is supposedly excellent for easing arthritis, joint pain, and other ailments. Some credit the lightly (and naturally) radioactive water; it's recommended to be in the water for only about 30 minutes at a time, punctuated by 30-minute breaks.

For a somewhat surreal spa experience, stop by Hévíz to take a dip (www.spaheviz.hu). You'll change in the locker room, then follow the walkways to the pavilion in the middle of the lake, where you can ease into the waters. Rent a pool noodle so you can slowly float and paddle your way around the lake. Weave between the lily pad lotuses as you glide in slow motion across the lake's tranquil surface. All around you, portly, aching, aging bodies bob in the steamy surf. If you want a break, stroll partway around the shoreline, and surrender to the allure of a sunbathing perch.

Herend Porcelain Factory

Set back from the north bank of Balaton, but an easy detour (about 20 miles/30 minutes' drive inland from the lakefront), is the Herend Porcelain Factory. Herend has been Hungary's main producer of fine porcelain since 1826, and supplied the Habsburg emperors as well as other royal families across Europe. Today they welcome visitors to their "Porcelanium" visitors center to explore their museum and tour the "minimanufactory," a small-scale factory designed to educate curious porcelain lovers about the manufacturing process (www.herend.com).

DAY TRIPS

LAKE BALATON'S SOUTH BANK

With the highest concentration of summer-fun tourist attractions (beaches, campgrounds, nightclubs), Balaton's largely flat south bank is less interesting for visitors. The M-7 expressway, which connects Budapest to Zagreb, Croatia, runs roughly parallel to Balaton's south bank, offering a peek. Siófok is the main town here, and the resort hub for all of Balaton. But unless you're truly on vacation Hungarian-style, I'd skip the south bank.

EGER

Eger (EH-gehr) is a county-seat town in northern Hungary, with about 60,000 people and a thriving teacher-training college. While you've probably never heard of Eger, among Hungarians, the town has various claims to fame. Its powerful bishops have graced it with gorgeous churches. It has some of the best and most beloved spas in this hot-water-crazy country (including the excellent Salt Hill Thermal Spa in the nearby countryside). And, perhaps most of all, Eger makes Hungarians proud as the town that, against all odds, successfully held off the Ottoman advance into Europe in 1552. This stirring history makes Eger a field-trip mecca for Hungarian school kids. If the town is known internationally for anything, it's for the surrounding wine region (its best-known red wine is Bull's Blood, or Egri Bikavér).

And yet, refreshingly, enchanting Eger remains mostly off the tourist trail. Egerites go about their daily routines amidst lovely Baroque buildings, watched over by one of Hungary's most important castles. Everything in Eger is painted with vibrant colors, and even the communist apartment blocks seem quaint. The sights are few but fun, the ambience is great, and strolling is a must. It all comes together to make Eger an ideal introduction to small-town Hungary.

Eger

To Firefighters Museum

LENKEY J. U.

HOSPITAL

KNEZICH KÁROLY

DAJKA G. U.

VECSEY SÁNDOR U.

WAXWORKS

GOTHIC COURTYARD

CHURCH RUINS

KOVÁCS J. U.

MARKET HALL

MINARET ⑮

CASTLE

3D MOVIE

GÁRDONYI'S GRAVE

POST

⑩

TICKETS

CSÍKY SÁNDOR U.   MACZKY V.   ZALÁR U.

KEPES INSTITUTE

DR. SÁNDOR MARKHÓTH

❸   ❷   ❺

⑰   ⑲

DOBÓ U.

❶

❻

BRÓDY SÁNDOR U.

ISTVÁN DOBÓ STATUE

Dobó Square

⑭   DR. HIBAY K. U.   ⑯   ❽

SYNAGOGUE GALLERY

ALMAGYAR

MENCSEY U.

❾   ④

SZENT JÁNOS U.

TOWN HALL

MINORITE CHURCH

GÓLYA U.

FOGLÁR U.   SZÉCHENYI UTCA

⑬

❶❶   ÉRSEK U.   ❼

ARCHBISHOP'S PALACE

BAJSCL.

JÓKAI U.

❶❷

ESZPERANTÓ SÉTÁNY

SWIMMING POOL BY MAKOVECZ

Bus Station

⑱

LYCEUM (CAMERA OBSCURA)

KOSSUTH LAJOS U.

EGÉSZSÉGHÁZ U.

TURKISH BATHS

BARKÓCZY U.

CATHEDRAL

TÖRVÉNYHÁZ U.

TÁRKÁNYI B. U.

FÜRDŐ U.

To Sirens' Valley

TELEKESSY U.

GÁRDONYI SZINHÁZ (THEATER)

SZÁLLODA U.

KLAPKA GY. U.

Eger Creek

THERMAL BATHS

ARANY JÁNOS U.   SÓHÁZ U.   SZTÁRENYI UT.   DEÁK FERENC

Bishop's Park (Érsekkert)

N

CSÁKÁNY U.

100 Meters

100 Yards

To Train Station

STADION U.

EGER

❶ Imola Udvarház Rooms
❷ Senator Ház Hotel & Rest.
❸ Offi Ház Hotel
④ Szent János Hotel
❺ Dobó Vendégház Rooms
❻ Imola Hostel
❼ HBH Restaurant
❽ Palacsintavár Rest.
❾ Szantofer Vendéglő Rest.
⑩ Elefanto

❶❶ Dobós Cukrászda Pastries
❶❷ Sárvári Cukrászda Pastries
⑬ Kürtőskalács Window
⑭ Bikavér Borház Wine Shop
⑮ Kopcsik Marzipan Museum
⑯ Hist. Exhibition of Weapons
⑰ Palóc Folklore Museum
⑱ Town Under the Town
⑲ Castle Entrance

PLANNING YOUR TIME

Mellow Eger is a fine side-trip from Budapest. It's a doable round-trip in a single day (about two hours by train or bus each way), but it's much more satisfying and relaxing to spend the night.

A perfect day in Eger begins with a browse through the very local-feeling market and a low-key ramble on the castle ramparts. Then head to the college building called the Lyceum to visit the library and astronomy museum, and climb up to the thrillingly low-tech camera obscura. Take in the midday organ concert in the cathedral across the street from the Lyceum (mid-May-mid-Oct only). In the afternoon, unwind on the square or, better yet, at a thermal bath (in Eger, or at the Salt Hill Thermal Spa in nearby Egerszalók). If you need more to do, consider a drive into the countryside (including visits to local vintners—get details at TI). Round out your day with dinner on Little Dobó Square, or a visit to Eger's touristy wine caves in the Sirens' Valley.

In July and August (when Hungarians prefer to go to Lake Balaton—described in the previous chapter), Eger is busy with international visitors; in September and October, around the wine harvest, most of the tourists are Hungarians.

Orientation to Eger

Eger Castle sits at the top of the town, hovering over Dobó Square (Dobó István tér). This main square is divided in half by Eger Creek, which bisects the town. Two blocks west of Dobó Square is the main pedestrian drag, Széchenyi utca, where you'll find the Lyceum and the cathedral. A few blocks due south from the castle (along Eger Creek) is Eger's thermal baths complex.

TOURIST INFORMATION

Eger's TI (TourInform) offers a town map, as well as piles of brochures about the city and region. They can help you find a room and are eager to answer your questions (mid-June-Aug Mon-Fri 9:00-18:00, Sat-Sun 9:00-13:00; Sept-mid-June Mon-Fri 8:00-16:00, closed Sat-Sun—except open Sat 8:00-16:00 in Sept-Oct; Bajcsy-Zsilinszky utca 9, tel. 36/517-715, www.eger.hu).

ARRIVAL IN EGER

By Train: Eger's tiny train station is a 20-minute walk south of the center. The baggage-deposit desk is out along the platform by track 1, between the WCs (daily 7:00-19:00, attendant often waits in the adjacent *büfé*). For those in need of Hungarian cash, the closest ATM is at the Spar grocery store just up the street (turn left out of station, walk about 100 yards, and look for red-and-white supermarket on your right; the ATM is next to the main door, around front).

Taxis generally wait out front to take new arrivals into town (1,000-1,200 Ft). Even in little Eger, it's always best to take a taxi marked with a company name and number.

To catch the **bus** toward the center, go a block straight out of the station. Buses #11, #12, and #14 cut about 10 minutes off the walk into town (tickets are 300 Ft from driver or 240 Ft at train station newsstand facing track 1—ask for *helyijárat buszjegy*). Get off the bus when you reach the big yellow cathedral.

To **walk** all the way, leave the station straight ahead, walk one block, take the hard right turn with the road, and then continue straight (on busy Deák Ferenc utca) about 10 minutes until you run into the cathedral. With your back to the cathedral entry, the main square is two blocks ahead of you, then a block to the left.

By Car: In this small town, most hotels will provide parking or help you find a lot. For a short visit, the most central lots are behind the department store on Dobó Square, or in the square surrounding the Lyceum.

By Plane: Low-impact Eger is a pleasant place to get over jet lag. For tips on getting to Eger from Budapest's airport, see page 305.

GETTING AROUND EGER

Everything of interest in Eger is within walking distance. But a taxi can be helpful to reach outlying sights, including the Sirens' Valley wine caves and the Salt Hill Thermal Spa in Egerszalók (taxi meter starts at 310 Ft, then around 250 Ft/km; try City Taxi, tel. 36/555-555, toll-free tel. 0680-622-622).

HELPFUL HINTS

Blue Monday: Note that the castle museums and the Kepes Institute are closed on Mondays, and the Lyceum is open on Monday only from May to August. But even on Mondays you can visit the cathedral (and enjoy its organ concert), swim in the thermal bath, explore the market, see the castle grounds, and enjoy the local wine.

Organ Concert: Daily from mid-May to mid-October, Hungary's second-biggest organ booms out a glorious 30-minute concert in the cathedral (800 Ft, Mon-Sat at 11:30, Sun at 12:30).

Local Guide: The TI can arrange a private guide to give you a tour of town (8,000 Ft/hour, tel. 36/517-715, eger@ tourinform.hu).

Tourist Train: A variety of hokey little tourist trains leave the main square regularly (at least at the top of each hour, and often at other times when it's busy). These trains do a circuit around town, then head out to the Sirens' Valley wine caves (800 Ft, 50-minute trip).

Sights in Eger

▲▲Dobó Square (Dobó István Tér)

Dobó Square is the heart of Eger. In most towns this striking, the main square is packed with postcard stalls and other tourist traps.

Refreshingly, Eger's square seems mostly packed with Egerites. Ringed by pretty Baroque buildings and watched over by Eger's historic castle, this square is one of the most pleasant spots in Hungary.

The statue in the middle is **István Dobó** (EESHT-vahn DOH-boh), the square's namesake and Eger's greatest hero, who defended the city—and all of Hungary—from an Ottoman invasion in 1552 (see his story in the sidebar). Next to Dobó is his co-commander, István Mekcsey. And right at their side is one of the brave women of Eger—depicted here throwing a pot down onto the attackers.

Dominating the square is the exquisitely photogenic **Minorite Church**—often said to be the most beautiful Baroque church in Hungary. The shabby interior is less inter-esting, but has some appealing details (free entry, daily 9:30-17:30). Notice that each of the hand-carved wooden pews has a differ-ent motif. Pay close attention to the side al-tars that flank the nave: The first set (left and right) are 3-D illustrations, painted to repli-cate the wood altars that burned in a fire; the next set are real. And looking up at the faded ceiling frescoes, you'll see (in the second one from the entrance) the church's patron: St. Anthony of Padua, who's preaching God's word to the fishes after the townspeople re-fused to hear him. The green, arcaded build-

ing to the right of the Minorite Church is the Town Hall, next to an old-fashioned pharmacy.

Use the square to orient yourself to the town. Behind the stat-ue of Dobó is a bridge over the stream that bisects the city. Just be-fore you reach that bridge, look to the left and you'll see the north-ernmost Ottoman **minaret** in Europe—once part of a mosque, it's now a tourist attraction. Across the bridge is the charming **Little Dobó Square** (Kis-Dobó tér), home to the town's best hotels, its outdoor dining zone, and a handy and atmospheric opportunity to sample local wines at the Bikavér Borház wine shop (see page 375). Hovering above Little Dobó Square is Eger Castle; to get there, hang a right at the Senator Ház Hotel and go up Dobó utca. (All of these places are described later in more detail.)

Now face the opposite direction, with the castle at your back. On your right is a handy supermarket (with an ATM by the door).

István Dobó and the Siege of Eger

In the 16th century, Ottoman invaders swept into Hungary. They easily defeated a Hungarian army—in just two hours—at the Battle of Mohács in 1526.

When Buda and Pest fell to the Ottomans in 1541, all of Europe looked to Eger as the last line of defense. István Dobó and his second-in-command, István Mekcsey, were put in charge of Eger's forces. They pre-pared the castle (which still over-looks the square) for a siege and waited.

On September 11, 1552—after a summer spent conquering more than 30 other Hungarian fortresses on their march northward—40,000 Ottomans arrived in Eger. Only about 2,000 Egerites (soldiers, their wives, and their children) remained to protect their town. The Ottomans expected an easy victory, but the siege dragged on for 39 days. Eger's soldiers fought valiantly, and the women of Eger also joined the fray, pouring hot tar down on the Ottomans...everyone pitched in. A Hungarian officer named Gergely Bornemissza, sent to reinforce the people of Eger, startled the Ottomans with all manner of clever and deadly explosives. One of his brilliant inventions was a "fire wheel"—a barrel of gunpowder studded with smaller jars of explosives, which they'd light and send rolling downhill to wreak havoc until the final, deadly explosion. Ultimately, the Ottomans left in shame, Eger was saved, and Dobó was a national hero.

The unfortunate epilogue: The Ottomans came back in 1596 and, this time, succeeded in conquering an Eger Castle guarded by unmotivated mercenaries. The Ottomans sacked the town and then controlled the region for close to a century.

In 1897, a castle archaeologist named Géza Gárdonyi moved from Budapest to Eger, where tales of the siege cap-tured his imagination. Gárdonyi wrote a book about István Dobó and the 1552 Siege of Eger called *Egri Csillagok* ("Stars of Eger," translated into English as *Eclipse of the Crescent Moon*, available at local bookstores and souvenir stands). The book—a favorite of many Hungarians—is taught in schools, keeping the legend of Eger's heroes alive today.

EGER

At the bottom end of this square, various pedestrian shopping lanes lead straight ahead two short blocks to Eger's main "walking street," Széchenyi utca (with the cathedral and the Lyceum at its left end).

▲Dobó Utca

This street, which leads from Little Dobó Square to the entrance of the castle, is lined with colorful shops and attractions. You'll encounter these sights in the following order from the main square (begin by heading up the street to the right of Senator Ház Hotel):

The **antique shop** (Régiségbolt, at #24) is worth a peek. If musty old things from the communist era—a painting of Lenin or a classic old radio—are cluttering your attic, you can sell them here.

The **wine-tasting courtyard** (#18) features a different local winery each week from May through October. Pop into the brightly lit, vaulted tasting room in the back to try a glass (200-600 Ft/glass).

A few steps down Fazola Henrik (on the right), the **Historical Exhibition of Weapons** (Történi Tárház) features centuries of Eger armaments: clubs, rifles, and everything in between (400 Ft, Tue-Sun 10:00-18:00, closed Mon, 300-Ft English book gives a full weapon-by-weapon tour).

The **Palóc Folklore Museum** (#12) displays a handful of traditional tools, textiles, ceramics, costumes, and pieces of furniture (200 Ft; open sporadically—likely May-Sept Tue-Sun 10:15-16:15, closed Oct-April and Mon year-round; no English information).

▲Eger Castle (Egri Vár)

The great St. István—Hungary's first Christian king—founded a church on this hill a thousand years ago. The church was destroyed by Tatars in the 13th century, and this fortress was built to repel another attack. Most importantly, this castle is Hungary's Alamo, where István Dobó defended Eger from the Ottomans in 1552—as depicted in the relief just outside the entry gate. These days, it's usually crawling with field-tripping schoolchildren from all over the country. (Every Hungarian sixth grader reads *Eclipse of the Crescent Moon*, which thrillingly recounts the heroic siege of Eger.) For those of us who didn't grow up hearing the legend of István Dobó, the com-

plex is hard to appreciate, and English information is sparse. Most visitors find that the most rewarding plan is simply to stroll up, wander the grounds, play "king of the castle" along the ramparts, and enjoy the sweeping views over Eger's rooftops.

Cost and Hours: While a 700-Ft "walking ticket" gets you into the castle grounds only, the 1,100-Ft ticket includes the big castle sights (history museum, art gallery, casements tour). The castle grounds are open daily (April-Aug 8:00-20:00, Sept until 19:00, March and Oct until 18:00, Nov-Feb until 17:00). The castle museums have shorter hours (April-Oct Tue-Sun 10:00-17:00, Nov-March Tue-Sun 10:00-16:00, closed Mon year-round).

Casements Tours: The underground casements and Heroes' Hall are only accessible by a one-hour tour in Hungarian (included in ticket price, tours depart frequently in summer, sporadically off-season).

Information: Tel. 36/312-744, www.egrivar.hu.

Getting There: To reach the castle from Dobó Square, cross the bridge toward Senator Ház Hotel, then jog right around the hotel, turning right onto Dobó utca (with its own set of attractions, described earlier). Take this street a few blocks until it swings down to the right; the ramp up to the castle is on your left.

Visiting the Castle: Buy your ticket at the lower gate, then hike up the entry ramp and through the inner gate into the main courtyard—with grassy fields, souvenir stands, and easy access to the ramparts. Straight ahead—through the corridor with the little information window—is a pink, Gothic-style courtyard, which contains two small museums. The **history museum** (in the top floor of the main building) is the best of its kind in town, with lots of artifacts and good English descriptions. The **picture gallery** (top floor of building to the left as you enter the courtyard) is worth a few minutes, with paintings giving you a look at traditional life in Hungary.

Exploring the **grounds,** you'll see the remains of a once-grand cathedral and a smaller rotunda dating from the days of St. István (10th or 11th century; at the far-right corner as you enter). The underground **casements** (tunnels through the castle walls, which include the Heroes' Hall with the symbolic grave of István Dobó) are accessible only by guided tour, but you can dip into the **dungeon** anytime with the museum ticket (to the left as you enter).

Other Castle Sights: The castle hosts a few privately run exhibits (with sporadic hours and prices).

The **waxworks,** or "Panoptikum" (500 Ft, daily April-Oct 9:00-17:00, shorter hours off-season; at far-left corner as you enter), while kind of silly, is fun for kids or those who never really grew up. Think of it as a very low-tech, walk-through *Ottomans of the Caribbean.* You'll see a handful of eerily realistic

EGER

heroes and villains from the siege of Eger (including István Dobó himself and the leader of the Ottomans sitting in his colorful tent). Notice the exaggerated Central Asian features of the Egerites—a reminder that the Magyars were more Asian than European. A visit to the waxworks lets you scramble through a segment of the tunnels that run inside the castle walls (a plus since it's not really worth it to wait around through the similar, Hungarian-language casements tour).

The **Eger 1552** **3-D movie** offers a fun little lesson in the town's history. Appropriately low-budget for this small town, the film's graphics are closer to a retro video game than a blockbuster, but it does a fine job of re-creating the medieval townscape. A second 3-D movie features a baby Tyrannosaurus rex (400 Ft for one movie, 600 Ft for both, 10 minutes each, English subtitles).

Additional sights include an **archery** exhibit (in summer, look for archers just to the right of the Gothic courtyard, and pay them for the chance to shoot old-fashioned bows and crossbows); and **temporary exhibits** in the ground floor of the Gothic courtyard. The castle also has a **café** and a **1552 Restaurant**.

ON SZÉCHENYI UTCA
▲▲Lyceum (Líceum)

In the mid-18th century, Bishop Károly Eszterházy wanted a university in Eger, but Habsburg Emperor Josef II refused to allow it. Instead, Eszterházy built the most impressive teacher-training college on the planet, and stocked it with the best books and astronomical equipment that money could buy. The Lyceum still trains local teachers (enrollment: about 2,000). Tourists also roam the halls of the Lyceum; they come to visit its classic old library and its astronomy museum, which has a

fascinating camera obscura. The library and museum are tucked away in the big, confusing building.

Cost and Hours: Library-800 Ft, museum-1,000 Ft; both open May-Aug daily 9:30-17:30; mid-March-April and Sept-Oct Tue-Sun 9:30-15:30, closed Mon; Nov-mid-March Tue-Sun 9:30-13:30, closed Mon; Eszterházy tér 1, at south end of Széchenyi utca at intersection with Kossuth utca, enter through main door across from cathedral and buy tickets just inside and to the left.

Visiting the Lyceum: First, visit the old-fashioned **library** one floor up (from the main entry hall, cut through the middle of the courtyard, go up the stairs to the next floor, and look for Room 223, marked *Bibliothek*—it's on the right side of the complex as

you face it from the entrance). This library houses 60,000 books (here and in
the two adjoining rooms, with several
stacked two deep). Dr. Erzsébet Löffler
and her staff have spent the last decade
cataloging these books. This is no easy
task, since they're in over 30 languages—
from Thai to Tagalog—and are shelved
according to size, rather than topic. Only
one percent of the books are in Hungarian—but half of them are in Latin. The
ticket-taker can give you an English in-

formation sheet highlighting the collection's most prized pieces.
The shelves are adorned with golden seals depicting some of the
great minds of science, philosophy, and religion. Marvel at the gorgeous ceiling fresco, dating from 1778. To thank the patron of this
museum, say *köszönöm* to the guy in the second row up, to the right
of the podium (above the entry door, second from left, not wearing
a hat)—that's Bishop Károly Eszterházy.

Turn right as you leave the library to find the staircase that
leads up the **Astronomical Tower** (*Varázstorony*, follow signs several flights up) to the **Astronomical Museum.** Some dusty old
stargazing instruments occupy one room, as well as a meridian line
in the floor (a dot of sunlight dances along this line each day around
noon). Across the hall is a fun, interactive **magic room,** where you
can try out scientific experiments—such as using air pressure to
make a ball levitate or sending a mini "hot-air balloon" up to the
ceiling.

A few more flights up is the Lyceum's treasured **camera obscura**—one of just two originals surviving in Europe (the other
is in Edinburgh). You'll enter a dark room around a big, bowl-
like canvas, and the guide will fly you around the streets of Eger
(presentations about 2/hour, maybe more when busy). Fun as it is
today, this camera must have astonished viewers when it was built
in 1776—well before anyone had seen "moving pictures." It's a bit
of a huff to get up here (nine flights of stairs, 302 steps)—but the
camera obscura, and the actual view of Eger from the outdoor terrace just outside, are worth it.

▲▲Eger Cathedral
Eger's 19th-century bishops peppered the city with beautiful
buildings, including the second-biggest church in Hungary (after
Esztergom's—see page 346). With a quirky, sumptuous, Baroque-
feeling interior, Eger's cathedral is well worth a visit.

Cost and Hours: 300-Ft donation requested (but you must
buy ticket if visiting before an organ concert, 11:00-12:00), open

EGER

Mon-Sat 8:30-18:00, Sun 13:00-18:00. The cathedral is the big, can't-miss-it yellow building at Pyrker János tér 1, facing the start of Széchenyi utca.

Visiting the Cathedral: Eger Cathedral was built in the 1830s by an Austrian archbishop who had previously served in Venice, and who thought Eger could use a little more class. The colonnaded Neoclassical **facade,** painted a pretty Habsburg yellow, boasts some fine Italian sculpture. As you walk up the main stairs, you'll pass saints István and László—Hungary's first two Christian kings—and then the apostles Peter and Paul.

Enter the cathedral and walk to the first collection box, near the start of the nave. Then, turning back to face the door, look

up at the ornate **ceiling fresco:** On the left, it shows Hungarians in traditional dress; and on the right, the country's most important historical figures. At the bottom, you see this cathedral, celestially connected with St. Peter's in Rome (opposite). This symbol of devotion to the Vatican was a brave statement when it was painted in 1950. The communists were closing churches in other small Hungarian towns, but the Eger archbishop had enough clout to keep this one open.

Continue to the transept, stopping directly underneath the main dome. The **stained-glass windows** decorating the north and south transepts were donated to the cathedral by a rich Austrian couple to commemorate the 1,000th anniversary of Hungary's conversion to Christianity—notice the dates: 1000 (when St. István converted the Magyars to Christianity), and 2000.

As you leave, notice the enormous **organ**—Hungary's second-largest—above the door. In the summer, try to catch one of the cathedral's daily half-hour organ concerts (800 Ft, mid-May-mid-Oct Mon-Sat at 11:30, Sun at 12:30, no concerts off-season).

Near the back-right corner, look for the statue of **Szent Rita,** a local favorite; the votive plaques that say *köszönöm* and *hálából* are offering "thanks" and "gratitude" for prayers answered.

Nearby: If you walk up Széchenyi utca from here, you'll see the fancy **Archbishop's Palace** on your left—still home to Eger's archbishop.

Just to the right of the steps leading up to the cathedral is the entrance to the **Town Under the Town** (Város a Város Alatt), a 45-minute guided tour of the archbishop's former wine-cellar network (950 Ft, generally departs at the top of each hour—schedule posted at door, 5-person minimum, you'll get a little English sprinkled in with the Hungarian, daily in summer 10:00-17:00, shorter hours off-season, last tour departs one hour before closing, tel. 20/961-4019, www.varosavarosalatt.hu).

NORTH OF DOBÓ SQUARE
▲Market Hall (Piaccsarnok)

Wandering Eger's big indoor market will give you a taste of local

life—and maybe some samples of local food, too. This ramshackle hall is a totally untouristy scene, with ugly plastic tubs piled high with an abundance of fresh local produce. Tomatoes and peppers of all colors and sizes are plentiful— magic ingredients that give Hungarian food its kick.

Hours: Opens daily at 6:00; while open weekday afternoons, it's best in the mornings.

Minaret

Once part of a mosque, this slender, 130-foot-tall minaret represents the century of Ottoman rule that left its mark on Eger and all of Hungary. The little cross at the top symbolizes the eventual Christian victory over Hungary's Ottoman invaders. You can climb the minaret's 97 steps for fine views of Eger, but it's not for those scared of heights or enclosed spaces. Because the staircase was designed for one man to climb to call the community to prayer, it's very tight. To avoid human traffic jams, they allow groups of visitors in about twice an hour.

Cost and Hours: 300 Ft, daily April-Sept 10:00-18:00, Oct 10:00-17:00, closed Nov-March; if it's locked, ask around for the key.

▲Kopcsik Marzipan Museum (Kopcsik Marcipánia)

Lajos Kopcsik is a master sculptor who has found his medium: marzipan. Kopcsik can make this delicate mixture of sugar dough, ground almonds, egg whites, and tempera paints take virtually any form. Pass through the entryway, filled with awards, to enter this surprisingly engaging little museum. You'll see several remark-

EGER

able, colorful examples of Kopcsik's skill: sword, minaret, gigantic wine bottle, suitcase, Russian stacking dolls, old-timey phonograph, grandfather clock, giant bell...and paintings galore (including Van Gogh's sunflowers and Picasso's musicians). Who'd have thought you could do so much with candy? Don't miss the "Baroque room"—furnished and decorated entirely in marzipan.

Cost and Hours: 800 Ft, no English information, daily 9:00-18:00, shorter hours off-season, Harangöntő utca 4, tel. 36/412-626, www.kopcsikmarcipania.hu.

▲Kepes Institute (Kepes Intézet)

This beautifully renovated, minimalist building—sitting proudly on Eger's main walking street, Széchenyi utca—has a permanent collection of György Kepes' works upstairs, and fills several other halls with good temporary exhibits of contemporary artwork. Hungarian-born György Kepes (1906-2001) later moved to the US, where he was a university professor in Chicago and at MIT in Boston. A painter and photographer, Kepes followed the very Hungarian, left-brained artistic tradition of Op Artist Viktor Vasarely, drawing inspiration from geometry—except that Kepes ventured deeper into abstraction (producing canvases reminiscent of fuzzy Abstract Expressionism). In typical left-brained Hungarian fashion, Kepes combined art with practical purpose as he helped design effective camouflage for the US military.

Cost and Hours: 1,200 Ft, Tue-Sat 10:00-18:00, Sun 10:00-16:00, closed Mon, Széchenyi utca 16, tel. 36/440-044, www.kepeskozpont.hu.

OTHER MUSEUMS

Eger has several other small museums that may be worthwhile for those with a special interest. Though Eger's Jewish population was wiped out during the Holocaust, one of its synagogues has been converted into the **Synagogue Gallery** (Zsinagóga Galéria), allowing you to see the roughly restored interior and peruse temporary exhibits on various topics (exhibits are generally not Jewish-focused; entry price changes based on exhibit, Tue-Sun 10:00-18:00, closed Mon, two short blocks straight ahead from castle ramp at Kossuth Lajos utca 17). The TI can give you information about the **Firefighters Museum** (Egri Tűzoltó Múzeum, a long walk north of downtown on Széchenyi utca, www.tuzoltomuzeum.hu), the **Sport Museum,** and more.

Experiences in Eger

AQUA EGER

Swimming and water sports are as important to Egerites as good wine. They're proud that many of Hungary's Olympic medalists in aquatic events have come from the surrounding county. The men's water polo team took the gold for Hungary at three Olympiads in a row (2000-2008), and speed swimmer László Cseh might have been a multiple gold medal-winner at Beijing in 2008 if he hadn't been swimming next to Michael Phelps. The town's Bitskey Aladár swimming pool—arguably the most striking building in this part of Hungary—is practically a temple to water sports.

Eger also has several appealing thermal bath complexes: one right in town, and two more a few miles away (near the village of Egerszalók). Budapest offers classier bath experiences, but the Eger options are more modern and a bit more accessible, and allow you to save your Budapest time for big-city sights. Before you go, be sure to read the Thermal Baths chapter.

Baths and Pools in Eger

Note that you can't rent a swimsuit or a towel at either of these places; bring both with you, along with shower sandals for the locker room (if you've got them).

Bitskey Aladár Pool

This striking swimming pool was designed by Imre Makovecz, the father of Hungary's Organic architectural style. Some Eger tax-

payers resented the pool's big price tag, but it left the city with a truly distinctive building befitting its love of water sports. You don't need to be an architecture student to know that the pool is special. It's worth the five-minute walk from Dobó Square just to take a look. Oh, and you can swim in it, too.

Cost and Hours: 1,050 Ft, Mon-Fri 6:00-21:30, Sat-Sun 7:30-18:00, follow Eger Creek south from Dobó Square to Frank Tivadar utca, tel. 36/511-810, www.egertermal.hu.

▲Eger Thermal Bath (Eger Thermálfürdő)

For a refreshing break from the sightseeing grind, consider a splash at the spa. This is a fine opportunity to try a Hungarian bath: relatively accessible (men and women are clothed and together most of the time), but frequented mostly by locals.

Cost and Hours: 1,900 Ft (cheaper Sun-Wed after 16:00), 1,300 Ft extra gives you access to sauna and Turkish bath for two hours; June-Aug Mon-Wed 8:30-19:00, Thu-Fri 8:30-21:00, Sat 8:00-21:00, Sun 8:00-19:00; May and Sept Sun-Wed 9:00-19:00, Thu-Sat 9:00-21:00; Oct-April daily 9:00-19:00; Petőfi tér 2, tel. 36/510-558, www.egertermal.hu.

Getting There: It's easy to reach and within a 10-minute walk of most hotels. From Dobó Square, follow the stream four blocks south (look for signs for *Strand*), then into a park; halfway through the park, look for the bath's entrance on your left, over a bridge.

Entry Procedure: After you pay, show your wristband to an attendant to get a key to a locker (1,000-Ft deposit per key; private changing cabins available in the locker room for no extra charge). Change, stow your stuff, and join the fun.

Taking the Waters: There's a sprawling array of different pools, each one thoughtfully described in English and labeled with its depth and temperature. The best part is the green-domed, indoor-outdoor adventure bath, right at the side entrance. Its cascades, jets, bubbles, geysers, and powerful current pool will make you feel like a kid again. Exploring the complex, you'll also find big and small warm pools, a very hot sulfur pool (where Egerites sit peacefully, ignore the slight stink, and supposedly feel their arthritis ebb away), a kids' pool with splashy-slide fun, and a lap pool (some of these are closed off-season).

Turkish Bath: Eger's recently refurbished Turkish-style bath is closer to the main entrance (to the left as you face the main gate; you can't enter directly from the main part of the bath). It costs 1,300 Ft in combination with the main bath, or 2,200 Ft by itself (Mon-Tue 16:30-21:00, Wed-Thu 15:00-21:00, Fri 13:00-21:00, Sat-Sun 9:00-21:00).

Baths near Eger, in Egerszalók

Two more thermal baths—Salt Hill and Demjén—sit in the countryside outside of Eger, flanking a rocky hill between the villages of Egerszalók and Demjén. While these baths lack the old-fashioned class of the Budapest options, they more than compensate with soggy fun.

Getting There: Both baths are about a mile outside the village of Egerszalók, which is itself about three miles from Eger. You can take a public **bus** from Eger's bus station to the baths (take bus going toward Demjén; for Salt Hill, get off at the *Egerszalók Gyógyfürdő* stop—tell the bus driver "EH-gehr-sah-lohk FEWR-dur"—just after leaving the town of Egerszalók; for the Demjén Baths, get off at the entrance to Demjén village and walk back to

Hungary's Organic Architecture

Hungary's post-communist generation has embraced a unique, eye-catching style of architecture, called Organic, which was developed and championed by Imre Makovecz (1935-2011).

As a young architect, Makovecz pursued a flowing style that was quite intentionally at odds with the rigid right angles of communist architecture. He was inspired by the Hungarian Art Nouveau of a bygone and "decadent" Golden Age, and by pioneering Organic architects from other countries (including American Frank Lloyd Wright, who had a more angular style but a similar aesthetic of making sure his works fit their surroundings).

After being blacklisted by the regime for his stubborn adherence to his architectural vision—and for his nationalistic politics—Makovecz ramped up his pursuit of something new. Because the authorities denied him access to modern building supplies, Makovecz made do with sticks, rocks, and other foraged building materials. He was also inspired by Transylvanian village architecture: whitewashed walls with large, overhanging mansard roofs to maximize attic space (resembling a big mushroom).

After the fall of the regime, Makovecz swiftly became Hungary's premier architect, but he still kept things simple. He believed that a building should be a product of its environment, rather than a cookie-cutter copy. Organic buildings use indigenous materials (especially wood) and take on unusual forms—often inspired by animals or plants—that blend in with the landscape. Organic buildings look like they're rising up out of the ground, rather than plopped down on top of it. You generally won't find this back-to-nature style in big cities like Budapest; Makovecz preferred to work in small communities such as Eger (see photo on page 371) instead of working for large corporations. Makovecz wanted his creations—from churches, thermal baths, and campgrounds to cultural centers, restaurants, and bus stations—to represent the civic pride of the local community. For more on Makovecz, visit www.makovecz.hu.

EGER

the baths; bus runs 9/day Mon-Sat, only 4/day Sun, 20-minute trip, 400 Ft). Check the return bus information carefully (especially on weekends, when frequency plummets). Or you can take a **taxi** from Eger (about 3,000 Ft; tel. 36/555-555 for a return taxi from Egerszalók). Here's a fun and very hedonistic afternoon plan: Take the bus or taxi to the spa, taxi back to Eger's Sirens' Valley for some wine-cave hopping, then taxi back to your Eger hotel.

Nearby Wineries: The village of Egerszalók has several fine wineries, including the excellent **St. Andrea**—fun to combine with your bath visit. For details, see page 375.

▲▲Salt Hill Thermal Spa

For decades, Egerites would come to this "salt hill" (a natural terraced formation caused by mineral-rich spring water running down the hillside) in the middle of nowhere and cram together to baste in pools of hot water. Then the developers arrived. Today, a giant new hotel and spa complex has been built nearby. With 12 indoor pools and five outdoor ones—many cleverly overlapping one another on several levels—these cutting-

edge baths are worth the trip outside of Eger. Take some time to explore the sprawling complex. Everything is labeled in English, and each pool is clearly marked with the depth and temperature. This complex uses the same system as at Eger's thermal baths: Press your wristband against a computer screen to be assigned a locker, change in the private cabin, then have fun.

Cost and Hours: In Sept-June, 4,500 Ft for all day, 2,100 Ft for 3 hours or less, 1,500 Ft after 17:00; all prices 1,000 Ft

more in July-Aug. You'll pay 1,500 Ft extra to access "sauna world," with five different saunas. Towel rental is 1,000 Ft; massages and other treatments also available. Open June-Aug daily 10:00-20:00, likely less off-season—call ahead to check; tel. 36/688-500, www.egerszalokfurdo.hu.

EGER

Demjén Thermal Baths (Demjéni Termál Völgy)

Just over the hill from Salt Hill Thermal Spa, Demjén Baths is a less glitzy complex of nicely rustic wooden buildings and pools that are similarly nestled in hills (minus the terrace formations). Thanks to its low prices and long hours, these baths attract more locals. It also offers fewer amusements: Jets, fountains, and other "adventure bath"-type features are rare, and the goal here is simply stewing in pools of warm water. (The aquapark section— open only in summer—does have waterslides and a diving pool, for an extra charge.) You'll pay, change in a cabin in the shared locker rooms, ask the attendant to assign you a locker (she'll tell you to remember your number, which you'll need to tell her when you're ready for her to unlock it for you), then go soak.

Cost and Hours: 1,400 Ft, plus 1,200 Ft for a "wellness" ticket that adds more saunas and spas, daily 9:00-24:00; aquapark costs

1,900 Ft extra and open summers only until 20:00; mobile 0630-853-7419, www.demjengyogytermal.hu.

EGER WINE

Eger is at the heart of one of Hungary's best-known wine regions, internationally famous for its **Bull's Blood** (Egri Bikavér). You'll likely hear various stories as to how Bull's Blood got its name during the Ottoman siege of Eger. My favorite version: The Ottomans were amazed at the ferocity displayed by the Egerites, and wondered what they were drinking that boiled their blood and stained their beards so red...it must be potent stuff. Local merchants, knowing that the Ottomans were Muslim and couldn't drink alcohol, told them it was bull's blood. The merchants made a buck, and the name stuck.

Creative as these stories are, they're all bunk—the term dates only from 1851. Egri Bikavér is a blend (everyone has their own recipe), so you generally won't find it at small producers. Cabernet sauvignon, merlot, *kékfrankos*, and *kékoportó* are the most commonly used grapes.

But Bull's Blood is just the beginning of what the Eger wine region offers. Although Eger is better known for its reds, 42 of the 62 regional varieties are white. (For details, see "Hungarian Wines" on page 252.)

Tasting Local Wine: While it would be enjoyable to drive around the Hungarian countryside visiting wineries (and I've recommended one great choice, **St. Andrea,** later), the most accessible way to get a quick taste of local wine is at a wine shop in town. I like the Kenyeres family's **Bikavér Borház,** right on Little Dobó Square (across from Senator Ház Hotel). In addition to a well-stocked (if slightly overpriced) wine shop, they have a wine bar with indoor and outdoor seating (six tastings and two cheeses for less than 2,000 Ft, wine also sold by the glass, some English spoken, menu lists basic English description for each wine, daily 10:00-22:00, possibly later in busy times, Kis-Dobó tér 10, tel. 36/413-262).

Sirens' Valley (Szépasszony-völgy)

When the Ottoman invaders first occupied Eger, residents moved into the valley next door, living in caves dug into the hillside. Eventually the Ottomans were driven out, the Egerites moved back to town, and the caves became wine cellars. (Most Eger families who can afford it have at least a modest vineyard in the countryside.) There are more than 300 such caves in the valley to the southwest of Eger, several of which are open for visitors.

The best selection of these caves (about 50) is in the Sirens' Valley (sometimes also translated as "Valley of the Beautiful Women"—or, on local directional signs, the less poetic "Nice Woman Valley"). While the valley can feel vacant and dead (even sometimes in the summer), if you visit when it's busy it can be a fun scene—locals showing off their latest vintage, with picnic tables and tipsy tourists spilling out into the street. At some places, you'll be offered free samples; others have a menu for tastes or glasses of wine. While you're not expected to buy a bottle, it's a nice gesture to buy one if you've spent a while at one cave (and it's usually very cheap). Most caves offer something light to eat with the wine, and you'll also see lots of non-cave, full-service restaurants. Some of the caves are fancy and finished, staffed by multilingual waiters in period costume. Others feel like a dank basement, with grandpa leaning on his moped out front and a monolingual granny pouring the wine inside. (The really local places—where the decor is cement, bottles don't have labels, and food consists of potato chips and buttered Wonder bread—can be the most fun.)

This experience is a strange mix of touristy and local, but not entirely accessible to non-Hungarian-speakers—it works best with a bunch of friends and an easygoing, sociable attitude. Hopping from cave to musky cave can make for an enjoyable evening, but be sure to wander around a bit to see the options before you dive in (cellars generally open 10:00-21:00 in summer, best June-Aug in the late afternoon and early evening, plus good-weather weekends in the shoulder season; it's sleepy and not worth a visit off-season, when only a handful of cellars remain open for shorter hours).

Getting to the Sirens' Valley: The valley is on the southwest outskirts of Eger. Figure no more than 1,000 Ft for a **taxi** between your hotel and the caves. During the summer, you can take an 800-Ft **tourist train** from Eger's main square to the caves (see "Helpful Hints" on page 361), then catch a later one back.

You can **walk** there in about 25 minutes: Leave the pedestrian zone on the street next to the cathedral (Törvényház utca), with the cathedral on your right-hand side. Take the first left just after the back end of the cathedral (onto Trinitárius utca), go one long block, then take the first right (onto Király utca). At the fork, bear to the left. You'll stay straight on this road—crossing busy Koháry István utca—for several blocks, passing through some nondescript residential areas (on Szépasszony-völgy utca). When you crest the hill and emerge from the houses, you'll see the caves (and tour buses) below you on the left—go left (downhill) at the fork to get there. First you'll come to a stretch of touristy non-cave restaurants; keep going past these, and eventually you'll see a big loop of caves on your left.

Wineries near the Baths in Egerszalók

The village of Egerszalók, near the Salt Hill and Demjén thermal baths (described earlier), has a variety of fun wineries. The most interesting, and well worth a visit for wine lovers, is **St. Andrea.** This slick, modern, Napa Valley-esque facility offers cellar tours and tastings of their excellent wines, which show up on fine restaurant menus across Hungary. They're evangelical both about their spirituality (hence the name) and their wine, and enjoy explaining everything in English. They make generous use of pinot noir grapes, and produce some good, pungent whites with volcanic qualities. While it may be possible to simply drop in for a tasting, it's better to call ahead and let them know you're coming (3,500 Ft/person, bottles for 2,500-5,500 Ft, Mon-Sat 10:00-18:00, closed Sun, Ady Endre út 88 in Egerszalók, mobile 0630-692-5860, www.standrea. hu). It's most practical with a car (or by taxi), but you can also walk there from the bus stop in Egerszalók's town center (about a half-mile; head down Ady Endre út, toward the baths).

Nightlife in Eger

Things quiet down pretty early in this sedate town. Youthful student bars and hangouts cluster along the main "walking street," Széchenyi utca (especially Fri and Sat nights). Older travelers feel more at home on Little Dobó Square, with schmaltzy live music until 21:00 or 22:00 in summer; the Bikavér Borház wine bar (described earlier) is the lively hub of activity here, and stays open later.

Sleeping in Eger

Eger is a good overnight stop, and a couple of quaint, well-located hotels in particular—Senator Ház and Offi Ház—are well worth booking in advance. The TI can help you find a room; if you're stumped, the area behind the castle has a sprinkling of cheap guesthouses *(vendégház)*. Elevators are rare—expect to climb one or two flights of stairs to reach your room. A tax of 400 Ft per person will be added to your bill (not included in the prices listed here). Most of these hotels are in pedestrian zones, so get detailed driving and parking instructions from your hotel; many offer free or cheap parking, but it's often a block or two away.

$$$ Imola Udvarház rents six spacious apartments—with kitchen, living room, bedroom, and bathroom—all decorated in modern Ikea style. They're pricey for this small town, but roomy and well-maintained, with a great location near the castle entrance. Their free on-site parking garage makes this a good choice for drivers (Sb-19,000 Ft, Db-23,000 Ft, 1,000 Ft more July-Aug,

3,000 Ft less in winter, extra person-3,000 Ft, air-con, Wi-Fi, Tírodi Sebestyén tér 4, tel. 36/516-180, www.imolaudvarhaz.hu, info@imolaudvarhaz.hu).

$$ Senator Ház Hotel is one of my favorite small, family-run hotels in Eastern Europe. Though the 11 rooms are a bit worn, this

place is cozy and well-run by András Cseh and his right-hand man, Viktor. With oodles of character, all the right quirks, and a picture-perfect location just under the castle on Little Dobó Square, it's a winner (Sb-13,200 Ft, Db-18,000 Ft, extra bed-6,000 Ft, 1,000 Ft more in July-Aug, less in winter, András offers 10 percent cash discount for Rick Steves readers who book direct and mention this book, air-con, Wi-Fi, Dobó István tér 11, tel. 36/411-711, www.senatorhaz.hu, info@senatorhaz.hu). The Cseh family also runs **Pátria Vendégház**—with two doubles (same prices as main hotel) and four luxurious apartments (Db-20,000 Ft, Tb-27,000 Ft).

$$ Offi Ház Hotel shares Little Dobó Square with Senator Ház. Its five rooms are classy and romantic, but a bit tight, with slanted ceilings. Communication can be tricky (German helps), but the location is worth the hassle (Sb-14,000 Ft, Db-17,500 Ft, Db suite-19,500 Ft, Tb suite-23,000 Ft, extra bed-5,000 Ft, 15 percent cheaper Nov-March, non-smoking, air-con, Wi-Fi, Dobó István tér 5, tel. 36/518-210, www.offihaz.hu, offihaz@t-online.hu, Offenbächer family).

$$ Szent János Hotel, less charming and more business-like than the Senator Ház and Offi Ház, offers a good but less atmospheric location, 13 straitlaced rooms, and a pleasant winter garden to relax in. Choose between the newly renovated rooms, which face a busy pedestrian street and can be noisy on weekend nights, or the still-good older rooms, which face the quieter back side—both for the same price (Sb-15,000 Ft, Db-18,000 Ft, extra bed-6,000 Ft, cheaper Nov-April, non-smoking, air-con, Wi-Fi, a long block off Dobó Square at Szent János utca 3, tel. 36/510-350, www.hotelszentjanos.hu, hotelszentjanos@hotelszentjanos.hu).

$ Dobó Vendégház, run by warm Marianna Kleszo, has seven basic but colorful rooms just off Dobó Square. Marianna speaks nothing but Hungarian, but gets simple reservation emails translated by a friend (Sb-10,500 Ft, Db-15,900 Ft, extra bed-4,500 Ft, cash only, air-con in some upstairs rooms, Wi-Fi, Dobó utca 19, tel. 36/421-407, www.dobovendeghaz.hu, info@dobovendeghaz.hu).

$ Imola Hostel, a big, modern, and comfy hostel, is basi-

Sleep Code

Abbreviations   (225 Ft = about $1, country code: 36, area code: 36)
S = Single, **D** = Double/Twin, **T** = Triple, **Q** = Quad, **b** = bathroom.
Price Rankings
  $$$ Higher Priced—Most rooms 20,000 Ft or more.
   $$ Moderately Priced—Most rooms between 15,000-20,000 Ft.
    $ Lower Priced—Most rooms 15,000 Ft or less.
Unless otherwise noted, credit cards are accepted, breakfast is included, Wi-Fi is generally free, and English is spoken. Prices change; verify current rates online or by email. For the best prices, always book directly with the hotel.
     Phone Tip: Remember, if calling Eger internationally, you'll have to dial 36 twice (once for the country code, again for the area code).

---

cally a college dormitory that welcomes travelers of any age into its dorm rooms in summer (July-Aug only). As there are 400 beds, finding a place should be easy (bunk in 2-3-bed room-3,300 Ft, includes sheets but no breakfast; a short hike up behind the castle or a 5-minute walk from the Old Town at Leányka utca 2; tel. 36/520-430, www.imolanet.hu/imolahostel, hostel@imolanet.hu).

Eating in Eger

HBH Restaurant (named for the Hofbräuhaus beer on tap) is doing its best to be classy in this small town. They offer traditional Hungarian dishes (including chalkboard specials) in an upscale environment (2,000-3,100-Ft main dishes, good wine list, daily 11:30-23:00, outdoor tables in summer, right at the bottom of Dobó Square at Bajcsy-Zsilinszky utca 19, tel. 36/515-516).

    Palacsintavár ("Pancake Castle"), near the ramp leading up to the castle, isn't your hometown IHOP. This cellar bar (which also has pleasant sidewalk seating) serves up inventive, artfully presented crêpe-wrapped main courses to a mostly student clientele. It's decorated with old cigarette boxes, and cutting-edge rock music plays on the soundtrack (meal-sized 2,000-2,500-Ft pancake dishes, daily 12:00-23:00, Dobó utca 9, tel. 36/413-980).

    Restaurant Senator Ház, on Little Dobó Square, offers the best setting for al fresco dining in town, with good Hungarian and international food (1,200-1,800-Ft light meals, 1,700-3,200-Ft main dishes). Sure, you're paying a bit extra for the setting—but it's worth it for the postcard-perfect outdoor seating, from which you can survey the Little Dobó Square action (open daily 10:00-22:00,

EGER

cheesy live music on summer evenings). Neighboring restaurants (such as Offi Ház) offer the same ambience.

Szantofer Vendéglő serves traditional Hungarian food at local prices to both Egerites and tourists. The good, unpretentious, fill-the-tank grub is designed for the neighborhood gang (1,800-2,500 Ft main dishes, daily 11:30-22:00, Bródy Sándor utca 3, tel. 36/517-298).

Elefanto, above the market hall, has a pleasant tree-house ambience. As it's outside of the cute zone, it attracts more locals than tourists. Sit indoors or enjoy covered terrace seating that's delightful in warm weather. The menu is mostly Italian, with pastas (1,300-1,600 Ft), pizzas (2,500 Ft), and main dishes (2,000-3,300 Ft), plus a few Hungarian standbys thrown in (daily 12:00-22:00, Katona István tér 2, tel. 36/412-452).

Dessert: Cukrászda (pastry shops) line the streets of Eger. For deluxe, super-decadent pastries of every kind imaginable, drop by **Dobós Cukrászda** (Mon-Sat 9:30-20:00, Sun 9:00-19:00, point to what you want inside and they'll bring it out to your table, Széchenyi utca 6, tel. 36/413-335). For a more local scene, find the tiny **Sárvári Cukrászda,** a block behind the Lyceum. Their pastries are good, but Egerites line up here for homemade gelato (Mon-Fri 7:00-18:00, Sat-Sun 10:00-18:00, Kossuth utca 1, between Jókai utca and Fellner utca). You'll spot several ice-cream parlors in this town, where every other pedestrian seems to be licking a cone. Another good option is the *kürtőskalács* **window** on Szent János utca, where you can step up and grab a piping-hot "pastry horn" that's slow-cooked on a rotisserie, then rolled in toppings (daily 9:00-19:30, Szent János utca 10).

Eger Connections

BY TRAIN

The only major destination you'll get to directly from Eger's train station is **Budapest** (every 2 hours direct to Budapest's Keleti/Eastern Station, 2 hours; more frequent and faster with a change in Füzesabony—see next). For other destinations, you'll connect through Füzesabony or Budapest.

Eger is connected to the nearby junction town of **Füzesabony** (FOO-zesh-ah-boyn) by frequent trains (13/day, 17 minutes). The very rustic Füzesabony station does not have lockers or an ATM; to find an ATM, exit straight from the station, walk about two blocks, and you'll find one on your right (just past the *Napcentrum*).

In Füzesabony, you can transfer to Budapest on either a slower milk-run train or a speedier InterCity train (a little pricier, as it requires an extra supplement, but gets you to Budapest in just under 2 hours total).

BY BUS

Eger's bus station (unlike its train station) is right in town, a five-minute uphill walk behind Eger's cathedral and the Archbishop's Palace: Go behind the cathedral and through the park, and look for the modern, green, circular building. Blue electronic boards in the center of the station show upcoming departures.

From Eger to Budapest: The direct Eger-Budapest bus service is about the same price as the train, and can be a bit faster (3,000 Ft, 2/hour, tickets generally available just before departure). Express buses depart Eger at :15 after each hour and make the trip in one hour and 50 minutes; slower regular buses leave at :45 after each hour and take 20 minutes longer. While Eger's bus station is closer to the town center than its train station, this bus takes you to a less central point in Budapest (near Budapest's Stadionok bus station, on the M2/red Metró line).

To the Thermal Baths near Egerszalók: Buses from the same station also connect Eger to the thermal baths near Egerszalók (Salt Hill and Demjén; see "Getting There" on page 372). However, buses marked for *Egerszalók* do not actually go to the spa; instead, you need a bus going *beyond* Egerszalók, marked for *Demjén*.

PÉCS

An established settlement for nearly 2,000 years, Pécs (pronounced "paych") is a historic, museum-packed, and oh-so-pretty city near Hungary's southern frontier. Cheerful, inviting Pécs, with colorful buildings dripping with lavish Zsolnay porcelain decoration, feels unusually proud and prosperous. Of course, it's a relative backwater, and compared to Budapest, its charms are modest...but they're also delightfully accessible. Pécs offers an unusually satisfying day of sightseeing for a city its size. And you'll hardly see another tourist, as this place is rarely visited by Americans.

Pécs' position as the major city of southern Hungary often placed it at the crossroads of cultures. Owing to the city's illustrious history, museum-going is fun and enlightening here. You'll gradually peel back the many layers of Pécs' past: Walk in the footsteps of Romans through ancient crypts, stroll the medieval trade-town street plan, explore some rare surviving artifacts of the Ottoman occupation, ogle colorful Baroque and Art Nouveau buildings... and enjoy the energetic bustle of one of Hungary's leading cities. The city's symbol—a mosque-turned-church—says it all.

The Mecsek Hills gently cradle the city, blocking out the colder weather from the north to give Pécs a mild Mediterranean climate closer to Croatia's than to Budapest's. It's no surprise that this bright and invigorating city has earned a reputation as a leading art colony. Its streets are lined with museums devoted to local artists both obscure and well-known (including Vasarely and Csontváry, two great figures of Hungarian art). Students love it, too. Hungary's first university was founded here in 1367, and today's U. of Pécs rivals Budapest's ELTE as the country's biggest university. More than 30,000 students give Pécs a youthful buzz. After a successful stint as European Capital of Culture in 2010, the city is proud and gleaming—and there's never been a better time to visit.

PLANNING YOUR TIME

One full day is plenty to get your fill of Pécs. It's barely doable as a long day trip from Budapest (three hours each way by train)—so it's worth spending the night. With the better part of a day in Pécs, go for a walk through town following my self-guided commentary (under "Sights in Pécs"), dipping into the museums that appeal to you. Nearly everything is within a few minutes' walk of the main square. The one exception—the Zsolnay Cultural Quarter, a 15- to 20-minute walk east—is interesting but skippable, or can be squeezed into any remaining time you have on a busy day (or the next morning).

Orientation to Pécs

With about 170,000 people, Pécs is Hungary's fifth-largest city. But it feels like a small town, right down to the convivial strolling atmosphere that combusts along its pedestrian zone. The Belváros, or Inner Town, is hemmed in by a ring road (the site of the former town wall, some of which still stands). You can walk from one end of this central tourist zone to the other in about 15 minutes. All roads lead to the main square, Széchenyi tér, marked by the pa-latial yellow Town Hall and giant mosque/church. Because Pécs is nestled up against a gentle hillside, you'll go gradually uphill as you head north.

TOURIST INFORMATION

The main TI—Pécs Infopoint—is in the pedestrian zone just below the main square, facing the yellow Town Hall building (daily 9:00-20:00, Széchenyi tér 7, tel. 72/213-315, www.iranypecs.hu). A second, seasonal branch is in a kiosk just below the cathedral, where Dom tér meets István tér (daily June-mid-Oct 10:00-18:00, closed off-season).

PÉCS

ARRIVAL IN PÉCS

By Train: The Pécs train station is three-quarters of a mile due south of the city center's Széchenyi tér. Inside, the station is long but straightforward (with ATM, lockers, and all the usual amenities).

A **taxi** to any of my recommended hotels should cost no more than 1,000 Ft.

You can **walk** from the train station to the town center in about 15 minutes: Exit straight ahead from the station and walk up the tree-lined, slightly angled Jókai út, which funnels you directly to Széchenyi tér. It's gently uphill the entire way.

Various **bus** lines (#4, #4Y, #38, #38A, #39, and #40) shave a few minutes off the walk downtown, taking you to the Árkád shop-

Pécs

MIKLÓS U.

NYIL U.

VILMOS U.

MECSEK U.

JUHÁSZ GY. U.

HUNYADI U.

To Mecsek Hills
& TV Tower

DAMJANICH U.

ARADI VÉRTANÚK ÚTJA

Bus #35
(Alagút)

KODÁLY Z. U.

CITY WALLS

LAPIDARIUM

ZSOLNAY
MUSEUM

MODERN
HUNGARIAN
ART MUSEUM

WALK
ENDS

CATHEDRAL

MARTYN
MUSEUM

KÁPTALAN U.

Bus #35
(Barbakán)

NEMES
MUSEUM

BARBICAN

BISHOP'S
PALACE

Dóm
tér

CAFÉ
KIOSK

VASARELY
MUSEUM

FORBÁT A. U.

CELLA SEPTICHORA
VISITOR CENTER

PADLOCKS

KLIMÓ GYÖRGY U.

SÁNC U.

Várkert

SZT. ISTVÁN TÉR

JANUS
PANNÓNIUS U.

István
tér

NEMES
MUSEUM

CSONTVÁRY
MUSEUM

YÖRÖSMARTY U.

CISZT

ALKOTMÁNY U.

APÁCA U.

SARACEN
PHARMACY

HUNGÁRIA U.

Kórház Tér

FERENCESEK UTCÁJA

MÁTYÁS KIRÁLY U.

GARAY U.

ZRÍNYI MIKLÓS U.

VÁRADY ANTAL

DISCHKA GYŐZŐ

POST

EÖTVÖS U.

RÁKÓCZI

ÚT

Zsolnay-Sobor

REF U.

SZABADSÁG U.

JÓKAI U.

To Train Station

PÉCS

1. Hotel Arkadia
2. Hotel Palatinus
3. Diána Hotel
4. Szinbád Panzió
5. Aranyhajó Fogadó
6. Hotel Főnix
7. Náp Hostel & Nappali Bar
8. Enoteca Corso
9. Oázis Gyros & Falafels
10. Cooltour Café
11. Egylet Restaurant
12. Jókai Bisztró & Elefántos Ház
13. Jókai Cukrászda

GAZI KASIM PASHA
MOSQUE/CHURCH

← BELL TOWER

Széchényi
tér

HOLY TRINITY
COLUMN

NÁDOR SZÁLLÓ

COUNTY
HALL

HUNYADI
MONUMENT

TOWN
HALL

NATIONAL
THEATER

WALK
BEGINS

JÓKAI
TÉR

ZSOLNAY
FOUNTAIN

Kossuth
tér

SYNAGOGUE

Bus #38, #38A,
#39, #40 & #43
(from train station)

ÁRKÁD
SHOPPING
MALL

To Zsolnay
Cultural
Quarter

To Zsolnay
Cultural
Quarter

PÉCS

50 Meters
50 Yards

Street names visible on map:
ISTVÁN U., SZŐLŐ U., KÁLVÁRIA U., CITY WALLS, PAPNŐVELDE U., MEGYE U., SZENT MÓR U., KIS FLÓRIÁN U., NAGY FLÓRIÁN U., MAJOROSSY IMRE, MAJOROSSY I. U., TETTYE U., ANNA U., JÓZSEF U., MÁRIA U., JÁNOS U., SZEPESSY IGNÁC, KIRÁLY U., KAZINCZY U., LICEUM U., PERCZEL MIKLÓS U., BOTTYÁN KÖZ, VÁROSH, KISFALUDY S., GÁBOR U., TOLDI M. U., FELSŐMALOM U., KÖZ, MUNKÁCSY MIHÁLY U., GOLDMARK U., FÜRDŐ U., BERCSÉNYI U., TÍMÁR U., ÚT, TERÉZ U., IRGALMASOK U., RÁKÓCZI, ZSINKÓ I. U., CITROM U., CZINDERY U., BAJCSY-ZSIL. U., ALSÓMALOM U., LISZT FERENC U., NAGY LAJOS KIRÁLY ÚTJA

ping center just south of the pedestrianized old center. As you exit the station, head down to the left end of the bus stops; you'll find these buses at the second row of bus stops (out in the parking lot, marked *VI;* buy 360-Ft ticket from driver, ride two stops to Árkád). From the Árkád bus stop, it's about a five-minute walk to the main square (backtrack a few steps up Rákóczi street, then angle diagonally through the long square called Kossuth tér and turn right up Irgalmasok utcája).

GETTING AROUND PÉCS

In compact Pécs, you could easily get by without using local buses—but they may come in handy for getting into the town center from the train station, reaching the Zsolnay Cultural Quarter, or heading up into the hills. A single ticket is 280 Ft when purchased in advance at a kiosk, or 360 Ft when bought on the bus (www.tukebusz.hu). If you buy it on the bus, the driver will likely stamp it to validate it for you. Otherwise, you'll need to validate it yourself: Stick the ticket in the slot, then pull the slot toward you.

HELPFUL HINTS

Pécs Outdoor Theater Festival: Each July through mid-August, the city hosts a festival (Pécsi Szabadtéri Játékok) with lots of concerts at reasonable prices (www.pecsinyariszinhaz.hu). If visiting in the summer, ask about it. The kiosk at the National Theater sells tickets to all festival events.

Shopping: The big, American-style **Árkád** shopping mall—with a supermarket, food court, and lots more—is just a block beyond the synagogue and Kossuth tér, at the southern edge of the Inner Town (shops open Mon-Sat 9:00-20:00, Sun 10:00-18:00, Bajcsy-Zsilinszky utca 11, www.arkadpecs.hu).

Tourist Train: A hokey tourist train does a 40-minute loop through the city center, and heads out to the Zsolnay Cultural Quarter (980 Ft one-way, 1,400 Ft round-trip, departs from in front of the mosque on Széchenyi tér, runs May-Sept, season extended in good weather, train cancelled in bad weather).

Sightseeing Pass: The 3,500-Ft **day ticket** *(napijegy)* saves you a little money if you're seeing the three main museums downtown (Csontváry, Vasarely, and Zsolnay). Simply buy it at the first museum you visit. Note that it does not cover the mosque/church, cathedral, Roman crypts, synagogue, or Zsolnay Cultural Quarter.

Local Guide: Brigitta Gombos is a knowledgeable guide who leads good tours of her hometown (17,000 Ft/3 hours, mobile 0670-505-3531, gerluc@freemail.hu).

Sights in Pécs

I've listed these sights roughly in the order of a handy self-guided orientation walk through town.

ZSOLNAY FOUNTAIN TO THE CATHEDRAL
• *Begin in front of the little church next to the Town Hall, at the...*

▲Zsolnay Fountain (Zsolnay-kút)

This fountain, an icon of Pécs, was a gift from the beloved local Zsolnay (ZHOL-nay) family. The family created an innovative

material called pyrogranite that allowed colorful, delicate-seeming porcelain to be made frost-proof and hard as steel—ideal for external building decoration. The ox heads—modeled after an ancient drinking vessel found in Pécs—are specially glazed with another Zsolnay invention, eosin. Notice how the iridescent eosin glaze glimmers with a unique range of colors. (Since this glaze compromises the pyrogranite, the fountain must be covered in winter.) Above the oxen heads are traditional symbols of Pécs. One is the shield with five tall churches, dating from the Middle Ages. (Germans still call the town Fünfkirchen.) This seal was appropriated by the Zsolnay family as a symbol of their porcelain. The other seal is Pécs' coat of arms: a walled city under vineyard-strewn hills.

This is the first of many gorgeous Zsolnay decorations we'll see all over town. But Pécs is just the beginning. In the late 19th and early 20th centuries, Budapest and cities all over Europe covered their finest buildings with decorations from this city's Zsolnay Porcelain Manufacture. (For more, see the "Zsolnay Porcelain" sidebar on page 400.)

• *Across the pedestrian street from the fountain, and 20 yards uphill, is the entrance to an enjoyable zone called...*

Jókai Tér

At the start of the street, notice the **game boards** on top of the little pillars. When this street was renovated in 2000—with funky benches and other playful elements—the designers wanted to remind locals to take time to relax.

On the right (a few doors down, at #2), notice the **Zsolnay porcelain shop.** Although the company was reduced to an industrial supplier under the communists, today Zsolnay is proudly reclaiming its role as a maker of fine art. Dipping into the shop, notice that some of the decorative items use the same distinctive eosin glaze as the fountain's oxen heads...and are priced accordingly (Mon-Fri 9:00-17:00, Sat 9:00-13:00, closed Sun).

Continuing to the corner, you enter a fine little square with a kid-pleasing fountain. At the far end of the square, look left down the street called **Ferencesek utcája.** When Pécs was a walled market town, this street—and Király utca to the east, also now pedestrianized—made up the main east-west road. At the house on the uphill corner, notice the elephant. This used to be a grocery store, which likely imported exotic Eastern goods, symbolized by the then-mysterious pachyderm.

Hang a right around the elephant house, noticing the former tram tracks preserved in the street. The yellow bricks were pretty standard in 20th-century Hungary. Imagine how unappealing this drag was when it was choked with tram and car traffic. At the corner (on the left), look for the old-time **Saracen Pharmacy** (marked with the words *Sipöcz István* and an African prince over the door). Its interior features gorgeous woodwork, little porcelain medicine pots, and a Zsolnay fountain. Now it's a tourist shop, selling wine, candy, soaps, and other local artisan products (Mon-Sat 8:00-15:00, closed Sun).

• *Continuing up the street, you'll emerge into the main square...*

▲▲Széchenyi Tér

In the Middle Ages, Pécs was a major trading crossroads, located at the intersection of two Byzantine trade routes. Széchenyi tér was a natural meeting point and market zone. Today the market is gone, but this square remains the bustling city center, where both political demonstrations and the annual New Year's Eve festivities percolate.

Let's get oriented. Stand at the base of the square (across from the McDonald's). Face the green-domed **Gazi Kasim Pasha Mosque** at the top of the square (described in detail later). On the right (housing the McDonald's), the giant yellow-and-white building with the tower is the **Town Hall** (Városház, 1908), strategically located here since the olden days to watch over the market activities.

The Town Hall's tower plays laid-back organ ditties throughout the day. (The **TI** is directly across the pedestrian street from the Town Hall.) Across the square is the gorgeous, red-roofed **County Hall** (Megyháza, 1898), frosted like a wedding cake with sumptuous Zsolnay decorations. Because the building was originally a bank, it's adorned with beehives (one at the very peak of the building, and two more between the top-floor windows). Industrious bees, who carefully collect and store away their golden deposits, are a common symbol for banking.

Farther up the square on the right is the pink **Nádor Szálló.** In the early 20th century, this hotel was a popular gathering place for artists and intellectuals; today, the gutted interior is an industrial-mod gallery space where the arts faculty of the local university showcases works by students and visiting artists. Peek inside to see what's on during your visit.

The square has two monuments. On the right is an equestrian statue of **János Hunyadi,** the war hero who fended off the Ottoman invaders at the 1456 Battle of Belgrade (described on page 175). Later those Ottomans took Pécs and built the mosque at the top of the square. But Hunyadi gets the last laugh: If you position yourself just right, Hunyadi's club smashes the crescent at the top of the mosque. (Try it.) This statue is a popular meeting point: Locals say, "I'll meet you under the horse's...tail." With perhaps unintended irony, Hunyadi—who died of the plague soon after that battle—shares the square with the **Holy Trinity Plague Column,** which townspeople built to give thanks to God after surviving a nasty bout of the plague in the late 17th century. Around its base are three saints known for protecting against disease or injury: Sebastian, who was killed by arrows (on left); Rocco, with his trusty dog and trademark leg wound (on right); and Anthony of Padua, who offers help recovering that which is lost—including health (behind the pillar).

• *We'll visit the mosque/church soon. But first, head down the street branching off to the right, next to the Town Hall...*

▲The Walking Street: Király Utca

This vibrant Technicolor people zone—combined with Jókai tér and Ferencesek utcája, across the square—bisects the city center.

Király utca ("Royal Street") is a delight to stroll. Walk its entire length, simply enjoying street musicians and people-watching, and noting its personality-filled architecture.

This street is lined with plenty of (largely

interchangeable) **restaurants.** The lineup shifts constantly, but I've mentioned a few specifics under "Eating in Pécs," later. As you stroll, peruse the posted menus and scope out a place for a meal later.

About a block down (on the left, at #5), keep an eye out for the gorgeous, horseshoe-shaped **Hotel Palatinus;** step into its lobby for a taste of genteel Secession architecture. The hotel's second wing is filled with a hoity-toity wine bar (Le Gourmet) in a nicely atmospheric, vintage setting. (One of Hungary's top wine-growing regions, Villány, is about 40 minutes' drive south of Pécs—and explained later in this chapter). While the prices in this wine bar are high, it's a nice chance to peruse vintages produced by local wineries (as well as from other parts of Hungary).

Soon you'll reach the square in front of the **National Theater,** built (along with most of the other houses on this square) for the Hungarian millennial celebrations of 1896 (see page 33). The decorations on the theater—including the stone-like statues—are all made of Zsolnay pyrogranite. This is a popular venue in this city of culture, and hosts the local philharmonic (their season runs Sept-May). Duck into the box office here (to the right of the big building) any time of year to see what's on, either here or elsewhere in town.

Farther along, you'll find a good ice-cream parlor (at #15, on the left); **Oázis Keleti Étterem,** a good spot for a quick gyro or falafel snack (at #17, on the left); a very cool ruin pub (the recommended **Cooltour**—the name is a wordplay on *kultur* or "culture"—with an inviting garden out back; at #26, on the right); and, finally, a contemporary Hungarian painting gallery (at #31, on the left).

While this part of Pécs appears wealthy and manicured, the region is struggling. In the early 1950s, Pécs had only about 50,000 residents. Coal and uranium mines kick-started the economy, causing the population to more than triple over the last 50 years. However, both mines are now closed, and while Pécs' university and business center continue to thrive, outlying communities are grappling with 30 percent unemployment.

• *Head back to Széchenyi tér to visit the...*

▲▲Gazi Kasim Pasha Mosque
(Gázi Kászim Pasa Dzsámija)/Inner Town Parish Church

It's rare to find such a well-preserved Ottoman structure in Hungary. The Ottomans—who began their 150-year stay in Pécs in

1543—lived here in the Inner Town, while the dwindling Hungarian population moved to the outskirts. The Ottomans tore down the church that stood on this spot and used the stones to build the structure you see today. After the Ottomans were forced out, the Catholic Church reclaimed this building and turned it into a church—which is why it's still intact today. Despite renovations over the years, it remains an offbeat hybrid of the Islamic and Christian faiths.

Cost and Hours: 1,000 Ft, Mon-Sat 9:00-17:00, Sun 13:00-17:00.

⊙ Self-Guided Tour: From the **outside,** notice the crescent moon of Islam capping the dome—but it's topped by the victorious Christian cross. The only decorations on the austere facade are the striped ogee arches over the windows. Before entering, notice the fig trees; locals are proud that their mild climate can support these heat-seekers.

Go **inside** and let your eyes adjust to the low light. Are you in a church, or a mosque...or both? The striped arches over the windows are even more apparent inside. Notice the colorful Islamic-style stalactite decorations at the tops of the corners. The painting on the underside of the dome seems to combine Christian figures with the geometric designs of Islam. To the right of the main altar is a verse from the Quran translated into Hungarian and used for Christian worship (a reminder that Islam and Christianity are founded on many of the same principles).

Looking back to where you entered, scan the back wall for gray patches with faint Arabic script peeking through—most were whitewashed over during the church-ification. In the middle of the wall, next to the door, is a large **prayer niche** (mihrab). This niche, which faces Mecca (southeast from here), indicated to Muslim worshippers the direction they had to face to pray. The holy water basin in the niche and the crucifix suspended above it make it clear who's in charge now.

Mentally erase these and other Christian elements, and imagine worshipping here during the Ottoman period. There were no pews, and carpets covered the floor. Worshippers—men in front, women segregated in back—stood and knelt as they prayed toward the mihrab. A step-stair pulpit, called a *mimber*, likely stood off to one side of the mihrab.

When the Christians reclaimed this building, they flipped it around, creating an entrance near the mihrab, and an altar at the former entrance. Much later, in 1940, they added the giant **apse** (semicircular area behind the altar). Explore this area, with its striking 1930s-style murals. The modern paintings depict Bible scenes and events in Hungary's Christian history. And the giant organ is an Angster (made by a local Hungarian organ-maker). In the corners, you'll see small stone basins. These once stood outside the building, where the Ottoman worshippers performed their ablution, or ritual washing before prayer.

Down in the **crypt,** you'll find an exhibit with interactive touchscreens that explain the three phases of this building's tumultuous history: church, mosque, church.

Exiting the building, head around back to find the latest addition to this constantly evolving structure: the modern **bell tower** and a concrete footprint that recalls the original church that preceded the mosque. The statue is St. Bartholomew, the patron of this church. Depicted (as he always is) with his skin peeling away, he steps on a serpent, representing victory over evil (Islam?). Every day at 12:00 and 19:00, the bell tower mechanically rises 40 feet into the air to play a tune. Viewing the church from back here, you can also appreciate how jarringly ugly the 1940 concrete addition is.

• *While interesting, this is not Pécs' main church. To see that (and a lot more), go down the street at the upper-left corner of the square...*

Janus Pannonius Utca

About a block down this street, watch (on the right) for a railing that's completely covered in **padlocks.** While this tradition has caught on in recent years along romantic bridges all over Europe, the people of Pécs are trendsetters—they've been doing it here since the 1980s. Some say it was a clever way for graduating students to get rid of the padlocks from their lockers. These days, the padlocks mostly belong to lovers who want to pledge themselves to each other.

Many of the locks are marked (or even engraved) with couples' names. Farther down the same block, the tradition continues at the padlock-covered gate. (Not missing a sales opportunity, guess what the nearby shop sells.)

• *Continue along the street until you emerge into the little square. In the pretty, white building on the left (with the gray roof), you'll find Pécs' best art museum...*

▲▲Csontváry Museum (Csontváry Múzeum)

This small but delightful collection showcases the works of beloved Hungarian painter Tivadar Csontváry Kosztka. Csontváry produced only 100 paintings and 20 drawings, and about half are collected here. For a crash course in this enigmatic painter, read the sidebar before visiting; the paintings are described in English.

Cost and Hours: 1,200 Ft, covered by 3,500-Ft day ticket, open Tue-Sun 10:00-18:00, closed Mon, borrow the English information sheet, Janus Pannonius utca 11, tel. 72/224-255.

Visiting the Museum: The museum is divided into five rooms. In Room 1 are Csontváry's art-school sketches, which capture people at unguarded moments and show the work of a budding genius. Rooms 2, 3, and 4 are mostly dedicated to Csontváry's many travel canvases. Room 2 has "postcards" from his trips to Sicily (Castellammare, Taormina) and Bosnia-Herzegovina (Mostar, Jajce), but the best canvas in here is from Hungary: *Storm over the Great Hortobágy* is a dynamic snapshot of life on the Great Hungarian Plain, where cowherds tend longhorn cattle. A storm brews on the horizon as a horseman races across the bridge. Notice the balance between movement and stillness, and between the yellow sky and the blue clouds. Room 3 covers Baalbek, the High Tatras (where Csontváry first had the epiphany that drove him to paint, and to madness), and a historical scene of Mary's well in Nazareth. In Room 4 is Csontváry's most acclaimed work, *Solitary Cedar:* a windblown tree on a ridge above the sea. The tree seems boldly independent even as it longs for companionship. The last room (5) displays Csontváry's final major painting, *Riders on the Seashore.* This haunting valedictory canvas, with an equestrian party pausing by an eerily deep-blue cove, hints at the troubled depths of Csontváry's own psyche. Other works in this room date from Csontváry's final days, when—in his worsening mental state—he sketched large-scale, absurdist scenes.

• *Leaving the museum, cross the street and continue left down the tree-lined, pedestrian-only path. Soon you'll see a beautiful yellow kiosk (on the right)—an inviting place for a coffee break. A few steps beyond that, look for the modern entrance to the...*

Tivadar Csontváry Kosztka (1853-1919)

Adored by Hungarians, but virtually unknown outside his home-land, the artist Tivadar Csontváry Kosztka had a life as fascinating as his paintings. Because of the time in which he lived and his struggles with mental illness, Csontváry (CHONT-vah-ree) is often compared to Van Gogh. While that's a bit of a stretch, view-ing Csontváry's works gives you a glimpse into the Hungarian psyche, and into his own fractured mind.

Tivadar Kosztka was born to an upper-class family, seemingly bound for a humdrum life. He didn't pick up a paintbrush until his 27th year. Idly sketching sleeping oxen while recovering from an illness, he had a revelation (or, perhaps, a psychotic episode): A voice told him that he was destined to become "the world's greatest *plein air* painter."

He adopted the pseudonym "Csontváry" and became driven by an almost pathologi-cal compulsion to prepare himself for his destiny. He worked as a pharmacist to finance his quest, and by age 41, he had saved enough to attend art school (in Munich and Paris). Seeking ideal subjects for his outdoor style, he traveled extensively in Europe and the Middle East: Italy, Croatia, Bosnia-Herzegovina, Greece, Egypt, Lebanon, Jerusalem, and the Tatra Mountains. By the time

▲Cella Septichora Visitor Center (Roman Crypts)

This unique, modern, well-presented museum allows visitors to take a peek inside some remarkably preserved Roman crypts. (Note: If you skip this museum, sneak a free look at the some of the ruins through the glass behind the yellow kiosk.)

Cost and Hours: 1,700 Ft; April-Oct Tue-Sun 10:00-18:00, Nov-March Tue-Sun 10:00-16:00, closed Mon year-round; Dóm tér, tel. 72/224-755, www.pecsorokseg.hu.

Discount with Zsolnay Cultural Quarter: If you'll definitely be visiting some of the museums in the Zsolnay Cultural Quarter, ask about combo-tickets that let you save more the more sights you visit (see museum descriptions on page 403).

Nearby: If you're interested in these sorts of ruins, ask about the "medieval university" that was recently excavated and restored nearby (covered by 400-Ft ticket; visit possible only with guided tour).

Tours: While my self-guided tour—and good posted English descriptions—cover the basics, Roman history buffs may be able to request or join a guided English tour (for details, call 72/224-755 or email info@pecsorokseg.hu).

Background: There was a Roman settlement in today's Pécs

PÉCS

he began painting in earnest, he had only six productive years (1903-1909).

Csontváry's rough, self-taught style reveals his untrained origins, but contains a depth of meaning that exceeded his technical skill. While classified as a Post-Impressionist, Csontváry forged a style all his own. Like his contemporary Marc Chagall, he worked in almost childlike bright colors with big, bold themes. His most common subjects were the destinations to which he traveled.

After exhibitions in 1909 and 1910 failed to win him the praise he so desperately sought, he became consumed by schizophrenia and created only bizarre, surrealistic works. He died in obscurity in 1919.

After Csontváry's death, his family nearly sold his works to wagon-makers, who wanted the valuable canvas (not the paintings themselves). Fortunately, a Budapest art collector bought them instead.

Csontváry remained largely unappreciated until the 1960s, when art lovers began to take notice. But one discerning eye for talent knew greatness when he saw it: Pablo Picasso reportedly discovered Csontváry's canvases at a 1949 exhibition, and proceeded to lock himself in the room with them for an hour. Finally emerging, he told his friend Marc Chagall that Chagall could never produce a work half as good as Csontváry's.

from the year A.D. 30, and by the second century it was a provincial capital called Sopinae. During that time, this part of town was a vast cemetery, which included the graves of early Christian martyrs. Later, after Christianity became the state religion in the early

fourth century, these tombs attracted pilgrims from afar. Wealthy Christian families were now free to build a double-decker structure to hold the remains of their relatives: a sealed crypt below ground (painted with Bible scenes and floral motifs), with a chapel directly above for remembering and praying for the dead. About a century later, Rome fell. Nomadic invaders lived in the chapels and raided the crypts (then carefully re-covered them). Today the remains of some of these crypt-chapels have been discovered, excavated, and opened to visitors.

PÉCS

⊙ Self-Guided Tour: Buy your ticket, borrow the English map of the sprawling underground complex, and head into the first area (under the glass roof), the foundation of a **giant chapel with seven apses.** (The exhibit is named for this—Cella Septichora means "seven-apsed chapel.") Experts believe that the crypt of a different martyr would have been placed in each apse, and pilgrims would come here to worship. However, the structure was never finished.

From here, follow signs (and your map) as you climb up and down through the subterranean exhibit to the highlights. Unlike Rome's famous catacombs, these crypts were not originally connected underground; modern archaeologists built the tunnels you'll pass through to allow visitors easier access to all the tombs.

Find the **Wine Pitcher Burial Chamber.** The model shows the two-tiered structure. Peer through the window to see the paintings that decorate the crypt. Its nickname comes from the wine jug and glass painted in the niche above the body. Romans used wine to toast to the memory of the departed (the Roman version of "pour one out for the homies who ain't here"). Climb up the stairs to what was ground level, where you can view the foundation of the chapel and look down into the crypt. From here, you'll see other paintings (representing paradise), as well as the drain at the bottom of the sarcophagus. The Romans, ever the clever engineers, provided drainage so that accumulating groundwater would not defile the body.

Retrace your steps back up the long hallway, then follow signs to the Peter and Paul crypt. Along the way, you'll pass through an area with several **smaller crypts.** Notice that these didn't have large chapels up top; rather, worshippers would kneel and look inside a small decorative chapel. In one, a hole in the floor of the chapel indicates where tomb raiders broke in to search for valuables. Turn right into the **octagonal chapel,** which—like the seven-apsed chapel—was likely designed to be a pilgrim church. Finally you'll pass another small crypt that's more intact, showing the barrel vaulting that once covered all of these.

Take the spiral stairs all the way down to the bottom to enter the **Peter and Paul Burial Chamber.** Standing under the painted tomb, you'll see faded Sts. Peter and Paul flanking the Christogram (an ancient Christian symbol). The side walls are painted with biblical scenes, while the ceiling features another Christogram, four portraits (possibly the Four Evangelists), and more nature motifs—plants and birds. (An artist's rendering of the original version is nearby.) Notice the little window above the body. Experts believe that a ribbon tied to the sarcophagus led through this window up into the chapel, so the faithful could have a tangible connection to the dead.

Retracing your steps on your way out, you'll pass through even more crypts (they've unearthed more than 20), as well as some simple brick sarcophagi used by poorer families to bury their dead.

• *Exiting the exhibit, turn right and continue down Janus Pannonius utca, which deposits you at...*

István Tér and Dóm Tér

These two squares—the lower István Square, which belonged to the people, and the upper Cathedral Square, which was the bish-

op's—used to be separated by a wall and moat. But later, the enlightened **Bishop Szepesy** turned them into one big park. In the statue that dominates the square, the bishop is stepping down from the pulpit clutching a Bible—a reminder that he's believed to have been the first priest to use Hungarian.

Walk up the stairs and into Cathedral Square. The brown, Neo-Renaissance building on the left is the **Bishop's Palace**—recently restored and opened to the public. It's possible to tour the interior, including the so-called "Texas passage" that leads to a hidden garden. But it's pricey, and you can only visit the facility on a guided tour (2,700 Ft, tours depart 3/day, get details at visitors center inside).

At the corner of the Bishop's Palace that faces the park, notice the engaging statue of **Franz Liszt** by popular 20th-century sculptor Imre Varga. Liszt was a friend of the bishop, and Liszt's visit here in 1846 is still the stuff of legend.

• *Now turn your attention to the massive, four-towered...*

▲▲Cathedral

With an imposing exterior and an elaborately decorated interior, Pécs' cathedral merits a close look. St. István established a bishopric

in Pécs in the year 1009, and this church building grew in fits and starts from then on. By the 14th century, it had roughly the same floor plan as today, and gradually morphed with the styles of the day: Romanesque, Gothic, Renaissance. The Ottomans preserved the building, using it first as a mosque and later as a stable, a grain store, and a library. Later, when it became the cathedral again, it got a Baroque makeover. Finally, in the 1880s, a bishop (likely hoping to be remembered as a visionary) grew tired of the architectural hodgepodge, gutted the place, and turned it into the Neo-Romanesque fortress of God you see today. The 12 apostles stand along the roofline, and the four distinctive corner towers anchor and fortify the massive structure. Meanwhile, the interior is a riot of finely executed and pristinely preserved golden decorations.

Cost and Hours: 1,200 Ft, Mon-Sat 9:00-17:00, Sun 13:00-17:00, can close for weddings Sat afternoons—especially in summer, tel. 72/513-057, www.pecsibazilika.hu.

Visiting the Cathedral: Outside, study the symbolic **bronze gate** from 2000. The vines, grapes, and branches are all connected, symbolizing our connection to God. If you look closely, you'll find animals representing good (birds) and evil (snake, scorpion, frog). On the left, St. István gives Pécs to the first bishop; on the right, Jesus offers his hand to St. Peter.

Stepping inside, you're struck by the rich Neo-Romanesque, 19th-century decor. It's clear that the renovating bishop did not subscribe to the "less is more" school of church decoration. Like the Matthias Church in Budapest (see page 76)—renovated at about the same time—every square inch is covered by a thick and colorful layer of paint. Along the **nave** are paintings depicting the lives of the church's patrons, Sts. Peter and Paul. Above the arches are biblical scenes. The coffered ceiling of the nave depicts the 12 apostles and (near the organ) John the Baptist.

The **altar,** with its highly decorated canopy, is a replica of the 13th-century original. The mosaic on the apse dome (behind the altar, not entirely visible from here) features Jesus flanked by Peter and Paul (on the right) and, on the left, Mary and István (the patron saint of Hungary).

Back in the main church, to the right of the altar are the stairs down to the **crypt.** This 11th-century forest of columns (redecorated like the rest of the church) is part of the original church building on this site. The bust at the front depicts the bishop who decided to renovate the church.

Your ticket also includes access to one of the cathedral's four **towers,** with sweeping views over Pécs.

Nearby: In addition to the Bishop's Palace (described earlier), the cathedral office also runs two more sights nearby: a **lapidarium** (collection of old stone sculptures and fragments) and a **treasury.** Both are skippable and covered by their own, separate 1,800-Ft ticket.

• *From in front of the cathedral, if you want to take a look at part of the old city wall, go down the stairs and turn right at the wide path, which will take you to a barbican (round tower) that helped fortify the walls. (For more on these walls, see page 402.) If you decide to visit the wall, on your way there—but just before the barbican and busy street—watch on the left for the gateway at #5 (marked Eoz!n Grillterasz Kultúrpark), which leads to a pleasant series of sleepy parks along the inside of the town wall, some modest views of the four cathedral steeples, and a near- "ruin pub" terrace serving drinks and grilled foods with views over the suburbs.*

Otherwise, after you exit the cathedral, walk about halfway down the square, turn left before the steps, pass through the archway, walk over the glassed-in Roman ruins (noticing the entrance to the cathedral lapidarium just uphill), and head down...

KÁPTALAN UTCA: "MUSEUM ROW"

A cluster of museums line tranquil Káptalan utca ("Chapterhouse Street," where priests once lived). A few of the smaller museums are skippable, but the Zsolnay and Vasarely museums are worthwhile (www.jpm.hu). Remember, these are covered by the same 3,500-Ft day ticket (see page 386). Nearby are museums that showcase the work of yet two more local artists—Ferenc Martyn and Endre Nemes—and the Modern Hungarian Art Museum.

PÉCS

▲Viktor Vasarely Museum (Vasarely Múzeum)

You might not know Viktor Vasarely (1908-1997), but you know his work. Think optical illusions, and the dizzying Op Art that inspired the psyche-delic 1960s. Here in his home-town, you can see a museum of Vasarely's eye-popping creations. Inspired by nature, Vasarely discovered that the repetition and slight variation of lines and forms can play with the viewer's brain to create illusions of depth and movement. In other words, black-and-white lines undulating across a canvas are trippy, baby. It's easy to get lost in Vasarely's

Zsolnay Porcelain

Thanks to the pioneering Zsolnay (ZHOL-nay) family of Pécs, buildings all over Hungary are slathered with gorgeously colorful porcelain.

Miklós Zsolnay (1800-1880) opened a porcelain factory in Pécs in 1853. But the real breakthrough came at the hands of his innovative son, Vilmos Zsolnay (1828-1900), who experimented with glazes and additives, and revo-

lutionized the use of porcelain in building materials. He invented pyrogranite—a type of weatherproof ceramic as resilient as steel, but which could be delicately sculpted and painted any color of the rainbow. Zsolnay pyrogranite made a splash at Vienna's 1873 World Exhibition, winning an avalanche of orders from all over Europe. The twists and curves that Zsolnay porcelain allowed were a perfect fit for the Art Nouveau style of the day. Exhibits at further world fairs added to the Zsolnay family's renown and wealth.

In 1893, Vilmos Zsolnay unveiled his latest innovation: eosin, a shimmering, almost metallic iridescent glaze that has the effect of light striking a precious gemstone or the glistening surface of a soap bubble. This eosin technique is exemplified by Pécs' Zsolnay Fountain (described on 387).

Boom time for the Zsolnays coincided with the 1896 millennial celebrations in Budapest (see page 33). The city's architects, who had ample resources and imagination, were striving to cre-

mind-bending designs—such as, in the first room, a pair of carpets with zebras—which make you go cross-eyed before you stumble up the stairs to see him add more color to the mix.

Cost: 1,200 Ft, covered by 3,500-Ft day ticket, Tue-Sun 10:00-18:00, closed Mon, Káptalan utca 3, mobile 0630-539-8069.

▲Zsolnay Porcelain Museum (Zsolnay Múzeum)

This museum, situated in the former mansion of the Zsolnay family, is as much a shrine to the family as a showcase of their work. (For more on the family and their legacy, see the "Zsolnay Porcelain" sidebar.) The collection is divided into two parts: architectural elements and decorative ware. Each room is well-described in English. In the architectural elements section (on the ground floor), you'll see impresate a unique Hungarian national style, and many adopted colorful pyrogranite tiles and other decorations as an integral part of that style. In Budapest alone, the Great Market Hall, Matthias Church and National Archives on Castle Hill, and Ödön Lechner's Postal Savings Bank and Museum

of Applied Arts are roofed with Zsolnay pyrogranite tiles. Zsolnay decorative elements also adorn the Hungarian Parliament and Gellért Baths, among other buildings. To this day, Zsolnay tiles are synonymous with Budapest (and Hungarian) architecture.

All of that porcelain generated a lot of work for the Pécs factory. By the time World War I broke out, the Zsolnay family business was the Austro-Hungarian Empire's biggest company. But the stripped-down modern styles that emerged in the 20th century had little use for the fanciful Zsolnay decorations. The factory was nationalized by the communists, the Zsolnay name was abandoned, and quality plummeted.

In the 1990s, private investors took over and have made great strides toward rehabilitating the Zsolnay name. All over Hungary, you'll see shops selling beautiful, innovative Zsolnay tableware. To keep up with our modern economy, Zsolnay also creates everyday items. In fact, they recently signed a big deal to make dishes for Ikea.

sively detailed and colorful decorations for the many buildings the Zsolnays were involved in renovating (including Budapest's Matthias Church and Parliament). You'll also see a playful duck fountain, with its colorful eosin glaze, and some beautiful pieces of the destroyed István Stove that once warmed Budapest's Royal Palace. Upstairs, the decorative-ware collection displays vases, sculptures, and other objects that demonstrate the evolution of porcelain style. Notice how trends came and went over time. A spinning table allows you to easily inspect each place setting of Zsolnay dinnerware. The "memorial room" is furnished as it would have been during the Zsolnays' day.

Cost: 1,200 Ft, covered by 3,500-Ft day ticket, Tue-Sun 10:00-18:00, closed Mon, Káptalan utca 4, tel. 72/514-045.

• *From Káptalan utca, you're just a block above the main square and our starting point. If you have more time, consider some of these sights...*

ELSEWHERE IN PÉCS

City Walls

Several segments of the city walls around the northern part of Pécs are still standing; a path leads around the outside of the wall that

still hems in the top of town. Built after the Tatar invasions of the 13th century, and beefed up in the 15th century, the walls were no match for the Ottoman invaders who took the town in 1543. Still standing just west of the cathedral area is the round, stout barbican defensive gate, which you can actually climb.

▲Synagogue (Zsinagóga)

Just south of the old center, overlooking the modern, beautifully renovated Kossuth tér, is Pécs' colorful synagogue. Dating from the 1860s but recently restored, this building is a powerful reminder of Pécs' Jewish heritage. The city had a thriving population of 4,000 Jews; only a few hundred survived the Holocaust.

Cost and Hours: 500 Ft, April-Oct Sun-Fri 10:00-17:00, Nov-March Sun-Fri 10:30-12:30, closed Sat year-round, Kossuth tér, tel. 72/315-881.

Visiting the Synagogue: The building feels like a humbler little sibling to Budapest's Great Synagogue, with wood-carved pews and a double-decker ar-
cade (where women worshipped, while the men gathered on the main floor). Its finest feature is the delicate ceiling decoration. The congregation here was Neolog (similar to today's "re-formed"); the organ at the front

of the building is a clear sign that this was not an Orthodox house of worship.

Like other Hungarian synagogues of this era, this building seems to be trying hard to feel like a church—at a time when local Jews were eager to feel integrated into the larger community. You can head upstairs, into the galleries (enter from outside—it's the door to the left of the main entrance) to find an exhibit about the history of local Jews, with good English descriptions and several actual artifacts (scrolls, postcards, personal effects) that characterize Pécs' Jewish community.

PÉCS

Mecsek Hills

Pécs is picturesquely nestled in the Mecsek (MEH-chek) Hills, a popular place to go for a hike. To get an aerial view of Pécs, ride bus #35Y about 30 minutes up to the Misinatető stop, near the TV tower that overlooks the city (catch this bus at the train station, or at the northern entrance to the city center). Ascend the 580-foot-tall TV tower for views over the town and surrounding region (950 Ft, daily 9:00-20:00).

ZSOLNAY CULTURAL QUARTER (ZSOLNAY KULTURÁLIS NEGYED)

The first and last name in Pécs industry, the Zsolnay porcelain-making family operated their major factory on the eastern edge of

town. Tucked in the middle of the sprawling brick industrial center were some fine villas and houses and a leafy park. Now this facility has been thoroughly restored and converted into a community cultural center with indoor and outdoor events venues, cafés, restaurants, children's play zones, and—of course—a collection of small museums celebrating the Zsolnay clan and their works. While it's out on the edge of things—a dull 20-minute walk or quick bus ride from downtown—the center is worth the trip if you've exhausted your in-town sightseeing interests and are curious to see another side of Pécs. And those taken with Zsolnay tiles may enjoy a pilgrimage to where they were created. (For more on the family and their legacy, see the "Zsolnay Porcelain" sidebar, earlier.)

Cost: It's free to enter the complex and explore the grounds. Each museum has its own admission price (listed later). It's worth buying all of your tickets at one ticket desk, as the more sights you visit, the bigger discount you get. Note that the excellent Cella Septichora Visitor Center participates in this discount deal (see page 394).

Hours: While the grounds are open daily 9:00-24:00, the individual sights are open substantially shorter hours: April-Oct Tue-Sun 10:00-18:00, Nov-March Tue-Sun 10:00-16:00, some sights stay open an hour later Fri-Sat, all closed Mon year-round. A few exceptions are noted in the individual listings.

Information: Tel. 72/500-350, www.zsn.hu.

Getting There: It's due east of the town center. You can **walk** there in about 20 minutes: Follow Király utca (the main walking street) to its end, then continue straight (as the road becomes Felsővámház utca) through residential neighborhoods about 10 minutes farther to the complex. Just head for the many tall smoke-stacks.

Multiple **buses** run to the complex. From in front of Árkád shopping center, catch bus #4, #20, #20A, #21, #27, #31, or #31A, and get off at the Zsolnay Negyed stop. From Búza tér, at the end of the traffic-free section of Király utca, catch bus #27 or #40 for the short trip to the Bóbita Bábszínház stop near the complex (though this saves you only an easy 10-minute walk). From the train station, take bus #4, #31, or #31A to Zsolnay Negyed; or bus #40 to Bóbita Bábszínház.

You could also hop on the **tourist train** from Széchenyi tér, but it's pricey (see "Helpful Hints," earlier). A **taxi** costs about 1,500 Ft.

Orientation: There are two main gates to the complex: the lower gate (just up from Zsolnay Vilmos út) and the upper gate (on Felsővámház utca). Once inside, you'll find a lower complex of buildings surrounding a small park with a short, colorful chimney. The modern building just uphill houses the **Visitors Center** (with ticket office, open daily April-Oct 9:00-19:00, Nov-March 9:00-17:00), a planetarium, a kids' play zone with hands-on scientific exhibits, and (downstairs) a funky café and the Pécsi Galéria (contemporary art installations). At the lower end of the park are the E78 Pyrogranite Courtyard (a modern indoor theater and outdoor live music venue, plus a tall smokestack with colorful Zsolnay tiles embedded in the base). Nearby is the Sikorski Villa, which houses the **Gyugyi Collection.**

More sights cluster up the small hill, in a long, sprawling mansion—here you'll find (in the right half of the building) the **Pink Zsolnay Exhibition** and the **Zsolnay Live Manufactory,** and (in the left half) the **Zsolnay Family and Factory History Exhibition.** The building also contains various eateries and, tucked back in a little courtyard (follow the signs), the **American Corner**—a service of the US Embassy that strives to educate Hungarians about American culture with an English lending library, special events on American holidays, English conversation clubs, and other resources.

Finally, up a few more steps to the top of the hill is another ticket office and the **"street of shops"**—basically a row of candy, chocolate, wine, and handicraft shops (generally open Tue-Sun 10:00-12:30 & 13:00-18:00, closed Mon). Leaving the gate by the ticket office, you'll turn right on Felsővámház utca and walk 200 yards to find the long staircase up to the **Zsolnay Mausoleum.** If you turn left on Felsővámház utca, you'll find the **Bóbita Puppet Theater** (Bóbita Bábszínház), which offers periodic performances for kids.

And, of course, the grounds are studded with pretty Zsolnay

decorations—fountains, pillars, and statues. Posted maps and directional signs help you find your way.

Planning Your Time: While it sounds like a lot—and Zsolnay enthusiasts could spend hours here—for the casual visitor, it's enough to simply stroll the colorful grounds; the only sights I'd pay to enter are the Gyugyi Collection (if you didn't get your fill at the Zsolnay Museum downtown) and the mausoleum. Below are brief descriptions of each sight to help you decide.

▲Gyugyi Collection (Gyugyi-gyűjtemény)

Dr. László Gyugyi fled Hungary after the 1956 Uprising and settled in the US, where he gradually amassed a breathtaking collec-

tion of sumptuous decorative Zsolnay objects. Now he has donated them to their hometown of Pécs, where they are displayed in a fine old villa at the heart of the complex. With a remarkable collection of Historicist and Art Nouveau items, beautifully displayed and well-

described in English on two floors, this is a better collection of decorative works than the Zsolnay Museum downtown—though unless you're a connoisseur, it may feel like a rerun, and it lacks the Zsolnay Museum's impressive collection of architectural features.

Cost and Hours: 1,400 Ft, see hours earlier.

Pink Zsolnay Exhibition (Rózsaszín Zsolnay Kiállítás)

Early on, the Zsolnay factory focused on producing everyday items in the then-in-vogue hue of pink. This modest collection shows

off more pink porcelain in one place than you'll see anywhere else. Unlike the finely detailed showpieces of the Gyugyi Collection, these are practical, unglamorous objects that were handmade, making them a bit rougher and with subtle imperfections. If it's fancy vases and plates you're hoping to see, skip it.

Cost and Hours: 1,000 Ft, see hours earlier.

Zsolnay Live Manufactory (Látványmanufaktúra)

This lets you peer through windows at Zsolnay potters hard at work. Posted English information briefly outlines the manufacture process, but it's tricky to appreciate since there's no practical English tour option.

Cost and Hours: 500 Ft, admission charged until 16:00—free after that because you won't see craftspeople at work; closed Sun.

Zsolnay Family and Factory History Exhibition (Család- és Gyártörténeti Kiállítás)

Displayed on two floors (factory downstairs, family upstairs), this exhibit traces—with dry English descriptions—the history of this complex and the people who built it. The museum doesn't add much to your visit here, and the few pieces on display are less striking than those in the Gyugyi Collection or the Zsolnay Museum downtown. For me, the offbeat highlight was the Zsolnay porcelain bust of Lenin dating from just after the factory was nationalized by the communists.

Cost and Hours: 1,200 Ft, see hours earlier.

▲Zsolnay Mausoleum (Zsolnay Mauzóleum)

A short walk from the rest of the complex, this hilltop perch is the final resting place of Vilmos Zsolnay, who founded the factory and enjoyed sitting on this hill to survey the family business. After his death in 1900, Vilmos' son Miklós commissioned this fine mausoleum (Miklós and his mother Terézia are also buried here)—entirely decorated in Zsolnay tiles, of course. Everything is now carefully restored and gleaming. From the road, you'll climb a staircase lined with 42 resting lions to reach the mausoleum itself. The entry doors (with eosin-glazed plaques depicting the 12 apostles) lead into a structure beautiful in its simplicity: a cylinder turned on end. Inside are an eosin altar and chandelier above an opening in the

floor where you can peer down at Vilmos' monumental tomb. Back outside, you can circle around back to find stairs down for a better look (through a grate).

Cost and Hours: 1,000 Ft, see hours earlier, but open until 19:00 in summer, possibly closed in bad weather.

NEAR PÉCS: THE VILLÁNY WINE REGION

The golden hillsides south of Pécs, draped with cornfields and vineyards, produce some of Hungary's best-regarded wines. Most of the production is centered near the village called Villány (VEE-layn), which sits just below the neatly cone-shaped Mount Szársomlyó. The area produces a variety of reds, whites, and rosés, using a range of grapes: merlot, cabernet sauvignon, pinot noir, Riesling, and *kékfrankos* ("blue Frankish"). For more on Hungarian wines, see page 252.

Drivers find Villány and the surrounding countryside easy to visit from Pécs—it's just a 40-minute drive south. (But remember that Hungary has a zero blood-alcohol level, so you're not supposed to drive even if you've had just a few tastes. Bring a designated driver.) You can also take a train from Pécs to Villány, then explore on foot from there (every 2 hours, 45 minutes).

In Villány and surrounding villages, cute little wine cellars line the main road, with picnic tables out front trying to lure in passersby for a taste. (*Pince* means "wine cellar.") This is a touristy scene, where the emphasis is not on top-quality wine but on the fun, folksy experience. Many of these places are endearingly humble, family-run affairs; they may offer you a few small tastes, hoping you'll buy a bottle, or give you a sample of their wine jelly—a tasty (and lightly alcoholic) addition to your cheese tray.

If you're more serious about wine, seek out one of the larger, more prestigious producers (Bock is perhaps the best-regarded, but also look for Gere, Sauska, Vylyan, Wunderlich, and Tiffán); some of these have tasting rooms in town, while others have big factories on the outskirts of town. For more information on Villány wines and wineries, see www.villanyiborvidek.hu.

The road leading from Villány west to Siklós is a popular wine road, which runs along the base of Mount Szársomlyó. You'll enjoy views of vines scampering up the hills, and pass a few vineyards where you can pull over for a taste.

Just past Siklós, where the wine road ends, is the larger town of **Harkány**—famous for its huge outdoor thermal spa (www.harkanyfurdo.hu). From here, highway 58 zips right back up to Pécs.

PÉCS

Sleeping in Pécs

Most of Pécs' city-center accommodations are affordable pensions with simple but sleepable rooms. Elevators are rare.

$$$ Hotel Arkadia is a minimalist, concrete place with 25 tight, modern rooms—the most stylish I've seen in Pécs—wonderfully located just a few steps above the mosque/church on the main square (Sb-16,500 Ft, Db-19,900 Ft, cheaper for stays more than 1 night and in mid-Oct–mid-April, air-con, elevator, guest computer, Wi-Fi, Hunyadi út 1, tel. 72/512-550, www.hotelarkadiapecs.hu, info@hotelarkadiapecs.hu).

$$$ Hotel Palatinus is your impersonal big-hotel option, with 94 rooms perfectly located right on the main walking street. You'll rarely find a more impressive facade, lobby, and breakfast

Sleep Code

Abbreviations (200 Ft = about $1, country code: 36, area code: 72)
S = Single, **D** = Double/Twin, **T** = Triple, **Q** = Quad, **b** = bathroom
Price Rankings

$$$ Higher Priced—Most rooms 16,000 Ft or more

$$ Moderately Priced—Most rooms between 10,000-16,000 Ft

$ Lower Priced—Most rooms 10,000 Ft or less

Unless otherwise noted, English is spoken, credit cards are accepted, breakfast is included, and Wi-Fi is generally free. The hotel tax (400 Ft per person, per night) is not included in these rates. Prices change; verify current rates online or by email. For the best prices, always book directly with the hotel.

room; the showpiece 1915 building (although not all of its bedrooms) has been painstakingly restored to its turn-of-the-20th-century glory. Though it's overpriced and less than charming (it's run by a big company), the location and public areas help compensate. Choose among the three room types: small, simple, communist-vintage "economy" (Db-18,500 Ft); lightly renovated "standard" with balconies on the walking street (Db-21,500 Ft); and nicely renovated and air-conditioned, but still not quite luxurious, "superior" (24,500 Ft; prices can vary with demand, elevator, Wi-Fi in lobby, free sauna, on-site underground parking-3,200 Ft/day, Király utca 5, tel. 72/889-400, www.danubiushotels.com/palatinus, palatinus.reservation@danubiushotels.com).

$$ Diána Hotel has 22 simple but comfortable-enough rooms on a side street facing the synagogue, between the town center and the Árkád shopping mall (Sb-11,000 Ft, Db-15,000 Ft, rates about 1,000 Ft cheaper if you pay cash, air-con-1,500 Ft, some street noise, guest computer, Wi-Fi, limited free parking or pay 2,000 Ft/24 hours at nearby garage, Tímár utca 4a, tel. 72/328-594, www.hoteldiana.hu, info@hoteldiana.hu).

$$ Szinbád Panzió is on a busy street in a dull urban area just outside the city wall. Though it has a labyrinthine floor plan, it feels more hotelesque than the other mid-range options in town: Its public areas are classy, the 26 rooms are nice and woody, and it's a short walk from the cathedral area (Sb-10,900 Ft, Db-13,900 Ft, Tb-16,900 Ft, extra bed-3,000 Ft up to 6 people, request quieter courtyard room, air-con, guest computer, Wi-Fi, free parking, Klimó György utca 9, tel. 72/221-110, www.szinbadpanzio.hu, info@szinbadpanzio.hu).

$$ Aranyhajó Fogadó ("Golden Ship Inn"), a lesser value, is ideally situated at the start of the Király utca pedestrian zone. In operation since the 18th century, the hotel's 18 rooms are old and a bit musty, with once-classy furniture. The front "standard" rooms are a bit bigger, noisier, and more expensive (Sb-11,000, Db-16,000); I'd request a quieter back "economy" room (Sb-9,000 Ft, Db-13,000 Ft; Wi-Fi, Király utca 3, tel. 72/210-685, www.aranyhajo.hu, hotel@aranyhajo.hu).

$$ Hotel Főnix has 13 dated rooms in a boldly artistic 1980s-vintage building that's ideally located just beyond the mosque/church at the top of the main square (Sb-8,000 Ft, Db-13,000 Ft, Tb-17,000 Ft, reception open 8:00-20:00, only 2 rooms with air-con, Wi-Fi, no parking, Hunyadi János út 2, tel. 72/311-680, www.fonixhotel.com, sales@fonixhotel.com).

$ Náp Hostel ("Sun") is colorful and well-run by Tamás. Hiding upstairs in an apartment building on the main walking street, its four bedrooms share three WCs and two showers. Enter through the Nappali bar on the main street and head up through the graffiti-slathered atrium (D-13,500 Ft, bunk in 8-bed dorm-3,000 Ft, in 6-bed dorm-4,000 Ft, in 6-bed dorm with balcony-4,600 Ft, no breakfast, Wi-Fi, kitchen, laundry service, Király utca 23-25, mobile 0630-277-0733, tel. 72/950-684, www.naphostel.com).

Eating in Pécs

ON THE PEDESTRIAN DRAG, KIRÁLY UTCA

The walking streets branching off from the main square are lined with restaurants and cafés that feature outdoor tables with ideal people-watching. Király utca (described earlier, under "Sights in Pécs") is Pécs' "restaurant row," with a fine variety of eating options. This is an ever-changing scene, with lots of turnover; it's a good strip to simply stroll and comparison-shop, noticing which places are popular right now. Here are a few worth tuning into (listed in the order you'll pass them):

Enoteca Corso, serving modern international (mostly French) cuisine, considers itself the finest dining establishment in town. Its upstairs dining room defines Hungarian pretense, with shag carpet, trendy music, a flatscreen monitor showing the chefs hard at work in the kitchen, an adult-contemporary vibe, and fine views on the National Theater. The main floor is more casual, with the same menu (2,500-4,500-Ft main dishes, daily 11:00-23:00 except Oct-April closed Sun dinner and all day Mon, Király utca 14, mobile 0670-222-2404).

Oázis is the place for a simple, cheap, fast, and good gyro or falafel. Grab one to go, or enjoy it at their outdoor tables on this main street (600-Ft sandwiches, daily 10:00-23:00, Fri-Sat until late, Király utca 17).

Cooltour Café is a ruin pub with a bohemian vibe and rickety tables strewn around its hidden garden, draped with twinkling Christmas lights. It's a fine place for a toasted sandwich, pastry, coffee, or drink (Király utca 26). Consider dropping by after dinner for a cocktail or beer (nightly until wee hours).

Nappali Bar, on the ground floor of a gorgeously restored townhouse, is a mecca for Pécs' hipsters and hipster tourists. While they serve only light food (basic sandwiches), this is a fine place for a pre- or after-dinner drink; they host live bands or DJs two nights a week in their bohemian interior (which displays works by local artists), and their outdoor seating is delightful (daily 9:00-late, Király utca 23-25, mobile 0630-277-0733).

ON JÓKAI TÉR AND NEARBY

The pedestrian strip on the opposite side of the main square has a few more good options. These are slightly less crowded and touristy than the zone listed above.

Egylet is a fun, casual, youthful hangout that combines two things and does them both well: a long list of Hungarian microbrews on tap; and a short but enticing menu of Balkan dishes (think grilled meats, like *ćevapi*—little minced-meat sausages, grilled on an open fire). Ramshackle tables decorated with old Yugoslav comic strips fill the cozy interior and the long, sunny alleyway, which has a tranquil Ottoman teahouse vibe. Order your beer (at the bar in front) and your food (at the bar in back), then find a seat (900-1,500-Ft dishes, daily 11:30-24:00, Ferencesek utcája 32, mobile 0620-350-8919).

Jókai Bisztró is working hard to bring some foodie sophistication to Pécs' culinary scene. The seasonally changing menu is an intriguing fusion of updated Hungarian and international cuisine, and most ingredients come from their own farm. While the results can be hit-or-miss, it's always inventive and reasonably priced. They also have a long wine list—including many by the glass—that focuses on local vineyards. The nondescript interior is fine but forgettable; it's especially pleasant to sit out on the delightful shopping square (1,600-3,200-Ft main dishes, daily 10:00-24:00, Jókai tér 6, tel. 72/213-915). Across the square, the same people run **Jókai Cukrászda,** a dessert and ice cream shop with a similar creative flair and modern setting (daily 10:00-21:00, Ferencesek utcája 6).

Elefántos Ház ("House at the Elephant"), next door to Jókai Bisztró, features decent, if overpriced, Italian fare, including pizzas from a wood-fired oven. The terrace tables are more inviting than the white-arched interior (1,600-2,800-Ft pizzas and pastas,

3,000-5,200-Ft meat dishes, daily 11:30-23:30, Jókai tér 6, tel. 72/216-055).

Pécs Connections

From Pécs by Train: For destinations in this book (including **Eger, Sopron,** and **Bratislava**), you'll generally change trains in Budapest. Direct trains connect Pécs and **Budapest** (every 2 hours direct, 3 hours; a few additional connections are possible with a transfer at the suburban Budapest-Kelenföld station). One handy train each afternoon (departing at 14:15) follows a different route, near the Croatian border, connecting Pécs directly to **Sopron** (5.5 hours).

SOPRON

Sopron (SHOH-prohn), nestled in the foothills of the Alps a stone's throw from Austria, is a picture-perfect little Baroque town jam-packed with historic buildings. Its square—watched over by the town's symbol, the Fire Tower—may be Hungary's most romantic. Because Austrians flock over the border to sightsee, sample the local wine, and get dental work done (at a fraction of the cost back home), then stumble home, the town's streets are lined with modest museums and dentist's offices.

Sopron, populated since Roman times, was a stop on the Amber Route of trade between the Adriatic and Baltic Seas. As a Hungarian backwater of Austria's Vienna, the town has long been a unique bilingual mix of Hungarian and Germanic culture. But it's always remained true to Hungary, most famously after World War I, when residents voted to stick with the Magyars rather than becoming part of Austria—earning it the nickname "the most loyal town." Even so, its proximity to Austria keeps Sopron in touch with its Germanic heritage. Today Sopron caters almost entirely to its German-speaking tourists (while English is in short supply).

Sopron is sleepy...sometimes *too* sleepy. After dark, the Main Square is magical—but deserted. Museum attendants react to your visit as though they've never seen a tourist before. With a little more restoration and liveliness in the Old Town, it could become a major draw. For now, this not-quite-ready-for-prime-time Hungarian burg is a delightful hidden secret.

PLANNING YOUR TIME

Sopron deserves a half-day. A few hours is more than enough time to exhaust its sightseeing options, and its sleepiness makes the initial "Oh, wow!" wear off quickly. Sopron fits perfectly on a trip between Budapest and Vienna (adding about an hour to your total train time between those cities). Consider arriving at midday, spending the afternoon here, then either taking a late train out, or spending the night and leaving the next morning.

On a brief visit, lock up your bag at the station and do a spin through the Old Town. With a little more time, explore the Ikva neighborhood northeast of town. If you're here for a while, head into the Lőver Hills.

Orientation to Sopron

Sopron, with about 60,000 inhabitants, is a manageable small city. The compact tourist zone of the Old Town (Belváros) contains

most of Sopron's attractions, and you can walk from one end to the other in less than 10 minutes. The retail district along the ring road (Várkerület) that follows the former outer walls surrounding the Old Town is much livelier, and the gently rolling Lőver Hills embrace the entire city.

TOURIST INFORMATION

Sopron's TI (called TourInform) hands out maps and brochures about the town and has free Internet access. It's in the big, yellow Franz Liszt Cultural Center at the southwest corner of the Old Town (Mon-Fri 9:00-17:00, Sat-Sun 9:00-13:00—except closed Sun Oct-April, Liszt Ferenc utca 1, tel. 99/517-560, www.turizmus.sopron.hu). The TI is next to the city's central box office, which has tickets and information on local cultural events.

ARRIVAL IN SOPRON

By Train: Sopron's compact little train station is situated an easy half-mile walk south of the Old Town. Stepping into the main lobby with your back to the tracks, you'll find luggage lockers (on left), an ATM (on right), an international ticket window (ahead on left), and a domestic ticket window (ahead on right).

Outside on the left is a **taxi** stand (about 1,300 Ft to hotels at the far end of town, taxi tel. 99/333-333). You can also hop a **bus** heading into town (#1, #2, #10, #10Y, #12, and #12A); all go directly to the Várkerület ring road that encircles the Old Town. Note: As you exit the station, the bus stop directly to your left is for buses going *away from* town; for buses *into* town, walk a half-block straight ahead and look for the stop on the right side of the street.

You can buy a ticket for 300 Ft from a kiosk, or pay 350 Ft to the driver.

It's a 10-minute **walk** into the Old Town—just go straight out of the station and head four blocks up Mátyás király utca toward the big yellow building in the distance (halfway there, you'll cross the long, skinny park called Deák tér). When you reach the park-like Széchenyi tér, cross into it, turn left at the flagpole (commemorating Hungarian uprisings throughout history), and look for the big, yellow building on the right (the Franz Liszt Cultural Center). The TI is inside, and the street next to it—Templom utca—is the main drag through the Old Town.

Sights in Sopron

OLD TOWN (BELVÁROS)

Sopron's Old Town is peppered with museums, but only a few are worthwhile (if tight on time or money, visit the Storno House and climb the Fire Tower, but skip the rest). Notice that these sights are ordered so they form a handy orientation walk (which begins where the "Arrival in Sopron" directions, earlier, leave off). While the Old Town is charming, it can feel pretty dead. The main business street, Várkerület, which arcs around the Old Town, makes up for this, and the square around the Fidelity Monument at the far side of town can be full of energy.

• *Begin exploring the town in front of the TI and the yellow...*

Franz Liszt Cultural Center

The huge building holds Sopron's main concert hall, TI, and central box office. The side facing Széchenyi tér is boldly marked with the words *Magyar Művelődés Háza* ("House of Hungarian Culture") to show up their Germanic rivals. Its current name honors the composer who was born in Sopron county (back when it was part of Austria) and performed his first-ever public concert here in Sopron in 1820, when he was only nine years old. Notice the bust (to the right of the entrance) honoring this favorite son. You'll see "Liszt played here" signs all over town.

• *Now head into the Old Town on...*

Templom Utca ("Church Street")

This was where important local bigwigs lived: mayors, lawyers, and intelligentsia. The town's sturdy wall spared it from being devastated by the Tatar and Ottoman invaders who reshaped much of Hungary. However, a fire, quickly spread by the strong winds that blow through this valley, consumed the town in 1676. Sopron was rebuilt in Baroque style (often over earlier Gothic cellars), which has left it colorful and tidy-looking. You'll notice that every other building has a *MŰEMLÉK* ("historical monument") plaque. Although lots

Sopron

① Hotel Wollner
② Pannonia Med Hotel
③ Palatinus Hotel
④ Erhardt Panzió Rooms & Rest.
⑤ Wieden Panzió Hotel
⑥ Jégverem Fogadó
  Hotel & Restaurant
⑦ To Csőszkunyhó Fogadó Rooms
⑧ Corvinus Restaurant
⑨ Papa Joe's Steakhouse
⑩ Nagymama Konyhája Cafeteria
⑪ Dömötöri Kávéház

of locally important people and events have graced Sopron, very little of this history is meaningful to visitors. Don't worry about the nitty-gritty of the town's past—just enjoy its ambience.

Notice the many fine passages leading to noble courtyards. For example, near the end of the first, very long block, at #12 (on the left), go into the Gothic passage (with pointy arches), which goes into a little courtyard with a Renaissance porch (with rounded arches), showing the evolution of the local architecture.

Back on the main street and a few steps down, the big church on the left is Lutheran. Because the local mayor protected the rights of religious minorities, Sopron was unusually tolerant, attracting groups who were persecuted elsewhere (such as Lutherans at the time of the Reformation). The first Lutheran congregation here was established in 1565, and the current building dates from 1782. Inside, the fine 1884 pipe organ and stately pulpit emphasize the Lutheran emphasis on preaching the word of God. The white-marble 1946 monument just outside the door memorializes the boarded-up windows of Sopron's Jewish ghetto; the local Jewish population was decimated during the Holocaust (we'll learn more about this dark time later).

• *When the road forks at the green building, stay left. In the next block on the left are two very modest museums, dedicated to Sopron's major industries. First, at #4, is the...*

Forestry Museum (Erdészeti Gyűjtemény)

While most of Hungary's geography consists of rolling plains and farmland, the area around Sopron is heavily wooded. This museum, part of the local Forestry College, celebrates that heritage, but has virtually no English information and is worthwhile only if you have a special interest. A second collection, upstairs, features the big- and small-game hunting trophies of Béla Hidvégi, a Hungarian sportsman who has traveled the world (a touchscreen provides information in English).

After the 1956 Uprising, there was an exodus of teachers and students from Sopron's Forestry College to Vancouver, British Columbia. To this day, Hungarians play a major role in the Canadian timber industry.

Cost and Hours: 800 Ft for each collection, 1,300 Ft for both; May-Oct Thu-Tue 10:00-17:00, Nov-Dec and Feb-April Thu-Tue 14:00-17:00; closed Wed year-round and likely closed in Jan; Templom utca 4, tel. 99/338-870.

• *Next door at #2 is the slightly more interesting...*

Central Mining Museum (Központi Bányászati Múzeum)

Displayed around a courtyard in the beautiful town house of a powerful local family, this museum explains the lives of miners and the history of Hungarian mining and coinage. It also features a life-size replica of a mineshaft and small-scale working models of mining equipment. Collections include decorative items made of metal, and rock and mineral samples. Look for the little dioramas-in-bottles, which were created by miners.

Cost and Hours: 700 Ft; April-Sept Tue-Sun 10:00-18:00, Oct Tue-Sun 10:00-17:00, Nov-March Tue-Sun 10:00-16:00, closed Mon year-round; Templom utca 2, tel. 99/312-667, www.kbm.hu.

• *At the end of the block, the street opens into the main square. Before exploring the square, visit the Gothic church on the right...*

Goat Church (Kecske Templom)

So nicknamed for the goat on the coat of arms over its door, this prominent Benedictine church is a Sopron landmark. While much

of the rest of Hungary was occupied by the Ottomans, this region remained in Hungarian hands—and this church was actually used for a few royal coronations and parliament sessions. The Gothic interior is adorned with wood-carved Baroque altars and a Rococo pulpit. Notice how the once-clean Gothic apse has been obliterated by the retrofitted Baroque altar—illustrating how little regard each era had for the previous one's art. On the right, find the plaque listing the ancestors of István Széchenyi who are buried here. (Széchenyi was a powerful 18th-century aristocrat who championed the rights of the poor and built, among other things, Budapest's Chain Bridge.) By the door, you can pop in a coin to light things up: 200 Ft for a little light, or 400 Ft for lots of light.

Other parts of the church require an additional admission fee (not worth it): the crypt, where various old graves and tombs have been consolidated into a tasteful modern mausoleum; a series of touchscreen terminals that offer additional information about specific church features; and the little cloister and chapter hall, where the carvings that top the columns represent human sins.

Cost and Hours: The church is open daily 8:00-19:00 (likely closes earlier in winter). During certain times when the touchscreen exhibition is open (Tue-Sun 10:00-12:00 & 13:00-17:00), you'll pay 400 Ft for the church or 800 Ft to also enter the crypt and chapter house; at other times, it's free to enter the church but the exhibition is closed.

• *Leaving the church, you're in the middle of Sopron's...*

▲▲Main Square (Fő Tér)

One of the most appealing Old World squares in Hungary, this area is dominated by the giant **Holy Trinity Column,** erected in 1701 to commemorate the 1695 plague. The wealthy local couple who survived the plague and commissioned the column kneel in thanksgiving at its base. Above them, the column corkscrews up to heaven, marked by Jesus, God the Father, and a dove representing the Holy Spirit. Gleeful cherubs, as if celebrating life after the plague, ride back down the column like kids on a waterslide.

Grand buildings surround the column. Orient yourself with the Goat Church to your back: On the left is the big, white, Neoclassical County Hall. To the right of it are three historic houses, two of which contain museums. The tall **Fire Tower** (described later) is the town's main landmark. Next to it is the vast, off-white 19th-century Town Hall, in the eye-pleasing Historicist style of the day. (Those interested in ancient history can walk behind the Town Hall to see fragments of Roman-era Sopron, with posted English information.) Across from the Town Hall, the little yellow building sticking out into the square houses a small **Pharmacy Museum** (Patika-Ház), which was a working pharmacy from 1642 to 1967 (you can see most everything from the door with a sweep of your head, or pay 500 Ft to examine the exhibits up close; Tue-Sun 10:00-14:00, closed Mon). In the early 16th century, local officials wanted to tear down this house to enlarge the square. But the king, who had visited Sopron earlier and enjoyed the square the way it was, decreed that it not be touched...making it Hungary's first government-protected building.

• *If you're ready for some museum going, consider the two collections in the pretty Baroque house with the corner turret overlooking the square.*

▲▲Storno House (Storno-Ház)

This prime real estate is marked with plaques celebrating visits by two big-league Hungarians: King Mátyás (Matthias) Corvinus and Franz Liszt. Today the building houses two exhibits: the Storno Collection and the "History without Borders" exhibition.

Cost and Hours: Storno Collection-1,000 Ft, history exhibit-700 Ft; both open April-Oct Tue-Sun 10:00-18:00, Nov-March Tue-Sun 9:00-17:00, closed Mon year-round; Fő tér 8, tel. 99/311-327, www.muzeum.sopron.hu.

Visiting the Museum: Sopron's best museum is the **Storno Collection** (Storno-Gyűjtemény), upstairs. Franz Storno, the son of a poor 19th-century Swiss family of chimney sweeps, showed prodigious talent as an artist at a young age and ultimately became quite a Renaissance man. He moved here to Sopron, married a chimney-sweep master's widow, and became a restorer of buildings for the Habsburg Empire.

Today, in his creaky old house, charming attendants direct visitors through a series of jam-packed rooms to look at a random but fun grab-bag of paintings, decorative items, and other bric-a-brac that Franz collected in his renovation work. While you can borrow an English leaflet for a room-by-room description, renting the cheap audioguide (200 Ft) makes the place much more meaningful—well worth the 30 minutes its narration takes. Following this forces you to take time to look around, and it highlights wonderful little details.

In the entrance hall, check out the panorama painting of 18th-century Sopron (high up on the wall). Later, the balcony room boasts a gorgeously painted, light-filled alcove with table and chairs (as well as more paintings of old Sopron). The old iron box in the middle of this room has a complicated secret-locking system. Passing through the painted door into the bedroom, look for the Biedermeier paintings on the ceilings. The antler chandelier shows a 3-D version of the family seal: chimney-sweeping brush in one hand, compass (for restoration work) in the other.

In the final room (the salon), you'll see square tables with hinged edges that can be brought up to make them circular. These were practical but also superstitious: It was considered bad luck for a young woman to sit at the corner of a table (either she'd never marry or have a difficult mother-in-law, depending on the legend), so this design ensured that would never happen.

Downstairs, the well-presented **"History without Borders"** (Határtalan Történet) exhibit, which traces the history of Sopron, is also worth a look (no audioguide, but good English information posted). In the final room, find the exhibit about the post-World War I referendum in which Sopron elected to remain part of Hungary instead of Austria. The referendum, which took place in December of 1921, asked citizens to vote with color-coded ballots whether they would join Austria or Hungary. As you can see from the bilingual posters announcing the results, Hungary won 15,334 votes to Austria's 8,227. This cemented Sopron's already-established reputation as being the "most loyal town." (Maybe it was because other Austrians would never let them live down the town's German name, Ödenburg, which roughly means "Dullsville.")

Nearby, you'll see propaganda trying to convince locals to vote one way or another—such as the unsettling poster of the skeleton, clad in traditional Hungarian folk costume, menacingly serenading the town on his violin.

• *Two buildings to the left of the Storno House is the...*

Fabricius House (Fabricius-Ház)

This historic mansion, once belonging to Sopron's most beloved mayor, is home to a pair of dull, skippable museums. The **Civic Apartments** (Polgári Lakások), basically a collection of old furniture, will appeal only to antique lovers. The **Archaeological Exhibit** (Régészet-Kőtár) is a very dry overview of the history of Sopron, especially relating to the Amber Road trade route that put the town on the map. The best part is the Roman Lapidarium in the cellar (same ticket)—a collection of Roman tombstones unearthed here, as well as the shattered fragments of three larger-than-life Roman statues.

Cost and Hours: Apartments-800 Ft, archaeological exhibit-700 Ft; both open April-Sept Tue-Sun 10:00-18:00, closed Mon and Oct-March, Fő tér 6.

• *Dominating the Main Square is Sopron's symbol, the...*

Fire Tower (Tűztorony)

A Roman watchtower once stood here, but the current version was gradually expanded from the 13th to the 18th centuries. Fire

watchmen would survey the town from the top of the tower, then mark the direction of a fire with colorful flags (by day) or a bright light (at night) to warn townspeople.

Cost and Hours: 1,150 Ft, May-Aug daily 10:00-20:00, April and Sept-Dec daily 10:00-18:0, shorter hours off-season, can be closed in bad weather, Fő tér 1, www.tuztorony.sopron.hu.

Visiting the Tower: Just above the passage through the gate is a stone carving depicting Hungária, the female embodiment of Hungary—given to the city to thank them for choosing Hungary during the 1921 referendum.

Buy your ticket and climb the 120 steps to the top. On the way up, pause at the landings to check out the exhibits. There are historic photos and drawings of the tower, and the original double-headed Habsburg eagle—with an "L" for the Emperor Leopold—that topped the tower's spire.

At the top, do a clockwise spin: First is a great view over the rooftops of the Old Town; beyond that, you can see the Lőver Hills, Sopron's playground. (While the name sounds romantic, *lőver* refers to master archers who defended the border from Tatar invasions in the 13th century.) Continuing around the tower and looking down, you'll see remains of the city wall defining the Old Town; an outer wall was once located on the outside of

today's ring road. Beyond the stadium lights is Austria. A bit farther to the right, the big steeple in the distance is St. Michael's, one of Sopron's historic churches. Farther to the right, the oddly shaped bulbous tower on the hill is a windmill missing its blades. This was used to garrison Habsburg troops after the 1848 Revolution.

• *Descending from the tower, continue through the gateway.*

Outside the Walls

Just on the other side of the tower, look for the giant **key monument** on the left, commemorating a "key" event in this loyal town's history. After presenting the Hungarian king with the key to their city when his rival was planning an invasion, Sopron was rewarded with free "royal town" status, which came with special privileges (in 1277). Just beyond is the entrance to the **City Wall Walk** (Várfal Sétány), where you can walk along part of the course of the surviving wall (not particularly scenic since it's outside the wall rather than on top of it; free, Mon-Fri 9:00-20:00, Sat-Sun 9:00-18:00).

Just outside the Old Town, you reach the ring road and a livelier zone. Look (on your left) for a modern **sculpture** with three figures, each one representing a time when Sopron demonstrated its fidelity: 1277, when the town sided with the Hungarian king (described earlier); 1921, when they voted to remain part of Hungary; and 1989, when the Iron Curtain fell (symbolized by the woman breaking the barbed wire). In August of that fateful year—before the communists had officially given up the ghost—the "Pan-European Picnic" took place in the hills near Sopron. Residents of various Central European countries—East Germany, Austria, and Hungary—came together for the first time in decades, offering a tantalizing taste of freedom.

Across the busy ring road from this sculpture, look for the **Golden Lion Pharmacy** (*Gyógyszertár Apotheke* sign), which has beautiful Art Nouveau Zsolnay porcelain decorations.

Looking back toward the Old Town, notice the **colorful little shops** that cling like baby animals to the protective town walls.

• *From here, you can backtrack to the Main Square and head down New Street to more sights (described next). Or keep going beyond the walls into the Ikva neighborhood (described in the "Ikva Neighborhood" section).*

To see more of the **Old Town**, *take the street to the left of the Pharmacy Museum (as you face it). This is...*

New Street (Új Utca)

This misnamed street is actually one of the oldest in town. Near the start of the street (a few steps down from the Main Square), the building at the fork has remains of the original **forum** of Sopron's Roman settlement in its basement (likely closed to the public except by prior reservation—but if you see a museum here and are interested in ancient ruins, drop in).

Continue to the right, down New Street—which used to be called **"Jewish Street"** (Zsidó utca) until the Jews were kicked out in 1526. After the 1848 Revolution, they finally returned...but for less than a century. When the Nazis took control of Hungary, they walled off both ends of this street and turned it into a ghetto. Some 1,840 Sopron Jews were eventually sent to concentration camps... where 1,650 of them died. Along the street, about one block down, are two synagogues. The first is the **New Synagogue** (Új Zsinagóga), in a modern office on the left at #11. It's not a museum, but if the door is open you can peek inside.

A few steps down, on the right at #22, is the **Old Synagogue** (Ó Zsinagóga), dating from the early 14th century (800 Ft, borrow English descriptions, April-Oct Tue-Sun 10:00-18:00, closed Mon and Nov-March, Új utca 22, tel. 99/311-327). Rediscovered in 1968, it has been renovated but still retains a few of its original elements (such as the Torah holder). Notice the two adjacent rooms, separated by narrow windows: Men worshipped in the main room, with the women in the smaller room. In the courtyard is a reconstruction of a ritual bath.

• *New Street ends at Ursula Square (Orsolya tér), watched over by the Church of St. Ursula and a statue of Mary that stands in the center of the square. If you double back to the left, you can head up the third of old Sopron's three parallel streets...*

St. George's Street (Szent György Utca)

This street is named for the red-and-white **Church of St. George** (halfway down the street on the right, free, daily 8:00-18:00). The beautiful, stuccoed Baroque interior hosted Lutheran services for a time, but the Lutherans were evicted during the Counter-Reformation. Head across the street and into the fine Renaissance courtyard at #12, where the Lutherans were forced to worship al fresco. Notice the stone pulpit carved into the upper balcony, and the metal rings used to secure a tarp that covered the service in bad weather.

• *St. George's Street will take you right back up to the Main Square, where—if you haven't already—you can head into...*

SOPRON

THE IKVA NEIGHBORHOOD, NORTHEAST OF THE OLD TOWN

With a little more time, venture into the workaday streets northeast of the Old Town—beyond the ring road and the Ikva brook (hidden here beneath the road). While lacking the storybook charm of the Old Town, this area is also historic. Back when wealthy aristocrats populated the Old Town, farmers and craftsmen lived here—giving it a rustic, lived-in ambience that's fun to explore. (It's also home to several recommended accommodations, and the good Jégverem restaurant—see "Sleeping in Sopron" and "Eating in Sopron," later.)

The main drag changes names as it twists through this neighborhood (first called Ikva híd, then Dorfmeister utca, then Szent Mihály utca). Eventually it leads up a hill to **St. Michael's Church** (Szent Mihály Templom) and the adjacent little Romanesque chapel. The church complex is surrounded by a cemetery.

• *Closer to the Belváros, but still in the Ikva neighborhood, is one final Sopron sight, the...*

▲Zettl-Langer Collection (Zettl-Langer Gyűjtemény)

A Bavarian art lover named Gustav Zettl came to Sopron in the late 19th century, set up a distillery, and became a pillar of the community. Today his descendants (usually his great-granddaughter, Ágnes Langer, who speaks English) lead tours of this fine old townhouse that's jammed with Gustav's eclectic private collection of furniture, porcelain, paintings, knick-knacks, and more. Ágnes will show you everything from a collection of ancient Roman vessels to fine inlaid furniture (find out why a "money changer's table" has a marble top) to delicately decorated windows to all manner of clever cup-boards with hidden panels and drawers.

It's similar in many ways to the excellent Storno Collection on the Main Square, but because the family still resides here, this is a unique opportunity to see a very lived-in home that feels like a museum (or vice versa). Each item on display has been in the family for generations, and Ágnes relishes telling their stories in as much detail as you'd like to hear. Near the end is Gustav's death announcement, in a frame that also holds a stack of dozens more. It must be both sobering and comforting for Gustav's descendants to know that their death notices will be added to the family stack someday. The public can only visit with a tour (generally about 40 minutes); it's smart to call ahead to let Ágnes know you're coming.

Cost and Hours: 1,000 Ft per person to enter, plus 2,000 Ft for the group for the mandatory tour; April-Oct Tue-Sun 10:00-12:00, closed Mon; Nov-March Fri-Sun 10:00-12:00, closed Mon-Thu; Balfi utca 11, tel. 99/311-136.

HIKING

With its forested hillsides and fresh air, Sopron is popular with hikers. To get to the best trailhead, take bus #1 or #2 from the Old Town to Lővér Körút, and get off at the giant-domed bath complex. From here, several trails lead through the hills. Before setting out, get advice from the TI (they can give you a free map, or sell you a better one).

Sleeping in Sopron

Few places have air-conditioning; even fewer have an elevator (I've noted those that do).

IN OR NEAR THE OLD TOWN

You'll pay a bit extra to be right in the Old Town. But it's worth it—not for the convenience, but for the romance of calling those floodlit cobbles home after dark.

$$$ Hotel Wollner, a top option in Sopron, has real class. This 600-year-old Baroque townhouse on the Old Town's main street is thoroughly renovated and rents 18 tastefully appointed rooms. An inviting terraced garden in the rear rounds out its appeal (Sb-23,000 Ft, Db-29,000 Ft, bigger superior Db-34,000 Ft, Tb-34,000 Ft, entirely non-smoking, free Wi-Fi, Templom utca 20, tel. 99/524-400, www.wollner.hu, wollner@wollner.hu).

$$$ Pannonia Med Hotel rents 79 rooms on the ring road just across from the Old Town. The large public areas recall Sopron's faded elegance, while the rooms are straightforward business-class and charmless. As you're paying a premium for its big-hotel services (such as a swimming pool and fitness center), it's a bit overpriced (rates vary based on demand, but the inflated "rack rates" are smaller "classic" Db with older furnishings-19,000 Ft, 2,500 Ft more for bigger and newer "comfort" Db with air-con; elevator, free guest computer and Wi-Fi, street noise—ask for quieter room, Várkerület 75, tel. 99/312-180, www.pannoniahotel.com, sopron@hotelpannonia.com).

$$ Palatinus Hotel is a soulless, tour-oriented place with

Sleep Code

Abbreviations   (225 Ft = about $1, country code: 36, area code: 99)
S = Single, **D** = Double/Twin, **T** = Triple, **Q** = Quad, **b** = bathroom.

Price Rankings

  $$$ **Higher Priced**—Most rooms 15,000 Ft or more.

   $$ **Moderately Priced**—Most rooms between 10,000-
           15,000 Ft.

    $ **Lower Priced**—Most rooms 10,000 Ft or less.

Unless otherwise noted, English is spoken, breakfast is included, credit cards are accepted, and Wi-Fi is generally free. The hotel tax (450 Ft per person, per night) is not included in these rates. Prices can change without notice; verify current rates online or by email. For the best prices, always book directly with the hotel.

31 rooms. But it's a good value—modern, well-priced, and ideally located in the heart of the Old Town (rates vary but typically Sb-9,000 Ft, Db-13,000 Ft, three floors with no elevator, non-smoking rooms, free Wi-Fi, parking-2,000 Ft/day—reserve ahead, Új utca 23, tel. 99/523-816, www.palatinussopron.com, info@palatinussopron.com).

NORTHEAST OF THE OLD TOWN

These four accommodations are just outside the ring road. While not as romantic as the Old Town, this appealing residential zone is also historic. The first three places are a five-minute, slightly uphill walk from the Old Town, while the fourth (the best value) is about five minutes farther up.

$$ Erhardt Panzió rents nine rooms above their upscale-feeling restaurant, in a nicely restored house on a quiet, if dingy, street (Sb-10,000 Ft, Db-14,000 Ft, air-con, Wi-Fi, Balfi utca 10, tel. 99/506-711, www.erhardts.hu, info@erhardts.hu).

$$ Wieden Panzió, run by the Fazekas family, has 15 basic but crisp, recently renovated rooms (Sb-8,000 Ft, Db-11,000 Ft, Tb-14,000 Ft, some very large rooms also available, Wi-Fi, some street noise—request quiet room on the courtyard, Sas tér 13, tel. 99/523-222, wieden@fullnet.hu).

$ Jégverem Fogadó ("Ice House Inn"), with a recommended restaurant, rents five cheap, simple, well-worn rooms upstairs from its busy eatery (Sb-7,400 Ft, Db-9,800 Ft, extra bed-2,000 Ft, breakfast extra, Wi-Fi, Jégverem utca 1, tel. 99/510-113, www.jegverem.hu, jegverem@jegverem.hu).

$ Csőszkunyhó Fogadó ("Field Guard's Shelter") sits across the street from St. Michael's Church, on a small hill near the Old

SOPRON

Town. Above this local restaurant are two beautiful, spacious, woody rooms—the nicest I've seen in Sopron in this price range. The catch: limited English is spoken (Sb-4,900 Ft, Db-6,900 Ft, Tb-9,300 Ft, cash only, Wi-Fi, Szent Mihály utca 35, tel. 99/506-588, www.csoszkunyho.hu, csoszkunyho@gmail.com).

Eating in Sopron

You might notice lots of bean dishes on the menu in Sopron. The thrifty Germans—who were responsible for most of the winemaking in the surrounding hills—would plant beans in the earth between their rows of vines. In fact, in local dialect, German residents are called "bean farmers." Sopron is also known for its local beer (called Soproni) and for its local wines.

Jégverem Fogadó ("Ice House Inn") serves up heaping plates of reliably tasty Hungarian food from a clever, descriptive menu. It's worth the five-minute walk outside the Old Town (near several recommended accommodations). The circular table in the middle of the cozy dining room peers down into a pit where ice was stored, to be sold through the hot summer months. In good weather, sit out on the inviting terrace. As portions are huge, consider sharing or ordering a smaller dish (1,700-2,800-Ft meals, daily 11:00-23:00, Jégverem utca 1, tel. 99/510-113).

Corvinus, across from the City Hall and in the shadow of the Fire Tower, is a no-brainer for a romantic al fresco dinner on the Main Square. With a traditional menu of good Hungarian classics and a few international dishes, the place sprawls into a wine cellar and its sister restaurant next door, the Generális café (1,400-2,900-Ft main dishes, also indoor seating, daily 11:30-22:00, Fő tér 7-8, tel. 99/505-035).

Papa Joe's, an American-style steakhouse, had my travel sensibilities crying, "No!"—but my stomach saying, "Hmmmm... maybe." Here's your chance to experience the Old West through Hungarian eyes. Done up to the nines like a cowboy saloon (including six-shooter-handle doorknobs and saddle barstools), this theme restaurant grills up steaks and other Tex-Mex dishes (such as baked beans). When locals want a break from Hungarian food, they come here (2,000-4,000-Ft main dishes, daily 11:00-24:00, Várkerület 108, tel. 99/340-933).

Erhardt Restaurant, in the Ikva neighborhood just outside the Old Town (a 5-minute walk away), serves Hungarian and international fare in a sophisticated-feeling, white-tablecloth, mellow dining room. They also have a wine shop and a lengthy wine list (2,500-4,000-Ft main dishes, daily 11:30-23:00, Balfi utca 10, tel. 99/506-711).

Fast and Cheap: **Nagymama Konyhája** ("Grandma's Kitchen") is your best option for a quick, no-frills meal. This small self-service cafeteria, filled with locals, specializes in savory and sweet crêpes (*palacsinta,* 600-900 Ft), but also offers other traditional Hungarian dishes. Just point to what you want, or ask to see the clear English menu (900-1,200 Ft for most meals, Mon-Sat 10:00-21:00, Sun 12:00-21:00, Várkerület 104, mobile 0620-315-8730).

Coffee and Cake: **Dömötöri Kávéház** is a pastry and coffee shop slinging a wide array of cakes and fancy ice-cream dishes—with seating in a classy interior, in an aristocratic upstairs, and out on a pretty square across from the big, yellow Franz Liszt Center. It's where locals satisfy their sweet tooth (500-Ft desserts, June-Aug daily 8:00-23:00, closes earlier off-season, Széchenyi tér 13, tel. 99/506-623).

Sopron Connections

From Sopron by Train to: Budapest (6/day direct, 3 hours, more with a transfer in Győr), **Eger** (about every 2 hours, 5-6 hours, transfer in Budapest and sometimes also in Füzesabony), **Pécs** (1/day direct in the morning, 5.5 hours; otherwise about every 2 hours, 5.5 hours, most transfer at Budapest's suburban Kelenföld station), **Bratislava,** Slovakia (hourly direct, 2.5 hours on RegionalExpress/REX; more with transfers at stations in downtown and/or suburban Vienna), **Vienna,** Austria (every 2 hours direct on RegionalExpress/REX, 1.5 hours; also 1-2/hour with transfer in Weiner Neustadt, 1.75 hours).

BRATISLAVA, SLOVAKIA

The Slovak capital, Bratislava (brah-tee-SLAH-vah), long a drab lesson in the failings of the communist system, has become downright charming. Its old town bursts with colorfully restored facades, lively outdoor cafés, swanky boutiques, in-love-with-life locals, and (on sunny days) an almost Mediterranean ambience.

The rejuvenation doesn't end in the old town. The ramshackle quarter to the east is gradually being flattened and redeveloped into a new forest of skyscrapers. The hilltop castle is getting a facelift. And even the glum commie suburb of Petržalka is undergoing a Technicolor makeover. Bratislava and Vienna have forged a new twin-city alliance for trade and commerce, bridging Eastern and Western Europe.

You sometimes get the feeling that workaday Bratislavans—who strike some visitors as gruff—are being pulled to the cutting edge of the 21st century kicking and screaming. But many Slovaks embrace the changes and fancy themselves as the yang to Vienna's yin: If Vienna is a staid, elderly aristocrat sipping coffee, then Bratislava is a vivacious young professional jet-setting around Europe. Bratislava at night is a lively place; its very youthful center thrives. While it has tens of thousands of university students, there are no campuses as such—so the old town is the place where students go to play.

Bratislava's priceless location—on the Danube (and the tourist circuit) smack-dab between Budapest and Vienna—makes it a very worthwhile "on the way" destination. Frankly, Bratislava used to leave me cold. But all the changes are positively inspiring.

PLANNING YOUR TIME

A few hours are plenty to get the gist of Bratislava. Head straight to the old town and follow my self-guided walk, finishing with a stroll along the Danube riverbank to the thriving, modern Eurovea development. With more time, take advantage of one or more of the city's fine viewpoints: Ascend to the "UFO" observation deck atop the funky bridge, ride the elevator up to the Sky Bar for a peek (and maybe a drink), or hike up to the castle for the views (but skip the ho-hum museum inside). If you spend the evening in Bratislava, you'll find it lively with students, busy cafés, and nightlife.

Note that all museums and galleries are closed on Monday.

Day-Tripping Tip: Bratislava can be done as a long side-trip from Budapest (or a short one from Vienna), but it's most convenient as a stopover to break up the journey between Budapest and Vienna. But pay careful attention to train schedules, as the Vienna connection alternates between Bratislava's two train stations (Hlavná Stanica and Petržalka). If checking your bag at the station, be sure that your return or onward connection will depart from there.

Orientation to Bratislava

Bratislava, with 430,000 residents, is Slovakia's capital and biggest city. It has a small, colorful old town *(staré mesto)*, with the castle on the hill above. This small area is surrounded by a vast construction zone of new buildings, rotting residential districts desperately in need of beautification, and some colorized communist suburbs (including Petržalka, across the river). The northern and western parts of the city are hilly and cool (these "Little Carpathians" are draped with vineyards), while the southern and eastern areas are flat and warmer.

TOURIST INFORMATION

The helpful TI is at Klobučnícka 2, on Primate's Square behind the Old Town Hall (daily May-Sept 9:00-19:00, Oct-April 9:00-18:00, tel. 02/16186, www.visitbratislava.eu). Pick up the free *Bratislava Guide* (with map) and browse their brochures; they can help you find a room in town for a small fee. They also have a branch at the airport.

Discount Card: The TI sells the €10 Bratislava City Card, which includes free transit and sightseeing discounts for a full day—but it's worthwhile only if you're doing the old town walking tour (€14 without the card—see "Tours in Bratislava," later; also available for €12/2 days, €15/3 days).

ARRIVAL IN BRATISLAVA
By Train

If you're choosing which of Bratislava's two train stations to use, consider this: Hlavná Stanica is far from welcoming, but it's walk-

Welcome to Slovakia

In many ways, Slovakia is the "West Virginia of Europe"—relatively poor and undeveloped, but spectacularly beautiful in its own rustic way. Sitting quietly in the very center of Central Europe, wedged between bigger and stronger nations (Hungary, Austria, the Czech Republic, and Poland), Slovakia was brutally disfigured by the communists, then overshadowed by the Czechs. But in recent years, this fledgling republic has found its wings.

With about 5.5 million people in a country of 19,000 square miles (similar to Massachusetts and New Hampshire combined), Slovakia is one of Europe's smallest nations. Recent economic reforms have caused two very different Slovakias to emerge: the modern, industrialized, flat, affluent west, centered on the capital of Bratislava; and the remote, poorer, mountainous, "backward" east, with high unemployment and traditional lifestyles. Slovakia is ethnically diverse:

In addition to the Slavic Slovaks, there are Hungarians (about 10 percent of the population, "stranded" here when Hungary lost this land after World War I) and Roma (Gypsies, also about 10 percent). Slovakia has struggled to incorporate both of these large and often-mistreated minority groups.

Slovakia has spent most of its history as someone else's backyard. For centuries, Slovakia was ruled from Budapest and known as "Upper Hungary." At other times, it was an important chunk of the Habsburg Empire, ruled from neighboring Vienna. But most people think first of another era: the 75 years that Slovakia was joined with the Czech Republic as the country of "Czechoslovakia." From its start in the aftermath of World War I, this union of the Czechs and Slovaks was troubled; some Slovaks chafed at being ruled from Prague, while many Czechs resented the financial burden of their poorer neighbors to the east.

After they gained their freedom from the communists during 1989's peaceful Velvet Revolution, the Czechs and Slovaks began to think of the future. The Slovaks wanted to rename the

able to some accommodations and the old town; Petržalka (in a suburban shopping area) is small, clean, and modern, but you'll have to take a bus into town. Frequent bus #93 connects the two stations (5-12/hour, 10 minutes; take bus #N93 after about 23:00). For public transit info and maps, see http://imhd.zoznam.sk.

Hlavná Stanica (Main Train Station): This decrepit and demoralizing station is about a half-mile north of the old town. It was still standing on my last visit...but barely. The city hopes to tear it country Czecho-Slovakia, and to redistribute power to give themselves more autonomy within the union. The Czechs balked, relations gradually deteriorated, and the Slovak nationalist candidate Vladimír Mečiar fared surprisingly well in the 1992 elections. Taking it as a sign that the two peoples wanted to part ways, politicians pushed through (in just three months) the peaceful separation of the now-independent Czech and Slovak Republics. (The people in both countries never actually voted on the change, and most opposed it.) The "Velvet Divorce" became official on January 1, 1993.

At first the Slovaks struggled. Communist rule had been particularly unkind to them, and their economy was in a shambles. Visionary leaders set forth bold solutions, including the 2003 implementation of a flat tax (19 percent), followed by EU membership in 2004. Before long, major international corporations began to notice the same thing the communists had: This is a great place to build stuff, thanks to a strategic location (300 million consumers live within a day's truck drive), low labor costs, and a well-trained workforce. Not surprisingly, multiple foreign automakers have plants here. Today Slovakia produces one million cars a year, making the country the world's biggest car producer (per capita) and leading the *New York Times* to dub Slovakia "the European Detroit."

The flat tax and other aggressively pro-business policies have not been without their critics—especially in the very impoverished eastern half of the country, where poor people feel they're becoming even poorer. With the rollback of social services and the proverbial cracks widening, many seem to have been left behind by Slovakia's bold new economy.

Even so, particularly if you zoom in on its success story around Bratislava, the evidence is impressive. Bratislava has only 3 percent unemployment. The standard of living (as it relates to local costs) puts Bratislava in 10th place among European cities. Slovakia joined the EU in 2004; in 2009, it adopted the euro currency. While most of Europe is struggling through difficult economic times, much of Slovakia seems poised for its brightest future yet.

---

down and start again from scratch. If those plans go forward, these arrival instructions could also become obsolete.

As you emerge from the tracks, the left-luggage desk is to your right (€2-2.50, depending on weight; look for *úschovňa batožín;* reconfirm open hours at the desk so you'll be able to get your bags when you need them). There are also a few €2 lockers along track 1.

Getting from the Station to Downtown: It's a 15-minute **walk** to the town center. Walk out the station's front door and follow the covered walkway next to the looped bus drive; it will bend right and lead to a double pedestrian overpass. Cross the near arch and head downhill on the busy main drag, Štefánikova (named for politician Milan Štefánik, who worked for the post-WWI creation of Czechoslovakia). This once-elegant old boulevard is lined with Habsburg-era facades—some renovated, some rotting. In a few minutes, you'll pass the nicely manicured presidential gardens on your left. Next comes the Grassalkovich Palace, Slovakia's "White House" (with soldiers at guard out front), which faces the busy intersection called Hodžovo Námestie. The old town is just a long block ahead of you now. You can cross the intersection at street level or find the stairs and escalators down to the underground passageway *(podchod)*. Head for the green steeple with an onion-shaped midsection. This is St. Michael's Gate, at the start of the old town (and the beginning of my self-guided walk, described later).

To shave a few minutes off the trip, go part of the way by **bus** #93 or #X13 (after 23:00, use bus #N93). Walk out the station's front door to the line of bus stops to the right. Buy a 15-minute ticket from the machines for €0.70 (select *základný lístok—platí 15 minút,* then insert coins—change given). Ride two stops to Hodžovo Námestie, across from Grassalkovich Palace, then walk straight ahead toward the green steeple, passing a pink-and-white church.

Tram #13 is another option from the station, if it's running again (the tracks have been closed for construction). Trams *(električky)* use the same tickets as buses; ride to the Poštová stop, then walk straight down Obchodná street toward St. Michael's Gate.

Petržalka Train Station (ŽST Petržalka): Half of the trains from Vienna arrive at this small, quiet train station, across the river in the modern suburb of Petržalka (PET-ur-ZHAL-kuh). From this station, ride bus #93 (direction: Hlavná Stanica) or #94 (direction: STU) four stops to Zochova (the first stop after the bridge, near St. Michael's Gate); after 23:00, use bus #N93. Buy a €0.70/15-minute *základný lístok* ticket (described earlier).

By Bus, Boat, or Plane

For information on Bratislava's buses, riverboats, and airport, see "Bratislava Connections," at the end of this chapter.

HELPFUL HINTS

Money: Slovakia uses the euro (€1=about $1.40). You'll find ATMs at the train stations and airport.

Language: The official language is Slovak, which is closely related to Czech and Polish—although many Bratislavans also speak English. The local word used informally for both "hi" and "bye" is easy to remember: *ahoj* (pronounced "AH-hoy," like a pirate). "Please" is *prosím* (PROH-seem), "thank you" is *ďakujem* (DYAH-koo-yehm), "good" is *dobrý* (DOH-bree), and "Cheers!" is *Na zdravie!* (nah ZDRAH-vyeh).

Phone Tips: To call locally within Bratislava, dial the number without the area code. To make a long-distance call within Slovakia, start with the area code (which begins with 0). To call from Hungary to Slovakia, dial 00-421, then the area code minus the initial zero, then the number (from the US, dial 011-421-area code minus zero, then the number). To call from Slovakia to Hungary, you'd dial 00-36, then the area code (minus the initial zero) and number.

Internet Access: Free Wi-Fi hotspots are at the three major old town squares (Main Square, Primate's Square, and Hviezdoslav Square). You'll see signs advertising computer terminals around the old town.

Local Guidebook: For in-depth suggestions on Bratislava sightseeing, dining, and more, look for the excellent and eye-pleasing *Bratislava Active* guidebook by Martin Sloboda (see "Tours in Bratislava," next; around €10, sold at every postcard rack).

Tours in Bratislava

Walking Tours

The TI offers a one-hour old town walking tour in English every day in the summer at 14:00 (€14, free with €10 Bratislava City Card; book and pay at least two hours in advance). Those arriving by boat will be accosted by guides selling their own 1.5-hour tours (half on foot and half in a little tourist train, €10, in German and English).

Local Guide

MS Agency, run by **Martin Sloboda** (a can-do entrepreneur and tireless Bratislava booster, and author of the great local guidebook described earlier), can set you up with a good guide (€130/3 hours, €150/4 hours); he can also help you track down your Slovak roots. Martin, who helped me put this chapter together, is part of the generation that came of age as communism fell and whose energy and leadership are reshaping the city (mobile 0905-627-265, www. msagency.sk, sloboda@msagency.sk).

BRATISLAVA

Bratislava Old Town Walk

This self-guided orientation walk passes through
the heart of delightfully traffic-free old Bratislava
and then down to its riverside commercial zone
(figure 1.5 hours, not including stops, for this
walk). If you're coming from the station, make
your way toward the green steeple of St. Michael's Gate (explained in "Arrival in Bratislava,"
earlier). Before going through the passage into
the old town, peek over the railing on your left
to the inviting garden below—once part of the
city moat.

• *Step through the first, smaller gate, walk along
the passageway, and pause as you come through the
green-steepled...*

St. Michael's Gate (Michalská Brána)

This is the last surviving tower of the city wall. Just below the gate,
notice the "kilometer zero" plaque in the ground, marking the
point from which distances in Slovakia are measured.

• *You're at the head of...*

Michalská Street

Pretty as it is now, the old center was a decrepit ghost town during
the communist era, partly because WWII bombing left Bratislava
a damaged husk. The communist regime believed that Bratislavans of the future would live in large, efficient apartment buildings.
They saw the old town as a useless relic of the bad old days of poor
plumbing, cramped living spaces, social injustice, and German
domination—a view which left no room to respect the town's heritage. In the 1950s, they actually sold Bratislava's original medieval
cobbles to cute German towns that were rebuilding themselves
with elegant Old World character. Locals avoided this desolate
corner of the city, preferring to spend time in the Petržalka suburb
across the river.

With the fall of communism in 1989, the new government
began a nearly decade-long process of restitution—sorting out who
had the rights to the buildings, and returning them to their original
owners. During this time, little repair or development took place
(since there was no point investing in a property until ownership
was clearly established). By 1998, most of these property issues had
been sorted out, and the old town was made traffic-free. The city
replaced all the street cobbles, spruced up the public buildings, and
encouraged private owners to restore their property. (If you see any

remaining decrepit buildings, it's likely that their ownership is still in dispute.)

The cafés and restaurants that line this street are inviting, especially in summer. Poke around behind the facades and outdoor tables to experience Bratislava's charm. Courtyards and passageways—most of them open to the public—burrow through the city's buildings. For example, a half-block down Michalská street on the left, the courtyard at #12 was once home to vintners; their former cellars are now coffee shops, massage parlors, crafts boutiques, and cigar shops. Across the street, on the right, the dead-end passage at #5 has an antique shop and small café, while #7 is home to a fashion design shop.

On the left (at #6), the **Cukráreň na Korze** chocolate shop is highly regarded among locals for its delicious hot chocolate and creamy truffles (Mon-Thu 9:00-21:00, Fri-Sat 9:00-22:00, Sun 10:00-21:00, tel. 02/5443-3945).

Above the shop's entrance, the **cannonball** embedded in the wall recalls Napoleon's two sieges of Bratislava (the 1809 siege was 42 days long), which caused massive suffering—even worse than during World War II. Keep an eye out for these cannonballs all over town...somber reminders of one of Bratislava's darkest times.

• *Two blocks down from St. Michael's Gate, where the street jogs slightly right (and its name changes to Ventúrska), detour left along Sedlárska street and head to the...*

Main Square (Hlavné Námestie)

A modest Town Hall square that feels too petite for a national capital, this is the centerpiece of Old World Bratislava. Cute little

kiosks, with old-time cityscape engravings on their roofs, sell local handicrafts and knickknacks (Easter through October). Similar stalls fill the square from mid-November until December 23, when the Christmas market here is a big draw (www.vianocnetrhy.sk).

Virtually every building around this square dates from a different architectural period, from Gothic (the yellow tower) to Art Nouveau (the fancy facade facing it from across the square).

Cafés line the square. You can't go wrong here. Choose the ambience you like best (indoors or out) and sip a drink with Slovakia's best urban view. The Art Nouveau **Café Roland,** once a bank, is known for its 1904 Klimt-style mosaics and historic photos of the days when the city was known as Pressburg (Austrian times)

Bratislava

1 Hotel Marrol's
2 Hotel Michalská Brána
3 Hotel Ibis
4 Penzión Virgo
5 Penzión Gremium
6 Downtown Backpackers Hostel
7 1. Slovak Pub
8 Bratislavský Meštiansky Pivovar
9 Lemon Tree/Sky Bar/Rum Club
10 Shtoor (3)
11 Coffee & Bagel Story;
Café Roland; Kaffee Mayer
12 Billa Supermarket

ULICA PALISÁDY
ŠTETINOVA
PANENSKÁ
TYČENJA
KOZIA ULICA
PODJAVOR
KONVENTNÁ
STAROMESTSKÁ
ZOCHOVA
DANKOVSKÉHO
ULICA PALISÁDY
ŠKARNICLOVA
SVORADOVA
Župné Nám.
KORENIČOVA
ZÁMOCKÁ ULICA
Zochova B
TVAROŽKOVA
ULICA
2 BAŠTOVÁ
ŽIDOVSKÁ
Fashion Courtyard
KLARISKÁ
KRÁTKA
STRELECKÁ
3
KAPITULSKÁ
PREPOŠTSKÁ
CASTLE
SUMMER RIDING SCHOOL
ENTRY
KNIGHTS HALL
STAROMESTSKÁ
OLD
VENTÚRSKA
VODNY
TREASURE ROOM
TICKETS
PARLIAMENT
WALK ENDS
ST. MARTIN'S CATHEDRAL
ZÁM. SCHODY
SCHODY PRI STAREJ VODÁRNI
HOLOCAUST MEMORIAL
NÁBR. ARMÁDNEHO GENERÁLA L. SVOBODU
Most SNP
(Bus stop under bridge) B
RÁZUSOVO NÁBR.

N

100 Meters
100 Yards

SNP BRIDGE

To Petržalka
"UFO" OBSERVATION DECK

or Pozsony (Hungarian times). The barista stands where a different kind of bean counter once did, guarding a vault that now holds coffee (Hlavné Námestie 5; the café may have a new name by the time you visit). The classic choice is the kitty-corner **Kaffee Mayer.** This venerable café, an institution here, has been selling coffee and cakes to a genteel clientele since 1873. You can enjoy your pick-me-up in the swanky old interior or out on the square (€3-3.50 cakes, small selection of expensive-for-Bratislava hot meals, daily 9:30-22:00, Fri-Sat until 23:00, Hlavné Námestie 4, tel. 02/5441-1741).

Peering over one of the benches on the square is a cartoonish statue of a **Napoleonic officer** (notice the French flag marking the embassy right behind him). With bare feet and a hat pulled over his eyes, it's hardly a flattering portrait—you could call it the locals' revenge for Napoleon's sieges. Across the square, another soldier from that period stands at attention.

At the top of the Main Square is the impressive **Old Town Hall** (Stará Radnica), with its bold yellow tower. Near the bottom of the tower (to the left of the window), notice another cannonball embedded in the facade—yet another reminder of Napoleon's impact on Bratislava. Over time, the Old Town Hall grew, annexing the buildings next to it and creating a mishmash of architectural styles along this side of the square. (A few steps down the street to the right are the historic apartments and wine museum at the **Apponyi House**—described later, under "Sights in Bratislava.")

Step through the passageway into the Old Town Hall's gorgeously restored **courtyard,** with its Renaissance arcades. (The **City History Museum**'s entrance is here—described later.)

Then, to see another fine old square, continue through the other end of the courtyard into **Primate's Square** (Primaciálne Námestie). The pink mansion on the right is the **Primate's Palace,** with a fine interior decorated with six English tapestries (described later). At the far end of this square is the **TI.**

• *Backtrack to the Main Square. With your back to the Old Town Hall, go to the end of the square and follow the street to the left (Rybárska Brána). On your way you'll pass a pair of...*

Whimsical Statues

Playful statues (such as the Napoleonic officer we met earlier) dot Bratislava's old town. Most date from the late 1990s, when city leaders wanted to entice locals back into the newly prettied-up center.

Just at the beginning of the street, as you exit the main square, you'll come to a jovial chap doffing his top hat. This is a statue of **Schöner Náci,** who lived in Bratislava until the 1960s. This eccentric old man, a poor carpet cleaner, would dress up in his one black suit and top hat, and go strolling through the city, offering gifts

to the women he fancied. (He'd often whisper *"schön"*—German for "pretty," which is how he got his nickname.) Schöner Náci now gets to spend eternity greeting visitors outside his favorite café, Kaffee Mayer. Once he lost an arm: A bunch of drunks broke it off. (It was replaced.) As Prague gets more expensive, Bratislava has become one of the cheaper alternatives for weekend "stag parties," popular with Brits lured here by cheap flights and cheap beer.

• *Continue down Rybárska.*

At the end of this block, at the intersection with Panská, watch out on the right for **Čumil** ("the Peeper"), grinning at pass-

ersby from a manhole. This was the first—and is still the favorite—of Bratislava's statues. There's no story behind this one—the artist simply wanted to create a fun icon and let the townspeople make up their own tales. Čumil has survived being driven over by a truck—twice—and he's still grinning.

• *Keep along Rybárska to reach the long, skinny square called...*

Hviezdoslav Square (Hviezdoslavovo Námestie)

The landscaping in the center of this square makes it particularly inviting. At the near end is the impressive, silver-topped Slovak National Theater (Slovenské Národné Divadlo). Beyond that, the opulent yellow Neo-Baroque building is the Slovak Philharmonic (Slovenská Filharmónia). When the theater opened in the 1880s, half the shows were in German and half in Hungarian. Today, it's a proud Slovak institution—typical of the ethnic changes that have marked this city's life.

Right in front of the theater (by the McDonald's), look down into the glass **display case** to see the foundation of the one-time Fishermen's Gate into the city. Surrounding the base of the gate is water. This entire square was once

City of Three Cultures: Pressburg, Pozsony, Bratislava

Historically more of an Austrian and Hungarian city than a Slovak one, Bratislava has always been a Central European melting pot. Everyone from Hans Christian Andersen to Casanova has sung the praises of this bustling burg on the Danube.

For most of its history, Bratislava was part of the Austrian Empire and known as Pressburg, with a primarily German-speaking population. (Only the surrounding rural areas were Slovak.) The Hungarians used Pozsony (as they called it) as their capital during the century and a half that Buda and Pest were occupied by Ottoman invaders.

By its turn-of-the-20th-century glory days, the city was a rich intersection of cultures—about 40 percent German, 40 percent Hungarian, and 20 percent Slovak. Shop clerks greeted customers in all three languages. It was said that the mornings belonged to the Slovaks (farmers who came into the city to sell their wares at market), the afternoons to the Hungarians (diplomats and office workers filling the cafés), and the evenings to the Austrians (wine producers who ran convivial neighborhood wine pubs where all three groups would gather). In those wine pubs, the vintner would listen to which language his customers used, then bring them a glass with the serving size expected in their home country: 0.3 liters for Hungarians, 0.25 liters for Austrians, and 0.2 liters for Slovaks (a distinction that still exists today). Jews (one-tenth of the population), and Roma (Gypsies) rounded out the city's ethnic brew.

When the new nation of Czechoslovakia was formed from the rubble of World War I, the city shed its German and Hungarian names, and took the newly created Slavic name of Bratislava. The Slovak population was on the rise, but the city remained tricultural.

World War II changed all of that. With the dissolution of Czechoslovakia, Slovakia became an "independent" country under the thumb of the Nazis—who all but wiped out the Jewish population. Then, at the end of the war, a Czechoslovakia reunited under the Soviet Russian thumb rudely expelled the city's

a tributary of the Danube, and the Carlton Hotel across the way was a series of inns on different islands. The buildings along the old town side of the square mark where the city wall once stood. Now the square is a lively zone on balmy evenings, with several fine restaurants (including some splurgy steakhouses) offering al fresco tables jammed with visiting European businessmen looking for good-quality, expense-account meals.

Stroll down the long art-and-people-filled square. Each summer, as part of an arts festival, it's ornamented with entertaining ethnic Germans and Hungarians in retribution for the misdeeds of Hitler and Horthy (Hungary's wartime leader).

Bratislava's urban heritage suffered terribly under the communists. The historic city's multilayered charm and delicate cultural fabric were ripped apart, then shrouded in gray. The communists were prouder of their ultramodern SNP Bridge than of the city's historic Jewish quarter—which they razed to make way for the bridge. Now the bridge and its highway slice through the center of the old town, and the heavy traffic rattles the stained-glass windows of St. Martin's Cathedral. Similarly, the city's Germanic heritage was deliberately obscured.

But Bratislava's most recent chapter is one of great success. Since the fall of communism, the city has gone from gloomy victim to thriving economic center and social hub. With a healthy market economy, it now has the chance to re-create itself as Slovakia's national capital. Its population of about 430,000 includes some 60,000 students (at the city's six universities), creating an atmosphere of youthful energy and optimism. Its remarkable position on the Danube, a short commute from Vienna, is prompting its redevelopment as one of Europe's up-and-coming cities.

Bratislava and Vienna have realized that it's mutually beneficial to work together to bring the Slovak capital up to snuff. They're cooperating in a new "twin city" commerce super-zone. In the coming years, foreign investors talk of erecting a Bratislavan skyline of 600-foot-tall skyscrapers and a clutch of glittering new megamalls. Bratislavans also have high hopes for revitalizing the city's transport infrastructure: The highway that barrels between the old town and the castle will be diverted underground (through a tunnel beneath the Danube); a bullet train will swoosh to a stop at a slick new train station; a new six-station subway line will lace the city together; and the entire riverfront will be transformed into a people-friendly park.

As the city pulls funding together, expect lots of construction during your visit. You'd never have guessed it a few years ago, but today calling Bratislava "the next Berlin on a smaller scale" is only a bit of a stretch.

---

modern art. After passing a statue of the square's namesake (Pavol Országh Hviezdoslav, a beloved Slovak poet), you'll come upon an ugly fence and barriers on the left, which mark the fortified US Embassy. Just past the embassy is the low-profile entrance to the **Sky Bar,** an affordable rooftop restaurant with excellent views (ride elevator to seventh floor; see "Eating in Bratislava," later). Farther along, after the giant chessboard, the glass pavilion is a popular venue for summer concerts. On the right near the end of the park, a statue of Hans Christian Andersen is a reminder that the Danish storyteller enjoyed his visit to Bratislava, too.

• *Reaching the end of the square, you run into the barrier for a busy highway. Turn right and walk one block to find the big, black marble slab facing a modern monument—and, likely, a colorful wooden reconstruction of a synagogue.*

Holocaust Memorial

This was the site of Bratislava's original synagogue. You can see an etching of the building in the big slab.

Turn your attention to the memorial. The word "Remember" carved into the base in Hebrew and Slovak commemorates the 90,000 Slovak Jews who were deported to Nazi death camps. Nearly all were killed. The fact that the town's main synagogue and main church (to the right) were located side by side illustrates the tolerance that characterized Bratislava before Hitler. Ponder the modern statue: The two pages of an open book, faces, hands in the sky, and bullets—all under the Star of David—evoke the fate of 90 percent of the Slovak Jews.

• *Now head toward the adjacent church, up the stairs.*

St. Martin's Cathedral (Dóm Sv. Martina)

If the highway thundering a few feet in front of this historic church's door were any closer, the off-ramp would go through the nave. Sad as it is now, the cathedral has been party to some pretty important history. While Buda and Pest were occupied by Ottomans from 1543 to 1689, Bratislava was the capital of Hungary. Nineteen Hungarian kings and queens were crowned in this church—more than have been crowned anywhere in Hungary. In fact, the last Hungarian coronation (not counting the Austrian Franz Josef) was not in Budapest, but in Bratislava. A replica of the Hungarian crown still tops the steeple.

It's worth walking up to the cathedral's entrance to observe some fragments of times past (circle around the building, along the busy road, to the opposite, uphill side). Directly across from the church door is a broken bit of the 15th-century town wall. The church was actually built into the wall, which explains its unusual north-side entry. In fact, notice the fortified watchtower (with a WC drop on its left) built into the corner of the church just above you.

There's relatively little to see inside the cathedral—I'd skip it (€2, Mon-Sat 9:00-11:30 & 13:00-18:00, Sun 13:30-

16:00). If you do duck in, you'll find a fairly gloomy interior, some fine carved-wood altarpieces (a Slovak specialty), a dank crypt, a replica of the Hungarian crown, and a treasury in the back with a whimsical wood carving of Jesus blessing Habsburg Emperor Franz Josef.

Head back around the church for a good view (looking toward the river) of the huge bridge called **Most SNP,** the communists' pride and joy (the "SNP" stands for the Slovak National Uprising of 1944 against the Nazis, a typical focus of communist remembrance). As with most Soviet-era landmarks in former communist countries, locals aren't crazy about this structure—not only for the questionable Starship *Enterprise* design, but also because of the

oppressive regime it represented. However, the restaurant and observation deck up top have been renovated into a posh eatery called (appropriately enough) "UFO." You can visit it for the views, a drink, or a full meal.

• *You could end the walk here. Two sights (both described later, under "Sights in Bratislava") are nearby. To hike up to the **castle**, take the underpass beneath the highway, go up the stairs on the right marked by the* Hrad/Castle *sign, then turn left up the stepped lane marked* Zámocké Schody. *Or hike over the SNP Bridge (pedestrian walkway on lower level) to ride the elevator up the **UFO** viewing platform.*

*But to really round out your Bratislava visit, head for the river and stroll downstream (left) to a place where you get a dose of modern development in Bratislava—**Eurovea**. Walk about 10 minutes downstream, past the old town and boat terminals until you come to a big, slick complex with a grassy park leading down to the riverbank.*

Eurovea

Just downstream from the old town is the futuristic Eurovea, with four vibrant layers, each a quarter-mile long: a riverside park, luxury condos, a thriving modern shopping mall, and an office park. Walking out onto the view piers jutting into the Danube and surveying the scene, it looks like a computer-generated urban dreamscape come true. Exploring the old town gave you a taste

of where this country has been. But wandering this riverside park, enjoying a drink in one of its chic outdoor lounges, and then browsing through the thriving mall, you'll enjoy a glimpse of where Slovakia is heading.

• *Our walk is finished. If you haven't already visited them, consider circling back to some of the sights described next.*

Sights in Bratislava

If Europe had a prize for "capital city with the most underwhelming museums," I'd cast my vote for Bratislava. You can easily have a great day here without setting foot in a museum. Focus instead on Bratislava's street life and the grand views from the castle and UFO restaurant. If it's rainy or you're in a museum-going mood, the Primate's Palace (with its cheap admission and fine tapestries) ranks slightly above the rest.

ON OR NEAR THE OLD TOWN'S MAIN SQUARE

These museums are all within a few minutes' walk of one another, on or very near the Main Square.

▲Primate's Palace (Primaciálny Palác)

Bratislava's most interesting museum, this tastefully restored French-Neoclassical mansion (formerly the residence of the arch-

bishop, or "primate") dates from 1781. The religious counterpart of the castle, it filled in for Esztergom—the Hungarian religious capital—after that city was taken by the Ottomans in 1543. Even after the Ottoman defeat in the 1680s, this remained the winter residence of Hungary's archbishops.

Cost and Hours: €3, Tue-Fri 10:00-17:00, Sat-Sun 11:00-18:00, closed Mon, Primaciálne Námestie 1, tel. 02/5935-6394, www.bratislava.sk.

Visiting the Museum: The palace, which now serves as a government building, features one fine floor of exhibits. Follow signs for *Expozícia* up the grand staircase to the ticket counter. There are three main attractions: the Mirror Hall, the tapestries, and the archbishop's chapel.

The **Mirror Hall,** used for concerts, city council meetings, and other important events, is to the left as you enter and worth a glance (if it's not closed for an event).

A series of large public rooms, originally designed to impress, are now an art gallery. Distributed through several of these rooms is the museum's pride, and for many its highlight: a series of six English **tapestries,** illustrating the ancient Greek myth of the tragic love between Hero and Leander. The tapestries were woven in England by Flemish weavers for the court of King Charles I (in the 1630s). They were kept in London's Hampton Court Palace until Charles was deposed and beheaded in 1649. Cromwell sold them to France to help fund his civil war, but after 1650, they disappeared. Centuries later, in 1903, restorers broke through a false wall in this mansion and discovered the six tapestries, neatly folded and perfectly preserved. Nobody knows how they got there (perhaps they were squirreled away during the Napoleonic invasion, and whoever hid them didn't survive). The archbishop—who had just sold the palace to the city, but emptied it of furniture before he left—cried foul and tried to get the tapestries back...but the city said, "A deal's a deal."

After traipsing through the grand rooms, find the hallway that leads through the smaller rooms of the archbishop's private quarters, now decorated with minor Dutch, Flemish, German, and Italian paintings. At the end of this hall, a bay window looks down into the archbishop's own private marble **chapel.** When the archbishop became too ill to walk down to Mass, this window was built for him to take part in the service.

On your way back to the entry, pause at the head of the larger corridor to study a 1900 view of the then much smaller town by Gustáv Keleti. The museum's entry hall also has grand portraits of Maria Theresa and Josef II.

City History Museum (Mestské Múzeum)

Delving into the bric-a-brac of Bratislava's past, this museum includes ecclesiastical art on the ground floor and a sprawling, chronological look at local history upstairs. The displays occupy rooms once used by the town council—courthouse, council hall, chapel, and so on. Everything is described in English, and the included audioguide tries hard, but nothing quite succeeds in bringing meaning to the place. On your way upstairs, you'll have a chance to climb up into the Old Town Hall's tower, offering so-so views over the square, cathedral, and castle.

Cost and Hours: €5, includes audioguide, €6 combo-ticket with Apponyi House, Tue-Fri 10:00-17:00, Sat-Sun 11:00-18:00, closed Mon, last entry 30 minutes before closing, in the Old Town Hall—enter through courtyard, tel. 02/5920-5130, www.muzeum. bratislava.sk.

Apponyi House (Apponyiho Palác)

This nicely restored mansion of a Hungarian aristocrat is meaningless without the included audioguide (dull but informative). The museum has two parts. The cellar and ground floor feature an interesting exhibit on the vineyards of the nearby "Little Carpathian" hills, with historic presses and barrels, and a replica of an old-time wine-pub table. Upstairs are two floors of urban apartments from old Bratislava, called the Period Rooms Museum. The first floor up shows off the 18th-century Rococo-style rooms of the nobility—fine but not ostentatious, with ceramic stoves. The second floor up (with lower ceilings and simpler wall decorations) illustrates 19th-century bourgeois/middle-class lifestyles, including period clothing and some Empire-style furniture.

Cost and Hours: €4, includes audioguide, €6 combo-ticket with City History Museum, Tue-Fri 10:00-17:00, Sat-Sun 11:00-18:00, closed Mon, last entry 30 minutes before closing, Radničná 1, tel. 02/5920-5135, www.muzeum.bratislava.sk.

BEYOND THE OLD TOWN

Bratislava Castle (Bratislavský Hrad)

This imposing fortress, nicknamed the "upside-down table," is the city's most prominent landmark. The oldest surviving chunk is the

13th-century Romanesque watchtower (the one slightly taller than the other three). When Habsburg Empress Maria Theresa took a liking to Bratislava in the 18th century, she transformed the castle from a military fortress to a royal residence suitable for holding court. She added a summer riding school (the U-shaped complex next to the castle), an enclosed winter riding school out back, and lots more. Maria Theresa's favorite daughter, Maria Christina, lived here with her husband, Albert, when they were newlyweds. Locals nicknamed the place "little Schönbrunn," in reference to the Habsburgs' summer palace on the outskirts of Vienna.

Turned into a fortress-garrison during the Napoleonic Wars, the castle burned to the ground in an 1811 fire started by careless soldiers, and was left as a ruin for 150 years before being reconstructed in 1953. Unfortunately, the communist rebuild was drab and uninviting; the inner courtyard feels like a prison exercise yard.

A more recent renovation has done little to improve things, and the museum exhibits inside aren't really worth the cost of admission (described next). The best visit is to simply hike up (it's free to enter the grounds), enjoy the views over town, and take a close-up look

at the stately old building (the big, blocky, modern building next door is the Slovak Parliament).

For details on the best walking route to the castle, see page 443.

Castle Museum

The newly restored castle has a few sights inside, with more likely to open in the future. Two small exhibits are skippable: the misnamed **Treasure Room** (a sparse collection of items found at the castle site, including coins and fragments of Roman jugs) and the **Knights Hall** (offering a brief history lesson in the castle's construction and reconstruction). You can also enter the **palace** itself. A blinding-white staircase with gold trim leads to the Music Hall, with a prized 18th-century *Assumption* altarpiece by Anton Schmidt (first floor); a collection of historical prints depicting Bratislava and its castle (second floor); and temporary exhibits (third/top floor). From the top floor, a series of very steep, modern staircases take you up to the Crown Tower (the castle's oldest and tallest) for views over town—though the vista from the terrace in front of the castle is much easier to reach and nearly as good.

Cost and Hours: €6 all-inclusive "Road A" ticket, €2 for pointless "Road B" ticket (covers only the less interesting parts of palace—the Treasure Room and Knights Hall); Tue-Sun 10:00-18:00, closed Mon; ticket office is right of main riverfront entrance—enter exhibits from passage into central courtyard, tel. 02/2048-3110, www.snm.sk.

▲▲The SNP Bridge and UFO

Bratislava's bizarre, flying-saucer-capped bridge, completed in 1972 in heavy-handed communist style, has been reclaimed by capitalists. The flying saucer-shaped structure called the UFO (at the Petržalka end of the bridge) is now a spruced-up, overpriced café/restaurant and observation deck, allowing sweeping 360-degree views of Bratislava from about 300 feet above the Danube. Think of it as the Slovak Space Needle.

Cost and Hours: €6.50, daily 10:00-23:00, elevator free if you have a meal reservation or order food at the restaurant—main courses steeply priced at €23-28, restaurant opens at 12:00, tel. 02/6252-0300, www.redmonkeygroup.com.

Getting There: The elevator entrance is underneath the tower. Walk across the bridge from the old town (there are pedestrian walkways on the lower level). If you take the downstream (old-town side) walkway, you'll pass historical photos of the bridge's construction, including the demolition of the city's synagogue and other old town buildings.

◉ Self-Guided Tour: The "**elevator**" that takes you up is actually a funicular—you'll notice you're moving at an angle. At the top, walk up the stairs to the observation deck.

Begin by viewing the **castle** and **old town.** The area to the right of the old town, between and beyond the skyscrapers,

 is a massive construction zone. A time-lapse camera set up here over the next few years will catch skyscrapers popping up like dandelions. International investors are throwing lots of money at Bratislava. (Imagine having so much prime, undeveloped real estate available downtown in the capital of an emerging European economic power...and just an hour down the road from Vienna, no less.) Most of the development is taking place along the banks of the Danube. In a decade, this will be a commercial center.

The huge TV tower caps a forested hill beyond the old town. Below and to the left of it, the pointy monument is **Slavín,** where more than 6,800 Soviet soldiers who fought to liberate Bratislava from the Nazis are buried. Under communist rule, a nearby church was forced to take down its steeple so as not to draw attention away from the huge Soviet soldier on top of the monument.

Now turn 180 degrees and cross the platform to face **Petržalka,** a planned communist suburb that sprouted here in the 1970s. The site was once occupied by a village, and the various districts of modern Petržalka still carry their original names (which now seem ironic): "Meadows" *(Háje),* "Woods" *(Lúky),* and "Courtyards" *(Dvory).* The ambitious communist planners envisioned a city laced with Venetian-style canals to help drain the marshy land, but the plans were abandoned after the harsh crackdown on the 1968 Prague Spring uprising. Without the incentives of private ownership, all they succeeded in creating was a grim and decaying sea of miserable concrete apartment *paneláky* ("panel buildings," so-called because they're made of huge prefab panels).

Today, one in four Bratislavans lives in Petržalka, and things are looking better. Like Dorothy opening the door to Oz, the formerly drab buildings have been splashed with bright new colors. Far from being a slum, Petržalka is a popular neighborhood for Bratislavan yuppies who can't yet afford to build their dream houses. Locals read the Czech-language home-improvement magazine *Panel Plus* for ideas on how to give their *panelák* apartments some style (browse it yourself at www.panelplus.cz).

Petržalka is also a big suburban-style shopping zone (note the supermall down below). But there's still some history here. The **park** called Sad Janka Kráľa (originally, in German, Aupark)—just downriver from the bridge—was technically the first public park in Europe in the 1770s and is still a popular place for locals to relax and court.

Scanning the **horizon** beyond Petržalka, two things stick out: on the left, the old communist oil refinery (which has been fully updated and is now state-of-the-art); and on the right, a sea of modern windmills. These are just over the border, in Austria...and Bratislava is sure to grow in that direction quickly. Austria is about three miles that way, and Hungary is about six miles farther to the left.

Before you leave, consider a drink at the café (€3-4 coffee or beer, €7-20 cocktails). If nothing else, be sure to use the memorable WCs (guys can enjoy a classic urinal photo).

Sleeping in Bratislava

I'd rather sleep in Budapest (or in Vienna)—particularly since good-value options in central Bratislava are slim, and service tends to be surly. Business-oriented places charge more on weekdays than on weekends. Expect prices to drop slightly in winter and in the hottest summer months. Hotel Michalská Brána is right in the heart of the old town, while the others are just outside it—but still within a 5-10-minute walk.

$$$ Hotel Marrol's, on a quiet street, is the town's most enticing splurge. Although the immediate neighborhood isn't interesting, it's a five-minute walk from the old town, and its 54 rooms

Sleep Code

Abbreviations   (€1 = about $1.40, country code: 421, area code: 02)
S = Single, **D** = Double/Twin, **T** = Triple, **Q** = Quad, **b** = bathroom
Price Rankings
  $$$ **Higher Priced**—Most rooms €100 or more.
   $$ **Moderately Priced**—Most rooms between €50-100.
    $ **Lower Priced**—Most rooms €50 or less.
English is spoken at each place. Unless otherwise noted, credit cards are accepted, rooms have no air-conditioning, breakfast is included, and Wi-Fi is generally free. Prices change; verify current rates online or by email. For the best prices, always book directly with the hotel.

are luxurious and tastefully appointed, Old World country-style. While pricey, the rates drop on weekends (prices flex, but generally Mon-Thu: Db-€160, Fri-Sun: Db-€120, Sb-€10 less, non-smoking, elevator, air-con, Wi-Fi, loaner laptops, free minibar, gorgeous lounge, Tobrucká 4, tel. 02/5778-4600, www.hotelmarrols.sk, rec@hotelmarrols.sk).

$$ Hotel Michalská Brána is a charming boutique hotel just inside St. Michael's Gate in the old town. The 14 rooms are sleek, mod, and classy, and the location is ideal—right in the heart of town, but on a relatively sleepy lane just away from the hubbub (Sb-€69-73, Db-€79-83, higher prices are for Mon-Thu nights, extra bed-€20, pricier suites available, non-smoking, air-con, elevator, Wi-Fi, Baštová 4, tel. 02/5930-7200, www.michalskabrana.sk, reception@michalskabrana.com).

$$ Hotel Ibis, part of the Europe-wide chain, offers 120 nicely appointed rooms just outside the old town, overlooking a busy tram junction—request a quieter room (Mon-Thu: Sb/Db-€85, Fri-Sun: Sb/Db-€69, rates flex with demand, you'll likely save €20 or more with advance booking on their website, breakfast-€10, elevator, air-con, guest computer and Wi-Fi, Zámocká 38, tel. 02/5929-2000, www.ibishotel.com, h3566@accor.com).

$$ Penzión Virgo sits on a quiet residential street, an eight-minute walk from the old town. The 11 boutiqueish rooms are classy and well-appointed (Sb-€61, Db-€74—but often discounted to around Sb/Db-€55, extra bed-€13, breakfast-€6, Wi-Fi, inexpensive parking, Panenská 14, tel. 02/3300-6262, www.penzionvirgo.sk, reception@penzionvirgo.sk).

$$ Penzión Gremium has six nondescript rooms and three apartments in a very central location, just a block behind the National Theater and a few steps from the old town. It's on a busy street with good windows but no air-conditioning, so it can be noisy on rowdy weekends (Sb-€60, Db-€70, Db apartment-€90, prices soft, breakfast-€7, elevator reaches some rooms, Wi-Fi, Gorkého 11, tel. 02/2070-4874, www.penziongremium.sk, recepcia@penziongremium.sk).

$ Downtown Backpackers Hostel is a funky but well-run place located in an old-fashioned townhouse. Rooms are named for famous artists and decorated with reinterpretations of their paintings (45 beds in 7 rooms, D-€54, bunk in 7-8-bed dorm-€18, bunk in 10-bed dorm-€17, breakfast-€3-5, Wi-Fi, free laundry facilities, kitchen, bike rental nearby, Panenská 31—across busy boulevard from Grassalkovich Palace, 10 minutes on foot from main station, tel. 02/5464-1191, mobile 0905/259-714, www.backpackers.sk, info@backpackers.sk).

Eating in Bratislava

Today's Slovak cooking shows some Hungarian and Austrian influences, but it's closer to Czech cuisine—lots of starches and gravy, and plenty of pork, cabbage, potatoes, and dumplings. Keep an eye out for Slovakia's national dish, *bryndzové halušky* (small potato dumplings with sheep's cheese and bits of bacon). For a fun drink and snack that locals love, try a Vinea grape soda and a sweet *Pressburger* bagel in any bar or café.

Like the Czechs, the Slovaks produce excellent beer (*pivo*, PEE-voh). One of the top brands is Zlatý Bažant ("Golden Pheasant"). Bratislava's beer halls are good places to sample Slovak and Czech beers, and to get a hearty, affordable meal of stick-to-your-ribs pub grub. Long a wine-producing area, the Bratislava region makes the same wines that Vienna is famous for. But, as nearly all is consumed locally, most people don't think of Slovakia as wine country.

Bratislava is packed with inviting new eateries. In addition to the heavy Slovak staples, you'll find trendy new bars and bistros, and a smattering of ethnic offerings. The best plan may be to stroll the old town and keep your eyes open for the setting and cuisine that appeals to you most. Or consider one of these options.

1. Slovak Pub ("1." as in "the first") attracts a student crowd. Enter from Obchodná, the bustling shopping street just above the old town, and climb the stairs into a vast warren of rustic, old countryside-style pub rooms with uneven floors. Enjoy the lively, loud, almost chaotic ambience while dining on affordable and truly authentic Slovak fare, made with products from the pub's own farm. This is a good place to try the Slovak specialty, *bryndzové halušky* (several varieties for €4-5; €4-12 main courses, Mon 10:00-23:00, Tue-Sat 10:00-24:00, Sun 12:00-24:00, Obchodná 62, tel. 02/5292-6367, www.slovakpub.sk).

Bratislavský Meštiansky Pivovar ("Bratislava Town Brewpub"), just above the old town behind the big Crowne Plaza hotel, brews its own beer and also sells a variety of others. Seating stretches over several levels in the new-meets-old interior (€7-15 main courses, Mon-Sat 11:00-24:00, Sun 11:00-23:00, Drevená 8, mobile 0944-512-265, www.mestianskypivovar.sk).

Lemon Tree/Sky Bar/Rum Club, a three-in-one place just past the fenced-in US Embassy on the trendy Hviezdoslavovo Námestie, features the same Thai-meets-Mediterranean menu throughout (€8-12 pasta and noodle dishes, €16-19 main courses). But the real reason to come here is for the seventh-floor Sky Bar, with fantastic views of the old town and the SNP Bridge. It's smart to reserve a view table in advance if you want to dine here—or just drop by for a pricey vodka cocktail on the small terrace. You've got the best seat in town, and though prices are expensive for Bratislava, they're no more than what you'd pay for a meal in Vienna (daily 11:00-late, Sun from 12:00, Hviezdoslavovo Námestie 7, mobile 0948-109-400, www.spicy.sk).

At **Eurovea** (the recommended end to my walking tour, 10 minutes downstream from the old town), huge outdoor terraces rollicking with happy eaters line the swanky riverfront residential and shopping-mall complex. You'll pay high prices for the great atmosphere and views at international eateries—French, Italian, Brazilian—and a branch of the Czech beer-hall chain Kolkovna. Or you can head to the food court in the shopping mall, where you'll eat well for €4.

Shtoor is a hip, rustic-chic café (named for a revered 19th-century champion of Slovak culture, Ľudovít Štúr) with coffee drinks and €3-5 sandwiches and quiches (takeaway or table service, open long hours daily). They have three locations: in the heart of the old town at Panská 23; just east of the old town (near Eurovea) at Štúrova 8; and inside a Barnes & Noble-type bookstore, Martinus.sk, at Obchodná 26.

Coffee & Bagel Story (a chain) sells...coffee and €3 takeout bagel sandwiches. The handiest location is on the town's main square at Hlavné Námestie 8, with picnic tables right out front.

Supermarket: Try **Billa,** in the Tatracentrum complex across the street from Grassalkovich Palace (Mon-Sat 7:00-22:00, Sun 8:00-20:00).

Bratislava Connections

BY TRAIN

Bratislava has two major train stations: the main station closer to the old town (Hlavná Stanica, abbreviated "Bratislava hl. st." on schedules) and Petržalka station (sometimes called ŽST Petržalka), in the suburb across the river (for full details, see "Arrival in Bratislava," earlier). When checking schedules, pay attention to which station your train uses.

From Bratislava by Train to: Budapest (7/day direct, 2.75 hours to Keleti Station, more with transfers; also doable—and possibly cheaper—by Orange Ways bus, 1-4/day, 2.5 hours, www. orangeways.com), **Vienna** (2/hour, 1 hour; buy the €15 round-trip EU Regio day pass, which is cheaper than a one-way fare; departures alternate between the two stations—half from main station, half from Petržalka), **Sopron** (at least hourly, 2.5-3 hours, usually 2 transfers—often at stations in downtown and/or suburban Vienna), **Prague** (5/day direct, 4.25 hours). To reach other Hungarian destinations (including **Eger** and **Pécs**), it's generally easiest to change in Budapest; for Austrian destinations (such as **Salzburg** or **Innsbruck**), you'll connect through Vienna.

BY BUS

Two different companies run handy buses that connect Bratislava, **Vienna,** and the **airports** in each city: Blaguss/Eurolines (www. blaguss.sk or www.eurolines.at) and Slovak Lines/Postbus (tel. 0810-222-3336, www.postbus.at or www.slovaklines.sk). You can book ahead online, or (if arriving at the airport) just take whichever connection is leaving first. The bus schedules are handily posted at www.airportbratislava.sk (find the "Navigation—From the Airport" tab).

The buses run about hourly from Bratislava's airport to Bratislava (15 minutes, stops either at the main bus station east of the old town or at the Most SNP stop underneath the SNP Bridge), continues on to Vienna's airport (1 hour), and ends in Vienna (1.25 hours, Erdberg stop on the U-3 subway line). They then turn around and make the reverse journey (€7.50-10, depending on route).

BY BOAT

Riverboats connect Bratislava to Vienna. Conveniently, these boats dock right along the Danube in front of Bratislava's old town. While they are more expensive, less frequent, and slower than the train, some travelers enjoy getting out on the Danube. It's prudent to bring your passport if crossing over for the day (though it's unlikely anyone will ask for it).

BRATISLAVA

The **Twin City Liner** offers three to five daily boat trips between a dock at the edge of Bratislava's old town, along Fajnorovo nábrežie, and Vienna's Schwedenplatz (where Vienna's town center hits the canal; €30-35 each way, 1.25-hour trip; can fill up—reservations smart, Austrian tel. 01/58880, www.twincityliner.com).

The competing Slovak **LOD** line connects the cities a little more cheaply, but just twice a day. These boats are slower, as they use Vienna's less-convenient Reichsbrücke dock on the main river, farther from the city center (€23 one-way, €38 round-trip, 1.5-hour trip, tel. 02/5293-2226, www.lod.sk).

BY PLANE

You have two options for reaching Bratislava: You can fly into its own airport, or into the very nearby Vienna Airport.

Bratislava Airport (Letisko Bratislava)

This airport (airport code: BTS, www.letiskobratislava.sk) is six miles northeast of downtown Bratislava. Budget airline Ryanair (www.ryanair.com) has many flights here. Some airlines market it as "Vienna-Bratislava," thanks to its proximity to both capitals. It's compact and manageable, with all the usual amenities (including ATMs).

From the Airport to Downtown Bratislava: The airport has easy **public bus** connections to Bratislava's main train station (Hlavná Stanica, €1.30, bus #61, 4-5/hour, 30 minutes). To reach the bus stop, exit straight out of the arrivals hall, cross the street, buy a ticket at the kiosk, and look for the bus stop on your right. For directions from the train station into the old town, see "Arrival in Bratislava," earlier. A **taxi** from the airport into central Bratislava should cost less than €20.

To Budapest: Take the bus or taxi to Bratislava's main train station (described above), then hop a train to Budapest.

To Vienna: Take either the Slovak Lines/Postbus bus, which runs to Vienna's Hauptbahnhof (every 1-2 hours, 2-hour trip, €7.70, www.slovaklines.sk or www.postbus.at) or the Blaguss/Eurolines bus to the Erdberg stop on Vienna's U-3 subway line, on which it's a straight shot to Stephansplatz or Mariahilfer Strasse (every 1-2 hours, 1.5-hour trip, €7.20, www.blaguss.sk or www.eurolines. at). A taxi from Bratislava Airport directly to Vienna costs €60-90 (depending on whether you use a cheaper Slovak or more expensive Austrian cab).

Vienna International Airport

This airport, 12 miles from downtown Vienna and 30 miles from downtown Bratislava, is well-connected both to both capitals (airport code: VIE, airport tel. 01/700-722-233, www.viennaairport. com).

To reach **Bratislava** from the airport, the easiest option is to take the Blaguss/Eurolines or Slovak Lines/Postbus bus described earlier (under "By Bus"). Ask the TI which bus is leaving first, then head straight out the door and hop on. After about 45 minutes, the bus drops off in downtown Bratislava, then heads to the airport. I'd skip the train connection, which takes longer and involves complicated changes (airport train to Wien-Mitte Bahnhof in downtown Vienna, S-Bahn/subway to Südbahnhof, train to Bratislava, figure 1.75 hours total).

HUNGARY: PAST AND PRESENT

The Hungarian story—essentially the tale of a people finding their home—is as epic as any in Europe. Over the course of a millennium, a troublesome nomadic tribe that was the scourge of Europe gradually assimilated with its neighbors and—through a combination of tenacity and diplomacy—found itself controlling a vast swath of Central and Eastern Europe. Since arriving in Europe in 896, the Hungarians adopted Christianity; fended off Tatars and Turks; lost, regained, then lost again two-thirds of their land; and built one of the world's great 19th-century cities.

Today, the Hungarians still perplex and amuse their neighbors with their bizarre Asian language, lovably quirky customs, and spicy cuisine. And yet, despite their mysterious origins and idiosyncrasies, the Hungarians have carved out a unique and vital niche in European life. Hungary is a place worth grappling with, and the persistent reap grand rewards here. Locals toss around the names of great historical figures such as Kossuth, Széchenyi, and Nagy as if they're talking about old friends. Take this crash course so you can keep up.

The story begins long, long ago and far, far away...

WELCOME TO EUROPE

The land we call Hungary today has long been considered the place—culturally and geographically—where the West (Europe) meets the East (Asia). The Roman province of Pannonia once extended to the final foothills of the Alps that constitute the Buda Hills, on the west side of the Danube. Across the river, Rome ended and the barbarian wilds began. From here, the Great Hungarian Plain stretches in a long, flat expanse all the way to Asia—hemmed in to the north by the Carpathian Mountains. (Geologists consider this prairie-like plain to be the westernmost steppe in Europe—

resembling the terrain that covers much of Central Asia.) After Rome collapsed and Europe fell into the Dark Ages, Hungary became the territory of Celts, Vandals, Huns, and Avars...until some out-of-towners moved into the neighborhood.

The seven Magyar tribes, led by the mighty Árpád (and, according to legend, guided by the mythical Turul bird), thundered

into the Carpathian Basin in A.D. 896. They were a rough-and-tumble nomadic people from Central Asia who didn't like to settle down in one place. (For more on this mysterious clan, see the "Who Were the Magyars?" sidebar.) And yet, after their long and winding westward odyssey, the Great Hungarian Plain felt comfortingly like home to the Magyars—reminiscent of the Asian steppes of their ancestors.

The Magyars would camp out in today's Hungary in the winters, and in the summers, they'd go on raids throughout Europe. They were notorious as incredibly swift horsemen, whose use of stirrups (an eastern innovation largely unknown in Europe at the time) allowed them to easily outmaneuver foes and victims. Italy, France, Germany's Rhine, the Spanish Pyrenees, all the way to Constantinople (modern-day Istanbul)—the Magyars had the run of the Continent.

For half a century, the Magyars ranked with the Vikings as the most feared people in Europe. To Europeans, this must have struck a chord of queasy familiarity: a mysterious and dangerous eastern tribe running roughshod over Europe, speaking a gibberish language, and employing strange, terrifying, relentless battle techniques. No wonder they called the new arrivals "Hun-garians."

Now planted in the center of Europe, the Magyars effectively drove a wedge in the middle of the sprawling Slavic populations of the Great Moravian Kingdom (basically today's "Eastern Europe"). The Slavs were split into two splinter groups, north and south— a division that persists today: Czechs, Slovaks, and Poles to the north; and Croats, Slovenes, Serbs, Bosniaks, and Bulgarians to the south. (You can still hear the division caused by the Magyars in the language: While Czechs and Russians call a castle *hrad*, Croats and Serbs call it *grad*.)

After decades of terrorizing Europe, the Magyars were finally defeated by a German and Czech army at the Battle of Augsburg in 955. The Magyars' King Géza—realizing that if they were to survive, his people had to put down roots and get along with their neighbors—made a fateful decision that would forever shape Hun-

Who Were the Magyars?

The ancestors of today's Hungarians, the Magyars, are a mysterious lot. Of all the Asian invaders of Europe, they were arguably the most successful—integrating more or less smoothly with the Europeans, and thriving well into the 21st century. Centuries after the Huns, Tatars, and Ottomans retreated east, leaving behind only fragments of their culture, the Hungarians remain a fixture in contemporary Europe.

The history of the Magyars before they arrived in Europe in A.D. 896 is hotly contested. Because their language is related only to Finnish and Estonian, it's presumed that these three peoples were once a single group, which likely originated east of the Ural Mountains (in the steppes of present-day Asian Russia, near Mongolia).

After the Magyars' ancestors spent some time in Siberia, climatic change pushed them south and west, eventually (likely around the fifth century A.D.) crossing the Ural Mountains and officially entering Europe. They settled near the Don River (in today's southwestern Russia) before local warfare pushed them farther and farther west. The Magyars began raiding European lands, eventually setting up camp in the Carpathian Basin—today's Hungary—in A.D. 896.

After the Magyars settled down and began to intermarry with Germans, Slavs, and other European peoples, their Asian features

gary's future: He adopted Christianity; baptized his son, Vajk; and married him to a Bavarian princess at a young age.

On Christmas Day in the year 1000, Vajk changed his name to István (Stephen) and was symbolically crowned by the pope (for more on István, see page 171). A Venetian missionary, Gellért, came to Buda to attempt to convert the Hungarians—and was martyred (and later sainted) for his efforts. The domestication of the nomadic Magyars was difficult, thanks largely to the resistance of István's uncles, but was ultimately successful. Hungary became a legitimate Christian kingdom, welcomed by its neighbors. Under kings such as László I, Kálmán "the Book Lover," and András II, Hungary entered a period of prosperity. (For more on these three kings, see pages 171-172.)

and customs mostly faded away. But the Europeans also took on the Hungarian language and some elements of the culture ("Magyarization"). Hungary became Central Europe's melting pot. After all these centuries, most Hungarians have lost track of the many tangled strains of their personal family histories. Many people who consider themselves "fully Hungarian" have last names that are obviously Polish, Jewish, German, Serbian, and so on—likely dating back generations. In fact, a recent genetic study found that Hungarians are the most ethnically diverse nationality on the planet.

But even though certain aspects of their Magyar heritage have been lost to time, the Hungarians have done a remarkable job of clinging to their Asian roots. They still do things their own way, making Hungary subtly but unmistakably different from its neighboring countries. And people of German-Hungarian, Slavic-Hungarian, and Jewish-Hungarian descent still speak a language that's not too far removed from the Asian tongue of those original Magyars.

Were the Hungarians (Magyars) descended from the Huns, a similarly aggressive nomadic tribe that lived in the same area centuries earlier? It has long been a popular romantic notion—for historians, but also in legends and among everyday people—to speculate about a tie between these two groups. But modern historians strongly doubt that the two ever had anything to do with each other. Even so, many Hungarians still take pride in the legendary link to the Huns...and Attila remains a popular name even today.

THE TATARS, THE OTTOMANS, AND OTHER OUTSIDERS (A.D. 1000-1686)

One of Hungary's earliest challenges came at the hands of fellow invaders from Central Asia. Through the first half of the 13th century, the Tatars—initially led by Genghis Khan—swept into Eastern Europe from Mongolia. In the summer of 1241, Genghis Khan's son and successor, Ögedei Khan, broke into Hungarian territory. The Tatars sacked and plundered Hungarian towns, laying waste to the kingdom. It was only Ögedei Khan's death in early 1242—and the ensuing dispute about succession—that saved the Hungarians, as Tatar armies rushed home and the Mongolian Empire contracted. The Hungarian king at the time, Béla IV, was left to rebuild his ruined kingdom from the rubble—creating for the first time many of the stout hilltop castles that still line the Danube. (For more on Béla IV, see page 173.)

Each of Béla's successors left his own mark on Hungary, as the Magyar kingdom flourished. They barely skipped a beat when the original Árpád dynasty died out in 1301, as they imported French kings (from the Naples-based Anjou, or Angevin, dynasty) to continue building their young realm. King Károly Róbert (Charles Robert) won over the Magyars, and his son Nagy Lajos (Louis the Great) expanded Hungarian holdings (for more on these two, see pages 173 and 174).

This was a period of flux for all of Central and Eastern Europe, as the nearby Czech and Polish kingdoms also saw their long-standing dynasties expire. For a time, royal intermarriages juggled the crowns of the region between various ruling families. Most notably, for 50 years (1387-1437) Hungary was ruled by Holy Roman Emperor Sigismund of Luxembourg, whose holdings also included the Czech lands, parts of Italy, much of Croatia, and more.

For more than 150 years, Hungary did not have a Hungarian-blooded king. This changed in the late 15th century, when a short-

age of foreign kings led to the ascension to the throne of the enlightened King Mátyás (Matthias) Corvinus. The son of popular military hero János Hunyadi, King Matthias fostered the arts, sparked a mini-Renaissance, and successfully balanced foreign threats to Hungarian sovereignty (the Habsburgs to the north and west, and the Ottomans to the south and east). Under Matthias, Hungarian culture and political power reached a peak. (For more on this great Hungarian king, see page 204.)

But even before the reign of "good king Mátyás," the Ottomans (from today's Turkey) had already begun slicing their way through the Balkan Peninsula toward Central Europe. (It's ironic that the two greatest threats to the Magyar kingdom came in the form of fellow Asian invaders: Tatars and Turks. Or maybe it's not surprising, as these groups all found the steppes of Hungary so familiar and inviting.) In 1526, the Ottomans entered Hungary when Sultan Süleyman the Magnificent killed Hungary's King Lajos II at the Battle of Mohács. By 1541, they took Buda. The Ottomans would dominate Hungarian life (and history) until the 1680s—nearly a century and a half.

The Ottoman invasion divided Hungary into thirds: Ottoman-occupied "Lower Hungary" (more or less today's Hungary); rump "Upper Hungary" (basically today's Slovakia), with its capital at Bratislava (which they called "Pozsony"); and the loosely independent territories of Transylvania (in today's Romania), ruled by

Hungarian dukes. During this era, the Ottomans built some of the thermal baths that you'll still find throughout Hungary.

Ottoman-occupied Hungary became severely depopulated, and many of its towns and cities fell into ruins. While it was advantageous for a Hungarian subject to adopt Islam (for lower taxes and other privileges), the Ottomans rarely forced conversions—unlike the arguably more oppressive Catholics who controlled other parts of Europe at the time (such as the monarchs of Spain, who expelled the Jews and conducted the Spanish Inquisition). Ottoman rule meant that Hungary took a different course than other parts of Europe during this time. The nation fully enjoyed the Renaissance, but missed out on other major European historical events—both good (the Age of Discovery and Age of Reason) and bad (the devastating Catholic-versus-Protestant wars that plagued much of the rest of Europe).

Crippled by the Ottomans and lacking power and options, Hungarian nobles desperately offered their crown to the Austrian Habsburg Empire, in exchange for salvation from the invasion. The Habsburgs instead used Hungary as a kind of "buffer zone" between the Ottoman advance and Vienna. And that was only the beginning of a very troubled relationship between the Hungarians and the Austrians.

HABSBURG RULE, HUNGARIAN NATIONAL REVIVAL, AND REVOLUTION (1686-1867)

In the late 17th century, the Habsburg army, starting from Vienna, began a sustained campaign to push the Ottomans out of Hungary in about 15 years. They finally wrested Buda and Pest from the Ottomans in 1686. The Habsburgs repopulated Buda and Pest with Germans, while Magyars reclaimed the countryside. Even 25 years after the Ottomans were kicked out, the combined population of Buda and Pest was less than 20,000—and most of them were Germans from other parts of the Habsburg Empire. As recently as the early 19th century, Hungary was considered practically beyond Europe; Vienna marked the end of the "civilized" European world. But that would soon change. The population of Buda and Pest grew nearly tenfold from the beginning to the end of the 19th century. The new Austrian rulers rebuilt Hungary in their favored colorful, frilly Baroque style. Even today, it seems every Hungarian town has a cheerfully painted church with a Habsburg-style onion dome.

The Habsburgs governed the country as an outpost of Austria.

Top 10 Dates That Changed Hungary

A.D. 896—The nomadic Magyars (a tribe from Central Asia) arrive in the Carpathian Basin and begin to terrorize Europe.

1000—King István (Stephen) accepts Christianity, marking the domestication of the Magyars.

1541—Invading Ottomans take Buda and Pest...and build thermal baths.

1686—The Austrian Habsburgs drive out the Ottomans, making Hungary part of their extensive empire (despite occasional rebellions from nationalistic Hungarians).

1867—A Golden Age begins, as Hungary gains semi-autonomy from Austria; Budapest, the new co-capital of a vast empire, booms.

1920—A loser in World War I, Hungary is stripped of two-thirds of its territory and half its population in the Treaty of Trianon...and they're still angry about it.

1945—Hungary allies with Germany for most of World War II. After the war, the Soviet Union "liberates" the country and establishes a communist state.

1956—Hungarians bravely revolt. A massive invasion of Soviet tanks and soldiers brutally suppresses the rebellion, killing 2,500.

1989—Hungary is the first Soviet satellite to open its borders to the West, sparking similar reforms throughout the Eastern Bloc.

2004—Hungary joins the European Union.

The Hungarians—who'd had enough of foreign rule—fought them tooth and nail. Countless streets, squares, and buildings throughout the country are named Rákóczi, Széchenyi, or Kossuth—the "big three" Hungarian patriots who resisted the Habsburgs during this time.

Transylvanian prince Ferenc Rákóczi led Hungarians in the first major rebellion against the Habsburgs, the War of Independence (1703-1711). While Rákóczi initially enjoyed great territorial gains, his war ultimately failed, he went into exile in the Ottoman Empire, and Habsburg rule continued. (For more on Rákóczi, see page 176.)

The early 19th century saw a thawing of Habsburg oppression. Here as throughout Europe, "backward" country traditions began to trickle into the cities, gaining more respect and prominence. It was during this time of reforms that Hungarian (rather than German) became the official language. It also coincided with a Romantic Age of poets and writers (such as Mihály Vörösmarty and Sándor Petőfi) who began to use the Hungarian tongue to create literature for the first time. By around 1825, the Hungarian National Revival was underway, as the people began to embrace the culture and traditions of their Magyar ancestors. Like people across Europe—from Ireland to Italy, and from Prague to Scandinavia—the Hungarians were rediscovering what made them a unique people.

In Hungary, the movement was spearheaded by Count István Széchenyi, who had a compelling vision of a resurgent Hungarian nation, and the wealth and influence to make it happen. Széchenyi funded grand structures in Budapest (such as the iconic Chain Bridge) to give his Magyar countrymen something to take pride in. But even as Széchenyi spurred Hungarian patriotism, he was savvy enough not to push for total Hungarian independence—knowing that the volatile combination of strong Habsburg rule and a complicated ethnic mix would make an independent Hungarian state unlikely. Rather, he sought some degree of autonomy within the empire. And it began to work, as the Habsburgs gave in to some Hungarian demands.

And yet, despite the "Reform Age" that was already brewing, the gradual progress was too little, too late for many Hungarians. In March of 1848, a wave of Enlightenment-fueled nationalism that began in Paris spread like wildfire across Europe, igniting a revolutionary spirit in cities such as Vienna, Milan...and Budapest.

In Hungary, it inspired a revolt against the Habsburgs. Széchenyi's slowly-but-surely patriotism was eclipsed by the militarism of popular orator Lajos Kossuth (pictured) and patriotic poet Sándor Petőfi. On March 15, the Revolution of 1848 began on the steps of the National Museum in Pest (see page 57).

For several tense months, the uprising led to little more than diplomatic wrangling (as the Habsburgs were distracted elsewhere). Meanwhile, minority groups inside Hungarian territory—most notably the Croats, led by Josip Jelačić—began to rise up against the Hungarians. That winter, Habsburg Emperor Ferdinand I abdicated, replaced by his young nephew, Franz Josef. One of his first acts was to officially condemn Hungarian independence.

In the spring of 1849, the Hungarians mounted a bloody but successful offensive to take over a wide swath of territory, including Buda and Pest. But in June, Franz Josef enlisted the aid of his fellow divine monarch, the Russian czar, who did not want the Magyars to provide an example for his own independence-minded subjects. Some 200,000 Russian reinforcements flooded into Hungary, crushing the revolution by August. After the final battle, the Habsburgs executed 13 Hungarian generals, then celebrated by clinking mugs of beer. To this very day, clinking beer mugs is, for many traditional Hungarians, just bad style.

For a while, the Habsburgs cracked down on their unruly Hungarian subjects. It was a time of shame for Hungary. Lajos Kossuth, now in exile, traveled the world to convince foreign leaders to take an interest in Hungary's plight (for more on him, see page 177). The now-forgotten Count Széchenyi spent his final years in a mental hospital, before committing suicide in 1860. The poet Sándor Petőfi—Hungary's answer to Lord Byron—disappeared while participating in an 1849 battle, and is presumed to have been killed in the fighting.

In the 1860s, a clever elder statesman named Ferenc Deák—in an attempt to seize on the spirit of reform and the liberalization of the time—began to advocate for a power-sharing arrangement with the Habsburgs. Deák believed that diplomacy, rather than unilateral military action, could be most effective. Deák's often-repeated motto: "Quiet persistence can succeed where violence fails." (In some ways, this could be the slogan for the whole of Hungarian history.)

After an important military loss to Bismarck's Prussia in 1866, Austria began to agree that it couldn't control its rebellious Slavic holdings all by itself. The Habsburgs found themselves governing a vast, sprawling empire in which their own ethnic/linguistic group—Germans—were a tiny minority. In order to balance out the huge Slav population, they took Deák's advice and teamed up with the Hungarians.

And so, just 18 years after crushing the Hungarians in a war, the Habsburgs handed them the reins. With the Compromise (*Ausgleich*) of 1867, Austria granted Budapest the authority over the eastern half of their lands, creating the so-called Dual Monarchy of the Austro-Hungarian Empire. Hungary was granted their much-prized "home rule," where most matters (except finance, foreign policy, and the military) were administered from Budapest rather than Vienna. The Habsburg emperor, Franz Josef, agreed to a unique "king and emperor" (*König und Kaiser*) arrangement, where he was emperor of Austria, but only king of Hungary. In 1867, he was crowned as Hungarian king in both Buda (at Matthias Church) and Pest (on today's March 15 Square). The insignia "K+K" (*König und Kaiser*)—which you'll still see everywhere—

evokes these grand days. (For more on Franz Josef and his wife Sisi, see page 320.)

BUDAPEST'S GOLDEN AGE (1867-1918)

The *Ausgleich* marked a precipitous turning point for the Hungarians, who once again governed their traditional holdings: large parts of today's Slovakia, Serbia, and Transylvania (northwest Romania), and smaller parts of today's Croatia, Slovenia, Ukraine, and Austria. To better govern their sprawling realm, in 1873, the cities of Buda, Pest, and Óbuda merged into one mega-metropolis: Budapest. But each part retained (and still retains) its unique character. Buda, which was more Germanic, Catholic, and pro-Habsburg, remains the traditional, conservative part of town. And Pest (with three times Buda's population), which was a hotbed of Magyar pride and the crucible of the uprisings of the mid-19th century, remains the more liberal, youthful, forward-looking part of town.

Serendipitously, Budapest's new prominence coincided with the 1,000th anniversary of the Hungarians' ancestors, the Magyars, arriving in Europe...one more excuse to dress things up. Budapest's long-standing rivalry with Vienna only spurred them to build bigger and better. The year 1896 saw an over-the-top millennial celebration, for which many of today's greatest structures were created (see page 33).

It was clearly Budapest's Golden Age. No European city grew faster in the second half of the 19th century than Budapest; in the last quarter of the 19th century alone, Budapest doubled in size, building on the foundation laid by Széchenyi and other patriots. By 1900, the city was larger than Rome, Madrid, or Amsterdam. During this time, among other claims to fame, Budapest was the world's biggest mill city—grinding grains from across Hungary and throughout the Balkans. The speedy expansion of the city garnered comparisons with Chicago, another boomtown of that era.

Budapest's most characteristic and most impressive architecture dates from this era. Today's palatial mansions and administra-

tive buildings—whether sooty and crumbling, or newly restored and gleaming—hint at this era of unbridled prosperity. Compelled to adopt the trends of the Habsburgs, but eager to distinguish their own, uniquely Hungarian style, local architects made creative use of Historicism—borrowing bits and pieces of past styles, injecting a healthy dose of bigger-is-better modernity, and finishing it all off with striking, unique flourishes. Miklós Ybl and Ödön Lechner were two of the most prominent architects of this era, designing banks, museums, churches, and municipal buildings around Budapest. It was during this time that many buildings were first decorated with the colorful Zsolnay tiles—pretty as porcelain but hard as stone—invented in the city of Pécs (see page 400). To this day, these colorful adornments are a defining characteristic of Hungarian architecture.

It was also a period of great artistic and creative achievement. Composers Franz Liszt (more Germanic than Magyar) and, later, Béla Bartók and Zoltán Kodály incorporated the folk and Roma (Gypsy) songs of the Hungarian and Transylvanian countryside into their music. As Magyar culture thrived, the traditions of the countryside flowed into the music salons of Budapest. (For more on these great musicians, see "Hungarian Music" on page 288.)

Observers at the time saw Hungarians as characterized by a strange combination of pessimism and optimism: pessimistic about their future, especially relating to the Habsburgs; and optimistic (or maybe even chauvinistic) about the influence of their culture—which, while thriving, remained on the fringe of mainstream Europe. Hungarian historians proposed outrageous boasts about Magyar heritage (including suggesting that Adam and Eve must have been Magyars, and "proving" connections between the Magyars and the Huns and ancient Greeks).

During its time of plenty, Hungary—which had for so long been an oppressed minority under the Habsburgs—became known for trampling its own minorities' rights. (Only a little more than half of the people in Hungarian territory were ethnic Hungarians.) Most signs were in Hungarian only, and the Magyar tongue was taught in every school in the realm. Minorities—who were given virtually no say in government—staged uprisings and revolts, and in 1868 Croatia was even granted semi-autonomy. (It wasn't enough—as early as 1890, Croats began grumbling with Serbs and other South Slavs to create their own Yugo-Slavia.)

However, this did have the intended effect of "Magyarization"—people from all ethnic backgrounds adopted the Hungarian language and culture, giving it an uncanny persistence for something so very foreign and so very old. Germans and Jews adapted their names to Hungarian. For example, the Hungarian communist leader Béla Kun was born Aaron Kohn.

Before long, the optimist in every Hungarian would be proven very wrong indeed—as the Golden Age came crashing to an end, and Hungary plunged into its darkest period.

THE CRISIS OF TRIANON (1918-1939)

World War I marked the end of the age of divine monarchs, as the Romanovs of Russia, the Ottomans of Asia Minor, and, yes, the Habsburgs of Austria-Hungary saw their empires break apart.

Pre-Trianon Hungary

Pre-Trianon Hungary (1920) — Current Hungarian Border

Hungary, which had been riding the Habsburgs' coattails to power and prominence for the past half-century, now paid the price. As retribution for their role on the losing side of World War I, the 1920 Treaty of Trianon (named for the palace on the grounds of Versailles where it was signed) reassigned two-thirds of Hungary's former territory and half of its population to Romania, Ukraine, Czechoslovakia, and Yugoslavia (parts of today's Slovenia, Croatia, and Serbia).

It is impossible to overstate the impact of the Treaty of Trianon on the Hungarian psyche—and on Hungarian history. Not unlike the overnight construction of the Berlin Wall, towns along the new Hungarian borders were suddenly divided down the middle. Many Hungarians found themselves unable to visit relatives or commute to jobs that were in the same country the day before. This sent hundreds of thousands of Hungarian refugees—now "foreigners" in their own towns—into Budapest, sparking an enormous but bittersweet boom in the capital.

To this day, the Treaty of Trianon is regarded as one of the greatest tragedies of Hungarian history. Like the Basques and the Serbs, the Hungarians feel separated from each other by circumstances outside their control. Today, more than two million ethnic Hungarians live outside Hungary (mostly in Romania)—and many Hungarians claim that these lands still belong to the Magyars. The sizeable Magyar minorities in neighboring countries have often been mistreated—particularly in Romania (under Ceauşescu), Yugoslavia (under Milošević), and Slovakia (under Mečiar). You'll see maps, posters, and bumper stickers with the distinctive shape of a much larger, pre-WWI Hungary...patriotically displayed by Magyars who feel as strongly about Trianon as if it happened yesterday.

Some Hungarians see the enlargement of the European Union as a happy ending in the big-picture sense: They have finally been reunited with Slovakia, Romania, and Croatia.

After Trianon, the newly shrunken Kingdom of Hungary had to reinvent itself. The Hungarian crown sat unworn in the Royal Palace, as if waiting for someone worthy to claim it. The WWI hero Admiral Miklós Horthy had won many battles with the Austro-Hungarian navy. Though the new Hungary had no sea and no navy, Horthy retained his rank and ruled the country as a regent. A popular joke points out that during this time, Hungary was a "kingdom without a king" and a landlocked country ruled by a sea admiral. This sense of compounded deficiency pretty much sums up the morose attitude Hungarians have about those gloomy post-Trianon days.

Adding insult to injury, in the mid-1940s Hungary's currency (the *pengő*) underwent the worst inflation spike in the history of money. At the lowest point of the crisis, the government issued a 100,000,000,000,000,000,000-*pengő* note. Their plan for a 1,000,000,000,000,000,000,000-*pengő* bill fell through when the note became worthless after they printed it, but before they had a chance to circulate it.

The mounting financial crisis, and lingering resentment about the strict post-WWI reparations, made Hungary fertile ground for some bold new fascist ideas.

WORLD WAR II AND THE ARROW CROSS (1939-1945)

As Adolf Hitler rose to power in Germany, some other countries that had felt mistreated in the aftermath of World War I—including Hungary—saw Nazi Germany as a vehicle to greater independence. Admiral Horthy joined forces with the Nazis with the hope that they might help Hungary regain the crippling territorial losses of Trianon. In 1941, Hungary (somewhat reluctantly) declared war on the Soviet Union in June—and against the US and Britain in December.

Being an ally to the Nazis, rather than an occupied state, also allowed Hungary a certain degree of self-determination through the war. And, while Hungary had its own set of anti-Semitic laws, the vast majority of its sizeable Jewish population was spared from immediate deportation to Nazi concentration camps. Winning back chunks of Slovakia, Transylvania, and Croatia in the early days of World War II also bolstered the Nazis' acceptance in Hungary.

As Nazism took hold in Germany, the Hungarian fascist movement—spearheaded by the Arrow Cross Party (Nyilaskeresztes Párt)—gained popularity within Hungary. As Germany increased its demands for Hungarian soldiers and food, Admiral Horthy resisted...until Hitler's patience wore thin. In March of 1944, the Nazis invaded and installed the Arrow Cross in power. The Arrow Cross made up for lost time, immediately beginning a savage campaign of executing Hungary's Jews—not only sending them to death camps, but butchering them in the streets. Almost 600,000 Hungarian Jews were murdered. (For more on this dark era of Hungarian history, see the Great Synagogue and Jewish Quarter Tour chapter.)

The Soviet Army eventually "liberated" Hungary, but at the expense of Budapest: A months-long siege, from Christmas of 1944 to mid-February of 1945, reduced the proud city to rubble. One in 10 Hungarian citizens perished in the war.

COMMUNISM...WITH A PINCH OF PAPRIKA (1945-1989)

After World War II, Hungary was gradually compelled to adopt Moscow's system of government. The Soviet-puppet hardliner premier, Mátyás Rákosi, ruled Hungary with an iron fist. Everyday people were terrorized by the KGB-style secret police, called the ÁVO and ÁVH, and intimidated into accepting the new regime. Non-Hungarians were deported, potential and actual dissidents disappeared into the horrifying gulag system of Siberia (and similar forced-work camps in Hungary), food shortages were epidemic, people were compelled to spy on their friends and families, and countless lives were ruined. Coming on the heels of Trianon and two devastating world wars, communist rule was a blow that Hungary is still recovering from. (For much more on life in Soviet-

controlled Hungary, see the House of Terror Tour chapter.)

Beginning on October 23, 1956, the Hungarians courageously staged a monumental uprising, led by Communist Party reformer Imre Nagy. Initially, it appeared that one of the cells on the Soviet Bloc might win itself the right to semi-autonomy. But Moscow couldn't let that happen. In a Tiananmen Square-style crackdown, the Soviets sent in tanks to brutally put down the uprising and occupy the city. When the dust settled, 2,500 Hungarians were dead, and 200,000 fled to the West. (If you know any Hungarian Americans, their families more than likely fled in 1956.) Nagy was arrested, given a sham trial, and executed in 1958. For more on these events, see the "1956" sidebar on page 112.

The Hungarians were devastated. They were frustrated that the Suez Canal crisis distracted the world from their uprising. Many felt betrayed that the US—which spoke so boldly against the Soviet Union—did not offer them military support (contrary to the promises of the US-based Radio Free Europe). While the US and its Western allies understandably did not want to turn the Cold War hot, the Hungarians (also understandably) felt abandoned.

Weeks after the uprising came the now-legendary "Blood in the Water" match at the Melbourne Olympics. Soviet satellite states were often ordered to "throw" matches to allow the USSR's athletes to prevail. On December 6, 1956, Moscow issued such a decree to the Hungarian men's water polo team in their semifinal against the Soviet Union. The Hungarians refused and played their hearts out, much to the delight of their fans (and the rest of the world). The game turned violent, and in one indelible image, a Hungarian athlete emerged from the pool with blood pouring from a gash above his right eye. The Hungarians won, 4-0, and went on to take the gold.

After the uprising, the USSR installed János Kádár—a colleague of Nagy's who was also loyal to Moscow—to lead Hungary. For a few years, things were bleak, as the secret police ratcheted up their efforts against potential dissidents. But in the 1960s, Kádár's reformist tendencies began to cautiously emerge. Seeking to gain the support of his subjects (and avoid further uprisings), Kádár adopted the optimistic motto, "If you are not against us, you are with us." While still mostly cooperating with Moscow, Kádár gradually allowed the people of Hungary more freedom than citizens of neighboring countries had—a system dubbed "goulash communism." The "New Economic Mechanism" of 1968 partly opened Hungary to foreign trade. People from other Warsaw Pact countries—Czechs, Slovaks, and Poles—flocked to Budapest's Váci utca to experience "Western evils" unavailable to them back home, such as Adidas sneakers and Big Macs. People half-joked that Hungary was the happiest barrack in the communist camp.

In the late 1980s, the Eastern Bloc began to thaw. And Hungary—which was always skeptical of the Soviets (or any foreign rule)—was one of the first satellite states that implemented real change. In February of 1989, the Hungarian communist parliament, with little fanfare, essentially voted to put an expiration date on their own regime. There were three benchmarks in that fateful year: May 2, when Hungary was the first Soviet Bloc country to effectively open its borders to the West (by removing its border fence with Austria); June 16, when communist reformer Imre Nagy and his comrades were given a proper, ceremonial reburial on Heroes' Square; and August 19, when, in the first tentative steps toward the reunification of Europe, Hungarians and Austrians came together in a field near the town of Sopron for the so-called "Pan-European Picnic." (Some 900 East Germans seized this opportunity to make a run for the border...and slipped into the West when Hungarian border guards refused their orders to shoot defectors.) On October 23—the anniversary of the 1956 Uprising—the truly democratic Republic of Hungary triumphantly replaced the People's Republic of Hungary.

Hungary's first post-communist president, Árpád Göncz, was a protester from the 1950s who was famous for learning English while in prison...a skill that later came in handy when he translated *The Lord of the Rings* into Hungarian. Fantasy was becoming a reality in Hungary. Change was in the air.

HUNGARY TODAY (1989-PRESENT)

The transition from communism to capitalism has been rocky in Hungary. While many Hungarians were eager for the freedom to travel and pursue the interests that democracy allowed them, many others struggled to cope with the sudden reduction of government-provided services. Hungary has had an even more difficult transition than some of its neighbors, as post-communist governments have attempted to preserve as many social services as possible while stepping down taxation—leaving Hungary with rampant inflation unmatched in Europe (and bringing back unpleasant memories of the *pengő* debacle of the 1940s).

The process of privatization (returning property once seized by the communist government to its original owners) has been messy. When possible, the government attempted to find the original owners of the property, and allow them to purchase it at a low price. But this was often difficult, or impossible, to do (especially considering that one in 10 Hungarians did not survive World War II). And so, in other cases, people were simply given the opportunity to purchase the apartment or house where they were living on the day of the transition. If you had a nice apartment, this was good news; if not, you were out of luck.

In 2004, Hungary took the monumental step of joining the European Union (along with nine other, mostly former-communist nations). Many of the new members demonstrated great ambivalence about joining the EU, fearing that they would lose their hard-fought autonomy. And EU membership has come with its

Viktor Orbán and Fidesz: Reshaping Hungary in the 21st Century

Prime Minister Viktor Orbán came of age during Hungary's transition from communism to democracy. Today he leads his party (Fidesz) and his nation with a populist authoritarianism that pleases his traditional supporters even as it outrages both Hungarian and international critics.

Born in the town of Székesfehérvár in 1963, Orbán had a varied career before entering the political realm: He got a law degree, played professional soccer, and studied political philosophy at England's Oxford University. In 1989, when he was just 25, an unkempt, rabble-rousing Orbán made his name when he delivered a stirring speech at Imre Nagy's ceremonial reburial on Heroes' Square. By that time, he had already co-founded the Fidesz party (the Federation of Young Democrats, later renamed the Hungarian Civic Alliance). Through the 1990s, this youthful, anti-communist party evolved into Hungary's dominant right-wing political institution, and in 1998, Orbán became prime minister of Hungary at age 35. He quickly moved to consolidate his power, tweaking the still-fledgling system of government to his advantage—a practice that his critics say has been typical of his entire political career.

In 2002, Fidesz lost power to a left-wing coalition. But Orbán continued to agitate in opposition, and watched as the Hungarian left imploded under Prime Minister Ferenc Gyurcsány. Fidesz won the 2010 elections in a landslide—giving Orbán not only the prime ministership, but a two-thirds majority in the parliament that he took as a mandate to completely remake Hungary:

share of heavy-handed regulation and convoluted bureaucracy. The question of whether Hungary is better off with or without the EU continues, as the ruling Fidesz regime is sternly Euroskeptic.

Hungary has often been in the international news over the last several years, as its fitful transition to democracy has taken some attention-grabbing turns. The Hungarian Socialist Party (MSzP), which took control of parliament in 2002, stubbornly maintained and even extended some social programs, despite worries that mounting public debt would bankrupt the country. After they won re-election in April of 2006, Prime Minister Ferenc Gyurcsány gave a shockingly frank "wake-up call" speech to his party's leaders. Al-adopting a new constitution, restricting media freedom, renaming streets and squares around the capital, reforming the educational system, and revising Hungarian history by tearing down old monuments and erecting new ones.

The plainspoken Orbán is famous for wearing a children's soccer backpack as a symbol of his down-to-earth connection to the people. He also considers himself the standard bearer of Hungary's Christian historical tradition. He takes advantage both of his faith and of hot-button Hungarian issues (such as lingering resentment over the loss of territory after World War I) to curry favor with his base.

Most Hungarians you'll likely meet (i.e., progressive urbanites in the tourist trade) have nothing good to say about Orbán or Fidesz, and you may wonder: Who's voting for these people? But Fidesz's base is similar to George W. Bush's in the United States, or Vladimir Putin's in Russia: traditional, proudly nationalistic, somewhat insular voters in small towns and the countryside who appreciate their leader's willingness to take a stand for their deeply held values.

Many international observers—who fear Hungary's very democracy is in peril—will be watching the 2018 elections carefully, while others write off Fidesz's rise as the natural pendulum swing of politics. Will Orbán's reign run its natural course? Or will his reforms prove successful enough to keep Fidesz enshrined in power in the long term, potentially threatening the very fabric of Hungary's democracy? Stay tuned.

though his remarks were intended to be kept secret, someone recorded it. A few months later, on September 17, Hungarians turned on their TVs to hear their prime minister detailing the ways he and his party had driven their country to the brink of ruin: "We have screwed up. Not a little but a lot. No country in Europe has screwed up as much as we have... We did not actually do anything for four years. Nothing... We lied morning, noon, and night." The release of the tape sparked protests—which occasionally turned violent—as furious demonstrators demanded Gyurcsány's resignation. He refused.

Rampant inflation continued to wrack the country. In late 2008, with Gyurcsány warning of "state bankruptcy" and a currency collapse, Hungary received a $25 billion bailout package from the EU, International Monetary Fund, and World Bank. Gyurcsány finally resigned in early 2009, acknowledging that he was getting in the way of Hungary's economic recovery.

Viktor Orbán, of the nationalistic, right-of-center Fidesz

Party, became prime minister in a landslide in May of 2010. Fidesz—a strange hybrid of populist and authoritarian—stands for traditional Christian and Hungarian values, economic interventionism, and a healthy skepticism toward European Union membership. Orbán has said his goal for Hungary is an "illiberal democracy." (For more on Orbán and Fidesz, see the sidebar.)

Orbán seized on his two-thirds majority to adopt a new, Fidesz-favorable constitution that stripped away checks and balances and entrenched party leaders in institutions that had previously been considered apolitical. Almost immediately, international observers—including the EU and US—grew concerned.

In early 2011, Orbán's party created a new FCC-like media authority with broad latitude for suppressing material that it considers inappropriate. Fidesz also extended Hungarian citizenship to people of Hungarian descent living in neighboring countries. This stoked century-old Hungarian resentment about the territorial losses from the post-World War I Treaty of Trianon. Orbán also insists on flying the flag of Transylvania (a part of Hungary that was lost in Trianon)—and not the EU flag—above the Hungarian Parliament.

Fidesz has a penchant for reinterpreting Hungarian history—rehabilitating some figures (such as Miklós Horthy, who led Hungary between the two World Wars—and forged an alliance with Hitler's Nazi Germany), while brushing other, less Fidesz-friendly figures under the rug. The party went on a renaming binge—rechristening more than two dozen streets, squares, and other features of Budapest—and have been aggressive about tearing down old monuments and erecting new ones. (For more on this, see the Leopold Town Walk chapter.)

On a positive note, Fidesz has also been proactive about funneling European Union funds into public-works projects, and Budapest has made stunning progress in renovating formerly dreary streets and squares. But this always seems to come with a Fidesz-approved aesthetic that evokes the party's values. Some critics have described these new spaces—vast and bombastic, as if designed to trumpet historical greatness and host military parades—as "fascistic."

Other Orbán and Fidesz policies have also been controversial—from nationalizing the school system (the same Fidesz-approved textbooks are now used in every school in Hungary) to proposing a per-use Internet tax. (That last one resulted in enormous public protests in the fall of 2014, and Orbán quickly backpedaled.) In 2014, Orbán spoke favorably about Vladimir Putin, whose authoritarian ruling style has been compared to his own.

Outrageous as Fidesz seems to younger, EU-supporting, highly educated Hungarians, the party pleased its base enough to easily retain its power in the 2014 parliamentary elections. (Fidesz's control of the media didn't hurt its chances either.) Many international observers worry that Fidesz's success could be the death knell for true democracy in Hungary. Whether Orbán can continue to ride his wave of popularity remains to be seen.

Fortunately, tourists visiting today's Hungary are scarcely aware of its political squabbles. The Hungarian people—relieved to be free of oppression, and allowed to pursue their lovably quirky customs with a renewed vigor—enthusiastically welcome and charm visitors. It's been a long road for the Hungarians from those distant, windblown steppes of Central Asia...but today they seem to be doing better than ever.

PRACTICALITIES

Contents

This chapter covers the practical skills of European travel: how to get tourist information, pay for purchases, sightsee efficiently, use technology wisely, and get between destinations smoothly. To study ahead and round out your knowledge, check out "Resources" for a summary of recommended books and films.

Tourist Information

The Hungarian National Tourist Office **in the US** is a wealth of information. Before your trip, contact their office to request brochures on topics or regions that interest you. Call 212/695-1221 or visit www.gotohungary.com.

In Hungary, Budapest has its own tourism organization, called Budapest Info (www.budapestinfo.hu), with several branches in the city (for details, see page 30). Other towns have their own local tourist information offices, which all belong to a large government agency called "TourInform"; these are marked by a white *i* in a green rectangle (www.tourinform.hu). Tourist offices vary in quality; those in some of the smaller towns (including Eger's) can be excellent, while Budapest's are hit-or-miss. Remember that tourist information offices are abbreviated "TI" in this book.

TIs are good places to get a city map and information on public transit (including bus and train schedules), walking tours, special events, and nightlife.

Travel Tips

Emergency and Medical Help: The all-purpose emergency number in Hungary is 112. You can also call 107 for police, 104 for ambulance, or 105 for fire. If you get sick, do as the Hungarians do and go to a pharmacy (*gyógyszertár* or *patika*) for advice. Or ask at your hotel for help; they'll know of the nearest medical and emergency services. Embassies can recommend English-speaking doctors (see contact information on page 511). Budapest also has a private, English-speaking medical center (see page 31).

Theft or Loss: To replace a passport, you'll need to go in person to an embassy or consulate (see page 511). If your credit and debit cards disappear, cancel and replace them (see "Damage Control for Lost Cards" on page 482). File a police report, either on the spot or within a day or two; you'll need it to submit an insurance claim for lost or stolen rail passes or travel gear, and it can help with replacing your passport or credit and debit cards. For more information, see www.ricksteves.com/help. Precautionary measures can minimize the effects of loss—back up your photos and other files frequently.

Borders: There are no passport checks when traveling between Hungary and the 25 other open-borders Schengen Agreement countries (including neighbors Slovakia, Austria, and Slovenia; Croatia is scheduled to join in 2016). At airports, by car, or by train, you'll simply zip through the border without stopping. (Hungary's southern and eastern neighbors—Croatia, Serbia, Romania, and Ukraine—have not yet joined Schengen, so you'll need to show your passport when entering any of those places.) Even as borders fade, when you change countries, you must still change telephone cards, postage stamps, and underpants.

Time Zones: Hungary is generally six/nine hours ahead of the East/West Coasts of the US. The exceptions are the beginning and end of Daylight Saving Time: Hungary and Europe "spring forward" the last Sunday in March (two weeks after most of North America), and "fall back" the last Sunday in October (one week before North America). For a handy online time converter, try www.timeanddate.com/worldclock.

Business Hours: Most stores are open Monday through Friday (roughly 10:00-18:00), with a late night on Thursday (until 20:00 or 21:00). On Saturday, shops are usually open only from

10:00 to 13:00 or 14:00. Sundays have the same pros and cons as they do for travelers in the US: Sightseeing attractions are generally open; shops, banks, and markets are closed; public-transportation options are fewer; and city traffic is light. Rowdy evenings are rare on Sundays.

Many businesses, as well as many museums, close on Good Friday, Easter, and New Year's Day. On Christmas, virtually everything closes down. Museums are also generally closed December 24 and 26; smaller shops are usually closed December 26.

Watt's Up? Europe's electrical system is 220 volts, instead of North America's 110 volts. Most newer electronics (such as laptops, battery chargers, and hair dryers) convert automatically, so you won't need a converter, but you will need an adapter plug with two round prongs, sold inexpensively at travel stores in the US. Avoid bringing older appliances that don't automatically convert voltage; instead, buy a cheap replacement in Europe.

Discounts: Discounts aren't listed in this book. However, many Hungarian sights offer discounts for youths (under 18) and students with proper identification cards (www.isic.org). Always ask. Some discounts are available only for citizens of the European Union (EU).

Online Translation Tip: While most Budapest-based websites have a built-in English version (just click on the "EN" or British flag), small-town Hungarian websites may be in Hungarian only. You can use Google's Chrome browser (available free at www.google.com/chrome) to instantly translate websites. With one click, the page appears in (very rough) English translation. You can also paste the URL of the site into the translation window at www.google.com/translate.

Money

This section covers advice on how to pay for purchases on your trip (including getting cash from ATMs and paying with plastic), dealing with lost or stolen cards, VAT (sales tax) refunds, and tipping.

WHAT TO BRING

Bring both a credit card and a debit card. You'll use the debit card at cash machines (ATMs) to withdraw local cash for most purchases, and the credit card to pay for larger items. Some travelers carry a third card, in case one gets demagnetized or eaten by a temperamental machine.

For an emergency stash, bring several hundred dollars in hard cash in $20 bills. If you need to exchange the bills, go to a bank; avoid using currency-exchange booths because of their lousy rates and/or outrageous fees.

Exchange Rates

Hungary still uses its traditional currency, the **forint** (abbreviated Ft, or sometimes HUF). Check www.oanda.com for the latest exchange rates.

225 Ft = about $1

To very roughly convert prices in forints to dollars, divide by two and drop the last two digits. For example, 1,000 Ft = about $5 (actually $4.50), 5,000 Ft = about $25 (actually $22), and 10,000 Ft = about $50 (actually $44.50). The exchange rate has fluctuated wildly in recent years—these are just rough estimates.

While Hungary is on track to adopt the Europe-wide **euro** currency, it likely won't happen for several years. However, you might already see some prices (especially hotel rates in Budapest) listed in euros for the convenience of international visitors. Even when you see prices listed in euros, locals gladly accept (and sometimes prefer) payment in forints. Hungary's neighbors Slovakia (whose capital, Bratislava, is included in this book), Austria, and Slovenia all use the euro:

1 euro (€) = about $1.40

To roughly convert prices in euros to dollars, add 40 percent: €20 is about $28, €50 is about $70, and so on.

So, that 1,500-Ft canister of paprika costs about $7, that €25 meal in Bratislava is about $35, and that 13,000-Ft taxi ride through Budapest is...uh-oh.

CASH

Cash is just as desirable in Europe as it is at home. Small businesses (mom-and-pop cafés, shops, etc.) prefer that you pay your bills with cash. Some vendors will charge you extra for using a credit card, and some won't take credit cards at all. Cash is the best—and often only—way to pay for cheap food, transit tickets, and local guides.

Throughout Europe, ATMs are the standard way for travelers to get cash. In Hungary, ATMs are called *bankjegy-automata* (BONK-yedge OW-toh-maw-taw). Most Hungarians also recognize the international term *Bankomat*.

To withdraw money from an ATM, you'll need a debit card (ideally with a Visa or MasterCard logo for maximum usability), plus a PIN code. Know your PIN code in numbers; there are only numbers—no letters—on European keypads. For increased security, shield the keypad when entering your PIN code, and don't use an ATM if anything on the front of the machine looks loose or damaged (a sign that someone may have attached a "skimming" device to capture account information). Try to withdraw large sums of money to reduce the number of per-transaction bank fees you'll pay.

When possible, use ATMs located outside banks—a thief is less likely to target a cash machine near surveillance cameras, and if your card is munched by a machine, you can go inside for help. Stay away from "independent" ATMs such as Travelex, Euronet, Moneybox, Cardpoint, and Cashzone, which charge huge commissions, have terrible exchange rates, and may try to trick users with "dynamic currency conversion" (described at the end of "Credit and Debit Cards," next).

Although you can use a credit card for an ATM transaction, it only makes sense in an emergency, because it's considered a cash advance (borrowed at a high interest rate) rather than a withdrawal. Try to withdraw large sums of money to reduce the number of per-transaction bank fees you'll pay.

While traveling, if you want to monitor your accounts online to detect any unauthorized transactions, be sure to use a secure connection (see page 497).

Avoid using currency exchange booths, which generally offer lousy rates and/or charge excessive fees. One exception is if you are traveling between countries that have different currencies (say, from Hungary to Slovakia or Croatia). Coins can't be exchanged once you leave the country, so try to spend them before you cross the border. But bills are easy to convert to the "new" country's currency. Regular banks have the best rates. Post offices and train stations usually change money if you can't get to a bank.

Pickpockets target tourists. To safeguard your cash, wear a money belt—a pouch with a strap that you buckle around your waist like a belt and tuck under your clothes. Keep your cash, credit cards, and passport secure in your money belt, and carry only a day's spending money in your front pocket.

CREDIT AND DEBIT CARDS

For purchases, Visa and MasterCard are more commonly accepted than American Express. Just like at home, credit or debit cards work easily at larger hotels, restaurants, and shops, but most prefer cash—and small vendors require it. I typically use my debit card to withdraw cash to pay for most purchases. I use my credit card only in a few specific situations: to book hotel reservations, to cover major expenses (such as car rentals, plane tickets, and long hotel stays), to buy theater tickets or other admissions online, and to pay for things near the end of my trip (to avoid another visit to the ATM). While you could use a debit card to make most large purchases, using a credit card offers a greater degree of fraud protection (because debit cards draw funds directly from your account).

Ask Your Credit- or Debit-Card Company: Before your trip, contact the company that issued your debit or credit cards.

• Confirm that your card **will work overseas,** and alert them that you'll be using it in Europe; otherwise, they may deny transactions if they perceive unusual spending patterns.

• Ask for the specifics on transaction **fees.** When you use your credit or debit card—either for purchases or ATM withdrawals—you'll typically be charged additional "international transaction" fees of up to 3 percent (1 percent is normal) plus $5 per transaction. If your card's fees seem high, consider getting a different card just for your trip: Capital One (www.capitalone.com) and most credit unions have low-to-no international fees.

• If you plan to withdraw cash from ATMs, confirm your daily **withdrawal limit,** and if necessary, ask your bank to adjust it. Some travelers prefer a high limit that allows them to take out more cash at each ATM stop (saving on bank fees), while others prefer to set a lower limit in case their card is stolen. Note that foreign banks also set maximum withdrawal amounts for their ATMs.

• Get your bank's emergency **phone number** in the US (but not its 800 number, which isn't accessible from overseas) to call collect if you have a problem.

• Ask for your credit card's **PIN** in case you need to make an emergency cash withdrawal or encounter Europe's "chip-and-PIN" system; the bank won't tell you your PIN over the phone, so allow time for it to be mailed to you.

Chip and PIN: While much of Europe is shifting to a "chip-and-PIN" system for credit and debit cards, Hungary still uses the old magnetic-swipe technology. (European chip-and-PIN cards are embedded with an electronic chip, and require the purchaser to punch in a PIN rather than sign a receipt.) If you happen to encounter chip and PIN, it will probably be at payment machines, such as those at toll roads or self-serve gas pumps. On the outside chance that a machine won't take your card, find a cashier who can make your card work (they can print a receipt for you to sign), or find a machine that takes cash. But don't panic. Most travelers who are carrying only magnetic-stripe cards don't run into problems. You can always use an ATM to withdraw cash with your magnetic-stripe card, even in countries where people predominantly use chip-and-PIN cards.

Dynamic Currency Conversion: If merchants offer to convert your purchase price into dollars (called dynamic currency conversion, or DCC), refuse this "service." You'll pay even more in fees for the expensive convenience of seeing your charge in dollars. "Independent" ATMs (such as Travelex and Moneybox) may try to confuse customers by presenting DCC in misleading terms. If an ATM offers to "lock in" or "guarantee" your conversion rate, choose "proceed without conversion." Other prompts might state, "You can be charged in dollars: Press YES for dollars, NO for forints." Always choose the local currency in these situations.

Damage Control for Lost Cards

If you lose your credit, debit, or ATM card, you can stop people from using it by reporting the loss immediately to the respective global customer-assistance centers. Call these 24-hour US numbers collect: Visa (tel. 303/967-1096), MasterCard (tel. 636/722-7111), and American Express (tel. 336/393-1111). European toll-free numbers (listed by country) can be found at the websites for Visa and MasterCard.

Providing the following information will allow for a quicker cancellation of your missing card: full card number, whether you are the primary or secondary cardholder; the cardholder's name exactly as printed on the card; billing address; home phone number; circumstances of the loss or theft; and identification verification (your birth date, your mother's maiden name, or your Social Security number—memorize this, don't carry a copy). If you are the secondary cardholder, you'll also need to provide the primary cardholder's identification-verification details. You can generally receive a temporary card within two or three business days in Europe (see www.ricksteves.com/help for more).

If you report your loss within two days, you typically won't be responsible for any unauthorized transactions on your account, although many banks charge a liability fee of $50.

TIPPING

Tipping in Hungary isn't as automatic or as generous as in the US. For special service, tips are appreciated, but not expected. As in the US, the proper amount depends on your resources, tipping philosophy, and the circumstances, but some general guidelines apply.

Restaurants: Tipping is an issue only at restaurants that have table service. If you order your food at a counter, don't tip.

Most Budapest restaurants automatically tack on a 10 to 12 percent service charge. Check for it as a line-item at the end of bill: Look for "service," "tip," *felszolgálási díj*, or *szervízdíj*. If you see this charge, an additional tip is not necessary for adequate service. However, if the service charge isn't included, most servers expect about a 10 percent tip (though a bit less is fine, if it rounds to a convenient total). More than 10 percent is reserved only for exemplary service, and 15 percent verges on extravagant. For example, for a 3,650-Ft bill with no service charge, I'd hand over 4,000 Ft (that's a 350-Ft tip, or a bit more than 9 percent—perfectly acceptable). If you're not sure whether your bill includes the tip, just ask. In smaller cities and towns outside Budapest, it's very rare for the service charge to be tacked on—rounding the bill up 10 percent is more than enough.

Taxis: For a typical ride, round up about 10 percent (for instance, if the fare is 1,350 Ft, pay 1,500 Ft). If the cabbie hauls your bags and zips you to the airport to help you catch your flight, you might want to toss in a little more. But if you feel like you're being driven in circles or otherwise ripped off, skip the tip.

Special Services: In general, if someone in the service industry does a super job for you, a small tip (200-400 Ft) is appropriate...but not required. If you're not sure whether (or how much) to tip for a service, ask your hotelier or the TI.

GETTING A VAT REFUND

Wrapped into the purchase price of your Hungarian souvenirs is a Value-Added Tax (VAT) of about 27 percent. You're entitled to get most of that tax back if you purchase more than 52,000 Ft (about $231) worth of goods at a store that participates in the VAT-refund scheme. Typically, you must ring up the minimum at a single retailer—you can't add up your purchases from various shops to reach the required amount.

Getting your refund is usually straightforward and, if you buy a substantial amount of souvenirs, well worth the hassle. If you're lucky, the merchant will subtract the tax when you make your purchase. (This is more likely to occur if the store ships the goods to your home.) Otherwise, you'll need to:

Get the paperwork. Have the merchant completely fill out the necessary refund document, called a "Tax-Free Shopping Cheque." You'll have to present your passport. Get the paperwork done before you leave the store to ensure you'll have everything you need (including your original sales receipt).

Get your stamp at the border or airport. Process your VAT document at your last stop in the European Union (such as at the airport) with the customs agent who deals with VAT refunds. Arrive an additional hour before you need to check in for your flight to allow time to find the local customs office—and to stand in line. It's best to keep your purchases in your carry-on. If they're too large or dangerous to carry on (such as knives), pack them in your checked bags and alert the check-in agent. You'll be sent (with your tagged bag) to a customs desk outside security, which will examine your bag, stamp your paperwork, and put your bag on the belt. You're not supposed to use your purchased goods before you leave. If you show up at customs wearing your new communist-kitsch T-shirt, officials might look the other way—or deny you a refund.

Collect your refund. You'll need to return your stamped document to the retailer or its representative. Many merchants work with services, such as Global Blue or Premier Tax Free, that have

PRACTICALITIES

offices at major airports, ports, or border crossings (either before or after security, probably strategically located near a duty-free shop). These services, which extract a 4 percent fee, can refund your money immediately in cash or credit your card (within two billing cycles). If the retailer handles VAT refunds directly, it's up to you to contact the merchant for your refund. You can mail the documents from home, or more quickly, from your point of departure (using an envelope you've prepared in advance or one that's been provided by the merchant). You'll then have to wait—it can take months.

CUSTOMS FOR AMERICAN SHOPPERS

You are allowed to take home $800 worth of items per person duty-free, once every 30 days. You can take home many processed and packaged foods: vacuum-packed cheeses, dried herbs or spices (like paprika), jams, baked goods, candy, chocolate, oil, vinegar, mustard, and honey. Fresh fruits and vegetables and most meats are not allowed, with exceptions for some canned items. As for alcohol, you can bring in one liter duty-free (it can be packed securely in your checked luggage, along with any other liquid-containing items).

To bring alcohol (or liquid-packed foods) in your carry-on bag on your flight home, buy it at a duty-free shop at the airport. You'll increase your odds of getting it onto a connecting flight if it's packaged in a "STEB"—a secure, tamper-evident bag. But stay away from liquids in opaque, ceramic, or metallic containers, which usually cannot be successfully screened (STEB or no STEB).

For details on allowable goods, customs rules, and duty rates, visit www.cbp.gov.

Sightseeing

Many of Budapest's museums are dusty and a bit old-fashioned. But with patience and imagination, and a solid background in the topic (provided by this book's descriptions, self-guided tours, in-depth sidebars, and the Hungary: Past and Present chapter), Budapest's sights come to life and become genuinely enthralling.

Sightseeing can be hard work. Use these tips to make your visits to Budapest's big sights meaningful, fun, efficient, and painless.

PLAN AHEAD

Set up an itinerary that allows you to fit in all your must-see sights. For a one-stop look at opening hours, see "Budapest at a Glance" on page 50. Most sights keep stable hours, but you can easily confirm the latest by asking the local TI.

Don't put off visiting a must-see sight—you never know when a place will close unexpectedly. On holidays (see list on page 512), expect reduced hours or closures.

To get the most out of the self-guided tours and sight descriptions in this book, reread them the night before your visit. A walk through the communist relics at Memento Park, for instance, is more meaningful if you've read up on the Soviet era the night before. When you arrive at the sight, use the overview map to get the lay of the land and the basic tour route.

When possible, visit key museums first thing (when your energy is best) and save other activities for the afternoon. Hit a sight's highlights first, then see the rest if you have the stamina and time. Going at the right time can also help you avoid crowds. This book offers specific tips on a few of Budapest's most crowded sights.

AT SIGHTS

Here's what you can typically expect:

Entering: Be warned that you may not be allowed to enter if you arrive 30 to 60 minutes before closing time. And guards start ushering people out well before the actual closing time, so don't save the best for last.

Some sights (including the Parliament, Great Synagogue, and Holocaust Memorial Center) have metal detectors that will slow your entry, while others require you to check daypacks and coats. (If you'd rather not check your daypack, try carrying it tucked under your arm like a purse as you enter.)

At churches—which often offer interesting art and a cool, welcome seat—a modest dress code (no bare shoulders or shorts) is encouraged.

Photography: If the museum's photo policy isn't clearly posted, ask a guard. Generally, taking photos without a flash or tripod is allowed. Some sights ban photos altogether.

Temporary Exhibits: Museums may show special exhibits in addition to their permanent collection. Some exhibits are included in the entry price, but most come at an extra cost (which you may have to pay even if you don't want to see the exhibit).

Once inside, you'll generally follow a confusing one-way tour route through a maze of rooms with squeaky parquet floors, monitored by grumpy grannies who listlessly point you in the right direction.

While most museums label exhibits in English, most don't post full descriptions; you'll have to buy a book, rent an audioguide (described later), or borrow laminated translations. In a few cases, none of these is available.

Expect Changes: Items can be on tour, on loan, out sick, or shifted at the whim of the curator. To adapt, pick up a floor plans as you enter, and ask museum staff if you can't find a particular item.

Audioguides: Some Budapest museums rent audioguides, which generally offer dry recorded descriptions in English. If you

PRACTICALITIES

bring your own earbuds, you can enjoy better sound and free your hands up (rather than having to hold the device to your ear). To save money, share one audioguide with your travel partner: Bring a Y-jack for your headphones, or listen cheek to cheek. Increasingly, museums are offering apps (often free) that you can download to your mobile device.

Services: Important sights may have an on-site café or cafeteria (usually a handy place to rejuvenate during a long visit). The WCs at sights are usually free and generally clean.

Before Leaving: At the gift shop, scan the postcard rack or thumb through a guidebook to be sure that you haven't overlooked something that you'd like to see.

Every sight and museum offers more than what is covered in this book. Use the self-guided tours in this book as an introduction—not the final word.

Communicating

"How can I stay connected in Europe?"—by phone and online—may be the most common question I hear from travelers. You have three basic options:

1. "Roam" with your US mobile device. This is the easiest option, but likely the most expensive. It works best for people who won't be making very many calls, and who value the convenience of sticking with what's familiar (and their own phone number). In recent years, as data roaming fees have dropped and free Wi-Fi has become easier to find, the majority of travelers are finding this to be the best all-around option.

2. Use an unlocked mobile phone with European SIM cards. This is a much more affordable option if you'll be making lots of calls, since it gives you 24/7 access to low European rates. Although remarkably cheap, this option does require a bit of shopping around for the right phone and a prepaid SIM card. Savvy travelers who routinely buy European SIM cards swear by this tactic.

3. Use public phones, and get online with your hotel's guest computer and/or at Internet cafés. These options work particularly well for travelers who simply don't want to hassle with the technology, or want to be (mostly) untethered from their home life while on the road.

Each of these options is explained in greater detail in the following pages. Mixing and matching works well. For example, I routinely bring along my smartphone for Internet chores and Skyping on Wi-Fi, but also carry an unlocked phone and buy SIM cards for affordable calls on the go.

For an even more in-depth explanation of this complicated topic, see www.ricksteves.com/phoning.

How to Dial

Many Americans are intimidated by dialing European phone numbers. You needn't be. It's simple, once you break the code.

Dialing Domestically Within Hungary

Like many things in Hungary, making domestic calls is uniquely confusing. You must dial different codes depending on whether you're calling locally or long distance within the country. The following instructions apply whether you're dialing from a Hungarian mobile phone or a landline (such as a pay phone or your hotel-room phone). If you're roaming with a US phone number, follow the "Dialing Internationally" directions described later.

To dial a number in the same city, simply dial direct, with no area code.

To dial long-distance within Hungary, add the prefix 06, followed by the area code (e.g., Budapest's area code is 1, so you dial 06-1, then the rest of the number).

For example, to call a hotel in Eger, I'd dial 411-711 if I was calling from within Eger; but from Budapest, I'd have to dial 06, then 36 (Eger's area code), then 411-711.

Dialing Internationally to or from Hungary

Always start with the **international access code**—011 if you're calling from the US or Canada, 00 from anywhere in Europe. If you're dialing from a mobile phone, simply insert a + instead (by holding the 0 key).

Dial the **country code** of the country you're calling (36 for Hungary, or 1 for the US or Canada).

Then dial the **local number.** Include the area code, if applicable (many countries require dropping the initial zero). The European Calling Chart lists specifics per country.

Calling from the US to Hungary: To call the Eger hotel from the US, dial 011 (US access code), 36 (Hungary's country code), 36 (Eger's area code), then 411-711.

Calling from any European country to the US: To call my office in Edmonds, Washington, from anywhere in Europe, I dial 00 (Europe's access code), 1 (US country code), 425 (Edmonds' area code), and 771-8303.

Dialing Mobile Phones and Other Unusual Numbers

Certain Hungarian phone numbers are particularly confusing to dial. Numbers beginning with 0620, 0630, or 0670 are mobile phones; those beginning with 0680 are toll-free; and 0681 and 0690 are expensive toll lines. The way you dial these numbers de-

Hurdling the Language Barrier

The language barrier in Hungary is no bigger than elsewhere in Europe. In fact, as a monolingual visitor, I find that it's actually easier to communicate in Hungary than in places such as Italy or France. Since Hungary is small and not politically powerful, the people here realize that it's unreasonable to expect visitors to learn Hungarian (which has only 12 million speakers worldwide). It's essential for them to find a common language with the rest of the world—so they learn English early and well. You'll find that most people in the tourist industry—and virtually all young people—speak fine English.

Of course, not *everyone* speaks English. You'll run into the most substantial language barriers in situations when you need to deal with a less highly educated clerk or service person (train station and post-office counters, maids, museum guards, bakers, and so on)—especially outside of Budapest. Be reasonable in your expectations. Museum ticket-sellers in Hungary are every bit as friendly and multilingual as they are in the US.

Luckily, it's relatively easy to get your point across in these places. I've often bought a train ticket simply by writing out the name of my destination; the time I want to travel (using the 24-hour clock); and the date I want to leave (year first, then month,

pends on where you're calling from, and whether you're calling from a fixed line or a mobile phone.

To call these numbers **from a fixed line within Hungary,** simply dial them direct, as they appear in this book.

To dial them **from a fixed line outside of Hungary,** you need to replace the initial 06 with other numbers: From the US, replace the 06 with 011-36. From other European countries, replace the 06 with 00-36. Then dial the rest of the number.

To dial them **from a mobile phone** (whether within or outside of Hungary), replace the initial 06 with +36, then dial the rest of the number.

So, to call my favorite Budapest guide from a fixed line inside Hungary, you'd dial 0620-926-0557; from North America, you'd dial 011-36-20-926-0557; and from another European country, you'd dial 00-36-20-926-0557. From any mobile phone, you'd dial +36-20-926-0557.

More Dialing Tips

The chart on page 490 shows how to dial per country. For online instructions, see www.countrycallingcodes.com or www.howtocallabroad.com.

Remember, if you're using a mobile phone, dial as if you're in that phone's country of origin. So, when roaming with your US then day). Here's an example of what I'd show a ticket-seller at a train station: "Eger, 10:30, 2016.8.15."

Hungarians, realizing that their language intimidates Americans, often invent easier nicknames for themselves—so András becomes "Andrew," Erzsébet goes by "Elisabeth," and István tells you, "Call me Steve."

There are certain universal English words all Hungarians know: "hello," "please," "thank you," "super," "pardon," "stop," "menu," "problem," and "no problem." While Hungarians don't expect you to be fluent in their tongue, they definitely appreciate it when they can tell you're making an effort to pronounce Hungarian words correctly or to use the local pleasantries. For pronunciation tips, see page 14. For survival phrases in Hungarian, see page 517.

Don't be afraid to interact with locals. Hungarians might initially seem shy, overly formal, or even brusque (a holdover from the closed communist society)—but usually a simple smile is the only icebreaker you need to make a new friend. You'll find that doors open a little more quickly when you know a few words of the language. Give it your best shot. The locals will appreciate your efforts.

phone number in Hungary, dial as if you're calling from the US. But if you're using a European SIM card, dial as you would from that European country. Note that calls to a European mobile phone are substantially more expensive than calls to a fixed line. Off-hour calls are generally cheaper.

USING YOUR SMARTPHONE IN EUROPE

Even in this age of email, texting, and near-universal Internet access, smart travelers still use the telephone. I call TIs to smooth out sightseeing plans, hotels to get driving directions, museums to confirm tour schedules, restaurants to check open hours or to book a table, and so on.

Most people enjoy the convenience of bringing their own smartphone. Horror stories about sky-high roaming fees are dated and exaggerated, and major service providers work hard to avoid surprising you with an exorbitant bill. With a little planning, you can use your phone—for voice calls, messaging, and Internet access—without breaking the bank.

Start by figuring out whether your phone works in Europe. Most phones purchased through AT&T and T-Mobile (which use the same technology as Europe) work abroad, while only some phones from Verizon or Sprint do—check your operating manual

PRACTICALITIES

European Calling Chart

Just smile and dial, using this key:
AC = Area Code, LN = Local Number.

European Country	Calling long distance within ...	Calling from the US or Canada to ...	Calling from a European country to ...
Austria	AC + LN	011 + 43 + AC (without initial zero) + LN	00 + 43 + AC (without initial zero) + LN
Belgium	LN	011 + 32 + LN (without initial zero)	00 + 32 + LN (without initial zero)
Bosnia-Herzegovina	AC + LN	011 + 387 + AC (without initial zero) + LN	00 + 387 + AC (without initial zero) + LN
Croatia	AC + LN	011 + 385 + AC (without initial zero) + LN	00 + 385 + AC (without initial zero) + LN
Czech Republic	LN	011 + 420 + LN	00 + 420 + LN
Denmark	LN	011 + 45 + LN	00 + 45 + LN
Estonia	LN	011 + 372 + LN	00 + 372 + LN
Finland	AC + LN	011 + 358 + AC (without initial zero) + LN	999 (or other 900 number) + 358 + AC (without initial zero) + LN
France	LN	011 + 33 + LN (without initial zero)	00 + 33 + LN (without initial zero)
Germany	AC + LN	011 + 49 + AC (without initial zero) + LN	00 + 49 + AC (without initial zero) + LN
Gibraltar	LN	011 + 350 + LN	00 + 350 + LN
Great Britain & N. Ireland	AC + LN	011 + 44 + AC (without initial zero) + LN	00 + 44 + AC (without initial zero) + LN
Greece	LN	011 + 30 + LN	00 + 30 + LN
Hungary	06 + AC + LN	011 + 36 + AC + LN	00 + 36 + AC + LN
Ireland	AC + LN	011 + 353 + AC (without initial zero) + LN	00 + 353 + AC (without initial zero) + LN
Italy	LN	011 + 39 + LN	00 + 39 + LN

European Country	Calling long distance within ...	Calling from the US or Canada to ...	Calling from a European country to ...
Latvia	LN	011 + 371 + LN	00 + 371 + LN
Montenegro	AC + LN	011 + 382 + AC (without initial zero) + LN	00 + 382 + AC (without initial zero) + LN
Morocco	LN	011 + 212 + LN (without initial zero)	00 + 212 + LN (without initial zero)
Netherlands	AC + LN	011 + 31 + AC (without initial zero) + LN	00 + 31 + AC (without initial zero) + LN
Norway	LN	011 + 47 + LN	00 + 47 + LN
Poland	LN	011 + 48 + LN	00 + 48 + LN
Portugal	LN	011 + 351 + LN	00 + 351 + LN
Russia	8 + AC + LN	011 + 7 + AC + LN	00 + 7 + AC + LN
Slovakia	AC + LN	011 + 421 + AC (without initial zero) + LN	00 + 421 + AC (without initial zero) + LN
Slovenia	AC + LN	011 + 386 + AC (without initial zero) + LN	00 + 386 + AC (without initial zero) + LN
Spain	LN	011 + 34 + LN	00 + 34 + LN
Sweden	AC + LN	011 + 46 + AC (without initial zero) + LN	00 + 46 + AC (without initial zero) + LN
Switzerland	LN	011 + 41 + LN (without initial zero)	00 + 41 + LN (without initial zero)
Turkey	AC (if there's no initial zero, add one) + LN	011 + 90 + AC (without initial zero) + LN	00 + 90 + AC (without initial zero) + LN

- The instructions above apply whether you're calling to or from a European landline or mobile phone.
- If calling from any mobile phone, you can replace the international access code with "+" (press and hold 0 to insert it).
- The international access code is 011 if you're calling from the US or Canada.
- To call the US or Canada from Europe, dial 00, then 1 (country code for US and Canada), then the area code and number. In short, 00 + 1 + AC + LN = Hi, Mom!

(look for "tri-band," "quad-band," or "GSM"). If you're not sure, ask your service provider.

Roaming Costs

"Roaming" with your phone—that is, using it outside its home region, such as in Europe—generally comes with extra charges, whether you are making voice calls, sending texts, or reading your email. The fees listed here are for the three major American providers—Verizon, AT&T, and T-Mobile; Sprint's roaming rates tend to be much higher. But policies change fast, so get the latest details before your trip. For example, as of mid-2014, T-Mobile waived voice, texting, and data roaming fees for some plans.

Voice calls are the most expensive. Most US providers charge from $1.29 to $1.99 per minute to make or receive calls in Europe. (As you cross each border, you'll typically get a text message explaining the rates in the new country.) If you plan to make multiple calls, look into a global calling plan to lower the per-minute cost, or buy a package of minutes at a discounted price (such as 30 minutes for $30). Note that you'll be charged for incoming calls whether or not you answer them; to save money ask your friends to stay in contact by texting, and to call you only in case of an emergency.

Text messaging costs 20 to 50 cents per text. To cut that cost, you could sign up for an international messaging plan (for example, $10 for 100 texts). Or consider apps that let you text for free (iMessage for Apple, Google Hangouts for Android, or WhatsApp for any device); however, these require you to use Wi-Fi or data roaming. Be aware that Europeans use the term "SMS" ("short message service") to describe text messaging.

Data roaming means accessing data services via a cellular network other than your home carrier's. Prices have dropped dramatically in recent years, making this an affordable way for travelers to bridge gaps between Wi-Fi hotspots. You'll pay far less if you set up an international data roaming plan. Most providers charge $25-30 for 100-120 megabytes of data. That's plenty for basic Internet tasks—100 megabytes lets you view 100 websites or send/receive 1,000 text-based emails, but you'll burn through that amount quickly by streaming videos or music. If your data use exceeds your plan amount, most providers will automatically kick in an additional 100- or 120-megabyte block for the same price. (For more, see "Using Wi-Fi and Data Roaming," later.)

Setting Up (or Disabling) International Service

With most service providers, international roaming (voice, text, and data) is disabled on your account unless you activate it. Before your trip, call your provider (or navi-

gate their website), and cover the following topics:
• Confirm that your phone will work in Europe.
• Verify global roaming rates for voice calls, text messaging, and data.
• Tell them which of those services you'd like to activate.
• Consider add-on plans to bring down the cost of international calls, texts, or data roaming.

When you get home from Europe, be sure to cancel any add-on plans that you activated for your trip.

Some people would rather use their smartphone exclusively on Wi-Fi, and not worry about either voice or data charges. If that's you, call your provider to be sure that international roaming options are deactivated on your account. To be double-sure, put your phone in "airplane mode," then turn your Wi-Fi back on.

Using Wi-Fi and Data Roaming

A good approach is to use free Wi-Fi wherever possible, and fill in the gaps with data roaming.

Wi-Fi is readily available throughout Europe. At accommodations, access is usually free, but you may have to pay a fee, especially at expensive hotels. At hotels with thick stone walls, the Wi-Fi signal from the lobby may not reach every room. If Wi-Fi is important to you, ask about it when you book—and be specific ("In the rooms?"). Get the password and network name at the front desk when you check in.

When you're out and about, your best bet for finding free Wi-Fi is often at a café. They'll usually tell you the password if you buy something. Or you can stroll down a café-lined street, smartphone in hand, checking for unsecured networks every few steps until you find one that works. Some towns have free public Wi-Fi in highly trafficked parks or piazzas. You may have to register before using it, or get a password at the TI.

Data roaming is handy when you can't find Wi-Fi. Because you'll pay by the megabyte (explained earlier), it's best to limit how much data you use. Save bandwidth-gobbling tasks like Skyping, watching videos, or downloading apps or emails with large attachments until you're on Wi-Fi. Switch your phone's email settings from "push" to "fetch." This means that you can choose to "fetch" (download) your messages when you're on Wi-Fi rather than having them continuously "pushed" to your device. And be aware of apps—such as news, weather, and sports tickers—that automatically update. Check your phone's settings to be sure that none of your apps are set to "use cellular data."

I like the safeguard of manually turning off data roaming on my phone whenever I'm not actively using it. To turn off data and voice roaming, look in your phone's settings menu—try checking

Internet Calling

To make totally free voice and video calls over the Internet, all you need are a smartphone, tablet, or laptop; a strong Wi-Fi signal; and an account with one of the major Internet calling providers: Skype (www.skype.com), FaceTime (preloaded on most Apple devices), or Google+ Hangouts (www.google.com/hangouts). If the Wi-Fi signal isn't strong enough for video, try sticking with an audio-only call. Or...wait for your next hotel. Many Internet calling programs also work for making calls from your computer to telephones worldwide for a very reasonable fee—generally just a few cents per minute (you'll have to buy some credit before you make your first call).

under "cellular" or "network," or ask your service provider how to do it. If you need to get online but can't find Wi-Fi, simply turn on data roaming long enough for the task at hand, then turn it off again.

Figure out how to keep track of how much data you've used (in your phone's menu, look for "cellular data usage"; you may have to reset the counter at the start of your trip). Some companies automatically send you a text message warning if you approach or exceed your limit.

There's yet another option: If you're traveling with an unlocked smartphone (explained later), you can buy a SIM card that also includes data; this can be far cheaper than data roaming through your home provider.

USING EUROPEAN SIM CARDS

While using your American phone in Europe is easy, it's not always cheap. And unreliable Wi-Fi can make keeping in touch frustrating. If you're reasonably technology-savvy, and would like to have the option of making lots of affordable calls, it's worth getting comfortable with European SIM cards.

Here's the basic idea: With an unlocked phone (which works with different carriers; explained next), get a SIM card—the microchip that stores data about your phone—once you get to Europe. Slip in the SIM, turn on the phone, and bingo! You've got a European phone number (and access to cheaper European rates).

Getting an Unlocked Phone

Your basic options are getting your existing phone unlocked, or buying a phone (either at home or in Europe).

Some phones are electronically "locked" so that you can't switch SIM cards (keeping you loyal to your carrier). But in some circumstances it's possible to unlock your phone—allowing you to replace the original SIM card with one that will work with a European provider. Note that some US carriers are beginning to offer phones/tablets whose SIM card can't be swapped out in the US but will accept a European SIM without any unlocking process.

You may already have an old, unused mobile phone in a drawer somewhere. Call your service provider and ask if they'll send you the unlock code. Otherwise, you can buy one: Search an online shopping site for an "unlocked quad-band phone," or buy one at a mobile-phone shop in Europe. Either way, a basic model typically costs $40 or less.

Buying and Using SIM Cards

Once you have an unlocked phone, you'll need to buy a SIM card (note that a smaller variation called "micro-SIM" or "nano-SIM"—

used in most iPhones—is less widely available.)

SIM cards are sold at mobile-phone shops, department-store electronics counters, and newsstands for $5–10, and usually include about that much prepaid calling credit (making the card itself virtually free). Because SIM cards are prepaid, there's no contract and no commitment; I routinely buy one even if I'm in a country for only a few days.

However, an increasing number of countries—including Hungary —require you to register the SIM card with your passport (an antiterrorism measure). This takes only a few minutes longer: The shop clerk will ask you to fill out a form, then submit it to the service provider. Sometimes you can register your own SIM card online. Either way, an hour or two after submitting the information, you'll get a text welcoming you to that network.

When using a SIM card in its home country, it's free to receive calls and texts, and it's cheap to make calls—domestic calls average 20 cents per minute. You can also use SIM cards to call the US—sometimes very affordably. Rates are higher if you're roaming in another country. But if you bought the SIM card within the European Union, roaming fees are capped no matter where you travel throughout the EU (about 25 cents/minute to make calls, 7 cents/minute to receive calls, and 8 cents for a text message).

While you can buy SIM cards just about anywhere, I like to seek out a mobile-phone shop, where an English-speaking clerk can help explain my options, get my SIM card inserted and set up, and show me how to use it. When you buy your SIM card, ask about rates for domestic and international calls and texting, and about roaming fees. Also find out how to check your credit balance (usually you'll key in a few digits and hit "Send"). You can top up your credit at any newsstand, tobacco shop, mobile-phone shop, or many other businesses (look for the SIM card's logo in the window).

To insert your SIM card into the phone, locate the slot, which is usually on the side of the phone or behind the battery. Turning on the phone, you'll be prompted to enter the "SIM PIN" (a code number that came with your card).

If you have an unlocked smartphone, you can look for a European SIM card that covers both voice and data. This is often much cheaper than paying for data roaming through your home provider.

LANDLINE TELEPHONES AND INTERNET CAFÉS

If you prefer to travel without a smartphone or tablet, you can still stay in touch using landline telephones, hotel guest computers, and Internet cafés.

Landline Telephones

Phones in your **hotel room** can be great for local calls and for calls using cheap international phone cards (described in the sidebar). Many hotels charge a fee for local and "toll-free" as well as long-distance or international calls—always ask for the rates before you dial. Since you'll never be charged for receiving calls, it can be more affordable to have someone from the US call you in your room.

While **public pay phones** are on the endangered species list, you'll still see them in post offices and train stations. Pay phones generally come with multilingual instructions. Most public phones work with insertable phone cards (described in the sidebar).

You'll see many cheap **call shops** that advertise low rates to faraway lands, often in train-station neighborhoods. While these target immigrants who want to call home cheaply, tourists can use them, too. Before making your call, be completely clear on the rates.

Internet Cafés and Public Internet Terminals

Finding public Internet terminals in Europe is no problem. Many hotels have a computer in the lobby for guests to use. Otherwise, head for an Internet café, or ask the TI or your hotelier for the nearest place to access the Internet.

European computers typically use non-American keyboards. A few letters are switched around, and command keys are labeled in the local language. Many European keyboards have an "Alt Gr" key (for "Alternate Graphics") to the right of the space bar; press this to insert the extra symbol that appears on some keys. Europeans have different names for, and different ways to type, the @ symbol. If you can't locate a special character (such as the

Types of Telephone Cards

Europe uses two different types of telephone cards. Both types are sold at post offices, newsstands, street kiosks, tobacco shops, and train stations.

Insertable Phone Cards: These cards can only be used at pay phones: Simply take the phone off the hook, insert the card, wait for a dial tone, and dial away. The phone displays your credit ticking down as you talk. Each European country has its own insertable phone card—so your Hungarian card won't work in a Slovakian phone.

International Phone Cards: While these cards are popular and easy to buy in some parts of Europe, they are still relatively rare (and more expensive) in Hungary. These prepaid cards can be used to make inexpensive calls—within Europe, or to the US, for 25-50 cents a minute—from nearly any phone, including the one in your hotel room. The cards come with a toll-free number and a scratch-to-reveal PIN code. If the voice prompts aren't in English, experiment: Dial your code, followed by the pound sign (#), then the phone number, then pound again, and so on, until it works.

PRACTICALITIES

@ symbol), simply copy it from a web page and paste it into your email message.

Internet Security

Whether you're accessing the Internet with your own device or at a public terminal, using a shared network or computer comes with the potential for increased security risks. Ask the hotel or café for the specific name of their Wi-Fi network, and make sure you log on to that exact one; hackers sometimes create a bogus hotspot with a similar or vague name (such as "Hotel Europa Free Wi-Fi"). It's better if a network uses a password (especially a hard-to-guess one) rather than being open to the world.

While traveling, you may want to check your online banking or credit-card statements, or to take care of other personal-finance chores, but Internet security experts advise against accessing these sites entirely while traveling. Even if you're using your own computer at a password-protected hotspot, any hacker who's logged on to the same network can see what you're up to. If you need to log on to a banking website, try to do so on a hard-wired connection (i.e., using an Ethernet cable in your hotel room), or if that's not possible, use a secure banking app on a cellular telephone connection.

If using a credit card online, make sure that the site is secure. Most browsers display a little padlock icon, and the URL begins with *https* instead of *http*. Never send a credit-card number over a website that doesn't begin with *https*.

If you're not convinced a connection is secure, avoid accessing any sites (such as your bank's) that could be vulnerable to fraud.

MAIL

You can mail one package per day to yourself worth up to $200 duty-free from Europe to the US (mark it "personal purchases"). If you're sending a gift to someone, mark it "unsolicited gift." For details, visit www.cbp.gov and search for "Know Before You Go."

The Hungarian postal service works fine, but for quick transatlantic delivery (in either direction), consider services such as DHL (www.dhl.com). Get stamps at the neighborhood post office, newsstands within fancy hotels, and some mini-marts and card shops.

Transportation

If you're focusing on Budapest, you definitely don't want a car. Even for side-trips into the countryside, virtually all of the attractions listed in this book (with the possible exception of Hollókő) are easily reachable by public transit. Even so, some areas—such as the Danube Bend and Hollókő—can be done more efficiently by car. Instead of hassling with a car of your own, consider splurging by hiring a local guide (see page 42) or a driver (see page 35).

TRAINS

Hungary's train network is run by MÁV (Magyar Államvasutak). From centrally located Budapest, train lines branch out across Hungary. Most connections between outlying cities aren't direct—you often end up having to go back through Budapest. While Hungary's trains are generally good, many are old and fairly slow; major routes use faster, newer, and slightly more expensive InterCity trains (marked with an "IC" or a boxed "R" on schedules). To ride an InterCity train, you must pay extra for a required reservation (which is printed on a separate ticket).

If traveling to international destinations such as Bratislava or Vienna, other trains are faster and more direct than the InterCity. Between Budapest and Bratislava, EuroCity (EC) trains are fastest and most direct—one train per day (in each direction) requires reservations, but the other six daily EC departures don't. If traveling from Budapest to Vienna, Austrian RailJet (RJ) trains are fastest and direct (seven trains a day), and don't require reservations.

Warning: Trains can be very crowded on weekends, when it's smart to book a reservation for any train trip.

For timetables, the first place to check is Germany's excellent all-Europe site, www.bahn.com. You can also check Hungary's own timetable website at http://elvira.mav-start.hu. For general rail information in Hungary, call 0640-494-949 (from outside Hungary, dial +36-1-444-4499).

Ticket prices are reasonable (1,500 Ft per 100 kilometers/62 miles). While **rail passes** can be a good deal in other countries, the low cost of point-to-point tickets in Hungary makes passes a lesser value here. However, if you're connecting multiple countries, a rail pass might be worth considering. For more detailed advice on figuring out the smartest rail pass options for your train trip, visit the Trains & Rail Passes section of my website at www.ricksteves.com/rail.

It's best to buy your ticket in advance at the MÁV ticket office in downtown Pest (see page 32). Be aware that ticket lines can be very long at the train stations; if you're buying a ticket there, it's smart to arrive with plenty of time to spare, and make sure you get in the correct line: international *(nemzetközi)* or domestic (signed "inland," *háztartási*).

RENTING A CAR

If you're planning to rent a car in Hungary, bring your driver's license. You're also required to have an International Driving Per-

mit—an official translation of your driver's license (sold at your local AAA office for $15 plus the cost of two passport-type photos; see www.aaa.com). While that's the letter of the law, I've often rented cars in Hungary without having this permit. If all goes well, you'll likely never be asked to show this permit—but it's a must if you end up dealing with the police.

Rental companies require you to be at least 21 years old to drive in Hungary and to have held your license for one year. Drivers under the age of 25 may incur a young-driver surcharge, and some rental companies do not rent to anyone 75 and over.

Research car rentals before you go. It's cheaper to arrange most long-term car rentals from the US. Call several companies or look online to compare rates. All of the major US rental agencies (including Avis, Budget, Enterprise, Hertz, and Thrifty) have offices in Budapest. Also consider the two major Europe-based agencies, Europcar and Sixt. It can be cheaper to use a consolidator, such as Auto Europe/Kemwel (www.autoeurope.com) or Europe

Hungary Transportation

by Car (www.europebycar.com), which compares rates at several companies to get you the best deal—but because you're working with a middleman, it's especially important to ask in advance about add-on fees and restrictions.

Regardless of the car-rental company you choose, always read the contract carefully for add-on charges—such as one-way drop-off fees, airport surcharges, or mandatory insurance policies—that aren't included in the "total price." You may need to query rental agents pointedly to find out your actual cost.

For the best deal, rent by the week with unlimited mileage. To save money on fuel, ask for a diesel car. I normally rent the smallest, least-expensive model with a stick shift (generally much cheaper than an automatic). An automatic transmission adds about 50 percent to the car-rental cost over a manual transmission. Almost all rentals are manual by default, so if you need an automatic, request one in advance; be aware that these cars are usually larger models (not as maneuverable on narrow, winding roads).

Figure on paying roughly $200 for a one-week rental. Allow

extra for supplemental insurance, fuel, tolls, and parking. Be warned that international trips—say, picking up in Budapest and dropping in Vienna—can be expensive (it depends partly on distance, but the extra fee averages a few hundred dollars).

As a rule, always tell your car-rental company up front exactly which countries you'll be entering. Some companies levy extra insurance fees for trips taken in certain countries with certain types of cars (such as BMWs, Mercedes, and convertibles). Double-check with your rental agent that you have all the documentation you need before you drive off (especially if you're crossing borders into non-Schengen countries, such as Serbia or Romania, where you might need to present proof of insurance). For more on borders, see page 477.

Big companies have offices in most cities; ask whether they can pick you up at your hotel. Small local companies can be cheaper but aren't as flexible.

Compare pickup costs (downtown can be less expensive than the airport) and explore drop-off options. Always check the hours of the location you choose: Many rental offices close from midday Saturday until Monday morning and, in smaller towns, at lunchtime.

When selecting a location, don't trust the agency's description of "downtown" or "city center." In some cases, a "downtown" branch can be on the outskirts of the city—a long, costly taxi ride from the center. Before choosing, plug the addresses into a mapping website. You may find that the "train station" location is handier. But returning a car at a big-city train station or downtown agency can be tricky; get precise details on the car drop-off location and hours, and allow ample time to find it.

When you pick up the rental car, check it thoroughly and make sure any damage is noted on your rental agreement. Find out how your car's lights, turn signals, wipers, radio, and fuel cap function, and know what kind of fuel the car takes (diesel vs. unleaded). When you return the car, make sure the agent verifies its condition with you. Some drivers take pictures of the returned vehicle as proof of its condition.

Navigation Options

When renting a car in Europe, you have several alternatives for your digital navigator: Use your smartphone's online mapping app, download an offline map app, or rent a GPS device with your rental car (or bring your own GPS device from home).

Online mapping apps used to be prohibitively expensive for overseas travelers—but that was before most carriers started offering affordable international data plans. If you're already getting a data plan for your trip, this is probably the way to go (see "Using Your Smartphone in Europe," earlier).

A number of well-designed apps allow you much of the convenience of online maps without any costly demands on your data plan. City Maps 2Go is one of the most popular of these; OffMaps, Google Maps, and Navfree also all offer good, zoomable offline maps for much of Europe (some are better for driving, while others are better for navigating cities on foot).

Some drivers prefer using a dedicated GPS unit—not only to avoid the data-roaming fees, but because a stand-alone GPS can be easier to operate (important if you're driving solo). The major downside: It's expensive—around $10-30 per day. Your car's GPS unit may only come loaded with maps for its home country—if you need additional maps, ask. Make sure your device's language is set to English before you drive off. If you have a portable GPS device at home, you can take that instead. Many American GPS devices come loaded with US maps only—you'll need to buy and download European maps before your trip. This option is far less expensive than renting.

Car Insurance Options

When you rent a car, you are liable for a very high deductible, sometimes equal to the entire value of the car. Limit your financial risk by choosing one of these three options: Buy Collision Damage Waiver (CDW) coverage from the car-rental company, get coverage through your credit card (free, if your card automatically includes zero-deductible coverage), or get collision insurance as part of a larger travel-insurance policy.

CDW includes a very high deductible (typically $1,000-1,500). Though each rental company has its own variation, basic CDW costs $10–30 a day (figure roughly 30 percent extra) and reduces your liability, but does not eliminate it. When you pick up the car, you'll be offered the chance to "buy down" the basic deductible to zero (for an additional $10-30/day; this is sometimes called "super CDW" or "zero-deductible coverage").

If you opt for **credit-card coverage,** there's a catch. You'll technically have to decline all coverage offered by the car-rental company, which means they can place a hold on your card (which can be up to the full value of the car). In case of damage, it can be time-consuming to resolve the charges with your credit-card company. Before you decide on this option, quiz your credit-card company about how it works.

If you're already purchasing a **travel-insurance policy** for your trip, adding collision coverage is an option. For example, Travel Guard (www.travelguard.com) sells affordable renter's collision insurance as an add-on to its other policies; it's valid everywhere in Europe except the Republic of Ireland, and some Italian car-rental companies refuse to honor it, as it doesn't cover you in case of theft.

For more on car-rental insurance, see www.ricksteves.com/cdw.

  AND LEARN THESE ROAD SIGNS

Speed Limit (km/hr)

Yield

No Passing

End of No Passing Zone

One Way

Intersection

Main Road

Freeway

Danger

No Entry

No Entry for Cars

All Vehicles Prohibited

Parking

No Parking

Customs

Peace

DRIVING

Road Rules: Be aware of typical European road rules; for example, many countries, including Hungary, require headlights to be turned on at all times (the lights of many newer cars automatically turn on and off with the engine). Seatbelts are mandatory in Hungary, children under age 3

PRACTICALITIES

must ride in a child seat, and it's illegal to drink any alcohol at all before driving. As in most other European countries, it's also illegal to drive while using your mobile phone without a hands-free headset. In Europe, you're not allowed to turn right on a red light, unless there is a sign or signal specifically authorizing it, and on expressways it's illegal to pass drivers on the right. In roundabouts, give way to the left. Ask your car-rental company about these rules, or check the US State Department website (www.travel.state.gov, search for your country in the "Learn about your destination" box, then click on "Travel and Transportation").

Toll Stickers: Hungary has a fine network of expressways, which always begin with "M" (e.g., the M-3 expressway runs east of Budapest toward Eger). To drive on Hungarian expressways, you'll need a toll sticker, called an *autópálya matrica* (also called a "vignette"; 2,975 Ft/week, 4,780 Ft/month, www.motorway.hu). Ask about this when you rent your car (if it's not already included, you'll have to buy one). It's not uncommon to be pulled over at an on- or off-ramp to be checked for a toll sticker; those caught without one are subject to a hefty fine. If you drive into Slovakia or Austria, you'll also need to buy a toll sticker to use their highways (Slovakia—*úhrada*, €10/10 days; Austria—*Vignette*, €8.50/10 days, €24.80/2 months). You don't need a toll sticker if you'll be dipping into the country on minor roads—only for major highways.

FLIGHTS

The best comparison search engine for both international and intra-European flights is www.kayak.com. For inexpensive flights within Europe, try www.skyscanner.com or www.hipmunk.com; for inexpensive international flights, try www.vayama.com.

Flying to Europe: Start looking for international flights four to five months before your trip, especially for peak-season travel. Off-season tickets can be purchased a month or so in advance. Depending on your itinerary, it can be efficient to fly into one city and out of another. If your flight requires a connection in Europe, see our hints on navigating Europe's top hub airports at www.ricksteves.com/hub-airports.

Flying Within Europe: If you're considering a train ride that's more than five hours long, a flight may save you both time and money. When comparing your options, factor in the time it takes to get to the airport and how early you'll need to arrive to check in.

Malév Hungarian Airlines went bust in 2012—leaving Hungary without an official national airline. But many major international lines (such as Lufthansa and Austrian Airlines) still serve Budapest, and the void has been capably filled by various low-cost airlines. The most prominent of these is Budapest-based **Wizz Air** (www.wizzair.com)—which also has hubs in the Polish cities of Warsaw, Gdańsk, and Katowice (near Kraków).

Well-known cheapo airlines include **easyJet** (www.easyjet.com), **Ryanair** (www.ryanair.com), and **germanwings** (www.germanwings.com).

If you're not finding the flight you want out of Budapest, consider flying out of **Bratislava,** Slovakia, instead—it's less than a three-hour train ride away (see the Bratislava chapter). Bratislava is served by several daily flights on the budget carrier Ryanair. **Vienna,** Austria—just three hours from Budapest by train—has cheap flights on germanwings.

Be aware of the potential drawbacks of flying on the cheap: nonrefundable and nonchangeable tickets, minimal or nonexistent customer service, treks to airports far outside of town, and stingy baggage allowances with steep overage fees. For example, Wizz Air's flights to Kraków actually arrive at Katowice, 50 miles away (but in most cases, the airline offers a relatively affordable shuttle bus into the main city). If you're traveling with lots of luggage, a cheap flight can quickly become a bad deal. To avoid unpleasant surprises, read the small print before you book.

Resources

RESOURCES FROM RICK STEVES

Books: *Rick Steves Budapest* is one of many books in my series on European travel, which includes country guidebooks (including Eastern Europe), city and regional guidebooks (including Prague & the Czech Republic and Vienna, Salzburg & Tirol), Snapshot guides (excerpted chapters from my country guides), Pocket guides (full-color little books on big cities), and my budget-travel skills handbook, *Rick Steves Europe Through the Back Door.* My phrase books—for German, French, Italian, Spanish, and Portuguese—are practical and budget-oriented. My other books include *Europe 101* (a crash course on art and history designed for travelers); *Mediterranean Cruise Ports* and *Northern European Cruise Ports* (how to make the most of your time

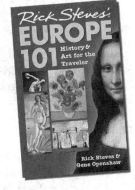

in port); and *Travel as a Political Act* (a travelogue sprinkled with tips for bringing home a global perspective). A more complete list of my titles appears near the end of this book.

Video: My public television series, *Rick Steves' Europe*, covers European destinations in 100 shows, including one on Budapest. To watch full episodes online for free, see www.ricksteves.com/tv. Or to raise your travel I.Q. with video versions of our popular classes, including a talk on the Czech Republic, Poland, and Hungary, see www.ricksteves.com/travel-talks.

Audio: My weekly public radio show, *Travel with Rick Steves*, features interviews with travel experts from around the world. All of this audio content is available for free at Rick Steves Audio Europe, an extensive online library organized by destination. Choose whatever interests you, and download it via the Rick Steves Audio Europe app, www.ricksteves.com/audioeurope, iTunes, or Google Play.

MAPS

The black-and-white maps in this book are concise and simple, designed to help you locate recommended places and get to local TIs, where you can pick up a more in-depth map of cities and regions (usually free). Map apps for your smartphone or tablet are also handy (see "Navigation Options," earlier).

Better maps are sold at newsstands and bookstores all over Hungary. Before you buy a map, look at it to be sure it has the level of detail you want. The Hungarian-produced maps by Cartographia are best (www.cartographiaonline.com). Train travelers can usually manage fine with the freebies they get at the local tourist offices. Hikers will find no shortage of excellent, very detailed maps locally. For drivers, I'd recommend a 1:450,000-scale map of Hungary.

RECOMMENDED BOOKS AND MOVIES

To learn more about Hungary past and present, check out a few of these books and films.

Nonfiction

Lonnie Johnson's *Central Europe: Enemies, Neighbors, Friends* is the best historical overview of Hungary and the surrounding nations. John Lukacs' *Budapest 1900* is a scholarly but readable cultural study that captures Budapest at its turn-of-the-20th-century zenith. Patrick Leigh Fermor's *Between the Woods and the Water* is the vividly recounted memoir of a young man who traveled by foot and

Begin Your Trip at
www.RickSteves.com

My **website** is *the* place to explore Europe. You'll find thousands of fun articles, videos, photos, and radio interviews on European destinations; money-saving tips for planning your dream trip; monthly travel news; my travel talks and travel blog; my latest guidebook updates (www.ricksteves.com/update); and my free Rick Steves Audio Europe app. You can also follow me on Facebook and Twitter.

Our **Travel Forum** is an immense yet well-groomed collection of message boards, where our travel-savvy community answers questions and shares their personal travel experiences (www.ricksteves.com/forums).

Our **online Travel Store** offers travel bags and accessories specially designed by me to help you travel smarter and lighter. These include my popular bags (rolling carry-on and backpack versions), money belts, totes, toiletries kits, adapters, other accessories, and a wide selection of guidebooks, journals, planning maps, and DVDs.

Choosing the right **rail pass** for your trip—amid hundreds of options—can drive you nutty. Our website will help you find the perfect fit for your itinerary and your budget: We offer easy, one-stop shopping for rail passes, seat reservations, and point-to-point tickets.

Want to travel with greater efficiency and less stress? We offer **tours** with more than three dozen itineraries and more than 800 departures reaching the best destinations in this book...and beyond. We offer an eight-day Prague and Budapest tour, and a 16-day Best of Eastern Europe tour that visits Budapest and Eger, along with highlights of the Czech Republic, Poland, Croatia, and Slovenia. You'll enjoy great guides, a fun bunch of travel partners (with small groups of 24 to 28 travelers), and plenty of room to spread out in a big, comfy bus when touring between towns. You'll find European adventures to fit every vacation length. For all the details, and to get our Tour Catalog and a free Rick Steves Tour Experience DVD (filmed on location during an actual tour), visit www.ricksteves.com or call us at 425/608-4217.

on horseback across the Balkan Peninsula (including Hungary) in 1933. András Török's irreverent *Budapest: A Critical Guide*, while technically a guidebook, offers more local insight (and wit) than any other source. Timothy Garton Ash has written several good "eyewitness account" books analyzing the transition in Central and Eastern Europe from the late 1980s through the 1990s, including *History of the Present* and *The Magic Lantern*. Tina Rosenberg's dense but thought-provoking *The Haunted Land* asks how individuals who actively supported communist regimes should be treated in the post-communist age. For information on Eastern European Roma (Gypsies), consider the textbook-style *We Are the Romani People* by Ian Hancock, and the more literary *Bury Me Standing* by Isabel Fonseca. And for a look at life during communist times—albeit not in Hungary—Croatian journalist Slavenka Drakulić has written a pair of insightful essay collections from a woman's perspective: *Café Europa: Life After Communism* and *How We Survived Communism and Even Laughed*. If you're going to Eger, consider reading Géza Gárdonyi's *Eclipse of the Crescent Moon*, an epic about the Siege of Eger that's read and beloved by every Hungarian grade-schooler.

Fiction

Imre Kertész, a Hungarian-Jewish Auschwitz survivor who won the Nobel Prize for Literature in 2002, is best known for his semi-autobiographical novel *Fatelessness (Sorstalanság),* which chronicles the experience of a young concentration-camp prisoner. Arthur Phillips' confusingly titled novel *Prague* tells the story of American expats negotiating young-adult life in post-communist Budapest, where they often feel one-upped by their compatriots doing the same in the Czech capital (hence the title). Joseph Roth's *The Radetzky March* details the decline of an aristocratic family in the Austro-Hungarian Empire. The Newbery Honor book *Zlateh the Goat* (Isaac Bashevis Singer) includes seven folktales of Jewish Eastern Europe.

Films

One of the more accessible films for an introduction to Budapest is *Sunshine* (1999, starring Ralph Fiennes, directed by István Szabó; not to be confused with Danny Boyle's very different 2007 film of the same name). Tracing three generations of an aristocratic Jewish family in Budapest—from the Golden Age, through the Holocaust, to the Cold War—*Sunshine* is an enlightening if melodramatic look at recent Hungarian history.

For Hungarian-language films, the surreal dark comedy *Kontroll* (2003) is about ticket inspectors on the Budapest Metró whose lives are turned upside down by a serial killer lurking in the shadows. *Fateless,* the 2005 adaptation of Imre Kertész's Nobel Prize-winning novel about a young man in a concentration camp, was scripted by Kertész himself. The 1998 Oscar-winning documentary *The Last Days* chronicles the fate of Jews when the Nazis took over Hungary in 1944. *The Witness* (*A Tanú,* a.k.a. *Without a Trace,* 1969), a cult classic about a simple man who mysteriously wins the favor of communist bigwigs, is a biting satire of the darkest days of Soviet rule. *Time Stands Still (Megáll Az Idö),* a hit at the 1982 Cannes Film Festival, tells the story of young Hungarians in the 1960s. *Children of Glory* (*Szabadság, Szerelem*, 2006) dramatizes the true story of the Hungarian water polo team that defiantly trounced the Soviets at the Olympics just after the 1956 Uprising.

Many American studios have taken advantage of Hungary's low prices to film would-be blockbusters in Budapest (such as the 2002 Eddie Murphy/Owen Wilson action-comedy *I Spy*—a terrible film that makes wonderful use of many real Budapest settings). More often, Budapest stands in for other cities—for example, as Buenos Aires in Madonna's 1996 film *Evita,* and as various European locales in Stephen Spielberg's 2005 film *Munich.*

Two German movies—while not about Hungary—are still excellent for their insight into the surreal and paranoid days of the Soviet Bloc. The Oscar-winning *Lives of Others* (2006) chronicles the constant surveillance that the communist regime employed to keep potential dissidents in line. For a funny and nostalgic look at post-communist Europe's fitful transition to capitalism, *Good Bye Lenin!* (2003) can't be beat.

APPENDIX

Contents

Useful Contacts

Emergency Needs
Any Emergency: Tel. 112
Police: Tel. 107
Ambulance: Tel. 104
Fire: Tel. 105

Embassies in Budapest
United States: Tel. 1/475-4400, emergency tel. 1/475-4703 or 1/475-4924 (Mon-Fri 8:00-17:00, closed Sat-Sun, Szabadság tér 12, district V, www.usembassy.hu).
Canada: Tel. 1/392-3360 (Mon-Thu 8:30-12:30 & 13:00-16:30, Fri 8:00-13:30, closed Sat-Sun, Ganz utca 12-14, district II, www.hungary.gc.ca); for after-hours emergencies, call collect to Canadian tel. 613/996-8885.

Embassies/Consulates in Bratislava, Slovakia
United States: Tel. 02/5443-0861 (Mon-Fri 8:00-11:45 & 14:00-15:15, closed Sat-Sun, Hviezdoslavovo Námestie 4, http://slovakia.usembassy.gov).
Canada: Tel. 02/5920-4031 (Mon-Fri 8:30-12:30 & 13:30-16:30,

closed Sat-Sun, Mostová 2, www.czechrepublic.gc.ca); for after-hours emergencies, call collect to Canadian tel. 613/996-8885.

Directory Assistance
Operator/Directory Assistance for Hungary: Tel. 198
Operator/Directory Assistance for International Calls: Tel. 199

Holidays and Festivals

This list includes selected festivals in Budapest, plus national holidays observed throughout Hungary. While nominally a Catholic country, most Hungarians are not very devout. Catholic holidays (such as Epiphany, Ascension, Corpus Christi, and the Assumption of Mary) are observed, but with less impact than in some other countries. Before planning a trip around a festival, verify its dates by checking the festival's website or TI sites (www.gotohungary.com). Many of Budapest's top festivals share a website (www.fesztivalvaros.hu).

Jan 1	New Year's Day
March 15	National Day (celebrates 1848 Revolution, closures)
April	Budapest Spring Festival (2 weeks, April 10-26 in 2015; opera, ballet, classical music)
Good Friday	(April 3 in 2015, March 25 in 2016)
Easter	(April 5 in 2015, March 27 in 2016)
May 1	Labor Day (and anniversary of joining the EU, closures)
Ascension	(May 14 in 2015, May 5 in 2016)
Pentecost	("Whitsunday"; May 24 in 2015, May 15 in 2016)
Whitmonday	(May 25 in 2015, May 16 in 2016)
Corpus Christi	(June 4 in 2015, May 26 in 2016)
June	Danube Carnival (3 weeks, June 6-26 in 2015, http://dunakarneval.hu)
June-mid-Aug	Outdoor Theater Festival, Pécs (outdoor evening performances, www.pecsiszabadteri.hu)
Late June	Early Music Days, Sopron (1 week, June 27-July 4 in 2015, www.filharmoniabp.hu)
Early July-late Aug	Szentendre Summer Festival (art festival with theater, concerts, film, activities, www.szentendreprogram.hu)

Mid-July	Bull's Blood Festival, Eger (4 days, July 9-12 in 2015, wine and traditional food, www.bikaverunnep.hu)
Late July	Formula 1 races, Budapest (July 24-26 in 2015, www.hungaroinfo.com/formel1)
Mid-Aug	Sziget Festival, Budapest (1 week, Aug 10-17 in 2015, rock and pop music, www.sziget.com)
Aug 15	Assumption of Mary
Aug 20	St. István's Day (also known as Constitution Day; fireworks, celebrations)
Late Aug-early Sept	Jewish Summer Festival, Budapest (2 weeks, Aug 20-Sept 4 in 2015, www.zsidonyarifesztival.hu)
Oct 23	National Day (remembrances of 1956 Uprising)
Mid-Oct	Café Budapest Contemporary Arts Festival (www.cafebudapestfest.hu)
Nov 1	All Saints' Day/Remembrance Day (religious festival, some closures)
Dec 24-25	Christmas Eve and Christmas Day
Dec 26	Boxing Day

Conversions and Climate

NUMBERS AND STUMBLERS

- Europeans write a few of their numbers differently than we do. 1 = 1, 4 = 4, 7 = 7.
- In Hungary, dates appear as year/month/day, so Christmas 2016 is 2016/12/25 (or sometimes using dots: 2016.12.25).
- Commas are decimal points and decimals commas. A dollar and a half is $1,50, and there are 5.280 feet in a mile.
- Hungarians usually list their surname first (for example, Bartók Béla instead of Béla Bartók).
- When counting with fingers, start with your thumb. If you hold up your first finger to request one item, you'll probably get two.
- What Americans call the second floor of a building is the first floor in Europe.
- On escalators and moving sidewalks, Europeans keep the left "lane" open for passing. Keep to the right.

METRIC CONVERSIONS

A kilogram is 2.2 pounds and 1 liter is about a quart, or almost four to a gallon. A kilometer is six-tenths of a mile. I figure kilometers to miles by cutting them in half and adding back 10 percent of the original (120 km: 60 + 12 = 72 miles, 300 km: 150 + 30 = 180 miles).

1 foot = 0.3 meter	1 square yard = 0.8 square meter
1 yard = 0.9 meter	1 square mile = 2.6 square kilometers
1 mile = 1.6 kilometers	1 ounce = 28 grams
1 centimeter = 0.4 inch	1 quart = 0.95 liter
1 meter = 39.4 inches	1 kilogram = 2.2 pounds
1 kilometer = 0.62 mile	32°F = 0°C

CLOTHING SIZES

When shopping for clothing, use these US-to-European comparisons as general guidelines (but note that no conversion is perfect).

- Women's dresses and blouses: Add 30
  (US size 10 = European size 40)
- Men's suits and jackets: Add 10
  (US size 40 regular = European size 50)
- Men's shirts: Multiply by 2 and add about 8
  (US size 15 collar = European size 38)
- Women's shoes: Add about 30
  (US size 8 = European size 38-39)
- Men's shoes: Add 32-34
  (US size 9 = European size 41; US size 11 = European size 45)

CLIMATE

First line, average daily high; second line, average daily low; third line, average days with some rain. For more detailed weather statistics for destinations in this book (as well as the rest of the world), check www.wunderground.com.

J	F	M	A	M	J	J	A	S	O	N	D
HUNGARY • Budapest											
34°	39°	50°	62°	71°	78°	82°	81°	74°	61°	47°	39°
25°	28°	35°	44°	52°	58°	62°	60°	53°	44°	38°	30°
13	12	11	11	13	13	10	9	7	10	14	13

APPENDIX

FAHRENHEIT AND CELSIUS CONVERSION

For Weather   For Health

*Europe takes its temperature using the Celsius scale, while we opt for
Fahrenheit. For a rough conversion from Celsius to Fahrenheit, double
the number and add 30. For weather, remember that 28°C is 82°F—
perfect. For health, 37°C is just right. At a launderette, 30°C is cold,
40°C is warm (usually the default setting), 60°C is hot, and 95°C is
boiling.*

Packing Checklist

Whether you're traveling for five days or five weeks, you won't need more than this. Pack light to enjoy the sweet freedom of true mobility.

Clothing

- ❏ 5 shirts: long- & short-sleeve
- ❏ 2 pairs pants or skirt
- ❏ 1 pair shorts or capris
- ❏ 5 pairs underwear & socks
- ❏ 1 pair walking shoes
- ❏ Sweater or fleece top
- ❏ Rainproof jacket with hood
- ❏ Tie or scarf
- ❏ Swimsuit
- ❏ Sleepwear

Money

- ❏ Debit card
- ❏ Credit card(s)
- ❏ Hard cash ($20 bills)
- ❏ Money belt or neck wallet

Documents & Travel Info

- ❏ Passport
- ❏ Airline reservations
- ❏ Rail pass/train reservations
- ❏ Car-rental voucher
- ❏ Driver's license
- ❏ Student ID, hostel card, etc.
- ❏ Photocopies of all the above
- ❏ Hotel confirmations
- ❏ Insurance details
- ❏ Guidebooks & maps
- ❏ Notepad & pen
- ❏ Journal

Toiletries Kit

- ❏ Toiletries
- ❏ Medicines & vitamins
- ❏ First-aid kit
- ❏ Glasses/contacts/sunglasses (with prescriptions)
- ❏ Earplugs
- ❏ Packet of tissues (for WC)

Miscellaneous

- ❏ Daypack
- ❏ Sealable plastic baggies
- ❏ Laundry soap
- ❏ Spot remover
- ❏ Clothesline
- ❏ Sewing kit
- ❏ Travel alarm/watch

Electronics

- ❏ Smartphone or mobile phone
- ❏ Camera & related gear
- ❏ Tablet/ereader/media player
- ❏ Laptop & flash drive
- ❏ Earbuds or headphones
- ❏ Chargers
- ❏ Plug adapters

Optional Extras

- ❏ Flipflops or slippers
- ❏ Mini-umbrella or poncho
- ❏ Travel hairdryer
- ❏ Belt
- ❏ Hat (for sun or cold)
- ❏ Picnic supplies
- ❏ Water bottle
- ❏ Fold-up tote bag
- ❏ Small flashlight
- ❏ Small binoculars
- ❏ Insect repellent
- ❏ Small towel or washcloth
- ❏ Inflatable pillow
- ❏ Some duct tape (for repairs)
- ❏ Tiny lock
- ❏ Address list (to mail postcards)
- ❏ Postcards/photos from home
- ❏ Extra passport photos
- ❏ Good book

Hungarian Survival Phrases

Remember, the letter *a* is pronounced "aw," while *á* is a brighter "ah." In the phonetics, *dj* is pronounced like the *j* in "jeans."

English	Hungarian	Pronunciation
Hello. (formal)	Jó napot kívánok.	yoh **nah**-poht **kee**-vah-nohk
Hi. / Bye. (informal)	Szia. / Hello.	**see**-yaw / "Hello"
Do you speak English?	Beszél angolul?	**beh**-sayl **awn**-goh-lool
Yes. / No.	Igen. / Nem.	**ee**-gehn / nehm
I (don't) understand.	(Nem) értem.	(nehm) **ayr**-tehm
Please.	Kérem.	**kay**-rehm
You're welcome.	Szívesen.	**see**-veh-shehn
Thank you (very much).	Köszönöm (szépen).	**kur**-sur-nurm (**say**-pehn)
Excuse me. / I'm sorry.	Bocsánat.	**boh**-chah-nawt
No problem.	Semmi gond.	**sheh**-mee gohnd
Good.	Jól.	yohl
Goodbye.	Viszontlátásra.	**vee**-sohnt-lah-tahsh-raw
one / two / three	egy / kettő / három	edj / **keh**-tur / **hah**-rohm
four / five / six / seven	négy / öt / hat / hét	naydj / urt / hawt / hayt
eight / nine / ten	nyolc / kilenc / tíz	nyolts / **kee**-lehnts / teez
hundred / thousand	száz / ezer	sahz / **eh**-zehr
How much?	Mennyi?	**mehn**-yee
local currency	forint (Ft)	**foh**-reent
Where is it?	Hol van?	hohl vawn
Is it free (no charge)?	Ingyen van?	een-**jehn** vawn
Where can I find / buy...?	Hol találok / vehetek...?	hohl **taw**-lah-lohk / **veh**-heh-tehk
I'd like / We'd like...	Kérnék / Kérnénk...	**kayr**-nayk / **kayr**-naynk
...a room.	...egy szobát.	edj **soh**-baht
...a ticket (to ___).	...egy jegyet (___-ig).	edj **yehdj**-eht (___-ig)
Is it possible?	Lehet?	leh-**heht**
Where is the ___?	Hol van a ___?	hohl vawn aw ___
big train station (in Budapest)	pályaudvar	**pah**-yood-vawr
small train station (elsewhere)	vasútállomás	**vaw**-shoot-ah-loh-mahsh
bus station	buszpályaudvar	**boos**-pah-yood-vawr
tourist information office	turista információ	**too**-reesh-taw **een**-for-maht-see-yoh
toilet	toalet / WC	**toh**-aw-leht / **vayt**-say
men / women	férfi / női	**fayr**-fee / **nur**-ee
left / right	bal / jobb	bawl / yohb
straight	egyenesen	**edj**-eh-neh-shehn
At what time...?	Mikor...?	**mee**-kor
...does this open / close	...nyit / zár	nyit / zahr
Just a moment.	Egy pillanat.	edj **pee**-law-nawt
now / soon / later	most / hamarosan / később	mohsht / **haw**-maw-roh-shawn / **kay**-shurb
today / tomorrow	ma / holnap	maw / **hohl**-nawp

In a Hungarian Restaurant

APPENDIX

English	Hungarian	Pronunciation
I'd like to reserve a table for one / two people.	Szeretnék foglalni egy asztalt egy / két fő részére.	seh-reht-nayk **fog**-lawl-nee edj **aws**-tawlt edj / kayt few **ray**-say-reh
Is this table free?	Ez az asztal szabad?	ehz oz **aws**-tawl saw-**bawd**
Can I help you?	Tessék?	**tehsh**-shayk
The menu (in English), please.	Kérem az (angol), étlapot.	**kay**-rehm oz (**awn**-gohl) **ayt**-law-poht
service (not) included	a számla a felszolgálási díjat (nem) tartalmazza	aw **sahm**-law aw **fehl**-sohl-gah-lah-shee **dee**-yawt (nehm) **tawr**-tawl-maw-zaw
"to go"	elvitelre	**ehl**-vee-tehl-reh
with / without	___-val / nélkül	___-vawl / **nayl**-kewl
and / or	és / vagy	aysh / vawdj
fixed-price meal (of the day)	(napi) menü	(**naw**-pee) **meh**-new
daily special	napi ajánlat	naw-pee **aw**-yahn-lawt
main courses	főételek	**fur**-ay-teh-lehk
appetizers	előételek	**eh**-lur-ay-teh-lehk
bread / cheese	kenyér / sajt	**kehn**-yayr / shayt
sandwich	szendvics	**send**-veech
soup / salad	leves / saláta	**leh**-vehsh / **shaw**-lah-taw
meat / poultry	hús / szárnyasok	hoosh / **sahr**-nyaw-shohk
fish	halak	**haw**-lawk
seafood	tengeri halak	**tehn**-geh-ree **haw**-lawk
fruit / vegetables	gyümölcs / zöldség	**jewm**-urlch / **zulrd**-shayg
dessert	desszert	**deh**-sehrt
vegetarian	vegetáriánus	**veh**-geh-tah-ree-ah-noosh
(tap) water	(csap) víz	(chawp) veez
mineral water	ásványvíz	**ash**-vawn-veez
milk / (orange) juice	tej / (narancs) lé	**tay**ee / (**naw**-rawnch) lay
coffee / tea	kávé / tea	**kah**-vay / **teh**-aw
beer / wine	sör / bor	shohr / bohr
red / white	vörös / fehér	**vur**-rursh / **feh**-hayr
sweet / dry / semi-dry	édes / száraz / félszáraz	**ay**-dehsh / **sah**-rawz / **fayl**-sah-rawz
glass / bottle	pohár / üveg	**poh**-hahr / **ew**-vehg
Cheers!	Egészségedre!	**eh**-gehs-sheh-geh-dreh
More. / Another.	Még. / Máskikat.	mayg / **mah**-shee-kawt
The same.	Ugyanazt.	**oodj**-aw-nawst
Bill, please. (literally, "I'll pay.")	Fizetek.	**fee**-zeh-tehk
tip	borravaló	**boh**-raw-vaw-loh
Bon appétit!	Jó étvágyat!	yoh **ayt**-vah-yawt
Delicious!	Finom!	**fee**-nohm

INDEX

MAP INDEX

Explore Europe

At ricksteves.com you can browse through thousands of articles, videos, photos and radio interviews, plus find a wealth of money-saving travel tips for planning your dream trip. And with our mobile-friendly website, you can easily access all this great travel information anywhere you go.

TV Shows

Preview the places you'll visit by watching entire half-hour episodes of Rick Steves' Europe (choose from all 100 shows) on-demand, for free.

your travel dreams into affordable reality

Radio Interviews

Enjoy ready access to Rick's vast library of radio interviews covering travel

tips and cultural insights that relate specifically to your Europe travel plans.

Travel Forums

Learn, ask, share! Our online community of savvy travelers is a great resource for first-time travelers to Europe, as well as seasoned pros. You'll find forums on each country, plus travel tips and restaurant/hotel reviews. You can even ask one of our well-traveled staff to chime in with an opinion.

Travel News

Subscribe to our free Travel News e-newsletter, and get monthly updates from Rick on what's happening in Europe.

Rick's Free Travel App

Get your FREE **Rick Steves Audio Europe™** app to enjoy…

- Dozens of self-guided tours of Europe's top museums, sights and historic walks

- Hundreds of tracks filled with cultural insights and sightseeing tips from Rick's radio interviews

- All organized into handy geographic playlists

- For iPhone, iPad, iPod Touch, Android

With Rick whispering in your ear, Europe gets even better.

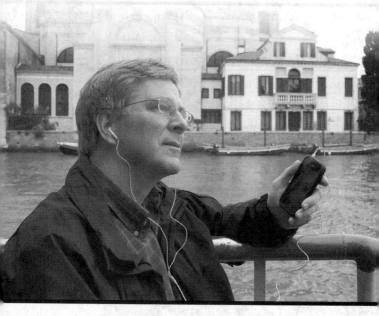

Find out more at ricksteves.com

Gear up for your next adventure at ricksteves.com

Light Luggage

Pack light and right with Rick Steves' affordable, custom-designed rolling carry-on bags, backpacks, day packs and shoulder bags.

Accessories

From packing cubes to moneybelts and beyond, Rick has personally selected the travel goodies that will help your trip go smoother.

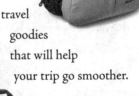

Shop at ricksteves.com

Experience maximum Europe

Save time and energy

This guidebook is your independent-travel toolkit. But for all it delivers, it's still up to you to devote the time and energy it takes to manage the preparation and logistics that are essential for a happy trip. If that's a hassle, there's a solution.

Rick Steves Tours

A Rick Steves tour takes you to Europe's most interesting places with great

with minimum stress

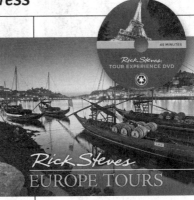

guides and small groups of 28 or less. We follow Rick's favorite itineraries, ride in comfy buses, stay in family-run hotels, and bring you intimately close to the Europe you've traveled so far to see. Most importantly, we take away the logistical headaches so you can focus on the fun.

customers—along with us on 40 different itineraries, from Ireland to Italy to Istanbul. Is a Rick Steves tour the right fit for your travel dreams? Find out at ricksteves.com, where you can also get Rick's latest tour catalog and free Tour Experience DVD.

Join the fun

This year we'll take 18,000 free-spirited travelers— nearly half of them repeat

Europe is best experienced with happy travel partners. We hope you can join us.

See our itineraries at ricksteves.com

EUROPE GUIDES

Best of Europe
Eastern Europe
Europe Through the Back Door
Mediterranean Cruise Ports
Northern European Cruise Ports

COUNTRY GUIDES

Croatia & Slovenia
England
France
Germany
Great Britain
Ireland
Italy
Portugal
Scandinavia
Spain
Switzerland

CITY & REGIONAL GUIDES

Amsterdam, Bruges & Brussels
Barcelona
Budapest
Florence & Tuscany
Greece: Athens & the Peloponnese
Istanbul
London
Paris
Prague & the Czech Republic
Provence & the French Riviera
Rome
Venice
Vienna, Salzburg & Tirol

SNAPSHOT GUIDES

Basque Country: Spain & France
Berlin
Bruges & Brussels
Copenhagen & the Best of
   Denmark
Dublin
Dubrovnik
Hill Towns of Central Italy
Italy's Cinque Terre
Krakow, Warsaw & Gdansk
Lisbon
Madrid & Toledo
Milan & the Italian Lakes District
Munich, Bavaria & Salzburg
Naples & the Amalfi Coast
Northern Ireland
Norway
Scotland
Sevilla, Granada & Southern Spain
Stockholm

POCKET GUIDES

Amsterdam
Athens
Barcelona
Florence
London
Paris
Rome
Venice

Rick Steves guidebooks are published by Avalon Travel,
a member of the Perseus Books Group.

NOW AVAILABLE:
eBOOKS, DVD & BLU-RAY

TRAVEL CULTURE

Europe 101
European Christmas
Postcards from Europe
Travel as a Political Act

eBOOKS

Nearly all Rick Steves guides are available as ebooks. Check with your favorite bookseller.

RICK STEVES' EUROPE DVDs

11 New Shows 2013–2014
Austria & the Alps
Eastern Europe
England & Wales
European Christmas
European Travel Skills & Specials
France
Germany, BeNeLux & More
Greece, Turkey & Portugal
Iran
Ireland & Scotland
Italy's Cities
Italy's Countryside
Scandinavia
Spain
Travel Extras

BLU-RAY

Celtic Charms
Eastern Europe Favorites
European Christmas
Italy Through the Back Door
Mediterranean Mosaic
Surprising Cities of Europe

PHRASE BOOKS & DICTIONARIES

French
French, Italian & German
German
Italian
Portuguese
Spanish

JOURNALS

Rick Steves Pocket Travel Journal
Rick Steves Travel Journal

PLANNING MAPS

Britain, Ireland & London
Europe
France & Paris
Germany, Austria & Switzerland
Ireland
Italy
Spain & Portugal

RickSteves.com 🅕🅣 @RickSteves

Rick Steves books and DVDs are available at bookstores and through online booksellers.

Photo © Patricia Feaster

Credits

CONTRIBUTOR
Gene Openshaw

Gene is a writer, composer, and lecturer on art and history. Specializing in writing tours of Europe's cultural sights, Gene has co-authored a dozen of Rick's books and contributes to Rick's public television series. As a composer, Gene has written a full-length opera *(Matter)*, a violin sonata, and dozens of songs. He lives near Seattle with his daughter, and roots for the Mariners in good times and bad.

ACKNOWLEDGMENTS

Many thanks to our Hungarian friends for sharing their invaluable insights: Péter Pölczman, Andrea Makkay, Elemér Boreczky, George Farkas, Etelka Parine Berecz, István Koteczki, and Eszter Bokros. *Köszönjük szépen!*

Avalon Travel
a member of the Perseus Books Group
1700 Fourth Street
Berkeley, CA 94710

Text © 2015 by Rick Steves
Maps © 2015 by Rick Steves' Europe, Inc.

Printed in Canada by Friesens. First printing March 2015

ISBN 978-1-63121-057-0
ISSN 1946-6161

For the latest on Rick's lectures, guidebooks, tours, public radio show, and public television series, contact Rick Steves' Europe, 130 Fourth Avenue North, Edmonds, WA
98020, tel. 425/771-8303, www.ricksteves.com, rick@ricksteves.com.

Rick Steves' Europe
Managing Editor: Risa Laib
Editorial & Production Manager: Jennifer Madison Davis
Editors: Glenn Eriksen, Tom Griffin, Cameron Hewitt, Suzanne Kotz, Cathy Lu,
Carrie Shepherd
Editorial & Production Assistant: Jessica Shaw
Editorial Intern: Stacie Larsen
Maps & Graphics: David C. Hoerlein, Sandra Hundacker, Lauren Mills, Mary Rostad

Avalon Travel
Senior Editor and Series Manager: Madhu Prasher
Editor: Jamie Andrade
Associate Editor: Maggie Ryan
Copy Editor: Patrick Collins
Proofreader: Janet Walden
Indexer: Stephen Callahan
Production & Typesetting: Rue Flaherty
Cover Design: Kimberly Glyder Design
Maps & Graphics: Kat Bennett, Mike Morgenfeld

Photo Credits
artin Moos/Getty Images
Palace © Cameron Hewitt
eron Hewitt
tt, Rick Steves, Gretchen Strauch (photos are
y of the original copyright owners).

s Group West, Berkeley, California

*le every effort to provide accurate, up-to-date
for loss, injury, bad goulash, or inconvenience*

Want More Eastern Europe?
Maximize the experience with Rick Steves as your guide

Guidebooks
Rick's Eastern Europe guide makes your trip smooth and affordable

Planning Maps
Use the map that's in sync with your guidebook

Rick's TV Shows
Preview Budapest with Rick's TV show

Free! Rick's Audio Europe™ App
Hear Budapest travel tips from Rick's radio shows

Small Group Tours
Rick offers great itineraries through Eastern Europe

For all the details, visit ricksteves.com